A Guide to
American Christian
Education
for the
Home and School

Logo: an original lithograph in watercolor used by permission of the artist, Ray Harm, America's contemporary field-naturalist. The American Eagle's aerie represents the governmental and educational responsibilities of parents, pastors, and pedagogues to "raise up the foundations of many generations" of men and nations for God's glory and Gospel purpose. (*Isa.* 58:12; *Psa.* 145:6)

"THOU SHALT RAISE UP THE FOUNDATIONS • OF MANY GENERATIONS" ISAIAH 58:12

A Guide to

American Christian

Education

for the Home and School

The Principle Approach

American Constitution Bicentennial Edition

by James B. Rose

Introduction by Rosalie June Slater

American Christian History Institute

Camarillo, California

Anno Domini 1987

First Edition

First Edition 1987
American Constitution Bicentennial
September 17, 1987
Copyright 1987 by James B. Rose

Published by
THE AMERICAN CHRISTIAN HISTORY INSTITUTE
1093 Beechwood Street
Camarillo, California 93010

Printed by Iversen-Norman Associates
Irvington on Hudson, New York

Designed by Gloria Difley
Studio 3 Graphics
San Rafael, California

Library of Congress Catalog Card Number 85-082560
ISBN Number 0-9616201-1-0

DEDICATION

VERNA M. HALL
American Christian Historian

Verna Hall devoted her life to documenting
the Christian History of America's Constitution.
She taught us to remember the
Providence of God in establishing Constitutional Liberty in America,
and by "thinking governmentally" to return the Biblical idea
of civil government to the Christian.
Miss Hall's love for God,
commitment to Jesus Christ, and her Christian Scholarship,
are her legacy to this and future generations
of American Christians.

ROSALIE J. SLATER
American Christian Educator

Building on the foundations established by Verna Hall,
Rosalie Slater defined the principles and leading ideas
of America's Christian history and government and joined them
to the educational goals of the American Christian home and school.
She restored the Biblical method of reasoning and writing
which characterized our Colonial education
and which support our American Constitutional Republic.
Miss Slater is reviving for us
the satisfaction of teaching our children
the Literature of Liberty.

REFERENCES AND ABBREVIATIONS

With few exceptions, this work is keyed to statements and documentation published by the Foundation for American Christian Education, San Francisco, California. The particular volumes quoted or referenced and the abbreviations used to refer the reader to them are as follows:

Teaching and Learning America's Christian History – *The Principle Approach*	T/L
The Christian History of the Constitution of the United States of America: *Christian Self-Government*	CHOC
The Christian History of the Constitution of the United States of America: *Christian Self-Government with Union*	SGW/U
The Christian History of the American Revolution: *Consider and Ponder*	C/P
Rudiments of America's Christian History and Government: *Student Handbook*	RUDIMENTS
American Dictionary of the English Language – Noah Webster 1828	WEBSTER 1828
The Bible and the Constitution of the United States of America	B/C

ACKNOWLEDGMENTS

The loving support, direction and example of Miss Verna M. Hall and Miss Rosalie June Slater, officers of the Foundation for American Christian Education, is gratefully acknowledged. Miss Hall and *The Christian History of the Constitution* were God's means of developing in me an appreciation and understanding of this country's Christian history and government. Miss Slater, author of *Teaching and Learning America's Christian History*, provided the fullest expression of the Principle Approach to American Christian education and the literature of liberty. The testimony of these two women, their scholarship and their Foundation's support helped me define and articulate both my calling and the content of this *Guide*.

My wife, Barbara, and our four children – Jason, Matthew, Deborah and Lydia – consistently warrant my esteem for bringing the sunshine of loving support and sacrifice to this work.

Pastor Elliott Paulsen and his wife, Janice, and the Board of Governors, teachers, parents and students involved in my administration of the pilot school in Hayward, California, from 1968 to 1979 were all used of God to instruct and chasten me in how to practically implement this philosophy in grades kindergarten through twelve.

The creative contributions and superior research and reasoning of Master Teacher and former associate, Miss Katherine Dang, have proven not only quickening but invaluable.

The practical and literary contributions of my good friend, Mr. William M. Hosmer, are gratefully acknowledged.

Mr. Adolph Schoepe has consistently supported both Christian education and the Republic. Thanks to him, I had time to initially research and record the vision for this *Guide*.

For their enthusiasm and support, I am deeply grateful to Esther and her late husband, Mr. George Roberts, who frequently said to his wife concerning their involvement with the Christian history educational program, *"This is our most important work!"*

If it was not for Mr. Charles Hull Wolfe and his professional skill in design and editorial assistance, and for being a most thoughtful, discerning and intelligent critic and friend, this book would have been delayed indefinitely.

My sincere thanks to Isobel R. Harper of Gardnerville, Nevada, for her professional proofreading skills and remarkable consistency.

Among the gracious volunteers who read and

commented on the content of the *Guide* during its early stages were Mrs. Dorothy Robbins, Mrs. Regina Hoff, and Pastor George Gunn.

Appreciation also goes to my Executive Secretary, Mrs. Maurine Sadoian, who conscientiously attended to innumerable details of production and promotion of the book with diligence and dispatch in order to assure that there would be a Bicentennial Edition.

Each of the following individuals have my deepest appreciation for their timely and generous contributions in making this volume possible and exercising great patience as numerous delays in publishing took place:

Mr. Howard Ahmanson

Dr. & Mrs. Ivan Bierly

Mr. & Mrs. Ralph Bullard

Dr. & Mrs. Donald DeLoach

Mr. & Mrs. Walter Dimmick

Dr. Gilbert F. Douglas

Mrs. Patricia Folker

Mr. & Mrs. Terry Fritts

Mr. & Mrs. Bruce Hooper

Mrs. Marsha Grunden

Mr. & Mrs. Billy High

Mr. & Mrs. Craige Humphreys

Mr. & Mrs. Keith Jones

Mr. & Mrs. Frank Kahl

Mr. & Mrs. Ron Kirk

Mr. & Mrs. Daniel Martin

Mr. & Mrs. Scott Meier

Mr. Tracy Pennock

Mr. & Mrs. J. F. Phangman

Mr. & Mrs. John L. Rose

Mr. Karl Sauter

Mr. & Mrs. William Schmelzer

Mr. & Mrs. Allen Smith

Miss Jeannette Smith

Gladys Soulé Trust

Mr. Jack Stopyra

Mrs. Eileen Waage

Mr. & Mrs. Jeff Walters

Mr. & Mrs. John White

To Mr. Ralph Bullard and the Governing Board of Christian Heritage Academy in Oklahoma City, Oklahoma, I extend my respect and appreciation for encouraging not only a fine faculty but the publication of this book.

Mr. John G. Talcott, Jr. and his dear wife, Rosalin are esteemed among the Christian history family for their love of America's Christian history and the educational goal of the American Christian home and school. I "thank God upon every remembrance" of their moral and financial support in publishing this volume.

Special credit is given to Mrs. Ruth Smith, Director and Master Teacher of the Pilgrim Institute, for not only her own contribution to the history curriculum, but for assisting other contributors in preparing their sections and for providing the sound counsel of an experienced consultant.

I am very grateful to my good friend, Martin Selbrede, who prepared the special Bible Index. It was his firm, Continental Typographics, Inc. of Chatsworth, California, who typeset this book.

Gloria Difley of Studio Three Graphics, San Rafael, California, was providentially prepared to be the Graphics Designer and Paste-up Artist of this book by virtue of her talent, expertise and commitment to excellence. Mrs. Difley, along with Mrs. Desta Garrett of San Francisco, a skillful typesetter and earnest student of Christian History, were esteemed "fellow laborers" in the final stages of this work.

Lastly, the author is indebted to the following master teachers who have contributed to the *Curriculum Division* of this *Guide* and have helped to make the Principle Approach truly practical for the Christian home and school:

Miss Belinda Beth Ballenger

Mr. Darold Booton

Miss Katherine Dang

Mr. David Holmes

Mr. James V. Kilkenny

Mrs. Lois Wehrman Miller

Mrs. Barbara B. Rose

Miss Rosalie June Slater

Mrs. Ruth J. Smith

Mr. Charles Hull Wolfe

James B. Rose

INTRODUCTION

BY ROSALIE JUNE SLATER

Thou shalt raise up the foundations of many generations. (Isaiah 58:12)

With the publication of *A Guide to American Christian Education for the Home and School, The Principle Approach*, the ministry of James B. Rose will become available to many thousands of American Christian parents, teachers, principals, and pastors.

Like our *Pilgrims* of the seventeenth century, James Rose has truly been a Pilgrim by his *faith and steadfastness* in identifying and establishing the foundations of American Christian character, conscience and curriculum, so needed in education today in order to preserve our Christian Constitutional Republic.

Like our *Puritans*, he has been a Scripturist, and has demonstrated *diligence and industry* in "looking to the Word of God as his sole and universal directory," the *source* and *seedbed* of every field of study.

Like our *Patriots* of the eighteenth century, James Rose has endeavored to provide the means by which parents and teachers might, by their *resistance to tyranny*, the tyranny of socially prescribed goals of education, become *obedient to God*, and accept God's historic purpose for our nation as a basic ingredient of American Christian Education.

And truly, like our nineteenth century *Pathfinders* and *Pioneers*, James Rose has been willing to take to the trail himself, *teaching* and *learning how to teach*, every area of American Christian Education in the home, church and school. Leading the way by precept and practice, both James and Barbara Rose can testify to the role which American families must accept – if home is to become once again the *educational center* of this nation.

This volume represents a unique effort in American Education which has been in progress for the past three decades. It is the effort to restore to American Christians the knowledge of America's Christian History and America's role in the History of Liberty. It is impossible to teach the historic impact of the Gospel upon our nation's *character, curriculum* and *Constitution*, by modern progressive teaching techniques. Therefore, the restoration of The Principle Approach is a major contribution of James Rose's ministry to Christians in America who wish to once again both learn and teach that Biblical philosophy of education which formed us "one nation under God."

This volume, *A Guide to American Christian Education for the Home and School, The Principle Approach*, also represents the *first three generations* of this program. The *first* generation appears in the documentation of America's Christian History and the relationship of Christianity to our character and our Constitution. The volumes compiled by Miss Verna M. Hall, *The Christian History of the Constitution of the United States of America, Christian Self-Government*, and *Christian Self-Government with Union*, and *The Christian History of the American Revolution, Consider and Ponder* comprise the first volumes of the series. The *first* generation of this program also appears in the identification of the Principle Approach as our historic method of Biblical reasoning and writing, as expressed in *Teaching and Learning America's Christian History, The Principle Approach*. The *second* generation appears in the ministry of Mr. Rose as he established the first pilot school for this program, taught parents and teachers across the nation, and defined a new role for administrators as Head Master Teachers. It was at this time that he began to *record* the results of his research on how to teach this program.

The *third* generation of the Christian History program appears in the work of the teachers represented in this volume, many taught by Mr. Rose. They have developed their subjects and have also been willing to learn how to record or write up their teaching in The Principle Approach. Many of these teachers head up schools or ministries of their own as a result of their *renewal* in American Christian Education. Most all of the associated teachers in this volume are parents first. Their individual concerns for their own children prompted them to accept America's Christian History as the *missing ingredient* which, once restored, enabled them to take dominion over the critical area of American Education, *source and seedbed* of the American character and Constitution.

When James Rose began to restore the foundations of American Christian Education he had the support and encouragement of a pastor and his wife who had established a Christian school in order to preserve the character of their own sons. Pastor Elliott Paulsen and Janice Paulsen gave many years of support and teaching to their school and were gratified with the results of character and learning which blessed their own family. When James Rose accepted the principalship of this school, he also accepted the challenge presented by his vision for an American Christian School, based upon his early study and work with America's Christian History. It was his love for God's Providential Hand in our history and his acceptance of the Principle Approach in our colonial education which provided him with a framework with which to begin.

Had James Rose been able to see the long road ahead of him, or had he ever imagined the degree to which our *original foundations* of character, conscience, curriculum and Constitution had been eroded, he might have hesitated at taking on such a large task. But God is merciful. He only asks us to take one step at a time – in faith. And if a man or a woman has "caught the vision" of their individual ministry, then, usually, they will go forward, waiting on their Great Deliverer and Restorer of paths, to guide and direct them. James B. Rose was such a man, and Barbara Rose, his faithful and supportive wife, was such a woman. Walking and working together in the pilot school for the Christian History Program, and ultimately adding the testimony of the work with their own children, Jim and Barbara have contributed a pathway of leadership for those willing to follow.

LAYING THE FOUNDATIONS OF THE PRINCIPLE APPROACH

The first division of *A Guide to American Christian Education* is properly entitled the *Rudiments* of the program. It is perhaps the most important section of this volume. Here James Rose carefully lays the foundations of The Principle Approach which must be restored if we are to see the continuance of this Republic. Until the individual American Christian learns America's Christian History and is willing, once again, to accept the stewardship of the civil and religious liberty which the Lord has placed in our hands – our homes, our churches, and our schools, he will not be prepared to develop the foundations of character and curriculum needed to insure the perpetuation of the world's first Christian Constitutional Republic.

The schools of a nation and its philosophy of government are inseparable. If a nation has a *totalitarian*, oppressive form of government, ruling from the supremacy of the state over the individual's life, liberty and property, it will require in its citizens a character of *subservience* and *dependence*. Fidelity to state goals – and the aggrandizement of the state, are achieved through education. State education must produce in its curriculum and methodology a *character* to support its philosophy of government. In a *democracy*, the will of the people may determine the decisions of government. In such nations education will work to produce a character of *cooperation* rather than *competition*, of *toleration* rather than *individualism*, of *group* values, rather than personal conviction.

In America, the world's *first* Christian Constitutional Republic, the Biblical foundations of liberty with law require a totally different kind of character. Since our form of government was designed to *preserve* the life, liberty, property and productivity of each individual, in order to function – we must have a character with the *capacity for self-*

government, productivity and *voluntary union.* How to achieve academically these two aspects of American Christian Constitutional government – the *external* goal of limited, representative government – the *internal* goal of American Christian character – is the subject of this book.

In Section One of this book, James Rose endeavors to define the Principle Approach – what it is – and what it is not. He also contrasts it philosophically with Child-Centered and Subject-Centered education. He provides us with a method of determining the Biblical and historical basis of the fundamental principles of America's Christian History. He demonstrates how our efforts to think and act governmentally as Christ-governed individuals, in our homes, churches, schools, business and professional fields, in all areas of our lives – reflect our educational philosophy. As James Rose takes us through the Christian History of America we learn how our Founding Fathers and Mothers were able to make the Bible their educational and political textbook. We learn how they researched, reasoned from, related and recorded, all that the Word could teach them, in every field.

The impact of Jesus Christ upon men and nations is evident when we learn that the Providential Approach to history is still in effect – just as it was along the Chain of Christianity moving Westward – just as it was when our nation was founded. This is what our Colonial Americans believed! This is what our Patriots and Pioneers believed! It is only in twentieth century America that we have diminished our view of the sovereignty of God. And as we have done this – we have also diminished our conviction of the power of Christ in our nation.

As James Rose explores the *rudiments* of each of the seven principles that identify both America's Christian Constitutional Republic and our individual capacity for self-government, property and voluntary union, we understand how important it is for each parent or teacher to lay a Biblical, historical, governmental and educational foundation *before* they build the superstructure of curriculum.

HOME GOVERNMENT WITH GRACE

Section Two of *A Guide to American Christian Education, The Principle Approach,* deals with America's most important institution – the home. God's first institution has always been our most critical institution. Early pastors were not afraid of stating unequivocally that the Christian home was a "preparation for both the state and the church." The Christian Home had its bearing upon "the prosperity of both." The Christian Home in America has as its role "the development of individual

character and happiness in the church and state, in time and eternity." Therefore, "home-training and nurture" are essential, for the Christian home "lays the foundation for civil and political character," "prepares the social element and taste" and determines "what we are as a nation as well as individuals." (Rev. S. Phillips, 1859, *The Christian Home*)

America's history reveals the distinction of the American Christian home in the formation of the character of the men and women who were God's instruments to bring forth civil and religious liberty. And never before has the role of *women* been so critical as in America. Our own Lydia – Lydia Sigourney, wrote in the nineteenth century:

"In our own republic, man, invested by his Maker with the right to reign...has generously lavished on women the means of knowledge... Demand of her as a debt the highest excellence which she is capable of attaining... Make her accountable for the character of the next generation ... Gird her with the whole armour of education and piety, and see if she be not faithful to her children, to her country, and to her God." *Christian History,* pp. 409-410

The role of teaching begins as soon as the child is conceived, and Barbara Rose's account of applying the Principle Approach in the raising of their children is inspirational, joyous, and most instructive. What an encouragement to other parents to *stand fast in the liberty wherewith Christ hath made us free!* Do not become *entangled again with the yoke of bondage* (Galatians 5:1) to the many *worldly* elements which seek to rob home of its *sacred* elements and its *serious devotion* to teaching children Biblically, historically, governmentally, and academically.

Barbara's delightful recording of the early years of raising a family with the help of the Principle Approach includes many areas not yet evident in the character of most American Christian children. Secular education, and secular patterns of conduct have brought so many *ungracious* and *thoughtless* habits into home life that have not been effectively replaced with Gospel government. Matthew Henry, the Prince of Commentators on the Holy Scriptures, reminds us of the purpose of home education in his commentary on 1 Peter 1:15,16:

"But as he which hath called you is holy, so be ye holy in all manner of conversation; Because it is written, Be ye holy; for I am holy." "Complete holiness is the desire and duty of every Christian...in all civil and religious affairs, in every condition, prosperous or reverse; towards all people, friends and enemies;

xv

in all our intercourse and business still we must be holy... The Old Testament commands are to be studied and obeyed in the times of the New Testament." (Henry, Vol. vi, page 1011.

The *graciousness* of our Lord Jesus Christ is a key to the tone of an American Christian home. Barbara Rose speaks of making the effort to teach children graciousness in speech, in manners, and in conversation, or life style. It is important that our children know the proper table manners – so that they will always be children of grace at meals. We need to help our children to pay attention to the adults that visit our home – to be genuinely interested in what they have to say and what their visit might contribute. We need to instruct our children in the proper and appropriate dress and attire for different occasions in the home. And what do we bring into our homes in the way of periodicals and current publications? Do these complement the fine libraries we are endeavoring to establish for their more formal education?

Also, this is a day of *thanklessness*. How many relatives and friends find themselves disappointed when they give gifts to the young. Can we teach our children the importance of correspondence – prompt letters written in response to gifts or invitations which have been received or enjoyed? The Christian home in America has a battle to exclude the heathen characteristics of secular homes.

Neither James nor Barbara Rose claim to have achieved the goal of a home totally "holy" in all its manners and conversation any more than any other parents in America can claim this accomplishment. In this section of their book they share their aspirations and record their individual struggles in their efforts to establish a truly American Christian home for these times.

In order to restore the Christian home in America to its role as the *educational center* of the nation, the application of the Principle Approach needs also to extend to the first instruction of children in the basic principles of America's Providential History. As they learn to accept their *God-given individuality* and are willing to work at developing and producing a responsible *property* of time and talents; as they understand their obligations under *home-government*, functioning according to the legislative, executive, and judicial functions of love ruling and obeying according to God's law; as they work joyfully without peevishness in *voluntary association* with the family members towards the goals of home – they will be expressing the capacity for *Christian self-government* so badly needed in this nation.

As the great Home School movement has accepted the scriptural heritage and admonition to educate their children in God's Word, what a heritage they have historically. What a witness America is to the impact of Jesus Christ upon men and nations! Can we afford to neglect this heritage as we construct curriculum? Should we continue to ignore the Hand of God in our history? Or should we build an American curriculum from the Christian treasury of our nation?

In the beginning of the section entitled "American Christian Education" from the volume compiled by Verna M. Hall, entitled *The Christian History of the American Revolution: Consider and Ponder,* occurs the following sermon, preached and recorded. These verses precede:

"He established a testimony in Jacob, and appointed a law in Israel, which he commanded our fathers, that they should make them known to their children. That the generation to come might know them, even the children which should be born, who should arise and declare them to their children. That they might set their hope in God, and not forget the works of God, but keep his commandments. (Psalm Lxxxviii, 5-7)

"The importance of the rising generation, has engaged the attention of the wise and good, in all ages... The inspired writer of this Psalm, impressed deeply with the subject, calls on us to attend to the words of his mouth, even the words which had been received from the fathers which, said he, we will not hide from their children, *'shewing to the generations to come the praises of the Lord, and his strength and his wonderful works.' (PSALM 78:4)"* Pastor Levi Hart, *The Importance of Parental Fidelity in the Education of Children,* 1792.

May we not approach the school in the home, with these words from Benson Lossing, historian of a century ago, when he pleaded:

"Above all, let our youth be instructed in all that appertains to the vital principles of our Republic ... They should be led by the hand of history into every patriotic council; upon every battle field; through every scene of trial and hardship, of hope and despondency, of triumph and defeat, where our fathers acted and endured so that when we

'Go ring the bells and fire the guns,
And fling the starry banner out –
Cry FREEDOM! till our little ones
Send back their tiny shout:'
Whittier

our children may not, in their ignorance, ask *'What mean ye by this service?' (Exodus 12:26),"* Consider and Ponder, p. 255

BUILDING CONSTITUTIONAL CHARACTER
AT HOME

Section three of James Rose's *A Guide to American Christian Education, the Principle Approach,* deals with the school developed at home in accordance with the Principle Approach. He proposes, through the subjects chosen and the methods described, to help you accomplish the following:

Develop in your students a character capable of acting from the Biblical principles of individual Christian self-government, property and voluntary union;

Become knowledgeable of Key Individuals in history who have made their contribution to civil and religious liberty;

Become knowledgeable of Key Institutions of government throughout history and of our distinctive American Christian Constitution; and

Become masters of those subjects which are basic to the perpetuation of the Christian idea of man in government in America.

Please refer to TOWARD BUILDING AN AMERICAN CONSTITUTIONAL CHARACTER in the Chart on p. xviii.

Mr. Rose begins this section with a discussion of what the Principle Approach can mean to home school education in America. He raises some questions which need to be answered as parents consider this program for their children. What can the Principle Approach add to what is already available in the "supermart" of home school education? In fact, the Principle Approach will take more time for it does require that parents do more than teach what has been pre-planned for them. They must learn the course content that they are going to teach. And in fact, as they help select this course content, they will find that they can make their own contributions to what their children will study. This is a natural consequence of learning principles, leading ideas, and their Biblical and historical origin. Once you begin to study from this approach you discover an inspiration and receive a satisfaction that no other educational program can offer. So, rather than less time, the Principle Approach is going to take more time, and parents need to consider what advantages they will gain by this investment.

Our lives today represent a choice of motion. Will we be moved by God or by man? Will we endeavor to accelerate the tempo, or "rate of speed" at which we try to teach and learn? Are we willing to slow ourselves down and get into the rhythm of God's universe? Can we discover God's laws of motion which should govern our lives? We in America today still incorporate much of the Pavlovian stimulus-response into our teaching and learning. But, our goal in the Principle Approach to home school learning is to produce a *reflective* character, one able to listen to the "still small voice" of conscience which enables us to act appropriately in any circumstance. This was true of David as he came to the camp of Israel where the Giant Goliath threatened. Yet, because he had been prepared by God, he was able to listen and to act in God's timetable. So, too, did many of the Biblical and historical characters who had learned to respond to the internal first, rather than to the external events of their lives.

In the Principle Approach we must indeed slow ourselves down, put off the old patterns of secular learning which sometimes seek to propel us into fast *"fact mastery."* The emphasis here is to put our learning into a framework of principles and leading ideas and then relate the facts to the unfoldment of those principles and leading ideas in the subject. We will become more effective learners as we teach ourselves to become more reflective.

DEVELOPING AN AMERICAN CHRISTIAN
CURRICULUM AT HOME, DISTINCTIVES OF
THE PRINCIPLE APPROACH

This chart represents the effort to put together some of the major elements of curriculum which should characterize your home school program as you begin to incorporate the Principle Approach. We are so used to looking at the pieces and parts of our education that it is not until we reach the end of formal learning in the secondary school, perhaps in preparation for college or university, that we look at the whole of what we have covered.

Again, as we are exhorted to see both the Alpha and Omega of Biblical truth, so here we seek to anticipate what should characterize our planning as we look at both elementary and high school learning. How does what is begun in the early years of schooling continue to deepen and to expand as we contemplate the Biblical purpose of each area of the curriculum? Also, we have not related the structure of courses to each other, and that is important, for, while we distinguish each subject, we also recognize the basic unity of all subjects in the setting of the Westward flow of His Story.

As we discussed in our review of the Kindergarten program, the restoration of academics to young learners allows them to enjoy the satisfaction and accomplishment which the "play" kindergarten does not emphasize. So, as we approach what should be the first year of formal school, the Kindergarten, we also become aware of what both parents and children can anticipate, for the academic

DEVELOPING AN AMERICAN CHRISTIAN CURRICULUM AT HOME
DISTINCTIVES OF THE PRINCIPLE APPROACH

CURRICULUM
The Academic Kindergarten Lays the Foundation for all Subjects

LITERACY

Reading, Writing, Grammar, Spelling Handwriting

"Queen" of the Curriculum

The preservation of Constitutional Liberty requires literacy

THE ART OF TYPING; COM-PUTER SCIENCE

Tools for developing Christian self-government, property and productivity

BIBLE

The American text-book for Christian self-government and education

For the Law was given by Moses, but grace and truth came by Jesus Christ. John 1:17

NATURAL SCIENCE

Unity of Biblical principles in the Works of God; history of sciences on the Chain of Christianity moving westward

ARITHMETIC

Learning by reasoning not by rote; how used in God's Providential History

ALGEBRA

Identifying the Biblical principles; number and the dominion mandate; mathematical links in the history of Liberty

ECONOMICS

Rudiments of an American Christian Economy; enterprise and character in our Christian Constitutional Republic

HISTORY

Elementary: Providential Links of Liberty, Creation to the Constitution

Junior High: Universal History, *Jesus Christ* focal point of History

Senior High: Six major periods contribute to civil and religious liberty in America

RUDIMENTS OF AMERICA'S CHRISTIAN HISTORY AND GOVERNMENT

A basic course in character and government

LITERATURE

The Bible, *Source of Literature and Liberty*

Our English Heritage of Literature and Liberty

Restoring the Literature and character of American Liberty

MUSIC

Music on the Chain of Christianity; American Christian Music and Liberty

GEOGRAPHY & CARTOGRAPHY

God's formation of the individuality of the continents and their function in nature and History

Map-making

THE ARTS

First principles of drawing, painting, design; contributions of American Christian Arts

METHODOLOGY

4 R-ING YOUR SUBJECT — INDIVIDUAL TEACHER AND STUDENT NOTEBOOKS — CLASS CONSTITUTIONS

TOWARD BUILDING AN AMERICAN CONSTITUTIONAL CHARACTER

BIBLICAL

Learning to act on principles of character and government

HISTORICAL

Study of key individuals and their contributions to civil and religious liberty

GOVERNMENTAL

Learning Key Institutions of Liberty as Christian self-government with union unfolds on the American Continent

ACADEMIC

Mastering subjects basic to perpetuating America's Christian Constitutional Republic

© Rosalie June Slater

Kindergarten lays the foundation for all subjects—and is instrumental toward building an American Christian Constitutional character.

How this is accomplished is well documented by Mrs. Miller's "An American Christian Kindergarten" on pages 163 through 199 of this volume.

It is not difficult to see that beginning in Kindergarten and continuing on through the primary grades "Literacy" would be a primary emphasis. It may also need to be re-introduced at the high school level when pupils appear not well-grounded in the basics of reading, writing, grammar, spelling, to say nothing of handwriting. One of the most striking contrasts between contemporary education and that of our Colonial and Constitutional periods was the ability of our Founding generations to read, reason and write or record. They were led by pastors who contributed greatly to the Christian literature of America in their sermons and often in their contribution to our state papers of government. So, the preservation of our Constitutional Liberty requires that our people become much more capable of handling prose in their reading and writing. The quality of American writing has declined drastically.

It follows that the use of tools of literacy, especially the typewriter, can be introduced in upper elementary, so that our students can enhance their written output as they pursue their studies. If the computer becomes a tool for reasoning and writing, then it also can be introduced at an earlier level, provided it does not fall into the uses of play and games which tend to be hypnotic.

Bible study in the Principle Approach will be greatly expanded beyond doctrinal instruction. It becomes part of every subject taught, and in history, literature and science, it plays a major role. It is taught in Literature every semester as the Source of Literary types and the foundation of characterization and plot themes. In history the English Bible is the source of our governmental principles. In the sciences, the early scientists sought to find the nature and character of God in their particular field. The history of America is inseparable from the history of the Bible.

The mathematical subjects once again bring us to consider the God who is Sovereign in the Universe and whose principles compel us to marvel how there is room for all that He has created. We can only begin to fathom God's immensity by measurement, and by understanding the principles which have unfolded from these subjects.

The practical uses of economics once again remind us of the mercies of God in allowing us to put to productive use our resources—both internal and external. Beginning with simple lessons in the early years, we have an opportunity to teach our children something of God's infinite resources and how others as well as ourselves can make prudent use of them in our diverse life styles and individual enterprises.

Providential History can be restored in one generation if we begin at home with the youngest child to teach our Biblical and historical heritage. While we enjoy the dramatic presentations of history in song, story, and picture, we must also communicate the serious nature of our American Constitutional Republic. The whole world looks to us to preserve this asylum of liberty—and we must once again accept the responsibility for stewardship of God's gift to us of its blessings and possibilities.

As we teach history—His Story—so we must teach the character which made us a nation. By our own life practice and by the many, many examples which exist in our original sources, we can restore the purpose and promise of this nation to each generation. The course on *Rudiments of America's Christian History and Government* is an individually designed course—for all levels and all ages. Take this student handbook and "wrought out" your own beginning course on how we should live and govern ourselves today in America. You will find great interest as you discuss contemporary challenges in the light of Biblical and historical principles.

We characterize Literature as the *handmaid* of history. What a joy to transform what we have called literature—simply because it was printed matter—into the great and little books which should become our companions for life. This is a joyous enterprise, one that can be enjoyed by your whole family together.

Music as it was brought to our shores has a unique heritage, for while we accepted the great composers of Christian Europe as foundational, it was the individual composer in America who brought forth the music of a new continent, founded upon Biblical principles of self- and civil government. The Moravians from Germany started off a century of great music. And we had our American hymns and patriotic songs, as well as the work of men like Stephen Foster, Edward McDowell, and others. So, we view our American contribution to music in the light of our Constitutional Liberty—by and for the individual.

In the arts, our children can begin to learn the first principles of how to see as an artist sees, so that drawing becomes representational of what is God's universe, not man's impressionism. And painting and design can be learned Biblically as well as historically. Our own early painters of both the Colonial and Constitutional periods painted character, painted historical events, painted what they learned from God's Word. We have some fine periods in American Art, like the Hudson River School. We have some excellent periods of architecture, like our Federal Period, still visible in the wonderful houses of Salem, Massachusetts, home of Nathaniel Bowditch. Every field of the American Arts is influenced by our Biblical beginnings and should be a joy to identify and recapture for our children. Do you know American needlework, American furniture design, or American pottery? Begin now to explore these fields and look for the "preeminence of Christ" in all fields.

We cannot ignore the fact that America is a nation made up of all nations. As one of our nineteenth century writers put it:

"(Here) the Englishman, the German, the Frenchman, the Italian, the Scandinavian, the Asiatic, and the African all meet as Equals. (Here) they are free to speak, to think, and to act. They bring the common contributions of character, energy and activity to the support and enlargement of a common country, and the spread of its influence and enlightenment through all the lands of their origin." *Christian History*, p. 8

God also blessed us with the kind of geography which was designed for a united people. As Arnold Guyot, first professor of geography in America, at Princeton, wrote:

"The structure of this continent is characterized by a unity and simplicity as striking as is the diversity of Europe... Its vast plains, overflowing with natural wealth, are turned towards Europe, and its largest rivers discharge into the Atlantic; while its lofty mountains, and less fertile lands, are removed far towards its western shores... Each continent has, therefore, a well-defined individuality, which fits it for an especial function... The conclusion is irresistible – that the entire globe is a grand organism, every feature of which is the outgrowth of a definite plan of the all-wise Creator for the education of the human family, and the manifestation of his own glory." *Christian History*, pp. 4–5

How wonderful to be free from the economic determinism of the secular historians who view geography as causative rather than a stage for Christ His Story of men and nations. So with geography we can once again both study the field of Cartography or map-making as it has come down to us through the ages and as it has been recorded by the explorers who came to the New World. And as we learn how to draw our own maps again, what an encouragement to our students who in their time will have much greater opportunity to travel and to study the land of liberty.

As we learn the methodology of the Principle Approach we can see that it is basically composed of Mr. Rose's 4 R-ing, which allows much individual teacher initiative, but provides for an orderly outcome of course content. The Notebook Approach for the teacher gives opportunity for unity of philosophy and diversity of individual teacher expression. For students the Notebook Approach enables them, with guidance from their teachers, to become productive researchers and writers. This program has the answer to the diversity of your students' abilities so that a parent can be teaching the same subjects but can provide for those children who would be able to go deeper or develop additional projects from the same basic philosophy and content.

And what about Class Constitutions as a method of the Principle Approach? In our Christian walk learning to be self-governed is a key to the self-government of the nation. When John Wyclif was led by the Lord to give the people of England their first English Bible, he wrote: "This Bible is for the government of the people." The Christian states: *I can of mine own self do nothing.* John 5:30, but *I can do all things through Christ which strengtheneth me."* Philippians 4:13

In the twentieth century even Christian homes and schools have relinquished the responsibility to teach the Biblical principles of government to their children. Pastor S. Phillips, writing on *The Christian Home* a century ago, reminds us of our Biblical obligation to this field of home government:

"Abraham instituted in his household a model system of home-discipline. 'I know him,' says God, 'that he will command his children and his household after him, and they shall keep the ways of the Lord to do justice and judgment.' He was not a tyrant; his comrades did not bear the rough sternness of a despot, neither did his power wear the scowl of vengeance. But these bore the firmness and decision of love tempered and directed by the law of Christian duty and responsibility... Hence, his children respected his station, venerated his name, appreciated his love, confided in his sympathy, and yielded a voluntary obedience to his commands; for they discerned in them the blessing; and when offenses came, they bent in the spirit of loving submission and pupilage, under his rod of correction, and kissed it as the means of their reformation and culture." *Teaching and Learning,* p. 28

Our children learn how to be self-governed at home and at school as we work together to determine our areas of responsibility. That is the purpose of the Class Constitution. From the earliest years teachers and students identify their individual goals of self-government. And as they, like the Pilgrims on board the *Mayflower,* agree to work towards certain goals of accomplishment, they can be reminded of these *recorded* goals, and of their consent to endeavor to achieve them. This is where parental guidance and instruction in God's Word helps us walk with the Lord in all things. Every classroom and every home school should compose their own Constitutions for their individual goals. See *Teaching and Learning,* The Christian Principle of Self-Government, especially the Key to this principle on pp. 184–190.

Lastly, the goal of American Christian Education is to choose and master the subjects basic to perpetuating the world's only Christian Constitutional Republic–the guardian of our liberties, both civil and religious. But, we are primarily concerned with the heart of the principal, the teacher, and the student–and those parents who have accepted the Lord's call to be the first two of these offices. That means character. But not just Christian character. By now we must have learned that God gave us as individuals living on this continent a special stewardship of government–directly dependent upon and related to the Gospel of Jesus Christ. Inasmuch as the whole world looks to us to be faithful to that stewardship and not to let the forces of godless tyranny prevail in the world, perhaps now we are ready to pick up our place on the Chain of Christianity, and forge new links to preserve and extend the Biblical principles of character and government necessary to preserve the blessings of liberty.

Less than one hundred years ago our pastors were among our best teachers of history. One of these pastors, David Gregg, wrote about our responsibility to America and to the world:

"We demand America for Christ for the world's sake.

". . . The responsibility laid upon her, therefore, is a double one; first and supremely, to keep the fountains of her own intelligence and virtue and religion pure for the sake of the native-born in the land; and, second, to ply with all the forces of Christian learning and religion the thousands of the unevangelized who have come to her shores, that they may send back to their old homes, in the form of letters and newspapers and earnest appeals, the blessed gospel of the Son of God to work as a regenerating and converting power in the different fatherlands across the sea.

"All this being true, it is the veriest truism to say that America taken for Christ means the nations of the world far and near taken for Christ;

America a Christian nation means a mighty witness for God among all lands of the earth.

"My fellow-men, our country is the battleground on which the conflicts of the ages are to be fought and decided. . . In the Christianizing of our nation the Republic has its life at stake, society its order, labor its reward, home its happiness, and the world its future." *Teaching and Learning,* pp. 44–45

As you begin to develop your American Christian Curriculum at home with the distinctives of the Principle Approach you will be, like Nehemiah of old, rebuilding the wall that has crumbled in America under the falling away of American Christians. Let us pray that we are now willing to accept our stewardship of "one nation under God," and that all of these courses in our home school will be designed for "the glory of God and the advancement of the Christian faith," protected by a revitalized American Christian Constitutional Republic.

LEADERSHIP IN BUILDING A LIVING CURRICULUM FROM THE CHRISTIAN TREASURY OF OUR NATION

Section Four of *A Guide to American Christian Education* is the practical achievement of the ministry of James Rose in his work with teachers and curriculum development in the Principle Approach. The teachers represented in this section are indeed like their Master Teacher. They have been willing to become *Pilgrims* in this program, taking the first steps in restoring to the academic curriculum its Biblical and historical foundations. Like our early *Puritans,* they knew that their title to the property of their subjects in the curriculum depended upon their individual mastery and productivity. In this they "cast off the yoke of anti-Christian bondage" of programmed learning and pre-fabricated curricula in which they had no contribution–a matter of their own Liberty of Conscience. In proportion as they became part of the character and content of their subjects their testimony to their students has had greater impact.

Again, like our *Patriots,* these teachers recognized that they needed to be *true representatives* of those Biblical and historical principles which built our nation. They have concluded that they could *no longer ignore* the Christian treasury of our nation in the construction of curriculum.

They have been willing *Pioneers* and *Pathfinders* in breaking trail, finding the needed resources, developing their individual subject presentations and mapping the route *in writing* for others. To each one of these individuals we would like to express our appreciation and to thank the Lord that He inspired and strengthened them for their ministries.

JAMES B. ROSE

We thank James Rose, who first caught the vision of making the Principle Approach a reality in the total curriculum. His work began with the development of his own courses of study in *Government, Economics*, in *Reading*, in *The Rudiments of America's Christian History and Government* and in *American Literature*. As he learned how to organize the essential ingredients needed to construct his courses in the Principle Approach he was able to lead his teachers into the Biblical and historical foundations which would enable them to understand how the knowledge of America's Christian History makes every subject distinct.

The greatest loss to teachers in American Christian schools has been the loss of their Head Master teachers. As the contemporary role of the principal has been transformed into that of an administrator, it has been necessary to call in supervisors—individuals other than the principal to assist teachers. James Rose has always been an *academic shepherd* of his flock. From the time of the first interview he worked with his teachers individually on a scheduled and regular basis, helping them to deepen their Biblical, historical and academic understanding of the program. With his total faculty, again on a regular basis, James Rose encouraged mutual presentations of the application of the Principle Approach by teachers to their subjects. In this way, by sharing with each other, teachers, from Kindergarten through High School, could see the relationship of all subjects to a basic philosophy of education. There was a *unity* of Biblical principles and Christian character and a *diversity* of subject applications.

Each summer Mr. Rose gave specific assignments so that his teachers might *redeem* their earlier education and *reclaim* it for the Lord by their individual research and writing. The Normal Schools and Teacher's Colleges have robbed the American teacher of the self-education and self-government which has always been basic to American education.

This entire volume is a testimony to Mr. Rose's determination to master for himself and for others the "art" of writing once again. We know that one reason why our students are so often bored with history is that historians have lost their "literary art." And the loss of writing in schools is now reflected in our loss of those thrilling historical novels which did so much to create an excitement about learning history. To restore the ability to

research, reason, relate and record with God's principle of individuality is a basic ingredient of The Christian History Program. To the degree that this has been accomplished here is largely through the patient guidance and persistent help of James Rose.

STEPS IN PRINCIPLE APPROACH CURRICULUM

Jim Rose leads us into a consideration of the Principle Approach as it is applied to the development of curriculum. What are the distinctions of this approach—especially in course content and in the methods of teaching and learning? A first step in the Principle Approach is always to consult Noah Webster's original *American Dictionary of the English Language*—"the 1828." As we look up the word CURRICULUM, we are encouraged to learn that it refers to the identification of *principles* in a subject field, to an *orderly method of proceeding*—and, most important, to *a way of life or conduct*. All three of these aspects are found in Mr. Rose's development of the Principle Approach. These steps as outlined in the PREFACE to Curriculum for an American Christian School, if followed consistently, allow teachers to become masters of what they teach. And this step by step approach will also yield the following:

1. The WHOLE view of a subject, not segmented;
2. The UNITY of all subjects in the curriculum, united Biblically, historically, governmentally;
3. GOD'S PROVIDENCE in the subject as the subject contributed to the History of Liberty—both civil and religious;
4. The opportunity to develop the Christian Character qualities which established and are needed to maintain our American Christian Republic—in both teachers and students.

Mr. Rose's *especially developed technique* in the Principle Approach is what he calls *How to 4 R a Subject*. This enables teachers, and parents becoming teachers, to proceed in an "orderly" manner in the researching, reasoning, relating, and recording of their subject fields. Mr. Rose patiently leads the student teacher, new or experienced, down a path, which if followed, brings immediate results. Jim Rose's method of 4 R-ing a subject also will make a change in *the way of life or conduct* of a teacher. It will have a new impact upon the lives of students who become the beneficiaries of inspired teaching. It is a dominion-oriented quality of both teaching and learning.

In order to exemplify the 4 R-ing practice, James Rose takes the subject of *Reading*. This is an excellent subject to begin with since reading ability, or the lack of it, has been a calculated defect in American education. Our nation first went off its Biblical standard of education in the nineteenth century, separating from the Providential history of America, and thus falling away from our stewardship of the civil and religious liberties entrusted to us by our forefathers and mothers. Our Lord prayed before his crucifixion: *"I pray not that thou shouldst take them out of the world, but that thou shouldst keep them from the evil. They are not of the world, even as I am not of the world. Sanctify them through thy truth: thy word is truth. As thou has sent me into the world, even so have I also sent them into the world. And for their sakes I sanctify myself, that they also might be sanctified through the truth."* John 17:15–19

The role of the pastor was the role of leadership in our Colonial history. These pastors were mindful of the fact that America was an asylum of liberty—both civil and religious. But those who fled here did not build a *segregated society* for religious liberty. Rather, they began immediately to translate the Christian idea of man into government, for the benefit of all Americans.

We go off the Biblical standard of American education when we *ignore* our Biblical past and the contribution which it made to those "blessings of liberty" which we still enjoy today. What has happened today in both *public* and *private* education is that America's Christian History has been left out of the curriculum. This means that, generally, Christians will not have accepted responsibility for the "one nation under God" which was formed on Biblical principles of government and depends for its proper functioning on Christian character.

How did this falling away from our Biblical heritage of self- and civil government affect our teaching of *Reading?* The role of the pastor in education became diminished as he pulled away from teaching and relating the Bible to all fields. So, in education we succumbed to a non-principled, non-phonetic teaching of reading. Since learning to research the Bible, reason from Biblical truths and principles, relate the Bible to all fields, and to always record one's findings, we did not make the Bible our first goal in learning to read. Mr. Rose documents how the "Look–Say" non-phonetic method of teaching children to read gradually replaced phonetic reading. The remarkable work of Noah Webster, Founding Father of American Christian Education, after the establishment of our Constitution, had given us a firm foundation in *Literacy,* in *Law,* or the understanding of Liberty with Law, and in *Literature.* Noah Webster is our character model for an American Christian educator. He knew the importance of teaching the principles of reading, spelling, and grammar, so that Americans might be actively engaged in making a contribution to the Republic. Without *Literacy* we lose our Constitutional character and begin to take on the *character for socialism.* Thus Noah Webster's spellers, grammars, and readers were all designed to perpetuate character qualities for a Republic.

Noah Webster's histories were also Bible based. His *History of the United States* began with Adam and Eve, and ended with a study of the Constitution of the United States of America. In the Preface to this history Noah Webster wrote: "The brief exposition of the constitution of the United States, will unfold to young persons the principles of republican government; and it is the sincere desire of the writer that our citizens should early understand that the genuine source of correct republican principles is the BIBLE, particularly the New Testament or the Christian religion."

In this same volume was added a section entitled ADVICE TO THE YOUNG. Here Noah Webster taught the first duties of children to God and their parents—obedience to God's commands. "The character of God, his holy attributes, and perfect law, constitute the only models and rules of excellence and true honor."

Noah Webster dealt also with the way of life or conduct appropriate to a republic—not extravagant—but productive. Then he discussed the importance of how to vote for those men who would hold public office for he said: "If a republican government fails to secure public prosperity and happiness, it must be because the citizens neglect the divine commands, and elect bad men to make and administer the laws. Intriguing men can never be safely trusted." *History of the United States,* p. 308. It also contained *A Moral Catechism,* or *Lessons for Saturday,* and *A Federal Catechism,* containing a short Explanation of the Constitution of the United States of America, and the Principles of Government.

But the Christians in America became careless of preserving those foundations of liberty which had made us "one nation under God." We lost our concern for the nation while we were enjoying personal liberties. So, when the new custodians of public education came into control of the schools, we did not provide a vigorous enough leadership to prevent the erosion of our Biblical, governmental, and finally our academic character—*a character for a republic.* What Horace Mann and others were able to accomplish, although it took them one hundred years, was to form a new secular character—*a character for socialism.* But this was only due to the "falling away" of Christians in our nation.

At this time, too, we began to exchange our excellent phonetic teaching of reading for a "Look–Say" approach, which each year brought down our level of literacy to our present situation of predominate functional illiteracy. Unfortunately, many Christian schools in America have incorporated the "Look–Say" method of reading. But for a Principle Approach educational program it is essential to start off with a reading program which will enable students to master the basic principles of phonetic reading and become dominion-oriented rather than to be frustrated by the inadequacies of a non-principled approach.

For this reason Mr. Rose presents us with two suggested reading programs: *The Little Patriots Series* by Guyla Nelson and Saundra Scovill, and *The Writing Road to Reading*, by Romalda Spalding. A brief summary of the former is given here and the latter is discussed in Lois Miller's Kindergarten Curriculum.

DR. GUYLA NELSON
Curriculum Director, Phonics Specialist

Miss Hall and I met Dr. Guyla Nelson in Denver, Colorado, when she and her husband, Dr. Ed Nelson, pastor of South Sheridan Baptist Church, founded Silver State Baptist schools. Guyla Nelson had for many years been concerned with the field of Literacy. Her own excellent education in English – grammar, spelling, composition and literature – and her experience in teaching these subjects, convinced her that teachers needed to receive special and particular preparation before they were ready to teach any of these areas of the curriculum. Beginning reading was the critical stage of learning. All other subjects would flow from a mastery of phonetic reading.

Dr. Guyla Nelson had expected that Christian schools and colleges would adequately prepare teachers for the subject of literacy, but it seemed as if the "Look–Say" method dominated what was being taught to teacher candidates. So, in the spirit of individual enterprise, and praying her way to an understanding of how to present the basics of the field, Dr. Nelson began to prepare her teachers to teach reading to the youngest children. During this time Mrs. Nelson attended Christian History seminars and studied the emphasis of "Biblical principles on the content and methodology of curriculum for American Christian schools."

For many years now Dr. Nelson has taught teachers not only in her own school, but in Christian schools across the nation. Her published two-volume work, *Phonics / Spelling Manual*, is a basic part of the *Little Patriot Series* of readers which she has developed with her Master Teacher and Supervisor of Elementary Education, Miss Saundra Scovill. We have watched the patience and persistence with which Mrs. Nelson has labored to instruct teachers and parents in the Home School field in the principles of literacy. We praise the Lord for the support of her husband, Rev. Ed Nelson, and her family who have helped her publish these invaluable materials. We also appreciate the time it has taken to make Christian school educators aware of the need for phonetic reading instruction – a cause which Guyla Nelson dedicated to the timing of the Lord. Now there is widespread acceptance for beginning early phonetic instruction with young children in order to establish the mastery of their own language, and to glorify the Lord by helping them gain the ability to read the Word of God for themselves.

SAUNDRA SCOVILL
Master Teacher and Supervisor

Perhaps Saundra Scovill is the most outstanding product of the teaching of Dr. Guyla Nelson. Saundra was a Kindergarten teacher in Silver State Baptist Schools and was early converted to the need to teach young Kindergartners to read phonetically. Under the care and supervision of Mrs. Ed Nelson she began to demonstrate the *liberty to learn* which children can have when they are instructed in the principles of phonetic reading. Saundra Scovill also caught the vision of teaching America's Christian History and its Biblical principles of self- and civil government to her Kindergarten students. What a joy to visit a classroom where children demonstrate their eagerness to learn and accomplish so much! Miss Scovill *demolished* many of the progressive educator's theories about young children. Her classes were often filled with up to fifty students. And many years she taught both a morning and an afternoon session of fifty students each. But, despite the numbers, there was time for individual attention and opportunity to help each one achieve the high standards of phonetic reading. Learning America's Christian History, memorizing facts of history, in poetry, song, hymns, and coming to know individuals of history, Miss Scovill gave her children a *head start* with their own accomplishment. Always a creative teacher, she produced many delightful programs in which the children and oftentimes parents participated. Often the teachers from other grade levels would come to her and ask – "what's left for us to teach, Miss Scovill?" As a supervisor, Miss Scovill helped teachers in the elementary level to become masters of the principles of phonics, grammar, spelling, and America's Christian History, and to discover the unopened treasury of learning which still awaited them. These early years can become tremendous years of learning.

Little Patriots Series, developed by Dr. Guyla Nelson and written by Saundra Scovill, is another fruit of teacher participation and productivity. How gracious is the Lord to raise up new seed in the teacher education field with individuals like Mrs. Nelson and Miss Scovill, lifting parents and teachers and students through a principled approach to learning into the capacity to spread the Good News of the Gospel and the Christian idea of man and government in all fields where the Lord leads them.

LOIS WEHRMAN MILLER
American Christian Kindergarten Curriculum

When James Rose began working with Reverend Elliott Paulsen to establish an American Christian school, the idea of an Academic Kindergarten was far from their minds. After all, this school was beginning at the Junior High level of learning. There was no demand by parents for those early grades which in the public schools were not producing readers, writers, or researchers. So, for a number of years the school continued without any elementary grades. Since the Christian History program had already been started in a number of other elementary schools, we wondered why the Lord had opened this pilot school without any of the early grades. But, in later years, we did learn why the delay, and again we marvelled at God's wisdom.

When the big surge for Christian schools became apparent in the 1960's, the majority of the Christian schools we worked with were still laboring under the philosophies and the limitations of *progressive education.* While some parents and teachers had discovered that children could learn much more than the public schools were teaching, few schools had escaped the "play" kindergarten concept, the "show and tell," the "group adjustment," and the "Look–Say" approach to reading. As the Christian History program was presented to schools it soon became evident that you could not teach America's Providential History, with all its inspiration and Biblical and academic consequences, without a better beginning in the basics of Literacy, and without a better philosophy of education.

After some years of working at both the Junior and Senior High School levels, it became apparent why the Lord had delayed the establishment of an Elementary school. For it took a number of years to raise the academic and scholarship level in the upper grades—and indicated how important the elementary years could be for achievement, not only of literacy, but in the acquiring of a love of learning—an *internal* commitment which would enable the student to become more and more responsible for his or her own performance in researching and recording Biblical and historical truths in all subjects.

It was discovered that high school students did not know the techniques of study and one of the teachers on the faculty, Mrs. Jan Humphrey, developed a *How to Study Manual.* Grammar and Composition were also found badly limited by the inability to read, write and spell adequately. So a search began for a comprehensive system for teaching reading, writing and spelling which would not ignore the basics but would be appropriate for the High School student's self-image. It was at this time that Mr. Rose began to research Reading in the United States and found that it was indeed in sad array. At a conference in San Francisco of the Reading Reform Foundation he came upon Romalda Spalding's *The Writing Road to Reading.* This succinct method seemed to correspond well with the Principle Approach to American Christian Education and so Mr. Rose set himself to learn the Spalding method and to teach it to all of his faculty.

As the High School began to emerge from its public school counterpart as a training ground for character, curriculum, and the living of those Biblical principles of government which formed our American Constitutional Republic, the need for an elementary school became apparent. There were now parents interested in seeing their younger children started in an academic Christian school which made America's Christian History—the outcome of the Chain of Christianity moving Westward—a centerpiece of the school. It was determined that no Social Studies courses would be taught so that from the earliest years students would have restored to them the heroes and heroines who had contributed to our Providential history as a nation. Since all of history is His Story, America's history began with Creation. Our early writers used to begin with the Garden of Eden and progress up to America's establishment as the world's first Christian Constitutional Republic. Now all of universal history could be introduced, following the History of Liberty, and the progress of the Gospel and government.

Literature too would once again find its way back into the elementary curriculum as the *handmaid* of history. And the sciences would be started with their most fundamental principles simply explained and illustrated. But, above all, the subject of phonics would once again become the *queen* of elementary learning. It was natural for Mr. Rose to chose teachers who would be willing to learn Mrs. Spalding's *The Writing Road to Reading.* Since most teachers were not trained in this field, this in itself was a discipline—an exercise in Christian self-government. But these same teachers soon discovered that the results of teaching the children to read by a principled phonics method brought results that excelled anything they had known before.

It was at this time that Mrs. Lois Miller appeared to teach the Kindergarten children. Mrs. Miller was an experienced teacher and had already been introduced to a philosophy of learning which was related to the Spalding phonics program. She became an expert teacher in this method and was able to incorporate it into her own Principle Approach to Kindergarten—a program which she worked on and developed in Mr. Rose's pilot school.

Mrs. Lois Miller entitles her academic Kindergarten an *American Christian Kindergarten Curriculum* and provides this section of Mr. Rose's volume with her *Overview.* In the Overview she discusses how to teach kindergarten children to read by the Spalding method. However, before beginning with reading, let us look at the foundation which Mrs. Miller first established before she identified her *fourteen* subject areas. This follows the path which all the other teachers have taken in the Principle Approach to American Christian education. Philosophy must precede product.

How soon can children of an early age begin to learn? This question is uppermost in the minds of most parents, and certainly in the minds of educators brought up on philosophies of education which emphasized *delaying* academic learning. As an individual Mrs. Miller is a very relaxed teacher in the classroom, so what she has proposed here is what she was able to carry out successfully over many years with young children. Once again it verifies what we have learned in the Principle Approach program, namely, that children taught by an orderly method, with an enthusiastic teacher who has a regard for the proper *pacing*, become eager learners and blossom as individuals.

These are the questions which Mrs. Miller raises and endeavors to answer philosophically and practically in the first pages of her Overview. The distinction of the Principle Approach with other Kindergarten programs is that the teacher's research and reasoning are key to the curriculum. And if a teacher recognizes that God has placed us here in America, with a special responsibility and stewardship for this nation, then we begin at an early age to include America's Christian History, character and government as basic to our program. This indeed elevates the role of the teacher and the goal of our educational product. It links up both teacher and student to the Chain of Christianity moving westward with liberty, responsibility and

productivity—for "the glory of God and the advancement of the Christian faith"—which includes the Christian idea of man appearing in government.

In the light of the above, many questions can be answered which might not have come up in a "play" and "adjustment," group-oriented Kindergarten. So Mrs. Miller discusses such incredible things as giving children of this age a notebook— and a big one at that! Can children of four and five years of inexperience handle a big binder? Yes! Over the years she found only one or two who ever caught their fingers in the fasteners!

Are there academic goals for a Kindergarten child? And how do character and curriculum fit into the goal of learning about America's Christian Constitution? The Christian History principles help bring about opportunities for the understanding and practice of God's government of each one of us—and what our responses to that government should be. Mrs. Miller also answers other questions such as grades and tests for small children.

The wholistic approach to all subjects means that in every grade teachers and students will be teaching and learning the same principles and deepening their knowledge of the subjects from year to year. In effect, Mrs. Miller is laying the foundation for all subjects which will be taught in the school. Beginning with the Bible, she is not only teaching its contents to her class, but she is also relating the Bible to our history, our literature and to our American Christian philosophy of government. In particular as she indicates in her Bible curriculum, "our elected representatives" listen to and participate in prayers for our nation by the Chaplain of the United States Congress, and are encouraged to read and study the Bible for their knowledge of government.

In her teaching of *The Writing Road to Reading,* Mrs. Miller incorporates some of the Christian History principles so that the children are not only learning the subject but are also learning how their own work habits, and attitudes, relate to character development. The principles of America's Christian History and government come to mean more when children can meet those Pilgrims, Patriots, and Pioneers, in story, song, plays and programs in which they can participate.

In each of her fourteen subjects, Mrs. Miller includes the Biblical purpose for learning the subject. Thus Physical Geography, American Christian Literature, Mathematics, Science, Music, Art, and Physical Training, all are unfolding aspects of the nature and character of God. And the Classroom Constitution enables these young children to become aware of those precious ideals of Life,

Liberty and Property which are so important to our American Christian philosophy of education and government.

In conclusion, Mrs. Miller overviews for us how to schedule the Kindergarten day so that it is balanced. She also discusses the Kindergarten Notebook so that we can follow her procedure and see how we can incorporate her steps with our own children. Finally, as we study carefully all that Mrs. Miller has researched, reasoned, related and recorded in her ministry with children and adults, we must indeed thank the Lord for opening up new horizons of inspired teaching. We pray that as parents and teachers gain not only encouragement for teaching their Kindergarten students, but also specific instruction for dealing with these children, that they too will have the satisfaction of teaching such a program and watching young minds, hearts, bodies grow in the Lord.

We thank you, Lois Miller, for your vision, your patience and persistence, and your willingness to implement this program when you yourself had to seek out and find almost all of your needed resources. May the Lord continue to bless your ministry and bring many new prospective teachers and students to you.

KATHERINE DANG

Among those teachers who worked in the pilot school shepherded by Mr. Rose was Miss Katherine Dang. It was a great encouragement to all of us at the Foundation for American Christian Education when our first link to the Chain of Christianity going ever westward appeared in the person of Katherine Dang, who found this program of American Christian education. It seemed to meet an inner desire of her heart to discover where she, as an American-born Chinese and a Christian, fit into God's plan for nations. From her own Biblical base and church affiliation she desired to minister to those with the ancient heritage of China and to prepare evangelists to carry the Chain of Christianity ever westward—with the message of the Gospel in its *full expression of civil and religious liberty.*

As Puritan pastor, George Herbert (1593–1633) wrote in his great poem of the westwardness of His Story:

The course was westward, that the sun might light
As well our understanding as our sight...

Religion, like a Pilgrim, westward bent,
Knocking at all doors, ever as she went...

Religion stands on tiptoe in our land,
Ready to pass to the *American* strand...

Then shall Religion to America flee:
They have their times of Gospel, e'en as we...

But as the Sun still goes both West and East,
So also did the Church by going West
Still Eastward go; because it drew more near
To time and place, where judgment shall appear.

How dear to me, O God, thy counsels are!
Who may with thee compare?

In her years of association with Mr. Rose, Katherine Dang spent considerable time in self-study. Her desire was to master the field of history utilizing those earlier sources where historians identified the Providence of God. Miss Dang also wished to assist her pastor, Louis Lightfoot of the Bay Area Chinese Bible Church in the establishment of a school for Chinese students. Today Miss Dang is the Administrative Director of the Chinese Christian Schools in San Leandro, California, a school largely brought about by her individual efforts in researching and teaching America's Christian History and education.

Miss Dang's contributions to this section on curriculum are many. First is the presentation of *Notebook Methodology—a declaration of independence* from the Workbook mentality and character of dependence. This historic tool of education is restored to us in this program and we have the step-by-step description of how to introduce this method to your students—and to yourself. You will be pleased with the examples drawn from our history of Americans who found this Notebook Method during their years of home schooling. You will discover other individuals who record the results of their study in this manner for their continued use. And you might find that the *Notebook Methodology* will become your favorite tool in education.

Miss Dang's second contribution is in the field of Geography. When we as American Christians lost our leadership in education—by our own default—we lost the unique relationship of Geography to His Story. The Social Studies homogenization of so many vital subjects like history, government, political science, and geography, had rendered these subjects neutral and of only passive interest. The foundational work of Dr. Arnold Guyot, the first Professor of Geography in an American University, Princeton in 1854, became the basis for restoring *God's Geography of Nature or Creation,* and the *Geography of Man,* the *Dominion Mandate.* How satisfying to teachers and students to discover the wondrous efficiency of our Creator in His plan for civil and religious liberty—in the structure of the Continents of History! How important also that in this age of travel throughout the world, our students can look at the earth through the eyes of understanding and comprehension of Geographic and Biblical principles, in both the Continents of History and the Continents of Nature.

Rudiments of America's Christian History and Government was designed as a Student Handbook, to help teachers, parents and students to break away from their *social orientation* to the subject of how men are governed. The course was intended for that period of young manhood and womanhood beginning at the Junior High School or Middle Years, and extending up into the first years of college. The course was open, to be structured by individual teachers. Mr. Rose, Miss Dang and Miss Ballenger have all added their contributions based upon their individual teaching of this subject. *Rudiments* has always proved to be the most *explosive* course in a school because it brings to the surface all the *misconceptions* of *character* and *government* which students have imbibed through their years of education. It is one of the most useful tools in the curriculum for helping teachers and students identify the qualities of character needed to perpetuate and extend our American Christian Constitutional Republic.

Finally, as her *piéce de resistance*, we have Miss Dang's *American Christian History Curriculum for Senior High School.*

God's Book, our textbook, begins with a first statement and indicates the whole subject of Creation.

"In the beginning, God created the heaven and the earth." Genesis 1:1

This is a statement of completion. The details of Creation are significant—because we know the completed whole. This approach to identifying a subject provides us with a standard for course construction. We *begin* with the *end*.

When we identify a subject from the completed whole we are able to know where we are going before we start our journey. Miss Dang begins her curriculum design for teaching and learning America's Christian History with the presentation of Six Major Themes. Her first theme reflects the goal of the course. It is our journey's destination. It is what we see appearing on the Chain of Christianity moving westward with the liberty and the responsibility of the individual.

THEME I.
AMERICA RESERVED BY GOD FOR CHRISTIAN
SELF-GOVERNMENT 1000–1620 A.D.

The Theme identifies our Biblical, historical, governmental and academic purpose for our study. It is the Providential Approach to history. It is our question: What in the world was God doing?

With each of her six themes, Miss Dang identifies for us *Key Individuals, Key Events, Key Institutions,* and *Key Documents, Speeches, Sermons* or *Essays.* These will complement each other as they will document the major ideas and principles. Now we have the map of our journey through American History. We know where we are going and some of the major periods we will visit in detail. We know what we are looking for as a philosophy of history and government and we look forward to becoming acquainted with *God's instruments* for carrying out each major theme.

A distinction of curriculum development in the Principle Approach is the restoration of the *individuality of the teacher.* Like a *Pathfinder* who has gone before the *Pioneers* who will follow, Miss Dang has provided us with the highlights of her own study and mapping. But, she does not presume to substitute her total course content for our own. If she did that we would once again have to accept a minor position in regard to our teaching on the subject. We would have to take the results of another teacher's study and endeavor. It is like teaching a journey which we have not travelled ourselves. We have had to do this many times in our educational program—so let us now begin to make this subject our own and allow the Holy Spirit to illuminate our individual teaching and learning.

But, we are not stranded if we do not have Miss Dang's total curriculum content. She has provided us with rich resources for our own research and lesson planning. In a special section, *Suggested Bibliography for Research and Lesson Planning,* we have the general readings she has used. In a *Bibliography* for each major theme she has given specific page references to the basic books published by the Foundation. She has listed books which can be found in the public library or can be purchased for work with students. Finally, in addition to Lesson Plan instruction, she has charted the teaching of some example in history for each of her KEY areas. And lastly, Miss Dang has included some special poems which express the spirit and literature of liberty. For all of this and for her trail-blazing efforts we thank her and pray for many more pioneers to follow until they too can become Pathfinders in the Christian History Program.

BELINDA BETH BALLENGER

Miss Belinda Beth Ballenger was the first teacher in James Rose's pilot school for the Christian History Program, to produce her own course of study in *Rudiments of America's Christian History and Government* in notebook form. She was therefore the first *missionary* sent out by the Foundation for American Christian Education during the summers to teach this course to other Christian schools across America. This proved to be an introduction to the Principle Approach for many.

Called to help establish an educational foundation in the Mid-West, Miss Ballenger discovered how important it was for parents to work with their children when given direction. Her unique one-day-a-month Pilgrim Academies enabled many parents and children to continue in their regular schools until they had mastered the rudiments of home teaching. It was during these years that Beth wrote her *Home Study Guide for Parents on the Life of George Washington "From America's Traditional Method of Biblical Reasoning"* – the Principle Approach. When we consider how much secular education has robbed us of our Founding Fathers and Mothers, this study is a blessing and enables parents and students to restore to their own minds and characters a man whom God raised up as His *special instrument* in the establishment of this nation.

We rejoice that Beth Ballenger has once again returned to California and pray that her plans to establish her own American Christian educational foundation will bring more laborers into the vineyard needed on this west coast. To continue steadfast in the Christian History Program requires many of the same qualities as our first seekers after liberty and responsibility. Like all of those who early caught the vision of the importance of restoring the *missing ingredients* in contemporary Christian education in America there have been many trials. We praise God for His Hand in sustaining all those who have loved this ministry and especially we thank Miss Ballenger for her persistence. In this volume her contributions are found in the *Rudiments* course which she helped pioneer in the first years of this program.

RUTH J. SMITH

Another star of American Christian Character in the Christian History constellation is Mrs. Ruth Smith. We first met Mrs. Smith when she was associated with another pilot school for this program, Silver State Baptist Schools in Denver, Colorado, presided over by Pastor Ed Nelson, his talented wife Dr. Guyla Nelson, and administered by Omer Perdue. When Mrs. Smith moved to Iowa to assist her pastor brother, Dr. Glen Jaspers, she began her ministry in the Principle Approach in the classroom working with students, and assisting teachers in re-establishing their educational foundations on a more Biblical base. Pastor Jaspers and Ruth wrote the first guide for *Restoring America's Heritage of Pastoral Leadership*. We value Pastor Jasper's efforts to challenge our ministers of the Gospel to return to their leadership role in this nation which has been sadly turned aside.

Ruth and Allen Smith established the *Pilgrim Institute* to extend the outreach of America's Christian History and Education to homes, churches and schools. In Indiana the Smiths now operate an elementary and high school, which serve as demonstration schools. Their *Collegiate Institute* for the training of teachers and administrators in the Principle Approach has just opened. But of special interest is the great response to Mrs. Smith's Consultant Program which has taken her into the South and Southwest, working directly with schools and homes. And, for those who cannot attend seminars, the Pilgrim Correspondence Course has proved to be most successful.

Ruth Smith's valuable contribution for James Rose's volume is her introductory course on *Teaching America's Christian History in the Elementary School*. For so many decades in this century we have been lured by the secular approach to curriculum for the elementary years, especially in the fields of history and literature. The "here and now" syndrome of the progressive, socially oriented educators turned our children from a knowledge of their own history to a study of social issues or to the contemplation of primitive societies. The "cultural concept" of character – the work of Dr. Margaret Mead and other anthropologists – led us into paths of accepting social and tribal adaptation as the key to successful living together, the goal of secular education. No wonder our children associate the idea of history with that which is too familiar to be interesting. The "here and now" of everyday living has not produced inspired teaching and learning.

Current efforts to return to our traditional history has brought little more than efforts to teach history as a series of events without a cause – other than economic or social. History is unrelated to the life of the student and to the individual's relationship to the Lord. Should not the study of all subjects in the school curriculum bring us closer to God's purpose, not only for the subject field or the nation in which we live, but for each of us as individuals? Should we not emerge from American Christian Education, whether in the home, the church, or the school, with a greater understanding of God's Sovereign rule of the universe and of all Creation, of all fields of study as well as all areas of life?

It becomes apparent that if history is not taught

as God's Providential Hand in the affairs of men and nations, then we as individuals, and as Americans, cannot truly see a relationship with the Lord. Nor can we credit God for America's role in His Story as the world's first Christian Constitutional Republic, unless we are willing to read the writings of our Founding generations who moved as the Lord directed them in fleeing the Old World's oppressions to endeavor to extend liberty and responsibility to all men—the Christian idea of man in government. That we have succeeded is due to the Hand of God. That we have not succeeded better is due to the nature of man.

In Ruth Smith's program for teaching America's Christian History to Elementary students, we discover that a major goal is to restore the ability to Biblically reason from *cause to effect*. It was this ability that enabled our American colonists, educated by their pastors for one hundred and fifty years, to think their way to the establishment of a nation. They had learned how easy it is to become *"entangled again with the yoke of bondage"*—the bondage of state control over the life, liberty, and property of the individual. Should we not teach our children how God was with our fathers and directed their efforts to maintain those Biblical principles for greater self- and civil government?

The setting for all subjects is the westward course of the Gospel, *The Chain of Christianity* as illustrated on page 6A of *The Christian History of the Constitution of the United States of America, Christian Self-Government*, compiled by Miss Verna Hall. Mrs. Smith has chosen some of the major links of the Chain of Christianity to teach during the Elementary years and she charts them out for us in her SUGGESTED OVERVIEW from Kindergarten through Sixth Grade.

Mrs. Smith has taken nine links, which are taught each year from Kindergarten through Sixth Grade and deepened and expanded. This is our method of Bible study, to continue to *deepen* and *expand* our study of God's Word and works. Mrs. Smith has given instruction on how to plan your course of study for each link. Suggestions for the Leading Ideas, and for Developing your Teacher's Notebook will enable you to form your own content and determine your own course or pace of teaching. Basic book references and resource books for your students are also indicated and many of these are available for purchase, or can be found in your local public library. Above all you will be leading your children into the Biblical and historical research of the impact of the Law and the Gospel of Jesus Christ as it directly affects America's Christian history, self- and civil government. You will be teaching them to reason from the cause of

God's Sovereignty in history to its effect on men and nations.

A special introduction has also been given of one link—*The Pilgrim, Seed of our American Christian Republic*. Mrs. Smith has identified the Seven Principles of America's Christian History in the Pilgrim Story, thus providing teachers and parents with an excellent example of how to include original source material in a unit. She also has examples of Lesson Plans and has provided many specific suggestions for the writing of students as they develop their notebooks under your direction.

The ability to research, reason, relate and record from the Bible is illustrated in the life of William Bradford, future Pilgrim Governor. At age twelve, in England, he found a Bible. As he studied it, and as he was led to attend a Separatist church, he began to reason. From his Bible he saw that the Church of England was not a church in any New Testament meaning of the word. "He set himself by reading, by discourse, by prayer, to learn whether it was not his duty to withdraw from the communion of the parish-assemblies, and engage with some society of the faithful, that should keep close unto the *written word* of God, as the *rule* of their worship." *The Hand of God in the Return of the Bradford Manuscript to America*, p. 145. The decision to separate from the Church of England began the Pilgrim story—one that took them from England to Holland and to America, on the *Mayflower.* What a consequence from the ability to read and reason from the Word of God. Should we not restore this ability in our children?

We thank Mrs. Ruth Smith for her efforts to awaken American Christian parents and teachers to the joy of teaching a curriculum which has consequences for their own Christian character and commitment. We pray that the efforts of Mr. and Mrs. Allen Smith and Pastor Glen Jaspers will also be a reminder to present-day pastors of the leadership role which they once had in this nation, and from which they have presently *turned aside*. One hundred years ago when our pastors were still preaching the History and Character of Liberty from the pulpits of America, one pastor, celebrating our first one hundred years of Independence, chose these words to close his sermon preached by invitation to the civil officers of government in the state of Massachusetts:

". . . Whatever is noble in the character of our people, or heroic in the annals of our history, is deeply grounded in their constant recognition of a Divine Providence in human affairs, and the immutability of moral law, —the one the object of their daily trust, the other the inspiration and rule of their daily life . . . "

The Lord our God be with us, as he was with our fathers; let him not leave us nor forsake us. (1 Kings 8:57) Consider and Ponder, p. 54

JAMES V. KILKENNY

The term *teacher burn-out* has become popular today to explain the condition of many in both public and private school education. Noah Webster in his 1828 *An American Dictionary of the English Language* defines this term—not as an adjective, but in its original verb form: *"To burn out,* to burn till the fuel is exhausted and the fire ceases."

The more one contemplates modern education and its inability to bring the individual's talents to focus on those areas of most interest and concern to one whom the Lord has led into teaching, the more one can agree that *burn-out* is indeed a *way-out* for the disappointed and frustrated. Yet, if one internalizes the above definition, one can readily agree that unless a teacher is vitally replenishing the fuel of scholarship by individual contributions to both content and curriculum design; unless a teacher is growing more confident in his or her ability to help students effect changes in individual character,—then indeed we can expect the "fuel" to be "exhausted," and the "fire" to go out.

Over the years of working with individuals engaged in the Christian History program, it has been satisfying to witness those who have, through their own application of the philosophy of the Principle Approach, grown into revitalized American Christian teachers. Truly these individuals have come to a closer walk with the Lord and have found many creative ways to unify their Biblical learning with their classroom teaching. This has certainly been the case with the ministries of James and Barbara Kilkenny. And how graciously the Lord prepares His own children for just such a work! Furnished with a classical education which seemed out of place for either public or private education, this background enabled them to "take to" the Basic Books with less anxiety than many. To Jim and Barbara these volumes were not a hurdle but a ready means to get into the quality of learning which they themselves had always believed to be essential for Christians in America. Today as they expand their school in Texas and enlarge their sphere of serving Christian homes and schools in consultation and conferences, they are each one deepening a number of subject areas which they teach. Barbara is working in languages as they relate to the westward course of Christianity and to America, and writing her study on how

to teach Spanish and Latin in the Principle Approach. She is also working in the field of American Christian Music and Literature.

James Kilkenny is represented in this volume in his *Teaching Arithmetic from the Principle Approach.* We might ask, how can arithmetic be improved through the Principle Approach? Isn't arithmetic a *duty* subject—one that every teacher and child faces daily as a necessary chore to learn and perform? How can arithmetic become inspirational? How can it be related to Biblical truth? And what has arithmetic to do with our history?

All of these questions and more are considered by James Kilkenny as he leads us into his fascinating Biblical, historical and governmental research of arithmetic. As he first introduces us to the subject he reminds us that *different* qualities of character are produced by different methods of teaching and learning. Learning arithmetic by rote—rather than by reason—makes the distinction between a dependent character and a character which can express Christian confidence and skill. Learning by rote will enable a student to get the right answers to his problems in arithmetic. But a student who learns to reason from principles will soon begin to express the mastery and understanding which enables one to explain what one is learning and its relationship to other mathematical functions and their applications.

Most importantly, with the emphasis which the Principle Approach makes in every subject field, learning arithmetic means also learning more about the nature and character of God. As Dr. Mark Fakkema indicated in his definition of Mathematics, the subject proclaims that:

1) God is unchangeable
2) God is a God of order
3) God is a God of system
4) *Dependability* is one of God's attributes
5) God's infinitude is perhaps more clearly revealed in mathematics than in any other school subject.

How many teachers can define the Rudiments or First Principles of arithmetic? How satisfying for both teacher and students to clearly identify these basics. Then it is easy to define Course Goals specifically and to follow James Kilkenny's path of reason as he indicates how to lead students to participate in the reasoning learning approach. Some of their contributions are included in this study.

In addition to his many practical tables and suggestions for organizing the Arithmetic Course, Mr. Kilkenny gives us some interesting information in his research into *Arithmetic and the History of Liberty.* Surely as every student in the elementary years has an opportunity to meet Nathaniel Bowditch, the Father of American Mathematics, he will perceive how an individual living in a Christian Constitutional Republic can develop a field with regard to the Christian idea of man. Indeed, the Key Individual for illustrating what qualities of character are needed for mathematics is Dr. Bowditch. He was a self-educated mathematical genius, whose contributions were honored throughout the world. And his work on navigation, *The American Practical Navigator,* is still used at our Naval Academy in Annapolis – a practical application of navigational principles for the individual.

A philosophy of education is a philosophy of government. The character we manifest as individuals results in the kind of government we produce and are able to maintain. Our Founding generations, educated by their pastors to be self-governing, productive and capable of working in voluntary association, enabled them to be used of God to establish the American Christian Constitutional Republic. But succeeding generations have allowed much of the *dependent* character of socialism to erode those earlier Christian foundations. Yet, if we are willing as American Christian educators, like James Kilkenny, to not only win our students to Christ, but also, to engage them in taking more responsibility and interest in their own education and character development – then perhaps we shall see a revival of the essential qualities needed to perpetuate our Christian Constitutional liberties. The character that America manifests in our own nation affects the world. Mr. Kilkenny's excellent application of the Christian History principles to the field of arithmetic gives us some understanding of how this everyday subject in the classroom can become a tool in the hands of a teacher to shape and form the character of the next generation – to be an honor to the Lord and to extend the "blessings of liberty." We thank Mr. Kilkenny for his inspirational teaching and recording of arithmetic which indicates why teachers and students need not anticipate *burn-out,* but can rather *turn-out* to experiences, both on the mountain-top of inspiration and the market-place of practicality.

CHARLES HULL WOLFE

At first glance it might seem strange to find a former Madison Avenue executive and Communications expert writing in this volume. But the Lord is no respecter of persons; all men must eventually sit at the feet of Jesus and let Him rearrange their lives. So it has been with Charles, for while his talents found considerable expression in the world of Communication, the Lord has had more significant fields for him to work and other ideas for him to communicate.

Charles Wolfe was the first individual to pioneer Christian History study groups while working with Leonard Read at the Foundation for Economic Education. This is still a field of major priority for it allows both young people and adults to learn how to study our Biblical and historic principles, and how to apply them to the consideration of today's challenges to American Christian Constitutional liberty. Charles Wolfe was also one of our first modern day Pilgrims, as he worked professionally with John G. Talcott, Jr., founder of Plymouth Rock Foundation, in preparing in 1970 a Christian celebration of the 350th anniversary of the Pilgrim landing in New England. John Talcott had moved from his native Connecticut, the Constitution state, to Plymouth, Massachusetts, because of his love for our Pilgrim History. Here where some of its most precious beginnings unfolded, John Talcott became a cranberry grower, walking the bogs where William Bradford, William Brewster, John Winslow and so many other Pilgrims had worked and prayed and endeavored to survive. Charles Wolfe in his work with John Talcott for the 350th Pilgrim celebration prepared and produced several commemorative events, most noteworthy of which was a dramatic Pilgrim service complete with music written by Charles. The Wolfe family appeared in the production as well. Charles' work with Pilgrim History led to his appearance annually with the Pilgrim Seminars which John Talcott inaugurated with F.A.C.E. in order to teach American Christian teachers the *missing ingredient* in education today. Charles' tours to historic Plymouth landmarks, and his unique research into the Pilgrim Economic history were always a highlight of these conferences.

Charles Wolfe's presentation in this volume, *The Principle Approach to American Christian Economics,* provides us with a significant opportunity to re-educate ourselves and our children in those Pilgrim principles which have been sadly neglected by many Christian organizations today. The American free enterprise system grew from a Biblical and Christian base as Charles Wolfe so ably demonstrates in this article. But we neglect to spend much time on a field which our Lord had to deal with many times. Throughout history, the life of the individual is involved in multiple economic decisions. This does not preclude the need for Christian virtues.

The *faith and steadfastness* of the Pilgrims did not preclude their *diligence and industry* as they worked many years to repay the original *Mayflower* debt to their English investors. In a world which has so often discredited Biblical standards of conduct, the field of economics represents the most critical character challenge for the American Christian. Perhaps with the help of Charles Wolfe and his program for American Christian Economics this challenge can be met, and Christian enterprises can meet Biblical standards of sound economics. Before presenting the content of his curriculum design for teaching economics in the home, church and school, Mr. Wolfe carefully introduces us to the individual's relationship to this field. He also indicates the uniqueness of American Economics—that free enterprise which flowed from the qualities of Christian character which were developed by our forefathers as they endeavored to overcome the material obstacles placed in their paths. The *externals* were met first *internally* as Bradford himself relates when he described the shock which the English Pilgrims had upon reaching the Netherlands on the continent.

"...For though they saw faire & bewtifull cities, flowing with abundance of all sorts of welth & riches, yet it was not longe before they saw the grime & grisly face of povertie coming upon them like an armed man, with whom they must bukle & incounter, and from whom they could not flye; but they were armed with faith & patience against him, and all his encounters; and though they were sometimes foyled, yet by Gods assistance they prevailed and got ye victorie... And first though many of them weer poore, yet ther was none so poore, but if they were known to be of yt congregation, the Dutch (either bakers of others) would trust them in any reasonable matter when yey wanted money. Because they had found by experience how carfull they were to keep their word, and saw them so painfull & dilligente in their callings; yea, they would strive to gett their custome, and to imploy them above others, in their worke, for their honestie & diligence..."

Christian History, pp. 189,191

Thus no economic system is greater than the character of the individuals engaged in it. If we are consistent in our obedience to Christ's demands of character and conscience, we must be able also to obey His economic principles.

Mr. Wolfe begins *The Principle Approach to American Christian Economics* by confronting us with the necessity of educating our children in a philosophy of government. First we must know and teach our children the *distinctions* of various political systems. We can only do this by first clearly teaching *America's Christian History* and government. Our students will be making economic decisions and they need to know whether they are making these decisions in light of our Biblical principles of government, or whether they are helping socialism "descend like a pall upon every facet of our economy and culture." *Christian History*, p. III

Our children will need to learn how the Christian idea of man in government, brought to fruition in the establishment of our American Christian Constitutional Republic, allowed for a burst of activity never before witnessed in the world. Why? Because, as one writer put it, under our philosophy of government and economics:

"Our people are busy using their liberties and energies, each for his individual benefit, as is quite right and proper; since the welfare of individuals makes the prosperity of the community." *Christian History*, p. 6

After demonstrating the "close correlation between a nation's civil government and its economy," Charles Wolfe then gives us a brief economic history so that we may learn why the American economy was once judged to be a "miracle." He also discusses succinctly what the "hampering influences" are upon our economy today and why nations who even "imitate" our Christian principles are being more successful than we are—because we have gone off the "gold standard" of our American Christian character.

For restoration Mr. Wolfe introduces us to *God's Answers* to economic problems and he proposes the Course of Study which parents may pursue with their children, and teachers with their students. An illustrative series of charted *Diagrams* give us some clear goals for teaching the Principle Approach to American Christian Economics. As Charles explains *The Rudiments of God's Economy* he also defines his Diagrams. We are presented with some marvellous terms which provide us with a Biblical foundation for teaching and learning this subject. And he expands the work of earlier economists by including the Christian base, i.e. *The Ten Pillars of Economic Wisdom* by Fred G. Clark and Richard S. Rimanoczy.

INTRODUCING CHILDREN TO ECONOMIC IDEAS

Mr. Wolfe will especially endear himself to parents and teachers in his practical ideas for Curriculum in home and school. Noah Webster identifies the field of Economics with "the regulation of household concerns." Our national economy is dependent upon his definition of *Economy* as 1. "Primarily, the management, regulation and government of a family" and 2. "The management of pecuniary concerns" and 3. "A frugal and judicious use of money; that management which expends money to advantage and incurs no waste; frugality..."

Our Founding Fathers knew that the success of our Republic depended upon our sound economic base. Article VI:1 of the Constitution began: "All debts contracted and engagements entered into before the adoption of this Constitution shall be as valid against the United States under this Constitution as under the Articles of Confederation."

This was a courageous step taken by the United States to entitle all creditors the right to the full payment of their debts as contracted by the government *before* the new Constitution was adopted. It was a surprise to the European nations who did not expect a new nation to honor her obligations. But it was true to the Biblical admonition: "Owe no man anything." *Romans 13:8.* Justice Joseph Story in his exposition on the Constitution in 1840 wrote:

"This can scarcely be deemed more than a solemn declaration of what the public law of nations recognizes as a moral obligation, binding on all nations, notwithstanding any changes in their forms of government." p. 249

The effect was in keeping with the obedience to God's command. "Almost immediately it started the wheels of industry and commerce turning again. As President Washington saw what was happening, he could scarcely believe it. He saw the bankrupt United States experience a miracle of recovery at a pace he never would have believed possible." *The Making of America, The Substance and Meaning of the Constitution,* by Cleon Skousen, 1985, p. 655

Our Founding Fathers and Mothers knew that as goes the family, so goes the nation. If homes are balanced economically, then we have hope that our nation can balance its national budget and economy. Samuel Adams, writing to his future son-in-law, had this to say: "For though it is acknowledged, that the Superiority is & ought to be in the Man, yet as the Management of a Family in many instances necessarily devolves on the Woman... I can trust to my Daughters Discretion if she will only promise to exercise it... I could dwell on the Importance of Piety & Religion, of Industry & Frugality, of Prudence, Œconomy, Regularity & an even Government, all which are essential to the Well being of a Family." *Consider and Ponder,* p. 82

The remarkable inside story of the economic success of the American Revolution can be attributed once again to the instruction of pastors in economics and the family's responsibilities in this regard. A sermon preached on the Day of the General Fast, April, 1769, by Pastor Amos Adams of Roxbury, Mass, stated:

"But without industry and frugality, no people in the world can flourish. If families live in idleness, if people go beyond their abilities in living, building, dress, equipage, and the like; if children are not carefully brought up to industry, there is no doubt they will be miserable, with the greatest and best advantages. It is therefore highly necessary, if considered only as the means of present public happiness, that children be trained up to useful business, that we retrench our superfluities, that we content our selves with the effects of our own industry. These things I urge, not merely or chiefly as being at this time peculiarly necessary for answering political purposes in Great Britain, but as now and always necessary to the life and prosperity of a people." *Teaching and Learning,* pp. 187–188

The *industry* of earlier days, Mr. Wolfe presents in one of his first lessons as *work*. The "goods and services" that people need must be earned. So work–and its specialization–become critical in the American Christian Home. Today the arguments against what God teaches us as *productivity,* have brought down the *quality* of American work. But the Boy Jesus was a good carpenter. How many things He must have made using His hands carefully and letting His tools smooth the wood and design the furniture, bowls, and other useful and needed articles for the Hebrew Homes of His day.

Mr. Wolfe also believes that children can learn the importance of *tools* at an early age. Tools separate man from the animal. Tools "multiply human energies, and make it possible to produce things that could not be made otherwise."

As the learning level of students progresses and as they build firmly on the foundations which Mr. Wolfe sets forth, then the intermediate grades will not have difficulty in understanding *The Wheel of Progress in a Christian Economy.* They will be able to *Study Economic History* and understand *Economic Freedom* and its relationship to our Christian Constitutional form of government.

Finally, during the High School years, those students who have been working at a Principle Approach Curriculum, will be ready to consider what it takes to establish individual enterprises; why the role of government is critical–either as a stumbling block or an aid to the free exercise of individual talent; and finally, why "free and independent" men and women from other nations find the American climate so compatible to the expression of individual talent.

With a fine bibliography and a description of educational organizations for helping you in your economic teaching, Charles leaves no excuse for ignorance or inertia on the part of American Christians in this field of teaching economics to young people. Thank you Charles Wolfe for being such a devoted Pioneer in American Christian Economics and following in the footsteps of the Pilgrims whose principles you espouse and practice. You have researched, reasoned, related and recorded the Principle Approach to American Christian Economics in your own inimitable style.

ELAINE M. WAINWRIGHT

Among the references listed by Mr. Wolfe in his *Educational Organizations that Can Help Enrich Your Teaching of Economics* is the name of Elaine M. Wainwright, a friend of many years to this program. Elaine's *Achievement Basics* is the first Christian teacher's efforts to teach young children some of the language and activities of our free, individual enterprise economy. Elaine has captured a joyous vitality in this "dismal science" and in her *Junior Business News* she has recorded many young entrepreneurs around the country in agriculture, commerce and junior businesses. How important it is to restore this field to young Christians so that perhaps we can find in the future solutions to the large economic problems in our country that are really based upon a return to the "gold standard" of Christian character and productivity.

RALPH BULLARD
Christian Heritage Academy of Oklahoma City

Like the American marines, "all we need is a few good men." Next to having an outstanding pastor in the establishment of an American Christian school, the *principal* is the key to a Principle Approach program. While Mr. Ralph Bullard is not represented in writing in Jim Rose's book on American Christian Education, he is responsible for an educational setting which helped produce two of the men whose work appears here. Ralph Bullard was introduced to the Principle Approach at one of the Pilgrim Seminars in Plymouth, sponsored by John and Rosalyn Talcott and beautifully hosted by them in their home. As Ralph writes:

"I became convinced that the Principle Approach would enable our school to accomplish several essentials of Christian education. First, I had a vision of the restoration of America's Gospel purpose as teachers, students, and their parents reclaimed their heritage as American Christians. The Principle Approach emphasizes Providential History and leads us to an understanding of the Hand of God in the establishment of our Christian Republic. I also saw that the Principle Approach could transform our teachers into Christian scholars and Master teachers, and they, in turn, would be able to produce a new generation of Christian scholars."

The first two years of the work with the Principle Approach did not immediately yield the results with his faculty envisioned by Mr. Bullard. So, he was tempted to *mix* what he knew of the philosophy of American Christian Education with some other programs prepared by Christian publishers and emphasizing another method. Like the Bible admonition—one cannot put new wine into old wineskins, nor endeavor to patch up an old garment with new cloth, the Christian History program cannot be taught by contemporary or even traditional methods of education. We have to go back to our Colonial and Constitutional periods when the method of Biblical and historical researching, the ability to reason from principles, knowledge in how to relate, and willingness to record or write down the results of learning, were taught by pastors from the pulpit. No wonder our forefathers and mothers were so highly educated in Christian Constitutional principles at the time of our establishment as the world's first Christian Republic.

Mr. Bullard's honest confession of yielding to discouragement is helpful—for it is typical of the age in which we live where "instant" solutions and accomplishments are sought. But, as he continues his testimony, he indicates that he realized that what was missing was his own in-depth study in order to master the Principle Approach so that he might truly be a shepherd to his own faculty. With this attitude and effort his school soon began to reflect the character and conviction of the administrator now turned Master Teacher. In fact, Mr. Bullard's school and teachers are no longer continuing just to attend Christian school conferences—*"ever learning and never coming to a knowledge of truth."* The school now has a *unified* philosophy of education which affects all school subjects. Now Mr. Bullard and many of his teachers contribute to Educational Conferences. They also put on their own special Christian History Conferences and have become a magnet school to attract teachers and students desirous of attaining Christian character and scholarship.

Best of all, and pertinent to this volume, Mr. Bullard has encouraged and supported the independent efforts of those of his teachers who would go forward on their own to research, reason, and record their own fields of study—for the "glory of God and the advancement of the Christian faith," and Constitutional government. Two such men have been actively working to perfect their individual ministries and their work is included in this volume.

DAROLD BOOTON

Miss Hall and I first met Mr. Booton at Ralph Bullard's school in Oklahoma City. It was gratifying to visit his classes and watch him work with his students teaching them to reason. But it was even more satisfying to learn that his interests were not just confined to the field of mathematics. Like the scholars of old, he was interested in many subjects and sought to educate himself broadly. Darold Booton had read many of the classics which I presented in Literature to other teachers. Over the years he has been willing to read many of the books I have proposed. He is constantly expanding his horizons of thought and understanding in all directions, from a solid Biblical foundation. His courses include history, government, economics, German, as well as his special field of mathematics.

The year we met Mr. Booton in Oklahoma, he became interested in Nathaniel Bowditch, America's first mathematician of worldwide fame. To our surprise and delight, that very summer, Mr. Booton travelled to Virginia, where he could research the original work of Bowditch and have access to his writings. Mr. Booton's research as a High School teacher enabled him to develop a teaching unit for Elementary teachers who were presenting Nathaniel Bowditch in Literature. In the biography by Jean Lee Latham, *Carry On, Mr. Bowditch,* there is reference to Bowditch's application of mathematics to measurement in navigation. Mr. Booton's unit was entitled *Of the Log-Line & Half Minute Glass,* an early method of measuring the rate of speed at which a ship was travelling. With definitions and illustrations, and explanations, Mr. Booton explained to Elementary teachers and students just how to construct this measuring device.

The unity of the philosophy of the Principle Approach and the mutual interest of all teachers in Key Individuals whom God has used in His Story, provide opportunities for teachers at both levels of learning, elementary and high school, to exchange talents and contributions. It is important to see some of the tangible contributions which men of science made and often science teachers can assist elementary teachers in inventions of this sort.

Mr. Booton travelled with Mr. and Mrs. Smith on their Pilgrim Institute tour of New England and visited many of the historical places mentioned in America's Christian History. Here too, as they visited Salem, Massachusetts, Mr. Booton was prepared to be impressed by the fine quality of American architecture as they walked down Chestnut Street and looked at the Federal style of houses. Salem as a port has an amazing history, "evidence of the outworking of the internal Christian liberty," he wrote to us.

The American Christian who can "expand" the horizon of his or her mind and heart to include more and more of America's Providential History in every subject, will soon find that the fascination for learning and for teaching which they are experiencing, will have an incalculable effect upon their students. Let's have more of this kind of attitude in American Christian Education.

TEACHING ALGEBRA FROM THE PRINCIPLE APPROACH

Darold Booton regards the science of mathematics as a new way of ". . . looking at the universe by studying God's nature, character, and works . . . Looking at the subject from the Principle Approach, we conclude that God is the Author of mathematics and has a purpose for it. The subject becomes far more interesting because we start from a core of principles."

This approach simplifies what must be initially learned because we are approaching the subject in an orderly way. And "Order" is one of the first characteristics of the nature of God. "LET THERE BE LIGHT or ENLIGHTENMENT" was God's first command in Creation. Mr. Booton's first admonition to teachers is: "DEFINE YOUR TERMS." If you know what makes up your subject—you can then research this vocabulary in the Scriptures to determine the BIBLICAL PURPOSE of mathematics. Using the 1828 first Dictionary of Noah Webster, which contains the root and seed of the meaning of each term, we then go to research the Biblical source and purpose of Algebra.

Now it may be asked: Does the Bible contain the *exact* terms used in mathematics? Yes, some exact terms used in mathematics are in the Bible. In other cases the meaning can be reasoned. Mr. Booton discovered that while the word mathematics is not in the Bible, the word is derived from the Greek word *mathano* to learn. And *disciple* and *discipline* come from the Latin root to learn. Both of these words are important in the New Testament and Mr. Booton reasons:

"A conclusion which may be drawn from this is that mathematics is a discipline to advance our knowledge of the creation. The general character of mathematics is problem solving—learning things not previously known." This is well illustrated in the life of Nathaniel Bowditch who solved problems of navigation and commerce, mathematically.

After identifying the *Terms of Algebra I*—which will have to be mastered mathematically by any student of the subject—Darold Booton looks at *The Principles of Algebra*. Among these are *The Principle of Order and Magnitude* and *The Principle of Substitution and Representation*. Each of these principles is discussed Biblically and documented. What a joy for American Christian teachers and students to find their subject of mathematics has been in operation in the Bible for thousands of years.

One of the most interesting charts which Mr. Booton has designed is that entitled: Expanding the Principles of Elementary Mathematics through Algebra (Part I and Part II). This is "an attempt to explain where various topics 'fit' in a principle approach algebra course." Mr. Booton suggests that "the principles given here suggest the *internal aspect* of the number system because they suggest the derivation of the numbers and their consequent operations from the Trinitarian nature of the Godhead." The young mathematician proceeds from a position of following God's command to "take dominion" of the earth for His greater glory."

Also included are the events or *links* in the mathematical Chain of Christianity moving westward with individual liberty, both civil and religious. As all subjects find a unity on this Chain of Christ's Gospel, what a solid feeling this conveys of a God whose Providential superintendence of the world includes all events of life, in all fields of human thought and endeavor. Mr. Booton also relates the seven principles of America's Christian History to the field of mathematics as another indication of their consistency with a philosophy of government and education.

With all of this background of Biblical, historical and academic RESEARCHING, REASONING, RELATING and RECORDING, Mr. Booton gives parents and teachers a Lesson Plan, one which he has taught, and some further explanations for making your own course of instruction. Resources are also provided of books and helpful materials.

We are so glad that Darold Booton, formerly of Christian Heritage Academy in Oklahoma City, now Director of Admissions and Professor at Pilgrim Collegiate Institute in Indiana, caught the vision of returning his teaching to the foundations of our Biblical *and historical origins*. For God is a God of Order and of Distinctions.

"How precious also are thy thoughts unto me, O God! how great is the sum of them. If I should count them, they are more in number than the sand . . ."

Psalm 139:17,18

THE STUDY OF SCIENCE IN THE AMERICAN CHRISTIAN CURRICULUM

On Saturday afternoon, July 14, 1787, the members of the Constitutional Convention in Philadelphia recessed so that members could visit the grounds and botanical garden of William Bartram (1739–1823) and his brother John. A month earlier George Washington had visited the garden on the west bank of the Schuykill River. Through his agent ". . . he obtained plants of 106 varieties from the Catelogue of Trees, Shrubs & Plants of Jno Bartram." *Diaries of George Washington, Vol. V,* p. 168

William Bartram, ". . . from the advantages . . . enjoyed under his father John Bartram, botanist to the king of Great Britain, and fellow of the Royal Society. . ." had followed in his parent's leading. "As America's first native-born artist-naturalist he had during the years 1773-1776 explored the coastlands of Carolina and Georgia, crossed westward through Florida, and even penetrated into the country of the Cherokee Indians in lower Georgia. His later published record of this journey is the most important and beautiful description of the southeastern United States during the eighteenth century." In the Introduction to his *Travels,* William Bartram wrote:

"This world, as a glorious apartment of the boundless palace of the sovereign Creator, is furnished with an infinite variety of animated scenes, inexpressibly beautiful and pleasing, equally free to the inspection and enjoyment of all his creatures.

"Perhaps there is not any part of creation, within the reach of our observations, which exhibits a more glorious display of the Almighty hand, than the vegetable world; such a variety of pleasing scenes, ever changing throughout the seasons, arising from various causes, and assigned each to the purpose and use determined." *Travels through North and South Carolina, Georgia, East and West Florida* by William Bartram, The Beehive Press, Savannah, Georgia, 1973

At the time of the Constitutional Convention ". . . trained naturalists did not exist in America —trained, that is, in the sense that they had pursued a course of study in college or university to prepare them for that specialization. Many of the naturalists of the day (or natural philosophers as they were often called), men like Benjamin Smith Barton, Caspar Wistar, John Godman, Thomas Jefferson, and Henry Muhlenberg, had been formally educated not as naturalists, but as physicians, lawyers, and preachers of the gospel. Their genuine, enthusiastic preoccupation with animals, plants, and other aspects of nature was purely avocational. Others, though professional men, had experienced no academic training in any field. For example, Alexander Wilson *(ornithologist)* was a weaver by trade, Thomas Nuttall *(botanist and ornithologist)* a printer, C. S. Rafinesque *(botanist and zoologist)* a merchant, Thomas Say *(entomologist)* an apothecary, George Ord *(naturalist)* a ships' chandler, and John Bartram *(botanist)* a farmer. All of these men had gained their knowledge of fauna and flora through their own efforts or from instruction provided freely by other self-taught individuals." *Lewis and Clark: Pioneering Naturalists,* Paul Russell Cutright, 1969, pp. 397–398

The energy and interests of free men found their expression in many fields after our Constitutional Republic was established. And the American Christian character had both *faith and steadfastness* and *brotherly love and Christian care*–an interest in benefitting others as they plumbed the depths of knowledge in every field. Nathaniel Bowditch's *American Practical Navigator* was built upon the critical need for accuracy when compiling mathematical navigational charts which ships depended upon for safe passage. He had found 8,000 errors in the navigation charts compiled by Nevil Maskelyne, the royal astronomer of England. Bowditch also wrote his *American Practical Navigator* so that every able seaman might understand the principles of navigation in order to advance himself to first mate or captain.

Matthew Fontaine Maury also was concerned for the *"paths of the sea,"* sea lanes for the safety of ocean-going vessels. And he too, through the principle of voluntary cooperation, was able to request of 1,000 American captains, working charts of winds and waves, so that these might be compiled and published for the benefit of other navigators who, lacking accurate knowledge, sailed their courses by trial and error. Coming at the time of the California Gold Rush, Maury's Wind and Wave charts shortened the voyage around Cape Horn by 40 to 44 days. "The average time of ships *not* using the *Wind and Current Charts* was 187½ days to California–only 144½ for those that did." *Matthew Fontaine Maury, Scientist of the Sea* by Frances Leigh Williams, 1963

The desire to investigate scientific fields in America was from the first based upon both interest in understanding the Creation and a desire to share this knowledge for the benefit of others. This is a major outcome of so much that has appeared as American. And it is simply due to our Biblical beginnings and the prevalence of the Christian idea of man in government.

A major purpose for the teaching and learning of the sciences in an American Christian school should be to *edify* and *instruct* both teachers and students in the *wholeness* and *unity* of God's wonderful works. In addition to the teaching of science by the Principle Approach as is demonstrated by David Holmes in the section following, we also need to search out and present our students with the *writings* of those early men of science who were able to capture the wonder of God's Creation. It is also important to read some of the writings of men who relinquished the Biblical account of Creation—men like Charles Darwin. These writings, in contrast to those of creationists, horrify rather then edify, for we see the lengths to which the human mind will go to avoid acceptance of a First Great Cause and a complete Creation.

The implications of the evolutionary theories of plant and animal life are not limited to the biological and zoological spheres. But they have implication for the *political* and *governmental* fields. The writings of Darwin spawned the field of social Darwinism as demonstrated by Herbert Spencer. And it is notable that Karl Marx wished to dedicate *Das Capital* to Darwin. John Dewey and the writers of progressive education also based their theories of education and the *new social order* upon many of the leading ideas which Darwin had postulated for the origin, descent, and elimination of species. In the following quotation we can discern the basis of some political ideas which have had consequences in our 20th century:

"Finally, it may not be a logical deduction, but to my imagination it is far more satisfactory to look at such instincts as the young cuckoo ejecting its foster-brothers,–ants making slaves,–the larvae of ichneumonidae feeding within the live bodies of caterpillars,–not as specially endowed or created instincts, but as small consequences of one general law leading to the advancement of all organic beings,–namely, multiply, vary, let the strongest live and the weakest die . . ." pp. 296–297

"In the survival framework of bones in the hand of a man, wing of a bat, fin of a porpoise, and leg of the horse,–the same number of vertebrae forming the neck of the giraffe and of the elephant,–and innumerable other such facts, at once explain themselves on the theory of descent with slow and slight successive modifications... It is so easy to hide our ignorance under such explanations as the *plan of creation, unity of design,* and to think that we give an explanation when we only re-state a fact . . ." p. 517

"As all living forms of life are the lineal descendants of those which lived long before the

Cambrian epoch, we may feel certain that the ordinary succession by generation has never once been broken, and that no cataclysm has desolated the whole world. Hence we may look with some confidence to a secure future of great length. And as natural selection works solely by and for the good of each being, all corporeal and mental endowments will tend to progress towards perfection . . ." p. 528

"Thus from the war of nature, from famine and death, the most exalted object which we are capable of conceiving, namely production of the higher animals, directly follows. There is grandeur in this view of life, with its several powers, having been originally breathed by the Creator into a few forms or into one; and that, whilst this planet has gone cycling on according to the fixed law of gravity, from so simple a beginning endless forms most beautiful and most wonderful have been, and are being evolved." pp. 528–529

The Origin of the Species,
Charles Darwin, 1859

While these statements will hardly edify the mind and heart of teachers and students they can prove to be most instructive.

By contrast, consider these words from one of the most widely read texts in American Science, *The Physical Geography of the Sea and its Meteorology* by Matthew Fontaine Maury, 1855, and republished by Harvard University's Belknap Press in 1963:

"There is no more worthy or suitable employment of the human mind than to trace the evidences of design and purpose in the Creator, which are visible in many parts of the creation. Hence, to the right-minded mariner, and to him who studies the physical relations of earth, sea, and air, the atmosphere is something more than a shoreless ocean, at the bottom of which his bark is wafted or driven along. It is an envelope or covering for the dispersion of light and heat over the surface of the earth; it is a sewer into which, with every breath we draw, we cast vast quantities of dead animal matter; it is a laboratory for purification, in which that matter is recompounded, and wrought again into wholesome and healthful shapes; it is a machine for pumping up all the rivers from the sea, and conveying the waters for their fountains on the ocean to their sources in the mountains.

"Upon the proper working of this machine depends the well being of every plant and animal that inhabits the earth; therefore the management of it, or its movement, or the performance of its offices, can not be left to chance. They are, we may rely

upon it, guided by laws that make all parts, functions, and movements of machinery as obedient to order as are the planets in their orbits.

"An examination into the economy of the universe will be sufficient to satisfy the well-balanced minds of observant men that the laws which govern the atmosphere and the laws which govern the ocean are laws which were put in force by the Creator when the foundations of the earth were laid, and that therefore, they are laws of order . . .

"The Bible frequently makes allusions to the laws of nature, their operation and effects . . . As our knowledge of Nature and her laws has increased, so has our understanding of many passages in the Bible been improved. The Bible called the earth 'the round world', yet for ages it was the most damnable heresy for Christian men to say the world is round; and finally, sailors circumnavigated the globe, proved the Bible to be right, and saved Christian men of science from the stake . . .

"Whenever I turn to contemplate the works of nature, I am struck with the admirable system of compensation, with the beauty and nicety with which every department is poised by the others; things and principles are meted out in directions the most opposite, but in proportions so exactly balanced and nicely adjusted, that the results the most harmonious are produced.

"It is by the action of opposite and compensating forces that the earth is kept in its orbit, and the stars held suspended in the azure vault of heaven; and these forces are so exquisitely adjusted, that, at the end of a thousand years, the earth, the sun, and moon, and every star in the firmament, is found to come to its proper place at the proper moment.

"Nay, philosophy teaches us, that when the little snow-drop, which in our garden walks we see raising its beautiful head to remind us that spring is at hand, was created, that the whole mass of the earth, from pole to pole, and from circumference to centre, must have been taken into account and weighed, in order that the proper degree of strength might be given to the fibres of even this little plant.

"Botanists tell us that the constitution of this plant is such as to require, that, at a certain stage of its growth, the stalk should bend, and the flower should bow its head, that an operation may take place which is necessary in order that the herb should produce seed after its kind; and that, after this, its vegetable health requires it that it should lift its head again and stand erect. Now, if the mass of the earth had been greater or less, the force of gravity would have been different; in that case, the strength of fibre in the snow-drop, as it is, would have been too much or too little; the plant could not bow or raise its head at the right time, fecundation could not take place, and its family would have become extinct with the first individual that was planted, because its 'seed' would not have been 'in itself' and therefore it could not reproduce itself.

"Now, if we see such perfect adaptation, such exquisite adjustment, in the case of one of the smallest flowers of the field, how much more may we not expect 'compensation' in the atmosphere and the ocean, upon the right adjustment and due performance of which depends not only the life of that plant, but the well-being of every individual that is found in the entire vegetable and animal kingdoms of the world? . . .

"Harmonious in their action, the air and sea are obedient to law and subject to order in all their movements; when we consult them in the performance of their offices, they teach us lessons concerning the wonders of the deep, the mysteries of the sky, the greatness, and the wisdom, and goodness of the Creator. The investigations into the broad-spreading circle of phenomena connected with the winds of heaven and the waves of the sea are second to none for the good they do and the lessons which they teach. The astronomer is said to see the hand of God in the sky; but does not the right-minded mariner, who looks aloft as he ponders over these things, hear His voice in every wave of the sea that 'claps its hands', and feel His presence in every breeze that blows?"

The Physical Geography of the Sea, M.F. Maury, LL.D., 3rd Ed., 1855, pp. 68-69; 94-96

Those who accept the evolving universe and its random patterns will find little comfort in being a chance creation. While they seek to escape God's Laws–they also miss God's Love. The field of Creation Science has grown professionally during this century, and their writings are numerous and impressive in Biblical scientific reasoning. Yet we still need to restore a quality of scientific literature which inspires us with the unity, diversity and beauty of God's Universe. This is the outcome of reflective learners who then become effective teachers–and perhaps writers of the same ability as Matthew Fontaine Maury, scientist of Oceanography, charterer of the sea.

"Thou madest him to have dominion over the works of thy hands; thou has put all things under his feet:
All sheep and oxen, yea, and the beasts of the field;
The fowl of the air, and the fish of the sea, and whatsoever passeth through the paths of the seas.
O Lord our Lord, how excellent is thy name in all the earth!"   Psalms 8:6–9

DAVID HOLMES

"Known unto God are all his works from the beginning of the world." Acts 15:18

When Miss Hall and I met Mr. David Holmes at Oklahoma Christian Heritage Academy, we were impressed with two things. First, Mr. Holmes impressed us with his character of quiet assurance, his obvious dedication to the ministry of teaching in a Christian school in America, and his willingness to listen to two ladies who were proposing an alternative plan for his teaching and learning. Secondly, we were impressed when Mr. Holmes confronted us with the massive textbooks of science which he was responsible to teach to students. Not only was Mr. Holmes responsible for most if not all the science courses in the High School; he was also required to find the methods of imparting a vast amount of knowledge to his classes.

As the school was a Biblically academic Christian school we knew that all of Mr. Holmes' courses stemmed from the Creationist position. But we also were aware of the vast changes in education which, even in Christian education, were still infusing a mass of learning without providing the historical or American perspective. Why should this be a concern in Christian schools? Once again, unless we wish to ignore the impact of the Gospel of Jesus Christ upon men and nations, we cannot disregard the historical appearing of America. America as the world's first Christian Constitutional Republic set free the church and the state externally. Each was designed to support the other as can be determined by the writings of our Founding generations. But, with the liberty which the Gospel brought about in civil government, men were free to develop every field–and most especially the sciences–according to a Biblical position.

One might ask what particular additions could be made to courses of study in the fields of science which were already founded on the Creationist approach? And as Mr. Holmes relates in his autobiography, for several years he sought to find the way to *take dominion* over his courses of study so that he might better reach the students with the relevance of what they were learning to their own lives and to that of the nation in which God had placed them. We appreciate his persistence and as we have watched him teach his present course of study–as presented in this volume–we find a thrilling change in the quality and character and content of his ministry as an American Christian teacher.

How can Mr. Holmes help other teachers to grow and become productive in the mastery of their science curriculum as he did?

In Part I of his American Christian Philosophy of Natural Science, Mr. Holmes begins by showing us how to define our terms so that we may "understand exactly what we are studying." To be able to identify one's field of study means that both teacher and students may reflect upon the meaning of words which they may have been using for many years without being able to really explain them. We are now dealing with the *Philosophy of Natural Science* from a Principle Approach.

The terms are not difficult but they should be part of a lesson which will not only be researched, but reasoned and related, before they are recorded in the student's notebook.

To determine what makes this philosophy both Christian and American, Mr. Holmes supplies us with his Key Terms, with an Historical Statement by a man of science, and he proceeds to Elucidate what this means in the light of his Leading Idea, that "God is the creator who brought into existence all things from nothing."

Mr. Holmes develops his Leading Ideas so that we become aware of the fact that there is a unity in His Story which includes the history of science, and is inseparable from civil and religious liberty.

In a helpful statement, Mr. Holmes explains the difference between trying to teach the Christian History principles as science, rather than teaching the Biblical principles of science, and seeking to produce in students by their productivity a character which is the product of embodying the Christian History principles.

Having established the philosophy or framework in which he is going to teach all subjects in science, Mr. Holmes then begins the development of his course in *Human Anatomy and Physiology*, Part II of his writing. Once again we can ask the question: Does the study of human anatomy have anything to do with history? If we believe that the Christian Idea of man was first presented to the world by our Lord Jesus Christ, then we must admit that the silent revolution caused by this idea affected how man is regarded—*internally* as well as *externally*. Thus as men reasoned their way out of the Dark Ages, and were freed by the Reformation and the scientific investigation of man, so did a *kinder* more *compassionate* regard for the individual bring forth "practical application of anatomy and physiology."

Time Lines are exciting when you are not only tracing men in a particular field of study, but also the events of history which allow the liberty of the individual to investigate that field. Mr. Holmes' Time Line is especially illuminating in this regard. To give us a flavor of how a *Key Individual* can be handled in biographical form we meet an American Christian physician, Dr. Benjamin Rush, who was active in the events of our American Revolution and a Signer of our Declaration of Independence. Mr. Holmes includes his ministry as both a physician and an American Christian patriot.

Now we come to the heart of Mr. Holmes' excellent presentation of *Applying the Principle Approach to Human Anatomy and Physiology.* He takes us through the necessary first steps of identifying the vocabulary and properties of the subject. You might be surprised at some of the vocabulary which he includes because he is taking into account what he has found of "the Biblical origin and purpose of the specific course content." The Bible does speak to us through this subject.

We can see from Mr. Holmes' Basic Principles for the course that while he will not deviate from the fundamentals of *Human Anatomy and Physiology*, he will include areas which other programs would not as yet consider, namely, the historical unfoldment of this subject, and its relationship to the Christian idea of man and government. There is a divine *coincidence* of men and events in His Story.

When we are introduced to Mr. Holmes' OVERVIEWS of his Course we learn that what is taught at the High School Level can be *well begun* at the Elementary Level of Learning. This is such an important concern in teaching any subject in an American Christian school. We do not wait until High School to present the Bible to our students. Nor do we hesitate to present them with the foundation of the Biblical and theological doctrines we wish to impart. But, as we progress through the years of education, the levels of learning and maturity are deepened and documented with further detail. Just so in the course *Human Anatomy and Physiology* presented here.

If we would have our students begin to consider how the Lord has created them, it is important in the Elementary years to bring them to a consideration of these words of the Psalmist: *"I will praise thee; for I am fearfully and wonderfully made: marvellous are thy works; and that my soul knoweth right well."* Psalm 139:14.

The property of our bodies is one of the basic principles of our American Christian History. During the early years we teach this Biblical principle:

I Am God's Property

God made me for His purpose
He fashioned me to be
An image for His glory,
Almighty Father He.

Teaching & Learning, p. 230

And as James Madison, often called the Father of our American Christian Constitution, wrote: "Conscience is the most sacred of all property." *Christian History* p. 248A. Our freedom to enjoy liberty and property is one of the "blessings" which our Constitutional Republic has allowed us.

A Sample Lesson Plan completes this excellent presentation by David Holmes. He teaches you how to set up your Basic Principles, Leading Ideas, and then identify which facts you will teach and the methods of demonstration. References and Assignments are also included to complete your plan. Lastly, a Bibliography of books is included so that you may understand some of his sources.

We appreciate the vision of Mr. Ralph Bullard of Oklahoma's Christian Heritage Academy who gave Mr. David Holmes the freedom and the encouragement to pursue his search and research in this important field of science. We rejoice too that now our students will have more teachers of the quality of Mr. Holmes who was willing to pioneer the Principle Approach to an American Christian Philosophy of Natural Science and to take us down the trail of one particular course so that we might in turn praise the Lord for His infinite Wisdom and Grace. We pray that many parents and teachers will be blessed and encouraged to produce their own courses of science study under the guidance and teaching of the Holy Spirit.

BARBARA B. ROSE
Typing in the American Christian Curriculum

When Barbara Rose began her study of typing in the Principle Approach, the program of American Christian History and education had just been launched in the pilot school of which James Rose was the Head Master Teacher. Barbara, too, soon became a Master Teacher. In fact, she was the first to record her findings so that her study might prove to be helpful to other teachers, no matter what subjects they taught.

A basic goal of American Christian education is the character development of students as they live out their Christian lives. In both home and school there are "arenas" for these character struggles to take place. Where better than in the use and mastery of the typewriter? And indeed, Barbara Rose immediately classifies her subject as being first of *internal* importance, secondly, "as an acquired neuro-muscular skill." She writes: "We believe that typing in an American Christian curriculum can and should contribute to the advancement of individual Christian character, self-government and property as well as a knowledge of the basic skills of the subject."

Barbara, as an obedient wife and a good teacher, identifies what the *4 R's* of her typing course will be. Then she identifies the *Course Aims and Goals* and presents us with *Course Overviews* for both first and second year students. It is always so satisfying in a course of study to know what you will be covering in content. However, before beginning with the machine—the typewriter, Mrs. Rose takes her students on a journey through history to discover how the field of "type" has played a role in the westward course of the Gospel and individual liberty. This should make every student sit up straight—even though posture has not yet been addressed. For, a subject becomes important through God's use of that subject.

After "setting the stage" for the course, the students begin to participate. Not only do they have their own Notebooks for lecture notes, handouts, exams, and all the other aspects of a Principle Approach course of study, but now they can keep a record of their own achievement. And they must face up to their machines—learn finger positions—practice—be accurate—develop speed. But what kind of materials will they record on their typewriters?

I first became aware of the uniqueness of Mrs. Rose's course in typing when she showed me that she was not just using those boring exercises to which all typing students are usually exposed. No. Barbara, following the admonition of Noah Webster, was enlarging the knowledge that her students had of America's Christian History. In her curriculum she has this quotation which prompted her to give her students excerpts from some of the rich original sources of our history of liberty:

"I consider it a capital fault in all our schools, that the books generally used contain subjects wholly uninteresting to our youth." What Noah Webster proposed was the following:

"In America it will be useful to furnish schools with additional essays, containing the history, geography, and transactions of the United States. Information on these subjects is necessary for youth, both in forming their habits and improving their minds. A love of our country, and an acquaintance with its true state, are indispensable."

So, as Barbara indicates in her Methods section, "students will use sections of State Papers, famous documents of America's Christian history, addresses and quotes of the Founding Fathers, as well as patriotic poetry for typing practice."

Now, you may say, these pieces of typing material could prove to be boring also. Yes, they could. But teacher enthusiasm can make the difference—

and presentation–and setting. Perhaps, as the entire school commemorates those days when the Continental Army came from death into life at Valley Forge, Barbara might choose something from that inspiring section in *Consider and Ponder,* which students can type as they practice their skills, and commit some memorable events of our history to heart and mind. One officer wrote about the men at Valley Forge:

"Naked and starving as they are, we cannot enough admire the incomparable patience and fidelity of the soldiery that they have not been ere this excited by their sufferings to a general mutiny and desertion." "Nothing can equal their sufferings," says the Committee, "except the patience and fortitude with which they bear them." And Thomas Wharton, Governor of Pennsylvania, wrote to General Washington, the Commander-in-Chief of this ragged army:

"The unparalleled patience and magnanimity with which the army under your Excellency's command have endured the hardships attending their situation, unsupplied as they have been through an uncommonly severe winter, is an honor which posterity will consider as more illustrious then could have been derived to them by a victory obtained by any sudden and vigorous exertion. 'I would cherish these dear, ragged Continentals, whose patience will be the admiration of future ages, and glory in bleeding with them' cried John Laurens in the enthusiasm of youth."

Continental Oration at Valley Forge, p. 62

In the restoration of the quality of American Christian education which we had in the establishment of this nation is it not an excellent idea to incorporate the content of some of our memorable Christian History into a typing class?

In Barbara Rose's *Biblical Vocabulary of Typing* we find that the word *type,* which refers to the piece of metal or wood which makes an impression, also provides us with another opportunity for character development. For if we trace the *mark* or *impression* made by type on paper or parchment, it suggests that what also leaves a *mark* or *impression* is the quality of *individual character* as it takes on each experience of life.

In tracing the history of *Type and the Typewriter* Mrs. Rose confronts us with the excitement which she experienced as she researched this aspect of her teaching program. Again, we marvel at the Hand of God in bringing so many elements together so that we might enjoy first, our Bible in English, second, the art of printing itself.

So, what remains is the mastery of the machine

and the skills it entails. Certainly, as each student in the typing class toils to perfect typing skills, it will require character. Dominion must be exerted over finger placement. A determination to be accurate must keep pace with speed. A straight back and a clear eye are also part of the repertoire of matching one's character to the task at hand.

Typing has been placed as the last course in this selection of Curriculum Content to illustrate the Principle Approach to American Christian Education. The *last* should indeed have been the *first.* Students need to begin typing shortly after they learn how to hand write, particularly now as the word processor and the computer have gained access to the American Christian home and school. Why wait? So many students regret that they did not take some of their summer time to gain this skill so that they could produce much, much more in their assignments and in the organization of their class notes in their notebooks.

We appreciate that Mrs. Rose was an encouragement both to her husband as she applied the Principle Approach to her field of typing, and to other teachers as she was willing to write up the record of her teaching and learning. We pray that many more teachers will take on their subjects in the spirit and purpose of Barbara Rose, now a teacher of her own children in the home.

GLORIA DIFLEY
Book Designer and Graphic Artist

It is appropriate to follow the section on *The Principle Approach to Typing,* by mention and appreciation of the tremendous task which Gloria Difley took on when she agreed to finish the design of Jim Rose's book. Typography is a field which has a governmental aspect in that it too, historically, is related to the westward course of the Gospel. Looking at the history of the styles of type, one can discern that as the Christian idea of man affected society, the "signs following" were visible in all fields.

This volume has been set in CASLON 540. William Caslon (1692–1766) was an English designer of type, perhaps the greatest. The individual letter forms, the grace of the numerals and italics, are all aspects of that appreciation of God's principle of individuality. No wonder that our Declaration of Independence, which was the first great national document embodying the Christian idea of man in government, was printed in Caslon. Caslon was a style much admired by our founders, and especially by Benjamin Franklin, former printer.

With Caslon as the type style to indicate the importance of individual character as the basis of our American Christian Republic, it is not surprising that all of the aspects relating to this volume relate to the character of those individuals who fulfilled their specialized tasks to bring it forth. Gloria Difley had been working on the Christian History volumes with our original designer for some years and in 1981 took over the program exclusively. She consented to complete Jim Rose's book design after it had already been started. But, however difficult it was to not have been able to begin the book design, she has made the spirit and the letter of the book come alive with her persistence and her professional skills. It has been important that all aspects of the book testify to both the *unity* and the *diversity* of the content and the many authors of the Principle Approach to American Christian Education. This means that it must reflect typographically the *unity* of philosophy and the *diversity* of the individual authors herein represented. Only thus could it truly represent the spirit and the letter of what has been presented.

Setting type is one field, but, putting together the many elements that make up a book, is another, namely Book Designing. It is both a professional and an artistic field. And it reflects the skill and vision of the book-designer. A book represents a philosophy of education and government, and it must have its own character reflected in the design as well as in the typography. The *external* appearance must reflect what is expressed within its covers — the *internal* message.

In this volume charts play a big role in identifying both curriculum content and the role of the Bible and history in all subjects. Mrs. Difley has worked out more than one hundred and twenty-five charts from many distinctive authors. Her goal was to achieve the unity and diversity which are expressive of the Principle Approach. As you can imagine, this kind of charting and drafting takes infinite patience for the detail is endless. It is indeed a tribute to Mrs. Difley's desire to express excellence in her field as tribute to the Lord — the Author and Founder of America's Christian History.

We are grateful that Gloria Difley has helped us appreciate what it takes to express in design and type the American Christian character of government and education. Thank you, Gloria, for your commitment to this task.

NOAH WEBSTER
Founder of American Christian Education
Writes on the Constitution

This book appears with the 200th national celebration of the Signing of the Constitution of the United States on September 17th, at the conclusion of the long hot summer of 1787. During this summer in Philadelphia — "the city of brotherly love" — fifty-five men, selected as delegates from their individual states, worked in secret session to bring forth that form of government which we know today has Providentially allowed for the greatest individual liberty the world has ever known.

The Constitution of the United States of America was the culmination of the Christian idea of man appearing in government. For seventeen hundred and eighty-seven years it had travelled westward, steadily unfolding liberty with law. It appeared first in seed form in the *Magna Charta* in England, in the *English Bill of Rights*, the *Mayflower Compact*, the *Massachusetts Body of Liberties*, and in the *Declaration of Independence*. It was evident in our one hundred and fifty years of practice in degrees of self-government within the thirteen original colonies. It was an idea which God had prepared in His Story which was to grow on American soil. It was the culmination of the Chain of Christianity's westward course of the Gospel of Jesus Christ and its impact on both the external as well as the internal aspects of government.

Twelve of the thirteen states sent representatives. Rhode Island refused. Out of seventy-three men selected, only fifty-five actually arrived in Philadelphia. And when the document was ready to be signed there were only thirty-nine signatures appended.

Presided over by George Washington, and recorded copiously by James Madison, the Convention was a gathering well representative of the quality of Biblical, historical and academic education which characterized the colonies during the 17th and 18th centuries. There were some names not present — though they still had an influence over the meeting. John Adams, an authority on the field of government, was serving as our American Minister to England. Thomas Jefferson was in Paris, serving as our American Minister to France. And John Jay, later to be celebrated in *The Federalist Papers*, was not at the Convention. Yet God had brought to the city of Brotherly Love a young man who, though not a delegate, became an articulate exponent of the American Constitution. Providentially, Noah Webster, the 29-year old Connecticut schoolmaster, was teaching in the city during the Convention. Noah Webster had already made himself known as interested in the Convention, for two years before he had visited George Washington at Mount Vernon with a proposal for a national form of government. There was something forceful about the young educator, for he was visited in his rooms by most of the outstanding delegates: George Washington, Benjamin Franklin, James Madison,

Rufus King, Edmund Randolph, Oliver Ellsworth, William Livingston, John Marshall and others. No wonder then that Thomas Fitzsimmons, a delegate from Pennsylvania, requested Noah Webster to prepare an essay in support of the completed document. Written in about six weeks time, Webster's essay was well received in both northern and southern colonies. It was in fact circulating throughout the land before the more famous *Federalist Papers*.

What can we learn from Noah Webster's *An Examination into the Leading Principles of the Federal Constitution proposed by the late Convention held at Philadelphia?* It is not our purpose here to set forth Noah Webster's reasoning on principles of government, but, rather, to make note of the fact that he was *capable* of writing such an essay. Noah Webster is called by secular educators as "the schoolmaster to the Republic." We identify him as "The Founding Father of American Scholarship and Education." Educated in the Constitution state of Connecticut, a direct descendant of William Bradford, Pilgrim Governor of Plymouth Plantation, Webster learned his philosophy of government from both church polity and the town meeting of Hartford. He was prepared for Yale College by his pastor, Nathan Perkins, a long-time pastor, evangelist, educator, who held his pulpit for more than fifty years. In other words, both the Gospel and Biblical principles of government were the major emphasis in New England education for more than two centuries. Uppermost in the minds and hearts of all the colonists was the reason for their presence on these shores. They knew that God had given them a new land of liberty. Both Pilgrims and Puritans recorded their recognition of the Providence of God in bringing them to America.

As this book, *A Guide to American Christian Education, the Principle Approach,* appears, just at the period when our nation is celebrating the 200th anniversary of our Constitutional Republic, it makes us pause to consider how important it is that we restore the *missing ingredient* from Christian education in America. What is that missing ingredient? It is the knowledge of our unique form of government and how God was with our fathers in bringing to fruition that which we call the American Constitution. At a time in world history when nations are falling back into darkness and tyranny, we need to accept our God-given stewardship of Liberty – Liberty both civil and religious.

Noah Webster concludes his "Examination into the Leading Principles of the Federal Constitution" with this paragraph:

"The constitution defines the powers of Congress; and every power not expressly delegated to that body, remains in the several state-legislatures. The sovereignty and the republican form of government of each state is guaranteed by the constitution; and the bounds of jurisdiction between the federal and respective state governments, are marked with precision. In theory, it has all the energy of the British and Roman governments, without their defects. In short, the privileges of freemen are interwoven into the feelings and habits of the Americans; *liberty* stands on the immoveable basis of a general distribution of property and diffusion of knowledge; but the Americans must cease to contend, to fear, and to hate, before they can realize the benefits of independence and government, or enjoy the blessings, which heaven has lavished, in rich profusion, upon this western world."

And in his *History of the United States*, a "little volume intended for the use of American youth," he wrote:

"The *Advice to the Young*, it is hoped will be useful in enlightening the minds of youth in religious and moral principles, and serve, in a degree, to restrain some of the common vices of our country. Republican government loses half of its value, where the moral and social duties are imperfectly understood, or negligently practiced. To exterminate our popular vices is a work of far more importance to the character and happiness of our citizens, than any other improvements in our system of education... Almost all the civil liberty now enjoyed in the world owes its origin to the principles of the Christian Religion." *New Haven,* 1832

*"If the foundations be destroyed,
what can the righteous do?"*

Psalms 11:3

CONTENTS
OF THE ENTIRE BOOK

PART I
RUDIMENTS OF AMERICAN CHRISTIAN EDUCATION

ELEMENTARY SCHOOL CURRICULUM*

ELEMENTARY AND HIGH SCHOOL CURRICULUM*

* There is a detailed Table of Contents at the beginning of each curriculum subject.

PART I
RUDIMENTS OF
AMERICAN CHRISTIAN
EDUCATION

BY JAMES B. ROSE

American Christian History Institute
Camarillo, California

A good man out of the good treasure of his heart
bringeth forth good things: and the evil man out of the evil treasure
bringeth forth evil things. (Matthew 12:35)

Inasmuch as Christian Liberty is individual, internal and causative,

does it not follow that there should be a societal,

external effect of this fact?

Verna M. Hall, *Consider and Ponder,* p. xxiv

America's Biblical Education produced America's Christian

History and Constitution. The method was the Principle Approach.

Let us restore the foundation of American Independence.

Rosalie June Slater, *Teaching and Learning,* p. 89

DEFINING THE
PRINCIPLE APPROACH

What is the Principle Approach to American Christian education and government, and how is this approach distinguished from other methods?

Just as God gave the Old Testament with its Moral Law and rules to govern Moses and the children of Israel – a comprehensive body of laws or principles by which they could direct their personal and national lives, and determine the rightness or wrongness of their choices and actions – so God gave the "whole counsel" of both the Law and the Gospel to both Jew and Gentile for the salvation and direction of all men and nations.

As God's eternal Word was translated into the English Bible, our American Christian forefathers discovered therein not only the way of salvation through Christ Jesus but the Biblical truths, laws or principles by which they too could direct or govern their individual and public lives; and they reasoned from these spiritual principles to determine everything from the right kind of education to the right form of government for America.

In its contemporary meaning, the Principle Approach refers to the re-discovery and re-statement of the historic truths or principles of God's Word on which the *character* of our original peace, order, liberty and prosperity, both individually and

corporately, were built. It refers also to the Christian method of reasoning from the Holy Bible (the proper and primary authority concerning our view or philosophy of life and living), and how to comprehend all subjects, inclusive of education and government in the home, church, school and society.

"Therefore, brethren, stand fast, and hold the traditions which ye have been taught, whether by word or by our epistle." (II Thessalonians 2:15)

America's traditional Biblical principles were first restored and explained in *Teaching and Learning America's Christian History – The Principle Approach* by Rosalie J. Slater. It summarizes this approach in seven key principles which may be concisely rendered as follows:

1. *God's Principle of Individuality* declares God's infinite individuality and diversity, and reveals that God created distinct and unique identities consistent with His nature and character. It exposes the error not only of secular collectivism but of any individualism separate from Christ.

3

2. *The Christian Principle of Self-Government* shows that man's capacity for governing himself, then his family, city, state and nation depends upon man's obedience to "the spirit of the law of Christ" in each expanding sphere of government. (Rom. 8:2)

3. *America's Heritage of Christian Character* is maintained when the attributes of God and His Son so mark the affections and actions of Christians, in conflict and contrast with the carnal world, that they express the same principle of Christian character revealed in the lives of the Pilgrims and Patriots.

4. *"Conscience is the Most Sacred of All Property"* sums up the traditional American conviction that the Christian citizen's most precious possession is his internal God-given sense of right and wrong, of the ultimate lawfulness or unlawfulness of his own actions and affections. He also has a God-given right to own external property, and a Christian responsibility for its stewardship.

5. *The Christian Form of Our Government* is revealed when we discover that America's civil government grew out of Biblical Law and the Gospel. The Biblical principles of self-government, conscience as property, and voluntary union gave rise to a Christian Republic based upon individual representation, separation of powers and federalism in both the states and the nation.

6. *How the Seed of Local Self-Government is Planted* is seen in America's Christian History: individuals planted and preserved the seed of Christian self-government and enjoyed the fruits of local sovereignty by teaching and practicing – in each sphere of local government – industry, charity and obedience to all laws not contrary to the Biblical principles of truth and righteousness.

7. *The Christian Principle of American Political Union* is the Biblical principle of voluntarism, which shows that God wants His children to cooperate and work together politically, commercially and in meeting community needs through voluntary consent, without compromising a Christian conscience or Scriptural separation.

Modern day Christians can agree with our Founding Fathers on the definition of the word *principle* in Noah Webster's 1828 American Dictionary of the English Language: "The source, origin or cause of a thing; that from which a thing proceeds." The more deeply contemporary Christians probe America's Christian history, turning to authentic source materials which are now readily available in the compilations by Verna M. Hall, the more confirmation they will find that an array of Biblical principles truly were "the source, origin or cause" of America's original philosophy of education and government.

And the more Christians today study America's Christian history – which for a century has been obscured and untaught – the more evidence they will see that this type of Biblical reasoning is indeed America's historic method of reasoning which distinguished the educational philosophy of learning of colonial Americans and which subsequently, under God's Providence, produced America's Christian history and, finally, its Constitution.

The Holy Scriptures and God's Providence, working in the hearts and minds of the American colonists – many of them earnest born-again Christians – produced the Principle Approach; and in turn, the Principle Approach, as a method of Biblical reasoning, produced these seven principles of America's Christian history and government.

OCCUPY TILL I COME

By the grace of God, this approach will be used by today's Christians, as the Lord tarries, to fulfill the command to "occupy till I come" (Luke 19:13), and to restore this Republic to its Gospel purpose: to spread the Gospel and its implications for both individual Christian liberty and the resulting civil liberty to *all nations* of the world and enable them to testify to the dominion or sovereignty of God through the Lord Jesus Christ.

The more the Principle Approach is understood and applied in contemporary America, the more God will be glorified. The more widely this approach is grasped and put to work by today's Christians, the more evidence we will see of American renewal, or the restoration of our Republic.

As vast numbers of unsaved Americans begin to perceive that this Bible-based Principle Approach – the application of Biblical wisdom to our educational and governmental choices and actions, and the solving of our social problems – comes directly from the Word of God, and meets urgent human needs which no worldly wisdom knows how to meet, they will have more reason to respect the supernatural wisdom of Christ and Biblical Christianity, and to turn to the Lord to be saved.

The more any individual studies the Principle Approach, the more reason he will have to search the Scriptures, and the more he will learn of the vastness of Biblical truth, and of its remarkable relevance to a surprisingly wide range of subjects

4

and aspects of life, including his own spiritual growth.

For example, the more anyone thoughtfully pursues the Principle Approach, the more he will learn about the real nature of government, of "the government that shall be upon His shoulder," upon the shoulder of the Prince of Peace, and the more he will understand why Isaiah said (Isa. 9:6–7) "of the *increase* of His government and peace there shall be no end..." In particular, the Christian who studies this approach will find that the same spiritual process that produces a self-governing *citizen* – learning how to know and do the will of God, and to be absolutely governed by Him – is inseparable from the process that produces a *saint*, i.e., a sanctified mature Christian.

PREPARING THE FREE AND INDEPENDENT INDIVIDUAL

This approach enables the individual to *think governmentally*, that is, to think in terms of "who" or "what" is controlling, restraining, directing or regulating; to discern whether the operations of government (direction, regulation, control, restraint) are being confirmed by, and exercised with, the operations of education. It compels one to ask, "Who is governing, first, internally – from the heart or mind?" Then, "Who is governing externally, in social and civil activities?"

The Honorable Robert Charles Winthrop (1809–1894), Massachusetts orator and legislator, explained why American Christians should think governmentally:

"All societies of men must be governed in some way or other. The less they may have of stringent State Government, the more they must have of individual self-government. The less they rely on public law or physical force, the more they must rely on private moral restraint. Men, in a word, must necessarily be controlled, either by a power within them, or by a power without them; either by the Word of God, or by the strong arm of man; either by the Bible, or by the bayonet."[1]

This approach enables the individual to extend Biblical principles of government and the doctrine of Providence into every sphere of life, that in all things Christ, the living Word of God, may have the pre-eminence, the rightful place, power and influence.

---

1. Address delivered at the Annual Meeting of the Massachusetts Bible Society, Boston, May 1849; *The Christian History of the American Revolution, Consider and Ponder,* p. 20, hereafter referred to as C/P.

THE 4 R'S

In method, the Principle Approach begins by restoring the four "R's" to teaching and learning.

RESEARCHING: studying God's Word to identify basic principles of life and living, and those principles which govern the "how" and "what" in teaching.

REASONING: reasoning from these Biblical principles so as to identify them for the student in each subject of the curriculum.

RELATING: expounding to each student the Bible Truth in the subjects of the curriculum; relating the truths of God's Word to individual Christian character, self-government and stewardship of God's gifts.

RECORDING: the use of writing, by both teacher and student, to account for and elucidate the way in which these principles are being applied to life and living, as well as to a given subject.

SEVEN DISTINCTIONS

The Principle Approach is distinguished from other approaches to education in at least seven ways:

1. It demonstrates that the history of Christianity and the history of America and her form of government cannot, and should not, be separated.

2. It restores our heritage of Christian scholarship and Biblical reasoning and writing which were characteristic of the Founding Father generation.

3. It brings both the student and the subjects of the curriculum into harmony with, and in subjection to, Biblical Truths.

4. It produces a unity of spirit and principle with a diversity of teachers and subjects, without denying the identity or individuality of either the subjects or the teacher in the home or school.

5. It helps identify the vocabulary and rudiments of a subject, both Biblically and historically, and recovers the Biblical origin and purpose of a subject in every grade level of education.

6. It unifies the Biblical principles of a subject with its correlative ideas and facts.

7. It enables both parent and teacher to produce the Christian character and scholarship necessary to support a Christian Republic, to separate from progressive and secular methods, and avoid producing a character ripe for governmental socialism and religious modernism.

Numerous Christian homes, churches, and schools throughout America have accepted the challenge and the responsibility to restore the Principle Approach and to implement it in the curriculum.

American Christians are urged to personally identify and document *Biblically, governmentally, educationally,* and *historically,* each of the seven principles of America's Christian history and government.

It took 1620 years from the birth of Christ, as the Chain of Christianity moved westward, before the seeds of Christian self-government, property, and unity and union were planted in America with the Pilgrim settlement. Then, for over 150 years, Colonial Christians used Biblical research, reasoning, relating and recording to produce an independent, Constitutional Federal Republic – one nation under God.

This calibre of Biblical reasoning must prevail again in order to restore what "the locusts have eaten" (Joel 2:25) through our own forgetfulness and ignorance. It will require a willingness on the part of Christian leaders to "*Remember* His marvellous works that He hath done, His wonders, and the judgments of His mouth;" (I Chr. 16:12), to patiently, "with all readiness of mind," search "the Scriptures daily, whether those things were so" (Acts 17:11) "that in *all* things," education and civil government as well, "He might have the pre-eminence." (Col. 1:18)

IN RETROSPECT

Before I expand this subject further, I would like to share with you some of my Christian history to explain how the Lord led me to embrace these convictions and the writing of this *Guide*.

As a mere lad of eight I asked Jesus Christ into my heart in response to a neighborhood evangelistic program; but while I attended church and was inspired by various Bible preachers and teachers, I was in fact a merely nominal Christian until my freshman year in college when I was compelled to search the Scriptures for a deeper understanding, and experienced a personal rededication and a new sense of God's plan and purpose for my life.

Shortly after that I met a fellow student whose parents were earnest Christians committed to relating their knowledge of Biblical truth to their responsibilities as citizens. Through this family I came to know a remarkable Christian historian and student of civil government, Miss Verna M. Hall, who introduced me to a study of America's Christian history.

After college, I became an officer in the United States Navy Supply Corps, and then a business-man; but all the while I continued my study of Christian history and became increasingly convinced that the Hand of God and Biblical Christianity had produced the exceptional degree of civil liberty that Americans had long enjoyed, and that for our freedom and prosperity to continue, it was imperative for the people of this country to regain an understanding of the Biblical principles on which America was built.

As a young businessman, I came to admire a Southern California pastor who often explained from the pulpit the relation between Biblical Truth and current political issues – a man who began to work with Miss Verna Hall and Miss Rosalie Slater in introducing America's Christian history into the curriculum of his Christian day school. This pastor invited me to become his administrative assistant, and gave me the opportunity to teach American Christian government in his Christian high school. I left the business world as part owner and operator of a small corporation and devoted myself full time to this Christian ministry in both church and school.

A few years later another earnest Christian pastor, who had been a special agent in the FBI and a counter-intelligence specialist before entering the pulpit, determined to start a Christian day school, with Miss Verna Hall and Miss Rosalie Slater of the Foundation for American Christian Education as curriculum consultants. In turn, I was asked to join the school's faculty and within a year became its Headmaster.

As I began to teach full time, I saw more clearly than ever that American Christian education is the bulwark of this country's religious and civil liberty and that only through restoring the Biblically-based Principle Approach to the Christian home, church and school could we perpetuate the vital relationship between this country's evangelical and political liberty.

I was further persuaded that the Principle Approach could restore and rebuild the foundations of the American Republic by implanting the Biblical view of God, man *and government*, and then by cultivating the character to be an American Christian, not just a Christian in America.

I desired to evangelize the lost and prepare Christians with the character and the scholarship to discern and distinguish the Christian purpose of a subject from the pagan purpose, to detect and deny socialism and modernism in education and government, as well as in religion. I hoped to help revive and restore an individual understanding of America's historic method of Biblical reasoning that it might be applied to all spheres of life, including America and her Christian form of government.

I sought to help prepare a generation of students who would be God's instruments or means for *revival*. Webster's 1828 Dictionary definition suggested the spirit of real revival. To me it meant to prepare a generation of students to be God's instruments to "return, recall and recover" indifferent, carnal, merely nominal Christians to new life in Christ; to "return, recall and recover to life" not only our homes and churches, but the American Christian purpose of education, civil government, and economics. I hoped to prepare teachers who would recall or recover America's Gospel purpose from languor, neglect and obscurity. I longed for teachers and students, parents and pastors who would be tempered and fit, quickened and refreshed with joy, hope and the aspirations of a spiritually and politically free and independent people.

There were many challenges I had to meet and many conflicts that I had to resolve in order to implement and administer the Principle Approach for the first time in a Christian day school. A Christian philosophy of education had to be identified and implemented. I had to begin within myself and think through and write out my own understanding of the *American Christian* philosophy of education before teaching teachers this approach. It meant taking leadership – to follow in advance of others the path of Biblical reasoning that had been identified by those Pilgrims and Pioneers who had gone before me.

NEED FOR DEFINITION

As I continued to study America's Christian history, I became increasingly aware of how insistent our Founding Fathers were in using key terms precisely and in explaining their ideas with maximum clarity.

I became convinced that such precision of thought was spiritually and intellectually sound, and represented a pattern of thinking and communicating that needs to be restored in this nation today. In turn, I sought to adopt this pattern of precise definition of terms in both my own study and in my teaching.

The one dictionary I chose for this purpose was Noah Webster's 1828 *American Dictionary of the English Language*, reprinted by the Foundation for American Christian Education. This primary resource, often called the world's first Christian dictionary, is preferred before all others for three reasons best declared by Miss Rosalie Slater in the title page of the facsimile edition. Miss Slater reasons that Webster's first edition 1) documents "the unique nature of our form of government and of our civil institutions which 'requires an appropriate language of the definition of words.'"; 2) demonstrates "'to the youth of the United States' the best American and English authors as authorities in the use and definition of language"; and 3) defines "to all Americans 'that the principles of republican government have their origin in the Scriptures.'" Hence, as Miss Slater summarily documents on pages 9-10 of the facsimile edition, Webster's 1828 Dictionary is needed to restore "Biblical definitions," "Christian Constitutional meanings," and "a standard for American Language."

APPROACH TO TEACHER TRAINING

The program I used to instruct teachers was as follows: First, I said American Christian Education had to be defined. I began with a definition of education and then defined *Christian* education. Secondly, I explained what constituted *American* Christian Education. Finally I explained the Principle Approach. I discussed government – internally and externally. I had to document and explain why a sound Christian philosophy of government constitutes a philosophy of education.

The emphasis upon government made some teachers uncomfortable. "After all," they asked, "what does government have to do with education?" The answer, I discovered, is that we are dealing first with the government of God through Christ in our lives, and then we are dealing with all other aspects of government – home, church, civil – which extend from that base or which are in opposition to it. The pagan and Christian views of government had to be explained and contrasted.

The basic philosophies of education in America – child-centered, subject-centered, Christ- or Bible-centered – had to be identified so the faculty could avoid becoming overly preoccupied with either child or subject, and learn how to bring both the child and the subject into harmony with Christ and the Bible. Jesus said, "You shall know the truth and the truth shall make you free." (John 8:32) It was essential to know the Biblical truth about our philosophy and approach to education in order to be "free" from evolutionary, progressive or secular humanistic approaches to education.

In any endeavor, the administrator should know his goals and the quality of the product he wants to produce. As Headmaster of a Principle Approach Christian day school, I defined for myself and for the teachers our educational aims and goals. What did we want to produce in our students when they had completed the curriculum?

We needed to know where we wanted to go.

Since we started with grades 7-12 and not an elementary school, every student needed to be taught the *Rudiments of America's Christian History and Government* (see *Curriculum*, p. 227). Yet I realized that few of my teachers had been taught the first principles of America's Christian history and government in their historical setting. Furthermore, I knew that this course was one of the best in the curriculum for developing American Christian character and scholarship, and the ability to think governmentally and Biblically concerning subject content. So the course was taught to the faculty as well as to the students.

When the school was about three years old, summer assignments were prepared for each teacher. The first project: to research each of the seven principles of America's Christian history and government. My conviction was that if each teacher researched these principles in the Scriptures to be assured they were truly Biblical, the Holy Spirit would encourage the teachers and bring a conviction to their hearts that these principles should be taught. After all, every individual has to come to this conviction voluntarily.

When the teachers had researched God's Principle of Individuality and the Christian Principle of Self-government in the Bible, they were requested to answer queries such as "Why is individualism separate from Christ as dangerous to mankind as any form of collectivism?" "At what level does Christian self-government begin?"

After the teachers had prepared thoughtful responses to these and other questions, they were asked to identify these principles of our heritage in history or literature. Soon the faculty began to demonstrate by their own scholarship that these truths were Biblical, practical, and could be identified to their students through a subject in the curriculum. This summer project also encouraged the faculty to continue on their own to take possession of each principle and subject Biblically, historically, and educationally.

Each faculty member was asked to work with the administration to write down the aims, goals, objectives, principles, and leading ideas they desired each student to learn in a subject. We worked together to write course aims or objectives and then course overviews consistent with the administrator's and school's philosophy of education and government.

The principle of local self-government and the dual form of government led us to write out *local classroom constitutions*, consisting of all the basic rules for individual classroom control and conduct – the organization and standards for notebooks, the handling of late work because of absences, late homework, the grading system, and so forth. Each teacher's classroom constitution was to be in harmony with the school constitution, the central "supreme law" of the school and campus.

One of the primary administrative duties was to direct and help teachers to "4 R" – research, reason, relate and record – their subjects and to find out where and how American Christian principles could be identified and related to the student in the subject content. This meant that my office was always open during and after school for any teacher to come in and talk about his or her curriculum.

It also meant that I had to spend time in the classroom observing and helping teachers implement the Principle Approach.

The weekly faculty meeting became a continuing in-service Principle Approach training program, and it meant that I had to expect production and progress, both from myself and from the teachers before the students could really achieve the hoped for Christian character and scholarship. When we restored one of the traditional elements in the Principle Approach educational methodology – use of the *Notebook* – we found that productivity increased immensely. Each teacher and student was required to keep a notebook. (Notebook Methodology is explained in the *Curriculum* section, p. 138)

Our methods of testing were reviewed and corrected to measure reflective learning rather than speculation and mere assimilation of data. The approach to grading was upgraded and amended to be more consistent with fixed Biblical principles and standards of accountability and productivity.

Step by step, more of the faculty and the program reflected the aspirations of our unique Bible-based approach. We were not a "model school," but had become a pilot and demonstration school for the Principle Approach.

THE PURPOSE OF THIS GUIDE

After some twenty-five years of studying this country's Christian history and government and after fifteen years of teaching and administrating it on the elementary, high school and college level, as well as implementing it at home, I became convinced that it would be helpful to others to summarize this experience and the lessons learned in a guide for Christian parents, pastors, teachers, and administrators – a book that would honor the Lord Jesus Christ and exalt the Word of God in every sphere of human experience.

The book is intended to help enlighten and

encourage the individual who is called of God to occupy the following vocations:

Parent: This *Guide* can help mothers and fathers teach their youngsters the Bible principles of self- and civil government. It will identify the rudiments of America's Biblical education and help parents understand the philosophy of government that will equip them to control the *direction* and *quality* of their children's schooling, and fit their boys and girls for a Christian Republic.

The *School at Home* section guides parents in how to instruct themselves in the American Christian philosophy of education, and how to start teaching their own children – at any age – with the aid of the curriculum guides in the book's *Curriculum* section.

Administrator: The Christian school administrator will find this book a guide to thinking through his own statement of a philosophy of government and education. It can also help him become something more than an administrator – a Head Master Teacher who can restore to his teachers the capacity to master their subjects and contribute creatively to building an American Christian curriculum. This *Guide* also suggests how the administrator may achieve a Biblical unity of principle with a diversity of subjects and teachers through the Principle Approach.

Teacher: Christian home or school teachers who are dependent upon text books and packaged programs can use this *Guide* to learn how to take possession of their subjects and gain confidence in using a greater variety of textbooks, references, and classic works of history and literature. Teachers can learn how to apply the Biblical principles of government in classroom control, and thus effect the blessings of self- and civil government in and outside of their school.

Pastor: The author hopes that this *Guide* will encourage clergymen to renew their leadership in *education* and *civil government* through a growing knowledge of the principles of America's Christian history and this nation's method of Biblical reasoning. In earlier times, it ws the pastor who proved to be best equipped to instruct and quicken the conscience of the Republic both in matters of religious and civil liberty. For over two hundred years, from 1620, it was the leadership and scholarship of our clergy that distinguished America's history and government:

"The clergy were generally consulted by the civil authorities; and not infrequently the suggestions from the pulpit on election days and other special occasions, were enacted into laws. The statute book, the reflex of the age, shows this influence. *The state was developed out of the church.*"[2]

---

2. Verna M. Hall, *C/P*, p. 191.

America's
Biblical Education

THE NEED FOR THIS PHILOSOPHY

"Examine yourselves, whether ye be in the faith; prove your own selves . . . " (II Cor. 13:5)

Where is one to find the philosophy or wisdom to exercise the functions of education – to instruct, discipline, enlighten, correct, form and fit? There can be only two choices for the source of such wisdom: God, as revealed in the Bible, or man. As Christians, we look to the Word of God to reveal "Christ the power of God, and the wisdom of God" (I Cor. 1:24) as the source and origin of our philosophy of education.

Occasionally a thunderbolt is needed to awaken Christians to examine whether their philosophy and methods are of Christ, and advancing His pre-eminence. Such a summons is issued by Miss Katherine Dang:

"In ignorance, Christians are aiding and abetting anti-Christianity in America. More than any other factor, it is the weakness of Christian character and scholarship that is responsible for this country's apostasy from its founding Christian principles of education, government and economics.

The pagan remains true to paganism. Spiritual backsliding is a believer's trait, not a pagan's. The dissolution of Christian character has resulted from generations of unbiblical education among *Christian* institutions of teaching and learning.

"Christians are duped to believe that the 'forces without' are mightier and inevitable; thus they isolate themselves, calling it separation, only to breed more cowards after their own kind.[1] The battle is within; the enemy is within the camp; that enemy is American Christianity's own ignorance to effect superior spiritual armaments.

"Impotent and unequipped to supplant or displace, Christians tacitly consent to creeping socialistic polities in their *own* institutions: homes, churches, and schools, advancing the kingdom of Satan.

"The need is for a soul-searching of content and methods in pastoring and teaching, to consider their implications for home, church, school and state.

---

1. There is, of course, a Biblical basis for separation – ecclesiastically, morally and socially (II Cor. 6: 14-18), but the emphasis here is on false isolation in the name of separation. The principle is discussed in more detail under *The Christian Principle of American Political Union*, p. 69.

"The need is for a generation of American Christians who know God and His Word, and by their own scholarship know how to implement their knowledge. It is the duty of Christian educators to lead in advance of their students, not only to stem the tide of anti-Christian socialism, but to seek an *effective alternative* in schooling parents, pastors, businessmen, *and statesmen.* American Christianity must first sanctify itself before this nation can be purged of her enemies and reclaimed for Christ.

"One of the aims of Christian education should be a Biblical mentality by which every sphere of activity is controlled. This mentality stems from a schooling in Biblical principles able to detect and reject everything contrary to Christ and Christianity.

"It was the Biblical reasoning of the Founding Father generation that produced the *only* historical alternative to tyranny and oppression of the individual, and which promoted the fullest expression of Christian liberty, rather than pagan license. The Biblical principles that founded America provided for unhindered propagation of the Gospel. Wisdom thus encourages Christians today to identify Biblical principles of civil government as a foundation of their warfare against secular humanistic reasoning.

"There are multitudes of principles within the Biblical realm, but not all such principles are applicable to extending Christianity's influence from the individual all the way into a nation's civil government. A comprehensive philosophy of education should include such a body of truth. These truths should govern every teacher in each class and department. Then, all that is effected in the Christian school or Sunday School would issue from a common spirit and vision.

"The greatest of these effects would be individuals equipped to walk independently with their God in a perverse and wicked generation.

"The strength of an institution, be it church school, Sunday School, club, missions committee, etc., lies largely in the unity of its constituents. Bound by an American Christian philosophy, a great bulwark would be raised for the church to advance Christ and His cause in *our* Jerusalem, and *then* to the uttermost parts of the world."[2]

THE BASIC VOCABULARY OF AMERICAN CHRISTIAN EDUCATION

God's word cautions the Christian concerning philosophy and philosophers in I Cor. 1:20-29,

Acts 17:18-20, and Col. 2:6-10. Is it Biblical to claim a philosophy of education? It depends on what the word philosophy really means.

Consider Webster's 1828 Dictionary definition of philosophy:

"Literally, the love of wisdom...Thus, that branch of philosophy which treats of God, &c. is called theology;...The objects of philosophy are to ascertain facts or truth, and the causes of things or their phenomena; to enlarge our views of God and His works, and to render our knowledge of both practically useful and subservient to human happiness."

Matthew Henry's *Commentary* on Colossians 2:8 is helpful in describing the positive and negative use of philosophy:

"There is a philosophy which is a noble exercise of our reasonable faculties, and highly serviceable to religion, such a study of the works of God as leads us to the knowledge of God and confirms our faith in him. But there is a philosophy which is vain and deceitful, which is prejudicial to religion, and sets the wisdom of man in competition with the wisdom of God, and while it pleases men's fancies ruins their faith."[3]

Philosophy may constitute a body of wisdom, knowledge or principles explaining the reason of things whose source and origin is *either* God, as revealed in Jesus Christ by the Holy Spirit in the Word of God, *or* the wisdom, reasoning and invention of man and the world "set in competition with the wisdom of God" who is Jesus Christ.(I Cor. 1:30)

EDUCATION

Consider Webster's 1828 Dictionary definition of education as most representative of historic American pedagogical thought:

"The bringing up, as of a child; instruction; formation of manners. Education comprehends all that series of instruction and discipline which is intended to...:
1. Enlighten the understanding
2. Correct the temper, and
3. Form the manners and habits of youth, and
4. Fit them for usefulness in their future stations."
The activity of education is to instruct, discipline, enlighten, correct, form and fit. By *defini-*

---

2. Katherine Dang, *A Sunday School Manual for the Oakland Chinese Bible Church*, December, 1977. Unpublished.

3. Matthew Henry's *Commentaries on the Bible*, Fleming Revell, vol. 6.

tion, however, education is neutral as Webster does not describe the product of education. Education, however, is never neutral as an instrument of a philosophy of government. Education will always have some purpose depending upon who or what is in control and the source of authority or power over the functions of education.

Education also deals primarily with the *inward* man, his understanding, temper, and character as revealed in his manners and habits of industry, diligence, patience, civility, etc.

CHRISTIAN EDUCATION

Education has been defined. But what distinguishes *Christian* education? Christian is used here as an adjective, not a noun, and literally means "of or pertaining to Christ; according to the Gospel, contained therein; relating to Christ, or to His doctrines, precepts and example."

Christian education should comprehend a philosophy, curriculum and methodology which *wholly* "testify of me," Christ Jesus, and are properly reasoned from the Word of God.

Consider Webster's definition of education and a correlative passage of Scripture which clearly modifies the intent and purpose of education to make it "Christian."

The following chart takes the components of Webster's definition of education and shows how II Timothy 3:16–17 corroborates and confirms the dictionary definition. The italicized words in either column have been defined in Webster's 1828 Dictionary to help explain the purpose of education in the contest of its Scriptural correlative.

NOAH WEBSTER'S DEFINITION OF EDUCATION CONFIRMED SCRIPTURALLY

"Education comprehends all that series of instruction and discipline which is intended to enlighten the understanding, correct the temper, form the manners and habits of youth, and fit them for usefulness in their future station."	"All Scripture is given by inspiration of God, and is profitable for doctrine, for reproof, for correction, for instruction in righteousness: That the man of God may be perfect, throughly furnished unto all good works." (II Timothy 3:16-17)
1. "*Enlighten* the understanding": illuminate, to instruct to enable to see or comprehend truth to illuminate with divine knowledge or knowledge of the truth	1. "*Doctrine*": truths of the gospel; teaching; learning knowledge (Isaiah 28:9)
2. "*Correct* the temper": disposition of mind; the constitution of the mind heat of mind or passion; irritation	2. "for *reproof*": to censure for a fault; blame expressed to the face to charge with a fault to the face, excite a sense of guilt "for *correction*": the act of bringing back from error or deviation, to a just standard as to truth, justice or propriety
3. "*form* the manners and habits of youth": to mold, model by instructions and discipline	3. "for instruction in *righteousness*": purity of heart, rectitude of life conformity of heart and life to divine law holy principles and affections
4. "*fit* them for usefulness in their future station": equip, furnish for a journey	4. "that the man of God may be perfect, throughly *furnished* unto all good works": supplied; fitted with necessaries

A philosophy of Christian education should have a distinctly Biblical and theological basis which separates it and its product from progressive, secular philosophies. Such a philosophy of education, if truly Biblical, has a universal application to all nations and peoples. It can be an instrument to evangelize and govern or disciple Christians in *any* nation. Hence, there may be a Biblical Christian education in Russia, China or Sweden which effectively wins souls to Christ and grounds them in the Word of God. However, if such a philosophy of education is not also reforming society and being reflected in civil government, it most certainly lacks a Christian philosophy of *government*.

Thus, a Christian philosophy of education that produces only internal, individual, spiritual regeneration and reformation without transforming governmental and economic relationships in homes, local communities and civil government, and finally in the nation and its form of government and economy, fails to achieve the full expression of the government of God internally and *externally*.

What hope have Chinese Christians, Russian Christians or Swedish Christians, et al., that a Christian philosophy of education or government could effect such a radical change in their respective societies and civil government? They can have great hope! If our traditional Biblical education produced our Christian history and Constitution then the universal Biblical principles and ideas that distinguish American Christian education, if taught universally, could not only restore this nation but extend the blessings of both Christian self-government and civil liberty to other nations consistent with God's "Dominion Mandate" (Gen. 1:26-28) and Great Commission. (Matt. 28:19-20)

AMERICAN CHRISTIAN EDUCATION

What distinguished this country's original Christian education? We begin to grasp the answer when we see the quality of Christianity that reached the North American continent in 1620, and the educational emphasis or focus of the Pilgrims and Puritans that subsequently permeated society and produced a form of government that protected the fullest expression of individual Christian liberty.

American Christian education emphasizes the following distinctions:

1. It teaches the Christian how to *think governmentally*, that is, to think:
   a. in terms of *who* or *what* is in control;
   b. in terms of the *internal* to the *external;*
   c. in terms of the Christian idea of God, man and *government;*
   d. in terms of a philosophy of education as a philosophy of government;
   e. in terms of every form of government having a philosophy of education.

2. It teaches the Providence or Hand of God in history, specifically the historical relation between Christianity and this nation. American Christian education is by no means synonymous with patriotism, Americanism, conservative politics, or our country's great leaders or heros. Rather, it is a Christian philosophy of God's continuing provision for individual liberty, self-government and dominion.

3. It teaches the Biblical principles that produced our Christian form of civil government, originally intended to preserve the greatest expression of individual liberty, property and voluntary union under a Christian Constitutional Republic.

4. It teaches what it means to be an American Christian: a steward of America's heritage of Christian character, self-government, property, union and form of government.

5. It teaches why this nation is *unique* in the history of Christianity, to the credit of Christ and His church. This uniqueness is not due to any personal, self-created righteousness in Americans of this or previous generations. We cannot say it is by "my power and the might of mine hand" that such liberty and prosperity has been produced, but it is the work of "the Lord thy God: for it is he that giveth thee power to get wealth." (Deut. 8:17-18) America's abundance and freedom were intended for God's glory, that He may establish His covenant, and set an example of what a Christian nation can be and achieve. Hence the story of how God has worked in America should provoke hope, not hatred, among the people of other nations and inspire them to seek out their own unique Christian histories.

6. It teaches how to perpetuate America's Gospel purpose: to extend the Gospel, *inclusive* of Biblical liberty with law, and Christian self and civil government.

THE PRINCIPLE APPROACH TO AMERICAN CHRISTIAN EDUCATION

"'The Principle Approach of teaching and learning is Biblical. It will restore the reasoning and writing of leading ideas and principles which we have deleted from present educational systems predicated upon secular philosophies. But it requires Christian courage to cut through the 'philosophy and vain deceit, after the tradition of men, after the rudiments of the world, and not after Christ.'" (Col. 2:8) [1]

There are two denotations of the Principle Approach, a general application and a specific definition.

The *general application* of the phrase, the Principle Approach, is to the *seven minimal Biblical principles* that explain the relationship between Christian character and America's history and government. (See *Teaching and Learning*, p. 63 or 111) This rendering is predicated upon the definition of *principle* in Webster's 1828 Dictionary:

PRINCIPLE: *n.* 1. In a general sense, the cause, source or origin of any thing; that from which a thing proceeds; 5. Ground; foundation; that which

supports…a series of actions or of reasoning.

Hence, *The Principle Approach* becomes a short title to *Teaching and Learning America's Christian History and Government* with reference to God's Providence in unfolding the seven specific Biblical principles that constitute the source or origin, ground or foundation of America's Christian character, history and government.

The *specific definition* of The Principle Approach to American Christian *Education* is found on page 88 of *Teaching and Learning:*

"The *principle approach* is America's historic Christian method of Biblical reasoning which makes the Truths of God's Word the basis of every subject in the school curriculum.

"The Principle Approach begins by restoring the 4 R's to their identification in the subjects of the curriculum…"

The following conclusions can be deduced from the above statement:

1. The Principle Approach is a *method*, a Christian method of Biblical reasoning. It is therefore a way

---

1. Rosalie J. Slater. *C/P*, p. 600d.

or manner of reasoning Biblically, then governmentally, historically and educationally.

2. It is *America's historic* method of Biblical reasoning, suggesting that there is historical evidence that American Christians made the Bible their primary textbook for every aspect of life and living, especially for both self and civil government.

3. The Principle Approach makes "the truths of God's Word the basis," the center and circumference, "of *every* subject in the school curriculum."

4. "It begins," but does not end, "by restoring the 4 R's to teaching and learning…"

The 4 R's may be paraphrased, defined and documented Biblically as follows:

RESEARCHING God's Word to identify the basic principles that govern the subject by searching the Scriptures for the vocabulary of the subject and deducing its Biblical source and purpose.
Webster's definitions of *research:*

1. To search or examine with continued care; to seek diligently for the truth.
2. To search again; to examine anew.
3. (*n*) Diligent inquiry or examination in seeking facts or principles; continued search after truth.

Biblical Basis: John 5:39; Acts 17:11; I Pet. 1:10

REASONING from Biblical principles/truths and identifying them to the student through each subject, thereby concluding from Scripture the Biblical significance and governmental importance of the subject.
Webster's definitions of *reason:*

1. To deduce inferences justly from premises.
2. (*n*) A faculty of the mind by which it distinguishes truth from falsehood, and good from evil, and which enables the possessor to deduce inferences from facts or from propositions.

Reasoning also builds upon truth researched, so that conclusions are anchored upon sound scholarship and doctrine.
Biblical Basis: Isa. 1:18; Acts 17:2; 24:25; I Pet. 3:15

RELATING of Biblical principles to each student through the subject; *expounding* or explaining thoroughly the meaning and application of Biblical truth to each student's Christian character, conscience and stewardship of God-given talents.
Webster's definitions of *relate* and *expound:*

1. To tell; to recite.
2. To restore.
3. To ally by connection or kindred.

Expound: To explain; to lay open the meaning; to clear of obscurity; to interpret; as, to expound a text of scripture; to examine; make clear to the understanding.
Biblical Basis: Acts 18:26, Luke 24:27, 32; Psa. 19:1-4

RECORDING or the written record by each teacher and student of the individual application of Biblical principles to the subject and to every aspect of human experience regarding the course content.
Webster's definitions of *record:*

1. To write or enter in a book or on parchment, for the purpose of preserving authentic or correct evidence of a thing;
2. To imprint deeply on the mind or memory;
3. To cause to be remembered.

Biblical Basis: Luke 1:1-4; I Jn. 5:10; III Jn. 12; Rev. 1:1-3; Hab. 2:2

The 4 R's are not necessarily ordered steps to a conclusion, but are exercised *simultaneously* to effect both Christian scholarship and liberty. Consider the following conclusions advanced by Miss Katherine Dang:

"Since America's Christian Republic came about as a consequence of Biblical scholarship and subsequent application, then the restoration of this Republic requires that there be a return to a similar American Biblical scholarship…

"Christian scholarship is individual and internal. Truth becomes the private possession of the individual by application of the 4 R's – researching, reasoning, relating and recording. Each one educates himself in the unchanging laws of God's Word, the primary source of all knowledge and wisdom. And within the text of Scripture is found the very means by which it is mastered…

"Self-education and self-government are close relatives. By means of individual Christian scholarship every sphere of human activity is brought under the subjection and authority of Biblical principles. The principles eliminate the gap between philosophy and practicality, Bible and subject, and the written Word and the living Word. That bridge is constructed from the purity of Christian scholarship." (I Jn. 1:1-4)[2]

For an explanation of How To 4 R a subject, see p. 145 of the *Curriculum* section.

---

2. Katherine Dang, *A Sunday School Manual for the Oakland Chinese Bible Church*, December, 1977. Unpublished.

WHAT THE PRINCIPLE APPROACH IS NOT

This philosophy of education says it is not enough for us simply to inform others of an abundance of factual material; it directs that we know and relate all useful facts and content to a Biblical philosophy that governs all of life, living and history.

It does not encourage the teacher to dominate the subject or the student, but to let Christ and Christian principles have first place in governing the teacher, student and subject.

It does not encourage administrators or teachers to copy what another school does, but to clearly identify and demonstrate for themselves local sovereignty through an independent curriculum and methods consonant with a philosophy of education which is demonstrably American Christian.

It does not exalt methodology above content or vice versa, but requires that both be subordinate to the truths of God's Word.

Christian education is not an attempt to coat the student with Christianity and knowledge. One master teacher had an opportunity to observe a number of Christian schools operating in a geographical area and made the observation that so many of them seem to be merely coating their students with Bible and content, like a "chocolate-covered banana, slick and sweet on the outside, but soft and mushy on the inside."

Our God is *All-in-all*, not just a cover-all for our students and over all our subjects. Christian education must work from the internal to the external and thus develop that integrity of character and conscience which, by the grace of God, is steadfast and unmovable in the face of trials and hardships, as contrasted with the education that produces an attractively coated Christian who melts under heat and gives under pressure – like a "chocolate-covered banana."

THE PRINCIPLE APPROACH IS EXPANSIVE, NOT EVOLUTIONARY

Teaching the principles of America's Christian history and government by the 4 R's is expansive, not evolutionary. Each teacher may simultaneously present the rudiments of every subject to every student through every grade in the context of a philosophy of education and government defined and illustrated by the Principle Approach. Thus, the instructor can expand the Biblical principles of each subject through the grades, showing God to be their Author and America the fullest expression of the expansion of these truths into the civil or political spheres.

This, I submit, is why Miss Slater speaks of "*expanding* principles of America's Christian History and Government" (*Teaching and Learning*, p. 111) and states that "there will never be a repetition of content for each teacher will bring out different aspects of the principles as they expand and amplify in meaning and in application. A principle must be defined clearly but it cannot be confined within a single subject, or grade level, and it will have universal application as it is understood."[3]

We must not adulterate our curriculum or Biblical truth with the contemporary view that if we make "secular" subjects conform to Christianity, or adapt Christian truth to "secular" subjects we can call ourselves a Christian school. I am apprehensive that many Christian schools simply mix Bible teaching with evolutionary, progressive methods which condition the student to look at his external environment – whether social, political, economic or religious – before he determines how to act. At the same time such schools tell the student he should live by faith, not by sight, apparently not realizing the contradiction in their dualistic approach.

FALSE DICHOTOMY

One wonders if we do not adulterate our Biblical convictions by believing academic subjects are inherently secular and only the Bible is Christian; that the subjects of government, economics, science and literature are inevitably of the world, worldly, while the subjects of prayer, evangelism, or missions alone are spiritual. Such a view of education serves to debase Christian education rather than distinguish it. How much better to identify and execute an approach to education that is so profoundly and pervasively Christian that it will enable us to "come out from among them, and be ye separate." (II Cor. 6:17)

Lastly, American Christian education cannot be packaged and sold as a program that requires little time and effort and gets "instant results." There is no expedient way to truly educate – no quick and easy method of producing the kind of character and scholarship able to withstand evil and "having done all, to stand!" (Eph. 6:13)

We know the power of Christ to regenerate individual lives, but are we witnessing the power of Christ, Biblical principles and sound reasoning, to renew and govern our methods, content and classroom? One can surely concur that it takes

3. Rosalie Slater, *Teaching and Learning America's Christian History*, p. 109, hereafter referred to as *T/L*. (See also *School at Home* section, p. 111)

years of diligent research and demonstration to produce a master teacher, a Christian philomath (lover of learning). Christian education demands the patience and perseverance of master teachers who work from a philosophy, curriculum, and method which wholly "testifies of me" – Christ and the Word of God.

CHILD AND SUBJECT-CENTERED PHILOSOPHIES CONTRASTED

The chart on page 18 entitled *Child and Subject-Centered Philosophies Contrasted With the Principle Approach* attempts to distinguish the essential ideas or emphasis of three views of education. The brief statements are not exhaustive but should prove helpful in identifying aspects of two dominant views of teaching and learning in contrast with how a teacher would reason from the Principle Approach to both the child and the subject.

Although the child-centered view described in the chart may embrace aspects of the rather short-lived philosophy advanced by professional educators in the 1930's, it is primarily intended to comprehend more contemporary views that make the child's nature, personality and desires the controlling emphasis in teaching and learning.

Most Christian educators desire a distinctly Christ or God-centered view of education in contrast to the progressive, child-centered approach on the one hand and an academic, scientifically rational but ungodly emphasis on the other hand. The goal, however, should be for a God-governed, Bible-wise teacher to bring both the child and the subject into loving obedience to Christ, the Truth and Principles of God's Word.

As the chart is inspected, the reader may consider studying one statement of the child-centered approach with its correlative subject-centered idea, then contrast these views with the Principle Approach. Finally, it is suggested that both the left-hand and the right-hand columns be read in their entirety. Then read the entire center column to discern the proper relation of the teacher, child and subject to Biblical Truth.

The following statement by John Dewey, philosopher of progressive education, may best summarize the secular child-centered view:

"The only true education comes through the stimulation of the child's powers by the demands of the social situations in which he finds himself... The educational process is psychological and sociological ...the child's own instincts furnish the material and give the starting point for all education...What a child gets out of any subject presented to him is simply the images which he himself forms with regard to it...The school is a social institution, and education, a social process and one's life should be in harmony with the group or society...each individual is to adjust to the social consciousness."[4]

The following excerpt from a guide published by the Council for Basic Education in Washington, D.C., entitled "What is Basic Education? A Model Curriculum" is submitted as a very positive statement of subject-centered (basic) instruction:

"Unlike some proponents of the 'Back to Basics' movement who are only concerned about the Three Rs, the Council advocates instruction in English (reading, writing, speech, and literature), mathematics, science, geography, government, foreign languages, and the arts. These subjects are fundamental in the sense that they are essential to life-long learning; therefore, mastery of the basic subjects should be the principal goal of schooling.

"Basic education, by developing the ability to think critically and independently, increases the capacity to learn still more.

"The basic academic subjects are the *means* schools use to achieve basic education. They are the building blocks on which all subsequent education rests; they enable people to learn whatever lessons life may present outside the classroom.

"In isolation, each basic academic subject has only limited value. In proper schooling, however, the knowledge and skills learned from the basic subjects are interdependent and mutually reinforcing. Newly acquired knowledge in one subject enlarges understanding of other subjects and provides an occasion for applying basic skills. Each skill is a medium for learning other skills and acquiring needed knowledge in the basic subjects. The value of a good curriculum exceeds the sum of its parts.

"Basic education strives for *mastery* of knowledge and skills, not mere awareness or appreciation. Mastery depends on study and practice, expectations of accomplishments, and explicit standards. Even 'exploratory' learning should strive for mastery.

"The balance of required basic subjects and electives should vary according to a student's mastery of the basic subjects... Electives should *augment* the basic subjects, not replace them, and should equal or surpass them in rigor."

4. John Dewey, "My Pedagogic Creed," *Three Thousand Years of Educational Wisdom,* edited by Robert Ulich, Harvard University Press, 1959, pp. 629-638.

CHILD AND SUBJECT-CENTERED PHILOSOPHIES CONTRASTED WITH THE PRINCIPLE APPROACH

CHILD-CENTERED	PRINCIPLE APPROACH To CHILD AND SUBJECT	SUBJECT-CENTERED
PHILOSOPHY		
Education is conceived as conditioning and stimulating the child to experience or adapt to his environment or circumstances, whether natural or artificial.	Education requires a teacher who knows the Biblical Principles that govern a subject, and can, by example, teach a student to reflect upon unchanging truth – in order to interpret and control his immediate environment and possess this nation for Christ and Christianity.	Education is conceived as transferring facts from books and teacher, and indoctrinating the student in what is seen as a secular subject and environment – void of Biblical truth and reasoning.
The child is of value as a part of the group, and is dependent upon the group's wishes and desires, and upon the collective expression of what is useful or important to learn or do.	The teacher reveals how God values the individual and subject, labors to cultivate the child's God-given capacity to take possession of a subject for Christ and advance Christian liberty and self-government in America.	The student's value is relative to his capacity to master a subject for merely personal achievement or to please the group apart from God.
CURRICULUM		
The teacher must adapt or adjust the curriculum (content) and methods to the physical and natural instincts of the child (or the group).	The teacher's Christian character and scholarship inspire the student to govern himself and to master the subject Biblically and historically as it fits in the Chain of Christianity moving westward to America.	The teacher makes the child adapt and conform himself to learning the facts of a subject through uninspired, rigidly academic methods.
The teacher and the subject must wait for "pupil readiness," and thus the teacher teaches only what the child is pleased to learn.	The teacher imputes to the student the God-given intelligence and faculty to learn the Biblical origin and purpose of a subject and become productive of good works in every sphere of government.	The child is required to depend upon and conform to whatever philosophy or viewpoint is contained in the textbook or expressed by the teacher.
METHODS		
The methods of instruction depend upon a socio-physio-psychological concept of the child's feelings and needs.	The teacher depends upon the Truths of God's Word, deduced through America's historic Biblical method of Education (4 R's), to develop the student's character and mastery over the principles and ideas of the subject.	The child depends upon the methodology of the textbook, the "program," its author(s) and dependent teachers.
The pupil chooses his own goals and does only what he is willing to do in the best way he knows how.	The teacher purposes to help the student comprehend a subject *wholistically* – by its Biblical purpose, principles and place in the Chain of Christianity moving westward to America.	Prefabricated, centralized curriculum or textbooks prescribe uniform methods and academic goals for the child and the teacher.

BRING STUDENT AND SUBJECT
INTO HARMONY WITH THE BIBLE

Christian education should not be predominantly child-centered or subject-centered. This is not to say it should ignore either the child's interests, desires, and wants or the demand to master subject content. But above all else, both child and student should be brought into harmony with God, the Principle (source, origin and first cause) of the creature and creation. True Christian education views the child and the subject as extensions of their Author and Governor, Christ Jesus, as opposed to the other views that hold to teaching the child and subject as an end in themselves.

HOW TO THINK GOVERNMENTALLY

Bible-believing people in all nations are encouraged to receive Jesus Christ not only as their Saviour but as the Lord who rules their lives. Born-again men and women everywhere are urged by Scripture to let their minds and hearts be governed by God, to be ever on guard, assessing what it is that seeks to control them, whether the Word and Spirit of God or the insinuations of Satan. *Thus, to some degree, Christians the world over are directed to think governmentally – to be alert to what is governing or controlling first, internally in their own thought-life, and then externally in what is governing their daily domestic, social, political, educational, and economic experience.*

But in traditional *American* Christian education there was always a *special* emphasis upon thinking *governmentally* – i.e., in terms of the flow of power and force. Who or what is in control internally *and* externally? Is God or Satan in control of our thoughts? Is civil government or individual self government directing our actions? Unfortunately, however, we do not find that inspired emphasis in most Christian homes, churches or schools today.

Contemporary Christian education is supposed to be at the leading edge of the movement to advance Christ, Christian liberty (salvation) and Christian truth; but for a great many years it has lacked the necessary correlative of true Christian liberty – the clearly, precisely-stated and boldly emphasized Christian idea of *government*.

When government is taught in most Christian homes and schools today, the emphasis is upon the external, the political functions, the machinery and the men who make, administer and judge the civil law. As necessary as this study is, it neglects the whole counsel of God concerning government, and the omission is dangerous.

To understand the constant presence and practice of the government of God on earth, to think governmentally, and to discern how one's philosophy of God, man and government constitutes one's philosophy of education, I believe the following ideas should be taught, illustrated and demonstrated:

1. God ordained three governmental institutions – the home, civil government and the church.
2. God ordained civil government for man's good, and not his harm.
3. The Christian idea of man is primary, and gives rise to the Christian idea of civil government, which protects man's God-given life, liberty and property.

4. A philosophy of education is based upon a philosophy of government, i.e., one's view of the principles of teaching and learning is determined by one's idea of who or what is exercising control and is the ultimate authority and source of Truth.
5. Every form of government is the result of a philosophy of education.

If Christian parents, educators and pastors omit – whether by ignorance or forgetfulness – the full expression of the Christian idea of God, man and *government* in America's history, our posterity will continue to be ill-equipped to detect and supplant wickedness on all levels of society and government, and will in their ignorance prevent the benefits of Christian liberty, self-government, private property and voluntary union from blessing this nation and subsequently *all* nations for Christ and Christianity. This ought not to be.

GOD'S THREE DIVINE GOVERNMENTAL INSTITUTIONS

There are three God-ordained institutions, divinely constituted for man to administer according to God's Law. Chronologically, they are the home or family (Gen. 2:24), civil government (Gen. 9:6), and the New Testament Church. (Matt. 16:18)

The home or family must be a Biblical institution with Biblical laws to govern it, if it is to be a Christian home. (Prov. 18:22; Heb. 13:4) Even if born-again Christian parents occupy the home, the government of that home is not Christian or Biblical unless the Will of God, i.e., His Law for the family, is administered and obeyed by Christian parents. (Col. 3:20; Gal. 4:1-2)

The family was established for the purpose of procreation with clearly defined governmental rules for the control and training of children. Its educational goal is to build Christian character that glorifies God and represents Christ and His plan and purpose for men and nations. (Deut. 6:6-7; Eph. 6:2,4; Prov. 22:6) According to God's Word, the education of children is the *exclusive* responsibility of the parents, not the state.

The New Testament church was ordained by the Lord Jesus Christ and commanded by Him to evangelize and teach or disciple the nations. (Matt. 28:19-20) Even if born-again Christians occupy the pulpit and the pew, that local church is Christian or Biblical only if it governs itself according to God's "perfect law of liberty" – the Word of God. (Eph. 2:20-21; 5:24-27; I Tim. 3)

Christian education is a *ministry* of the local church (Matt. 28:19) in support of the Christian home, church and civil government. Christian education is not a function of the state nor subject to its control. The *educational* goal of the Christian church is to teach and perpetuate both the Law and the Gospel of the Lord Jesus Christ. (Matt. 28:18-19) To the extent it does this, it will develop the Christian conscience and character to support a Christian Republic.

GOD ORDAINED CIVIL GOVERNMENT FOR OUR GOOD

Civil government was ordained by God. (Gen. 9:6; Rom. 13:1) God made the individual citizen responsible for the functions, conduct and quality of the administration of those men who exercised the God-given authority or power to fulfill God's purpose for civil government. The Biblical purposes of civil government include:

1. Being the "minister of God" – a servant of God – "to thee for *good*," not our harm. (Rom. 13:4)
2. Valuing (praising) and protecting individual God-given (not government granted) life, liberty and property so we can prayerfully "lead a quiet and peaceable life in all godliness and honesty..." (I Tim. 2:1-3)
3. Executing "wrath upon evil doers" and administering the death penalty upon convicted murderers in civil society. (Rom. 13:4; Gen. 9:6)

Civil government can be called Christian if the form or arrangement of its functions and parts is Biblical. It is emphatically Christian, of course, if the participants – citizens and officials – are expressing Christian self-government, character, stewardship of property, and voluntary union and relating these principles to their political decisions and actions. Note, however, that even if "born again" Christians exercise the functions of government – legislative, executive, judicial – *the consequences of their administration may not be Christian unless the individual is governed by the Biblical idea of God, man and government.*

THE CHRISTIAN VS. PAGAN VIEW OF MAN AND GOVERNMENT

Ideas or "images in the mind" have their consequences because the internal is causative of the external. As a man "thinketh in his heart, so is he:..." (Prov. 23:7) The people's idea of God determines the *form* of their civil, political, religious and social institutions, and that idea of God

21

must necessarily include man and government.[1]

Consult the chart on page 24 on how the Christian idea of God and man gives rise to a Biblical view of government. Pages 1 and 2 of *Christian History of the Constitution* also contrast the pagan versus Christian idea of man and government.

The *Pagan Idea of Man and Government*, on page 25, was prepared by Miss Katherine Dang of San Leandro, California. This chart represents false ideas which are first embraced within the internal, causative sphere of thought. They then manifest themselves and effect their own form and quality of external self- and civil government.

A PHILOSOPHY OF EDUCATION IS A PHILOSOPHY OF GOVERNMENT

What one believes about God, man, *and government* constitutes a philosophy of education.

What relationship does one's view of God and man have to one's philosophy of education? The answer would be self-evident, except many Christians believe that their statement of faith is *sacred* and their philosophy of education is *secular.* Such a belief is not Biblical. (Prov. 1:1–7; Psa. 2:10–12)

Christ and Christianity should not be separated from why, how, and what is taught. A school's philosophy of education must be consistent with its doctrinal statement of faith.

The relation between education and government is discerned by reasoning governmentally. The term government has traditionally been reserved for political or civil functions, but if we think of the idea of government in a more philosophical way, we can see it has broader applications, and is indeed related to education.

Study carefully the definitions of the words "govern" and "government" from Webster's 1828 Dictionary or as reprinted on pages 184–185 of *Teaching and Learning.* Consider the relationship between the functions of government – by definition, to direct, regulate, control, restrain – and the functions of education, by definition to instruct, discipline, enlighten, correct, form, and fit. The moment a teacher steps into the classroom to educate he is going to express *who* or *what* is governing him and *how* and *by what authority* the curriculum will be taught.

Consider that there are three basic functions of government: legislative, executive, and judicial. A Christian teacher exercises these three functions of government whenever a subject – any subject – is taught. He plans (prepares), executes (presents), and judges the propriety of the lesson plan and presentation by the governmental principles of God's Word. Self-education requires self-government.

The source and origin of the *wisdom* applied in exercising these three functions of government in education determines one's philosophy of education. Every subject has a philosophy of government at its base. Either one reasons from, hence is governed by, the Word of God, and lays Christ, the supreme Governor (Psa. 22:18; Isa. 9:7) "at the foundation of all sound knowledge and learning," – or man, his reason and imagination are in control.

Webster's definition of education suggests how education deals with the government of the inward man: his understanding, temper, and manners and habits (i.e., character). The Christian view of government conceives government as first internal, causative, then external, with Christian civil government the effect as each individual acknowledges the sovereignty of God through Christ by the Holy Spirit.

Education is first an internal activity and is governed by whatever body of wisdom or knowledge the individual accepts as his authority. Thus, as the home is the first sphere of civil government, so the classroom is a correlative sphere of civil government. These relationships are seldom acknowledged.

Consider how Christian education determines and constructs the character of both self- *and* civil government. (See *Teaching and Learning*, pp. 106–108) When an individual or a nation is *increasing* in the knowledge and application of the Word of God, there will be an increasing *reliance* upon the indwelling Spirit and government of God through Christ for every human need. In contrast, when an individual or nation is *decreasing* in a knowledge of the Word of God, there will be increasing reliance on the external, upon man and civil government for one's needs.

If the individual is not specifically identifying and expressing the Christian view of man and government in every area of life and living, then he is liable to be used as a tool of anti-Christian, humanistic ignorance. (Rom. 6:16) Christian government is elementary, simple in statement, but difficult to live out. Human government, divorced from God's Word, is complex, complicated and difficult in its statement, but in one sense simple for the individual to live under – i.e., while bureaucratic regulations and paperwork may not seem simple, under either a totalitarian government or

---

1. Verna M. Hall, Preface to *Christian History of the Constitution of the United States of America*, p. II (hereafter referred to as *CHOC*)

in anarchy, the citizen is relieved of the difficult challenges of Christian self-government.

"The scriptures were intended by God to be the guide of human reason. The Creator of man established the moral order of the Universe; knowing that human reason, left without a divine guide or rule of action, would fill the world with disorder, crime and misery...

"The principles of all genuine liberty, and of wise laws and administrations are to be drawn from the Bible and sustained by its authority. The man therefore who weakens or destroys the divine authority of that book may be accessory to all the public disorders which society is doomed to suffer."[2]

EVERY FORM OF GOVERNMENT HAS ITS PHILOSOPHY OF EDUCATION

As one learns to think governmentally, one's conscious concept of government shapes one's philosophy of education. Reasoning from cause to effect, an internal governmental view of education directs the individual in what to teach, and how to teach. The effect of a philosophy of government and education will be manifested as the practical form and quality of education and subsequently of civil government. This same idea is illustrated in the diagram below entitled "Every Form of Government Has Its Philosophy of Education."

Reasoning governmentally from effect back to cause, every form of government and every form of education has its philosophy of education and government. For example, socialism has a form and philosophy of education predicated upon man's autonomous control and authority separate from God. Consider what philosophy and form of education the communists in either Russia or mainland China insist upon to sustain pagan, totalitarian government. In contrast consider what philosophy of government and education produced the world's first Christian Republic in America.

"America's Biblical Education produced America's Christian History and Constitution. The method was the Principle Approach. Let us restore the foundation of American Independence."[3]

EVERY FORM OF GOVERNMENT HAS ITS PHILOSOPHY OF EDUCATION

INTERNAL (Causative)		EXTERNAL (Effect)	
Philosophy of GOVERNMENT (the source of authority or power)	⇒ *determines* ⇒ Philosophy of EDUCATION (the wisdom in teaching and learning)	⇒ *produces* ⇒ Form & Quality of EDUCATION (the practice and product of education)	⇒ *shapes* ⇒ Form & Quality of GOVERNMENT (the form and functions of government)

2. Noah Webster, "Preface to the Holy Bible...," *C/P*, p. 21b,d.

3. Rosalie J. Slater, *T/L*, p. 89.

The author, in collaboration with Master Teacher, Miss Belinda Ballenger, suggests a further refinement of the *Christian Idea of Man and Government* in the chart below. The premise behind this chart is that if one accepts the Christian idea of man in the left column, his internal idea will tend to produce the Christian idea and form of civil government expressed in the right column.

THE CHRISTIAN IDEA OF MAN AND GOVERNMENT

CHRISTIAN IDEA OF MAN INTERNAL⟩————————————➤ (Causative)	CHRISTIAN IDEA OF GOVERNMENT EXTERNAL (Effect)
1. By the law of God, all mortal men have sinned and need a Saviour: man's nature is corrupted.	1. Civil government is ordained of God to restrain sinful man and to "praise" or *value* those that do good.
2. God created individuals with an independent, distinct and special value; man is equal before God's law and love.	2. Man is superior to the state he constructs to protect his God-given value. Men are equal before the laws they make.
3. Liberty is first internal and spiritual as God governs man by the Holy Spirit through the "perfect law of liberty." (Jas. 1:25)	3. Christian (spiritual) liberty of conscience gave rise to religious, civil and economic freedom protected by law.
4. Christian self-government is God governing by the consent or supernatural response of the governed.	4. Christian civil government is a reflection of Christian self-government and local self-governing homes, churches and communities.
5. As Christ represents saved man before God, so man is God's representative on earth. Christianity is representative in its doctrine and essence.	5. Christian civil government is representative of the governmental spirit and form of its constituent homes, churches and schools.
6. Man exercises all three God-ordained functions of self-government and "shall be judged by the law of liberty." (Jas. 2:12)	6. The three functions of civil government are separated and limited by "settled, known and established laws" consistent with God's moral law.
7. God's government is by covenant with Christ and man's supernatural voluntary consent. Divine authority is delegated and flows from God to man under God's law.	7. Christian civil government is a voluntary compact between consenting citizens; political power flows from self-governing men to elected representatives limited by law.

The pagan view of man, which is first embraced within the internal, causative sphere of thought, manifests itself and effects its own form and quality of external government. The following brief statement will identify the pagan view of man and government:

THE PAGAN IDEA OF MAN AND GOVERNMENT

PAGAN IDEA OF MAN INTERNAL⟶ (Causative)	PAGAN IDEA OF GOVERNMENT ⟶ EXTERNAL (Effect)
1. Man is a higher form of animal, a product of evolution.	1. Man is governed according to animal, natural, physical instincts.
2. Man is incomplete, having neither a whole nor distinct existence, but is a temporal, passing species having no identity with the past or with the future.	2. Man is governed according to the moment, the current fashion, the present, without vision and foresight, only to be gradually conditioned to circumstances.
3. The stronger of the species survive and adapt.	3. Man is governed by a supreme elite in an inequitable society organized to eliminate the weak or nonconformist; he has no liberty of conscience; might makes right by the rule of the majority; society legislates, not representatives under law.
4. Man appears to move up the chain of sophistication: from polytheism to monotheism, from monotheism to eventual atheism.	4. Man is governed according to man's primary need: welfare for the physical, material existence in the Welfare State.
5. Man is a social creature and being with the "herd instinct" for his livelihood and security.	5. Man is governed by a search for the benevolent dictator to lead the group or collective; union is by force.

THE PROVIDENTIAL VIEW OF HISTORY

The Providence of God in history is distinctly a Biblical doctrine. It permeated the literature of the theologians and historians of England and America for over 500 years until the 20th Century. The following selected excerpts suggest how this important doctrine has been identified by theologians and scholars since the 16th Century and its relevance to the Christian citizen today:

John Calvin: *The Institutes of the Christian Religion,* 1536; "Chapter XVII, Sections:
"I. Summary of the doctrine of Divine Providence. 1. It embraces the future and the past. 2. It works by means, without means, and against means. 3. Mankind, and particularly the Church, the object of special care. 4. The mode of administration usually secret, but always just. This last point more fully considered.
"II. The profane denial that the world is governed by the secret counsel of God, refuted by passages of Scripture. Salutary counsel.
"III. This doctrine, as to the secret counsel of God in the government of the world, gives no countenance either to the impiety of those who throw the blame of their wickedness upon God, the petulance of those who reject means, or the error of those who neglect the duties of religion.

"IV. As regards future events, the doctrine of Divine Providence not inconsistent with deliberation on the part of man..."

John Gill, *A Body of Divinity,* 1769-70:
"The next eternal work of God is *Providence;* by which all the creatures God has made are preserved, governed, guided, and directed...The government of the world, and the ordering and disposing of all things in it, are attributed to him, without the counsel and direction of others: (Isa. 40:13-14)."

Noah Webster, *An American Dictionary of the English Language,* 1828:
"*Providence:* In theology, the care and superintendence which God exercises over his creatures. He that acknowledges a creation and denies a providence, involves himself in a palpable contradiction; for the same power which caused a thing to exist is necessary to continue its existence. Some persons admit a general providence, but deny a particular providence, not considering that a general providence consists of particulars. A belief in divine providence, is a source of great consolation to good men. By divine providence is often understood God himself."

Merrill F. Unger, *Unger's Bible Dictionary*, 1979. (Bible references written out):
"*Providence*, a term which in theology designates the continual care which God exercises over the universe which He has created. This includes the two facts of preservation and government.

"1. The doctrine of providence is closely connected with that of creation. That God could create the world and then forsake it is inconceivable in view of the perfection of God. Accordingly, in the power and wisdom and goodness of the Creator, declared in the Scriptures, we have the pledge of constant divine care over all parts of His creation. This idea finds expression in various places in both the Old and New Testaments..."
Psalm 33:13: "The Lord looketh from heaven; he beholdeth all the sons of men."
Isaiah 45:7: "I form the light, and create darkness: I make peace, and create evil: I the Lord do all these things."
Acts 17:24-28: "God that made the world and all things therein, seeing that he is Lord of heaven and earth, dwelleth not in temples made with hands; Neither is worshipped with men's hands, as though he needed anything, seeing he giveth to all life, and breath, and all things; And hath made of one blood all nations of men for to dwell on all the face of the earth, and hath determined the times before appointed, and the bounds of their habitation; That they should seek the Lord, if haply they might feel after him, and find him, though he be not far from every one of us; For in him we live, and move, and have our being; as certain also of your own poets have said, For we are also his offspring."
"2. Belief in providence, while agreeable with, and supported by reason, has its strongest ground in the truth of special divine revelation."
Joshua 1:8: "This book of the law shall not depart out of thy mouth;...for then thou shalt make thy way prosperous, and then thou shalt have good success."
I Corinthians 2:9: "But as it is written, Eye hath not seen, nor ear heard, neither have entered into the heart of man, the things which God hath prepared for them that love him."
"3. The Scriptures bearing upon this subject are very numerous and of great variety and force (see Nave's Topical Bible, re: *God, Divine Providence*)...aside from the large number of particular passages, the historical parts of the Bible are throughout illustrative of the great reality. In brief, it may be said that according to

the Scriptures;
(1) The providence of God is unlimited (Psa. 145:9-17)...Things seemingly of only slight importance or accidental are under his overruling power (e.g., I Kings 22:34; Esth. 6:1; Matt. 6:26; 27:19; Luke 12:6,7; Acts 23:16).
(2) ...there is ground in Scriptures, as in reason, for the distinction between general and particular and special providence...the people of God, the faithful servants of his kingdom, are the objects of his special love and care (e.g., Matt. 6:25-32; Psa. 91:11,12; Acts 14:16, 17; Rom. 8:28-39).
(3) The constant and final aim of God's providence is the fulfillment of his purpose in creation...nothing less than the complete establishment of an all-embracing kingdom of God, under the rule of the Lord Jesus Christ (e.g., Eph. 1: 9-11, Col. 1:19,20).
(4) The particular steps in this divine process are often unintelligible to us, but the purpose of God is independent and eternal, and is certain of its realization (e.g., Psa. 97: 2; Rom. 11:33; Eph. 1:4,5)..."

Most historians who wrote before 1900 viewed history from the Providential approach. Abundant evidence of this fact is revealed in the excerpts of historians referred to in the Christian History volumes identified in this *Guide*. (See the Bibliography of *Christian History, Christian Self-Government with Union*, and *Consider and Ponder*)

IMPORTANCE OF KNOWING CHRIST, HIS STORY

The American Christian philosophy of education and government is predicated upon the teaching of the Providential view of history. The imperative for restoring this Biblical view of history into the Christian curriculum and the consequences for Christians and American Christianity if it is ignored are compellingly advanced by Miss Verna M. Hall:

"Young American Christians know something of Christ's saving grace as the central theme of Christianity, but know little, so very little about how God brought forth this nation, America, for His purpose and for His glory. It is tragic, and an indictment upon Christian education for many years past, that so many American Christians know almost nothing about the Hand of God in America. The young people in our Christian colleges are at the peak of their youthful idealism, and yet, by and large they have never heard of the Hand of

God in relation to America, and therefore have no real love for America and her uniquely Christian institutions. If they do not know the Hand of God in our nation's past, how can they be sure of it in the present, or the future? As a consequence, they would not know *how important they are to God in respect to His government of men and nations*, nor would they know *what a responsibility they have, not only to those sacrificing Christians who have gone before, but to themselves and to their own posterity.* Most young Christians want to have a goal toward which they can work with God's help; they want to have a purpose and a hope. But if they have not been taught the Hand of God in history, they enter the work-a-day world *not realizing their importance as Christians in directing the course of human events.* They will not think it important to make decisions predicated upon Biblical principles of government in *all* fields of endeavor, for they will assume they are Christians in a secular world governed by secular rules and concepts. Somehow, someway in the last one hundred years particularly, America and Christianity have become separated in the mind and heart of the Christian, and he now lives in two worlds, the Christian inner world, and the secular outer world; whereas the Pilgrim and the Puritan lived in one world, the world of God, the creator of heaven and earth, and *all* that therein is... (emphasis added)

"The American Christian seldom thinks of America in the way the Pilgrims, the Puritans and the founding fathers of our nation thought. Instead, he has divided himself into two major categories, outside of denominationalism, for this twofold division runs right through all denominations. I might describe the division I mean in this way; one side is known for attempting to make Christianity more human, and more like secular institutions in attempting to solve our national problems. Indeed it is difficult to tell where this type of Christianity leaves off and good humanism begins. The other group have become so concerned with endeavoring to defend the faith itself, that they have withdrawn almost completely from the affairs of man in his daily walk. What is the result? The age-old tactic of Satan is to divide and conquer, and because of this division Christianity is no longer the leading influence in this nation, but is rather the follower of secularism, or the mere criti-

cizers of worldliness. Forgetting or forsaking the Hand of God in history, forgetting that God does rule in the affairs of men, forgetting or forsaking the Word of God as our American political textbook, our economic textbook, our social, cultural, educational textbook; this alone has produced the results we have in our nation today."[1] (emphasis added)

"...Who *causes* the human events which have taken place through the centuries, *God* or man? We have only these two choices. The *humanist* or *atheist* knows that man is causative. The secular textbook sets forth the facts of a subject in its causal relations, making *man* the *cause* – politically, sociologically, economically, ethnologically, etc. Should Christian educational institutions do the same? I submit they should not; they should structure *all* of their subjects from the *providential approach,* 'God's Causal relations,' and write their own course content and textbooks."[2] (emphasis added)

Further documentation on how the Hand of God in history was acknowledged and applied by the clergy and historians in America's Christian history may be found by researching the Index to *The Christian History of the American Revolution: Consider and Ponder.*

The Providential View of history is important because it is true, because it is Biblical, and because it challenges and supplants the prevailing secular social studies approach to history and government. The curricula of most schools and colleges omit this emphasis. Furthermore, understanding the Hand of God makes the lessons of history immediately individual and implants *hope* into the daily life of the teacher and student in the home, church, or school.

All of the preceding material identifies the philosophy and setting for teaching the seven principles of America's Christian history, government and education. The foregoing was also intended to establish the attitude, spirit and posture of a teacher in any sphere of governmental activity – home, church, school, business.

The following explanation of the seven principles – the Principle Approach – is applicable to every sphere of Christian activity.

---

1. Verna M. Hall, Excerpts from an address to the First Pilgrim Seminar, Plymouth, Mass., Nov. 18, 1971.

2. *Ibid.,* Excerpt from an address to the Second Pilgrim Seminar, November 18, 1972.

THE SEVEN PRINCIPLES

A KEY TO UNDERSTANDING
THE PRINCIPLE APPROACH

Miss Slater emphasizes on page 92 of *Teaching and Learning* that "as we understand Christian education to begin with *salvation* – the internal commitment of heart and mind to the saving grace of Jesus Christ – then we are concerned as to whether we are extending the Christian approach – *internal* – to our methods of teaching." The Christian approach to teaching and learning begins with the internal. What is the significance and relation of internal and external to the American Christian philosophy of history, government, and education?

The seven principles of America's Christian history and government may be understood and explained in the context of the diagram at the bottom of the page.

Consider Webster's 1828 Dictionary definitions of the terms "internal" and "external":

Internal: (adj.) inward; interior;…not external …pertaining to the heart.
Internally: (adv.) inwardly; beneath the surface. Mentally. Intellectually. Spiritually.

External: (adj.) Outward; exterior; opposed to internal…not being within; visible.
Externally: (adv.) Outwardly, on the outside. In appearance; visibly.

THE PRINCIPLE APPROACH SHOWS
HOW THE INTERNAL GIVES RISE TO THE EXTERNAL

INTERNAL >	→ EXTERNAL
Causative	Effect
Primary	Secondary
Invisible	Visible
Unseen	Seen

Research the following references concerning the Biblical basis and primary emphasis God places upon the *internal* as being primary, causative and invisible to all but God:

Proverbs 4:23: "Keep thy heart with all diligence; for out of it are the issues of life."
Proverbs 23:7: "For as he thinketh in his heart, so is he:…"
Matthew 15:18: "But those things which proceed out of the mouth come forth from the heart; and they defile the man."
Luke 6:45: "A good man out of the good treasure of his heart bringeth forth that which is good; and an evil man out of the evil treasure of his heart bringeth forth that which is evil: for of the abundance of the heart his mouth speaketh."
Romans 10:10: "For with the heart man believeth unto righteousness; and with the mouth confession is made unto salvation."
Eph. 3:16; II Cor. 3:3; Heb. 8:10; I Sam. 16:7

Educationally, the significance of the *internal* as causative in teaching and learning may be amplified as follows: The teacher endeavors to both discover and aim for the "heart." For example, one must discover the heart of the subject, the rudiments to which the facts are subordinate, and cultivate the heart of the student, his affections, character and will, of which his environment, circumstances and society are but effects.

Governmentally, the Christian approach impels the teacher to provide for the growth of Christian self-government whereby government – the flow of power and force from God indwelling and controlling the individual by the Holy Spirit – is causative and superior to the external and collective life. The correlative of Christian self-government is a Christian character and conscience (internal) whereby the individual student is both responsible and accountable to the internal demands of God's law written on the heart. The effect is a self-governed, free and independent man among men, who reasons from God's Word rather than adapts to his environment or acts without reflection.

Historically, as Master Teacher Katherine Dang has documented in her study of Universal History, men and events in all history are discerned by their spiritual, internal causes and their social,

external effects. Hence, a person's vertical relation to God or gods governs his horizontal and physical relation with men and things. Therefore, a study of the character and conduct of mankind throughout history demonstrates that the qualities and attributes of men are either of God or Satan, either holy or unwholesome, thus betraying their spiritual, mental and invisible origins.

Recalling Miss Slater's observation that "while it might look as if we were dealing with the subject of Christian government, actually, we are teaching principles which are basic to every Christian in every area of life. For what constitutes the Constitution is what constitutes the life and character of the people."[1] The seven principles that distinguish the character of every American Christian in every area of life and which produce an American Christian Republic are:

1. GOD'S PRINCIPLE OF INDIVIDUALITY
2. THE CHRISTIAN PRINCIPLE OF SELF-GOVERNMENT
3. AMERICA'S HERITAGE OF CHRISTIAN CHARACTER
4. CONSCIENCE IS THE MOST SACRED OF ALL PROPERTY
5. OUR CHRISTIAN FORM OF GOVERNMENT
6. HOW THE SEED OF LOCAL SELF-GOVERNMENT IS PLANTED
7. THE CHRISTIAN PRINCIPLE OF AMERICAN POLITICAL UNION.

RELATING INTERNAL AND EXTERNAL TO THE SEVEN PRINCIPLES

The discussion that follows explains four concepts necessary to teach the seven principles of America's Christian history and government:

1. How *internal* and *external* are related to the seven principles.
2. How God's Principle of Individuality is the primary principle of American Christian history, government and education.
3. How the other six principles are an extension of God's Principle of Individuality.
4. How each principle is expounded Biblically, educationally, historically and governmentally.

---

1. Rosalie Slater, *T/L*, p. 92.

GOD'S PRINCIPLE OF INDIVIDUALITY

ELUCIDATING THE PRINCIPLE

Consider God's infinity, diversity and individuality in nature. A snowflake always has six points with perfect sixty degree angles between the points, but each and every snowflake that has fallen since creation has a separate and distinct design or identity. No two snowflakes are ever alike, yet there is a sameness or oneness to them. Only God, Who changeth not (Mal. 3:6), Who is the same yesterday, today, and forever (Heb. 13:8) can make a snowflake of such infinite individuality and never repeat Himself.

The snowflake is but a representative and infinitesimal part of a creation wherein "Everything in God's universe is revelational of God's *infinity*, God's *diversity*, God's *individuality*. *God* creates distinct individualities. *God* maintains the identity and individuality of everything which He created."[1] How wonderful this is! What significance this principle has upon Christian education!

The principle may be explained and illustrated in a number of ways. Each individual should restate the principle or paraphrase it to his own satisfaction. For example:

God creates and maintains the identity and individuality of everything He made. God works through individual entities, and every being has a well defined existence which fits it for a special purpose.

God's Principle of Individuality gives rise to the Christian idea of man and government. All God made is revelational of His character and control. God creates and keeps, so as not to lose or surrender, everything He has made.

God is the one source, origin, cause – the ground or foundation – of a separate and distinct existence.

God is the Principle and foundation for unity with diversity; oneness among many; uniqueness without disparity; wholeness without conformity; completeness without contrariety.

A DIAGRAM OF THE PRINCIPLE:
"What Shows That I Am 'Me'?"

God's Principle of Individuality and the remaining six Christian history principles may be taught and explained using a diagram to show cause and effect and sometimes contrast. Diagram I applies the first principle to the individual. (*See page 32*)

In diagram I. *God's Principle of Individuality*, consider what things outwardly identify nearly everyone. Each person's fingerprints are unique from any other individual's; the whole theory of fingerprinting is predicated upon this fact. God made each person with his own footprint (Job 13:27: "Thou settest a print upon the heels of my feet"), profile, voice, signature and scent (consider how a bloodhound can distinguish the particular scent of one man from all others).

Then reason from the external back to the internal, from effect back to cause. For example, a person's conduct may be characterized as some visible kind of deportment, action, conversation, etc. Internally, one's character, inclusive of the *quality* of one's heart, conscience, consent, etc. is causative to the peculiar kind of conduct.

As every person has his own outward identity, so every person has an inward individuality, a separate and distinct existence. People may have kindred thoughts, motives and attitudes, but God's Principle of Individuality causes each individual to be absolutely unique, "like no one else you see, a witness to His diversity." (See *Teaching and Learning*, p. 155)

Consequently, each individual is responsible and accountable for his own choices and actions. Biblically we discover that salvation and service are individual, not collective; that the degree of spiritual liberty within the individual is causative of the peculiar quality of external, individual freedom we experience.

Furthermore, "man looketh on the outward appearance, but God looketh upon the heart." (I Sam. 16:7) The *heart* of the individual constitutes the inward man and is God's primary concern because "out of it are the issues of life"; what issues forth from man's heart is the visible effect, and of secondary importance. This fact supports Mercy Otis Warren's observation that "History . . . requires a just knowledge of *character*, to investigate the sources of action; . . ." (*Consider and Ponder*, p. 358c)

---

1. Rosalie Slater, *T/L*, p. 113.

1. GOD'S PRINCIPLE OF INDIVIDUALITY
HOW THE INTERNAL GIVES RISE TO THE EXTERNAL

INTERNAL > ►EXTERNAL	
Causative Primary Invisible	Effect Secondary Visible
Internal Individuality Thoughts, convictions, motives, opinions, affections, ideas, tastes, attitudes, disposition, temper.	*Outward Identity* Fingerprints, footprints, profile, voice, handwriting, scent, posture, countenance.
Internal Character Heart, Conscience, Consent, Soul, Mind, Will, Spirit.	*External Conduct* Deportment, Actions, Conversation, Gestures, Reputation, Demeanor, Walk.

The following chart, *Two Contrasting Approaches to Individuality*, suggests that individualism separate from Christ characterizes much of the secular world as some of the contemporary cliches indicate. In *contrast*, Christian individuality, in which the individual is found whole and complete by grace through faith in Christ, is characterized by entirely distinct sentiments, such as those uttered by some of the early prophets, apostles and Jesus.

TWO CONTRASTING APPROACHES TO INDIVIDUALITY

CHRISTIAN INDIVIDUALITY "CHOOSE YE..." HUMAN INDIVIDUALISM	
(separate, distinct, and revelational of God in Christ) *Eph. 2:10:* "We are His workmanship" *Eph. 4:6:* "One God...in you all" *Phil. 4:13:* "I can do all things through Christ..." *Mark 14:36:* "Thy will be done." *Acts 9:6:* "Lord, what will you have me to do?"	(either singular and selfish or conformed to man without God or Christ) "Look out for No. 1" "If it feels good, do it" "To each his own" "Get high on yourself" "My will be done" "Do your own thing" "Whatever makes you happy"

BIBLICAL BASIS FOR GOD'S PRINCIPLE OF INDIVIDUALITY

• *God's Infinity:* (Without limits; unbounded; boundless; not circumscribed; applied to time, space and qualities. That which will have no end; endless or indefinite ONE; fills all space)
Deuteronomy 4:39: "Know therefore this day, and consider it in thine heart, that the Lord he is God in heaven above and upon the earth beneath; there is none else."
Psalm 139:7–8: "Whither shall I go from thy spirit? or whither shall I flee from thy presence? If I ascend up into heaven, thou art there: if I make my bed in hell (sheol), behold, thou art there."
Jeremiah 23:24: "Can any hide himself in secret places that I shall not see him? saith the Lord. Do not I fill heaven and earth? saith the Lord"
I Kings 8:27: "will God indeed dwell on the earth? behold, the heaven and heaven of heavens cannot contain thee; how much less this house that I have builded?" (II Chr. 2:6; 6:1, 18)
Psalm 147:5: "Great is our Lord, and of great power; his understanding is infinite."

• *God's Diversity:* (Difference; dissimilitude; unlikeness. Variety; distinct being, as opposed to identity)
I Corinthians 4:7: "For who maketh thee to differ from another? and what hast thou that thou didst not receive? now if thou didst receive it, why dost thou glory, as if thou hadst not received it?"
I Corinthians 15:41: "There is one glory of the sun, and another glory of the moon, and another glory of the stars: for one star differeth from another star in glory."
Isaiah 46:9: "Remember the former things of old: for I am God, and there is none else; I am God,

and there is none like me, ... " (Ex. 15:11; I Sam. 2:2)

Jeremiah 10:6: "Forasmuch as there is none like unto thee, O Lord; thou art great, and thy name is great in might." (Isa. 40:18, 25; 46:5)

● *God's Infinite Individuality* (Unity with diversity)

Romans 11:36: "For of him, and through him, and to him, are all things: ... "

Colossians 1:16–19: " ... all things were created by him, and for him: and he is before all things, and by him all things consist."

Ephesians 4:6: "One God and Father of all, who is above all, and through all, and in you all."

1 Corinthians 12:4–6: "Diversities of gifts ... same Spirit ... differences of administration ... same Lord ... diversities of operations ... same God."

One will be quickened in his mastery of this first principle if he defines from Webster's 1828 Dictionary every significant word in the "Statement of the Principle" and the "Words related to Individuality" on page 113 of *Teaching and Learning* — then researches the words, their definitions and synonyms to see how they are used in the Bible.

APPLIED EDUCATIONALLY

● As surprising as it might seem at first, I believe that every subject taught in the Christian curriculum can reflect — and should reflect — a well-defined Biblical source and origin, a Christian history and government, and a Biblical end and purpose for the subject to be representative of God's Principle of Individuality. Every scriptural principle is fixed but infinite in its expression and identity. Hence, the Christian educator who acknowledges the Bible as the anchor of his research and scholarship can develop a unity of Biblical principles with a diversity of teachers and subjects.

Teaching from principles, inclusive of the rudiments of the subject as well as its Biblical origin and purpose, is expansive and produces a diversity of expression without inconsistency. As Noah Webster confirms in his 1828 Dictionary definition of "diversity" and "contrariety," *"There may be diversity without contrariety."* In turn, contrariety is defined as "opposition, in fact, essence, quality or principle ... inconsistency; quality or position destructive of its opposite."

On page 141 of *Teaching and Learning,* Miss Slater points out how the subjects of the school curriculum have become collectivized resulting in "loss of identity and importance of individual subjects ... " Consider how the following collectivized subjects have absorbed and lost the identity of the subjects on the right:

Social Studies	vs.	History: Ancient, Middle, Medieval, Modern. American Geography: Physical, Political. Government; Economics.
Language Arts	vs.	Grammar, Composition, Reading, Penmanship, Spelling, Literature.
Speech	vs.	Oratory, Rhetoric, Debate, Drama, Recitation.

Consider the emphasis suggested by God's Principle of Individuality in the home or school classroom:

Student's work in groups at tables	vs.	Use of individual desks
Workbooks, group projects	vs.	Individual notebooks, projects
Report cards with collectivized headings	vs.	Report cards listing particular subjects and specific qualities of character and self-government
Study of anthologies	vs.	Study of whole, complete works and individual authors
Group responsibility for school property, tools and equipment	vs.	Individual accountability for personal and assigned tools and equipment

The application of God's Principle of Individuality to specific subjects at various grade levels will be demonstrated in the *Curriculum* section.

REVEALED HISTORICALLY

This principle can be demonstrated historically. Evidence of it appears as individual links on the Chain of Christianity identified on page 6A of *Christian History* and expanded in *Teaching and Learning,* pages 158–183. This view of history is further elaborated in *Consider and Ponder,* pages 45a, 67a, 68a, 77b and 538c and in the *Curriculum* section, pp. 201 and 287.

APPLIED GOVERNMENTALLY

Christian Individuality can be contrasted with the extremes of human individualism on one hand

and the extremes of collectivism or centralization on the other hand. The student may consider and document the degrees of deviation from the Biblical standard in the center of the chart below called *God's Principle of Individuality – Contrasted With Two Extremes*.

Biblical examples of the ancient (and modern) forms of anarchy or tyranny in contrast with the Biblical basis for balance in the civil government, a manifestation of Christian Individuality, may be studied in the chart titled *Biblical Examples of Three Approaches to Civil Government* on page 35.

For example, the Bible references in the left-hand column describe a state of near anarchy, individualism separate from Christ, where the people rebel against the "law of the Lord," "trust in themselves," "despise others," "cease not from their own doing," and so forth. In the opposite right-hand column, Scripture describes a kind of tyranny or pagan individualism, despots who rule "over another to his own hurt," who arbitrarily *take* the property of others and make them servants, who denude or "legally plunder" the nation, and so forth. The middle column reflects Christian individuality, the government of God through Christ in both the individual "ruler" and citizen. In this balanced view, rulers are "ministers of God" for the good, not the harm, of God's people: they offer themselves "as servants, not masters," of the people and faithfully execute the law on "evil doers" – implying a *Biblical* standard for good and evil. They assure a "quiet and peaceable life" for those who "do well," and so forth. The people prayerfully submit unto righteous governors and are prepared in good conscience to obey God supremely rather than men who compel God's people to violate the "perfect law of liberty."

GOD'S PRINCIPLE OF INDIVIDUALITY CONTRASTED WITH TWO EXTREMES

ANARCHY – FREEDOM RUN WILD (EXTREME INDIVIDUALISM)	CHRISTIAN INDIVIDUALITY – BALANCE (LIBERTY WITH ORDER)	TYRANNY – ORDER WITHOUT FREEDOM (EXTREME INDIVIDUALISM)
Self-centered man	Christ-centered individual	Self-centered "king"
My will be done	"Thy will be done"	My will be done
Anarchy – do as one pleases with impunity	Authority with Responsibility	Tyranny – do as ruler pleases "or else"
License – an excess of freedom, no restraint	Christian self-government with rule by consent	Slavery – no freedom under arbitrary law
Lawlessness – each one a law unto himself	Liberty with Law	Bondage – lawful coercion or plunder; dictatorial
Rugged individualism separate from God or society	Self-government with Unity	Individual of value only as a part of the state
Nihilism: insurgency, insurrection, rebellion – social, moral, political	Local self-government with Union	Socialism – centralization of power in hands of one or a few
Individual determines amount of freedom and property exclusive of all others	Government by Consent of the Governed	Central government determines amount and extent of freedom, property, union
RESULTING FORMS OF GOVERNMENT:	RESULTING FORM OF GOVERNMENT:	RESULTING FORMS OF GOVERNMENT:
Anarchy to Democracy	Christian Constitutional Federal Republic	Bureaucracy to Dictatorship

BIBLICAL EXAMPLES OF THREE APPROACHES TO CIVIL GOVERNMENT

ANARCHY—FREEDOM RUN WILD (EXTREME INDIVIDUALISM)	CHRISTIAN INDIVIDUALITY—BALANCE (LIBERTY WITH ORDER)	TYRANNY—ORDER WITHOUT FREEDOM (EXTREME INDIVIDUALISM)
Isa. 30:9: "...this is a rebellious people...children that will not hear the law of the Lord."	*Rom. 13:3a,4a:* "For rulers are not a terror to good works, but to the evil... For he is the minister of God to thee for good."	*Eccl. 8:9:* "...there is a time when one man ruleth over another to his own hurt."
Luke 18:9: "And he spake this parable unto certain which trusted in themselves that they ...despised others..."	*Judges 5:9:* "My heart is toward the governors of Israel, that offered themselves willingly among the people..."	*I Sam. 8:17:* "He will take the tenth of your sheep: and ye shall be his servants."
Judges 2:19: "...when the judge was dead...they...corrupted themselves...in following other gods; ...they ceased not from their own doings, nor from their stubborn way."	*I Pet. 2:13-15:* "Submit yourselves unto every ordinance of man for the Lord's sake; ...as unto them that are sent by him for the punishment of evildoers, and for the praise of them that do well."	*II Chron. 28:19:* "For the Lord brought Judah low because of Ahaz king of Israel; for he made Judah naked, and transgressed sore against the Lord."
Gal. 1:10: "For do I now persuade men, or God? or do I seek to please men? for if I yet pleased men, I should not be the servant of Christ."	*I Tim. 2:1-4:* "I exhort therefore, that, first of all, supplications, prayers, intercessions, and giving of thanks, be made for all men; For kings, and for all that are in authority; that we may lead a quiet and peaceable life in all godliness and honesty. For this is good and acceptable in the sight of God our Saviour; Who will have all men to be saved, and to come unto the knowledge of the truth."	*Neh. 9:34-37:* "Neither have our kings, our princes, our priests, nor our fathers, kept thy law, nor hearkened unto thy commandments.... For they have not served thee in... the large and fat land which thou gavest before them, neither turned they from their wicked works. Behold, we are servants this day, and for the land that thou gavest unto our fathers to eat the fruit thereof and the good thereof, behold, we are servants in it: And it yieldeth much increase unto the kings whom thou hast set over us because of our sins: also they have dominion over our bodies, and over our cattle, at their pleasure, and we are in great distress."
Jer. 18:12: "And they said, There is no hope: but we will walk after our own devices, and we will every one do the imagination of his evil heart."	*Acts 5:29:* "Then Peter and the other apostles answered and said, We ought to obey God rather than men."	*Matt. 2:16-18:* "Then Herod...was exceeding wroth, and sent forth, and slew all the children that were in Bethlehem...."

THE CHRISTIAN PRINCIPLE OF SELF-GOVERNMENT

ELUCIDATING THE PRINCIPLE

On page 119 of *Teaching and Learning* there appears a statement by Hugo Grotius, the 16th century Dutch Doctor of Laws who systematized the subject of the Law of Nations. Grotius, "that learned and persecuted friend of liberty," as Alexander Hamilton viewed him, is quoted to explain the principle of Christian Self-Government:

"He knows not how to rule a kingdome, that cannot manage a Province; nor can he wield a Province, that cannot order a City; nor he order a City, that knows not how to regulate a Village; nor he a Village, that cannot guide a Family; nor can that man Govern well a Family that knows not how to Govern himselfe; neither can any Govern himselfe unless his reason be Lord, Will and Appetite her Vassals; nor can Reason rule unlesse herselfe be ruled by God, and (wholy) be obedient to Him." Hugo Grotius, 1654

Grotius' statement is analyzed from the governmental terms and spheres he uses, and reasoned from effect back to cause, from the external to the internal in diagram 2a, *Christian Self-Government Begins With God.*

Diagram 2a illustrates that if God is not indwelling and controlling the individual, then man's reason, will and appetite are the origin of the flow of political power and force that guides the home, city, county, state and nation. From the Christian perspective, however, God "ordained" civil government for the good of mankind, and made man the responsible vessel or instrument for the direction of the flow of power and force necessary to exercise the functions of government for our good or our harm. If God governs the individual, and man reasons from God's revelation, the Holy Bible, then the government of God and His Word will flow through that individual and manifest itself in the life of the individual, his home (and we might add, the local church) and in each expanding sphere of civil government to which,

2a. CHRISTIAN SELF-GOVERNMENT BEGINS WITH GOD

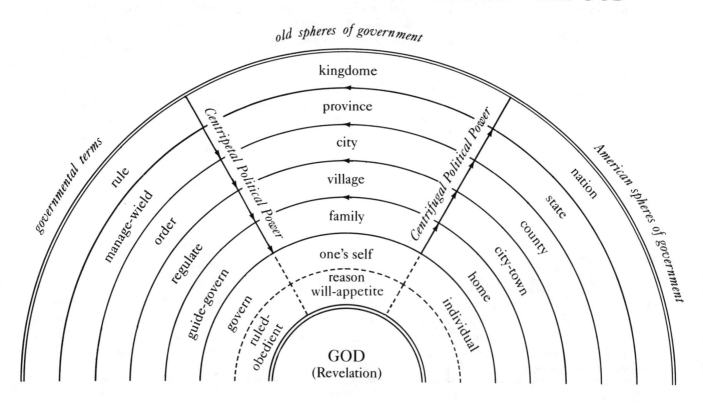

humanly speaking, man acts upon and responds to, subject to God's Providence.

The political force flowing *from* the individual to each sphere of government is *centrifugal*, wherein man and his concept of God, man and government is the center or the source of power. The political power that *acts upon* the individual, and *appears* to come from the national, state or local legislative, executive or judicial branches of government, is *centripetal* and a *reflection* of the active or passive power and force either expressly delegated or silently surrendered by each individual citizen.

Examples of *active* centrifugal constitutional political force flowing from the individual citizen are one's vote, instructions to representatives (letters, telegrams, telephone calls, petitions, etc.), support of responsible representatives, participation in administering the functions of government, and use of due process of law and judicial proceedings to contest or correct the actions of civil government. In addition, an individual's passive, tacit consent and indifferent attitude and actions also give force to civil government, with far more sinister consequences.

Centrifugal and centripetal political powers were actively demonstrated in America's first century by the two parent colonies – New England, and the Old Dominion in Virginia. The annotated diagrams on pages 270B to 270E in *Christian History of the Constitution* describe how these powers were exercised under two distinct systems of government, one where God's Law in the "free and independent man" was the center and source of political power, the other where the external church and state was the source of authority and power over the colonist.

DIAGRAM OF THE PRINCIPLE

A diagram of the foregoing principle shows those outward, visible things that should be controlled by the individual, and the constituents within each individual that should be governed.

In diagram 2b, *The Christian Principle of Self-Government*, the heart of man embraces the conscience, character, will, thoughts, etc. and is primary and causative to the external actions, deportment, conversation, conduct, etc. of man. Consequently, if the Law of God and His Love are published and man hears and heeds the Gospel-Law, that man can be properly self-governed. The effect is revealed in the individual's walk and deportment [*walk* is a figurative term often used in Scripture for actions and conduct which are conformed to God's will with the aid of the Holy Spirit (II Cor. 5:7; Gal. 5:16; I John 1:6)] and in his capacity to exercise dominion (authority, control) over the earth and his environment – whether social, political, economic, moral or otherwise.

2b. THE CHRISTIAN PRINCIPLE OF SELF-GOVERNMENT
ANSWERS THE QUESTION: WHAT WILL BE GOVERNED?

INTERNAL > ⟶ ►EXTERNAL	
Causative Primary Invisible Unseen	Effect Secondary Visible Seen
To Be Governed: Heart: conscience, character, will, thoughts, motives, affections, attitudes, convictions, ideas.	*To be Governed:* Actions, deportment, conversation, conduct, demeanor, posture, walk. Body: hands, feet, etc. Private property.
Conclusion: God's Law and Love, accepted and obeyed by the individual heart, governs the inward man.	*Conclusion:* Christian self-government is revealed in the individual's walk, deportment and dominion.

In scripture: A tree is known by it's fruit.

TWO VIEWS OF SELF-GOVERNMENT

Self-government has also been rendered as human self-discipline, self-control, and so forth, but the adjective *Christian* so modifies the origin and purpose of "self-government" that it represents one who is saved by "the washing of regeneration, and renewing of the Holy Ghost," (Ti. 3:5) enabling the new man to "walk in newness of life" and "serve in newness of spirit." (Rom. 6:4, 7:6) The chart below describes two contrasting views of self-government.

BIBLICAL BASIS FOR CHRISTIAN SELF-GOVERNMENT

The following two references are only representative of the hundreds of verses which elucidate this principle. The commentaries that follow suggest how expositors related the verses in different centuries.

Proverbs 16:32: "He that is slow to anger is better than the mighty: and he that ruleth his spirit than he that taketh a city."

"This recommends the grace of meekness to us...Observe the nature of it. It is to be slow to anger...It is to have rule of our own spirits, our appetites and affections, and all our inclinations, but particularly our passions, our anger, keeping that under direction and check, and the strict government of religion and right reason."[1]

"One that has the command of this temper, that can govern himself, and not suffer his passions to exceed due bounds, is superior in strength to him that can storm a castle or take a fortified city...but it requires the grace of God and the assistance of His Spirit, thoroughly to do the other."[2]

Acts 24:25: "And as he (Paul) reasoned of righteousness, TEMPERANCE, and judgment to come, Felix trembled, and answered, Go thy way for this time; when I have a convenient season, I will call for thee."

"TEMPERANCE: A Noun...occurs in Acts 24:25; Gal. 5:23; II Peter 1:6 (twice), in all of which it is rendered "temperance;" the R.V. marg. "self-control" is the preferable rendering, as temperance is now limited to one form of self-control. The various powers bestowed by God upon man are capable of abuse; the right use demands the controlling power of the will under the operation of the Spirit of God; in Acts 24:25 the word follows "righteousness," which represents *God's claims, self-control being man's response thereto;* (emphasis added) in II Peter 1:6, it follows knowledge suggesting that what is learnt requires to be put into practice."[3]

See also references to *sober* (self-controlled): I Tim. 3:2, Tit. 1:8; 2:2; to *meek* and meekness – (noun: meekness is that temper of spirit in which we accept His dealings with us as good, and therefore without disputing or resisting... W.E. Vine): Gal. 5:23, I Pet. 3:4. Meekness has also been defined as "strength or power under control."

PAGAN SELF-GOVERNMENT

God would not have us ignorant of the deceitfulness of sin or its consequences in self-centered

---

1. Matthew Henry, *Commentaries,* Vol. III, 1705.

2. John Gill, *Commentaries,* Vol. IV, 1810.

3. W.E. Vine, *An Expository Dictionary of New Testament Words,* Royal, 1939.

TWO CONTRASTING APPROACHES TO SELF-GOVERNMENT

"Choose ye..."	
Christ-centered	Self- or group-centered
God-governed	Materialistically self-governed
"Thy will be done"	"My will be done"
i.e.	i.e.
Christian self-government results when the individual yields his heart and mind to the government of Christ as defined by God's Word through the Holy Spirit.	Pagan self-government – rule of the individual either through fear of the state or by merely personal self-discipline or aggressive will-power.

government, and therefore reveals and illustrates the results of pagan self-government in the history of Israel. For example:

Judges 17:6: "In those days there was no king in Israel, but every man did that which was right in his own eyes."

Isaiah 53:6: "All we like sheep have gone astray; we have turned every one to his own way; . . ."

Psalm 10:4: "The wicked through the pride of his countenance, will not seek after God: God is not in all his thoughts."

Jeremiah 9:5: "And they will deceive every one his neighbour, and will not speak the truth: they have taught their tongue to speak lies, and weary themselves to commit iniquity."

Isaiah 47:8: "Therefore hear now this, thou that art given to pleasures, that dwellest carelessly, that sayest in thine heart, I am, and none else besides me; . . ."

CHRISTIAN SELF-GOVERNMENT RELATED EDUCATIONALLY

• "The Christian Educator needs to teach students first, that the source of all authority, law and government are found in God and defined in His Word; second, that Christian self-government makes God's Law the requirement of the heart — internal — and this is the basis of our American Christian Constitution."[4]

As Miss Slater has pointed out, the Christian Principle of Self-Government is the basis of the Christian Republic. It is also the foundation of both individual and collective Christian classroom control. (Study *Teaching and Learning*, pp. 102-106, 186-189)

IDENTIFIED HISTORICALLY

To understand and trace the development of the idea of individual and Christian self-government historically, from ancient civilizations to America, with its correlative expression in voluntary union, the student is directed to Volume II of *The Christian History of the Constitution: Christian Self-Government With Union.* For a detailed analysis of the outworking of this principle in the two parent colonies, Virginia and Plymouth, study *Teaching and Learning*, pp. 189-203, and pp. 363-366 for insights as to how this principle was tested up to 1776.

---

4. Rosalie Slater, *T/L*, p. 103.

AMERICA'S HERITAGE OF CHRISTIAN CHARACTER

ELUCIDATING THE PRINCIPLE

The perfect standard and principle of Christian character is Christ Jesus, the "express image" of God, the Father. (Heb. 1:3)

By the promises and "power of God," (I Cor. 1:24) individuals can become partakers of "the divine nature" (II Pet. 1:4) — the character and image of the Father — and thereby fulfill His commands, and "walk as children of God, in the midst of a perverse generation."

The expressly peculiar stamp, mark, or character of Christ engraved upon the individual is causative. An effect is the history and heritage of those individuals whose Christian faith and life endured both external and internal conflict and trials.

The character to be properly self-governed in response to God's "law of liberty," and to wisely, yet voluntarily, work with others constitutes the enduring basis of local self-government with union.

Let us understand the vocabulary of this principle through the following definitions:

Christian: adj. Of or pertaining to Christ, the Word of God.

Character: n. The peculiar qualities impressed by nature, habit or God upon a person which distinguish him from others.

Pagan: n. A heathen; an idolator; originally, an inhabitant of a country who worshipped false gods, heard the gospel, refused to receive it, and returned to his idols.

DIAGRAM OF THE PRINCIPLE

Diagram 3, *America's Heritage of Christian Character*, shows how Augustus Neander's statement of Christian character (*Teaching and Learning*, p. 210) is analyzed for the phrases that apply to the inward man and those that explain the external effect as recorded under part I, *The Source of Our Heritage of Christian Character.*

Part II of the diagram, examples of *How the Individual Reveals the Supernatural Christian Character and Conscience to Sustain a Christian Constitutional Republic*, suggests the quality and standard of character in conflict that characterizes Christian self-government and produces the necessary choices and actions, however uncomfortable and in conflict with society, which maintain a Christian form of government – a civil government limited to protecting private property, securing the general welfare (not the welfare of special classes of citizens), and guaranteeing a republican form of government to every state in the union. This is the character that should be the distinguished product of American Christian education and preaching and teaching the Gospel in the Christian home, church and school.

One may deduce from this diagram that a God-governed, individual "divine nature" which is overcoming sin by God's grace and truth, Jesus Christ, (John 1:17) produces a self-governed (peculiar) people and holy nation refined in conflict with the world.(I Pet. 2:9)

3. AMERICA'S HERITAGE OF CHRISTIAN CHARACTER
HOW THE INTERNAL GIVES RISE TO THE EXTERNAL

INTERNAL >————————————————▶ EXTERNAL
(Cause)   (Effect)

I. The Source Of Our Heritage of Christian Character

The "Power of the Gospel" . . . . "revealed itself to the heathen in the lives of Christians..."

The "Virtues of Him" . . . . "enabled them to walk as the children of God, in the midst of a perverse generation" (*T/L*, p. 123, Augustus Neander)

II. Some Examples of How the Individual Reveals the Supernatural Christian Character and Conscience to Sustain a Christian Constitutional Republic

(Causative – a conflict within)	(Effect – a conflict without)
Seeks to honestly, conscientiously examine and prove (try, test) himself by the Word of God. (II Cor. 13:5, I Tim. 3:16-17)	Perceives and corrects errors in his own conduct as a citizen even when both friends and public officials praise his conduct.
Evaluates the rectitude of his own character and conduct according to the law of God written on his heart, regardless of the pressure and conduct of the group.(Psa. 119:11, 139:23).	Refuses to share or participate in a government program simply because it will benefit some group – geographic, racial, age, etc. – to which he happens to belong.
Judges the rightness or the wrongness of each of his thoughts and actions by an absolute standard, Bible-derived – and thus is in a state of internal conflict with the world, which is resolved through the power and practice of Christian self-government.(Psa. 119:105, Matt. 22:36-40).	Does the right thing as a citizen even when most people are doing the wrong thing, and even when doing the wrong thing would meet a person's urgent human need, and won't result in being apprehended.
Looks to the law of God as well as the law of man (where consistent with God's Law) in determining whether any individual or corporate action is truly lawful.(Acts 5:29, Rom. 6:16-18).	Refuses to take special privileges, benefits, or subsidies even when the law of the land offers them to the individual or a special group.

BIBLICAL BASIS OF CHRISTIAN CHARACTER

Abundant examples of Christian character in contrast to pagan attributes are summarily identified in *Nave's Topical Bible*, under *Character, Of Saints* and listed in the chart below, *Christian vs. Pagan Character.*

One foundation of Christian character is the Biblical concept of *virtue.* (II Peter 1:1-9) Webster's 1828 Dictionary defines virtue as "Strength; Moral goodness; The practice of moral duties from sincere love to God and his laws, is virtue and religion. In this sense it is true, 'Virtue is nothing but voluntary obedience to truth.' (Dwight); A particular moral excellence; as the virtue of temperance, of chastity, or charity."

Miss Slater points out on page 251 of *Teaching and Learning*, that (Peter) defines virtue: as "the righteousness of God and our Saviour Jesus Christ." *Righteousness* in I Peter 1:1 is "the character or quality of being right or just" which is a "virtue" of God, or a "manifestation of His divine power." (See Vine's *Expository Dictionary of New Testament Words* for the Greek rendering of *righteousness* and *virtue*) Conscious of this standard and origin of virtue, the American Christian can esteem Samuel Adams' concern in 1779:

"A general Dissolution of Principles and Manners will more surely overthrow the Liberties of America than the whole Force of the Common Enemy. While the People are virtuous they cannot be subdued; but when once they lose their Virtue they will be ready to surrender their Liberties to the first external or internal Invader...If Virtue and Knowledge are diffused among the People, they will never be enslaved. This will be their great Security."[1]

CHRISTIAN CHARACTER APPLIED EDUCATIONALLY

It has already been observed that one of the unique benefits of American Christian education is that it produces the kind of Christian character needed to maintain a Christian Republic – the complete, spiritually-rounded character that expresses the wide range of attributes called for in God's Word. While Christian character building may be considered a primary goal of many Christian homes and schools, the emphasis tends to be only on those character traits needed to share the Gospel and live the Christian life in a rather narrow conventional sense, which perceives how men

---

1. Rosalie Slater, *T/L*, pp. 250–251.

CHRISTIAN VERSUS PAGAN CHARACTER

CHRISTIAN CHARACTER		PAGAN CHARACTER	
Attentive to Christ	John 10:3-4	abominable	Rev. 21:8
Blameless, harmless	Phil. 2:15	alienated from God	Eph. 4:18
Bold	Prov. 28:1	blasphemous	Luke 22:65
Devout	Acts 8:2	blinded	2 Cor. 4:4
Faithful	Rev. 17:14	boastful	Psa. 10:3
God-fearing	Acts 10:2	conspiring	Neh. 4:8
Godly	Psa. 4:3	corrupt	Psa. 14:1
Guileless	John 1:47	covetous	Mic. 2:2
Holy	Deut. 7:6	deceitful	Rom. 3:13
Honest	Rom. 12:17	disobedient	Neh. 9:26
Humble	Psa. 34:2	froward	Prov. 21:8

can behave virtuously or successfully in their strictly personal or private lives, but not in their lives as responsible citizens. This essentially incomplete and superficial approach to character building cannot, and does not, produce the needed correlative, compelling, and convicting effect in society and civil government.

Perhaps even more important, this sadly limited and restricted view of Christian character development, which has allowed millions of American Christians to sin without knowing it in their conduct as voters, politicians, employees, employers, etc., also has failed in a strictly spiritual sense – has failed to encourage and guide the kind of vigorous, multi-faceted spiritual growth that God wants Christians to experience, and that could help win unsaved multitudes to Christ.

America's heritage of Christian character can be identified by teachers to students through the curriculum in *every* way. Here are a few examples:

Curriculum:

1. Construct curriculum that reveals and teaches Christian character or the lack of it through the history and literature of the individuals God used to discover and advance the subject being taught.

2. Endeavor to have the subject so "rooted and grounded" in Biblical Truth with its Christian history that the student's love for God, for His Word, and for learning will be strengthened by the teacher's own scholarship and love for the subject as God revealed it.

Teachers:

1. Lead the way in demonstrating the character for Christian self-government, love of learning, moral rectitude, and productivity.

2. Teach models of character through a subject's history and literature, identifying the people God used to advance the subject from a Christian perspective.

3. Construct assignments, tests, and methods of teaching that challenge and strengthen the student's character for reasoning, relating and writing instead of merely guessing, filling in the blanks, or exercising rote memory without reflection.

Students:

1. Provide opportunities for students to exercise authority with responsibility as the teacher's or the class's representative in some specific task; provide opportunities to exercise certain choices and actions over assigned equipment or tools within both written and *unwritten* laws of conduct; administer clearly defined standards of writing, speaking, penmanship, spelling, grammar, et al., and expect students to answer for their own achievements in these areas.

2. Enable and expect students to give reasons and assign causes *within one's own character,* rather than blame one's circumstances or conditions at home and elsewhere, for the success or failure to meet deadlines, complete assignments, or maintain quality workmanship.

RELATED GOVERNMENTALLY

Discerning character as causative and the conduct and quality of the American Republic as effect, the American Christian knows why Christian character is important in a republic. It is essential that one teach why the character of the *electorate* is so necessary to maintaining our civil liberty under a limited constitutional government.

Noah Webster knew that "Men in republics are as wicked, and as selfish as in monarchies, and with far more power to introduce disorders, both into legislation and into the administration of the laws...The corruption of the electors is the first step towards the ruin of republics; and when the *sources of power* are corrupted, the evil hardly admits of a remedy."[2]

This is why it is so vital to explain to new teachers and those who are uncomfortable with thinking governmentally that "while it might look as if we were dealing with the subject of Christian government – actually, we are teaching principles which are basic to every Christian in every area of life. For what constitutes the Constitution is what constitutes the life and *character* of the people."[3] Hence the conclusion that "The qualities of a good ruler (effect) are also the qualities of those who are governed (cause) in a republic." (*Teaching and Learning,* p. 247)

Consider, then, the Biblical basis and practical application of Christian character to the principle of representation discussed in *Teaching and Learning,* page 322, and in *Christian History,* pp. 376-379, 396-397. Rev. Payson and Samuel Willard respectively suggest the following attributes of good leadership which have their inspiration and definition in the Word of God:

Fidelity: faithfulness; careful and exact observance of duty, or the performance of obligation; honesty, veracity; adherence to truth. Luke 16:10-12; I Cor. 4:2; Col. 3:22.

---

2. *Rudiments of America's Christian History and Government: Student Handbook,* p. 23, F.A.C.E. (Hereafter referred to as *Rudiments*).

3. Rosalie Slater, *T/L ,* p. 92.

Moral honesty: love righteousness, hate iniquity. Ex. 18:21; Ezek. 18:5-9; II Cor. 8:21; I Pet. 2:12.
Able: Having strong or unusual powers of mind, or intellectual qualifications; competent strength or fortitude; sufficient knowledge or skill; competent moral power. Ex. 18:21, 25; I Chr. 9:13; 26:8.
No respecter of persons: Deut. 1:17; 16:19.
Ruleth in the fear of God: Ex. 18:21; II Chr. 19:6.
Bear testimony against sin: Deut. 19:18; Rom. 13:3; I Pet. 2:14.
Promote true religion, piety: 2 Sam. 23:3; Prov. 29:2; Josh. 7-8; I Kgs. 3:28.

IDENTIFIED HISTORICALLY

Consider the premise that "The whole life of the Christian, from the beginning to the end, is a *conflict* with the world and the powers of darkness, a conflict *within* and *without...*"[4] Conflict is defined as "a struggle with difficulties; a striving to oppose, or overcome; a struggling of the mind."[5] Such conflicts in the context of afflictions and adversities are too numerous to list in the Bible, but two New Testament references may best characterize the nature of the Christian warfare:

4. *Ibid., T/L,* p. 123, Augustus Neander.
5. *American Dictionary of the English Language,* Noah Webster, 1828 (Hereafter referred to as *Webster 1828*).

"For what glory is it, if, when ye be buffeted for your faults, ye shall take it patiently? but if, when ye do well, and suffer for it, ye take it patiently, this is acceptable with God." (I Peter 2:20)

"Giving no offense in any thing, that the ministry be not blamed: But in all things approving ourselves as the ministers of God, in much patience, in afflictions, in necessities, in distresses, in stripes, in imprisonments, in tumults, in labours, in watchings, in fastings; ...As unknown, and yet well known, as dying, and, behold, we live; as chastened, and not killed; as sorrowful, having nothing, and yet possessing all things." (II Cor. 6:3-5, 9-10)

The Christian character God used to forward His Story through Peter and Paul's conflicts, is again honored by God in the trials and tribulations of the Pilgrims as documented by William Bradford's *History of Plymouth Plantation.* On page 216, *Teaching and Learning,* Miss Slater details some of the specific trials and conflicts which called forth the earliest and finest model of American Christian character.

The testing of character is the prevailing theme of the eight years of the American Revolution. The richness of the story is taught in *The Christian History of the American Revolution: Consider and Ponder:* refer to the Index of Leading Ideas.

"CONSCIENCE IS THE MOST SACRED OF ALL PROPERTY"

ELUCIDATING THE PRINCIPLE

During America's colonial and federal periods, when Biblical ideas exercised a profound influence over civil government and the economy, the term *property* was seen as embracing not only the right to possess or enjoy a thing but to dispose of it – to control it, i.e., to determine how it will be used, and this right was seen as God-given.

As Noah Webster put it in his 1828 Dictionary:

Property: n. The *exclusive right* of possessing, enjoying and *disposing* of a thing; ownership. In the beginning of the world, the Creator gave to man dominion over the earth, (Gen. 1:26-30), over the fish of the sea and the fowls of the air, and over every living thing. This is the *foundation* of man's property in the earth and in *all its productions...* (emphasis added)

Most Americans today are aware that there are many forms of economic property, but few people – even few Christians – realize that the creation and use of external private property is simply the manifestation of certain internal mental qualities, which should be qualities of Christian faith, character and understanding.

But is it not true that evil-doers also can prosper? (Psa. 73:3-9; 37:35-36; Job 12:6) From a Christian perspective, we see that various external forms of private property can result from *erroneous* mental qualities – i.e., from greed, egotism, materialism, fear, a desire for worldly power or display. This not only displeases the Lord and thwarts spiritual growth, but can cause harm to others and often is not an enduring form of wealth. (Prov. 1:32; Mark 4:19; I Tim. 6:9-10) By contrast, property produced God's way by expressing righteous qualities of thought and character, as indicated by Charles Wolfe, a teacher of the Principle Approach to economics, in diagram 4a, *The Christian Principle of Private Property,* p. 45, is pleasing to God, is not detrimental to the individual's spiritual growth, and is actually desirable from a Biblical viewpoint. (Isa. 3:10; 65:22; Deut. 29:9; Eccl. 8:12). It fulfills the Dominion Mandate to take possession of the earth – of land, wages, savings, profit, etc. – and provides evidence of God's supply and the income that can further the Gospel, the work of the Church and of voluntary charitable ministries.

Many Americans, and certainly most Christian Americans, would agree that it is vital for those who would live righteously to deliberately maintain a lively, sensitive, and uncompromised conscience – that state of mind which decides whether something is morally right or wrong. But to earlier generations of American Christians, conscience was much more highly regarded than it is today. Through the teaching and preaching of colonial clergymen, and by the exposition of God's Word in the colonial Christian home and school, the vast majority of early Americans were educated in Biblical law which quickened a conscience "dead in trespasses and sins" (Eph. 2:1) by clearly and boldly defining sin – what pleases and what displeases God.

By contrast today, most individuals – even those seeking to live Christian lives – are conditioned by the prevailing, carnal, worldly culture which blurs the distinction between right and wrong, determining conduct according to prevailing popular views, based on what the majority is doing, and what one can "get away with." Rather than looking to the internal demands of a Bible-based Christian conscience, the individual is encouraged to look at the external situation – what most people are doing and saying. Rather than turning inward to examine oneself in the light of God's Word, the individual turns outward, extends his mental antenna, and is satisfied if his actions are in tune with the times, with prevailing mores.

An earlier generation of Americans felt that Christian conscience was a distinct *possession,* and that it was given to the individual by God Himself, and thus it was vital not to lose it, or let it be diminished, violated or trespassed upon. The believer was convinced that Christian conscience was, in a word, a kind of property – valuable property. As James Madison said, "...*Conscience is the most sacred of all property.*"[1]

Consider how conscience was understood by the Founding Fathers over 150 years ago:

Conscience: n. "Internal or self-knowledge: or judgement of right and wrong. The faculty, power or principle within us which decides upon the lawfulness or unlawfulness of our own actions and affections and instantly condemns or approves them. Conscience is first occupied in *ascertaining our duty,* before we *proceed to action,* then in *judging of our actions* when performed." (Webster's 1828 Dictionary)

To Christians of America's first two centuries, conscience applied both to their affections and actions (i.e., internal and external) in every aspect of their lives. By the same token, Christians of the Founding Father generation understood that the term property applied both to the internal and external – the seen and the unseen – and related to much more than physical property, *per se.*

As James Madison wrote, in the limited conventional sense, "a man's land, or merchandise, or money, is called his property." But in a broader, deeper sense, he pointed out that property is also internal: "A man has a property of peculiar value in his religious opinions and in the profession and practice dictated by them...He has an equal property in the free use of his faculties and free choice of the objects on which to employ them. In a word, as a man is said to have a right to his property, he may be equally said to have a property in his rights...Conscience is the most sacred of all property."[2]

DIAGRAM OF PRINCIPLE

This broad sense of the Christian idea of property, as embracing both the internal and external, is summed up in diagram 4b, *Conscience Is the Most Sacred of All Property,* on page 46. Implicit in this diagram is the Christian truth that God's property is "all that was made," visible and invisible, by right of creation and redemption, and that private property among men is a stewardship from God to be protected, not regulated, by civil government.

It is equally true that the liberty and property of an individual conscience quickened by God's law and Holy Spirit is the workmanship of God. This "new creation" acknowledges the sovereignty of God over all possessions *and* the trustees of them.

---

1. *CHOC,* p. 248A.

2. *Ibid.*

4a. THE CHRISTIAN PRINCIPLE OF PRIVATE PROPERTY
THE INTERNAL INDIVIDUAL QUALITIES THAT GIVE RISE TO EXTERNAL ECONOMIC PROPERTY

INTERNAL >	▶EXTERNAL
Love of Christ, devotion to the local church, *concern* for the poor and needy; *willingness* to sacrifice; acceptance of *responsibility* as God's steward.	Property in the form of GOD'S TITHE AND VOLUNTARY CHARITY
Appreciation for the beauty of the earth as God's creation; *acknowledgement* that God wants man to take possession of the earth and exercise dominion over it; *recognition* of the individual independence and security that comes from private ownership of land, whether used for a home, church, school or a business.	Property in the form of LAND
Self-discipline and *conscientiousness* to perform assigned duties; *brotherly love* required to work cooperatively with others; *faith* in God's supply.	Property in the form of WAGES
Self-denial required to forego the satisfaction of immediate consumption of the fruits of one's labor; *diligence* to produce in excess of one's immediate needs; *character* to stay out of debt; individual *responsibility* to avoid economic dependence on the state.	Property in the form of SAVINGS
Self-denial required to save; *courage* required to risk one's savings in uncertain investments; *intelligence* to invest in business activities that will prove profitable; *patience* to wait until others – employees and suppliers – are paid before receiving payment in the form of profit.	Property in the form of PROFIT
Recognition and utilization of one's God-given creative and inventive talents; *faith* to undertake a creative task with the confidence that God will meet the need for ideas, language, invention, etc.	Property in the form of ROYALTIES
Loving concern for the economic well-being of others, especially one's family and those who have been faithful friends.	Property in the form of AN ESTATE WHICH OTHERS INHERIT

BIBLICAL BASIS OF PROPERTY

God's ownership of the natural world:

Exodus 19:5: "...for all the earth is mine:"
Leviticus 25:23: "The land shall not be sold for ever: for the land is mine; for ye are strangers and sojourners with me."

I Chronicles 29:11: "Thine, O Lord, is the greatness, and the power, and the glory, and the victory, and the majesty: for all that is in the heaven and in the earth is thine; thine is the kingdom, O Lord, and thou art exalted as head above all."
Psalm 24:1: "The earth is the Lord's, and the fullness thereof; the world, and they that dwell therein."

Psalm 50:10, 12: "For every beast of the forest is mine, and the cattle upon a thousand hills."
"...for the world is mine, and the fulness thereof."
Haggai 2:8: "The silver is mine, and the gold is mine, saith the Lord of hosts."

God's ownership of the souls of men:

Deuteronomy 32:6: "...Is not he thy father that hath bought thee? hath he not made thee, and established thee?"
Ezekiel 18:4: "Behold, all souls are mine; as the soul of the father, so also the soul of the son is mine:..."

God owns man by right of redemption:

I Corinthians 3:23: "And ye are Christ's: and Christ is God's."
I Corinthians 6:20: "For ye are bought with a price: therefore glorify God in your body, and in your spirit, which are God's."
Ephesians 2:10: "For we are his workmanship, created in Christ Jesus unto good works, which God hath before ordained that we should walk in them."

The Biblical Basis of Private Property:

Genesis 1:26: "And God said, Let us make man in our image, after our likeness: and let them have dominion..."
Exodus 20:15: "Thou shalt not steal."
Exodus 22:12: "And if it be stolen from him, he shall make restitution unto the owner thereof."
Deuteronomy 19:14: "Thou shalt not remove thy neighbour's landmark, which they of old time have set in thine inheritance, which thou shalt inherit in the land that the Lord thy God giveth thee to possess it."
Matthew 20:15: "Is it not lawful for me to do what I will with mine own?"
Acts 5:4: "Whiles it remained, was it not thine own? and after it was sold, was it not in thine own power?"
Ephesians 4:28: "Let him that stole steal no more: but rather let him labour, working with his hands the thing which is good, that he may have to give to him that needeth."
Titus 2:10: "Not purloining, but shewing all good fidelity; that they may adorn the doctrine of God our Saviour in all things."
I Peter 4:15: "But let none of you suffer as a murderer, or as a thief, or as an evildoer, or as a busybody in other men's matters."

4b. "Conscience Is the Most Sacred of All Property"

The Broad Application of the Principle As It Applies Not Just to Economic Property But to All That One Possesses

INTERNAL PROPERTY (Cause)	EXTERNAL PROPERTY (Effect)
Invisible properties:	*Visible possessions:*
Liberty of conscience and consent;	Physical possessions
Convictions, opinions, thoughts, affections, talents, gifts, ideas;	Fruit of one's labor Health: bodily Reputation: name, productions Freedom: movement, speech, assembly
Will, soul, spirit, mind.	Estate: condition or circumstances Signature
Conclusion: Individual liberty of conscience is God's property governed by His Law.	*Conclusion:* The conscientious stewardship of private property as established and protected by Law – Biblical and civil.

APPLIED EDUCATIONALLY

How does the principle of property, both internal and external, apply to both the teacher and student? The diagram below suggests some of the elements of our dual stewardship.

The Biblical principle of private property can be taught through every subject in the curriculum in a number of ways. It can be identified and applied to students through an examination of the choices and actions of individuals who are part of the history and literature of the subject studied. It can be applied as a correlative of the *methods* to teach the subject whereby the demands upon each student's property of conscience, consent, time, and labor are constantly exercised through student notebooks and written assignments, consignments of equipment or supplies, and use of delegated authority and responsibility.

CONSIDERED GOVERNMENTALLY

As already discussed, the first sphere of government is individual and internal. We know that God governs the Christian through the operation of His Holy Spirit in the heart and the conscience of the individual, and that our stewardship over God's property – our conscience and body – is exercised through *consent*. Webster's 1828 Dictionary defines *consent* as "to *yield* to what one has the power, the right, or the disposition to withhold, or refuse to grant," as illustrated in Prov. 1:10, 15; Rom. 6:16; 7:16.

Our consent is expressed one of two ways: *tacitly* – passively, perhaps in a cowardly manner, yielding without objection, or "surrender by silence"; or *expressly* – plainly, actively by word and/ or deed. Ponder which kind of consent – tacit or active – is expressed in the following verses: Job 31:34-35 and Psa. 50:18.

God expects our express or active consent to His saving grace. (Rom. 10:9-10). Neither passive resistance nor "surrender by silence" should char-acterize any Christian, and certainly not the American Christian. (Rom. 10:13; Jas. 4:7; 5:12) Study pages 229 and 232 of *Teaching and Learning.*

Concerning external civil government, representative government is by *consent* of the governed, and the end and purpose of civil government is the preserving and protecting of individual property. This was articulated forcefully by John Locke, the "Philosopher of the American Revolution." Study *Christian History,* p. 95:138 and 96:140 as well as *Teaching and Learning,* p. 238.

THE BIBLICAL PRINCIPLE OF PROPERTY IN HISTORY

Recall that Noah Webster declared in his 1828 Dictionary that the foundation of private property is found in Genesis 1:26-30, which says that God created man in His image and likeness, gave them dominion over the earth, and directed them to subdue it. However, among the pagan nations in ancient times, private property was the exclusive possession of the strongest, most warlike and powerful king and/or priest. Private property was obtained by coercion and maintained by force of arms, not through mutual compact, individual enterprise or voluntary consent.

The Bible alone clearly made property an individual, exclusive possession and responsibility in the Old Testament; and an individual, internal as well as external, possession and responsibility in the New Testament. Study the historical discussion of "Property in General" by Marshall D. Ewell on pages 225-227 of *Teaching and Learning.*

The Christian concept of property is advanced here as the greatest security and protection to the possession, use and disposing of one's exclusive interests. Some Christians may wonder, however, that if all things are God's property, how can individuals have a private property in God's creation.

The Biblical view that man, inclusive of all creation, is God's property by right of creation as well as redemption does not abrogate the concept of

TEACHER AND STUDENT EXERCISE OF PROPERTY

INTERNAL >	►EXTERNAL
1. Consent to school rules and classroom law. 2. Conscientiously use one's time, talents, and faculties. 3. Choose to obey or disobey directions of those in authority. 4. Decide to learn through one's own labor of mind and heart.	1. Stewardship over school property: desks, textbooks, keys, equipment. 2. Stewardship of individual possessions: time, labor, reputation, things. 3. Accountability for property entrusted by others: notes, books, clothing, supplies.

private property among men: we are God's property in relation to God, but God commanded that we enjoy private property in relation to *other men* and things.

The reader is urged to study and teach others the historic contribution of John Locke to the foundation of, title to, and the use and measure of property. Locke's conclusions should be reasearched and reasoned Biblically, of course. See *Christian History*, pp. 63–70 and *Teaching and Learning*, pp. 232–236, 356–362.

James Madison's conclusion that "Conscience is the most sacred of all property..." is a most significant concept in America's Christian history. The individual's property in his conscience is the historic foundation of the concept of Liberty of Conscience. "Thus we can see the Christian inheritance of property – from the first century when "liberty of conscience" became more important to men than their very lives. We remember the Pilgrims fleeing from England, rather than submitting to infringement of their rights of conscience..."[3]

LIBERTY OF CONSCIENCE BASIC TO CHRISTIAN SELF- AND CIVIL GOVERNMENT

Carefully consider the function of *consent* with regard to conscience as explained by Miss Slater under the heading "Consent is my Title to Conscience" in *Teaching and Learning*, p. 232. Reflect upon the right or wrong activity of consent in the following verses:

Proverbs 1:10: "If sinners entice thee, *consent* thou not."
Psalm 50:18: "When thou sawest a thief, thou *consentedst with him.*"
Acts 8:1: "... and Saul was *consenting* unto his (Stephen's) death, ..."
Romans 7:16: "If then I do that which I would not, I *consent* unto the law that it is good."

I Timothy 6:3–5: "If any man teach otherwise and *consent* not to wholesome words, even the words of our Lord Jesus Christ, and to the doctrine which is according to godliness; He is proud, knowing nothing... supposing that gain is godliness: from such withdraw thyself."

Liberty of Conscience, then, appears to be exercised when one consents to be governed by God through Christ by grace through faith, and when

one refuses to yield to that which violates God's Perfect Law of Liberty, whether the test is internal (inordinate desires, wrong-thoughtedness) or external (unbiblical social, political or religious coercion).

The Founding Fathers acknowledged that the consent inherent in one's liberty of conscience was essential to securing one's Christian and civil liberty, and protecting the free exercise of Christian self-government under a Christian form of government. Consider the following chronologically rendered statements concerning the relation between *consent, conscience*, and *government:*

"For the power that can invade Liberty of Conscience, can usurp civil Liberty."[4]

"Imposition, Restraint, and Persecution... enthrones Man as King over conscience, the alone just claim and privilege of his Creator; whose thoughts are not as men's thoughts; but has reserved to Himself that empire from all the Caesars on earth ... For if men, in reference to souls and bodies, things appertaining to this and the other world, shall be subject to their fellow-creatures, what follows, but that Caesar (however he got it) has all, God's share, and his own too? And being Lord of both, both are Caesar's and not God's."[5]

"No Action is a religious Action without Understanding and Choice in the Agent. Whence it follows, the Rights of Conscience are sacred and equal in all, and strictly speaking unalienable... And whoever invades this Right of another, be he Pope or Caesar, may with equal Reason assume the other's Power of Thinking, and so level him with the Brutal Creation..."[6]

"As the Happiness of the People is the sole End of Government, so the Consent of the People is the only Foundation of it, in Reason, Morality, and the natural Fitness of Things: And therefore every Act of Government, every Exercise of Sovereignty, against, or without, the Consent of the People, is Injustice, Usurpation, and Tyranny."[7]

"The gospel sets conscience above all human authority in matters of faith, and bids us to 'stand fast in that liberty wherewith the Son of God has

---

3. Rosalie Slater, *T/L*, p. 228.

4. James Harrington, 1611-1677, in *The Christian History of the United States of America: Christian Self-Government With Union*, p. 178 (Hereafter referred to as *CSG/U*).

5. William Penn, "The Great Case of Liberty of Conscience," 1670, in *CSG/U*, p. 94.

6. Elisha Williams, "The Essential Rights and Liberties of Protestants," 1744, in *C/P*, p. 187b.

7. By the Great and General Court of the Colony of Massachusetts Bay, A Proclamation." January 23, 1776, in *C/P*, p. 208.

made us free.' (Gal. 5:1) . . . At the same time that it commands us to submit to every ordinance of men, it also directs us to act 'as free, and not using liberty as a cloak of maliciousness, but as the servants of God.'" (I Pet. 2:13–16)[8]

The doctrine of liberty of conscience should be researched and understood as it developed in the Chain of Christianity. The following Biblical references may help further explain this first principle

---

of property and Christian government: Jos. 24:14-15; Psa. 119:102; Acts 4:19, 5:29; 23:1; Rom. 6:16; Heb. 13:18.

"No matter what may be the fashions of the hour or the common custom of his fellows, one whose heart beats true to God will not do anything knowingly against conscience: his language will ever be, 'whether it be right in the sight of God to hearken unto you more than unto God, judge ye.'"[9]

8. "A Sermon on American Affairs" by John J. Zubly, 1839, in *CIP*, p. 519b.

9. W. E. Vine, *An Expository Dictionary of New Testament Words*, Royal Publishers.

THE CHRISTIAN FORM OF OUR GOVERNMENT

FIRST AMENDMENT PROTECTION

Of the seven principles embraced in the Principle Approach to America's Christian history and government, probably the one that raises most questions is the fifth, which states that there is a Christian form to American civil government, specifically, a *Christian Constitutional Federal Republic*.

To a considerable extent, this skepticism is the net result of a full century of secular revision of American history, which has progressively removed evidences of tangibly Christian influences in the shaping of this nation's form of government – national, state and local.

In the past generations, this skepticism has been heightened by a much-repeated misinterpretation of the first clause of the First Amendment to the Constitution. The assertion that "Congress shall make no law respecting an establishment of religion, or prohibiting the free exercise thereof" was intended to *protect* both Christianity and individual liberty of conscience by guaranteeing toleration of *all* religious convictions, so long as they are not subversive of civil order or society.

This opening clause of the First Amendment did not reflect indifference to religion, a desire to hamper the Christian church, or to minimize or regulate the "free exercise" of Christianity. Justice Joseph Story, Associate Justice of the U.S. Supreme Court for 34 years by President James Madison's appointment, wrote in 1833 concerning the First Amendment:

"The promulgation of the great doctrines of religion, the being, and attributes, and providence

of one Almighty God; the responsibility to Him for all our actions, founded upon moral accountability; a future state of rewards and punishments; the cultivation of all the personal, social, and benevolent virtues; – these never can be a matter of indifference in any well-ordered community. It is, indeed, difficult to conceive, how any civilized society can well exist without them. And, at all events, it is impossible for those, who believe in the truth of Christianity, as a Divine revelation, to doubt, that it is the especial duty of government to foster and encourage it among all the citizens and subjects. This is a point wholly distinct from that of the right of private judgment in matters of religion, and of the freedom of public worship, according to the dictates of one's conscience.

"Probably, at the time of the adoption of the Constitution, and of the amendment to it, now under consideration, the general, if not the universal, sentiment in America was, that Christianity ought to receive encouragement from the State, so far as such encouragement was not incompatible with the private rights of conscience, and the freedom of religious worship. An attempt to level all religions, and to make it a matter of state policy to hold all in utter indifference, would have created universal disapprobation, if not universal indignation."[1]

The "separation of church and state" was never for a moment intended to separate government

1. Joseph Story, *A Familiar Exposition of the Constitution of the United States*, 1840.

from the benign influence of Christ and Christianity as defined in the Bible, nor was that phrase ever conceived to imply that our form of government came into being historically as a result of merely secular convictions, separate from the Word of God and Biblical doctrine concerning both church and civil government.

The concept of the separation of church and state was intended solely to protect the church and its members and ministries from any kind of domination or control by the general government. Political control of the church had been an ominous problem not only for the Pilgrims and Puritans in England, but for a variety of Protestants, Catholics and Jews who sought and found in colonial America a measure of freedom from religious persecution, which was enlarged under the umbrella of law established by the National Constitution.

BIBLICAL AND GOVERNMENTAL WISDOM

The wisdom of this policy, instituted by Bible-believing American Christians in colonial times, and confirmed in the U.S. Constitution, has been verified by history. The threats to religious freedom today come not only from the Communist countries, whose governments disavow all evangelical Christian religion and make atheism their official national belief, but from allegedly free societies which have established one denomination as the state church.

For example, in Sweden, where the Lutheran church is the official state institution, the clergy are so much under the thumb of the socialist state that they dare not voice their opposition to pagan socialism from the pulpit.

Although the Founding Fathers had state tax supported churches, they did not establish a national church, and thereby pressure all Americans for all generations to be Episcopalians, Congregationalists, Presbyterians, Methodists, Baptists or whatever. This was, in itself, a sign of their spiritual wisdom, and an implication of the spirit of our Christian form of government. A government derived from Biblical principles must recognize that true worship must always be voluntary, that in their institutions of worship, and in the Christian walk and conversation, true believers must practice *separation* from unbelievers in matters that pertain to Bible doctrine and morality. Christ-centered men must always be assured sufficient *independence* to rebuke severely and publicly the errors of civil leaders even as the God-appointed Old and New Testament prophets rebuked the wayward ways of Israel's kings and the prelates of Rome and their appointed high priests.[2]

The historic American Christian conviction that the church – redeemed individuals who constitute the body of Christ as governed by the Word of God – was God's instrument to produce a Christian nation to advance the Gospel and a civil government to protect, not presume or prey upon, the church, required a specific form of government that was most harmonious with Biblical principles and most representative of the diverse colonial views of church government. The Pilgrim and Puritan divines searched the Scriptures for wisdom concerning, first, ecclesiastical (church) government, and then extended their conclusions to civil government. The resulting *form* of civil government was as Biblical and as balanced as their knowledge and practice of Bible doctrine permitted.

---

2. New Testament examples of a prophet and Jesus rebuking Kings and state appointed priests:

John the Baptist: beheaded because he rebuked Herod Antipas for marrying his brother's wife and "for all the evils which he had done."

Christ Jesus reproved Herod Antipas as "that fox" in Luke 13:32.

Paul denounced Ananias, the high priest appointed by Herod, King of Chalcis, with the statement "God shall smite thee, thou whited wall." (Acts 23:3)

Old Testament examples of the Prophets rebuking the Kings of Israel, Judah or other nations:

Samuel reproved Saul for rejecting "the word of the Lord." (I Sam. 15:23)

Samuel "hewed Agag" the king of the Amalekites for making "women childless." (I Sam. 15:33)

The prophet Nathan rebuked King David for killing Uriah, in order to take Uriah's wife, Bathsheba. (II Sam. 11:7, 9.)

The prophet Ahijah rebuked King Jeroboam for his idolatries. (I Kgs. 11:31-39; 14:6-16)

Jehu, prophet of Judah, rebuked Baasha, successor to Jeroboam, for making "my people Israel to sin." (I Kgs. 16:1-2)

Elijah reproved Ahab for "forsaking the commandments of the Lord," (I Kgs. 18:17-18) and for selling himself "to work evil in the sight of the Lord." (I Kgs. 21:20)

Elisha rebuked Jehoram for the same sins of his father, Ahab. (II Kgs. 3:3, 13)

The prophet Shemaiah censured Rehoboam and the Kings of Judah and Israel for forsaking God. (II Chr. 12:5)

Hanani rebuked Asa, King of Judah, for relying on the King of Syria, not God, for military support. (II Chr. 16:1-3, 7, 9)

Azariah the priest, with 80 other priests, "withstood Uzziah the king for usurping the role of the priests" and, as king, burning incense unto the Lord. (II Chr. 26:17)

Daniel rebuked King Belshazzar for his idolatry. (Dan. 5:23)

HOW CAN THERE BE A CHRISTIAN FORM OF GOVERNMENT?

A DEFINITION

The question arises: Is there such a thing as a Christian form of government? Form is defined as (a) Manner of arranging particular things; (b) Manner; system; (c) Disposition of the component parts; (d) Stated method; established practice (Webster's 1828 Dictionary). Can there be a visible, Biblical system or way of arranging the component parts or functions of government? Many evangelical Christians would call their form of church government *congregational;* others would define their form of church government as *episcopal* or *presbyterian.* There are proponents for each historic form who are persuaded, and for good reason, that their system is Biblical. Bible scholars concur that all three constitute Christian forms of church government, and Christian historians have observed that elements or components of all three forms were applied by our Founding Fathers in constructing a Christian form of *civil* government.

The officers, functions and practices of either home, church or civil government are identified and described in the Bible. The *way* man uses the particulars of government and to what *end* or *purpose* they are used depends on whether or not the men using them are God-governed Christians. For example, the components of civil government – both the officials, such as judges, law-givers, magistrates (legislative, executive and judicial), policemen, ambassadors, and such elements as taxes, penalties, states, and constitutions – have a Biblical origin and purpose.

The Scriptures, as well as history, describe how pagans and believers used these components both before and after Jesus came. However, from the Christian point of view, it requires the Christian principle of self-government, property and voluntary union to make the external form or framework of government work for the good, and not the harm, of man.(Rom. 13:4)

ELUCIDATING THE PRINCIPLE

As men and as Christians we have a dual form of government under one sovereign Law of Liberty: As Christians we consent to King Jesus and the "Law of the Spirit of Christ" (Rom. 8:2) or Gospel Law; as men, God the Father is sovereign and we consent to the Truths of God's Word as our "reasonable service." (Rom. 12:1)

Both Biblically and in Christian civil government, the law or principles of representation

(Deut. 1:13; Ex. 18:21), three functions of government (Isa. 33:22), and two spheres of power (Matt. 22:36-40) are fundamental to the structure of a Christian Republic. This form of government, however, cannot long endure without God's gracious power to effect an individual character for Christian self-government, property of conscience, and Christian unity and union. Both the Law and the Gospel are constituents of a Christian Republic.

THE CHRISTIAN ORIGINS OF OUR GOVERNMENT

To understand how distinctly Christian is the form of America's civil government, as framed in the Constitution, we need to systematically examine its philosophical roots, which can be clearly discerned from a study of our Christian history. These Christian roots, and their fruition or form in our civil government as expressed in the Constitution, are summarized in diagram 5a, *The Christian Roots of America's Form of Government*, page 52.

Briefly, we can say that the origins of our form of government lie in a series of Christian convictions beginning with the Sovereignty of God, the belief that the Lord desires a covenantal relationship with men, and wants men to be ruled by His Law. Again, our Founding Fathers believed that the Creator is a God of liberty and order, and that both can be achieved when men practice Christian self-government, and limit the role and power of their civil government.

Our Founders were also vividly aware of man's fallen nature, which causes him to abuse the privilege of exercising governmental powers, and that a pure democracy or an absolute monarchy is not only impractical but ungodly because of the ignorance and selfishness of unredeemed men. However, they also saw that there is a Christian alternative to a secular monarchy or democracy – a Christian Republic, based on the Biblical principles of representation, separation of powers, and a dual form of government.

THE PRINCIPLE GOVERNMENTALLY AND HISTORICALLY EXAMINED

As summarized in diagram 5b, *The Christian Form of Our Government*, page 53, the internal sphere – the spirit, nature and essence of our government, is primary and causative of the letter, the external structure and framework. A genuine, practicing Christian understands and lives the principles on the left hand side of the diagram –

i.e., those that constitute the *spirit* of our civil government. If he truly loves God and has received Jesus as Lord and Savior, he will quite spontaneously be practicing Christian self-government, he will be a good steward of the property God has entrusted to him, and he will feel impelled to come together in voluntary union with like-minded men and women.

Many men and women understand and practice these principles in their personal lives, but do not see that these principles express themselves, logically and inevitably, in a certain form of civil government that is implicitly Christian.

The Christian Principle of Self-Government is the essential principle as both Miss Hall and Miss Slater have indicated:

"Each religion has a form of government, and

Christianity astonished the world by establishing self-government."[3]

"For this idea they [the Pilgrims] were driven from their native land and came, at last, to these shores to found the great governing principle of Christianity – Christian self-government, which became the basis of our American Constitutional government."[4]

"The individual with his Bible opened, became the root to America's Christian form of civil government – a Christian republic."[5]

---

3. Verna M. Hall, *CHOC*, p. III.
4. Rosalie Slater, *T/L*, p. 326.
5. Verna M. Hall, *C/P*, p. xxvii, Col. 1.

5a. THE CHRISTIAN ROOTS OF AMERICA'S FORM OF GOVERNMENT

INTERNAL > ————————————➤ EXTERNAL	
(GOD and the Government of the Individual)	(GOD and the Government of the Nation)
1. Only God is Sovereign; Only Christ is King.	1. No man can be King; no civil government can be Sovereign.
2. God wants us to covenant with Him – to Love Him supremely and our neighbor as ourselves.	2. In a series of American Covenants, the people pledged their faith to God and to one another.
3. God framed a fundamental Law – the Decalogue – for the government of men and the protection of their lives and property.	3. Our Founding Fathers framed the Constitution as America's fundamental law in keeping with the Law of God to protect life, liberty and property.
4. Maximum self-government results when man yields to the government of Christ.	4. Minimum civil government is effected – adequate to maintain order – when men are properly self-governed.
5. Natural man's fallen nature causes him to abuse the functions or powers of government.	5. Because of man's sinfulness, righteous government must be based upon the separation of functions.
6. Those who represent Christ are servants of God to man and hence are qualified to represent men.	6. Knowledgeable representatives balance the interests of their constituents with the provisions of the Constitution and the well-being of the entire people.
7. The Christian principle behind Christ's two great commandments is practical when men have the character to work together voluntarily while they obey God supremely.	7. American federalism – the dual form of our government – is maintained by the character that assumes responsibility for local self-government, yet will voluntarily unite as Americans and respect the law of the land.

The reader may want to reread and research the Biblical basis and application of each of the three internal principles as discussed in this *Guide* (see pages 36, 43, and 69).

The three minimal external principles of our Constitution will be amplified governmentally and historically as follows:

PRINCIPLE OF REPRESENTATION

Those who study civil government from a Biblical perspective often cite the experience of Moses in taking Jethro's advice, and sharing the overwhelming burden of government – and in the process, decentralizing government – by delegating responsibility to carefully qualified local officials. The passage that most clearly suggests this is Exodus 18:25-26. But this passage does not make it plain whether the local officials were selected solely by Moses, at his own initiative, or whether they were chosen by the people themselves.

Were the local officials truly representatives of the people? Is this event the Biblical precedent that gave rise to representative government in New England, framed in a written constitution? If the only passage we consult is Exodus 18:25, 26, there will be no clear answer to those questions. But the events depicted in Exodus 18 are recounted and clarified in Deuteronomy 1:13: "*Take you* wise men, and understanding, and known among your tribes, and I will make them rulers over you" (emphasis added).

This passage, which most able Bible scholars and Bible commentaries agree is simply a remembering and recapitulation of the events of Exodus 18, makes it clear that Moses charged the *people to elect their own qualified representatives* and he confirmed them in their office.

Over 3000 years later, Rev. Thomas Hooker cited this passage, Deuteronomy 1:13, in a sermon which commended the principle of representation as a fundamental of Christian civil government. In turn, Rev. Hooker's sermon in 1638 inspired the first constitution in America, the Fundamental Orders of Connecticut.[6]

Actually, in God's Providence representative government had appeared in America well before the framing of the Fundamental Orders – even though at first its Biblical justification was neither understood nor acknowledged. The first legislative assembly was held in Virginia in July 1619. But the call for this assembly was initiated by Governor Yeardley, not the people; just as the Governor granted the privilege of choosing representatives, he subsequently revoked it.[7]

A more Biblical basis for representative government appeared a year later, hundreds of miles to the North. In 1620, Pastor John Robinson advised the Pilgrims concerning the choice of representatives in the New World and consequently they elected John Carver the first governor of Plymouth Plantation.[8]

Then in 1638, a General Court, consisting of representatives from each of the three towns in the Connecticut River Valley, met to frame a body of laws for the permanent government of Connecticut colony. As already mentioned, their meeting to draft the Fundamental Orders of Connecticut was inspired by a sermon on Deuteronomy 1:13 by Rev. Thomas Hooker.[9]

Nearly 150 years later, the Connecticut Resolution of 1787 provided for a U.S. Congress consisting of two houses, a Senate and a House of Representatives.

---

6. Verna Hall, *CHOC*, pp. 250-251.
7. *Ibid.*, p. 164, 168.
8. *Ibid.*, p. 200, 205.
9. *Ibid.*, pp. 250-251.

5b. The Christian Form of Our Government

INTERNAL > Spirit Nature and Essence	EXTERNAL Letter Structure and Framework
Christian Self-Government	Principle of Representation (Deut. 1:13; Ex. 18:21)
Christian Principle of Private Property	Separation of Powers (Isaiah 33:22)
Christian Principle of Voluntary Union	Dual Form of Our Government (Matt. 22:36-40)

The Congress was an expression not only of the Biblical principle of representation but of its correlative, the principle of delegation of power. In the Scriptures, we discover a delegation of power from God to His Son, Jesus Christ, by the Holy Spirit, thence to men as ambassadors for Christ: Psa. 62:11; Matt. 28:18; John 1:21; II Cor. 5:20; Eph. 6:20; I Cor. 7:22. The Biblical idea of delegated power was understood and taught by the early American clergy as the following excerpt from Rev. Phillips Payson's Election Sermon of 1778 illustrates:

"The qualities of a good ruler may be estimated from the nature of a free government. Power being a delegation, and all delegated power being in its nature subordinate and limited, hence rulers are but trustees, and government a trust;..."[10]

Further documentation and direction concerning the principle of representation and the republicanism of Christianity is found in *Teaching and Learning*, pp. 317-321.

SEPARATION OF POWERS

All three powers or functions of government are identified in Isaiah 33:22 and are found to be originally in one God but not separated. Indeed, because God and Christ are perfect, and incapable of abusing their power – as mortal men so readily do – there is no need for their three governmental powers to be separated; and because even the three persons of the Trinity constitute one infinite divine Being, there is no possibility that these three governmental powers of God could be separated.

All three functions of God's government are explicitly exercised by Jesus Christ Who is described as our Lawgiver, Judge and King:

Matthew 28:18: "...all power is given unto me in heaven and in earth."
James 4:12: "There is one *lawgiver*, who is able to save and to destroy: who art thou that judgest another?"
II Timothy 4:1: "I charge thee therefore before God, and the Lord Jesus Christ, who shall *judge* the quick and the dead at his appearing and his kingdom;..."
Acts 17:7: "Whom Jason hath received: and these all do contrary to the decrees of Caesar, saying that there is another *king*, one Jesus."

All three functions of government have their source and origin in God as performed by Jesus Christ through the Holy Spirit. Man, made in God's image and likeness, exercises all three functions within himself as Miss Slater explains on page 244 of *Teaching and Learning*. When men enter into civil society, however, and consent to other men representing them or "ruling" over them, history records the danger and harm of permitting one (or more) sinful mortal man to exercise the power to make laws, execute them and judge right or wrong conduct according to his own laws. Witness the tyrannical reign of the kings of Assyria, Babylon or even some of the wicked kings of Israel such as Rehoboam,(II Chr. 11-12; I Kgs. 12-14) and the arbitrary reigns of the Caesars of Rome.

Probably the first positive body of law to limit the powers of a king of England was the Magna Charta in 1215. (See *Teaching and Learning*, pp. 344-346) The next successful limitation on English kings and the further dispersion of political power – by request – came in 1628 with the English Petition of Right. The Petition of Right "struck at prerogative taxation, which was the power of the king to exact taxes without the *consent* of Parliament;..."[11] The fullest unilateral declaration limiting the power of the kings of England and guaranteeing individual liberties is contained in the English Bill of Rights of 1689. (See *Teaching and Learning*, p. 347)

The first full American expression of the separation of powers was declared in what has been called the first American constitution – the Fundamental Orders of Connecticut in 1638 – followed by the Massachusetts Body of Liberties in 1639. (See *Christian History*, pp. 252-261)

It was Baron DeMontesquieu's *Spirit of Laws*, published in 1748, that articulated the principle of separation of powers most conclusively. (See *Christian History*, pp.131-138)

Miss Slater points out that the three functions of government are exercised by each individual conscience as explained by J. M. Mason in Webster's 1828 Dictionary definition of *conscience*. (See also *Teaching and Learning*, p. 229) In civil government, these separate but correlative powers of government are clearly defined in Articles I, II and III of the Constitution of the United States of America.

DUAL FORM OF GOVERNMENT

Dual – two levels or spheres – of government

---

10. *CHOC*, p. 379.

11. Rosalie Slater, *T/L*, p. 346.

or power and force are first illustrated in Matthew 22:36-40, Christ's two great commandments. Notice the dual governmental relation between God and men, and man and his neighbor, wherein the "vertical" relation is primary and inclusive of the horizontal sphere with God's Law being sovereign over all. This concept is expressed in Christian Constitutional government as two independent spheres within one sovereign sphere with one supreme law (The Constitution) over all.

In its fullest expression, this principle is unique to America. No other nation in the history of the world has developed and articulated the delicate balance between the sovereign limited powers and functions of a national government and the resident, reserved powers and functions of state and local government. Articles IV, V and especially the ninth and tenth amendments to the Constitution articulate this principle. James Madison, the Father of the Constitution, clearly explains and elaborates this delicate balance in the *Federalist Papers*, Nos. 39, 47 and 48.

THE LAW AND THE GOSPEL AS THE BASIS OF OUR FORM OF GOVERNMENT

When American Christians reflect on how much God's Moral Law is the origin and standard for whatever we plan, do and judge as Christians and citizens, and how much the Spirit of God is needed to successfully fulfill what He requires of us, we realize just how much the Law and Gospel determine the *quality* of American Christian self- and civil government.

THE LAW

Consider the following highlights of the nature and purpose of God's Law in relation to the intent and purpose of our civil laws.

The Law of God is described in the Bible as being holy, just, good, and spiritual. (Rom. 7:12, 14) God's commandments are also characterized as perfect, as light and as truth. (Psa. 19:7; Prov. 6:23; Psa. 119:142) Then consider the *purpose* of God's law in the light of its divine attributes:

Romans 3:20: To know what sin is...
Romans 5:20: To know what offends God...
Romans 7:7: To expose the works of the flesh...
I Timothy 1:9: Made for the lawless and disobedient...
Galatians 3:19: To expose transgressions until Christ should come...

Galatians 3:24: A schoolmaster, to bring us unto Christ...

The English and American Puritan divines understood the harmony between the Law and Gospel-Grace and sought to extend their convictions into an American Christian commonwealth. For example, in a little book called *Moral Law*, Ernest Kevan elaborated on the work of Anthony Burgess entitled *Vindiciae Legis*, or *A Vindication of the Moral Law*, first published in 1646. Mr. Kevan summarizes the purposes of the Law to the ungodly and to the believer. Consider his comments relative to the purpose of Christian civil law.

"So far as the ungodly are concerned the Law has two purposes: first, to restrain sin, and second, to condemn the sinner. As to the former of these, it is not possible to go so far as saying that the Law is capable of changing men's hearts, but it nevertheless performs a valuable service as an external instrument by means of which they are kept in a kind of outward conformity to what is right. By its positive instruction and its solemn warning, it keeps men back from much flagrant evil, and it was this use of the Law which made the apostle say that the Law 'was added because of transgressions.' (Gal. 3:19). The second purpose of the Law toward the ungodly is to condemn them for their transgressions of it. The curse of the Law is the sore displeasure of God, and this accompanies every breach of it.

"The purpose of the Law to the believer is fourfold. It stimulates resistance to sin, it reveals inward corruption, it destroys self-righteousness, and it increases esteem of Christ. Although it is true that 'the law is not made for a righteous man' (I Tim. 1:9), yet, because no believer is perfectly righteous, and because there is no one who does not need to confess the weakness of his love for God and the feebleness of his delight in holy things, it becomes a fact of spiritual experience that the Law of God, by commanding, stirs the believer to a resistance of evil and a zealous seeking after godliness...

"Paul writes to the Romans (7:7-25) about the continuing corruption in the heart of the believer, and he explains that in his own case he discovered this when the light of the Law shone into the secret places of his heart,...It was for this reason that Paul writes, 'I had not known sin, but by the law' (Rom. 7:7), meaning by this that the Law of Nature was so obliterated that it could not show a man even the least part of the corruption of his heart. The Law is the mirror in which the believer is permitted to see himself.

"The effects of this revelation to the believer of the sinfulness of his own heart are seen in a deep sense of shame and humility. When the believer perceives that his very best attainment comes short of the requirements of the Law, that the earth is not more distant from heaven than he is from righteousness, this drives him to abandon all confidence in his performance of religious good works..."

"In the wonderful wisdom of God the law is an instrument of grace, and the Holy Spirit by the Law reduces the believer to this deep shame and humility only to lead him to value the person and work of the Lord Jesus Christ the more highly...The Law constantly strips the believer of his self-righteousness and so increases his esteem for the righteousness which is to be found in Christ."[12]

From a Christian idea of government, is not the historic purpose of American civil law in regard to the lawless remarkably similar to the purpose of the Moral Law for the ungodly?

Consider the observations of the great English Jurist, William Blackstone, on the superiority of God's Law over human laws (1765):

"Law of Nature – This will of his Maker is called the law of nature..."

"Upon these two foundations, the *law of nature* and the *law of revelation, depend all human laws; that is to say, no human laws should be suffered to contradict these.*"[13]

Then consider John Locke, Philosopher of the American Revolution, on the end and purpose of the Law in his second essay *Of Civil Government*:

"So that, however it may be mistaken, *the end of Law is* not to abolish or restrain, *but to preserve and enlarge Freedom*. For in all the states of created Beings capable of Laws, *where there is no Law, there is no Freedom*. For *Liberty* is to be free from Restraint and Violence from others; which cannot be, where there is no Law: For Freedom is not, as we are told, *A Liberty for every Man to do what he lists* [likes]: (For who could be Free, when every Man's Humour might domineer over him?) But a *Liberty* to dispose, and order as he lists, his Person, Actions, Possessions, and his whole Property, within the Allowance of those Laws, under which he is, and therein not to be subject to the Ar-

bitrary Will of another, but freely follow his own."[14]

Lastly, the reader is urged to consider the concluding comments of Miss Slater on how the law becomes the *effect* of individual, internal salvation as explained in *Teaching and Learning*, p. 105.

THE GOSPEL

The following references are offered in explanation of how God's love and Holy Spirit are both *indwelling* and *outworking*:

John 13:34-35: "A new commandment I give unto you, That ye love one another; as I have loved you, that ye also love one another. By this shall all men know that ye are my disciples, if ye have love one to another."

Romans 3:31: "Do we then make void the law through faith? God forbid: yea, we establish the law."

Romans 8:2-4: "For the law of the Spirit of life in Christ Jesus hath made me free from the law of sin and death. For what the law could not do, in that it was weak through the flesh, God sending his own Son in the likeness of sinful flesh, and for sin, condemned sin in the flesh: That the righteousness of the law might be fulfilled in us, who walk not after the flesh, but after the Spirit."

II Corinthians 3:3: "Forasmuch as ye are manifestly declared to be the epistle of Christ ministered by us, written not with ink, but with the Spirit of the living God; not in tables of stone, but in fleshly tables of the heart."

Hebrews 8:10: "For this is the covenant that I will make with the house of Israel after those days, saith the Lord; I will put my laws into their mind, and write them in their hearts: and I will be to them a God, and they shall be to me a people:..."

The chart on page 57 is a summary of the foregoing thesis explaining how both the *Law and the Gospel are the basis of our government*.

CHRISTIAN LIBERTY – BOTH EVANGELICAL AND POLITICAL

Analogous to the Law and the Gospel as basic to the spirit and letter of civil government is the enlightening idea that "Christian liberty is *both* evangelical and political." How is Christian liberty political as well as evangelical?

---

12. Ernest Kevan, *The Moral Law*, Sovereign Grace Publishers, 1971.
13. Verna M. Hall, *CHOC*, p. 141, 143.
14. *Ibid.*, p. 72:57.

The Law	
INTERNAL: Written on "fleshly tables of the heart" – spiritual, holy, perfect Law.	EXTERNAL: Written on "tables of stone" – moral, social, and civil laws.

The Gospel	
INTERNAL: Indwelling – believed and received thus governing the affections and motives of the heart through the Holy Spirit.	EXTERNAL: Outgoing – evangelical and political, bringing both individual and civil government in consonance with the Gospel and the Law of Christ.

Evangelical: (a) According to the gospel; consonant to the doctrines and precepts of the gospel, published by Christ and his apostles. Contained in the gospel.
Political: Pertaining to policy, or to civil government and its administration; pertaining to a nation or state; public.[15]

Now consider the following excerpts from *Teaching and Learning,* in series: (emphasis added)

"Christian History of the Constitution of the United States of America traces Christianity as the basis of the American idea of Local Self-Government, beginning in the first century with the government of the primitive churches, as local, independent bodies. This concept of government only became possible with the advent of our Lord whose gospel of salvation began with the redemption of individuals and challenged the *external law* to be superseded by the *internal law.*"[16]

"Christianity alone brings true liberty and it establishes as the basis of government – the Christian idea of man. The *Gospel* brings forth a higher standard of liberty than *external law* – rather that *internal law* of the Two Commandments of our Lord. Christianity's government is self-government – and he that accepts the Gospel is willing 'to bring into captivity every thought to the obedience of Christ.' (II Cor. 10:5)."[17]

"When Wickliffe first translated the Bible into English he began the Reformation. This was the impetus which, by opening the Bible to the individual, launched the recognition of *evangelical liberty* and *political liberty.* As the Pilgrims found evidence in Scripture for the local self-governing church of the New Testament, they were impelled to break with the centralized Church of England and to count the cost of liberty of conscience."[18]

"Because their love of liberty was first *evangelical liberty,* second *political liberty,* the Pilgrim Separatists, in fleeing from the despotism of a centralized church, did not reject a government of laws. But they recognized that law must spring from an *internal conviction* rather than derive its sanction from the force of *external control.*"[19]

"At the age of 28 years, writing in the year 1750, Samuel Adams had already perceived that man's *political liberty* relates to *spiritual freedom* under the *law of God.*"[20]

Christian liberty, the liberty whereby "Christ hath made us free from the law of sin and death" (Rom. 8:2) is individual and internal and "consonant to the doctrines and precepts of the gospel" – evangelical. Christian liberty became causative to the achievement of political liberty. Individuals liberated from internal bondage to sin and governed by the law of God before men finally sought and won political liberty.

Political liberty is reflected in a government where external written laws and "policy" are legislated and administered to secure and protect individual God-given property from the lawlessness and tyranny of man or the state. But the *quality* of civil or political liberty rests upon individual love and regard for Gospel liberty with law. "Christian liberty *is* both *evangelical* and *political.*"

EDUCATIONAL APPLICATION OF A CHRISTIAN FORM OF GOVERNMENT

The Christian principle of Our Christian Form of Government is applicable to *all* levels of school government: board, administration, faculty, classroom and student discipline. Every level and of-

---

15. Webster's 1828 Dictionary.
16. Rosalie Slater, *T/L* , p. 185.
17. *Ibid.,* p. 159.
18. *Ibid.,* p. 245.
19. *Ibid.,* p. 261.
20. *Ibid.,* p. 252.

fice of the Christian school should reflect some degree of the administration of the Law and the Gospel.

Miss Slater suggests some practical applications of how to teach and practice representation, separation of powers and dual form of government for the classroom teacher on pages 243-245 of *Teaching and Learning*.

To elaborate on the extent and the application of one of the more difficult principles, consider how the Dual Form of Government can be identified and exercised in a school. There are "federal" and "national" spheres of government – or more simply vertical and horizontal domains – in a school just as there are within civil government.

For example, in civil government cities or towns have a "federal" relationship with each other in relation to their country; counties in one state have a "federal" relationship to the sovereign state government. The states of the union have a federal or covenant relationship to the national government. The flow of political power in civil government is from the "bottom-up," from the individual citizen and state to the national government and back. In school, although the flow of power or authority is from the "top-down," there are still dual levels of responsibility and authority.

The most elementary "federal" or horizontal governmental relationship in a school is between students and their federal head, the teacher. The teachers in a school have a federal or covenant relation with their administrator(s). The administrator(s) have a federal relationship to the school board or perhaps to a pastor. In civil, institutional, ecclesiastical or even home government, there are dual levels of government, vertical and horizontal, "national" and "federal." No matter what type of government, each level of authority reveals to some extent *two sovereign spheres within one sovereign body of law*. On each level the philosophy of government should be to regard the individuality and sovereignty of each person with respect to the proper authority of the federal head, and to instruct each individual on every level of government in Christian self-government and voluntary union.

Concerning the Law and the Gospel, both are essential to Christian school, church and home government. For example, a class constitution with written and published standards (rules) must be administered with the spirit of compassion, mercy and sometimes grace. School rules must be administered with loving discipline and discernment. The orderliness of a church is often a reflection of its written covenant and constitution as fulfilled by the diligence and faithfulness of Spirit-led members. The Christian home, the "first sphere of government," requires both law and love as opposed to either despotism or libertinism. (See *Teaching and Learning*, p. 23-29)

In conclusion, the Christian form of government embraces dual levels of government, and requires both the Law and the Gospel, and is best manifested primarily as Christian Self-Government, with voluntary union in a Christian Republic.

How the Seed of Local Self-Government Is Planted

LOCAL SELF-GOVERNMENT IN AMERICA

Visitors to America from other so-called "free countries," such as England and Scotland, sometimes are surprised to discover how vigorous and significant is local government in the United States.

In Great Britain, they point out, the central government is much more pervasive, the local governments tend not to have as much power to shape their own affairs, make their own laws, and really make a difference between living in one town or region versus living in another.

Even in this country, many people are discovering for the first time how the American tradition of local self-government is creating genuine differences between one city and another, and one state and another. One state, with high taxes and heavy welfare costs, may be losing business and suffering unemployment; an adjoining state, with lower taxes and more modest welfare expenditures, may be prospering. One city, with a conscientious, responsible, confident and imaginative citizenry, may be experiencing a vigorous renewal; another city not far away, with somewhat similar history and general circumstances, but a lackadaisical, uninvolved citizenry, may be slipping downhill.

America's heritage of local self-government is not only unique but it continues to create significant differences between living in one place and living in another. What brought this vital American institution about and how does the Christian principle of local self-government work?

America began not as a nation with a central government on this continent, but as a series of separate towns — first Jamestown, then Plymouth, then Salem and Boston, then many others, each essentially separate and three thousand miles from the central government of England. While some settlements were more under the control of royal governors or proprietors than others, eventually each town or county had to govern itself on a day-to-day basis, or it had no effective government at all. And even when broader geographic areas developed into counties and then colonies with governments embracing many towns, the institution of local town government remained vigorous.

LOCAL SOVEREIGNTY

The historian, legislator and editor Richard Frothingham, in *The Rise of the Republic of the United States* (9th Ed., 1905), pp. 22-28, tells why the elements of individual liberty and self-government gave rise to an immediate dominion over local affairs:

"It was early urged, that the inhabitants of a colony were the best informed of its circumstances, and therefore were the most qualified to make its laws ... It was considered, that the inhabitants of a district or town could act more intelligently in reference to its affairs than any others...

"But whether the municipality was called parish, borough, town, city, district, or county, the principle was alike recognized that the body of residents, according to prescribed rules, should manage their own local affairs. In each the voters chose their own officers; each had its courts and justices; each, in relation to its peculiar local interests, had a jurisdiction as wide as its territorial limits. In this way, each locality provided for the concerns of social comfort and of police, of education and of religion. *This work was never done for the people, but always by them:* they tested their own decisions, and could correct their own judgments. *The municipality was the unit in the system of local self-government. In it the citizen began to take a part in public affairs, and was trained for the wider field of the representative assembly.* And thus it fostered a public spirit and a public life. What has been called a "bureaucracy," which has had so repressive an influence in France, *is not seen in a single colony.* I do not know of the creation, by an American Legislature, of such an anomaly as a self-perpetuating municipal council.

"...The natural product of this self-government was a cluster of thirteen distinct and essentially *free* communities, composed of a *population who appreciated the value of their rights, and felt a personal concern in their preservation.* They had prejudices against each other, rivalries, and sharply defined provincialisms. But, however antagonistical might have been special circles of impulses and objects, however different the tendencies of their social systems, and however strongly the raw diversity might have ruled in their development for a century and a half, yet, in due time, all the colonies fell under the influence of a *spirit of union,* and each contributed to promote the design of *providence* in the formation of a great Republic in America." (Emphasis added) (See *Christian History of the Constitution,* p. 435 for a biographical sketch of Richard Frothingham)

To further understand and trace the development of the idea of individual and Christian self-government historically, from ancient civilizations to America, with its correlative expression in voluntary union, the reader is directed to Volume II of *The Christian History of the Constitution: Christian Self-Government with Union.* For a detailed analysis of Christian self-government in the two parent colonies, Virginia and Plymouth, study *Teaching and Learning,* pp. 189-203, and pp. 363-366 for how this principle was tested up to 1776.

An excellent outline on how the principle of local self-government was practiced in America is found on page 260 of *Teaching and Learning.* This page corresponds with a study of the chart on page 239 and a thorough evaluation of pages 282A to 370 in *Christian History.*

THE COMMITTEE OF CORRESPONDENCE

In *Teaching and Learning,* page 257, Miss Rosalie Slater emphasizes the "importance of *ideas* in overcoming tyranny" and on pages 250-258 relates how God raised up a Christian patriot with the character and vision to unite the colonists in constitutional principles through an instrument that depended upon the 150 years of self-government practiced by the American colonies. Miss

Slater explains Sam Adams' contribution:

"Samuel Adams was unceasing in his efforts to promote the course of independence. His concern was to educate his fellow Colonists to reason out their political convictions from the standpoint of their Christian rights. He knew that, in the tradition of freemen, they must *discuss, dispute* and *debate* the implications of their position ... It was particularly through his own vigorous participation in the Boston Town Meeting that he encouraged public discussion as well as private correspondence as a means of self-education...

"In 1772 Samuel Adams proposed *Committees of Correspondence*, in an educational effort to unite the colonies in knowledge, sentiment and purpose. His idea was for each town to express itself and to write to other towns. Thus town by town, and colony by colony, each individual could not only become informed and educated, but could inform and educate others. 'If each town would declare its sense of these matters, I am persuaded our enemies would not have it in their power to divide us.' But it takes a long time to educate in matters which require thought and consideration..."[1]

The vital role the Committees of Correspondence played in promoting independence and continuing to sow and reap the principle of local self-government in Colonial America suggests a very practical instrument of enlightenment today. A 1902 Government Printing Office pamphlet on the "Committees of Correspondence of the American Revolution" by Edward D. Collins, observes:

"The principle is very simple, and very fundamental. It was correspondence, with cooperation at the terminal points, that brought about the Revolution. As a starting point for the study we may take November 2, 1772, and say that then, for all practical purposes, the committee of correspondence began its life as a *local* institution of the Revolution, and that Samuel Adams was its promoter...It initiated measures, and its activities comprehended legislative, executive, and judicial functions. It was the germ of government.

"In its inception, this government in embryo which Samuel Adams set going was purely a *local affair*... and local conditions created its characteristic features in the different colonial communities.

"Constitutional questions were raised and discussed, and arguments disseminated, a thing of some importance when the colonies were feeling their way toward a common basis of opposition to the crown which should have at least a semblance of rationality and consistency...More important still had been the demonstration that a body could be created which might continue to act in successful opposition to the crown when the royal governors dissolved or prorogued the assemblies.

"A committee of correspondence was, to repeat, essentially a local agent. In this fact lay its revolutionary power, for *revolution was a local affair in its inception.* A committee of correspondence simply could not act unless something occurred which touched the interests of its own commuity. It was functionless if there was nothing to correspond about. To work up a successful revolution the correspondence must show the identity of various local interests or create a fictitious identity. The needed stimulus came in successive acts of parliament, giving at first something to *talk about* and eventually something *to do*. The two phases of activity are well reflected in the correspondence."[2]

Today, local, self-governing, independent Christian homes, churches, and schools might well consider the value of corresponding with each other in an educational effort to unite these constituents of Constitutional liberty in Christian self-government with union so that we all may act *lawfully* and in *concert* against the ignorance and tyranny of our mutual adversaries.

ELUCIDATING THE PRINCIPLE

Consider how any seed is planted, cultivated, and nourished in order to grow and bear fruit. *Seed* is defined by Noah Webster as "first principle, orginal; that from which anything springs." The seed of local self-government is Christian self-government, whereby the individual is properly self-governed when he is governed by God through Christ. The seed or principle of local self-government is *planted* (sowing) first internally by *educating individuals in principles* which bear fruit (reaping) externally through the practice of those principles.

The Union, consisting of a general government, and local governments, in order to remain free, impartial and righteous, must be sustained by the conscious capacity of individuals for self and local self-government. Local self-government, ex-

---

1. Rosalie J. Slater, *T/L*, pp. 254, 258.

2. From the Annual Report of the American Historical Association for 1901, Vol. I, pages 253-271. See also *SG W/U*, pp. 490-527.

pressed as a body of individuals within a community, county and state managing and financing their own affairs, finds its seed or source and origin in the "perfect law of liberty" – God's Law and Gospel – being taught and practiced individually and then collectively.

The "rulers" or representatives and appointed officers of civil government, taught the Biblical principles of truth and righteousness, must govern (legislate, administer, and judge) in the practical fear of God's Law and Gospel, and the people obey the laws of their own representatives according to the solemn covenants and compacts of self- and civil government.

What makes self-government *local?* Consider Webster's 1828 definitions of *local.* (1) Pertaining to a place, or to a fixed or limited portion of space. (2) Limited or confined to a spot, place or definite district; as a local custom. (3) In law, local actions are such as must be brought in a particular county, where the cause arises;..." *Locality:* (3) Position; situation; place; particularly, geographical place or situation..." Hence we understand a local self-governed *church* to be a body of believers in a limited or confined geographical area who meet, govern and finance their own ministry exclusive of any other church.

In the same manner, a local self-governed township, community or county consists of a body of citizens which meets personally or acts through their own representatives to legislate, execute, and judge its own affairs and needs and to finance them itself. Such a municipality should have little or no dependence upon the people and the taxes collected from other geographical areas.

As the lowest section of diagram 6, *How the Seed of Local Self-Government Is Planted*, p. 62, indicates, the foundation of local self-government is *the revelation of* God's law and love for man. As the individual responds internally to God's law and love with a love for God and His Word, the external effect should appear in such vigorous mental activities as researching, reasoning, relating and recording from God's Word, as the diagram shows. As the result of these endeavors, individuals become more Biblically knowledgeable and self-governing, and more capable of expressing the mature and effective love of family and home government indicated on the next-to-lowest section of the diagram — an authentic, responsible Christian love which should manifest itself in the home in the evangelizing, educating, worshipping, working and administering activities shown in the chart.

In turn, such growth in meeting one's responsibilities in the American Christian home enables one, as the next highest level of the diagram suggests, to express a genuine, effective love of the brethren in a local self-governing church through evangelizing, teaching, assembling, volunteering, tithing, exhorting and administering church government.

Finally, the individual prepared by such Christian character and activities in the home and local church should quite spontaneously extend his care and concern to his neighbors and immediate town, city, county, state, and national government as indicated in the highest level of the chart, by engaging in such activities of local self-government as educating neighbors, attending town meetings, volunteering, voting, and running for public office.

THE BIBLICAL BASIS OF LOCAL SELF-GOVERNMENT

The idea of local self-government was wrought out in the New Testament Church and simply extended into the civil sphere when it came to America. The Biblical basis for a local self-governing church is the Biblical *principle* for a local, self-governing community. As George Walker comments in his *History of the First Church in Hartford – 1633-1883*: "The interest of the subject, as connected with this church survey now in hand, is two fold: It is, first, *that the form of civil government here established was simply an extension to the domain of secular affairs of the principles already adopted in religious matters* — the mutual covenant and agreement of those associated, as under God the ultimate law. And, second and more particularly, because of the agency in leading into the establishment of this principle in the Fundamental Laws of this Colony, of the wise and farsighted *Pastor* of this church."[3]

The student of Christian civil government is obliged to study the history and doctrine of church government, "because," as Miss Verna Hall argues, "the church is the assembly or congregation of believers, whatever is reasoned from Scripture regarding church polity or government, is the precursor of civil polity of government. Thus it can also be said that the *history of church government* is the *history of Christian civil government*."[4]

Furthermore, Miss Hall makes the original observation that "The uniqueness of the American Constitution is due, in part, to its inclusion of aspects of the counterpart in the civil sphere of *each* of these classical forms of church government."[15]

---

3. Verna Hall, *CHOC*, p. 250.
4. Verna Hall, *CI P*, p. xxiv.
5. *Ibid*, p. 89, Col. 1.

6. How the Seed of Local Self-Government Is Planted

INTERNAL (sowing) >━━━━━━━━━━━━━━▶ EXTERNAL (reaping)

How God's law and love expands from the level of individual Christian
self-government to government of the home, church and community

LOCAL COMMUNITY
(county, state and nation)

Love (Care & Concern) for one's Neighbor and Local Civil Government	Educating neighbors in Christian principles to resolve local, state, and national issues.
Matt. 22:39: "Love thy neighbor as thyself."	Attending local town meetings.
Rom. 10:13: "Love worketh no ill to his neighbour."	Volunteering time, labor, materials for local projects.
Lev. 25:35: "And if thy brother be waxen poor...then thou shalt relieve him."	Assuming financial responsibility for needs in the community.
Rom. 13:4: "For he is the minister of God to thee for good."	Voting in local elections.
	Reproving public error boldly.
	Running for and administering local civil government offices.

LOCAL CHURCH

Love of the Brethren and Christian Church Government	Evangelizing the community.
John 15:12: "This is my commandment, That ye love one another."	Teaching, discipling the brethren.
	Assembling, worshipping together.
I Peter 1:22: "Obeying the truth through the Spirit unto unfeigned love of the brethren, see that ye love one another with a pure heart."	Volunteering labor, materials and time to build a church or to help a brother or neighbor.
	Tithing and offering money.
I John 5:2: "By this we know that we love the children of God, when we love God, and keep his commandments."	Exhorting, reproving by the Word of God.
	Participating in and administering local church government.

HOME

Love of Family and Christian Home Government	Evangelizing one's family.
Eph. 5:28: "So ought men to love their wives as their own bodies."	Educating, discipling oneself and one's children.
	Worshipping together.
Deut. 6:7: "And thou shalt teach them diligently unto thy children."	Laboring, producing goods and services in the home.
I Tim. 3:4; Titus 2:4; Isa. 43:13	Administering home government.

INDIVIDUAL

Love of God and His Law: Christian Self-Government	Researching God's Word
	Reasoning from His Truth
Deut. 6:5: "And thou shalt love the Lord thy God with all thine heart."	Relating Biblical principles
Psa. 119:13, 16, 47; II Cor. 5:14	Recording – writing out how Wisdom is applied to life and living.

GOD'S LAW AND LOVE FOR MAN

Deut. 6:24-25: "And the Lord commanded us to do all these statutes, to fear the Lord our God, for our good always, that he might preserve us alive, as it is at this day. And it shall be our righteousness, if we observed to do all these commandments before the Lord our God, as he hath commanded us."	*Rom. 5:8:* "But God commendeth his love toward us, in that, while we were yet sinners, Christ died for us."
	Eph. 2:4: "But God, who is rich in mercy, for his great love, wherewith he loved us..."

Hence, what the Bible teaches about *ecclesiastical polity* or a Christian form of church government, becomes a primary and original source for deducing and extending the Christian idea of a local, self-governing, independent *civil* body politic.

"The development of Christian civil government in America in the colonial period and in the formation of the American Christian Constitution, is dependent upon comprehending these three forms of church government; i.e. their arrangement of authority, representation, union, flow of power, etc., for all three forms are represented in the structure of our constitution and account for its delicate balances, and need self-governing Christians to make it operate properly."[6]

The three historic forms of church government are congregational, presbyterian and episcopal. The history and contribution of each form of church polity to both American religious and civil liberty is further documented in *The Christian History of the American Revolution: Consider and Ponder.* A brief description of the distinctions between congregational and episcopal church government is also found in *Teaching and Learning*, pp. 328–329.

There are advocates for each form of church government and whether we agree with the Biblical or philosophical presuppositions of one or another of the three systems, it is important to discern that in God's Providence, each form of church polity had its place and made its peculiar contribution in American history and in the development of our constitutional, federal republic.

What is the Biblical and rational basis for each historic form of church government? The following excerpts suggest how *each* system is defined and contrasted with other forms by one of its proponents.

CONGREGATIONAL FORM OF CHURCH GOVERNMENT

Rev. John Robinson

"As this church was the reservoir through which Congregationalism has chiefly flowed, by two diverging streams to the old and new world, it may be acceptable to my readers to have presented in a connected and condensed form the leading principles and doctrines of the Leyden church."[7]

"Power of the Church. – Touching 'the proper subject' of the power of Christ, he tells Bernard,

Where the Papists plant it in 'the Pope;' the Protestants in 'the Bishops;' the Puritans, as you term the reformed churches and those of their mind, in 'the Presbytery;' we, whom you name 'Brownists,' put it in 'the body of the congregation, – the multitude called the Church;' odiously insinuating against us, that we do exclude the Elders in the case of government where, on the contrary, we profess the Bishops or Elders to be the only ordinary governors in the church, as in all other actions of the church's communion, so, also, in the censures. Only we may not acknowledge them for 'lords over God's heritage.' I Pet. 5:3, as *you* would make them, – 'controlling all, but to be controlled by none;' much less essential unto the church, as though it could not be without them; least of all, the church itself, as you would expound Matt. xviii. But *we* hold the Eldership, as other ordinances, given unto the church for her service; and so, the Elders or Officers, the servants and minister's of the church, II Cor. 4:5, Col. 1:25; the wife, under Christ her husband...

"Church Polity. – Wise men, having written of this subject, have approved as good and lawful, three kinds of polities, – monarchical, where supreme authority is in the hands of one; aristocratical, when it is in the hands of some few select persons; and democratical, in the whole body or multitude. And all these three forms have their places in the Church of Christ. In respect for Him, the Head, it is a monarchy; and respect of the Eldership, an aristocracy; in respect of the Body, a popular state.

"Authority of Church Officer. – Ministers and church-governors have no such authority tied to their office (as civil magistrates have), but merely to the Word of God. And as the People's *obedience* stands not in making the Elders their lords, sovereigns, and judges, but in listening to their godly counsels; in following their wise directions; in receiving their holy instructions, exhortations, consolations, and admonitions; and in using their faithful service and ministry; so neither stands the Elder's *government* in erecting any tribunal-seat or throne of judgment over the People, but in exhorting, instructing, comforting, and improving them by the Word of God, II Tim. 3:16; and in affording the Lord and them their best service. But here it will be demanded of me, If the Elders be not set over the Church for her guidance and government? Yes, certainly, as the physician is set over the body, for his skill and faithfulness to minister unto it, to whom the patient, yea, though his Lord or master, is to submit; – the lawyer over his

---

6. *Ibid*, p. xxvii, Col. 2.
7. George Punchard, *History of Congregationalism from about A.D. 250 to 1616*, 1831.

cause, to attend unto it; – the steward over his family, even his wife and children, to make provision for them; – yea, the watchmen over the whole city, for the sake of safe-keeping thereof. Such and none other, is the Elders', or Bishops' government.[8]

Authority of the Brethren. – In the church, all and every ordinance concerns every person, as a part of their communion, – without the dispensation of necessity, – for their use and edification, I Cor. 3:22, 14:26; all the Officers to be chosen by suffrages and consent of 'the multitude,' Acts 1:15, 23, 25; 6:1-3, 5; 14:23; 15:2, 3; II Cor. 8:19, 23. The Brethren are to admonish their brethren of every violation of God's commandment; and so, in order, to 'tell the church,' Matt. 18:15, 17, 18, and to see the parties reformed: to observe and to take notice of the Officers' carriage to thy ministry that thou hast received of the Lord, that thou fulfil it, the spirit of profaneness, heresy, idolatry, or atheism, to censure, depose, reject, or avoid them, Matt. 18:17; Rom. 16:17,18; Gal. 5:12; I Tim. 6:3-5; II Tim. 3:1-5; Tit. 3:10, 11; otherwise they betray their own souls, and salvation."[9]

PRINCIPLE OF REPRESENTATION

"*Elders Representatives?* – But you will say, as learned men used to do, that these *Elders* sustain the person of the whole multitude, and supply their room, for the avoiding of confusion; and so are rightly, as commonly, called 'The church-representatives.' – I answer, first, No godly, no, nor reasonable man, will affirm, that this representation is to be extended to all the acts of religion, or indeed to others than these which are exercised in the governing of the church. What is it then? The Elders, in ruling and governing the church, must represent the People, and occupy their place. It should seem then, that it appertains unto the People, – unto the People primarily and originally, under Christ – to rule and govern the church, that is, themselves. But who will so say of a government not personal, but public, and instituted, as the church's is? If the Elders, in their consistory, represent the church, then whatsoever they either decree or do agreeing to the Word of God, whether respecting faith or manners, that also the church decreeth and doth though absent; ...this being the nature of representations, that what the representing doth, within the bounds of his com-

mission, that the represented doth primarily, and much more as but using the other for his instrument:..."[10]

DEMOCRACY?

"*Democracy.* – Lest any should take occasion, either by the things here spoken by us, or elsewhere of us, to conceive that we either exercise amongst ourselves, or would thrust upon others, any popular or democratical church-government; may it please the Christian reader to make estimate of both our judgment and practice in this point according to these three declarations following: first, We believe that the external church-government, under Christ the only Mediator and Monarch thereof, is plainly aristocratical, and to be administered by some certain choice men; although the state, which many unskilfully [sic] confound with the government, be, after a sort, popular and democratical. By this it appertains to the People freely to vote in elections, and judgments of the church; in respect of the other, we make account it behoves [sic] the Elders to govern the People, in their voting, in just liberty given by Christ whatsoever. Let the Elders publicly propound and order all things in the church, and so give their sentence on them: let them reprove them that sin, convince the gainsayers, comfort the repentant; and so administer all things according to the prescript of God's Word. Let the People, of faith, give their assent to their Elders' holy and lawful administration, that so the ecclesiastical elections and censures may be ratified, and put into solemn execution by the elders... Secondly, We doubt not but that the Elders both lawfully may, and necessarily ought, and that by virtue of their office, to meet apart, at times, from the Body of the church, (Acts. 20:18) to deliberate of such things as concern her welfare, as for the preventing of things unnecessary, so for the preparing, – according to just order, – of things necessary, so as publicly and before the People, that they may be prosecuted with most convenience... Thirdly, By the People, whose liberty and right in voting we thus avow and stand for in matters truly public and ecclesiastical, we do not understand, – as it hath pleased some contumeliously to upbraid us, – women and children; but only men, and them grown and of discretion: making account, that as children by their nonage, so women by their sex,

8. John Robinson, "A Justification of Separation from the Church of England, 1610," *History of Congregationalism from about A.D. 250 to 1616*, George Punchard (Salem, 1841) pp. 329-330.

9. John Robinson, *ibid.*

10. John Robinson, "A just and necessary Apology of certain Christians...called 'Brownists,' 1625" in *History of Congregationalism from about A.D. 250 to 1616*, by George Punchard (Salem, 1841), pp. 344-348.

are debarred of the use of authority in the church."[11]

WHAT IS CONGREGATIONALISM?

"Congregationalism is that system of church government, in which the Scriptures are recognized as the only infallible guide respecting the church order and discipline; – and which maintains, that, according to the Scriptures, a church is a company, or congregation, of professed Christians, who, having voluntarily convenanted and associated together to worship God and to celebrate religious ordinances, are authorized to elect necessary officers, to disciple offending members, and to act, authoritatively and conclusively, upon all appropriate business, independently of the control of any person or persons whatsoever."[12]

PRESBYTERIAN FORM OF CHURCH GOVERNMENT
Rev. Charles Hodge

"Brethren: – We are assembled this evening as a Presbyterian Historical Society. It has occurred to me that it would not be inappropriate to discuss the question, What is Presbyterianism? You will not expect from me an oration. My object is neither conviction nor persuasion; but exposition. I propose to occupy the hour devoted to this address in an attempt to unfold the principles of that system of Church polity which we, as Presbyterians, hold to be laid down in the word of God.

"Setting aside Erastianism, which teaches that the Church is only one form of the State; and Quakerism, which does not provide for the external organization of the Church, there are only four radically different theories on the subject of Church Polity.

"1. The Popish theory, which assumes that Christ, the Apostles, and believers, constituted the Church while our Saviour was on earth, and this organization was designed to be perpetual. After the ascension of our Lord, Peter became his Vicar, and took his place as the visible head of the Church. This primacy of Peter, as the universal Bishop, is continued in his successors, the Bishops of Rome; and the apostleship is perpetuated in the order of Prelates. As in the Primitive Church, no one could be an apostle who was not subject to Christ, so now no one can be a Prelate who is not subject to the Pope. And as then no one could be a Christian who was not subject to Christ and the apostles, so now no one can be a Christian who is not subject to the Pope and the Prelates. This is the Romish theory of the Church. A Vicar of Christ, a perpetual College of apostles, and the people subject to their infallible control.

"2. The Prelatical theory assumes the perpetuity of the apostleship as the governing power in the Church, which therefore consists of those who profess the true religion, and are subject to apostle-bishops. This is the Anglican or High-Church form of this theory. In its Low-Church form, the Prelatical theory simply teaches that there was originally a three-fold order in the ministry, and that there should be now. But it does not affirm that mode of organization to be essential.

"3. The Independent or Congregational theory includes two principles; first, that the governing and executive power in the Church is in the brotherhood; and secondly, that the Church organization is complete in each worshipping assembly, which is independent of every other.

"4. The fourth theory is the Presbyterian, which it is our present business to attempt to unfold. The three great negations of Presbyterianism – that is, the three great errors which it denies are – 1. That all church power vests in the clergy. 2. That the apostolic office is perpetual. 3. That each individual Christian congregation is independent. The affirmative statement of these principles is – 1. That the people have a right to a substantive part in the government of the Church. 2. That presbyters, who minister in word and doctrine, are the highest permanent officers of the Church, and all belong to the same order. 3. That the outward and visible Church is, or should be, one, in the sense that a smaller part is subject to a larger, and a larger to the whole. It is not holding one of these principles that makes a man a Presbyterian, but his holding them all.[13]

THE CHURCH –
A SELF-GOVERNING SOCIETY

"I. The first of these principles relates the power and rights of the people. As to the nature of Church power, it is to be remembered that the Church is a theocracy. Jesus Christ is its head. All power is derived from him. His word is our written constitution. All Church power is, therefore, properly ministerial and administrative. Everything is to be done in the name of Christ, and in accordance with his directions. The Church, however, is a self-governing society, distinct from the State, having its officers and laws, and, therefore, an

---

11. John Robinson, *ibid.*

12. Punchard, George, *History of Congregationalism from about A.D. 250 to 1616.* Salem, 1841, p. 35.

13. Rev. Charles Hodge, *What is Presbyterianism?*, Philadelphia, Presbyterian Board of Publication, 1855. pp. 3-11.

administrative government of its own. The power of the Church relates: 1. To matters of doctrine. She has the right to set forth a public declaration of the truths which she believes, and which are to be acknowledged by all who enter her communion. That is, she has the right to frame creeds or confessions of faith, as her testimony for the truth, and her protest against error. And as she has been commissioned to teach all nations, she has the right of selecting teachers, of judging of their fitness, of ordaining and sending them forth into the field, and of recalling and deposing them when unfaithful. 2. The Church has power to set down rules for the ordering of public worship. 3. She has power to make rules for her own government; such as every Church has in its Book of Discipline, Constitution, or Canons, etc. 4. She has power to receive into fellowship, and to exclude the unworthy from her own communion.

WHERE IS POWER VESTED?

"Now, the question is, Where does this power vest? Does it, as Romanists and Prelatists affirm, belong exclusively to the clergy? Have they the right to determine for the Church what she is to believe, what she is to profess, what she is to do, and whom she is to receive as members, and whom she is to reject? Or does this power vest in the Church itself – that is, in the whole body of faithful? This, it will be perceived, is a radical question – one which touches the essence of things, and determines the destiny of men. If all Church power vests in the clergy, then the people are practically bound to passive obedience in all matters of faith and practice; for all right of private judgment is then denied. If it vests in the whole Church, then the people have a right to a substantive part in the decision of all questions relating to doctrine, worship, order, and discipline. The public assertion of this right of the people, at the time of the Reformation, roused all Europe. It was an apocalyptic trumpet, i.e. a trumpet of revelation, *tuba per sepulcra sonans*, calling the dead soul to life; awakening them to the consciousness of power and of right; of power conveying right, and imposing the obligation to assert and exercise it. This was the end of Church tyranny in all truly Protestant countries. It was the end of the theory that the people were bound to passive submission in matters of faith and practice. It was deliverance to the captive, the opening of the prison to those who were bound; the introduction of the people of God into the liberty wherewith Christ has made them free. This is the reason why civil liberty follows religious liberty. The theory that all Church power vests in a divinely constituted hierarchy, begets the theory that all civil power vests, of divine right, in kings and nobles. And the theory that Church power vests in the Church itself, and all Church officers are servants of the Church, of necessity begets the theory that civil power vests in the people, and that civil magistrates are servants of the people. These theories God has joined together, and no man can put them asunder. It was, therefore, by an infallible instinct, the unfortunate Charles of England said, "No bishop, no king;" by which he meant, that if there is no despotic power in the Church, there can be no despotic power in the State; or, if there be liberty in the Church, there will be liberty in the State."[14]

PROTESTANT EPISCOPAL ECCLESIASTICAL POLITY
Bishop William Seabury

PERMANENT CHIEF OFFICE

"That our Lord transmitted to the Apostles the authority which He administered on earth, appears to be involved in the relation in which the Apostles stood, as those who were manifestly in training for the due execution of a trust to be reposed in them after His departure; as well as from particular texts, which have already been in part considered.

"It is recorded that after having by His preaching gathered disciples, and having by His miracles given them such evidence of His Divine authority as was needed to establish their faith in Him, our Lord went out into a mountain to pray, and continued all night in prayer to God. When it was day He called His disciples; and of them He chose twelve, whom also He named Apostles. (St. Luke 6:12-16) These Apostles, enumerated by name, are sometimes called 'the twelve,' sometimes 'the twelve disciples,' sometimes 'the disciples,' and 'His disciples; but the distinction between them and the company of disciples is as plain as between that company and the multitude. Unto the twelve Apostles St. Luke relates that He said: 'I appoint unto you a kingdom, as My Father hath appointed unto me.' (St. Luke 22:29-30) St. Mark says: 'He ordained twelve, that they should be with Him, and that He might send them forth' (St. Mark 3:13-19) – enumerating them. According to St. Matthew, who also enumerates them. He gives them various instructions, (St. Matt. 10) sends them to preach to the lost sheep of the

---

14. Rev. Charles Hodge, *ibid*.

house of Israel, (St. Matt. 10:5-7) and tells them: 'He that receiveth you receiveth Me, and he that receiveth Me receiveth Him that sent Me.' (St. Matt. 10:40) promises them that when the Son of Man shall sit on the throne of His glory, they also shall sit on twelve thrones judging the twelve tribes of Israel; (St. Matt. 19:28) and bids the eleven (after the defection of Judas) go and disciple all nations, baptizing and teaching them to observe all things which He had commanded them. (St. Matt. 28:19, 20) In the narrative of the Institution of the Eucharist, St. Matthew (St. Matt. 26:20) and St. Mark (St. Mark 14:17) record the commission to commemorate His sacrifice as spoken to *the twelve*, St. Luke (St. Luke 22:14) to the *twelve Apostles*. St. John, who does not relate the Institution, records that which follows it, and represents our Lord as saying to the disciples, 'Ye have not chosen Me, but I have chosen you, and ordained you.' (St. John 15:16) As there is no evidence of any addition to the number present at the Institution, it is a matter of course that these words were spoken to the Apostles.

"These texts are sufficient evidence of an official character given by our Lord to the Apostles involving authority as well as ministerial function. They would be sufficient even if they were not corroborated by that passage which many have regarded as the chief evidence of our Lord's commission to them; that, namely, which occurs in St. John 20:21-23, and the interpretation of which controls the interpretation of St. Matt. 16:19 and 18:18; and certainly if there were any reasonable ground of doubt about the application of this passage to the Apostles, that doubt should be settled in accordance with the plain meaning of other passages, and not be suffered to overbalance them. That there is no reasonable ground for this doubt, may perhaps be justly inferred from the unanimity with which it has been understood in the Church that the act of breathing and the accompanying words were directed to the Apostles alone: insomuch that it is not great venture to say that, prior to the present generation, and perhaps its predecessor, there is no defender to the Apostolic Succession who even so much as gives a reason or offers an argument for the propriety of this interpretation, so entirely is it taken for granted as a matter of course. It is strange, if the doubt have any reasonable foundation, that it should not have been discovered until, under the influence of the genius of popular sovereignty in the State, men began to cast about for evidence that the source of power in the Church also was in the Body and not in the Head. It is not, indeed, to be wondered at that under this influence men should altogether scout the doctrine of Apostolic Succession; but that men who profess an adherence to that doctrine should seek to accommodate it to the prejudices of its opposers by bringing it in circuitously in the guise of a grant from the people, is a process more commendable for its ingenuity than for its rectitude; though the attempt to appropriate this passage to their purposes is less injurious than plausible."[15]

THE HISTORICAL BASIS OF LOCAL SELF-GOVERNMENT

The Bible reveals that historically the idea of local self-government was non-existent before God gave the Moral Law to the nation of Israel about 1440 B.C. (Ex. 20; Deut. 5) Through the Mosaic laws – moral, civil, judicial and ecclesiastical – God commanded every individual Hebrew to hear and obey His commandments in the context of their own local home and tribe. (Deut. 4:6-9; 6:3-25). Whenever the people spurned their responsibility to remember God and His laws and mercies, they subsequently required a judge or demanded a king to rule over them. (Jud. 2:11-19; I Sam. 8:7, 19, 20) This irreverence and irresponsibility did not absolve them from their duty as individuals to keep the Law of God and govern themselves, their homes and tribes by it, even though it was a covenant of works which they could not keep because of recurring, inherent sin.

The history of Babylonia, Egypt, Assyria and other pagan nations reveals that political power was centralized in a king and flowed from a man-god to his few appointed princes and prelates who altogether controlled every aspect of national and local religious, political and economic life. (Example: Ex. 1:8, 6:27) The history of Israel in the Old Testament is the exception because of their acceptance of *one* God and each individual's duty to be governed by His Laws with its consequences for the home, tribe and finally the nation.

The principle of individual and local self-government continues in the New Testament. When the New Testament church was established by the Lord Jesus Christ, the body of believers – the ecclesia – assembled as distinctly local, independent self-governing churches. These "little republics" maintained the primitive Christian spirit of local self-government for nearly three centuries, but under persecution, authority and responsibility gradually tended to flow to one or more bishops

---

15. Seabury, William Jones, *An Introduction to the Study of (Protestant Episcopal) Ecclesiastical Polity*, New York: R. W. Crothers, 1911, pp. 97-99.

The Seven Great Exchanges In Modern History

"OLD WORLD" Pagan Idea of Man and Government	"NEW WORLD" Christian Idea of Man and Government
1. Infallibility of the church and its hierarchy – the idea that man's organizations, whether social, ecclesiastical or political, can be absolutely depended upon to make correct choices for others.	1. The infallibility of the Scriptures: *II Tim. 3:16; II Pet. 1:20-21; Acts 1:16*
2. Sovereignty of the king or pope over man – the idea that one political party or one church or denomination can dictate to man.	2. The sovereignty of God in the free and independent individual governed by God: *Rom. 8:1; 8:21; I Cor. 7:22-23; Gal. 5:1; Acts 17:28*
3. Class hierarchy and structure in government and society – the idea that there is inequality – artificial, contrived inequality – by either divine appointment or political fiat, and man can only advance in rank or authority by appointment of king or priest.	3. Equality of the individual before God's Law and civil law – laws for the lawless, liberty for the righteous under/with the Law: *Rom. 3:9-10; Rom. 3:22-23; Rom. 10:12; Prov. 22:2; Gal. 3:28; Acts 16:37-38.*
4. Centralized world church – centralized one-world government, totalitarian government in church and state.	4. Independent, local, self-governing church; local self-governing republics: *Acts 15:6, 28; I Cor. 7:17; I Tim. 3:4; Eph. 1:22, 4:15, 5:23; I Pet. 5:3; II Cor. 4:5; Col. 1:25; Acts 1:15, 23, 26; Acts 6:1-2, 5*
5. The flow of power and force is from man, from the top down, from king or priest to the individual – power flows through appointees.	5. All government is God, indwelling the individual believer by grace through faith; the *power* of God flows from inside-out, from "bottom to top," and is *delegated* to "ambassadors": *Psa. 62:11; Matt. 28:18; John 1:12; Acts 1:8; II Cor. 5:20; Eph. 6:20*
6. Limited freedom or privileges granted by priest or prince; liberty of the few over the many – liberty is government-granted, whether ecclesiastical or civil.	6. Liberty is inalienable; it is *God-given*, not government or church-granted; liberty of the individual is protected by law, covenant or constitution: *Rom. 8:1; Gal. 5:1; II Cor. 3:17; I Cor. 6:11-12*
7. Forced conformity and uniformity to the dictates of king or priest through coercion or force – union through conformity and uniformity to men and man's laws – external.	7. Voluntary unity with union; unity with diversity, churches and nations constituted by the *voluntary consent* of diverse individuals; liberty of conscience under God's Law: *I John 1:7; I Pet. 2:13-18; Acts 2:44, 46; Acts 4:23-31; Acts 5:11-14.*

until the spirit and framework of episcopacy was dominant.

"A tendency to monarchy begins to be developed in what was at first a simple republic. The principle of equality and fraternity begins to be superseded by the spirit of authority and subordination. This may be noted as the first departure from the simplicity of the primitive polity...".[16]

The episcopal form of church government, so comfortable with and allied to the political centralization that characterized Rome and subsequent medieval empires, was finally challenged

---

16. *CHOC*, p. 20.

when the Bible was translated for the use of individuals. Then the regeneration and reformation of men, churches and civil government commenced.

The Reformation, a direct result of God restoring the Bible as the supreme authority in matters of faith and practice, effected *The Seven Great Exchanges in Modern History* found on p. 68. The shift from the "Old World" view of man and government to the "New World" idea based upon the Christian principle of individual self and local self-government finally found its fullest expression in the world's first Christian Republic by 1787.

EDUCATIONAL IMPLICATIONS

Parents and teachers plant the seed of local self-government in the way they minister to their students and labor *with them* to elevate their Christian scholarship and effect a free and independent man. Indeed, the seed of Christian self-government is sown in the student as the educator inspires and cultivates that Biblical intelligence and responsibility that delights in answering to God and the leading of the Holy Spirit. For instance, specific instruction in how to use and account for one's time, tools, tasks and talents will help an individual take dominion over his environment and become both the "Lord's freeman" as well as "Christ's servant." (I Cor. 7:22) (How this principle is applied to the Christian home and family is further explained on p. 95.)

THE CHRISTIAN PRINCIPLE OF AMERICAN POLITICAL UNION

ELUCIDATION OF THE PRINCIPLE

"Till we all come in the unity of the faith, and of the knowledge of the Son of God, unto a perfect man, unto the measure of the stature of the fulness of Christ:" (Eph. 4:13)

America's Christian history documents that as the Bible became available to the individual, a voluntary spiritual unity (or oneness of the separate parts), consisting of a common faith and knowledge of Christ's love and law, eventually produced both the spirit and fact of American political union. When the unity of Christian faith and practice reached America with the Pilgrims, their spirit of voluntary association became the foundation of voluntary political union by covenant or compact, inspired by "the Pilgrim ideal of a 'single covenanted body of Christians, united for *civil* as well as *spiritual* purposes.'"

DIAGRAM OF THE PRINCIPLE

Diagram 7, *The Christian Principle of American Political Union* (p. 70), outlines the various internal and external aspects of Christian unity and union. It must be understood that each statement pertaining to internal unity presupposes a quality of unity and union consistent with the Biblical doctrine of separation. Otherwise the same statements could be taken out of this Biblical context and used to justify a voluntary but ungodly governmental union.

"Can two walk together except they be agreed?" (Amos 3:3) can be rendered wrongly to justify two thieves voluntarily agreeing to rob a bank or even a professing Christian and a pagan willfully consenting to some sinister partnership. However, the verse may also define the principle whereby two Christians may voluntarily consent before God to form a wholesome business venture. What is advanced in this principle is that Christ and Biblical Christianity have fundamentally required that any internal agreement and external cooperation must be based upon *voluntary consent* consistent with God's "law of liberty" and not upon any form of coercion, force or duress by man.

BIBLICAL SEPARATION
IS NOT ISOLATION

Recalling the terse challenge on page 10 of this *Guide* concerning Christians who "isolate themselves, calling it separation, only to breed more cowards after their own kind," any positive discussion of the implications of Biblical unity and union must necessarily advance the Biblical principle of separation. There are theologians and pastors who have correctly and comprehensively circumscribed this doctrine, but the essential teachings could be identified as follows.

Internal separation: This refers to a state or condition of spiritual holiness or sanctification whereby the individual is "dead," un-responsive, "to sin" (Rom. 6:1-18) and set apart unto Christ Jesus' plan and purpose for mankind, "that God in all things may be glorified through Jesus Christ, to whom be praise and dominion for ever." (I Pet. 4:11) Such holiness requires that our minds be renewed (Rom. 12:2) and, through an internal spiritual warfare, a "conflict within and without," we cast down "every high thing" or thought "that exalteth itself against the knowledge of God, and bringing into captivity every thought to the obedience of Christ;..." (II Cor. 10:5)

External separation: This refers to the visible Christian life, walk or conversation caused by the power and promises of Christ and His Word indwelling the individual by grace through faith. Hence, by the grace of God, the Christian can and should be set apart from evil associations, and "be not *unequally* yoked together with unbelievers" (II Cor. 6:14), nor associate with immoral people:

"I wrote unto you in an epistle not to company with fornicators;...or with the covetous, or extortioners, or with idolaters... Therefore put away from among yourselves that wicked person." (I Cor. 5:9, 10, 13)

"How blessed is the man who does not walk in the counsel of the wicked, nor stand in the path of sinners, nor sit in the seat of scoffers! But his delight is in the law of the Lord, and in His law he meditates day and night." (Psalms 1:1-2)

Separation, whether personal or ecclesiastical, is not isolation from the world nor its many problems – moral, political, economic, cultural and so forth. Indeed, Paul counsels that we cannot so detach or insulate ourselves from the world that we stop all association with the wicked or immoral or unbelieving person, "for then you would have to go out of the world." (I Cor. 5:10)

Jesus taught in the Sermon on the Mount that His disciples were to be the "salt of the earth" and "the light of the world." (Matt. 5:13, 14) One of the great contemporaries of the Founding Fathers, Rev. Matthew Henry, an English Bible commentator, wrote of this teaching:

"The prophets, who went before them, were the salt of the land of Canaan; but the apostles were the salt of *the whole earth*, for they must *go into all the world to preach the gospel.* It was a discouragement to them that they were so *few* and so *weak.* What could they do in so large a province as the *whole earth*? Nothing, if they were to work by force of arms and dint of sword; but, being to work silently as salt, one handful of that salt would diffuse its savour far and wide; would go a great way, and work insensibly and irresistibly as leaven, (Matt. 13:33). The doctrine of the gospel is as *salt;* it is penetrating, *quick*, and *powerful* (Heb. 4:12); it reaches the *heart*, (Acts 2:37). It is cleansing, it is relishing, and preserves from putrefac-

7. THE CHRISTIAN PRINCIPLE OF AMERICAN POLITICAL UNION

INTERNAL > (Causative)	⟶ EXTERNAL (Effect)
Christian Unity:	*Christian Union:*
1. Expresses the unseen, vertical, internal governmental relation between God and man. (John 17:21,23) This relationship is based on *voluntary consent.*	1. Manifests the visible, horizontal, external social and governmental relation between man and man. (Eph. 4:3,6,13,16) This relationship is also based on *voluntary consent.*
2. Expresses a kindred, common spirit, faith and doctrine, and shared affections, hopes, motives, aspirations, interests, purposes, and tastes.	2. Manifests itself in cooperative action – efforts, associations, organizations, societies and fellowships. In America, voluntary union manifests itself in three sectors of society: *political* (communities, towns, counties, states, nation) *commercial* (proprietorships, partnerships, cooperatives, corporations) and *independent* (homes, churches, schools, clubs, a variety of non-profit organizations).

tion. We read of the *savour of the knowledge of Christ* (II Cor. 2:14); for all other learning is insipid without that. An everlasting covenant is called a *covenant of salt* (Num. 18:19); and the gospel is an everlasting gospel...

"*Ye are the light of the world*, (v. 14). This also bespeaks them useful, as that former *(Nothing is more useful than the sun and salt)*, but more glorious. All Christians are *light in the Lord* (Eph. 5:8), and must *shine as lights* (Phil. 2:15)...

"The disciples of Christ must not muffle themselves up in privacy and obscurity, under pretense of contemplation, modesty, or self-preservation, but *as they have received the gift*, must *minister the same*, Luke 12:3...They must be to others for instruction, direction, quickening, and comfort, Job 29:11."

In conclusion, it was Jesus who prayed: "I do not ask Thee to take them out of the world, but to keep them from the evil one" (John 17:14, 15), even as John subsequently revealed through divine inspiration that "for this purpose the Son of God was manifested, that he might destroy the works of the devil." (I Jn. 3:8)

BIBLICAL BASIS OF CHRISTIAN UNITY AND UNION

Psalm 55:14: "We took sweet counsel together, and walked unto the house of God in company."
Psalm 133:1: "Behold, how good and how pleasant it is for brethren to dwell together in unity!"
Amos 3:3: "Can two walk together, except they be agreed?"
Acts 4:32a: "And the multitude of them that believed were of one heart and of one soul:..."
I Corinthians 1:10: "Now I beseech you, brethren, by the name of the Lord Jesus Christ, that ye all speak the same thing, and that there be no divisions among you; but that ye be perfectly joined together in the same mind and in the same judgment."
I Peter 3:8: "Finally, be ye all of one mind, having compassion one of another, love as brethren, be pitiful, be courteous:"
Matt. 23:8; Rom. 12:16, 15:5-6; I Cor. 12:20, 27; II Cor. 13:11; Eph. 4:3-4; Phil. 1:27, 3:16-17

A TIME TO UNITE AND A TIME TO SEPARATE

Great wisdom and discernment is necessary to determine when one should unite with another or separate. The Christian principle of voluntary union is still applicable to such a "time" of deci-sion. When would a Christian unite with others who may be unbelievers, perhaps very worldly, immoral, even vulgar people?

"To every thing there is a season, and a time to every purpose under heaven: ...a time to embrace, and a time to refrain from embracing;" (Eccl. 3:1, 3:5b) Consider the following "times" when one may "embrace" or include another in some common cause, and the "times" one may choose to come apart.

A TIME TO EMBRACE...

1. To affiliate as parents to support a Christian school, P.T.A. or P.T.F. project, school athletic team or social event.
2. To associate as citizens of a community project to clean up litter, administer "neighborhood watch" programs, cooperate to stop pornography, etc.
3. To work together in the market place as employees, laborers, businessmen or customers for production and sales.
4. To join together as republicans, democrats, or independents on policy, political action or legislation.
5. To unite as Americans in defense of our country.

AND A TIME TO REFRAIN FROM EMBRACING...
Ecclesiastes 3:1; 3:5b

1. By carefully choosing who one's friends are, who will be an invited guest in the home, and what associations and organizations one should join.
2. By not compromising the Christian principles of discipline, child training, domestic finances, and marital relationships.
3. By separating in the church as it pertains to doctrine, worship, or church government.
4. Discriminating as to tastes in art, music, or types of entertainment or sports.
5. Differing as to political means or methods and the execution or administration of policy or philosophy of government.

EDUCATIONAL IMPLICATIONS

Apply the principle to choosing friends. In the Student Handbook of *Rudiments of America's Christian History and Government*, (F.A.C.E. Publication), Noah Webster's counsel on choosing friends is quoted:

"In forming your connections in society, be careful to select for your companions, young men of good breeding, and of virtuous principles and habits. The company of the profligate and irreligious is to be shunned as poison. You cannot always avoid some intercourse with men of dissolute lives; but you can always select, for your intimate associates, men of good principles and unimpeachable character. Never maintain a familiar intercourse with the profane, the lewd, the intemperate, the gamester, or the scoffer at religion. Towards men of such character, the common civilities of life are to be observed – beyond these, nothing is required of men who reverence the divine precepts, and who desire, to 'keep themselves unspotted from the world.'" (p. 20)

One way to delineate Webster's counsel would be to contrast the character qualities of a person with whom one could unite or wisely avoid, as suggested in the chart, *Whom Should Our Companions Be?*

What should one's relations be toward those one should avoid? Webster counsels to "observe only the *common civilities of life*," i.e., to be:

Polite: courteous, gracious
Courteous: polite, civil, graceful.
Gentle: not rough, harsh or severe, treating with mildness
Kind: disposed to do good to others, and to make them happy by...supplying their wants or assisting them in distress; having tenderness or goodness of nature. ("God is kind to the unthankful, and to the evil." Luke 6:35)

Apply the principle to membership in associations. Webster's "Letter to a Young Gentleman Commencing His Education" (*Rudiments Handbook*, pp. 21-23) articulates the application of the historic American Christian principle of unity and union to other kinds of associations. He counsels to:

1. Never become a member of any secret associations.
2. "Associations for intellectual improvement, for executing useful undertakings, and for combin-

ing and giving effect to exertions of benevolence, are highly laudable" but to "beware" of the purpose and practice of other parties...

3. "When the fundamental *principles of government or our holy religion are assaulted, good men must unite* to defend them." But *avoid* those associations, political or religious...
   a. that "spring from private ambition and interest";
   b. that forms out of "speculative opinions in politics";
   c. that emphasize the "externals of religion";
   d. that are disposed to "exalt one class of citizens and depress another";
   e. that attempt to "exclude one class of citizens from any control in legislation over the property which their industry has acquired."

4. Finally, "Accustom yourself from your youth to consider all men as your brethren (a physical brotherhood, Deut. 32:8; Mal. 2:10), and know no *distinction* between fellow *citizens*, except that which they make themselves, by their *virtues* or their *vices;* by their *worth* or their meanness."

Webster defined *distinction* as "Difference made; a separation or disagreement in kind or qualities, by which one thing is known from another; eminence; elevation of character..."

Noah Webster clearly states that Americans should know no legislated, administrated or judicial distinction or difference between citizens who have (a) equal rights and property before the law and (b) equal claims to a share in the management of that property (through the formation and administration of laws that protect and secure individual property).

However, individuals should make a *moral* separation or distinction from those citizens whose character, conscience and want of self-government is manifested as vicious, mean actions and conduct. (Ezek. 44:22; Jude 22)

Vicious: "addicted to vice; corrupt in principles of conduct; depraved; wicked."

WHOM SHOULD OUR COMPANIONS BE?

Seek People Who Are:	Avoid People Who Are:
Of good breeding	Profligate
Of virtuous principles	Irreligious
Of virtuous habits	Leading dissolute lives
Of good principles	Profane, Lewd
Of unimpeachable character	Intemperate
Who reverence divine precepts	Gamesters
Who keep themselves unspotted from the world	Scoffers of religion

Vice: "Any voluntary action or course of conduct which deviates from the rules of moral rectitude ...every act of intemperance, all falsehood, duplicity, deception, lewdness and the like, is a vice; depravity or corruption of manners."
Meanness: "Want of dignity...or excellence of any kind; rudeness; lowness of mind; want of honor. All dishonesty is meanness; sordidness."[1]

CHRISTIAN UNITY AND UNION: IDENTIFIED HISTORICALLY/GOVERNMENTALLY

In contrast to Christian unity and union is Ancient History's record of political union by coercion of the few based upon the spiritual ignorance of the many. Master Teacher, Katherine Dang, best analyzed this period of history.

"Ancient History, dating as far back as 3500 B.C., records man's earliest efforts at *social organization through centralization.* Man's control over man extends from the primary family and tribal unit to a union encompassing the whole, known world. Civilization is wrought out with *political force* and *military might.* One supreme state is succeeded by one greater, which is overcome by another still greater. Imperial largeness and intrinsic greatness *seem* synonomous...

"Ancient History, from the creation to 50 B.C., reveals mankind fallen, spiritually impotent to regain Adam's lost liberty. Universal political slavery was the result of universal spiritual bondage to sin and its author, Satan, who purposes to supplant God's dominion, if not over the angels in Heaven, then over the individual on earth...

"External law and force were required to check the inclinations of man's barbaric heart. Depraved humanity ruling depraved humanity is harsh and cruel. Asiatic monarchs purposed to seat themselves at the top of empires where they alone might possibly experience liberty..." (Emphasis added)[2]

The Ancient and Middle periods of history, from Creation to 476 A.D. are characterized by two forms of union, or "nation-making": the Oriental Method and the Roman Method. John Fiske summarizes these two pagan methods of union in *Christian History,* pp. 11-12.

However, the cause and inspiration for the Christian principle of American political union is the Bible, and its first full expression was in the New Testament church polity:

"In the beginning, Christianity was simply Gospel. Ecclesiastical organization was not the cause, but the *effect* of life. Churches were constituted by the spontaneous association of believers. Individuals and families, drawn toward each other by their common trust in Jesus the Christ, and their common interest in the good news concerning the kingdom of God, became a community united, not by external bonds, but by the vital force of distinctive ideas and principles. New affections became the bond of a new brotherhood, and the new brotherhood, with its mutual duties and united responsibilities, became an organized society... Their new ideas and new sympathies and hopes were a bond of union;...

"...Their unity was their one faith and hope. It was the unity of all common ideas and principles distinguishing them from all the world besides – of common interests and efforts of common trials and perils, and of mutual affection."[3]

The diagram of the above quotation on p. 74, *Primitive Church Polity,* reveals clearly the cause of unity and the effect called union in the Christian Church polity which finally became the cement of American political union 1620 years later.

One of the finest essays articulating the nature and development of the idea of voluntary union is found in the *Preface* to *Christian Self-Government With Union* by Miss Verna Hall (F.A.C.E., 3rd Ed., 1979, pp. II-VI) In this volume, Miss Hall documents "how Christianity eventually produced the scriptural alternative to compulsory union – voluntary union, with its flowering in America. Prior to the settling of America by the Pilgrims, mankind had known only one form of cooperative civil action – compulsory union.

"The world's best example of how to maintain Christian self-government and achieve voluntary union among diverse individuals occurs in America between 1620 and 1789, from the Pilgrims through the Patriots, from the Mayflower Compact to the Constitution."

"How to maintain Christian self-government and achieve voluntary union among diverse individuals" was explained to the Pilgrims by their pastor, John Robinson, before they came to America. Perhaps this one excerpt is the key to demonstrating Christian self-government *with* union:

"Now next after this heavenly peace with God & our owne consciences, we are carefully to provide for peace with all men what in us lieth, espetially with our associats, & for yt watchfullnes

---

1. *Webster's 1828.*
2. An *American Christian Approach to Teaching and Learning Universal History,* Miss Katherine Dang, Oakland, California. Unpublished Manuscript.

3. Leonard Bacon, *CHOC,* pp. 16-17.

must be had, that we neither at all in our selves doe give, no nor easily take offence being given by others... Neither yet is it sufficiente yt *we keepe our selves by ye grace of God from giveing offence, excepte withall we be armed against ye taking of them* when they be given by others." (emphasis added)[4]

The documentation and explanation of the development and expression of that "unity of spirit with diversity of people" from 1620 to 1775 is clearly delineated by Miss Slater in *Teaching and Learning,* pp. 267-268, and 363-366. Her statement on page 268 is perhaps the most conclusive:

"Evidence of American unity – a *unity* which flowed from *individual recognition* of the *invasion of rights* which had consequence for every citizen – *a union* based upon the *Christian tradition of voluntary association* – the Pilgrim ideal of a "single covenanted body of Christians, *united for civil* as well as *spiritual* purposes."

HISTORICAL VOLUNTARISM IN THE POLITICAL, ECONOMIC AND INDEPENDENT SECTORS OF AMERICA

PILGRIMS ILLUSTRATE VOLUNTARY UNION

Charles Hull Wolfe, a former senior staff member of the Foundation For Economic Education who served as the Executive Director of the committee that celebrated the 350th anniversary of the landing of the Pilgrims in Plymouth, Massachusetts, and has been an executive with the Volunteer Center of Los Angeles, encourages people to look upon the Pilgrims as the first group in America to practice the principle of voluntary union in its varied aspects.

In a short essay written for this volume, Mr. Wolfe says:

"The more deeply one studies American history, the more evidence one finds that this Biblical principle of voluntary union expressed itself not only in the political realm but also in the commercial or business sphere, and in an array of organized voluntary activities, neither commercial nor governmental to meet community needs.

"Of special interest and importance is the evidence that in all three sectors, the political, the commercial, and the non-profit voluntary action sector, the people's understanding of and commitment to this Christian principle of voluntarism was so great it was instrumental in producing new and exceedingly beneficial forms of social organization: the world's first Christian Republic, the world's largest and most productive common market, and the world's most vital and well-organized 'independent sector,' meeting needs which the people believed government *should* not and business *could* not meet.

"All three expressions of voluntary union continued to develop throughout the colonial period, and then were specifically enhanced and

4. *CHOC,* p. 199.

PRIMITIVE CHURCH POLITY

CHRISTIAN UNITY Internal >	Form of UNION ➤ External
Voluntary internal unity of:	
Gospel Life.	. . Ecclesiastical Organization
Common: *Trust* in Christ Jesus	Spontaneous association
Interest in the good news of God's Kingdom	A community united
United by the:	
Vital force of *distinctive ideas* and *principles* and *affections*	New brotherhood or society
Mutual: *duties, responsibilities*	Bond of Union
Kindred: *sympathies* and *hopes*	Distinct community with a life of its own
Unity of: one *faith* and *hope*	Distinguishing them from all the world besides
Common: *interests* and *efforts*	Common trials and perils

strengthened by the United States Constitution which strictly limited the power and extent of national government; but each of these sectors appeared from the beginning of colonization, and each was dramatically illustrated in the experience of the Pilgrims.

VOLUNTARY POLITICAL UNION

"While the spiritual and intellectual insights that gave rise to the Mayflower Compact occurred to a relatively small group of Pilgrim leaders, the Compact could not have had its practical effectiveness as Plymouth Plantation's fundamental charter for civil self-government had it not been well understood, *voluntarily* accepted and truly adhered to by the *entire body* of settlers – not only by all the Pilgrims or "saints" as they came to be known, but also by all the "strangers," who actually *outnumbered* the Pilgrims.

"Apparently the 'strangers,' some of whom were on the verge of rebellion against all authority before the Compact was signed, were deeply touched by the Pilgrim leaders' Biblical reasoning concerning the need for such a covenant, its Scriptural soundness and its respect for the God-given rights of *all* the settlers. And it could well be that in God's Providence, He had chosen a group of 'strangers' with above-average receptivity and capacity for self-government, that allowed them to appreciate the Pilgrims' integrity and wisdom, and in turn, voluntarily join with them in accepting and *obeying* the Compact, for their 'better ordering and preservation' in the Massachusetts wilderness. (See *Christian History*, p. 204)

VOLUNTARY ECONOMIC UNION

"This Pilgrim achievement, the *political* manifestation of the principle of voluntary union, has been described by many authors; but not so well known is the unique way the Pilgrims expressed the same Christian principle in their *economic* experiences.

"By contrast, the Pilgrims – both because of their own understanding of the Christian principle of voluntarism, and because of the way God's Providence worked in their lives – enjoyed a mutually beneficial exchange of expertise and goods with the neighboring Indians, with whom they joined in voluntary economic union shortly after their arrival in the wilderness of Plymouth. And just a few years later, this union was expanded to include the Dutch traders in New Amsterdam, and then the Puritan settlers in Salem and Boston.

"Because the Pilgrims met the Indians in a spirit of faith and Christian love, the Indians showed the settlers how to plant native corn in the thin, sandy soil, and how to hunt in the woods, and thus kept the Pilgrims from starving to death. In turn, the Pilgrims exchanged with the Indians various English-made products that the Indians appreciated, nursed sick Indians back to health, and ground the Indians' corn for them in the Pilgrim grist-mill.

"In 1627, the Pilgrims built a trading post at Aptucxet, in the town now called Bourne. At Aptucxet, the Pilgrims happily engaged in a three-way trade – a free and peaceful exchange between themselves, the Dutchmen from Manhattan, and the Indians from Cape Cod. In the 1630's, with the arrival of the Puritans some 40 miles north of Plymouth, the Pilgrims greatly expanded their trading activities.

"While the Pilgrims might easily have felt too fearful or hostile to join in economic union with the Indians, or too self-sufficient or aloof to trade with the Dutch or the Puritans, or at least might have sought to set up some kind of tariff barriers to protect themselves in trade, instead they saw these peoples as neighbors with whom they could exchange in a free market to mutual advantage. Thus they experienced Christian voluntary union in the economic realm.

VOLUNTARY CHARITABLE EFFORTS

"Even though the Pilgrims were highly productive, thanks to their Christian work-ethic, their utilization of man's God-given ability to invent and use tools, and their switch from communal to private agriculture, some of their members from time to time were in acute want. Had the Pilgrim leaders been hard-hearted advocates of the survival of the fittest, they might have simply chided their impoverished neighbors, telling them to 'stand on your own two feet.' Or, if the Pilgrims had been statist-minded, believers in coercion, they might have taxed all the productive settlers, and set up a government fund for the poor.

"Instead, the Pilgrim set a pattern of organized *voluntary* charity for later generations to follow. In the early 1620's, Deacon Robert Cushman, preaching in the Plymouth fort-meeting house, urged his fellow Pilgrims 'not to seek only your own interest, ...but to seek still the wealth of one another, and inquire, as David did, 'How liveth such a man? Is his labor harder than mine? Surely I will ease him. Hath he no bed to lie on? Why, I have two; I'll lend him one. Hath he no apparel? Why, I have two suits; I'll give him one of them.

Eats he coarse fare, bread and water, and I have better? Why, surely we will part stakes.'

"For a century and a half, succeeding generations of colonists built on the Pilgrim example of Christian voluntary union – in the political, commercial and 'independent' sectors of colonial society.

"In the *political* realm, many of the other colonies took the Biblical covenant idea of the Mayflower Compact as a prototype for their own civil covenant or constitution, which the settlers voluntarily agreed to ratify and obey.

"In the *economic* realm, progress toward voluntary union, as expressed in free markets, was more erratic, owing to the English settlers' background, and especially their Mother Country's allegiance to the economic system called mercantilism, a species of authoritarianism that sought to use governmental authority to direct economic activities toward the acquisition of national wealth.

"The most numerous and influential group of settlers in the seventeenth century, the Puritans, at first tried an idealistic form of mercantilism, using governmental authority to direct the economic affairs of Massachusetts Bay toward the concepts of fairness and justice. Thus the Puritans enacted subsidies and bounties, and tried to set 'just' prices, wages and profits.

"But gradually the Puritans, and the settlers in other colonies discovered that such government interventions in the economy did not work, that they were all instances of 'man playing God' and led to turmoil and poverty, while they violated the settlers' economic freedom. Gradually, the colonists began to conclude that God had created a natural order in economics, in which there was a minimum of governmental intervention, a prohibition of coercion by either buyer or seller of goods or services, and a maximum of voluntary exchange.

"Thus the colonists began to come together in the kind of voluntary economic union known as the free market, where civil government's role is restricted to the prevention and punishment of theft and fraud, and the providing of judicial services, and where exchanges are made only when both buyer and seller view them as beneficial.

VOLUNTARY UNION ENHANCED
BY THE CONSTITUTION

"But despite progress toward total economic union, on a strictly voluntary basis within each of the colonies, the thirteen colonies still acted as if they were *separated countries*, protecting themselves from each other with tariff barriers, until the United States government, under the Constitution, prohibited such obstacles to free trade, and thereby made possible the greatest common market in all history, which proved to be a cornerstone in American prosperity.

"During the colonial era, the colonists increasingly expressed the Christian principle of voluntary union, not only in the political and economic realms, but in *independent*, non-commercial organized activities to help the less able and to solve community problems. Out of their keen sense of Christian brotherhood, they joined together in barn-raising, house-raising, quilt-making, corn-husking, flax-scutching, ice-cutting, well-digging, and a vast variety of other activities – from launching schools to launching ships bearing missionaries and food supplies for people overseas.

"Knowledgeable observers concluded during the nineteenth century that no other country had developed such a vital private sector in which volunteers teamed up without the coercion of government or the incentive of profit to meet community challenges.

"The renowned French observer, Alexis de Tocqueville, wrote in 1835, 'Whenever at the head of some new undertaking you see the government in France (or) a man of rank in England, in the United States you will be sure to find an association [of individuals].'

"During the mid-1700s, volunteer aid societies were formed for nearly every imaginable purpose: to help widows, orphans, immigrants, blacks, debtors, poor students, prisoners, the aged, drunks, gamblers, juvenile delinquents and others.

"As the American Revolution approached, the spirit of voluntarism prompted volunteers from neighboring colonies to smuggle food into blockaded Boston (*Teaching and Learning*, p. 264). It also allowed George Washington to recruit 'a band of casually gathered, haphazardly armed amateurs' who, in God's Providence, defeated the British Army, then the world's most powerful. After the war, the framers of the Constitution could confidently restrict the powers of the central government, aware that voluntary efforts were meeting community needs.

"A century ago, British historian Lord James Bryce wrote, 'In works of active benevolence, no country has surpassed, perhaps none has equaled, the United States. Not only are the sums collected for all sorts of philanthropic purposes larger relatively to the wealth of Americans than in any European country, but the amount of personal effort devoted to them seems to a European visitor to exceed what he knows at home.'"

A RECAPITULATION

In the foregoing pages, each of the seven Biblical principles of America's Christian history and government has been introduced separately, diagrammed, scripturally referenced and elucidated governmentally, historically and educationally. The summary diagram, *A Recapitulation of the Seven Biblical Principles* on page 78, suggests how all seven principles may be viewed wholistically and how they relate to and buttress one another to constitute a Christian philosophy and form of self- and civil government in the Chain of Christianity.

Each principle and its idea is identified first internally, as causative, primary and unseen in the human heart, constituting the real spirit, nature and essence of the American Christian idea of man and government. This Biblical body of wisdom and knowledge has a *Christian and civil* expression, a social, political and economic effect which is secondary and seen, and which constitutes the letter, framework and structure of the historic Christian *form* of civil government in America.

Further insight into the sequential relationship between each of the seven principles is submitted by permission of the discoverer, Miss Katherine Dang. She has astutely analyzed each "Statement

of the Principle" in *Teaching and Learning* and deduced the following conclusions:

1) The subject of "God's Principle of Individuality" is *GOD*, His character, creation and government. 2) Subsequently, "The Christian Principle of Self-government" reveals that *man's relationship with God is governmental* – first indwelling, in man's heart, then outworking in the social, ecclesiastical and finally the civil spheres of life. 3) "America's Heritage of Christian Character" emphasizes that *man's relation with man in civil society must be discriminative* – must constantly discriminate between worthy and unworthy attributes and right and wrong conduct. 4) "Conscience is the Most Sacred of All Property" suggests the *purpose* for which men covenant and combine into a civil body politic. They unite in a civil, not an ecclesiastical, union for the purpose of mutually preserving and protecting their God-given liberty of conscience, a key to the proper use of external property. 5) "Our Christian Form of Government" – *a Christian Constitutional Federal Republic*, best preserves man's property in his conscience and physical possessions. 6) "How the Seed of Local Self-Government is Planted" indicates the *method*

A RECAPITULATION OF THE SEVEN BIBLICAL PRINCIPLES

INTERNAL >————————————————————▶ EXTERNAL

Causative, primary, unseen	Effect, secondary, seen
Spirit, nature, essence	Letter, framework, structure

The Biblical Principle	The Christian Idea	The Christian Idea Expressed
I. GOD'S PRINCIPLE OF INDIVIDUALITY	God's Character and Individuality are reflected in the Christian liberty, conscience and virtue of the individual Christian.	The quality of man's government – self, home, church and civil – is primarily determined in his heart.
II. THE CHRISTIAN PRINCIPLE OF SELF-GOVERNMENT	Christian self-government expands as God's Law and Love are accepted and obeyed in the individual heart.	Local self-governing homes, churches and communities are maintained by properly self-governed individuals.
III. AMERICA'S HERITAGE OF CHRISTIAN CHARACTER	A God-governed individual expresses the "divine nature" through such Pilgrim qualities as faith, courage and brotherly love.	Only a self-governed (peculiar) people, refined by conflict within and with the world, can maintain a Christian Republic.
IV. CONSCIENCE IS THE MOST SACRED OF ALL PROPERTY	As God's property, individuals have a God-given right (a just claim) to the most sacred of all property – Liberty of Conscience and of Consent.	Conscientious stewardship of private property, with its fruits, is protected by just, written laws established by the consent of the governed.
V. OUR CHRISTIAN FORM OF GOVERNMENT	The divine flow of spiritual power and force is manifested in individual Christian self-government and character, liberty of conscience, and wisdom to know when to unite and when to separate as an American Christian.	A Christian Republic is a form of government in which self-governing citizens protect their God-given rights through elected representatives who must act in obedience to a fundamental law, covenant or constitution which provides for federalism-decentralization of power into two sovereign spheres – and prevents concentration of power through separation of governmental functions.
VI. HOW THE SEED OF LOCAL SELF-GOVERNMENT IS PLANTED	Christian self-government begins with evangelism and education in God's Law and Love for man, and is expressed as individual care and concern for family, brethren, neighbors and community.	Local self-government reflects an individual application of Biblical Law and Love in governing one's self, one's home, church and town and an education in the principles of lawful action.
VII. THE CHRISTIAN PRINCIPLE OF AMERICAN POLITICAL UNION	The unity of God and man expands in the spirit of Christian fellowship. Shared convictions can form an invisible voluntary common bond among countrymen without compromising Biblical principles of separation.	The visible voluntary union of fellow citizens in a Christian Republic manifests itself in three sectors: *political* (governmental), *commercial* (economic) and *independent* (home, church, school, and organized voluntarism to meet individual and community needs).

of building a Christian Republic – teaching and learning the importance of local responsibility and sovereignty. 7) "The Christian Principle of American Political Union" is the *effect* of God's Principle of Individuality and the subsequent five principles.

The following outline simplifies still further this sequential relationship between the seven principles:

THE LEADING IDEAS BEHIND EACH PRINCIPLE AND THEIR SEQUENTIAL RELATIONSHIP

1. *GOD* – and His individuality.
2. *Man* – and his relationship to God's government.
3. *Christian Character* – it is needed to maintain right relationships between man and man.
4. *Private Property* – a right relationship between men requires protection of both internal and external property.
5. *Civil Government* – the form that best protects both internal and external property is a Christian Constitutional Federal Republic.
6. *Local Self-government* – this must be practiced in order to maintain a Christian Republic.

7. *Voluntary Union* – this results when works through men with the Christian character ι love their neighbors, respect their property, and live under just law in a Christian Republic.

These seven minimal principles explain America's Christian *history*, constitute a philosophy of American Christian *government*, and distinguish American Christian *education*.[1] These principles, as Miss Slater states in *Teaching and Learning*, page 62, are "'measuring rods' for current problems."

Once the individual becomes informed and aware of the problems of the times, it then becomes critically important to take effective action to correct, *to* reconstruct, *to* rebuild *Constitutional liberty. This cannot be accomplished by merely uncovering a problem. With awareness must come constructive knowledge in order to deal intelligently and effectively with every challenge to individual liberty and to the freedom of these United States of America. Human knowlege and human reason are not able to provide the insight and wisdom needed. Unless one understands the Christian history of this nation and the Christian Principles of our form of government, one is not equipped to deal with today's challenge to the freedom of mankind...*"[2]

---

1. Further insight into how these principles may be applied *educationally in the home* is given on page 91 in this *Guide*.
2. Rosalie J. Slater, *T/L*, pp. xvi-xvii.

Some Questions Answered

The following questions have been asked concerning the American Christian Philosophy of Education and the Christian History program. The answers are brief and not exhaustive, and are intended only to offer direction for further consideration and study.

QUESTION: This approach to education and teaching America's Christian history appears to take so much time to learn and implement. There just doesn't seem to be time to restore the Christian scholarship necessary to rebuild the foundations of American Christian education and government before Christ returns in glory.

ANSWER: Indeed, I too am looking for Jesus Christ to "come quickly," as He promised. But regardless of when Christ comes, each Christian educator must decide if he is responsible to God to learn and live by Biblical Christian principles of education and government *now*, as the Lord tarries. Our philosophy, curriculum, and methods of education today will determine the character and scholarship of our students now, and the Lord Jesus Christ will hold us accountable for the children He has entrusted to us.

The real question is, as the Lord tarries, will I use my time to make the truths of God's Word the basis of *every* subject in the curriculum and so forward Christ, His Story, and the Gospel purpose of America in the Chain of Christianity? I submit that in this dispensation, the time or duration permitted us is subjective, or relative to the subject which we *choose* to spend time on. I've found that this argument of time is prompted by an attitude or disposition in me – and I'm certain shared by others – of either *irresponsibility* or *ignorance* of the need and importance of understanding Christian civil government; of *inertia*, or an active resistance to move on a right idea or Biblical command; of *ineptitude*, a feeling of being unfit or not inclined or qualified to be governed by Christ and his commandments *right now*.

The Bible teaches us "to so number our days that we may apply our hearts to wisdom" (Psa. 90:12) and to "walk in wisdom toward them that are without, redeeming the time" (Col. 4:5), i.e., buying it up, rescuing from loss, captivity or bondage that which is in bondage or servitude to Satan and the world. My authority for how to use my time is Christ and Biblical Christianity, and my responsibility as a Christian teacher is to claim every subject for Christ "that in *all* things He might have the preeminence" (Col. 1:18)

Time has nothing to do with our continuing stewardship over the light we have been given, both in terms of God's work and the Biblical principles of government entrusted to us which is our heritage as Americans as well as Christians. What are the consequences, the effects, if we don't redeem the time and rescue or liberate our subjects, methods and views? What kind of a product will we produce? It is my conviction that I am not only responsible for redeeming the lost through the power of the Holy Spirit and Biblical reasoning, but also for redeeming such subjects as history, government, economics, science and literature from the worldly philosophies and inventions of man.

I have struggled with the use of my time, too. I have had to learn how to use my time more diligently. I had to choose whom I will serve; to stay home more so I could read and research; to reduce my traveling and rushing about smartly when it wasn't accomplishing much; to stop talking or making lingering calls when I had nothing to say and little to accomplish. I had to choose whether I would lead in implementing the Principle Approach to America's Christian history, government and education by following in the footsteps of the Pilgrims and other pioneers of this approach and by conscientiously devoting my time to this task, *or to pursue other interesting but less significant endeavors.*

My time is God's and I am persuaded that as one comes to the conviction that the Principle Approach to American Christian education can be God's means of rebuilding the foundations, should the Lord tarry, that one will find the time to claim and apply this approach.

The Scriptures command that we "occupy till I come." (Luke 19:13) Who or what will occupy our time and thus control or govern our subjects and our methods as well as our homes and churches? Will Biblical principles and reasoning occupy or govern the church and home, but *not the civil*, the political, economic or cultural spheres of life in America?

Are the areas of government, history, economics, art, etc., of the world, worldly and not of or pertaining to Christ or Christianity? It is *time* that Christians see the unity of knowledge between *every* subject in the curriculum and Christ, Christianity, and the Word of God. American Christians should acknowledge responsibility *now* for claiming and perpetuating this precious heritage.

Lastly, it is improper and unbiblical to divorce our subjects from the Bible or conveniently divide the world into sacred and secular, Christian or worldly. We must not only *discern* if a subject is being taught from a secular or sacred viewpoint, but deliberately teach from the position that all subjects and objects of God's universe have a Christian principle and purpose governing them. Without this conviction, something else is in control – with the consent of the Christian parent, teacher or pastor.

QUESTION: We need a manual, a packaged program to tell us how to implement this approach. I've got to be shown how.

ANSWER: There are those who have pioneered this approach who will help you. There are Master Teachers who are writing down their curriculum, and administrators who are recording their own experience in teaching teachers; but the *principles* of America's Christian history and education have been identified and restored to all of us, and the cause of Christ and Christian education demands your own unique expression and contribution.

More detailed instructions and examples of how to teach subjects in an American curriculum are reprinted in the school curriculum section of this *Guide*; but the danger is that many educators will be too lazy to make this method of Biblical reasoning their own, or they may continue to be dependent upon the Christian scholarship of others.

The challenge is to individualize and internalize this approach and this history for ourselves by applying our own labor to it. As John Locke said in his treatise of civil government, it "is by the labor that removes (a thing) out of that Common State Nature left it in, that makes it his property who takes *pains* about it."[1]

QUESTION: There is too much emphasis on the past, upon history, especially on America's history. Also, why are these principles you speak of uniquely American principles? Are not these principles applicable to any other nation? Why should a missionary learn the Principle Approach to America's Christian history and education?

ANSWER: Without a philosophy of history or a knowledge of the history of your subject, one can understand neither its source nor origin. The history of our subjects will reveal the Hand of God in using men and nations to discover and apply the principles and blessings of each aspect of the curriculum.

---

1. John Locke, "Second Essay on Civil Government," *CHOC*, p. 65, para. 30 and p. 64, para. 27.

The view that too much emphasis is placed upon the past, especially America's Christian history, is a *feeling* (not a fact) that history is dead and has nothing to teach us concerning the character of men and nations and the power of Christ in *all* ages.

We are *not* glorifying America or the past more than the Bible or God, but only showing that God or the power of Christ in individual lives and nations produced or caused the progress of Christian liberty, self-government, property and unity and union in history and in America.

Indeed, the unveiling of America and our Christian history is to the credit of Christ and the Christians who were used of God to educate posterity in the Christian principles of self-government, property and liberty which became the basis of a form of civil government that provided for the greatest expression of individual liberty the world has ever known.

We are Americans and not of another nationality. This is no accident. As *Christians*, how will you and I account for America being so blessed with a government of law, whose spirit and letter, in its original context and purpose, secured so much more freedom to the individual than *any* other nation in the world? No other nation has the heritage of a Bible-living, Bible-believing people who were prepared by God to *extend* Christian principles into civil government and other areas of life and living. It is our ignorance of the Providence of God in our nation from 1620 to 1820 that makes us liable to the error of separating Christ and Christianity from America and its form of government. "No other nation has consciously and purposely based its institutions upon Christian Biblical principles. There would be no America if there were no Christianity."[2]

To deny this point and speculate as to what would have happened if America were settled and developed by either the Scandinavian explorers, the French Hugenots, the Jesuits, or the Spanish explorers, et al., is a suppositional question which ignores and even denies the power of Christ and the impact of the Word of God in our nation. But who is telling us just what our heritage is as Americans and Christians? What textbooks tell the story? Which teachers know it? Where did you hear it – if you have? No one has destroyed the record – we still have the original sources of our history. If you take time to research our Christian history, it will testify of the Hand of God.

If the record reveals the Hand of God in America and its civil government, then should not

Christians claim it as a part of their stewardship in order to perpetuate both its *roots* and its *fruits* to their children?

The people of all nations are welcome to accept the challenge of learning and implementing the principles of America's Christian history, government, and education. They are uniquely American principles because America, until about 1830, was the fullest expression, so far, of these principles in both the civil and religious spheres of activity. To what other nation or civilization may other peoples look to see how they work and what fruit they can bear? Other nations may use these same principles of government, internal and external; but to do so they must accept the Christ and the Bible from which they spring, and they must accept the Savior and the Lord that produced the character necessary to implement and defend them.

Lastly, American missionaries, at home or abroad, *also* need to know and teach the Biblical principles of civil government and education because America's Christian history is a *testimony* of the power of Christ and Biblical reasoning in shaping the government of a whole nation. And the Principle Approach to American Christian education is a method of educating others in understanding that Christian liberty is not only *Biblical*, pertaining to the Word of God, and *ecclesiastical*, pertaining to the church and its discipline and government, but also *political*, pertaining to civil government and its administration in respect to individual God-given rights.

Hence, America's Christian history, government and education is a *testimony*, an *example*, and a *hope* of what *all nations* can enjoy if they will *educate their people as Americans were educated 200 years ago.*

Again, what nation testifies to, or is an example of ever having established a Christian form of civil government as a result of the Christian philosophy of education embraced in that nation's homes, churches and schools? I submit that every missionary from America should claim this heritage and story of what *God's grace* has given us and thereby be enabled to give the same Gospel hope and purpose to the peoples of other nations.

QUESTION: Must all of the seven principles of America's Christian history and government be taught through my subject or in the curriculum? Are we not straining to fit the subject to the principles or vice versa? Also, these seven principles appear to be too limiting. Are there not other principles to be emphasized?

ANSWER: The Principle Approach is liberating, not limiting! This approach tells *how* to approach

---

2. *Rudiments Handbook*, p. 1.

or reason about a subject, and the seven principles of America's Christian history identify a Biblical view of God, man and government to emphasize to the student through the subject.

The Principle Approach to *education* is a method of teaching every subject in the curriculum by applying the 4 R's with the truths of God's Word. It explains how to reason governmentally from the internal to the external, from cause to effect, from the primary to the secondary, from the unseen to the seen. (See *Teaching and Learning*, pp. 92-94)

The seven principles are intended only to be the *minimal* principles or foundation of America's Christian character, history and government. These seven principles produced America's Christian history, and explain the relationship between America and Christ in Christian history. They define and declare what it means to be an Ameri-can Christian and how individual character influences history and government. The seven principles, unlike other principles of history, government, and education, are comprehensive of the whole scope of Christian life and living including the basis of *how* to supplant socialism and maintain a Christian civil government. (See also Preface to *Curriculum* section, page 135, and *Recapitulation*, page 77)

The Principle Approach is by invitation. You are invited and encouraged to research the principles of America's Christian history and government in the Word of God and prove them. Don't try to force them into your curriculum or impress them on subjects or on your students. The Christian approach to education is first internal and voluntary, then externally expressed; it is not imposed, contrived or impressed, and cannot be.

PART II

EDUCATION FOR THE AMERICAN CHRISTIAN HOME

BY JAMES B. ROSE AND BARBARA B. ROSE

American Christian History Institute
Camarillo, California

The educational goal of the
American Christian home in a republic is to build the foundation
of American Christian character. p. 3

As Christian parents restore the 'family altar' to their homes
they will also be able to rekindle the watchfires of an enlightened patriotism.
This Christian patriotism includes a recognition and understanding
of America's unique function in the Chain of Christianity
and a knowledge of the Christian principles
of America's Christian History. p. 4

Rosalie June Slater, *Teaching and Learning*

Home is a preparation for both the State and the Church.

Rev. S. Phillips, *Teaching and Learning*, p. 4

DEVELOPING AMERICA'S CHRISTIAN CHARACTER

For many years I have been deeply impressed by the wisdom of this statement by Rosalie J. Slater: "The educational goal of the American Christian home in a republic is to develop America's Christian character"—the hearts of the people out of which come the "issues of life." (Prov. 4:23)

This goal does not vitiate any of God's commands to parents to win their children to Christ and disciple them in His Word, but simply expands that *primary* purpose to the education of youth in America's heritage of Christian character, the Providence of God, and the Biblical principles of self and civil government.

What does this goal mean to me?

It suggests to me a *lifetime*: taking time throughout my life to value the grace of God to me and America; taking time to *remember* the "wonderful works of God" in blessing me with a Christian home and family, and giving American citizens more liberty, private property and unity than any people today! It means taking time to *discover* and *cultivate* the talents, affections and character of my children so they might love the God who gave us life and liberty under a Christian form of government, and learn to voluntarily add to the "increase of His government." (Isa. 9:7)

This goal also requires *love*: loving the labor and responsibility of struggling with my own character and the conscious daily choices and actions of my wife and children so that we might better preserve the "blessings of liberty unto all generations."

Finally, developing America's Christian character means hard *labor*: conscientiously working out from a position of God-given salvation and dominion a life that glorifies God, draws my children to Him, and consequently makes an evangelical and political difference in my church, community, state and nation.

The lifetime of love and labor required of me is exercised first in my home, then among the body of Christ, and ultimately in all levels of civil government. The Christian character needed to govern myself according to God's "perfect law of liberty" is the foundation of America's Christian character and constitutional government.

And this is a goal, a mark, that I have *not* wholly achieved, but have set my eyes upon, "Not as though I had already attained, either were already perfect: but I follow after, if that I may apprehend that for which also I am apprehended of Christ Jesus" (Phil. 3:12) knowing also that "The

Lord will perfect that which concerneth me; thy mercy, O Lord, endureth forever; forsake not the works of thine own hands:" (Psa. 138:8)

To help effect the goal of developing America's Christian character in the home, this section of the *Guide* has two objectives:

I. To confirm Biblically and historically that the *home is the first sphere of education and civil government* in a republic.

II. To suggest how parents can use the Principle Approach to *make home the first school* for developing the individual character to advance the Gospel and the Biblical principles of America's Christian history and government.

I
BIBLICAL BASIS FOR THE HOME

The family is a divine institution as confirmed in Genesis 2:23-24 and Matthew 19:3-6. It is one of three God-given spheres of external government. (See *Guide*, p. 21)

Matthew Henry, an English Bible commentator much enjoyed by our Founding Fathers, reasoned from these verses that:

"Marriage and the Sabbath are the most ancient of divine ordinances. (Gen. 2)

"Though marriage be not peculiar to the church, but common to the world, yet being stamped with a divine institution, and here ratified by our Lord Jesus (Matt. 19) *it ought to be managed after a godly sort*, and sanctified by the Word of God and prayer."[1]

HOME IS THE FIRST
MINISTRY OF EDUCATION

The Christian home is where God's Providence should be taught and wise instruction and discipline in Biblical principles should begin. Giving such instruction is a Biblical mandate:

Exodus 13:8: "And thou shalt shew thy son in that day, saying, This is done because of that which the Lord did unto me when I came forth out of Egypt."

Exodus 13:14: "And it shall be when thy son asketh thee in time to come, saying, What is this? that thou shalt say unto him, By strength of hand the Lord brought us out from Egypt, from the house of bondage: ..."

---

1. Matthew Henry, *Commentaries*, Vol. V, p. 269.

Deuteronomy 4:9: "Only take heed to thyself, and keep thy soul diligently, lest thou forget the things which thine eyes have seen, and lest they depart from thy heart all the days of thy life: but teach them to thy sons, and thy son's sons;...."

Deuteronomy 6:7: "And thou shalt teach them diligently unto thy children, and shalt talk of them when thou sittest in thine house, and when thou walkest by the way, and when thou liest down, and when thou risest up."

Joshua 4:20-22,24: "And those twelve stones, which they took out of Jordan, did Joshua pitch in Gilgal. And he spake unto the children of Israel, saying, When your children shall ask their fathers in time to come, saying, What mean these stones? Then ye shall let your children know, saying, Israel came over this Jordan on dry land ... That all the people of the earth might know the hand of the Lord, that it is mighty: that ye might fear the Lord your God forever."

Psalm 78:4: "We will not hide them (see vs. 2-3) from their children, shewing to the generation to come the praises of the Lord, and his strength and his wonderful works that he hath done."

John 21:15: " ... Feed my lambs."

II Timothy 3:15: "And that from a child thou hast known the holy scriptures, which are able to make thee wise unto salvation through faith which is in Christ Jesus."

Galatians 4:1-2: "Now I say, That the heir, as long as he is a child, differeth nothing from a servant, though he be lord of all; But is under tutors and governors until the time appointed of the father."

HOME IS THE PRIMARY SPHERE OF
GOVERNMENT

The first sphere of government, as well as education, is the individual heart or mind, of which the home is the immediate extension. Government is first internal, invisible, and individual as daily choices are made concerning who or what will govern one's thoughts and attitudes. Hence, the individual is the vehicle or instrument of authority—God's or some counterfeit's—that determines whether one's relationship with others in the home and the nation will be savage, or civil, discordant or harmonious.

Civil, by the way, is an adjective, and is defined as "relating to the community, or the policy and government of the citizens ... of a state" as in *civil government*. Civil therefore describes man's relation to man with respect to external deportment or government. One who is civilized acts civilly, or with civility, and is literally "reclaimed from a savage (wild, untaught, barbarous) state."[2] Hence, to live up to its potential, government needs the civilizing influence of Biblical Christianity because it is uniquely effective in reclaiming men from their savage, unregenerate state.

"What nation since the commencement of the Christian era, ever rose from savage to civilized without Christianity?"[3]

The home or family is a primary sphere of civil government according to the Bible. Christians generally understand that the home is responsible for developing *individual* self-government, but they should also realize that according to the Bible, the home must develop the *character for civil government*. For example, it is in the family that the qualities of *integrity* (Gen. 18:9; Job 31:5-6), *independence* (Phil. 4:12; II Thess. 3:11-12) and the attitudes of *reverence* (fear mingled with respect and esteem) (Ex. 20:12; Eph. 6:2), of *obedience* (Luke 2:51; Col. 3:20) and *respect* for the just authority of others (Gen. 18:19; I Cor. 11:3; Eph. 5:22; Col. 3:18-24; I Tim. 3:2; 5:1-3) are first taught and learned. Indeed, the character qualities developed in the home and needed by a "good ruler" or representative were described with great perception by Rev. Samuel Willard in 1694.[4] Also consider diagram 3, "America's Heritage of Christian Character" on page 40 of this *Guide*.

Consider how Rev. S. Phillips in 1861 perceived Christian home government as the necessary preparation for civil government:

"Home is a little commonwealth jointly governed by parents. It involves law. The mutual relation of parent and child implies authority on the one hand, and obedience on the other. This is the principle of all government. Home is the first form of society. As such it must have a government. Its institution implies the prerogatives of the parent and the subordination of the child. Without this there would be no order, no harmony, no training for the state or the church.

"The principle of home government is love— love ruling and obeying according to law. These are exercised, as it were, by the instinct of natural affection as taken up and refined by the Christian life and faith. This government implies reciprocity of right,—the right of the parent to govern and the right of the child to be governed. It is similar in its fundamentals to the government of the state and church. It involves the legislative, judicial and executive functions; its elements are law, authority, obedience, and penalties. The basis of its laws is the Word of God . . .

"Parental authority is threefold, legislative, judicial and executive.

"Parents are magistrates under God, and, as His stewards, cannot abdicate their authority, nor delegate it to another. Neither can they be tyrants in the exercise of it. God has given to them the principles of home-legislation, the standard of judicial authority, and the rules of their executive power. God gives the law. The parent is only deputy governor,—steward, 'bound to be faithful.' Hence the obligation of the child to obey the steward is as great as that to obey the Master. 'Where the principal is silent, take heed that thou despise not the deputy.'"[5]

THE CHARACTER OF CHURCH AND STATE IS FORMED IN THE HOME

"Home is a little commonwealth . . ." so Rev. Phillips suggested. Noah Webster declared in 1828 that "a commonwealth is properly a free state; a representative government; a republic . . . The word signifies strictly, the common good or happiness; and hence, the form of government supposed best to secure the public good."[6]

The idea of home as a little commonwealth does not repudiate the authority of father or mother over their children; rather it suggests the Biblical mandate that parents have absolute authority to *represent* the government of God. In the process, as Rev. Phillips has implied, parents will be preparing their children for effective participation in the government of the church as well as state.

The conclusion here is that the Christian home is the first sphere of both civil and ecclesiastical government, of both the civil state and the local church. Conversely, for the Christian home to flourish and be safe, it must have the ministry of the local church and the protection of property expected of civil government. From a Christian view, this protection includes legal safeguards for the parents' right to control the education of their children.

Again, the "home is a preparation for both the state and the church" and the church and state are a reflection of the quality of conscience and authority implanted at home.

Ponder these conclusions of Rev. Phillips:

"In this age of extreme individualism, we have almost left out of view the mission of the home as

---

2. *Webster 1828 Dictionary*.
3. *Ibid*, E.D. Griffith.
4. *CHOC*, pp. 396-397.

5. Rev. S. Phillips, "The Christian Home," *T/L*, pp. 23, 24.
6. *Webster's 1828*.

the first form of society, and the importance it has upon the formation of character.[7]

"The Christian home can have existence only in the sphere of the church . . .[8]

"As the family is a divine institution and a type of the church and of heaven, (Eph. 5:23; Psa. 127:3) it cannot be understood in isolation from Christianity; it must involve Christian principles, duties and interests; and embrace in its educational functions a preparation for not only the State, but also the Church.[9]

" . . . the development of individual character and happiness in the church and state, in time and in eternity, *starts with, and depends upon, home-training and nurture.*"[10] (Emphasis added)

Early American pastors, patriots and educators were fully persuaded that the character of representative government has its roots in the character of home education. The first colonial treatise on child training was written by Rev. Thomas Cobbett in 1656 when he was pastor of the church at Lynn, Massachusetts, and entitled "A Fruitful and Useful Discourse Touching the Honour Due from Children to Parents, and the Duty of Parents Towards Their Children." He taught that:

"The original then of state and church being the family, they are both, in that respect, concerned in it; yea as the family is an original to states and churches, in their essentials, so also in their morals, in their manners. As that nursery is better or worse, and the plants thereof of more or less worth, so are both the orchards of state and church, which are thence stored with trees, better or worse, and their fruits more or less wholesome; if *that school* be but well ordered, and the lesser scholars in it well principled and grounded, (Prov. 4:4.) those which afterwards come to be made use of, for more eminent use and service, in state and church, they will be the more precious ornaments to them both."[11]

Dr. Elias Boudinot, the President of the Continental Congress in 1783, reiterated Cobbett's emphasis in an oration given to the New Jersey Society of the Cincinnati on July 4, 1793:

"Good government generally begins in the family, and if the moral character of a people once degen-erate, their political character must soon follow."[12]

Homemaker and educator, Lydia H. Sigourney, admonished mothers in 1851 through her "Letters to Young Ladies" that:

"The strength of a nation, especially of a republican nation, is in the intelligent and well ordered homes of the people. And in proportion as the discipline of families is relaxed will the happy organization of communities be affected, and national character become vagrant, turbulent, or ripe for revolution."[13]

Perhaps these few excerpts from America's Christian history will encourage parents not only to teach their children how to grow spiritually and think Biblically, but to first teach them at home *why* and *how to think governmentally.* (See *Guide,* p. 20)

Church and state must indeed be separated in their God-given functions—the state and national government should be "the minister of God" to bear the "sword" of the law, (Rom. 13:3-4) and the church should "go . . . teach all nations . . . whatsoever I have commanded you." (Matt. 28:19-20). However, if the seed of the church and the state are in the home – the God-consciousness of the parents – then the Christian home is the one place where church and state should *not* be separated. The Christian idea of the church and the state should be united in the home because that is where the Biblical principles governing all three divine institutions should be taught and practiced.

II
APPLYING THE PRINCIPLE APPROACH AT HOME

This section of the *Guide* is intended to help parents use the Principle Approach to make their home the first place where the character of America's Christian history and government is cultivated and remembered.

As we have explained in the *Rudiments* section, beginning on page 3, the Principle Approach refers primarily to the *Seven fundamental principles derived from God's Word"* which are "*amplified and expanded through the text,* Christian History. *They become standards of reference for understanding both the founding of this nation and its maintenance as a Christian Republic.*"[14]

7. Rev. S. Phillips, *T/L,* p. 4.

8. Ibid, *T/L,* p. 5.

9. Ibid, *T/L,* p. 6.

10. Ibid, *T/L,* p. 5.

11. Lawrence Cremin, *American Education, The Colonial Experience 1607-1783,* pp. 52, 113.

12. Elias Boudinot, *C/P,* p, xxxii.

13. Lydia H. Sigourney, *CHOC,* P. 410.

14. Rosalie J. Slater, *T/L,* p. xxii.

THE SEVEN PRINCIPLES
ILLUSTRATED IN THE HOME

Every parent should be aware that the seven principles of America's Christian *history and government* are the essentials of an American Christian philosophy of *education* and just as important for parents as for teachers. Furthermore, these seven principles, if carefully considered or "4 R'd," will help you "train up a child in the way he should go" and enable him to make a godly difference in his community and nation. Now let us consider how these principles apply to the total training of your children.

GOD'S PRINCIPLE OF INDIVIDUALITY

This principle confirms that God's infinite individuality (the idea of ONE GOD manifesting Himself in the infinite diversity and individuality of His creation) is reflected in individual talents, gifts, skills and ministries. It also affirms that God has a special, unique purpose, form and place for each individual.

If a child's specific talents and purpose are not immediately apparent, the parent and child can observe what productive activities the child finds most interesting, what he does best—and then pray for God's guidance in identifying and developing the child's gifts. If it seems that one child is less confident or less talented, or compares himself unfavorably with others, you can affirm to yourself and your child that God bestows His gifts upon everyone, then deliberately magnify and cultivate whatever special abilities may appear.

God's Principle of Individuality or Identity challenges the idea of conformity in response to group or peer pressure, coercion or force. It challenges the tendency toward over-specialization, the limitation of individual interests and abilities, and confining oneself into narrow, self-inflicted boundaries—whether intellectual, physical or spiritual.

THE CHRISTIAN PRINCIPLE OF SELF-GOVERNMENT

Noah Webster explained that "self is sometimes used as a noun, noting the individual subject to his own contemplation or action, or noting identity of person. *Consciousness makes every one to be what he calls self.*" As Pope wrote, "A man's self may be the worst fellow to converse with in the world." Although self-government denotes control of or *by* oneself, the Supreme Original or Biblical Principle of Christian self-government was declared by the Lord Jesus Christ in *John 5:30:*

"I can of my own self do nothing; as I hear, I judge: and my judgement is just; because I seek not mine own will, but the will of the Father which hath sent me."

How can we demonstrate proper self-government and train up our children in the government of God through Christ? How can we plan, do and judge by "the will of the Father which hath sent me" and raise up a generation with the same capacity that many of the Founding Fathers manifested to effect and maintain a Christian Republic? The spiritual and practical application of this one principle is surely most important.

Christian self-government in the home does not mean surrendering authority to our children. It does involve *delegating* authority to a child to accomplish a *well defined* task or assignment and expecting a response-ability for the trust or confidence given. Daily opportunities to "be faithful over a few things" and to voluntarily accept authority with responsibility, liberty with law (clearly stated demands or rules of conduct) is necessary to enable a child to become "ruler over many things." (Matt. 25:21)

Miss Rosalie Slater has pointed out that "Fortunately, God has provided parents, adults, teachers to help boys and girls learn how to make decisions which are responsible. There may be mistakes, but if the lesson is pointed out, then Christian self-government has been strengthened. It is always easier and more efficient to do tasks which would provide practice for our youngsters— so, think about your own surrender of "job opportunities" at home which might provide teaching and learning experiences for your own family. Charity begins at home and so does the "job corps."[15]

Growing children frequently ask for more freedom to do as they please, assuring their parents that "you can trust me," and in frustration petulantly kick against the parental law that binds their will. When will a child be free of external laws legislated and executed by their parents? As Christians we know that reason separate from God's Revelation is a "miserable guide," but we also know the God-given reason applied by faith to His Revelation, the Bible, is what the Lord requires of us. With this in mind, consider philosopher John Locke's answer to the hypothetical question "When shall I be free from the laws of my parents?"

"What makes him Free of that Law? What gave him a free disposing of his Property, according to his own Will, within the compass of that Law? I answer; a State of Maturity wherein he might be supposed capable to know that Law, that so he might keep his Actions within the Bounds of it. When he has acquired that State, he is presumed to know how far that Law is to be his Guide, and how far he may make use of his Freedom, and so comes to have it; 'till then, somebody else must guide him, who is presumed to know, how far the Law allows a Liberty. If such a State of Reason, such an Age of Discretion made him Free, the same shall make his Son Free too.

"The Freedom then of Man, and Liberty of acting according to his own Will, is grounded on his giving Reason, which is able to instruct him in that Law he is to govern himself by, and make him know how far he is left to the Freedom of his own Will. To turn him loose to an unrestrain'd Liberty, before he has Reason to guide him, is not allowing him the privilege of his Nature to be Free; but to thrust him out amongst the Brutes, and abandon him to a State as wretched, and as much beneath that of a Man, as theirs. This is that which puts the Authority into the Parents hands to govern the Minority of their Children. God hath made it their business to employ this Care on their Off-Spring, and hath placed in them suitable Inclinations of Tenderness, and concern to temper this Power, to apply it, as His Wisdom designed it, to the Children's good, as long as they should need to be under it."[16]

AMERICA'S HERITAGE OF CHRISTIAN CHARACTER

As Rosalie J. Slater has written:

"America's real gold is the gold of Christian Character and we need to restore our capital. You as parents make the most significant contribution to your children's bank account of character. If they learn character through you 'as living epistles' of Christ because of what is written in your hearts and is "known and read of all men," this is their finest teaching. It will have more impact upon them than words—then 'precept upon precept' will have the weight of gold."[17]

The one quality that should distinguish American Christian character above other attributes is *faith*, "the faith of our fathers," the unseen, causative quality that "cometh by hearing . . . the Word

---

15. Rosalie J. Slater, *A Family Program*, F.A.C.E. Monograph.

16. John Locke, "Of Civil Government," *CHOC*, p. 72, para. 59; 73:63.

17. Rosalie J. Slater, *Family Program*.

of God" (Rom. 10:17); the quality of heart and mind which is the inward "substance" and produces the outward "evidence" of the very mark or character of Christ.(Heb. 1:3) For in God's Providence, parents must still raise up a generation "who through *faith* subdue kingdoms" and "turn to flight the armies of the aliens," (Heb. 11:33, 34) or who may again have to endure the "trial of cruel mockings and scourgings, yea, moreover of bonds and imprisonment," and still obtain "a good report through *faith*" at the cost of their mortal life. (Heb. 11:36, 39)

One of the primary functions of home education is to "form the manners and habits of youth." For example, the following qualities can be taught at home first, then confirmed at church or school: the character to start or finish on time a task *before* a parent asks; to read or heed instructions and deduce conclusions justly *without supervision*; or to voluntarily seek God's or another's forgiveness for offences given *without* prior reproof. Note that to develop character takes more than teaching, it takes *training* which involves continued observation and discipline of the child's conduct until the child shows the character and results of following a transformed way of life.[18]

CONSCIENCE IS THE MOST SACRED OF ALL PROPERTY

In every home, children are surrounded with "things," objects of some value that belong to others or to themselves. Conscientious parents often talk to their children and discipline them to respect those unseen fences around the physical possessions parents want left in place, unbroken or kept clean. As necessary as this kind of training is, especially in infancy, it should become secondary to parental instruction in the Biblical principle that property is first internal, then external.

"We learn from our Founding Fathers that property begins with individual responsibility and individual productivity. This means 'stewardship' first and 'ownership' second. It also means that one values one's Christian conviction and conscience above all external possessions—even life itself. This understanding of property goes back to first century Christianity when men were willing to be put to death rather than surrender their property of Christian commitment and conscience."[19]

Notice that stewardship of property is primary and ownership is secondary. This is deduced from the principle that God owns everything that was made by Him, including man. (See *Guide* p. 100) When God made the "earth, the sea, and all that therein is" (Psa. 146:6) and told man to "subdue it" and "have dominion" over it, (Gen. 1:28) man became a manager responsible for using and keeping what belongs to God Who sovereignly retained *title* or absolute right of possession. Man's stewardship of God's Property precedes his ownership and title to private property in relation to other men. (See *Guide* p. 47)

The task of educating children to understand that their Christian convictions and conscience (internal property) are to be valued and protected above their external possessions begins with the first words, songs, or sermons concerning the unseen Spirit or God who made all things. It is sustained when a child's thoughts, feelings, imagination and sentiments are identified and both rooted and refined in Biblical truth. As a child witnesses the convictions and values of parents, and reads about individuals in history and literature that felt so deeply about a cause that they sacrificed their person or possessions to keep "a conscience void of offense toward God and man," (Acts 24:16) he will then behold those models in thought by which to govern his own life.

THE CHRISTIAN FORM OF OUR GOVERNMENT

This principle suggests more for the home than the clear Biblical teaching concerning the "chain of command" where the father is the head of the wife and the children are in subjection to the parents. It also means that a chief end of Christian home government is to raise up self-governing children who require little or no external legal restrictions by the state or nation other than what is necessary to protect the lawful and restrain the lawless.

Consider the importance of individuals exercising the following three principles that constitute the framework and structure of Christian home-government and influence the way the state and nation finally will be governed.

THE DUAL FORM OF GOVERNMENT—THE FEDERAL PRINCIPLE: Christianity's form of government is Christian self-government. The Christian principle of self-government is manifested as geographically local self-governing homes, churches, non-profit agencies, businesses, and civil governments which respectively care for the *immediate welfare* of individuals. The Biblical law of Christian self-government and local civil government

---

18. See Richard Fugate, *What the Bible Says About Child Training*, pp. 63-69.

19. Rosalie Slater, *A Family Program*.

93

reserves local sovereignty under God to the individual home and local church under the protection of the magistrate. Hence a self-governing people within each state constitute one of two sovereign spheres of civil government—the other being all the American people in all the states under their national government.

Under our unique system of American federalism, local spheres of government properly limit and balance the specific, limited powers delegated or ceded to the national government by the Constitution. In America, the delicate balance between these two sovereign spheres of power is secured by the capacity of the people to practice local self-government with voluntary union beginning in their homes, then churches and states under God's Law, the Principle of all righteous government.

Dual levels of government are found in the home. Christ's two great commandments (Matt. 22:36-40) are implemented when one man and one woman covenant together with God to establish a Christian home. (See *Guide* p. 58) A federal relationship exists between man and wife and their federal head, Jesus Christ. As God blesses with children, the levels of government are expanded to include relationships between brothers and sisters and their parents under God and His Law.

Hence, the principle of federal (horizontal) and national (vertical) governmental relationships are implicit in the family. And although the flow of power in the Christian home is from God's Word indwelling parents who then minister God's Law and Love to and between the children, it is intended that God's will be done on all levels of government—child to child, child to parent, parent to parent, parent to God to the end that the children too are regenerated and learn to walk independently with their God by His Word.

THE LEGISLATIVE, EXECUTIVE AND JUDICIAL FUNCTIONS OF GOVERNMENT: As individuals made in God's image and likeness, we exercise these three functions of government moment by moment in our daily lives. For example, we "legislate" when we "make and enact a law or laws" or *plan* an action or *determine how* or by what means or manner to carry out an action.

When one plans to arise in the morning and plan a meal, make appointments, submit an agenda, prepare a lesson, outline a speech, or decide on the route home, one is legislating or enacting a plan or rule by which one will be governed. Father may be considering whether to mow the lawn or take a nap. Mother may be wondering whether to try out a new recipe or ask father to take the family out instead. A child about to take a spelling test may be deciding whether to exercise the principles of phonics or just guess at the word.

The *legislature* of our lives—that which most influences us—could be the words and actions of the television dramas and cartoons, or, by the grace of God, a godly *conscience* and heart that rejoices with the Psalmist that "in the volume of the book it is written of me, I delight to do thy will, O my God; yea, *thy law is within my heart.*" (Psa. 40:7-8)

When we *execute* our plans, we carry out our decisions, revealing whether one is "exercising a conscience void of offense toward God and toward man" or is moved to do what feels good or expedient at the time. Will we be found the kind of executives (whether parents or business men) that cry "the good that I would, I *do not*" (Rom. 7:19) or "I *can do* all things through Christ which strengtheneth me." (Phil. 4:13)

Judicial review was a function of Christian self-government before it was ever assumed by the Supreme Court. *How* you carry out any action, the *propriety* of the deed, can be reviewed in your judicial function. Was the discipline administered in anger and haste, or was it ministered with the spirit of God's Law and Love? Did the finest of labor and materials go into the project or was the workmanship indifferent, the timbers or fabric used inferior? What kind of letter was it? Was the tone Christian or did it testify of intemperance and ignorance of the truth?

The Scriptures urge that we take our judicial function most seriously: "Examine yourselves, whether ye be in the faith; prove your own selves" (II Cor. 13:5); "Judge not according to the appearance, but judge righteous judgment," (John 7:24) "for we shall all stand before the judgment seat of Christ." (Rom. 14:10)

"Whatever the action, it was governed in some way by how it was carried out—the legislative, executive and judicial functions. If the action is thought of as a mirror of Christian self-government, Christian character and Christian property, then one begins to see how much or how little of God's government was evident in our individual lives. Multiply and extend this and you have a picture of the nation. The Christian's Constitution begins with his Bible, and if he consults this book he will fulfill all obligations in a manner pleasing to the Lord; he will also make the American Christian Constitution work as it was originally intended by our Founding Fathers."[20]

THE PRINCIPLE OF REPRESENTATION: If the goal of the American Christian home in a *Republic*

---

20. *Ibid.*

94

is to develop America's Christian character, consider what the principle of representation can mean to your home.

Miss Slater points out in *Teaching and Learning*, p. 322, that "the government of a nation rests upon the qualities of character which represent us . . ." The principle of representation is as practical for the home as it is for the nation. Home government, like that of the nation, rests upon the qualities of character represented by the decisions and actions of the parents. The quality of parental leadership, listening and loving will either represent the character—the express image—of Christ or something else.

Is there a contradiction in the principles behind American civil government and Christian home government? No. Admittedly, representatives in our civil government are chosen democratically, by the voice of the people – and parents are not. But both the elected officials and parents are intended to be representatives – ambassadors for Christ.

It is the Christian view that both public officials and parents exercise delegated power, and are limited and directed by God's constitution as expressed in the Bible. If the parents adequately represent Christ in the home, then the children will grow up with the kind of character and conscience needed for them to elect, as adult citizens, their own righteous representatives in their civil government.

Home-government "implies a reciprocity of right—the right of the parent to govern and the right of the child to be governed."[21] This supreme "right" to rule is limited however, and parents must prayerfully train their children to *voluntarily consent* to Christ's "law of liberty" or risk developing an involuntary and mechanical obedience to the letter of the law.

"Parents are magistrates under God, and, as His stewards, cannot abdicate their authority, nor delegate it to another. Neither can they be tyrants in the exercise of it. God has given to them the principles of home-legislation, the standard of judicial authority, and the rules of their executive power. God gives the law. The parent is only deputy governor,—steward, 'bound to be faithful.' Hence the obligation of the child to obey the steward is as great as that to obey the Master..."[22]

HOW THE SEED OF LOCAL SELF-GOVERNMENT IS PLANTED

The epitome of local self-government, the most typical representative of its principle and idea, is the home. The Christian home, particularly, should be most representative of how authority and responsibility, independent of any other outside power, provides and pays for the individual's daily needs and wants.

To establish local self-governing homes, then churches and communities, the seed, or principle of Christian self-government must be taught and practiced daily in the smallest spheres of *individual* activity.(See *Guide*, p. 62)

This principle emphasizes the importance of the individual—the *one* among many separate links on the Chain of Christianity. Parents may illustrate this fact by demonstrating and teaching that salvation, service and accountability are always individual. Each child can be given a vision of his importance to God and to the welfare of his home, church, state and nation.

"Our people are busy using their liberties and energies, each for his individual benefit, as is quite right and proper; since the welfare of individuals makes the prosperity of the community."[23]

Children may be included when the family prays for local authorities as well as state and national representatives. Youth should be involved in discussions which seek to resolve current issues according to the governing principle and its effect on the home and community. As mother and father explain their political decisions and involvement, their children will observe how individuals can keep the power to protect and pay for the cost of government at the local level of the town, county or state.

"There is a phrase today 'corporate socialism' which means that no one person takes either the responsibility or the blame in a group situation. Thus, often, it is difficult to discover and correct errors. In our American Christian Republic, each link counts and is identified, and we are no stronger than the weakest link. It is interesting to note that strong links cannot keep a weak link from breaking—another lesson in true Christian individuality."[24]

THE CHRISTIAN PRINCIPLE OF AMERICAN POLITICAL UNION

Mothers and fathers will readily appreciate the need of unity with diversity in even the smallest families. How can parents cultivate the individual tastes, gifts and talents of their children over the years and still maintain a unity of affection, concern and effort? The prevailing trend is too much

21. Philips, *T/L*, p. 23.
22. *Ibid.*, p. 24.

23. Charles Bancroft, *T/L*, p. 6.
24. Rosalie Slater, *A Family Program*.

mere human individualism and not enough voluntary union. Can we hope to establish homes that express an enduring and harmonious union despite differences of interests and needs?

A spirit of sustained union, cooperation and Christian care within a family is effected as each individual voluntarily consents to the law and love of *one God* and the Lord Jesus Christ. To achieve this spirit, parents should lead their children in love of a common faith, and a Biblical intelligence that reflects upon "sound doctrine." If, over the years, our youth are provided clearly defined American Christian standards of reference that apply to every situation, then Christian self-government is built in to the individual—and it is built around God's unchanging Word.

Tyranny in home, church and civil government characterizes much of history. However, voluntary Christian unity can defeat Satan's attempts to coerce and enslave. The effect of such unity is seen at various times in American history. The most dramatic expression came in 1775 when three million colonists refused to be divided and subdued by Britain. (See *Teaching and Learning*, pp. 262-265) Despite differences in religion, language, education, wealth, and national background, the colonists were Providentially united by their common Christian commitment, and more united in fundamental principles of government than they were divided by the distinctions of particular issues. We can learn a lesson for our homes and nation from the consequences of their enlightened spirit of Christian love and support when Boston was being economically strangled.

Miss Rosalie Slater suggests how an education in unchanging Biblical principles of government can preserve family unity when teenagers begin to assert their independence:

"Parents are often concerned because there comes a time during the 'teens' when it would seem that individuals in their home have literally declared a Declaration of Independence from the family. Many efforts are made to *compel* a unity within the family and often without success, and often with greater separation. It is suggested that these times which do indeed try the soul of a fam-

ily be preceded by many years of laying a foundation of principles, convictions and ideals, so that despite *external* evidences to the contrary, ultimately this *internal* bond will be asserted by the young people. (Prov. 22:6)

"We all recognize that the period of 'trying one's own wings' of 'cutting loose from the apron strings' will come and it is important that the *constitution* of every home permit a proper amount of such independence. Properly supported and directed this can be an educational experience for all concerned.

"Unfortunately today the emphasis is upon *negative* teaching in the home, thus lending fuel to rebellion. The entire program of family devotion to teaching and learning America's Christian History and form of government is to encourage families to teach with a *positive* emphasis upon which is right, true and changeless . . .

"Take the time to build clearly defined foundations—Christian principles which changelessly turn to the compass-point regardless of which direction the individual faces. This will demand of you the vision which keeps you making the sacrifice of time and more time, to think through the lessons which you would teach and the principles which you would define and redefine by many examples and illustrations.

"If you, dear parents, will do your work painstakingly well, your reward will indeed be in evidence. While your offspring may challenge the world, they will *not challenge* you, and you too will experience that wonderful unity of the spirit which the patriots of Boston felt when supported by their sister colonies. 'Stand fast therefore in the liberty wherewith Christ hath made us free, and be not entangled again with the yoke of bondage.'" Galatians 5:1.[25]

As you and your children grow in your capacity to explain the seven principles, and how they have been manifested in our government, you should be inspired with the hope that Christ will continue to bless your faith and your God-given ability to keep His Word internally. You should see increasing outward signs of His Grace and Providence in the life of your family and your community.

25. *Ibid.*

A PERSONAL APPLICATION
OF THIS APPROACH
IN TRAINING CHILDREN

Just how do American Christians go about the challenging but rewarding task of applying the Principle Approach in raising and educating their children from the time of their birth? This is a question that parents constantly ask; and of course, there is no one specific, detailed answer that applies in every case. God's Principle of Individuality insists that every parent seeking to apply the Principle Approach will have a different experience, even though all worship the same God, study the same Bible, are seeking to apply essentially the same Biblical principles, and want to relate them to the same country—as well as to the lives of their children.

Perhaps the best way to be specific in answering the question, "How do you apply the Principle Approach in training a child in the first seven years of his life?" is to cite a particular case history, and the one I know best is my own—the experience my wife and I have had with our four children, Jason, Matthew, Deborah and Lydia—"the children which God hath graciously given [his] servant." (Gen. 33:5) Fortunately my wife, Barbara, has been a serious student of America's Christian history and Biblical principles for years. She had joined with me in this study long before our first

child was born, and vividly remembers how we sought to put these Scriptural truths to work.

As we recall our own experiences in training our children, our hearts' desire is simply to share the fruit of what we have considered and pondered in putting America's Christian principles to work in our own home, fully realizing that we frequently fall far short of the Christian ideal—in our attitudes, our conduct and our relationships. The Roses are not a model family; but we do have a perfect model, a Biblical standard, an underlying set of Biblical principles to guide us, and which we seek to demonstrate as stewards of God's "heritage." (Psa. 127:3-5)

It may even seem, as we narrate various positive incidents, that we felt we achieved perfection. Such is not the case. We suffer conflicts within and without. Such trials of our own and the children's character constantly confirm God's faithfulness to forgive and to renew our strength and resolve. A parent's only sure hope of success is God's promise that if a child is trained in Truth, "he will not depart from it." (Prov. 22:6)

Here is how Barbara recalls our experience as parents:

A MOTHER'S RECOLLECTIONS

From the time I knew I was pregnant with our first child, Jim and I wanted to hold in thought the qualities of Christian character that we prayed would distinguish this child. We started making a notebook, based on the Bible and the Principle Approach, of the positive Christ-like character qualities that a child could have. We called it "Rosebud's Book of Character." We would write down positive character qualities alphabetically as we researched them, such as able, courageous, honest, humble, loving, industrious—everything from alert to zealous; and for each attribute we would try to write down definitions (from Webster's 1828 American Dictionary) as well as synonyms and Biblical examples and references where these qualities were expressed.

We believed that the state of mind or mental conception of the parents, and especially of the mother, during pregnancy, exerted an influence on the baby growing in the womb, and we knew that God wanted that influence to be positive. We wanted to be obedient to Paul's instruction to the Philippians, "Finally, brethren, whatsoever things are true, whatsoever things are honest, whatsoever things are just, whatsoever things are pure, whatsoever things are lovely, whatsoever things are of good report; if there be any virtue, and if there be any praise, think on these things." *Philippians 4:8*

NO ACCIDENTS

We held in our thoughts and our prayers the conviction that God had created our child, that it was not an accident, that it was ordained by God, that the Lord was the child's source and origin.

"I will praise thee; for I am fearfully and wonderfully made: marvellous are *thy works*; and that my soul knoweth right well. My substance was not hid from thee, when I was made in secret, and curiously wrought in the lowest parts of the earth. Thine eyes did see my substance, yet being unperfect; and in thy book all my members were written, which in continuance were fashioned, when as yet there was none of them." (Psa. 139:14-16) Jim and I believed that this Scripture spoke to us, and to all Christian couples expecting a child, and that it was our assurance that we had nothing to fear, that the child God creates is "wonderfully made" with *all* his members. There are no accidents in His plan and story of each child.

Jim and I hoped and prayed for *ten years* to have our first child, and we were confident that God was answering our prayers just as He had answered Hannah's prayer thousands of years ago,

and that our child would be whole and complete, just as Hannah's child Samuel was. This proved to be the case, and spreading the news of Jason's birth, we had inscribed on the announcement card the words of *I Samuel 1:27-28*, "For this child I prayed; and the Lord hath given me my petition which I asked of him: Therefore also I have lent him to the Lord; as long as he liveth he shall be lent to the Lord . . ."

4 R-ING THE BABY

To use the language of the Principle Approach, one could say, of my husband and myself, that "we were 4 R-ing the baby in the womb." That is, we were *researching* God's Word to identify principles and qualities that were pertinent to our unborn child; *reasoning* from these principles and attributes, and *relating* them to this child's mind and body, health and character; then *recording* or writing down what we had researched, thought and prayed about. This 4 R-ing process continued before the birth of each child.

AMERICAN CHRISTIAN NAMES

In choosing our first child's name, as in choosing the names of the other three children, we sought names with positive meanings from both a Biblical and American perspective. We called our first-born Jason Bradford Rose. We called him Jason because we thought it was a unique name, a Biblical name that means "healing" in the Greek, and that is what he was to us—a healing of a decade of childlessness. His middle name is Bradford, after the splendid Christian leader of the original Plymouth colony, governor William Bradford. We have used his name as an instrument to teach him Christian History. Jason has Bradford memorabilia and his own copy of Bradford's *History of Plymouth Plantation*. Many of his birthday parties have centered around a Pilgrim theme or have been an excursion to some historical site or exhibit.

The second boy was named Matthew, which means "gift of God," after Matthew, the Apostle, and James for both his Dad and James Madison, the "Father of the Constitution." The first girl was Deborah Jean. Deborah was the Bible's "patriotic woman" and we hope she will be one of America's, too. Jean was for both her Mother and grandmother. The last girl was Lydia Joy, representative of Paul's first convert in Europe—Lydia, the seller of purple—and of Lydia Sigourney, 19th century American Christian author and educator. The Joy was for Mom's spiritual victory during a difficult pregnancy and for the happiness our new "bundle of joy" brought to the family.

APPROACH TO DISCIPLINE

Jim and I sought to express a balanced, principled sense of love and authority. We cradled and caressed the children but we also set a standard of discipline which is needed for the development of character and a capacity for self-government. We were helped by the excellent book, "My First 300 Babies, and How They Grew" by Gladys Hendricks, and were impressed by such statements as "It's not what the baby does, for at times he would seem unpredictable—it's what *you* do about it that counts." We found this sentiment—and much more—in agreement with our own philosophy of education that the parent, expressing the government of God through Christ, must be in control, and not the child.

Certainly this applies, first of all, to feeding, which we did on schedule, every three or four hours. As we saw it, it's not what the child demands, it is what you decide is right. The point was, if a child cried and it was wake time and he did not need to be fed or changed but went on crying, instead of indulging him, we put him in his bed and let him resolve the matter for himself. Furthermore, every child should have certain wake times during the day when he is alone on his own, to work out his own problems or explore his surroundings, rather than constantly being "indulged."

EXPRESSING LOVE AND LAW

Discipline should begin at the cradle. It includes giving the child firm commands. If wanton crying—"Hush!," or as Susanna Wesley told her children *"Cry softly!"* It involves the inner attitude that recognizes your God-given authority, and the need to manifest that authority in the look on your face, the tone of your voice, the consistency of your conduct—and never threatening correction or punishment without implementing it.

Discipline also means a firm, consistent schedule—for nap time, meal time, bed-time, wake-up time. The fact that *you* have done the scheduling means that you're in control.

We started this view of Christian discipline, expressing the love of a tender-hearted but principled heavenly Father, from the cradle, and it has paid off, not only for Jason but for the other three children that followed. All were usually disposed to do things on their own, to go to their rooms, to be happy looking at their books or playing with their toys, without constantly being dependent on their parents to amuse them.

The Principle Approach to discipline will be further amplified under "Liberty With Law." p.104

"GOD MADE ME SPECIAL"

The children learned early how God made them special, like no other person. They were created by God for His good pleasure and for His plan and purpose. Each memorized Miss Slater's poem in *Teaching and Learning*, p. 155:

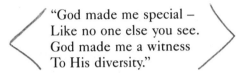

"God made me special –
Like no one else you see.
God made me a witness
To His diversity."

Another way we taught God's Principle of Individuality was to have the children make their hand prints in dough-art and hang them up on the kitchen wall by age. We also inked their feet and had each make a footprint, with their names underneath. As the Scriptures say, "Thou settest a print upon the heels of my feet." (Job 13:27)

Audio tapes were made of some of the children's first efforts to speak, just to identify their own way of self-expression. And even though we have limited skills as artists, we were able to make good silhouettes of each child's profile by shining a light on one side of his or her face, drawing an outline on a piece of white paper taped on the wall, then placing it over a piece of colored paper and cutting out the final silhouette.

Certainly such silhouettes vividly demonstrate that each child is a separate and distinct individual. God's Principle of Individuality teaches that our heavenly Father made each one special and unique, and we emphasized that they were special as members of the Rose family, just as other children are unique as members of their families.

In our case, we traced the Rose family-tree as far back as we could, to Mayflower and Revolutionary ancestors on their mother's side, and to German, Scottish and even American Indian ancestors in their father's family. (Tracing genealogy is even more instructive if you can teach something about your forebears, such as their positive character traits, contribution to American liberty, or how God worked in their lives.)

• Your children are special as individuals, as members of your family, as Christians, and as American Christians; so you teach them their individual history, including their family history, then their Christian History and their American Christian history. Each is a link on the Chain of Christianity moving westward and can learn to appreciate how important he is to His Story of Christian and civil liberty. (See *Curriculum* Section, History, p. 201)

"What doth the Lord thy God require of thee, but to fear the Lord thy God, to walk in all his ways, and to love him, and to serve the Lord, thy God with all thy heart and with all thy soul." (Deut. 10:12) We fear God in the right way, we revere and we obey Him, not only by serving Him and loving others but by respecting our own God-created individuality, and the God-created individuality of our children. To the extent we do that, we are unlikely to experience what psychologists call an "identity crisis."

GOD'S INFINITE DIVERSITY

God's Principle of Individuality is also demonstrated in the rest of His beautiful and infinite creation. The children have enjoyed leaf, rock, shell, insect, flower and seed pod collections showing the uniqueness of each item. They are learning to observe detail and diversity in color, texture, form and outline. To the small child, God's universe is full of wonder. Parents can help children to discover the marvelous things God has created for all of us to enjoy.

GOD'S PROPERTY

In teaching the children the concept of property, we began with the idea that since God created them, they are His property. We taught them Miss Slater's poem (*T/L*, p. 230):

I Am God's Property

"God made me for His purpose
He fashioned me to be
An image for His glory,
Almighty Father He."

A child's thoughts, hands, feet, eyes, tongue – all need to glorify God— "... for ye are bought with a price, therefore glorify God in your body, and in your spirit, which are God's." (I Cor. 6:20)

The marvelous hymn "Take My Life and Let It Be Consecrated, Lord to Thee" was a teaching tool for all our children to learn that their members are "always, only, for my King." (See *Teaching and Learning*, p. 230)

We often reasoned with the children about controlling the use of their hands, where their feet walk, how they talk, what their ears hear, and what thoughts they think.

"CONSCIENCE IS THE MOST SACRED OF ALL PROPERTY"

As boys and girls learn to be self-governing in response to Bible truths and the Holy Spirit's control of their will, thoughts, and emotions, they realize that in their conscience they have the property of consent. To what do they voluntarily, willfully, yield themselves? Do they choose to accept what their peers think is right, or what they know is right or wrong because they conscientiously reflect upon God's Word and what their parents tell them?

Often Jason and Matthew visit in friends' homes. There have been occasions when the music on the friend's radio or the program on their TV is not acceptable by our standards. The boys know this and in good conscience have endeavored to divert attention from such entertainment. There have been times when they haven't and have been challenged to have a conscience void of offense toward God, their parents and their friends.

DISCIPLINE OF PRIVATE PROPERTY

Discipline is particularly necessary in teaching the small child God's principle of private property. As soon as the child begins to walk, can pull himself up and reach for things, you can start building the concept of property and learning respect for the just claims of others.

When our children would reach for something that was not theirs, Jim or I would say, "No!," give a little slap on the hand, and add, "No, it's not yours, it belongs to so-and-so!" In this way, pointing out who owns the thing, and thus is entitled to control its use, you are teaching the positive meaning of property, not just the discipline of "No!"

Our job as American Christian parents is to help each of our children take charge of his possessions: they're still in control even when they invite others to share them. It's a case of voluntary consent. The owner is making the invitation, and learning wisdom and love in responding to requests, learning when to say Yes, and when to say No. By the same token, the other child, the non-owner, is learning when he *can* and when he *can't* use other people's property; he is learning self-denial, self-discipline, and the spirit of cooperation.

Our oldest daughter, Deborah, had a tea set. Sometimes her little sister, Lydia, would grab the dishes and say, "Mine!" I not only would explain to Lydia that the tea set belonged to Debbie, but urged Debbie to have a tea party, invite Lydia to come, and share her tea service with her.

Any toy of the children that another breaks must be replaced out of respect for the property of others. Restoring another's damaged or destroyed property from their own money confirms just how valuable one's time and labor are. In the grocery store, children must not pick things off the shelves or floor. They may assure the parent that it is all right, but we say, "No, it's not ours, it belongs to the store; please put it back!" (Once more, the principle of property.)

If a group of children play together, sharing with one another in an orderly way their personal property, this is a microcosm of a society built on voluntary union.

PRINCIPLES OF PROSPERITY

We wanted to develop in our children those principles of Christian economics that lead to prosperity, both for individuals and nations—principles that produce a greater capacity for self-government, respect for property, and the character of independence, self-sufficiency and initiative. We asked the Lord for a "cottage industry," an idea that would help our two eldest children (our sons) develop the capacity for business responsibility, to be conscientious and reliable in serving their neighbors, and to learn some principles of free enterprise economics.

We knew it would be desirable for our boys to learn to use simple tools, to offer a desired service at a price their customers could afford, to keep financial records, to tithe and save from their income, become good stewards, and to be responsible for what they earn. We wanted Jason and Matthew not only to learn how to make money but how to save it, how to spend it, and why and how to tithe.

PRODUCTION FOR PROFIT

We looked around our neighborhood and saw an unmet need which we felt our boys could meet—which suggests a basic principle for launching any new enterprise. The local garbage truck came around once a week in the morning, and most of the unsightly garbage cans were standing around all day, until the neighbors, returning from work in the evening, could bring them in.

It seemed to us that here was an opportunity for Jason (then age six) and Matthew (nearly five) to provide a service and learn some Biblical principles of economics. We typed some business cards for J & M Enterprises, offering a "Neighborhood Beautification Service." The boys went up and down the block (as far as we would allow them to go), and offered, for just five cents a can, to put their neighbor's empty cans back in their proper place on garbage collection day. The service included cleaning up anything that had spilled, making sure the cans were returned with their lids on, and making the collections just twice a month.

Our eldest, Jason, was the "boss," and in effect employed Matthew, at a wage of five cents a house (at first)—paying him from the collections and keeping the rest. These two young lads have been engaged in this business for over a year, and it has been well received. They earn good "profits" because usually they are paid more than they charge, receiving tips of ten to twenty-five cents on the grounds that they are so "cute" and diligent.

After each collection day, the oldest boy has to record in a journal what they earned from each house, which varies according to the number of cans and the size of the tip. He posts his receipts, totals what is owed, and writes out invoices every two weeks. Jason, as the senior entrepreneur and employer had to learn how to pay his "help" (employee) first, how to calculate ten percent of his income to tithe, save another ten percent for his future needs, and live off the rest, spending to satisfy his immediate needs and wants as a customer.

At first, but just for a few weeks, we supervised the boys; since then they've been on their own. Thus they are learning self-government as well as the importance of individual labor and basic free enterprise and business principles.

For some months, while she was still three, our daughter, Deborah, watched her brothers in their "beautification" business, and wanted to be a part of it. Just before she turned four, Debbie substituted for one brother. Her first day out she earned 30 cents and Matthew considerably more. Now she wants to go "full-time"!

SOWING BEFORE REAPING

Are we producing more than we consume? Economic educators, including many college professors with a Ph.D. in economics, are convinced that the one basic lesson most important for Americans to learn—and which they should begin to learn at an early age—is that we cannot continue to consume more than we produce, without suffering the consequences. (This, of course, is the attempt to "reap" more than the American people have "sown," which has produced the enormous deficits that give rise to more inflation, higher taxes and

and unusually high interest rates.)

Because the deficit-producing character pattern is so ingrained in the people, it is important that Christian parents and Christian educators encourage the development of the opposite character trait—a highly *productive* nature that knows how to restrain its consumption of what *others* have produced.

INVENTION AND CONSTRUCTION

Most children today are excessively dependent upon television, video games, amusement parks, and other non-productive and non-reflective activities for their entertainment. They are also too dependent upon purchased toys of all sorts for their recreation.

God gives to children the ability to create their own entertainment which also develops their initiative and imagination. Thus it is good for Christian parents and educators to encourage youngsters to invent more recreational activities, more games, toys and devices, and to be less dependent on what has been professionally produced by others. This we must do in order to teach young people to become good stewards of their time and talents, and to become more producer-oriented and less consumer-oriented.

This constructive approach should have diverse manifestations. We should help our children build their *structure of knowledge* in informal ways, above and beyond their regular schoolwork, by such means as memorizing more Scriptures and more poems. We should read more books to our children, and then encourage the older one to read to the younger, to develop their love of literature, their reading talents, and to enlarge their bank of ideas and their storehouse of wholesome sentiments. We should encourage children to make up and present little skits and shows.

We should make more toys for our children, and then guide them in making their own toys and simple gifts for others. Youngsters love to see Dad construct things with a saw, hammer, and nails. In raising our two boys, Jim would give them scraps of wood, cardboard and empty containers, show them how to use the basic cutting and pounding tools, and then how to use their own imaginations and create their own toys. If a new appliance arrived in a big shipping carton, we would encourage Jason and Matthew to make something out of it—a house, an airplane or whatever. Without minimizing the father's role, other men in the family,—a grandfather, uncle, or friend—can also work with boys in this way. So can neighbors who have a leaning toward carpentry or other skills. We

knew a man who had a good array of machine tools, and taught his sons how to use them. When they grew up, they were excellent at home repairs and the various facets of engineering.

LOCAL SELF-GOVERNMENT

As a child is properly self-governed, he can contribute to a righteously governed home, neighborhood, community, state and nation. How does a parent teach a child to participate in, to constructively influence, these expanding spheres of government? There are many ways. In conducting their Neighborhood Beautification Program, our sons were contributing to the well-being of their street, and thus reaching out to some extent to their community. They also learned to distinguish between the functions performed by the so-called "public sector" (in this case, local government, with its garbage collection trucks) and the "private sector" (in this instance, J & M Enterprises).

By the same token, we taught our children to be actively involved in the Neighborhood Watch Program, by being watchful of strangers on the street. Again, this was an opportunity to identify the duties of the "public sector" (i.e., local government with its police force), and what has been called the "independent sector" or "voluntary sector" (i.e., organized voluntary community action, neither governmental nor commercial, in this case the Neighborhood Watch Program).

Such experiences provide a solid base of understanding, from which the child can learn to distinguish between the government services rendered by the town, state and national governments, and to distinguish between the public (i.e., government), private (i.e., commercial) and independent (i.e., voluntary) sectors. (See *Rudiments* section, p. 70)

GOD AND GOVERNMENT

How does a child learn to influence the state? Biblically, he can pray by name for those in authority—for the President of the United States, Congressional representatives, the Governor of his state, the Mayor of his town and the members of the City Council, or whatever the local governing body may be called. Pictures of all these people can be placed on the child's own bulletin board, and the parent can pray with the boy or girl for these various persons "in authority" over them, and encourage the youngster to say his own prayers for these public officials.

Our son Matthew, (at the age of two) largely at

his own initiative, prayed for the President of the United States nightly for an entire year.

Through posting the President's picture on the family prayer board and encouraging regular prayer, we encourage the children to become distinctly conscious that there are those in authority who make decisions which affect all of us for good or evil, that help or hurt us, and that we can do something to upgrade their performance, both through prayer and through communicating with these officials. Thus, when we have phoned or written to our Assemblymen, Congressman or Senators, whenever possible we have exposed our children to what we were doing, and pointed out that they will also have such opportunities to express their views to those in authority.

We also would take our children with us when we went to the polls. They waited outside while we went into the voting booth. Then we would tell them for whom we voted and why and remind them that, as American Christians, one day it will be their duty, also, to vote and determine the quality of their civil government.

TEACHING VOLUNTARY UNION

The Christian principle of American political union encourages voluntary union. One advantage of a family with at least three or four children is that they form the microcosm of a community, and can learn from actual experience the obstacles to voluntary union and how to overcome them—how to achieve voluntary unity of goals, effort and action. In our family, with two brothers and two sisters, we encouraged all four to work and play together constructively from the time they were small. Whenever there was a brawl, any kind of irreconcilable disagreement, in addition to whatever correction was warranted, we would recite to them, and then have them recite Isaac Watt's poem, "*Love Between Brothers and Sisters*":

> Whatever brawls disturb the street,
> There should be peace at home;
> Where sisters dwell, and brothers meet,
> Quarrels should never come.

> Birds in their little nests agree,
> And 'tis a shameful sight,
> When children of one family
> Fall out, and chide, and fight.

> Hard names at first, and threatening words,
> That are but noisy breath,
> May grow to clubs and naked swords,
> To murder and to death.

> The devil tempts one mother's son
> To rage against another!
> So wicked Cain was hurried on,
> Till he had kill'd his brother.

> The wise will let their anger cool,
> At least before 'tis night!
> But in the bosom of a fool
> It burns till morning light.

> Pardon, O Lord, our childish rage,
> Our little brawls remove;
> That as we grow to riper age,
> Our hearts may all be love.

By the time he was six, our oldest boy, Jason, had memorized four of the six stanzas. If the two boys got into a fight, in addition to showing them that they have to repent for offending God as well as one another, we would point out that God's plan and purpose for them is to contribute to the peace of the home, which they can do only as they live in voluntary unity.

Sometimes when we were working on a project, like building a fort or baking a cake, we would point out that we want the children helping us to be of one mind, to share the same purpose and goal, to understand why we are working together, in order to achieve a common objective (internal) so we can have a union of effort, of action, to meet that jointly-held vision.

As parents, we realize that it is important to explain why we are involved in a project, what the end result will be, why we are working together to achieve the same goal. Thus we help produce the understanding that inwardly felt, voluntarily agreed upon, mutual goals are expressed outwardly as effective actions and successful, achieving organizations.

When we have suggested to one brother that he make the other brother's bed—because of lack of time, or one boy was ill or whatever the reason—the boys were learning not only voluntary cooperation but brotherly love. At first, they helped each other in such ways because they were *told* to, but as they learned the lesson in a true Christian sense, the desire to be helpful became internal, spontaneously coming from within, and they *volunteered*.

We found this did happen with Jason and Matthew, even though they tended to brag about their good deed at first: "I made my brother's bed this morning! He can make mine tomorrow!" Certainly this is not the ultimate either in brotherly love or voluntary cooperation, but to voluntarily do the other boy's chore is still a step in the right direction.

Finally, we need to teach our children the lesson of when to unite and when to separate. Again and again, boys and girls have to answer the question: When should I play or walk with somebody, and when should I not? As Christian parents, we need to show them there is a Biblical principle that can tell them whom to avoid, and whom to embrace. (See *Rudiments* section, p. 72)

The boys attended '*Awana*' (a Christian youth program). Jason reported that the language of one of his teammates was bad and he was upset by it. His Dad discussed *I Corinthians 15:33* with him and explained what it meant to be "deceived," and how "evil communications"—bad thoughts and words expressed to another—"corrupt good manners," i.e., change good conduct to bad. This doctrine was a basis for separating himself from further communication with the teammate if it were necessary and his supervisors did not reprove such talk.

We showed the children pictures of oxen, pointed out how they were yoked, and suggested, "You don't want to be yoked to the wrong kind of friends any more than these oxen want to be yoked together (or to the plow). You may meet peers who will take you away from God," so "come out from among them and be ye separate!" (II Cor. 6:14-18) We frequently discussed this concept at an early age, so our children were more at ease with the idea that they would be doing things differently from some people.

THREE FUNCTIONS OF GOVERNMENT

Even something as seemingly complex as teaching the Christian form of our government can be introduced to small children at home—not in the literal, academic way but in an elementary manner that combines a little thoughtful instruction while doing ordinary things with your children.

The form of government that appeared in America, in response to Christian influences, involved three branches—the executive, legislative and judicial—and parents can introduce this concept through any activity that requires planning, doing and judging. For example, we can teach this three-phased concept in the kitchen, when children help with cooking or baking.

In working with my children in the kitchen, I would systematically divide the governmental task into three steps, starting with the legislative function, the *planning* and discussing of what we were going to make, for what occasion it would be used, and what recipe would be best. Then I would explain the executive function, the *doing*, and we would get all our ingredients together, measure, stir and bake. Finally, we came to the judicial function, *judging* the finished product; we would determine whether it was made properly by examining the texture, shape and color, and best of all, by tasting.

Just as mothers can illustrate the legislative, executive and judicial functions of government with their daughters in the kitchen, fathers can do the same, working with their sons on building projects. And either parent can do it with boys or girls in planting a vegetable garden, a project which Jim and I, and our children have found rewarding.

GOVERNING A GARDEN

To start the legislative planning, take a piece of paper, on which you and your children can draw to approximate scale the land you are going to use and mark out the areas where you are going to plant the corn, the zucchini, or whatever. You can also make a list of what tools you are going to need, and your children can learn to use the dictionary and your concordance to the Bible to find out what these books say about these tools or the vegetables you are going to raise.

Then you move into the executive aspect, the actual doing, as you and your youngsters prepare the soil, plant and tend the garden. You end up again with the judicial function, judging the fruits of your joint labors by the size, appearance and taste of the vegetables you and your children have grown.

Of course, just how much is accomplished educationally in any of these projects, in preparing your children to grasp the Biblical principles behind a Christian Republic, depends to a considerable extent on the parent's ability to draw the needed comparison between the three phases of the project and the three separate but concurrent powers of a righteous civil government.

LIBERTY WITH LAW

One of the most fundamental needs of all human beings is the need for order, for a reasonable, organized existence—the opposite of anarchy and chaos. If order comes from within, a person can enjoy freedom; if it must be imposed from without, his liberty will be lost. Hence the importance of educating children, from the beginning of their lives, in the Christian self-government that produces order and restraint from within.

But how do we teach our little ones this spiritual sense of order? As Judges 13:12 asks, "How shall we order the child?" We order the child by teaching him to love and do what is right, according to fixed rules or laws. "Even a child is known by his doings . . ." (Proverbs 20:11) We helped establish our children's doings by framing the laws of the home in the form of a written Home Constitution.

A HOME CONSTITUTION

Such a constitution is desirable in every Christian home; it obliges the parents to "4 R"—to research, reason, relate and record the Biblical principles and rules by which their home will be governed. It is also helpful because it teaches the children to read and reason from the written law or will of their parents, just as they are expected to reason from God's written Word. And it avoids a very typical problem—constantly repeating (and changing) the basic rules of family conduct.

A home constitution should be brief. It should declare who will exercise the three functions of government (the parents), what the sovereign law of the home is (the Word of God), and the constitution's basic purpose (to advance the Law and the Gospel, and to regulate the home for His Name's sake). It could contain a summary of the home "Bill of Rights" such as the "right of the parent to govern and the right of the child to be governed." (Rev. S. Phillips, *Teaching and Learning*, p. 23)

A home constitution should not be simply an extended list of do's and don'ts, but should lay down the fundamental *principles* of home government. However, children do need specific rules, and parents should be explicit and consistent in administering these rules.

Our children are expected to abide by some of the rules of civility that George Washington learned as a child, including such discipline as "accept corrections thankfully, think before you speak, be attentive when others speak, be not obstinate in supporting your own opinion, and let your recreations be manful, not sinful." (William H. Wilbur, *The Making of George Washington*, pp. 116-123)

THREE STAGES OF DISCIPLINE

Before Christian parents can write the right kind of rules for their home, and establish the right kind of discipline, they must know what discipline really is. It is not primarily spanking, or any other kind of punishment. According to Webster's 1828 Dictionary, discipline is first of all education, instruction, including instruction in morals and manners, and in due subordination to authority; and this primary meaning makes sense, since "discipline" comes from the Latin word meaning *to learn.*

Discipline also means establishing and teaching the rules of government. Only after the teaching has been done, and the rules established, does a second meaning of discipline—the correction or chastisement to correct errors—come into play; and that correction is done to teach your children Christian self-government—to control themselves not by mere human will or out of fear of punishment but out of love for Christ and submission to Him. The third step of discipline is punishment—the pain of the rod if correction is not heeded.

"Children, obey your parents in all things: for this is well pleasing unto the Lord," (Col. 3:20) or as Ephesians 6:1 puts it, "Children, obey your parents in the Lord: for this is right." By the same token, children should be taught to obey their parents *because it is right*, and by learning to obey their parents, they will learn, as they grow up, to obey God—and to obey Him without question.

When we, as Christian parents, discipline our children, it's because we love them, and want them to learn to do what is right. This is what will make them happy, when they are in right governmental relationship to God, and to each other.

For one whole year, I had to paddle one of our children almost daily, week after week—for lying or whining or directly disobeying. Now this child is loving, wants to obey, desires to do what is right, is gracious and giving to others, rarely whines and would not lie. And since this time of punishment, the child has accepted Christ, Who has given him a greater desire to do what is right and to be properly self-governed.

CHRISTIAN SELF-GOVERNMENT

Those who are studying America's Christian history and Biblical principles usually place strong emphasis on individual self-government, and this is certainly right. But we must always be sure, in our own lives and in the instruction of our children, that we make the distinction between mere *human* self-government and *Christian* self-government. What the world calls self-government is simply the human self trying to be in control.

This is better than running wild, but it is not what we aspire to as Christians. Human self-discipline can be a beginning, until our children are old enough to understand the rudiments of the Gospel, until they reach the age of accountability, and become responsible to God for their actions which is their "reasonable duty."

Once they understand and then receive Christ as their Saviour and Lord, they can advance from mere human self-government to Christian self-government and yield themselves to the government of Jesus Christ. (I Jn. 1:8-9)

All of us, both parents and children, can practice true Christian self-government to the extent that Christ lives—and reigns—in us. As Paul wrote, "I am crucified with Christ; nevertheless I live; yet not I, but Christ liveth in me: and the life which I now live in the flesh I live by the faith of the Son of God, who loved me, and gave himself for me." (Gal. 2:20)

CORPORAL PUNISHMENT

The philosophy of child-raising based on loving discipline comes straight from the Word of God. One of the finest statements on home government is Rev. S. Philips' address in *Teaching and Learning*, pp. 4-37. Various other Christian authors have also discussed child training and discipline in depth, including the question of just when—and how—the Christian parent should correct the child with corporal punishment. You will find excellent insights in two sources that Jim and I found useful: *What the Bible Says About Child Training* by Richard Fugate and *Under Loving Command* by Al and Pat Fabrizio. How long should corporal punishment last? If both parents are in authority and under God's control, it has to last until the child exercises self-government in response to God's claims.

TEACHING CIVILITY

If we, as American Christian parents, are going to fulfill our potential in restoring our culture as well as our government, we must recognize the importance of civility; we must see how good manners have eroded in this century, and work to restore them in our children. Our Founding Fathers placed great stress on proper *manners* or "respectful deportment," to use one definition of Webster's 1828 Dictionary.

That dictionary reflects an awareness of the close connection between Chrisitan conduct and good manners, with two quotations: "Evil communications corrupt good manners (I Cor. 15)," and "Shall we, in our applications to the great God, take that to be religion which the common reason of mankind will not allow to be manners? (South)."

In our own study, Jim and I have been convinced that manners are an aspect of Christian self-government, and have their Biblical basis in Paul's instruction, "And be ye kind to one another

. . ." (Eph. 4:32) and in his amplification, "Be kindly affectioned one to another with brotherly love; in honour preferring one another. . ." (Rom. 12:10)

TABLE MANNERS

In training our children, we have kept in mind that manners relate to many aspects of life, from saying "Please" and "Thank you" to writing thank-you notes, and apply to many different areas—at the table, at church, at school, at play, when visitors come, and when the family goes out. When we go to restaurants, waitresses and others frequently tell us what a beautiful family we have; they notice the quietness, the orderliness, the way our children eat, their proper use of utensils, and the respectful, reverent way they listen when Jim says grace.

Understandably, our children's table behaviour is less than perfect, whether we are eating out or at home. At times a child may act up at the table, at home, and we will send him or her back to their room until they can be quiet. The basic idea we convey is that it's a privilege to be together, not a time of giggling and foolishness—that it is a time of sharing ideas, or listening to Dad's or Mother's counsel, of reviewing the day's events, of discussing what the children learned in school or Sunday School, or having devotions after the morning meal.

If anyone is playing with their food or becomes disruptive, they are disciplined, sent to their room or removed and reproved, until they are behaving properly and can come back with the right attitude and a sincere apology.

From age two, we began teaching each of the children how to hold their fork, what to do with their napkin, how to handle utensils properly. From age three, we showed them how to set the table, how to clear, how to serve from the correct side, to ask for items to be passed instead of reaching, and to say "thank you" or "no thank you," the importance of asking to be excused with permission, of sitting correctly, not playing with their food and finishing what's on their plate.

At the same early age, they were also taught that when an item is placed on the table, they are to pass it to others first, and not to grab what they like most for themselves. We read our children a story about a little boy who always took the biggest and best food on the table for himself and how his mother dealt with this problem. One day he took the biggest piece of pie—only to discover, to his dismay, that it was hollow inside. Another time, this greedy, unmannered lad grabbed a luscious-looking piece of fruit—only to find it was rotten inside.

We also told our four little ones the story of Slurpy Sam, who always made a mess of his face, and the table; and we concluded the tale with positive instruction about how to eat neatly, and how to cut things properly.

WHAT MANNERS REVEAL

One reason we discuss the importance of table manners, as we point out to our children, is that many people observe just the outward things about you; people make superficial judgements, and if your manners are poor, their judgements will be negative. Your manners do, in fact, state something about the kind of person you are. They are the outward signs of something that you are inside.

We've trained our children to believe they are going to be leaders, which we think all Bible-believing parents should do, especially if they are studying America's Christian history and teaching their children the Biblical principles of leadership. Certainly anyone who serves Christ is a testimony, and should be the best that he can be, in every aspect of life, whether he is alone with his thoughts, fellowshipping with his family, or entertaining guests.

From about the time they were four years old, we taught our children to join with us in being hosts and hostesses when visitors came. We taught them to greet the guests, the boys to shake hands, both the boys and girls to be courteous, to know when it's proper to engage in conversation, when it's more suitable to listen quietly or for the children to go play by themselves without interrupting the adults.

TEACHING WITH PICTURES

None of the five senses is more important in the learning process, and in uplifting the mind, than the sense of sight, not only because it is necessary in reading and writing but because it enables us to perceive pictures, which can inform and inspire. Hence we should carefully select pictures for our homes, especially for our children's rooms, which are instructive and which elevate the thought—which cause one to contemplate wholesome and constructive ideas, and to learn about great people and historic events.

In our family we began to explain the pictures in children's books to Jason—and to Matthew, Debbie and Lydia—before they were a year old. We used pictures in the children's rooms, and would point out items of special interest.

For example, in the boys' room we have a beautiful photograph of Washington kneeling in prayer at Valley Forge. Like our Forefathers, we wanted "our children to come up from their cradles . . . to contemplate this picture that it may . . . meet the early vision and affect the young heart of every child who may breathe the free air of freedom."—'*Washington is at prayer*'. This is what an American author wrote in Family Circle Magazine in 1945 explaining why children should behold this inspiring picture of Washington at Prayer. Then he concluded by saying "as we honor him and teach our children to give him honor, may we also love and honor, and teach our children to acknowledge the God of our Fathers, Who alone giveth the victory." (*Consider and Ponder*, p. *x*)

Studying the picture with the children, we would say, long before they could really understand the words, "George Washington is praying. He is worshipping God. George Washington loved the Lord, and you will love the Lord, too."

We were communicating on two levels: on the more obvious, sensory level, focused on what the child was looking at, we were seeking to impart knowledge, but we were also seeking to impart sentiments and feelings, and especially reverence for the Almighty through the tone of our voices and our very spirit.

READING ALOUD

Jim and I also believed that every child, since he is made by God in His own image and likeness, has the innate capacity to appreciate, to some degree, the spirit of the Word from the time of birth. Thus we started to read to them from the Scriptures and fine children's literature, believing we did not have to wait until they could actually understand the words.

When our children were as young as three years old, we were reading to them not only Bible stories but biographies of the Pilgrims, the Puritans, Pocahontas, Paul Revere, Benjamin Franklin, Noah Webster, Abigail Adams, Abraham Lincoln, Katherine Lee Bates, William McGuffey and many others.

We were reading such biographies to our children steadily until they were seven or could read for themselves. All the while we encouraged our boys and girls to look at the character of these heroes, and to see how God used these men and women in building America. We also helped our children identify, not only the *people* but the *places* of early American history—Jamestown, Plymouth, Boston, Lexington, Concord, Philadelphia—and the *symbols* of our country, such as the Liberty Bell, the eagle and the flag.

A LOVE OF COUNTRY

Like other Christian families, we take our children to church on Sunday mornings and evenings, on Wednesday nights and on special church occasions, but we also make it a point to take them regularly to patriotic commemorations, to Fourth of July celebrations, to parades, to Memorial Day ceremonies and campaign rallies. Before or after—and sometimes during these occasions—we talk with our children about the meaning of these events.

On patriotic occasions, we have our own flag-raising ceremony. We go out in our own front yard, raise the flag, pledge allegiance, and sing the National Anthem. Usually we try to have pictures on the bulletin boards in the children's rooms that relate to the occasion, such as illustrations of Lexington and Concord on April 19th, of signing the Mayflower Compact on November 11th, of the landing of the Pilgrims on December 20, of the Pilgrims and Indians eating together on Thanksgiving.

On Thanksgiving Day our children would dress in Pilgrim and Indian costumes, and stage a little program for all the relatives gathered at our home. Each child would be given the role of a particular Pilgrim (such as Governor Bradford, Elder Brewster or Priscilla Alden) or a particular Indian (such as Hobomack, Squanto or Chief Massasoit) and tell the family whom they represent and what that person did. The older children would memorize Psalm 100 and sing "We Gather Together" or "Harvest Home."

In February, we would celebrate the birthdays of Washington and Lincoln with a birthday cake, and the older children would be asked to memorize something that these great men said. We would also celebrate Constitution Day in September with a program. One year Jason learned and recited the Preamble to the Constitution, and the table centerpiece was a replica of our national charter.

Does this sound as if the Rose household was a bit over-balanced on the side of patriotism and American history? Actually, whatever we did in this regard was more than balanced out by our devotions, Bible-readings and church participations, which involved all our children; and in everything we did relating to the nation we always placed primary attention on Biblical principles of self- and civil government.

PREPARATION FOR LEADERSHIP

One of the most precious things we can give our children is a vision for their future. We know that God has a plan and purpose for them as Christians—for leading others to the Lord, and for restoring America. It is our task as parents to prepare them to fulfill God's plan for their lives. Why are they learning about their country? Why are they learning the character of George Washington and the other early American heroes, as well as Bible heroes? To prepare them for Christian leadership. The older children know they have a responsibility not only to their Lord and Savior, Jesus Christ, but to America to claim America's heritage of Biblical reasoning and to be faithful about extending Christian principles of government into their own homes, community and state for His sake.

LOVING TO WORK

God loves a cheerful giver; He also loves a cheerful *worker*; and the attitude of loving to work, and the habit of working cheerfully, and conscientiously, must be learned early. In the Rose home, all the children were assigned household chores: making their beds, taking out the trash, doing the dishes, vacuuming, helping with yard work, etc.

Our children did not get an allowance for doing their *regular* chores, the necessary things that were needed to maintain the home, to make it a nice place for all of us to live in. They were paid only when they did an extra amount of work. Jim and I never felt it was right to give them money for doing things which they should do anyway. But if it was a big, special job, like cleaning up the back yard or vacuuming the whole house, we would gladly give them money for that.

FAMILY DEVOTIONS

After breakfast, we have family devotions. Jim would use a chapter from book of Proverbs for each day of the month. We picked out just one or two verses to read to the children, instead of reading the entire chapter. We would relate those verses to the children's lives, and ask them to cite examples of how the passages applied to them. Then we would go round the table and each child would choose a favorite hymn or chorus.

We would follow this with a round of prayer. Each one would pray, including three-year-old Debbie. Even little Lydia, as a two-year-old, would pray, "Thank You, God!" That's a very small prayer, but she's being trained; she's learning to pray by listening to the prayers of her brothers and sister, as well as the prayers of her parents.

J.B. Williams wrote in his wonderfully instructive book, "The Lives of Phillip and Matthew Henry," that Phillip, Matthew Henry's father, "managed his daily family worship so as to make it a pleasure and not a task for his children and his servants; the variety of their duties made it more pleasant, so that none who joined with him had ever any reason to say, "Behold what a weariness it is!"

Jim and I sought to learn from that, and make our family devotions equally enjoyable. You want to make it a happy time; you want to make "worship a most sweet and amiable employment," to use Phillip Henry's words.

KEEPING THE SABBATH

We also made it a practice in the Rose family to keep the Sabbath in a somewhat traditional way, to make it a day that is special, not only by going to Sunday School and church but by making it a day of rest and of reading Bible story books, centering the day around the Lord. Often we would emulate Matthew Henry's father, who recalled that his common salutation to his family and friends on the Lord's Day in the morning was that of the primitive Christians, "The Lord is risen; He is risen indeed!" He made it his chief business on that day to celebrate the morning of Christ's resurrection, and would sometimes observe "Every Lord's Day is a true Christian's Easter Day!"

TELEVISION AND INDEPENDENCE

As far as TV is concerned, we never went as far as some Christian parents; we never eliminated TV altogether; but our children were limited, and directed, as to what they could watch. In our house the TV was not a baby-sitter. Many days they did not watch anything. They were allowed to watch programs we considered wholesome and instructive, like *Little House on the Prairie*, nature and wild life films, previously read classic books made into movies, and some sports programs. We always tried to see these programs with our children so they could benefit from our counsel.

In most families, even some Christian families, children spend all Saturday morning in front of the television. We have not had that pattern. Our children were taught from an early age to occupy themselves with some rewarding activity, and not to be dependent upon the TV for their entertainment. They would build things with Lincoln Logs or blocks, play Revolutionary war games, read books, or act out books they had read—like Swiss Family Robinson or Bible stories.

Jim and I observed that frequently other children from Christian homes, (when they came over to visit) would play happily enough outside for an hour, then get bored, and want to come in and watch TV.

Also, our children were not allowed to go to the movies. Their heroes were not movie stars. Most movie and TV heroes are secular humanist by definition. In these shows, evil *man* is always the problem, and good *man* is always the answer. There is no hint of the real conflict between God and Satan, Christian character and sin, or between sound principle and false beliefs.

ENTER VHS

The gift of VHS portable video equipment which allows Jim to tape his and other teachers' presentations, as well as family activities, was both a blessing and a liability. We were blessed with a tool for self-instruction, but one that could be misused. The children knew its uses, too, and asked if they could rent movies they had heard about. There were some video movies we let them see— the same or similar to those shown in church groups or socials with separated standards. The key was always "Who or what is in control?" and the answer is "Mom or Dad, as we practice the government of God's 'perfect law of liberty.'"

APPRECIATING GOOD MUSIC

Education for the young child should embrace more than his Christian faith, reading, writing, arithmetic, history and drawing; it should include music, which is part of God's plan for man's inspiration and spiritual enrichment. We had Jason study in the Suzuki Piano School, using the "mother-tongue method"—by hearing music, children learn to play it. This trains their ear for the kind of music you want them to love. Jim and I wanted our children to esteem good Christian music, classical music and traditional American music. Our boys and girls don't listen to rock music or "Christian Rock."

When Jason was six years old, he would go with me to concerts. His teachers gave recitals twice a year—piano, organ, cello, flute—and little Jason loved it. No doubt other six-year-olds, properly prepared, would love it too. These performances brought Jason and me a real joy. We would spend a lovely afternoon together, and he was thrilled to hear the different instruments. He didn't feel it was overly long or boring, but really enjoyed it as an expression of God's musical creation.

One day when Lydia was only two, all the children went to a Mozart and Brahms concert. They were fascinated by the use of the various instruments and jubilant in response to the richness of sound.

As soon as the oldest child starts taking piano lessons, it should awaken the desire of the younger ones to learn also. Because Jason was playing, Matthew and Debbie wanted to study (even little Lydia loves to try her hand at the piano). All the children come and sit at the piano, and try to play. On Saturday mornings, they will listen to good music instead of turning on the TV. They'll stay in their rooms, and listen to selected records or cassettes, or put on Bible story records.

God gave us music to praise Him, to delight the ear, and to appreciate the beauty of harmony.

ENJOYING DRAMA

In the town of Claremont, California, we took the children to the Annual Pilgrim Pageant put on by retired Christian missionaries. Even though the children were small, they found the pageant rewarding because we had been teaching them the Pilgrim story among their first lessons.

We also took them to a Shakespeare play, "Cymbelline," mainly because we wanted to go, but we found the two boys, at ages seven and five, were excited, and not the least bored. They certainly didn't understand the complicated plot, but got enough out of the drama to enjoy it. We went to the Ashland Shakespearean Festival in Oregon, which featured an old Elizabethan-type theatre (a replica of the ancient Globe Theatre that Shakespeare first acted in). The boys were intrigued by the building itself, by the old Elizabethan instruments, the costumes, the dramatics; and they are eager to go back again.

OUR ASPIRATIONS

The reader may rightfully ask my husband and me, "What is the end product you are aiming for? What is the ultimate purpose you have in mind? What do you want your children to know—and to become—fifteen or twenty years after these experiences have occurred?"

To some extent, these questions are answered in various places earlier in this book, but to sum it up here: We aspire to train a child who understands how God's love enables one to fulfill His Word—"the perfect law of liberty"—which commands us to "love the Lord thy God with all thy heart, and with all thy soul, and with all thy mind" and to "love thy neighbour as thyself." (Matt. 22:36) Our goal is to train a child to esteem all Scripture as "inspired of God, and ... profitable for doctrine, for reproof, for correction, for instruction in righteousness," so the child may become "the man of God ... perfect (mature), throughly furnished unto all good works." (II Tim. 3:16-17)

We aim to train a child who will have the Christian character and understanding necessary to demonstrate both *Christian self-government* (for the individual, his home and church) and *Christian civil government* (for America). Such a character and conscience will enable the child to decide issues and resolve difficulties according to American Christian principles. At the same time, we want the child to be able to extend those principles to the home, the school, the church, the economy, and the various levels of civil government—local, state and national.

With God's help, we would hope to inspire a generation whose Christian convictions and Biblical way of thinking can and will *penetrate* the world and displace and supplant evil, whether it appears as secular humanism in the world of education, socialism in the world of work, or corruption in the systems of government and society. As a net result of our efforts to "train up a child in the way he should go," (Prov. 22:6) we want to see a young man or woman quietly determined and able to express God-given dominion, a Christian who will be light in the world (and not isolated from it), who will be salt to the earth (not subdued by the environment).

We pray our children, as adults, will be God's instruments not only for bringing others to Christ but for helping to bring revival to Christianity, and Christian reconstruction to America. High aspirations, but we are happy to start with small beginnings, knowing that "He which hath begun a good work in you, will perform it until the day of Jesus Christ." (Phil. 1:6)

Imperfect parents have this hope, "The Lord will perfect that which concerneth me: thy mercy, O Lord, endureth forever: forsake not the works of thine own hands." (Psa. 138:8)

PART III

THE AMERICAN CHRISTIAN SCHOOL AT HOME

BY JAMES B. ROSE
American Christian History Institute
Camarillo, California

Christian parents! . . . magnify your office as a teacher;

be faithful to your household as a school.

Rev. S. Phillips, *Teaching and Learning*, p. 21

One hundred years ago we took education out of the home

where it had raised up men and women

who were God-fearing, Christ-honoring, Bible-loving people.

People who were willing to count the cost

of Christian liberty . . . p. xiii

As Christian teachers and parents draw upon their love of Christ

and country they will discover many new ways in which

to build a living curriculum from

the Christian treasury of the founding of our nation. p. xiv

Rosalie June Slater, *Teaching and Learning*

INTRODUCTION

PRINCIPLE APPROACH HOME SCHOOLERS

One of the fastest growing movements in American education is seen in the expansion of the home school. It is estimated that over one million children now are being taught at home – the great majority from a consciously Christian viewpoint.

It has been observed that the swift growth of home schools, rooted in Christian convictions, may be God's way of quickening parents in the task of restoring the home as the first sphere of government and education, and to subsequently insisting that the Christian school and finally the church begin to reflect the governmental and educational integrity of the godly home.

This is especially apt to happen when parents launch a home school based on the Principle Approach. Why are growing numbers of believers starting home schools based on America's traditional Christian principles and method of Biblical reasoning?[1]

---

1. The Principle Approach is introduced on p. 3 and explained on pp. 14-19 of the *Rudiments* division of this *Guide*.

We asked a variety of parents now conducting Principle Approach home schools, "What prompted you to start teaching your children at home?"

One mother said simply, "I have a desire to train my children in the ways of the Lord, and have not yet seen a school actually doing this, so I prayerfully decided to try!" (M.G., Texas)

An unusually thoughtful couple answered, "Through our own Biblical research, we became aware of our role and responsibility for the education of our children. We had a growing dissatisfaction with the Christian school our children were attending as we changed our philosophy about how to teach, the nature of accountability, and academic success. Lastly, we were uncomfortable with the character produced in this school's students." (K&D.J., Oregon)

A particularly articulate woman explained her experience this way: "We saw disturbing signs in our oldest daughter, a very bright child. Her grades began dropping, and there were discernible inroads into her personality. She became moody, underweight, expressed poor self-esteem, desired peer companionship at all cost, and sacrificed her grades to be popular.

"I started to look up every Scripture related to education, teaching, instructing, children, parents, etc. What I found left no doubt in my mind as to who was responsible for educating His children. As I compared the teachings of the Word of God with the public school where my child attended, I felt that I was sacrificing my children to another god – the god of humanism.

"Our decision was made to withdraw our daughter and teach her at home, and I deeply regret not having taken her out – or rather, kept her out – altogether. At first, like many other Christians today, I felt that the involvement of believers would change the public school system. Now I realize that it can never be changed until individuals are changed internally. Only then will we see the needed external change in our schools." (T.F., Florida)

WHY THE PRINCIPLE APPROACH?

Many parents, while determined to proceed with home-schooling, are puzzled as to how to go about it, and not at all sure at first what is a comprehensive, sound Christian philosophy of education. Then they discover something of America's Christian history and of this nation's original approach to education. Increasingly, such parents are starting Principle Approach home schools, finding it a clearly Biblical way to teach their boys and girls – a way that proved itself, most convincingly, in educating earlier generations of American Christians in literacy, liberty and local self-government.

When we asked "Why did you decide to use the Principle Approach to teach at home?" we received straightforward answers such as this one: "We could see that the Principle Approach made God's Word the basis for every subject in the curriculum, and as the child learned this fact, he could become a vital part of God's providential plan for this earth. By mastering each individual subject, we saw that our children could begin to take dominion for God's glory. We became very excited to see that God's Word could be applied to more of life and living than we previously had been taught." (K&D.J., Oregon)

Another parent wrote, "I wanted our children's education to have the Bible as its source, and move out from inward Christian convictions into the subject matter. I wanted our children to learn about real people in American history and to understand America's Christian heritage.

"As I prayed and searched and fasted, asking for God's will, I was introduced to Rose Weiner's book, *Friends of God*. I checked the footnotes and discovered the quotations were from the 'Red Books.' I sent for these books, by Miss Hall and Miss Slater, and every time I read a quotation from or reference to these books or to the Principle Approach, I seemed to feel God saying, 'This is the way, walk in it!'" (T.F., Florida)

Still another parent who had attended a seminar said, "I decided to use the Principle Approach because I discovered that the Lord is in each subject naturally, after I 4 R'd it.[2] Also I found that the children learn to deduce things on their own and discover how to reason correctly. Furthermore, I wanted the educational experience for myself that the Principle Approach provides; I wanted to learn our American Christian heritage along with my children." (M.G., Texas)

Finally, a young couple with four children explained, "As we began studying, we realize that education comprehends much more than the facts pertaining to reading, writing, and arithmetic. It includes all instruction necessary to prepare our children for their adult life. We chose to implement the Principle Approach because it is a reasoning approach – it requires both teacher and student to think. The whole of the subject is imparted from the heart of the teacher to the heart of the student, and students are inspired to do their best." (S&K.S, Oregon)

THE CHALLENGE OF HOME SCHOOLING

In our correspondence with Principle Approach home schoolers, we have asked, "What were the most challenging obstacles you encountered in using this method in your Home School? One capable mother summed it up with great brevity: "I would say the most challenging obstacles were a lack of time to do the research, and an intense desire to use the Principle Approach *now*, when I had an incomplete understanding of it. Furthermore, my children lacked a solid foundation in basic skills, so I had to spend a year rebuilding these skills in writing, reading, (other than graded readers and grammar), in math facts, and in thinking from cause to effect." (T.F., Florida)

Another woman spelled out the challenges she faced in arresting detail. "Most difficult for me was finding the time to be able to read and study enough to develop a correct philosophy of education, and to really comprehend what we had read. Raising four children, preparing meals, helping a husband in a new business, and keeping up a

---

2. The 4 R's are introduced on p. 5 and explained in detail on p. 15 of the *Rudiments* division.

home – doing all this at once does not allow much time for study and writing. And trying to teach four children of different grades (one through nine) makes it difficult to do the type of oral and written reasoning required of a Principle Approach teacher and student." Yet this woman persevered, even though she "had to struggle mastering ahead of time whatever I taught, rather than hand the student a work-book and then go on to other activities of my own." She demonstrated the Christian character that brought her victory, buttressed by the conviction that "nothing reaches a child's heart like another person, especially father and mother." That is why, she said, "my own sense of responsibility would not let me give my children a prepared or packaged curriculum, any more than absolutely necessary." (K&D.J, Oregon)

REWARDS OF PERSEVERANCE

Any parent, who conscientiously perseveres in home schooling with the Principle Approach, will develop his or her own capacity to think in a deeply Christian way about a vast range of subjects, including current political and economic issues, and he will also experience significant growth in Christian character.

Parents are clearly aware that this method helps educate them as well as their offspring. One woman says, "The Principle Approach helps me learn a subject thoroughly; I must master it, and not just give my children a workbook to fill in the answers." (M.G., Texas)

Why are Principle Approach home-schooling parents so determined to stick with it? One parent writes, "Because the Principle Approach is reasoned from a sound foundation of the Word of God, from Biblical absolutes which put God in control and make the parent an effective steward. With this approach we can govern our children's education, we can exercise control over the methodology, content and character we want to see produced. It is also an inspiration and help to others to see us educating our children in this way." (K&D.J, Oregon)

Principle Approach home schoolers who succeed despite obstacles generally do it with the recognition that, "I can of mine own self do nothing" (John 5:20) yet "I can do all things through Christ which strengtheneth me." (Phil. 4:13) They are convinced that the Lord, who *wants* them to do it, will *enable* them to do it, that they can advance a little each day in the right direction, and that the Lord will compensate for their inadequacies with His adequacy.

If you have struggled with yourself, and, with God's help, have learned to overcome your fears, apathy and adverse circumstances, and have found the time to teach yourself, then you are equipped with the Christian character you need to learn any subject, and it will be the kind of character you want to see in your children.

How do we explain that throughout history there have been parents who did not have a college education, yet, who produced children who greatly excelled in academic disciplines? My own Dad never went to college, but he feared nature's God, was an avid reader, disposed to teach himself, and always kept a healthy curiosity about things and how they worked. This is an attitude toward learning that can readily be communicated to a child, and can lead him to greatly surpass his parent's academic achievement.

PREPARATION AND DEDICATION

From time to time we meet parents who have been exceedingly studious and systematic in preparing to be Principle Approach home schoolers. When asked, "What sources and books did you use in preparing yourself for home schooling?" one woman replied. "I attended two in-depth Principle Approach seminars at the Pilgrim Institute in Indiana.[3] My husband attended a comprehensive 18-day course sponsored by the American Christian History Institute in California. We have studied *Teaching and Learning America's Christian History* by Rosalie Slater for three years, and began 4 R-ing history, reading, literature, government, Providence and other topics.

"Besides, we have purchased many nineteenth century history books mentioned in the bibliographies of the FACE books.[4] These resource books have been so interesting that I teach from them constantly." (K&D.J, Oregon)

Admittedly, such dedication and application is exceptional. Many have succeeded with far less preparation. Another successful Principle Approach home schooler writes, "Unfortunately, I did not find any books which truly prepared me for home-schooling. I read Raymond Moore's fine books but they did not really give me the answers I was seeking because my philosophy of education was very different from his. Paul Jehle's *Go Ye*

---

3. The Pilgrim Institute in Granger, Indiana, conducts teacher-parent training Institutes, a consultation program, and offers a correspondence program and practical educational publications based on the Principle Approach for Christian homes, schools and churches throughout the country.

4. The Foundation for American Christian Education (F.A.C.E.) is located in San Francisco, California.

Therefore and Teach really helped to explain this approach. But aside from these resources, and encouragement from my husband, home schooling demanded that I turn to God and seek His will and guidance!" (T.F., Florida)

SCHEDULING TO STUDY AND TEACH

Earnest home schoolers seek the Lord's direction in scheduling their time. The couple who was so systematic and thorough in preparing to teach, and took seminars and studied America's Christian history in depth, quoted in the few previous paragraphs, wrote: "We scheduled the school day from 9:30 a.m. to 1:30 p.m. and gave written assignments in the afternoon so that I might have time to prepare and study. To study at least thirty minutes daily is a goal for which I am striving, as "line upon line" I identify and reform my philosophy of education. Just before retiring for the night we spend some time in Bible study and reading from the F.A.C.E. books.

"We live far from town, so the time we spend traveling provides opportunity to clarify each other's thinking. As we see evidences of the seven principle of America's Christian history, and signs of God's Providence, or discover aspects of the Biblical basis of certain subjects in the world around us, we point these out to our four children, and thereby deepen our own understanding. The foremost method of comprehending the Principle Approach has been through verifying its elements from the Bible." (K&D.J., Oregon)

How does this mother meet the challenge of simultaneously teaching children of considerably different ages? She meets this challenge by mastering Biblical principles, and allowing her own natural gift of communicating with her children to lead her in interpreting each principle in ways most appropriate to each child. "In order to teach divergent grade levels, I have taught the same basic principles of the subjects to grades five, six and nine, doing a little extra research, writing and reasoning in response to the age and abilities of each student." (K&D.J., Oregon)

NEEDED TRANSITION PERIOD

Some home schoolers point out that just as they need a preparation period before they start their first semester, their children may need a transition period before they are fully in tune with the demands of American Christian education.

One mother tells us, "I first had to prepare my children for the greater demands of the Principle Approach, and take a year to wean them from workbooks, worksheets and fill-in-the-blanks. I also had to master the 'red books' myself with the help of the *Rudiments Handbook*,[5] the Pilgrim Institute correspondence course, and finally the excellent seminars offered by the Pilgrim Institute. I use evening hours after the children are in bed to study, and most of Saturday and Sunday afternoon. Since we are expecting our *fifth child* in October, I feel an added pressure to work ahead as much as possible." (T.F., Florida)

Home schoolers do not hide from us the fact that they have faced a difficult challenge, but they also make plain that they have found real rewards. A home schooling parent in Texas says, "If I hadn't believed and understood that a little correct philosophy of government and education could take me a long way through my subjects, I never would have attempted home schooling my two children.

"It breaks my heart when people give up on the Principle Approach because they think it is too hard. I would emphasize that as parents learn to have patience in studying this method, the child will learn that same patience from them. Stress taking one subject at a time and 4 R-ing it. That way they will just naturally move out of interest, curiosity and understanding on to the next subject, and 4 R that!" (E.W., Texas). (For directions on "How To 4 R," see *Curriculum* division, p. 145)

DOMINION OVER TIME

A frequently-voiced concern of those contemplating Principle Approach home schooling is that they will not have enough time each day to prepare and teach the lessons. Just as God can give us dominion over our fears about the adequacy of our own formal education, so He can give us dominion over our anxieties about time. *God is giving us the time* to do whatever He wants us to do, and as we draw closer to Him, He will show us how to make increasingly better use of our minutes, hours and days. (See *Some Questions Answered*, p. 80)

Admittedly, the time problem can appear overwhelming to anyone who has no prior background in America's Christian history and who seeks to suddenly plunge into the task of teaching several children who are widely separated in their levels of understanding. In such a situation, what is the best procedure for parents to start teaching Ameri-

---

5. An overview of the *Rudiments of America's Christian History* – "Rudiments Handbook," is found on p. 277 of the *Curriculum* division of this *Guide*.

116

ca's Christian history, government and education – the Principle Approach?

A BIBLICAL PHILOSOPHY IS NECESSARY

The constituents of a Christian school at home, in a church or independent setting are the same: parents, teachers and students governed by a well-defined American Christian *philosophy, curriculum, methods and goals* (results you wish to effect).

Why should parents have at least a Christian philosophy of education when they can simply gather materials and ideas from many contemporary Christian sources, or just buy a packaged program or curriculum? A Christian view of education is needed because so many of the prevailing ideas and materials about teaching and learning are a mixture of Christian, secular, and pagan views. A Biblical philosophy of education is vital "lest Satan should get an advantage of us; for we are not ignorant of his devices." (II Cor. 2:11) Secular, humanistic and unbiblical presuppositions prevail in so much of the psychological, sociological, anthropological, and physiological views of education today and are passed along as true and beneficial. (See *Child and Subject Centered Philosphies* chart, p. 18)

A precisely stated Christian philosophy of home schooling should be written out for at least three reasons: 1) It will be a memorial to remind you of *why* you are teaching and what your *goals* are. 2) It could help other parents to understand the "reason for the hope that lies within you." (I Pet. 3:15) 3) And if necessary it could help define and defend your convictions legally should your home school be challenged deliberately or ignorantly by local school or civil authorities.

AN EXAMPLE

Parents are urged to refine their view of education, its purposes and product, into one brief statement of a page, or less. For example, consider the philosophy of education that appeared in the annual, *The Record*, of the Chinese Christian Schools of San Leandro, California. In it, Miss Katherine Dang comprehends the basic elements of an American Christian philosophy of education for either a private or home school:

"For other foundations can no man lay than that which is laid, which is Jesus Christ." (I Cor. 3:11)

"The educational goal of Chinese Christian Schools is to build in its students the Christian character required for Christian self-government and Christian civil government – a character of such strength and distinction as to enable one to rule himself by godly principles and extend them into the home, church and state, and into his business and the various fields of the arts and the sciences.

"The rudiments of individual subjects are introduced in the earliest years and expanded upon throughout the elementary grades. Reflection and reasoning from the rudiments are developed according to the natural capacities of the students. Subject content and teaching methods conform to those principles which instruct and inspire faith, patience, steadfastness, diligence, industry, liberty of conscience, and Christian love and care for others. Thus, the philosophy of education at Chinese Christian Schools is predicated upon Biblical principles of self- and civil government so that individuals are equipped to lay Christ, the Truth, at the foundation of every sphere of their lives. From these future generations, it is hoped America may once again promote and support the Gospel in its institutions, which would supply and send forth into the world effective ministers and missionaries of the Gospel."

Now, begin to develop your own philosophy of history, government and education, respectively, for the following reasons: 1) Your view of history – literally your story "of events in the order they happened, with their *causes and effects*," will reveal to your children your idea of God's power for good, *today* as well as in the past. 2) Your concept of government is really your idea of who, or what, is the *supreme authority* in your life, either man and the state, or God and His Word; your idea of government, as your concept of history, reveals *where* you receive your direction, regulation, control and restraint for teaching and learning how to think and act. 3) Lastly, your idea of education – of instructing, disciplining, enlightening, correcting, forming and fitting your children for life and living – will reflect either the sovereignty of Christ, His Story and government, or man's story and rule instead.

USING THE GUIDE

This section of the *Guide* is the shortest, yet, this book contains more materials than it may seem of practical help to the home schooler in learning the Principle Approach. The entire *Guide*, from beginning to end, is useful to parents who teach their children at home. In particular, the *Rudiments* section helps you develop your understanding of the American Christian philosophy of history, government and education, and the *Curriculum* section tells you how to teach specific subjects. It is helpful to think of these two sections as part and parcel of this unit on the home-school, as the following course of action suggests.

How To Begin

Study the following twelve steps and keep notes on your conclusions as you prepare to record your own expression of the Principle Approach to American Christian education.

1. Study pp. 29-30 of this *Guide* and learn the "Key to Understanding the Principle Approach" – how to reason from the internal to the external or from cause to effect, and to discern how that which is seen so often has an unseen cause. Research the Bible references given for the significance of man's *heart* as truly "causative" to human experience, i.e., how the heart of man affects all aspects of life as a cause.

2. Read pp. 3-5, and pp. 14-19 to discover how the Principle Approach is defined, and, how it is summarized as seven Biblical principles and the 4 R's.

3. Study pp. 5-6 to learn how this approach is set apart from other methods of education in at least seven ways.

4. Read page 16 and reflect on *What the Principle Approach Is Not.* Consider how this method is "expansive," not evolutionary, because it guards against the liability of teaching a subject in bits and pieces, in ignorance of its Divine Author and purpose, and the principles that expand and govern the whole subject through the grades.

5. Read pp. 20-25 on *How To Think Governmentally.* This section will explain how to be alert to what is controlling one's daily domestic, social, political and educational experience. It will also describe why one's philosophy of government is a philosophy of education.

6. Consider the *need* for an American Christian philosophy of education beginning on page 10. Outline or excerpt the phrases that explain the reasons for our "national apostasy" and what American education needs to do in response.

7. Describe the specific purpose and fruit of *education, Christian* education, and finally *American* Christian education respectively by studying and outlining pp. 11 to 13. Declare your own reasons for a) the need for Christian home schooling, b) how an American Christian education would shape or give new form to your home school, and c) how your application of the Principle Approach could affect the nation.

8. Study pp. 31-79 to understand how each of the seven Biblical principles of American Christian history, government and education are defined and diagrammed. This section, the longest, may be consulted often as you think through these truths.

9. Consider pp. 85-96 in the *Home* section of this *Guide* for further amplification of these principles. Each of the seven principles have an important relation to each other and all combine into *one body of wisdom* as explained in pp. 77-79.

10. Read pp. 145-152 of the *Curriculum* section to learn how to 4 R a subject. Study an example of how this method is applied to the subject of *Reading* beginning on page 148.

11. Consider the importance of the *Providential View of History* to yourself and your country. Beginning on p. 26, reflect on just how preeminent the Providential approach has been since the 16th century, how it is defined, and why this view of history should be restored. Your view of history will reveal your idea of God and how you will live and learn today.

12. Lastly, ponder the chart on page 18 which contrasts the Principle Approach with child-centered and subject-centered views of education. This chart outlines a standard that may keep us from drifting into dangerous extremes.

Summarize the leading ideas deduced from reading and researching the foregoing references, and draft a concise declaration of your view of American Christian education – the Principle Approach.

Do not assume that your friends (or disputants) will understand your distinctions, especially since your vocabulary may seem so "quaint" or extraordinary to the contemporary ear if you have followed the twelve preceding steps. The vocabulary of this approach restores what Miss Slater calls the "primary Biblical, Christian and constitutional meanings of words" through the only American dictionary "to utilize God's written Word as a key to the meaning of words" – the Webster 1828 Dictionary.

The next step is to develop specific course goals, objectives, and overviews consistent with the Principle Approach.

Developing An American Christian Curriculum

Specific examples of how Master Teachers have developed their own expression of an American Christian curriculum for selected subjects are reprinted in the fourth division of this *Guide*, *Curriculum for the American Christian School*. These overviews are not intended to be textbooks, nor do they prescribe *daily* step-by-step directions. They are designed to be *guides* to help you take possession of a subject. They provide Biblical, academic, historical and practical landmarks for you to observe as you develop *your own expression* of the course.

God's Principle of Individuality directs that each teacher work from the same basic principles and come to essentially similar conclusions, but the manner of expressing and demonstrating the principles, ideas, and product is unique to each laborer. There is true liberty in this conviction.

CURRICULUM GOALS AND OBJECTIVES

Curriculum, or *course* as defined by Webster, refers to a way of life as well as a course of studies. The following statements briefly summarize possible course goals and specific objectives useful in an American Christian home school curriculum.

KINDERGARTEN: A proven and practical American Christian approach to a one year five-year old kindergarten curriculum embracing the Biblical purpose, basic premises, essential vocabulary, and useful resources in at least ten different subjects, from Bible to science, is presented by Mrs. Lois Miller on page 163 of the *Curriculum* division of this *Guide*. Specific suggestions for classroom control, scheduling, use of a notebook and other practical directions are included.

READING: Read, write, spell and speak distinctly the phonetic sounds of letters found in English words and sentences, and discover how Bible literacy undergirds individual liberty and self-government in America. Specific emphasis: The principles of intensive phonics, manuscript and cursive writing, including simple, dependable spelling rules which require reasoning. (See the *Curriculum* section, "How to 4 R Reading," p. 145, "Your Reading Program" with the suggested approach to teaching literacy, pp. 153 to 160, and the *Kindergarten* section, p. 172.)

BIBLE: John Wycliffe declared that his first handwritten English translation of the Bible was "for the government of the people, by the people, for the people." Our Founders in America considered the Bible as the American political textbook, a fact confirmed by the 200 year history of Artillery-Election Sermons and the three national acts of the Continental Congress in behalf of the Bible.[6] The Bible was also the textbook of education, of economics, of the arts and sciences — the foundation of all fields of knowledge, based upon man's relationship to God and to his fellowman.

The Hebrew prophets established a standard of statesmanship which our Founders looked to. Just as we today are confronted with the misconception that the Bible has "nothing to do with modern life," so were the Hebrew prophets challenged. They were "preachers of righteousness" — and set us a platform for dealing with all the sins of society. It is still the "virtue of the people" which is most needed in our American Christian Republic. Thus the Bible needs to be taught historically as well as doctrinally. Students need to learn how to reason from God's Truths or Principles, so that they may be prepared to successfully relate God's Word to their individual lives and to the nation in which God has placed them.

The Bible curriculum should also develop an appreciation and understanding of "all the counsel of God" (Acts 20:27) which reveal the recurring principles that govern man's relation to God, men and nations in Christian history. Specific emphasis: Daily instruction in the structure, authors and basic doctrines of the Bible with emphasis upon learning how to reason from and relate the Truths of God's Word to individual life and civil society.

The reader may want to consider Miss Rosalie Slater's excellent observations on "Restoring the Greatest Classic in the English Language — the English Bible" in the *Curriculum* section, beginning on page 331. See also Overview I of her Literature Program, page 334.

---

6. For a history and an example of the Election Sermon, see *C/P*, pp. 191b, 193 as well as *CHOC*, pp. 372-390 and *T/L*, pp. 338-341.

HISTORY (Elementary): Identifies the Christian idea of man and government, and God's plan and purpose for men, nations and continents in the Chain of Christianity moving westward. Specific emphasis: The Providence of God, operating from creation to America through at least nine important links in the development of spiritual and, subsequently, civil liberty. (See *Elementary Christian History* curriculum, by Ruth Smith, p. 201)

Objectives to Teach

What is History and Why Study It?
The Hand of God in History.
The Chain of Christianity Moving Westward.
God's Sovereignty and Man's Responsibility in Nine Links of the Chain of Christianity:

Creation	Paul	Pilgrims
Moses	Bible in English	Patriots
Christ Jesus	Columbus	Pioneers

HISTORY: RUDIMENTS OF AMERICA'S CHRISTIAN (Junior High): The first principles of America's Christian history are introduced in a published Student Handbook which may be used in both Junior and Senior High School. An overview of the course, teaching suggestions and an annotated outline with commentary on how to use this basic handbook is found on page 277 of the *Curriculum* section.

Objectives to Teach

Christian Idea of Man and Government
    Christian Character and Contributions of Noah Webster
    Identifying the Principle Approach in Webster's "Letter"
    Two Views of Life: Created or Evolved
Chain of Christianity Moving Westward
    Why Study History? Definitions
    Moses and the Moral Law
    Greece and Rome's Contribution
    Christ Jesus: Focal Point of History
    Two Systems of Law
    Reformation of Religion
    Bible in English
    Christian Philosophers of America's Constitutional Republic
    God's Providence and Pilgrim Character

HISTORY, AMERICAN CHRISTIAN (Senior High School): A timeline introduces how each of the four major periods of history lend elements which contribute to the spiritual and political liberty of men. America's Christian history is summarized by six major themes with a list of the key individuals, events, institutions, and documents, sermons, speeches, or essays which support each theme. Four approaches to teaching particular aspects of each of the six themes are explained. (See p. 287, *American Christian History Curriculum*, by Katherine Dang)

Objectives to Teach

How God established a form of civil government in America predicated upon the Christian liberty of the individual through six major themes and time periods:

   I. America reserved by God for Christian self-government (1000–1620 A.D.)
  II. One hundred fifty years of local self-government practiced (1620–1770 A.D.)
 III. The American Christian Revolution (1765–1783 A.D.)
 IV. The American Christian Constitution and Republic (1783–1789 A.D.)
  V. America, "the fullest expression of a Christian civilization" (1789–1830 A.D.)
 VI. America's falling away: the corruption and the correction of a Christian Republic (1830 to present)

GEOGRAPHY: The first professor of geography in an American university was Arnold Henry Guyot, appointed by Princeton University in 1854. Guyot was the first to link the formation and structure of the earth with the history of Liberty – His Story. He wrote: "The physical world has no meaning except by and for the moral world."

Guyot believed that "the *Earth . . . in itself*, may be regarded as a masterpiece of Divine workmanship, perfect in all its parts and conditions. In *its purpose*, as the abode of Man, the scene of his activity, and the means of his development." He stated that it must be studied in the light of the "Geographical March of History" – and man's civil and religious liberty and responsibility.

God created this world to accomplish what he purposed for history. The geography of the earth happened according to Divine plan. The three great oceans, six (habitable) continents and a geographical study of each continent are emphasized. "The sea is his, and he made it, and his hands formed the dry land." Psalms 95:5 (See p. 257, *Geography*, by Katherine Dang)

Objectives to Teach

Biblical Purpose for Teaching and Learning Geography.

The Geography of Nature
  The Earth as a Whole
  The Three Great Constituents of the Globe
  The Character of Organic Life Support by the Globe
  The Provisions for Human Life and Social Progress
The Geography of Man
  The Human Family
  Physical Structure and Individuality of the Southern Continents
  Physical Structure and Individuality of the Northern Continents
  State Geography
  Instructions for Map Work

LITERATURE: THE CHRISTIAN HISTORY LITERATURE PROGRAM

A twelve-year program set in the Chain of Christianity moving westward to America with civil and religious liberty.

A continuous program beginning with "Learning the Literature of the Bible," *Source and Seedbed of Literature and Liberty*. This foundational course for the study of literature is to be taught in every grade, all semesters, every year.

The Christian History Literature Program is dedicated to identifying the study of literature as the character of a nation. As Christianity traveled westward with the Gospel of Liberty with Law, the New World provided a haven for those who sought civil and religious freedom. With the establishment of the world's first Christian Constitutional Federal Republic in America, the fruitage of the Christian idea of man and government was reflected in the history and literature of this new nation "under God." (See p. 323, *The Christian History Literature Program*, developed by Rosalie June Slater)

*Objectives To Teach**

THE CHRISTIAN HISTORY LITERATURE PROGRAM
A 12-year program K-12

LEARNING THE LITERATURE OF THE BIBLE
Source and Seedbed of Literature and Liberty

---

* See charts, pp. 343-351.

A foundational course for the study of literature, taught in every grade, all semesters, every year.
  Establishes a standard from the Bible of language, style, expression
  Identifies Literary Types from the Bible
  Identifies Literary Elements from the Bible
  Adopts a Biblical standard of Character and Life from the Bible's Literature of Liberty

RESTORING THE LITERATURE AND CHARACTER OF LIBERTY – Elementary Years

In order to lay the proper foundation of Literature and Character for the elementary years, parents and teachers must begin to master the key elements of the twelve-year Christian History Literature Program. This can start in the Christian Home, for the study and enjoyment of Literature begins with the baby. The Principle Approach of every subject includes its alpha and omega.
  Learning the Literature of the Bible: Laying Foundations
  Studying our English Heritage of Mother Goose
  An Introduction to English and American Poets of Liberty
  A Study of the Individuality of Nations: Contrasting Folklore and Fairy Tales with Heroes and Heroines of Liberty
  History as Literature: Literary Authors of Historic Individuals and Events
  Notebook Studies:
    America's Heritage of Liberty
    Key nations and Key Classics on Christianity's Chain
    America's Establishment of Liberty
    Key Classics of America's Christian History and Character

CONTRASTS BETWEEN THE PAGAN AND CHRISTIAN IDEA OF MAN AND GOVERNMENT IN LITERATURE. A Two-Year program for Junior High Years

  Learning the Literature of the Bible: Biblical Foundations for Heroes and Statesmen
  Pagan History and Literature
  The Christian Era in History and Literature
  Literary Types in the History of Liberty
  Catching Up on the Classics

TRACING THE NOBLER STREAM OF LIBERTY IN ENGLISH LITERATURE. A Two-Year Program for the 9th and 10th grades
  1st *Learning the Literature of the Bible: Identify-*
  Year *ing the Literary Elements*

English Preparation for America:
Our Anglo-Saxon Heritage of self-government, language, character
The Norman Conquest and Magna Charta: first written liberties
Wycliffe and Chaucer: An English Bible for the Individual
English Reformation and the Bible Translators
Elizabethan Age and Colonization of the New World
The Puritan Age and a "People of the Book"

2nd *Learning the Literature of the Bible: Adopting*
Year *a Biblical Standard of Character and Life*
Biblical Influences on English Life and Literature
Restoration of Monarchy and Persistence of Puritanism
The Eighteenth Century and Ideas in Prose
Romanticism, Individualism, Reformation of Society
The Victorian Age: Christianity Challenged
The Twentieth Century. Return of the Reformed Faith

THE LITERATURE OF THE AMERICAN REPUBLIC: A Two-Year Program for 11th and 12th Grades

1st *Learning the Literature of the Bible: Biblical*
Year *Foundations of Government*
Prologue and Preparation for America: Wycliffe's Bible and a New Continent for Liberty
Colonial Character and Literature: English Colonies and Christian Writers
The Literature of the American Revolution: Patriots, Pastors and Women Write
First Fruits of the Republic in Literature: A New Era in Writing

2nd *Learning the Literature of the Bible: Biblical*
Year *Foundations of Life*
Christian Constitutional Government Reaches the Pacific: Pioneers and Pastors Carry the Gospel and Government Westward
Regional Writers of America: America's Unity of Principles and rich Diversity of Character
God Preserves the Union of American States: Civil War Literature

The "New" Literature of the 20th Century, Internationalism in Literature
Twentieth Century Character and Literature: Heroes and Heroines in all fields of endeavor
Reviewing the Literature and Character of American Liberty: America's Stewardship

ARITHMETIC: This subject is viewed as expressing God's infinite individuality, orderliness and dependability.
Specific emphasis: Counting, number line, and reasoning from expanding principles and functions of basic mathematics to problem-solving skills. (See p. 229, *Arithmetic*, by James Kilkenny)

Objectives to Teach

The Vocabulary of Arithmetic
Biblical Origin and Purpose of Arithmetic
The Principles of Counting, Order and Magnitude, Representation, and Plan for Problem Solving
Table of the Skills of Counting
K-8 Course of Study

ALGEBRA: Algebra is viewed as both a science and an art that reflects the character of God and His dominion mandate. As a science, algebra emphasizes the principles of mathematics to study the properties of numbers; as an art, algebra provides a method of using numbers to find an unknown quantity. (See p. 425, *Algebra*, by Darold Booton)

Objectives to Teach

The Vocabulary of Algebra
Biblical Foundations of the four Principles of Algebra
How to Use the Order of Operations
Basic Skills in Solving Linear and Quadratic Equations
Solve Word Problems
The History of Algebra on the Chain of Christianity

SCIENCE: Identifies and records the expanding principles of God's orderly universe and the Hand of God in raising up scientists to advance greater liberty for the individual. Specific subjects may include astronomy, botany, human anatomy/physiology and a biography of a leading scientist and observer of God's handiwork. (See p. 451, *Natural Science and Human Anatomy/Physiology*, by David Holmes)

Objectives to Teach
(For Human Anatomy)

The Marvel of God's Creation
Science in the Chain of Christianity
How the Body Works
Individual Stewardship Over the Body
Life of Benjamin Rush, American Christian
Physician
Chemicals and Cells of the Body
Nutrition and Digestion
Framework of the Body: Skin, Muscles and
Skeleton
Body Systems

ECONOMICS: An American Christian view of economics – the way men use God-given natural resources, tools, and human energy to produce goods and services with maximum efficiency. Specifically emphasizes the Christian history and seven Biblical principles of the American free-market economy. (See p. 393, *Economics*, by Charles Hull Wolfe)

Objectives to Teach

The Rudiments of God's Economy
    The factors of production
    Production in a secular, slavish culture
    Production in a Christian free society
The Wheel of Progress in a Christian Economy
    God-given liberty with law and stewardship
    Individual enterprise
    Economic self-government
    Christian character
    Private property
    Christian constitutional form of government
    Local business
    Voluntary union
A Christian View of the Ten Pillars of Economic
    Wisdom
Two Economic Blessings of God's Word
Want-Satisfaction Chain in Two Kinds of Society

ART: This is a subject area which our children love. It has been relegated to *drawing* without instruction, to *coloring* without observation, to *modeling* without purpose. The study of the life of Benjamin West, Father of American Painting, is helpful. He learned his first lessons of shading, line, and perspective by his own efforts. These are principles which we will enjoy teaching our students – and the use of pencil, crayon, brush. In the American wilderness Benjamin West learned from his Indian friends, who dug out their colors from the earth, or ground up mussel shells, mixing with bear grease, until they had reds and yellows.

His mother gave him a stick of "blue indigo dye" so that Benjamin had the basic colors. She said to him: "With red and yellow from the earth and with blue from my dye pot, thee can blend all the tints in the rainbow."

We need to teach the first principles of drawing, design, of Christianity's influence upon furniture, architecture, crafts of weaving and pottery, and the understanding of sculpture. Our students should learn their rich heritage of the westward movement of the arts. The balance achieved and the harmony attained all reflected the Christian Idea of Man and Government. The Fine Arts are foundational to all education, even as language and literature form the basis for the unity and diversity of all peoples.

MUSIC: CHRISTIAN MUSICIANSHIP was the first field of study developed for the American Christian History Institute by Mrs. Regina Hoff. She is currently upgrading this course of study as she ministers to her own children in home education and will be available for consultation.

America's Heritage of the Songs of Liberty – from the Scriptures – and from our own creating – is one of our most neglected fields. The principles of music which our Founders and their successors applied to song, and to hymns, and to instruments need to find their way back into one of the most joyous and most challenging areas of our children's education.

BASIC TOOLS NEEDED

Learning can take place anywhere in or around your home, but one particular, well-lighted and properly ventilated place in a certain room where one can keep books, teaching tools and supplies is best. A desk or separate chair and table of the proper size and height for each student reflects the principle of personal property and individual stewardship. Having his own desk helps make the student responsible for the neatness, organization and location of his own equipment, such as notebooks, paper, ink or colored pens, pencils (lead and colored), ruler, eraser, compass, scissors, glue-stick, paper clips, etc.

A 4' x 6' chalkboard or white board is important for recording the results of your lesson preparation and presentation. It is also an excellent tool to demonstrate the student's and your best manuscript or cursive writing, spelling, grammar and punctuation. It also helps the student to focus on one subject at one place as you outline it on the board, and to read and reason with you. (Review Luke 1:1-4 as one Biblical reason behind *recording*)

YOUR CLASSROOM SETTING

Even in your own home the classroom setting should be distinct. It is a "setting" for teaching and learning. Not only light, heat, and good desks and blackboards are needed, but your room decoration should include "beauty, grandeur, order." The "setting" will reflect "the religious, mental, moral, social and emotional" conditions of your educational program. It should be a place where both teachers and students *want* to be and it should also reflect the interests of both. Since the *internal* elements are of first importance, it will be how your classroom looks "overall," and how it "feels" that will reveal your own love of learning.

Under *external* aspects of your classroom setting what should first communicate the individuality of your educational center? Will it be *maps* – to entice the minds of your students as they study the Hand of God in history and His formation of the structure of the earth for His Story? What objects from God's Universe will find a place in your room?

Will your *Calendar of Liberty* suggest your emphasis upon the identification and documentation of the appearing of the Christian Idea of man and government – the liberty, responsibility and productivity of the individual?

Will your *Bulletin Boards* dealing with Principles, Persons, Providences, or Places, from some distinct area of your subject fields, indicate the vitality of the teaching and learning which you anticipate will take place in your educational setting?

An outstanding Principle Approach educator, Mrs. Ruth Smith, of the Pilgrim Institute in Indiana, suggests that the home or school classroom should provide a place for the following items:

1. The American and Christian *flags*. In no other nation can you find the symbols of Christianity and country so closely allied, representing the fact that without a people prepared to remember their God and Saviour, there could not be "one nation under God, indivisible."
2. A large monthly *calendar*, not only to keep children from constantly asking what day and date it is, but "to teach us to number our days, that we may apply our hearts to wisdom" in time and history. (Psa. 90:12)
3. A *clock*, with numbers and sweep hands, suggesting "a time to every purpose under the heaven." (Eccl. 3:1)
4. *Letter guides* – models and reminders for making letters distinct and separate, and as standards for

imprinting the mark of our Christian character" on whatever we write. (See *Teaching and Learning*, p. 102)
5. A *globe*, to discover the individuality and relationships of each continent, "every feature of which is the outgrowth of a definite plan of the all-wise Creator for the education of the human family, and the manifestation of His glory." (See *Christian History*, p. 5 and *Teaching and Learning*, p. 144)
6. *Maps*. A good atlas and wall maps of the world, the nation and your state are very useful in teaching the "geography of nature" and then the political "geography of man" in His Story. (See *Geography* in the *Curriculum* section, p. 257.) Relief maps made from a paste of flour, salt and water are also helpful.

If you are intent on winning your children to a "love of learning," you will carefully and prayerfully plan for a Setting to inspire and to encourage feelings and attitudes that will help them become eager and diligent learners and producers. Now that so many children are learning at home we need to pay special attention to the distinct setting which will restore confidence and joy in both teaching and learning. All should be blessed – of every age.

TEACHER AND STUDENT NOTEBOOKS

The teacher's and student's notebooks are tools for self-education and dominion over a subject. The 'Notebook Methodology for American Christian Scholarship' is explained in detail by Katherine Dang beginning on page 138 of the *Curriculum Division* and is followed by a summary of recommended standards for "demonstration" notebooks.

Each notebook (three ring, minimum 1½ inch binder, with 8½ x 11 inch wide or narrow ruled paper appropriate to the student) should contain the following items:

1. A title page identifying who owns the notebook, the name of the teacher, the school and the year. These elements should be proportionally centered on the page.
2. Dividers for each subject. Primary grade (K-3) students may have five or more labeled dividers, one for each subject, all in one or at the most two binders.
3. An assignment page may follow each subject divider or one sheet for all assignments could follow the title page. An assignment sheet may be arranged as follows:

MATH ASSIGNMENT SHEET

Date Due	Date Given	Assignment	Grade
2/9	2/10	Memorize definitions of multiply and multiplication. Do rows 1-3 on page 30 (or from the chalkboard)	

The teacher should *write out* each assignment on the chalkboard for the student to copy onto the assignment sheet. Older students may be ready to record homework by dictation.

4. Each page of notes should be dated. Notes for one subject taken from the chalkboard and from discussion (depending upon the student's capacity) would be recorded on *one side* of a sheet in chronological order.

5. Handouts, graded homework, tests and quizzes can either be put under a subject divider by date following the class notes, or separated in each subject's notebook by a) classnotes, b) handouts, c) homework, d) tests/quizzes.

6. Consider grading each notebook quarterly for a) *completeness* (all notes, assigned work, tests and handouts are accounted for) b) *neatness* (let the student's best work be the standard), c) *organization* (title page, assignment sheets, notes, homework are all where they should be and in chronological order). The notebooks *could* constitute one-third of the grade, tests one-third and homework one-third. Other factors and different weights are certainly allowable.

7. Each quarter the teacher or student can purge the binder and keep only the classnotes, the best tests, and the homework with the most important handouts. Parents can discard or save what is removed.

THE HOME SCHOOL SCHEDULE

Home schooling parents who are implementing the Principle Approach report that on the average they take a minimum of two hours and a maximum of four hours to work directly with their students. Some begin at 8:30 a.m. or 9 a.m. They approach two, or at the most, four subjects each day and/or alternate with other subjects every other or every third day (depending upon state requirements, if any).

Home schools need to maintain a *consistent daily minimum schedule*, but they have the liberty to take more time studying and discussing a topic if a child begins to show greater interest or to reflect the teacher's enthusiasm for a subject. Some parents schedule at least thirty minutes per subject to begin their program and then regulate their time according to how well they have prepared to meet the student's needs, interests and the child's natural aptitude for learning.

PREPARING FOR THE SCHOOL YEAR

How can a parent prepare a year's overview for a half dozen subjects so that there is a unity and relationship of principles and ideas in the curriculum? Mrs. Karla Stecker of Portland, Oregon, explains how she has effectively implemented the Principle Approach to prepare for the year and then week by week:

"Each summer I decide which subjects to teach myself using the Principle Approach and which subjects must be introduced through the best available textbooks. Then I try to 4 R one subject using the Bible and Webster's 1828 dictionary. I deduce the principles and Biblical origin and purpose of that subject which then allows me to formulate course goals. Although my desire is to teach all subjects, being the mother of four (soon to be five) does not allow me the study time that would be necessary. At this point I am able to study and teach history, geography and literature using this approach.

"Each year I prepare a year's overview in graph form. With my teacher's plan book, the school months are listed down the left side of the page and the subjects across the top. In this way, I am able to plan the emphasis of each subject month by month and see its relationship to what is being taught in the other subjects at that time. For instance, I could choose to teach the biography of Noah Webster, Father of American Christian Education, for literature, while we are studying the United States Constitution in history. I refer to this overview as I am planning my weekly schedule. Although circumstances often force us to go off this yearly schedule or get behind, it still is a reminder of my year's goals and I am able to adjust and rearrange as necessary.

"Admittedly, finding time to study is one of the greatest challenges that faces most home schoolers, myself included. For me, the best time seems to be on Sunday afternoon and night. Sunday is generally reserved as a quiet day at home with our family, and I can usually squeeze out several hours of study and planning between other activities. It is worth it to me to feel organized and ready on Monday morning, even if it means staying up late occasionally on Sunday night.

PLANNING THE WEEK'S LESSONS

"As I plan my week, subject by subject, I try to

think of poems, quotes, illustrations, stories, etc. that will add to what I am teaching. I also fill out a weekly assignment sheet for each child and make a list for myself of any library books, supplies or photocopies of classroom handouts necessary. In my plan book, I record not only what I plan to teach, but also what I will have the children record in their notebooks. In this way I am able to have maps and hand-outs ready when they are needed. Many home teachers may not find it necessary to organize their week in this way, but I find that I do a better job teaching when I feel well prepared."

TEACHING CHILDREN OF DIVERSE AGES

Typically in a classroom, there are children the same age but with varying abilities and interests, and sometimes with widely different skills in reading, writing and reasoning. Home-schooling parents often feel they have greater diversity within the family than there is in a typical graded classroom. So parents naturally ask how the same subject can be taught to children of different ages and capacities and this poses a real teaching challenge.

Usually teachers and parents will work with one or more children of the same age while they give another child a separate assignment. What if there is a subject the parent wants to teach all the children simultaneously? How would the Principle Approach help?

SAME PRINCIPLES IN EVERY GRADE

One of the advantages of the Principle Approach is that is emphasizes the same, unchanging, recurring principles and ideas of a subject, and *expands* them through the grades. Thus you can simultaneously teach children of different grade levels the same subject at the same time emphasizing the same principles and ideas, but amplifying them in more or less detail and complexity according to each child's level and your own preparation and knowledge.

In *Teaching and Learning*, page 109, Miss Slater discerns that "The message of salvation is not presented in an evolutionary manner by degrees, or part by part, nor progressively. The means by which the youngest may 'also obtain the salvation which is in Christ Jesus' is presented *full and complete from the first* ... The 'little child' learns the *same gospel* as the advanced student of theology. This message is amplified and expanded as the individual heart, mind and understanding opens more and more fully to Christ." "In Christian education beginning from the *wholistic* position of

Christ as the center and source of all subjects we proceed to find the unity of all knowledge in Him." (Col. 1:18-19)

Then in her explanation of how the same principles can be taught in every grade, she explained that "The effort has been made to *preserve the unity of the subject and not to break it down into specific grades*." (emphasis added)

Miss Slater then explains how the same principles can be taught in every grade through a *wholistic* approach:

"The effort has been made to preserve the unity of the subject and not to break it down into specific grades´... "Thus a school can be *teaching the same principles in every grade* and at *every grade level*." " ... there will never be a repetition of content for each teacher will bring out *different aspects of the principles* as they expand and amplify in meaning and in application. A principle must be defined clearly but it cannot be confined within a single subject, or grade level, and it will have universal application as it is understood." (*Teaching and Learning*, p. 109)

SOWING SEED

The Principle Approach views the parent-teacher as a sower going forth bearing precious seed. (Luke 8:5) For best results, seed should be implanted in the mental soil although it can be sown or scattered in handfuls on all kinds of ground. (Matt. 13:18-30) The seed which bears the most fruit is that which is set in prepared soil, in a receptive heart.

"But he that receiveth seed into the good ground is he that heareth the Word, and understandeth it; which also beareth fruit, and bringeth forth, some an hundredfold, some sixty, some thirty." (Matthew 13:23)

The manner in which God brings forth fruit in nature is by infixing (setting in) seed – representative of *whole, complete principles*. Seed is whole and complete in itself. It contains within itself the whole of the parts that constitute the grown plant bearing fruit. God works from the whole to the separate individual and distinct parts. He first created the heavens and the earth, then whole, complete individual elements of the earth (including the chicken *bearing* the egg) until all things were ready for God's man to possess it for his Creator.

Consider the Bible doctrine concerning seed as an analogy to the infixing of the principles and rudiments of a subject:

"And God said, Let the earth bring forth grass, the herb yielding seed, and the fruit tree yielding *fruit* after his kind, *whose seed is in itself.*" (*Genesis 1:11–12, 29*)

God conceived of the *whole tree* with fruit containing seed that embraced everything necessary for another separate and complete tree, except for soil and water.

There is a lesson in the way God creates and hence the way in which the subjects of God's creating can be taught. Identify the seed or the first principles of the subject – the rudiments that never change and are always recurring as the subject is expanded and illustrated through the grades. God is unchanging, and His principles and purpose for a subject do not change, whether a child is just discovering the subject or an adult is exploring its depths. Reduce each subject to its "seed," its first principles, and "infix" them in the mind and affections of the student as the parts of the subject are identified and unfolded. "Let the Light of God's Word appear to the student in every subject." (*Teaching and Learning*, p. 95)

We must grind several cups of wheat kernels to make a loaf of bread for an adult, but *one kernel can be a whole meal for a little chick.*

The conclusion is this: we do not have to "sow" or teach all the facts of the subject, but the "whole" of the subject can be taught through the principles and ideas from which it springs. The principles of a subject are usually few, are unchanging and govern the multitude of facts. Consequently, it is far easier to comprehend the volume of facts or phenomena of any discipline through an understanding of its fundamental and expanding principles. Paul illustrates this point in the context of the resurrection when he explained:

"...that which thou sowest, thou sowest *not that body that shall be, but bare grain* ... But *God giveth it a body* as it hath pleased him, and *to every seed his own body.*" (*I Corinthians 15:37–38*)

When we teach the principles of God's Word, the rudiments or "bare grain" of any subject, we do not know how the individual will mature or how the body of wisdom and knowledge implanted will be expressed by future generations. But, we are assured that if we teach whole, complete principles, and "sow" them in the good ground of a diligent student, that these seeds – will produce fruit after their own kind, and God will give them a *body* – an identity and individuality – that pleases Him. Careful sowing, watering and weeding cultivates the Truth sown.

PREPARING ONE LESSON FOR SEVERAL GRADES

The question then arises, How would the same principles and leading ideas of just one subject be presented, for example, to children in grades one, three and six in the same lesson?

The answer lies with the teacher who identifies first the seed of the subject – the unchanging, recurring vocabulary and rudiments of the discipline and then its leading ideas. Leading ideas take thought back to the principles of the subject and help us understand its subordinate facts. Leading *ideas* (objects of thought that lead to a principle which the multitude of facts explain or illustrate) are exemplified by the index of a book, an excellent example being the "Index of Leading Ideas" as prepared and explained by Rosalie Slater in *Christian History of the American Revolution*, pp. 597-598, and 617-698.

Mr. Booton and Mr. Kilkenny explain in this *Guide* how to teach the *principle* of counting in algebra and arithmetic, then they elucidate the *leading idea* of a numberline and counting forward and backward in order to understand the number *facts* with the thousands of possible combinations that follow. (See *Curriculum*, p. 425 and p. 229)

On the subject of reading, the author identifies the *principles* of phonetics and the *leading idea* of self-government in order to control the *facts* represented by thousands of combinations of letters which make words. (See *Curriculum*, p. 148)

Mrs. Ruth Smith applies one or more of the seven principles of America's Christian history to the subject of the Pilgrims and then expands the idea of Thanksgiving followed by the historical facts that illustrate the principles and ideas. (See p. 201)

The seven Christian History principles with their leading ideas can be exemplified in the teaching of various key classics in literature as explained by Miss Slater beginning on page 323 of this *Guide*.

One more illustration concerning how to teach the whole subject to a diversity of students. Prepare your lesson (in outline form) for yourself and the older student or the higher grade. Identify the governing principles of the subject (including any of the seven principles in the Principle Approach to history) for yourself, and organize the pertinent facts according to the leading ideas you chose to emphasize. As the lesson is presented and outlined on a chalkboard, and the facts and ideas discussed, illustrated or documented, require the younger students to write down only the primary points (I, A, B; II, A, B, C, etc.) and the older

Leading Ideas

students to record more of the detail (and discussion) according to their capacity to listen, read and write. In this manner, you will be comprehending the whole subject in some detail for the mature student, while helping the younger students learn to be accountable in writing, or at least orally, for the primary sequence of principles and ideas as they hear and share in the fullness and spirit of your own love and vision for the subject.

PRACTICAL SUGGESTION

Often, your own knowledge of a subject can readily be supplemented by ordering specific educational materials suggested in the bibliography attached to each curriculum overview in the *Curriculum* section. You may feel, for example, that you need more background or educational materials in the subject of economics, and may want to order some of the publications recommended in the related bibliography.

The mastery of facts is not the primary goal in teaching any subject, but rather identifying the philosophy and character which can utilize the subject to the glory of God and the greater self-government of the individual. Actually, in placing a subject in the setting of the Westward course of the Gospel and civil and religious liberty, we soon find that we can master more facts because we can see the linkage of every subject with the appearing of the Christian idea of man and government.

Your own love of the Lord, and your love of learning, are more important than any degree in higher learning that you may or may not have when it comes to instructing your children in the principles of life and the subjects of the curriculum.

WHAT YOU CAN ACHIEVE

You will find inspiration as a home schooling parent if you keep in mind what it is you aspire to attain, what result you expect to produce. We asked successful Principle Approach Home Schoolers, "What are you hoping to achieve in your American Christian home school?" Here are some of their spirit-lifting answers:

"I would like my children to know God and to follow His Holy Spirit. Of most importance to my husband and me is molding their character by leading them in the 'way they should go.' I would like them to become knowledgeable in their Christian heritage. I desire that their identities and individualities be strong and distinct, and not like everybody else's." (T.F., Florida)

Another home schooling parent answered, "We hope to develop in our children an individual, independent Christian character governed by God's law, and capable of taking dominion over this earth to God's glory! (Quite a tall order!) At the end of their formal education we pray that they will be the kind of citizens who are capable of promoting and supporting a Christian Federal Republic, and that in maintaining this Republic they will have a vision for the spreading of the Gospel to the rest of the world. Finally, we hope to give our children a sense of American Christian roots and purpose, and the reasoning ability to identify problems, resolve their source, and to solve them!" (K&D.J., Oregon)

A third parent, asked what she hoped to achieve in her Principle Approach home school, replied: "I am hoping to build American Christian character in our sons and daughters, and to lay a firm foundation upon which they can continue to build in educating themselves. I hope to instill in them Christian love of liberty – a liberty of conscience – that they might be strong enough to pay the price of maintaining their liberty of conscience before Almighty God." (M.G., Texas)

Such aspirations – and achievements – can be yours as you study this *Guide* and lean on God for guidance in the Christian education of your children! Go forth with the mental and spiritual attitude that says, "God is going to use me to make a difference in my students when I teach, whatever the subject may be. With God's help, and the knowledge of Biblical principles, my ministry as a teacher is going to be more important than the textbook, the workbook, or whatever we use as a tool!"

You can rightly reassure yourself with this conviction: Because the American Christian philosophy of government instructs me concerning the importance of developing the character, conscience and the capacity to govern one's self before God and His Word, as I learn the subjects of His creating, I can be the inspired and effective teacher that God wants me to be! I thank You, Lord, that with Your help I can produce in my children American Christians who know how to think governmentally, who see the Providence of God in the history of this nation, who are equipped with the Christian scholarship necessary to advance the Gospel, and to maintain individual liberty and property in a Christian Republic!

PART IV

CURRICULUM FOR THE AMERICAN CHRISTIAN SCHOOL

When for the time ye ought to be teachers,
ye have need that one teach you again which be the first principles
of the oracles of God. (Hebrews 5:12)

Our purpose . . . to ask ourselves how
and to what degree can we establish Christian standards
so that the *philosophy,* the *curriculum* and
the *methods "testify of me" – Christ.*

Because the documentation is so rich and so abundant
it is our purpose to demonstrate through
the development of an *American Christian Educational Program*
how present-day Christians can once again teach Christian principles
which relate to every subject in the school curriculum.

Rosalie June Slater, *Teaching and Learning,* p. 91

CURRICULUM DIVISION CONTENTS

INTRODUCTION

PREFACE

•

NOTEBOOK METHODOLOGY

•

HOW TO 4 R

•

YOUR READING PROGRAM

LITTLE PATRIOTS SERIES KINDERGARTEN PROGRAM

THE WRITING ROAD TO READING

PREFACE

OBJECTIVES FOR AN AMERICAN CHRISTIAN CURRICULUM

What is the American Christian approach to developing a curriculum for any grade level? How will the Principle Approach make a difference in the content of the curriculum, methods and in the opportunity of the teacher and student to master the subject?

The Father of American Christian Education, Noah Webster, defined curriculum as a "course of studies," specifically, a "*systemized order of principles in arts or sciences for illustration or instruction.*" Webster also explained that "a stated or orderly *method of proceeding,* the order pursued by a student,*" and "*a way of life or conduct*" further defines one's course.[1]

The foregoing definition of curriculum recommends four objectives for developing an American Christian curriculum consistent with the Principle Approach:

1. Begin with the *wholistic* position. Teach, illustrate and demonstrate to the student a "*regular union of principles* or parts forming *one entire*" subject.[2] A *whole* subject can be systematically comprehended in and by its rudiments or "first principles." Also discover how each subject complements the other subjects in the entire curriculum through the Principle Approach.

2. Deduce the *Biblical source and purpose* of the whole subject. This goal is achieved by 4 R-ing a topic and "thinking governmentally." (See *How To 4 R*, p. 145)

3. Follow your own course "*with joy*" (Acts 20:24) thereby making the curriculum you prescribe for others enjoyable. Cherish within yourself some expectation of good, of God-at-work, as you labor to teach and learn a subject. Keep alive the reason and purpose for such self-education as you aim to make it possible for the students to take pleasure or delight in the possession or mastery of the art or science studied.

4. Identify the Christian history of the subject or where it fits on the Chain of Christianity moving Westward to America. Links on the Chain of Christianity consist of individual men, events and nations God prepared and used in His timetable to

---

1. *Webster's 1828 Dictionary* definition of "course."

2. *Ibid,* definition of "system."

135

forward the Gospel and His government over men and nations. The Providential View of History *embraces the subjects of the curriculum*, too.

The following questions may be researched by the teacher to discover how a subject is linked to the westward movement of the Gospel:

1. When were the essential principles, ideas and facts of the subject discovered and by whom in God's Providence?

2. What part did this subject, and the character of the individuals who advanced it, have in promoting the Gospel and liberty?

DEVELOPING CURRICULUM WITH THE PRINCIPLE APPROACH

Each of the foregoing objectives is illustrated in this section of the *Guide* to help you develop your own expression of the Principle Approach to a subject. Our hope is that you will not only learn what distinguishes an American Christian curriculum, but will be encouraged to claim a subject for yourself and learn to teach it with confidence and joy, "as one having authority."

When the Principle Approach—America's Biblical method of education, was reintroduced, it was discovered that the "new wine" of individual learning could not be placed in the old wine skins of workbooks. When individual teachers and students do their own researching, reasoning, relating and recording from the Biblical and historical principles of a subject, they need an individualized accounting of their own productivity. Thus, the Notebook came back into its own. Katherine Dang explains how the *Notebook Methodology* was one of the primary *tools* of America's historic Christian method of developing a character for Christian scholarship and independence. (q.v., p. 138)

Learning to read has to precede any practice of the 4 R's, hence it was necessary to select intensive phonetic reading programs consistent with the Principle Approach. Only two approaches are recommended as most effective in producing literacy and its correlative, individual liberty. (q.v., p. 159) *Reading* is used to explain how to 4 R a subject to discern its Biblical principle and purposes. (q.v., p. 148)

How soon can the Principle Approach be taught? The author and his wife feel that the philosophy and methodology of America's Christian history, government and education can make a significant difference in child training from birth. (see pp. 85-110) And if we are willing to keep our children home and under the loving spirit and discipline of this approach, they will be ready for an academic kindergarten. *An American Christian Approach to Kindergarten* by Mrs. Lois Miller displaces the erroneous idea of kindergarten as a mere social experience. She presents an academic curriculum that is readily taught according to the maturity and capacity of the five year old student. (q.v., p. 163) The Biblical purpose, premises, vocabulary, content and resources to teach over a dozen subjects are outlined with a well defined approach to classroom government and even how to teach a kindergarten student to assemble and maintain his own notebook.

The Bible instructs the believer to "remember the mighty works of God" through the ages. In an *Elementary Christian History Program*, Ruth Smith demonstrates how to teach children nine key links on the Chain of Christianity and to help students discover and remember the providences, principles and persons God used to advance liberty to America. (q.v., p. 201) The leading ideas of each key link are expanded through the grades with step by step instruction on how to introduce the program, develop a teacher notebook, and organize a history course with the aid of sample lesson plans.

You can teach children not only to count but how arithmetic helps us to know God and make Him known. James Kilkenny's *Teaching Arithmetic from the Principle Approach* explains how to discover the Biblical origin and purpose of arithmetic as well as how to organize a course of study around its four fundamental principles, evaluate arithmetic textbooks, and successfully train up "students who have confidence, creativity and skill with numbers." (q.v., p. 229)

A basic subject to be restored in the Christian history program is geography. The Swiss-born Arnold Guyot (1807-1884), who later became a Creation Scientist and professor of geography and geology at Princeton University, New Jersey, was the first natural scientist to identify the individuality and function of the continents in the advancement of Christianity and liberty. Katherine Dang uses Guyot's compound conception of the Earth as "a master-piece of Divine workmanship," "for the education of the human family, and the manifestation of His glory," to develop a wholistic approach to *Geography* on page 257.

PLACING A SUBJECT ON THE CHAIN OF CHRISTIANITY

Belinda Ballenger, Katherine Dang and James Rose have assimilated over three decades of classroom experience teaching the relationship between character and government as documented in the course called *Rudiments of America's Chris-*

tian History and Government, developed by the Foundation for American Christian Education. An introduction to the course, and a detailed outline of the 76-page *Student Handbook* used in grades 7-12 with a commentary on how to teach it from specific references to the supporting textbooks, including this *Guide*, begins on page 277.

The *Senior High School American History* curriculum prepared by Katherine Dang explains how to research and develop six major themes that distinguish America's Christian History from 1000 A.D. to the present. (q.v., p. 287) Four approaches to thoroughly teach key individuals, events, institutions and original documents that have contributed to or tested the integrity of this Republic are illustrated with detailed examples of each method of study. A careful reading of just the six themes will surely quicken you runderstanding of God's providence in America better than any contemporary textbook.

Rosalie June Slater's *Christian History Literature Program* explains why "The field of literature deals with the consequences of history and deepens the *study of character*" and how to educate yourself and the rising generations, from Elementary through High School, in "the history, literature and character of liberty." (q.v., p. 323) A splendid piece of educational prose itself, her curriculum identifies the leading ideas and specific authors and works which distinguish the character and progress of liberty from its Divine source, the Bible, to the twentieth century. This course also explains the Notebook Approach to studying key classics and nations on the Chain of Christianity moving to America.

If our children are to function effectively on this earth, they will need to understand the rudiments of God's economy. In *An American Christian Approach to Economics*, beginning on page 393, Charles Hull Wolfe introduces the first principles of economics, facts that are so basic that a little child can understand them. He also demonstrates how the seven Biblical principles of America's Christian history and government are the spirit and basis of "The Economic Wheel of Progress in a Christian Economy."

Consider God's Hand in the life of Thomas Harriot, an English mathematician who introduced the equal sign in Algebra and was also Providentially used to explore and write an account of Virginia which the Pilgrims consulted prior to coming to America. This insight is only part of a Biblical, historical and practical study of mathematics by professor Darold Booton in *Teaching Algebra from the Principle Approach*, page 425.

In *An American Christian View of Natural Science*, David Holmes explains that "God's providential Hand can be seen in the preparation of individuals to discover the scientific advancements needed for the movement of the Gospel Westward." (q.v., p. 451) A partial list of the men and events God used to meet human needs for better health and dominion over the body, and to enable medical missionaries to show the love of Christ to the sick and sinful in heathen lands is found on page 460. Observe, too, how major medical advancements and the timing of America's founding are concurrent.

Read the wonderful story of how type and the typewriter contributed to the history and literature of liberty on the Chain of Christianity in Barbara Rose's discussion on *The Principle Approach to Typewriting*. (q.v., p. 479) What some teachers may consider as basically a secular, neuro-muscular skill for business or personal use, does, in fact, have a Providential heritage that documents why the history of Christian liberty and government is also the history of the printed Word of God. In the hands of a virtuous and free people, the typewriter and its more sophisticated cousin, the computer-word processor, is still used to advance the Gospel, "with signs following." Mrs. Rose also explains how the character and government of men in each of the three continents of history – Asia, Europe and North America – made a significant difference in the progress of type and printing and consequently the degree of individual liberty enjoyed.

THE SPIRIT OF AMERICAN CHRISTIAN EDUCATION

The struggle with one's self to be free from Satan's deceitful suggestions of ignorance, inertia, ineptitude or irresponsibility is a wonderful opportunity to demonstrate the Spirit and Power of God. Like Paul, you can take possession of one or more subjects in the curriculum and finish your "course with joy" – without sharing Paul's tribulations! There are hundreds of individual men and women "of like passions with you" (Acts 14:15) who have witnessed how God renewed their love of learning and transformed their minds as they applied the Principle Approach to American Christian Education to teaching and learning.

In each of the following curriculum overviews, consider the testimonies of the Christian parents and teachers who contributed to this division of the *Guide* and encourage yourself with their story of how God enabled them to "give an answer to every man that asketh . . . a reason of the hope" in them for their own labor, their family and their nation through the Principle Approach.

NOTEBOOK METHODOLOGY

BY KATHERINE DANG

American Christian educators may well be nullifying all that is Christian in their curriculum by using erroneous methods. A philosophy of education necessarily comprehends the manner in which doctrine is taught, and while Christian educators may decry and expose the evils of secular humanism or humanistic and evolutionary doctrines, some of these same educators are inconsistently advocating and adopting humanistic and evolutionary methods in their Christian classrooms. Consequently, modern Christian scholarship suffers for lack of integrity and loss of quality and credibility as well.

The Notebook Methodology, as defined here, suggests not only a physical, external separation from secular education by Christian schools and homes, but an internal separation unto a philosophy of education which reverses and overturns the pagan practices in the modern Christian classroom.

Notebook Methodology, on the surface, seems no more than 1½″ three-ring binders filled with 8½ x 11″ college-ruled paper. For purposes of classroom instruction, little more is required. Notebook Methodology is in direct contrast with the contemporary "workbooks" filling the educa-

tional bookshelves. In these workbooks, students do little work. They will answer true or false, or fill in blanks, or choose from a multiple of answers or connect dots. They do not have to reflect or think upon what is within themselves. They are required only to react to selected, controlled external stimuli.

Notebook Methodology would bring to the surface students' powers of response, memory, and reasoning. For as they work, so by their notebooks should their labors be known. Students, in their work, are required to answer, in writing and in oral recitation, with truths learned from rote and discovered by reasoning. Complete sentence answers and essays are the means used for expressing independent and original thought.

THE WORKBOOK APPROACH

By contrast, workbook approaches are predicated upon a philosophy of education and government that is not reasoned from the Scriptures. This philosophy deduces man to be the highest form of beast, which, as an organism, though complex, learns by conditioning, by stimulus and response. The student is taught to automatically act or react, without reflection, as arbitrarily desired. Emphasis is heavily placed upon audio and visual teaching instruments to provide strong physical stimuli which can motivate desirable behavior. This Pavlovian approach to teaching results in irresponsible, ignorant and inert mentalities which have well served as the foundation for slavish and dependent states and nations.

Notebook Methodology lends itself as a Biblical alternative to conditioned learning. Reasoning from the Scriptures, the notebook approach regards each student as a specially created being, made in God's moral likeness, with the faculty of reason. It is the faculty of reason which separates man from the bestial creation. Reason is the channel through which man is able to commune with and comprehend God. Although we know, from God's Word and Revelation of Truth, that mankind is universally fallen, the individual can be regenerated in spirit, soul, and mind. Biblical truth taught Biblically will test and put to task the student's own fallen intellect and character.

With notebook methods, the emphasis is primarily upon the student's reasoning from, and his productivity in accordance with, Biblical principles. Notebook Methodology aims to produce self-teaching students equipped with their own texts for learning. In effect, the self-teaching student will become the self-governing "freeman," the fundamental unit and support of America's Christian Republic.

DEMAND ON THE TEACHER

While contemporary workbook methods require instruments for teaching that are essentially mechanical and sterile in character, America's traditional notebook methods strive for inspirational teaching which in its character is spiritual and quickening. Workbook methods demand little of teachers and less of students in the way of scholarship and individual mastery of subject material.

If there is to be reformation in American Christian education, let it originate with the present generation of Christian educators, beginning with where they are. (Most students will progress no farther than where they are being led by their teachers. Christian teachers must demand of themselves what they envision for their students.) Notebook Methodology sets Christian educators free from prescription scholastics, and encourages them to exercise original, Biblical scholarship of the caliber which resulted in the world's first Christian Republic.

In Notebook Methodology, the teacher is the text. Teachers are the expositors of divine principles and the examples of right reasoning. It is their individuality, productivity, industry, self-government, progress, and accountability which are reflected upon and imitated by students. Students will record in their minds and hearts, as well as on paper, the teacher's posture, words, thoughts, arguments, and wisdom. Indeed, students are made subject to the subject as their minds are captivated by Christian excellence and original scholarship. The subjects at hand need not be warring foes, but friends to both teacher and students, fashioned by God to assist in and enhance man's earthly existence.

THE PRINCIPLE APPROACH TO NOTEBOOKS

Displacing workbooks with notebooks opens the classroom to Christian government of that classroom and its individual students. With Notebook Methodology, government of the classroom and students is republican. The chief controls stem from the ministry of teacher to students, within, not from without as coming in the form of packaged curriculum. Notebook Methodology is suited for the restoration of America's Biblical principles of civil government by the professing and the practicing of these principles. The seven principles of America's Christian history and government developed by Miss Rosalie Slater in *Teaching and Learning America's Christian History* catch the spirit and vision of Notebook Methodology.

God's Principle of Individuality requires notebooks for each student. Every boy and girl is expected to exercise integrity of individual labor and responsibility. Collective work and group projects violate this primary principle of Christian government. Nor should the separate subjects be confused with each other. Rather, students should use subject dividers in the elementary grades and each subject with its own division in a notebook or even a notebook for each subject in the high school. The fountain of productivity and progress is the individual's own initiative and willingness to work.

Without *Christian Self-Government*, teacher and students lack discipline and power in overcoming obstacles and fears when confronted with the challenges of self-education. Self-education cannot be realized until there is an internal, voluntary consent and commitment to overcome one's ignorance and possess a mastery of the subject for himself. *God's Principle of Individuality* places the burden of learning and labor directly upon the scholar. Without yielding to the authority of God in and over him, teacher or student will be enslaved by sloth, expressing itself in painless efforts for superficial gains. Notebooks demand upkeep, maintenance, corrections, re-writes, and attention, all of which reflect either Christian self-government or the absence of it.

America's Heritage of Christian Character came out of a tremendous struggle with evil forces, within and without. And so Noah Webster, Founding Father of American Christian Education and Scholarship, as historian Chauncey A. Goodrich wrote,

" ... felt that children should learn to acquire knowledge by severe effort; that the prevailing disposition to make everything easy is unphilosophical and wrong; that the great object of early training is to form the mind into a capacity of surmounting intellectual difficulties of any and every kind ... He wished ... at this early period of ready memory and limited comprehension to store the mind with many things which would afterward be found of indispensable use; things which are learnt with the utmost reluctance, or rather, in most cases, are not learnt at all, in the more advanced stages of intellectual progress. He felt that there must necessarily be much of drudgery in the formation of a thoroughly educated mind." (Chauncey A. Goodrich, as cited in *Teaching and Learning America's Christian History*, p. 294)

If the world is to witness a revival of the Christian character which founded our Republic, educators must not fail to equip our future homes and churches; they must not rob students of opportunities to do battle with and have victory over their evil dispositions and inclinations.

The rigor sometimes arising from the notebook approach of classroom instruction, especially in the beginning, will test teacher and students in diligence, industry, endurance, perseverance, patience and faithfulness. Yet by such classroom government, the marks made in grades are more approximate with the individual's development of Christian character. Too often, grades are the result of a student's natural abilities and talents alone, and scholastic achievement and Christian character become separated and unrelated entities, which reflects unsound educational doctrine. The cause for such incongruity lies in erroneous judgment of work, which does not include submission to principles of quality workmanship, attention to detail and diligence to obey standards of purity. Having correct written answers is not necessarily work well done.

The Christian Principle of Private Property is taught and maintained in Notebook Methodology. By conscientious effort, students will reap the fruits and joys of their own labor. Notebooks are a student's property; he has invested in them his time, labor, and intellect, and they express his capacities for stewardship. Notebooks are records of individual progress. No one can take away knowledge a student lays claim to by application of his own labor. The student is in competition with his own standard of excellence which he establishes himself from work representative of his most conscientious effort. With his God-given faculties and talents, each student pursues the fullest degree of achievement he can. Students are encouraged, and expected always to do and manage more than they have done or managed before.

Underlying Notebook Methodology is a Christian form of classroom government, patterned in principle after *America's Form of Christian Civil Government*. Here the teacher seeks to "think governmentally" through the various aspects of instruction: lectures and chalkboard notes, charts and diagrams, homework and examination schedules, vocabulary and memory work, essay questions, notebook organization, textbook selection and use, discipline and deportment, etc.

The teacher first settles on what might be called "the law of the classroom" which manifests the spirit and posture he will try to maintain. Upholding a dignity equal to his love for his courses, the teacher should establish his standard of scholarship, order, and deportment by a Class Discipline, printed and given to each of his students, for which he is accountable. This Class Discipline is, essentially, a classroom constitution, a form of external government designed to lay a foundation for good scholarship.

It should prove burdensome only to the student disposed to resist learning; it offers liberty and peace to the student who is seriously pursuing Christian scholarship. In accordance with Biblical government, classroom laws and grading standards are *fixed*, without respect of persons, weak or strong. Grading by class curve is at enmity with the Biblical concept of law; however, the teacher shows himself gracious and just to make his directions clear and explicit, to make his expectations known, and to make himself available to assist students with love and compassion, in reaching the standard set. Every student is given hope of success, because he is assured the teacher has gone in advance and is able to lead his students rightly.

Secondly, the teacher sees the notebook as a *representation* of his and his students' scholarship. Student notebooks reflect the teacher's reasoning and government, and speak for the teacher in each of the children's homes. Since the notebook is a record of student responsibility and productivity, it represents student character and self-government, and challenges teacher and students to greater levels of academic achievement as they become dissatisfied with their own mediocrity.

Another aspect of the *Christian form of American Government* that can be expressed in classroom management is the *dual form of government*. In the classroom, this relates to the principle of federalism: the "local" self-governing student voluntarily consents to be obedient to the "central" authority of a teacher. Both teacher and student are under one sovereign law, administered by the teacher.

In his system of classroom control, the teacher seeks to administer the law for both individual students and the entire class. He seeks to embrace and comprehend all the diverse elements, dispositions, and histories represented in the classroom through the execution of a supremacy of centralized, Biblical law, which checks licentiousness and pagan individualism and which allows the liberty to express God-given individuality. Independent reasoning and activity are never permitted to violate the biblical principle of Christian self-government. When it does violate this principle, it becomes lawlessness that offends the individual property of conscience. Each student is, thus, under law to be at liberty to develop as an individual — an individual who works in willing subjection to the law and authority of the teacher and in considerate cooperation with his fellow students.

Lastly, a Christian form of classroom government deliberately exercises the *three functions of power* — establishment of law, execution of law, and judgment in accordance with law. The teachers should seek not only to delineate the fine points of internal, Christian self-government, but to demonstrate those points in external classroom management and student government. The right use of power on the lowest of levels — classroom or school government — can serve as the students' model of Christian civil government.

The Seed of Local Self-Government is planted as individual teachers minister to each student, speaking with him, correcting him, and responding to his questions and answers with faith and conviction. Teachers transmit to their students the Biblical principles of every subject and should expect from the students, in turn, as Noah Webster states in *A Letter to a Young Gentleman Commencing His Education*, "satisfactory reasons for every opinion" they embrace. Students are viewed as eventual governors of their own domains, churches and states. The teacher views himself as a missionary for Christian self-government. His wisdom is built on the foundation of Jesus Christ and the Gospel and his call is to cultivate a Biblical mentality and intelligence that need not be ashamed when called upon to give a good account.

The Christian Principle of American Political Union can be realized in the classroom and in the total school system when the constituents of each body — students and departments — voluntarily consent to the spirit of Notebook Methodology. Regardless of the number of students in a classroom, Notebook Methodology helps bring the whole into oneness. Classroom union is evidenced by attentive recording and the quiet productivity of mental exertion. This union is the uniting of individual efforts to conscientiously comprehend the teacher's instruction. It is the instruction which unites each individual into a union — a body of working students. Biblical reasoning works the body, mind, and spirit of the individual. His focus of attention — his center of activity — is upon the teacher's reasoning, as the teacher speaks and writes upon the chalk board.

THE UNDERGIRDING SPIRIT

The undergirding spirit of Notebook Methodology is America's Christian history and government, a recognition that a philosophy of education is a philosophy of government. This internal bulwark — America's Christian history and government — consistently taught throughout the system with a corresponding methodology — Notebook Methodology — will fortify America's Christian schools. The internal unity which results from such consistency will provide a strong defense against all external elements of educational decline or deterioration of moral principles.

Many of today's Christian educators who are turning away from workbooks to the scholarship demands of Notebook Methodology, find themselves starting anew with self-education. Discovering how little they know of their subject fields, they begin to teach themselves what they know their students ought to learn. Despite their fears of inadequacy, they become faithful to the light which God gives them. As teachers return to the scholarship of Notebook Methodology, so gradually, might America return to the Biblical foundations of her Republic.

STANDARDS FOR DEMONSTRATION NOTEBOOKS

In the elementary years children are guided, directed, established, and made ready for those advanced stages of life when "the intellectual faculties expand and the reasoning power gains strength," when he, as an individual, must stand independent with his own researches and reasoning from Biblical principles. For slavish reliance upon and blind confidence in the opinions of others breeds "ignorance, inertia, and irresponsibility."

The notebook is a physical tool applied as a means to a spiritual end. The demands, discipline, and apparent drudgery of the elementary notebooks will form in children the internal supports for Christian scholarship and self-government.

"The first principles are often difficult to beginners; but when you have over come the first difficulties, your progress will be more easy and pleasant."[1]

It is Biblical to raise an equal standard for all levels and ages. All *strive* toward the same mark. Demonstration notebooks exercise and urge particular attributes of character, arts, and skills which fit individuals for Christian maturity and "usefulness in their future stations."

Those desirable attributes of character which may be represented in the notebooks are: neat, tidy, clean, orderly, conscientious, precise, accurate, responsible, diligent, industrious, and careful.

Listening, writing, organizing and managing property, consistency, and self-criticism are the *arts* exercised by Demonstration Notebooks. Criticism, as applied here, is "the art of judging with propriety of the beauties and faults of a literary performance, or of any production in the fine arts; ..." (Webster, 1828)

Skills counted as essential to master in the use of the notebook are: reading, spelling, handwriting, research, observation, and quickness.

As the present generation is given to train, so tomorrow's generation is given to obey. The notebook is a training tool of an American Christian school. A child's measure of progress is determined not by his capabilities, but by his willingness to obey instruction and correction.

"Children, obey your parents in the Lord, for this is right." *Ephesians 6:1*

"... in the first stages of life, our confidence in parents must be implicit—and our obedience to their will, complete and unreserved."[2]

"An earthly parent is more with his helpless and ignorant children, than with those who have experience. The first duty which he teaches them, is implicit obedience to his will; and when he finds them wayward and disobedient, he chastises them, and sometimes, with severity."

Emma Willard, *Universal History*, 1843

LAWS GOVERNING NOTEBOOKS

Notebook production is a craft useful for self-education and self-government. Here are laws which may be applied throughout the grades to effect consistent training and facilitate the advancing of students from one level to the next.

Prescribed For Every Notebook:
1. A three-ring binder
2. Paper size, 8½ x 11″ only
3. Dividers, labeled with subject names, homework, tests
4. Title pages for each binder with names of subsubject or subjects, student's name and/or grade and school.
5. Assignment sheets to record all homework and classwork with dates assigned and dates due

Handwriting and Written Assignments:
1. Words, letters, and numbers are kept on the paper's ruled lines.
2. Complete words are written in cursive with proper upsweep.
3. Dot all i's accurately. Cross all t's completely.
4. Printed letters are erect and uniform.
5. Writing remains *within* the red marginal line at the left.

---

1. Noah Webster, "Letters to a Young Gentleman," *Rudiments*, p. 28.

2. *Ibid.*, p. 7.

6. Words do not crowd or run off the page; some right margin is made.

7. All assignments include student's first and last names in the heading and the titles of assignments may be centered and underlined as follows:

LAST, FIRST NAME   DATE
SUBJECT   ASSIGNMENT

TITLE OF ASSIGNMENT

8. Questions are answered individually. Questions are copied before they are answered. Questions are answered with complete sentences.

9. Errors are not rewritten upon nor blacked out. Instructions for erasing penciled errors and crossing out inked errors are given to preserve the general cleanliness and overall neatness.

10. A minimum of errors is acceptable per page of notes. Papers exceeding the acceptable minimum are recopied.

11. When underlining is required, a ruler is used.

12. As soon as practical, ink is used in note-taking.

Spelling Corrections:

1. Each misspelled word is rewritten correctly in a vertical column.

2. Words are numbered down the first column along the left margin. Separate words run across the page in their individual columns.

3. Corrections are checked by the teacher.

4. Misspelling in corrections warrant a rewriting of the entire column or columns rewritten with correct spelling.

Science and Math Work:

1. Math problems are evenly spaced across the page.

2. Numbers are correctly formed on the ruled lines of the paper.

3. Lines are drawn with straight edges.

4. Questions to word problems are written out. The work for each answer is shown. The answer is given in written form in a sentence answer.

Art Work:

1. Drawings and diagrams are done upon unruled paper.

2. Technical drawings and diagrams are finished in ink or felt-tip pen. All pencil lines are erased clean off the paper.

3. Titles are lettered and centered on the paper.

4. An art folio may be provided.

STANDARD FOR GRADING NOTEBOOKS

The student's best written pages serve as the standard by which a grade is given. Periodic checks by the teacher to see that all written work is done, as well as the student's best notebook pages, will help to administer student consistency and improvement.

HISTORICAL EXAMPLES OF NOTEBOOKS

THE NOTEBOOKS OF GEORGE WASHINGTON

"… His manuscript schoolbooks, from the time he was thirteen years old, have been preserved. He had already mastered the difficult parts of arithmetic and these books begin with geometry.

"… But many pages of the manuscript in question are taken up with copies of what he calls Forms of Writing, such as notes of hand, bills of exchange, receipts, bonds, indentures, bills of sale, land warrants, leases, deeds, and wills, written out with care, the prominent words in large and varied characters in imitation of a clerk's hand.

"… the manuscripts fill several quires of paper, and are remarkable for the care with which they were kept, the neatness and uniformity of the handwriting, the beauty of the diagrams, and a precise method and arrangement in copying out tables and columns of figures.

"These particulars will not be thought too trivial to be mentioned, when it is known, that he retained similar habits through life. His business papers, daybooks, ledgers, and letterbooks, in which before the Revolution no one wrote but himself, exhibit specimens of the same studious care and exactness. Every fact occupies a clear and distinct place, the handwriting is round and regular without interlineations, blots, or blemishes; and, if mistakes occurred, the faulty words were so skillfully erased and corrected, as to render the defect invisible except to a scrutinizing eye. The constructing of tables, diagrams, and other figures relating to numbers or classification, was an exercise in which he seems at all times to have taken much delight. If any of his farms were to be divided into new lots, a plan was first drawn on paper; if he meditated a rotation of crops, or a change in the mode of culture, the various items of expense, labor, products, and profits were reduced to tabular forms; and in his written instructions to his managers, which were annually repeated, the same method was pursued."[3]

THE NOTEBOOKS OF JOHN QUINCY ADAMS

An excerpt from a letter to John Adams from his son, John Quincy, age ten, June 2, 1777:

"P.S.—Sir, If you will be so good as to favor me with a blank-book I will transcribe the most remarkable occurrences I meet with in my reading, which will serve to fix them upon my mind."

Excerpt from a letter introducing John Quincy Adams, age 18, to Harvard University, dated April 24, 1785, from tutor John Adams:

"If you were to examine him in English and French poetry, I know not where you would find anybody his superior; in Roman and English history, few persons of his age. It is rare to find a youth possessed of so much knowledge. He has translated Virgil's Aeneid, Suetonius, the whole of Sallust, and Tacitus's Agricola, his Germany, and several books of his Annals, a great part of Horace, some of Ovid, and some of Caesar's Commentaries, in writing besides a number of Tully's orations. *These he may show you*; and although you will find the translations in many places inaccurate in point of style, as must be expected at his age, you will see abundant proof that it is impossible to make those translations without understanding his authors and their language very well."

These excerpts, part of a brilliant essay by Miss Rosalie J. Slater entitled *The Education of John Quincy Adams*, may be read in *The Christian History of the American Revolution: Consider and Ponder*, pp. 602-606.

---

3. Jared Sparks, *The Life of George Washington*, 1855

How To 4 R

On page 5 of the *Rudiments* section of this *Guide*, the 4 R's were introduced as a method of teaching and learning and were paraphrased, defined and documented Biblically on page 15.

The following pages outline and explain seven basic steps in the process of 4 R-ing any subject in preparation to teaching it. The first four steps alone would enable one to discover for himself the vocabulary, first principles, and Biblical source and purpose of a subject more quickly, efficiently and thoroughly than taking most college courses on the discipline.

Beginning on page 148, the author illustrates how to 4 R the basic subject of *reading* in the American Christian curriculum. Each step of the suggested process is repeated and applied to the task of comprehending literacy—reading and writing—skills that must be learned even before 4 R-ing! School administrators, teachers and parents are then challenged to consider if their reading program is developing American Christian character and scholarship. Lastly, several published reading programs consistent with the Principle Approach are recommended.

PURPOSE OF THE 4 R'S

One might well ask why a person should 4 R a subject. What is the purpose or the fruit of this method of Biblical researching, reasoning, relating and recording? The answer: this method gives both teacher and student direction and dominion. The Principle Approach shows *how* to take possession of the Biblical truths that *control* the subject in His Story.

Headmaster Ronald Kirk of The Master's School in Camarillo, California, has clearly summarized the purpose of this method:

1. It enables one to find God's purpose for the subject—to discover how God defined the subject and used it in His Word and world.

2. This method helps one to discover the personal character demanded by the subject—those qualities required to master and use it Biblically and practically.

3. It helps one to organize the subject and

teach it from the whole to the part, from the rudiments of the discipline by definition and Biblical precept to the parts that make the whole discipline.

4. This method also enables one to evaluate correctly the emphasis, philosophy, and direction suggested by other authors and their works.

A WORD OF CAUTION

One should *not* 4 R a subject and expect to find the seven principles of America's Christian history and government. Every subject has its *own principles* and its *own vocabulary* which can be discovered through the Principle Approach.

The 4 R's embrace both the letter and the spirit of the Principle Approach. *How to 4 R is the letter.* The need is not primarily for the letter, but for the *spirit*—the conviction that there are vital principles to be discovered and taught. There are students of this approach who could testify that they nearly killed their love for a discipline and for the Principle Approach by being so conformed to the literal method of 4 R-ing that they thought the *process* would never end and almost gave up.

There are some subjects, such as reading, which are quickly 4 R'd. And although one could tackle the whole discipline of science or music with this method and finally comprehend more of its vocabulary, principles and ideas, the work may become tedious and time consuming. If you are new to this approach, we recommend that first you study the conclusions of those who have applied the 4 R's to the subjects presented in the *School Curriculum* section and then use the 4 R's to take possession of a part or a *unit* of one subject as you teach it.

For example, in Natural Science as presented by Mr. David Holmes, you may want to develop a complete, self-contained unit on just *respiration*. Use the 4 R's to define that one topic, deduce the vocabulary and research the Biblical purpose and revelations concerning the breath of God and man. Then use whatever textbooks or resources you want to complement your Biblical conclusions and share *your own understanding* of the "breath of life."

HOW TO 4 R A SUBJECT

I. *Define the vocabulary and the properties which constitute the rudiments of the subject.*

Define the general subject in Webster's Dictionary of the English language. In the facsimile edition of Webster's 1828 Dictionary published by the Foundation for American Christian Education,

Miss Rosalie June Slater gives three good reasons for using this first American dictionary as a primary resource for defining particular disciplines. In addition, a brief examination of the meanings used to circumscribe a word will compel the reader to thoroughly appreciate the comprehensive scholarship of Noah Webster and his contribution to American Christian education and government.

One may start with a broad topic such as science, mathematics, language, art, or take a more delimited subject like agriculture, addition, grammar, or the "polite" area of poetry. Excerpt the general definition of the subject and then underline the key words used to identify the properties of the discipline. Define the underlined words, underscoring in each new definition the qualities and ideas that unfold. Continue defining and underlining until the vocabulary needed to explain the principles and ideas of the subject are identified to one's satisfaction. Indeed, one can hardly teach anything with authority without dominion over the words necessary to communicating its leading ideas to thought.

Compile and list the properties or leading ideas of the subject. From this list deduce the rudiments which comprise the substance or "seed" of the subject, the essence of which can be taught to a small child or greatly expanded and applied for a mature student.

When the rudiments of a subject, by definition, have been concluded, the teacher may want to incorporate these elements into the *first* draft of the course goals and objectives (see step VI). The next step is to discover what the Bible says about the subject.

II. *Research the vocabulary and leading ideas of the subject in the Word of God.*

Use an exhaustive Bible Concordance to look up the vocabulary of the subject as defined from the dictionary. Consider any synonyms to the list of words which may be more peculiar to the Bible you use, such as the King James Version.

Write down the references from the concordance that *best represent the context of the vocabulary of the subject.* If Strong's Exhaustive Bible Concordance is used, note the appended number in either the Hebrew and Chaldee or the Greek Dictionary in the back of the concordance. These dictionaries are excellent resources for the roots and significance of words in the context of selected passages.

Write out the vocabulary word, the reference and the passage that *best explain the subject in the context of the Scripture.* The object is to develop correct views of both the *subject* and the *Bible.*

III. *Deduce the Biblical principle and purpose of the subject from the Scripture's use of the definitions.*

"Reasoning is nothing but the faculty of *deducing* unknown truths from principles already known." (John Locke, in Webster's 1828 Dictionary definition of *deduce*)

Working from the presupposition that the Divine Person, God, is the "principle"—the first source, origin and cause—of any subject created by Him for the *good* of man, deduce and discern the *source and origin* of the subject as found in the Truth of God's Revelation to man, the Bible. Discover how Biblical references to the vocabulary of the subject lead one back to the Author of it and reveal God's infinite individuality and diversity. Consider if it is true, indeed, that "of Him, and through Him, and to Him, are *all things*: to whom be glory for ever." (Romans 11:36)

Deduce the *Biblical end and purpose of the subject.* Every subject, from a Christian point of view, must have God as its author and have a Divine purpose consistent with God's plan for man and the universe, otherwise, the subject has no place in a Christian curriculum.

As one researches, reasons and relates the *manner* in which the Bible uses or explains the properties of the subject, consider the following questions:

a) What is my responsibility for the subject, as a Christian?

b) How does the Bible reveal the way that God uses the subject to instruct and govern man?

c) How does the Bible reveal the way man uses the subject to help take possession of God's Word and His world?

IV. *Identify the Christian history of the subject.*

Every subject God made has a Christian history. Recall that history reveals cause and effect in the events of man and nations through time. The Christian history of a subject includes *who* discovered, explained and developed aspects of the discipline, *where* the subject was used, and *how* it revealed "God's causal relations" and His government of men and nations as the Chain of Christianity moved westward.

First, research the history of the subject in relation to the history and progress of the Word of God, Christianity, and the Gospel. For example, make a timeline of the history of the Bible and include the major events of God's Providence in the Old and New Testament. Use the links of the Chain of Christianity identified on page 6A of *Christianity History of the Constitution* to start with. There are books on Bible Chronology that document in great detail the history of the Old and New Testaments or one might refer to "History, Old and New Testament" in Unger's Bible Dictionary for a useful chronology.

Second, research the history of the subject in any comprehensive contemporary resource such as an encyclopedia and history books written before 1900 (most authors still wrote from a Providential point of view before 1900). Then draw a second time-line parallel with the first, and record on it *who* discovered and advanced the subject, *when*, and on *what continent*. Consider any cause-effect relationship between what God has done to advance Gospel liberty on the first timeline and how the subject has advanced *accordingly*.

Finally, discover if, indeed, the rudiments of the subject originated in Asia for the benefit of a few, were developed in Europe for the advancement of the Gospel and the blessing of many, and finally had their fuller expression and use for the good of the individual in America—the world's first Christian Republic. Furthermore, draw conclusions from the sublime viewpoint of God's Providence in the history and chronology and spiritual and religious liberty for the individual with its correlative expression of political and economic freedom. Reason from cause to effect; the progress of *Gospel liberty* for individuals and nations being causative, and the discovery, development and use of the *subject* for the furthering of the Gospel and Christian self-government for the individual being the effect.

V. *Identify the course goals and objectives of the subject.*

Emphasize the Biblical significance and purpose of the subject, and its place on the Chain of Christianity moving westward. Include your own conclusions concerning the relation between the history of the subject and the progress of individual liberty.

At this point, an understanding of the seven Biblical principles of America's Christian history, government and education will greatly enhance one's ability to choose what properties of the subject to emphasize, and how to organize the course to relate the subject to the character, capacity for self-government, and stewardship of the student.

VI. *Review and refine your course goals and overviews each year as your mastery of the Principle Approach to the subject develops.*

Study the course goals and overviews of the subjects included in the School Curriculum section of this Guide. An example of how to conclude course goals from 4 R-ing the subject of Reading is found on page 148, following the next section.

HOW TO 4 R READING

Now let us take the single most important subject in the school curriculum and illustrate how it can be 4 R'd. Note how the following outline exactly parallels steps I-VI in the foregoing narration—how it defines the vocabulary and principles of reading, researches them in the Bible, deduces the Biblical principle and purpose of reading, and summarizes the conclusions of the 4 R-ing method in the subject's course goals and objectives.

(NOTE: Step V, Identifying the Christian history of reading is *not* included in this section)

I

Define the vocabulary and the properties which constitute the rudiments of the subject.

VOCABULARY OF READING

READ: *v.t.* NOTE: the etymology of the Saxon word *redan* is to read, *decree*, to *command*, to *rule* or *govern*. The capacity to read gives one the ability to rule or govern well oneself and a subject, hence, to have dominion over a thing.
The primary sense of read is to *speak, to utter*, that is, to push, drive or advance. This is also the primary sense of *ready*, that is, prompt or advancing, quick.
1. To utter or *pronounce* written or printed *words, letters* or *characters* in proper order; to repeat the *names* or utter the *sounds* customarily annexed to words, letters or characters;
2. To inspect and *understand* words or characters; to *peruse* silently;
3. To *discover* or understand by characters, *marks* or features;
4. To learn by observation;
5. To *know* fully.
v.i. To perform the act of reading (Neh. 8:8)
6. Instructed or knowing by reading, versed in books, learned. Well read...

DECREE: *n.* to judge, to divide.
1. Judicial decision.
2. In the civil law, a determination or judgment of the emperor on a suit between parties.
3. An edict or law...for regulating any business.
4. In general, an order, edict or law made by a superior as a rule to govern inferiors. (Luke 12)
5. Established law or rule. (Job 28)
6. In theology, predetermined purpose of God; the purpose or determination of an immutable Being, whose plan of operation is, like himself, unchangeable.

v.t. To determine judicially; to resolve by sentence.
2. To determine or resolve legislatively; to fix or appoint; to set or constitute by edict or in purpose. (Job 22)

COMMAND: *v.t.* 2. to govern, lead or direct; to have or to exercise supreme authority over.
3. To have in power; to be able to exercise power or authority over;...
6. To have or to exercise a controlling influence over.
v.i. To have or to exercise supreme authority; to possess the chief power; to govern;...
2. The power of controlling; governing influence; sway.

RULE: Sax. regol, to govern, that is to stretch, strain or to make straight.
1. Government: control; supreme command or authority.

GOVERN: 2. To regulate; to influence; to direct.
3. To control; to restrain; to keep in due subjection.
4. To direct; to steer.
v.i. To exercise authority;
2. To maintain the superiority; to have the control.

SPEAK: *v.i.* pret. spoke, pp. spoke, spoken. It. spiccar le parole, to speak distinctly; spiccare, to shine, that is, to shoot or thrust forth; (Eth. sabak, to preach, to teach, to proclaim.) The Sw. has spa, Dan. Spaer, to foretell.
1. To utter words or articulate sounds, as human beings; to express thoughts by words.

UTTER: *v.t.* To speak; to pronounce; to express; as to utter words, to utter sounds.
2. To disclose; to discover; to divulge; to publish.

READY: *a.*j (Sax. raed, from the *root* of *read*; bereder, to prepare)
1. Quick, prompt; not hesitating;
2. Quick to receive or comprehend;
5. Prepared; fitted; furnished with what is necessary, or disposed in a manner suited to the purpose; adv. In a state of preparation, so as to need no delay.

PRONOUNCE: *v.t.* 1. To speak; to utter articulately.
4. To speak; to utter,
5. To declare or affirm.
v.i. To speak; to make declaration; to utter an opinion.

WORD: *n.* (Sax. word or wyrd; Ir. abairim, to speak. A word which is uttered or thrown out.)
1. An *articulate* or vocal sound, or a *combination* of *articulate* and vocal *sounds*, uttered by the human voice, and by custom *expressing an idea* or ideas;
2. The letter or letters, written or printed, which *represent a sound or combination of sounds*.
3. A short discourse.
4. Talk; discourse.
6. *Language*; living speech; oral expression.
8. Signal; order; command.
9. Account; tidings; message.
10. Declaration; purpose expressed.
11. Declaration; affirmation.
v.t. To express in words. Take care to word ideas with propriety.

LETTER: *n.* 1. A mark or character, written, printed, engraved or painted; used as the *representative of a sound*, or of an articulation of the human organs of speech. By sounds, and articulations or closures of the organs, are formed syllables and words. Hence, a *letter* is the *first element of written language*, as *a simple sound is* the *first element of spoken language or speech*. As sounds are audible and communicate ideas to others by the ear, so letters are visible representatives of sounds, and communicate the thoughts of others by means of the eye.
2. A written or printed message; or epistle; a communication made by visible characters from one person to another at a distance.
3. The verbal expression; the literal meaning.
5. Letters, in the plural, learning; erudition; Dead letter, a writing or precept, which is without authority or force. The best law may become a dead letter.

CHARACTER: *n.* 1. A mark made by cutting or engraving, as on stone, metal or other hard material; hence, a mark or figure made with a pen or style, on paper, or other material used to contain writing; a letter, or figure used to form words, and *communicate ideas*. Characters are *literal*, as the letters of an alphabet; *numeral*, as the arithmetical figures; *emblematical* or symbolical, which express things or ideas; and abbreviations, as C for centum, a hundred; lb. for libra, a pound; A.D. Anno Domini, etc.
3. An account, description or representative of anything, exhibiting its qualities and the circumstances attending it.

NAME: *n.* That by which a thing is called; the sound or combination of sounds used to express an idea, or any material substance, quality or act; an appellation attached to a thing by customary use, by which it may be vocally distinguished from other things.
2. The letters or characters written or engraved, expressing the sounds by which a person or thing is known and distinguished.
v.i. 1. To set or give to any person or thing a sound or combination of sounds by which it may be known and distinguished.

SOUND: *n.* 1. Noise; report; the *object of hearing*; that which strikes the ear; or more philosophically, an *impression* or the effect of an impression made on the organs of hearing by an impulse or vibration of the air,
v.i. To make a noise; to utter a voice; to make an impulse of the air that shall strike the organs of hearing with a particular effect.
2. To exhibit by sound or likeness of sound.
v.t. To cause to make a noise;
2. To utter audibly;
4. To order or direct by a sound;
6. To spread by sound or report; to publish or proclaim.

UNDERSTAND: *v.t.* The sense is to support or hold in the mind.
1. To have just and adequate ideas of; to *comprehend*; *to know*;
2. To have the same ideas as the person who speaks, or the ideas which a person intends to communicate.
3. To receive or have the ideas expressed or intended to be conveyed in a writing or books; to know the meaning.

PERUSE: *v.t.* 1. To read, or to read with attention.
2. To observe; to examine with careful survey.

DISCOVER: *v.t.* 1. Literally, to uncover; to remove a covering.
2. To lay open to the view; to disclose; to show; to make visible; to expose to view something before unseen or concealed.
4. To espy; to have the first sight of.
5. To find out; to obtain the first knowledge of; to come to the knowledge of something sought or before unknown.
6. To detect.

MARKS: A visible line made by drawing one substance on another.

KNOW: *v.t.* 1. To perceive with certainty; to understand clearly; to have a clear and certain perception of truth, fact, or anything that actually exists. To know a thing precludes all doubt or uncertainty of its existence.

2. To be informed of; to be taught.

3. To distinguish.

4. To recognize by recollection, remembrance, presentation or description.

8. To learn. Prov. i.

11. To commit; to have.

v.i. To have clear and certain perception; not to be doubtful.

2. To be informed.

ARTICULATE: *a.* Formed by jointing...of the organs of speech; sounds *distinct, separate* and modified by joining the organs of speech.

LANGUAGE: Human speech; the expression of ideas by words or significant articulate sounds for the communication of thoughts.

DISTINCT: 4. So separated as not to be confounded with any other thing; clear; not confused.

SEPARATE: *v.t.* 1. To disunite; to divide; to sever; to part, ... A compound body may be separated into its constituent parts.

2. To cleave; to open.

PROPERTIES OF READING

The properties of reading—the peculiar qualities inherent or naturally essential to a subject—which may be deduced from the foregoing definitions, are:

1. Articulate (separate, distinct) sounds.

2. Combination of articulate sounds.

3. Letters, characters, words representative of distinct sounds.

4. To know fully thoughts and ideas.

5. To express or communicate thoughts and ideas.

6. To form language.

7. To rule, to govern, to command.

RUDIMENTS OF READING

The rudiments of reading—the governing principles or elements deduced by definition which are to be learned first and applied whenever one reads are:

1. The articulate sounds of letters and combinations of letters with their names.

2. Knowing again the thoughts and ideas of one person communicated to another through spoken and written language.

3. The command, rule or government of oneself and one's language through reading and reasoning.

II

Research the vocabulary and leading ideas of the subject in the Word of God, and

III

Deduce the Biblical principle and purpose of the subject from the Scriptures' use of the definitions.

BIBLICAL PURPOSE OF READING

In the following Scriptures that relate to reading, we have often included the Hebrew and Greek meanings of key terms derived from Strong's *Bible Concordance.*

A. READ.

1. *Exodus 24:7.* "And he (Moses) took the book of the covenant, and *read* in the audience of the people: and they said, All that the Lord hath *said* will we do, and be obedient."

Conclusion: Moses read God's Word publicly to effect obedience to God's Law among the people who heard and comprehended the Truth.

2. *Deuteronomy 17:18-19.* "And it shall be, when he sitteth upon the throne of his kingdom, that he (the King of Israel God would choose) shall write him a copy of this law in a book out of that which is before the priests the Levites: and it shall be with him, and he shall read therein all the days of his life: that he may learn to fear the Lord his God, to keep all the words of this law and these statutes, to do them: ..."

Conclusion: Kings and governors are to write their own copy of God's Law and read it daily so they may govern in the fear of God and carry out God's will for His nation.

3. *Nehemiah 8:7-8.* "...and the Levites caused the people to understand the law: and the people stood in their place. So they *read* in the book of the law of God *distinctly,* and *gave the sense,* and caused them to *understand the reading ...*" (See understand)

Conclusion: Since the Hebrew word for *distinctly* means "to separate," and the phrase *gave the sense* means to "give intelligence or understanding," we conclude that the Levites read God's Law so plainly and with such understanding that the people could also discern (or separate mentally) God's will and purpose for them. This reference is unique: it reveals Biblically both why to read and *how*.

4. *II Corinthians 1:13*. "For we write none other things unto you, than what ye *read* or *acknowledge;* and I trust ye shall acknowledge even to the end."
Conclusion: The Greek meaning of the word "read" means "to *know again*," confirming Webster's fifth definition of the meaning of read—"To know fully." Therefore, we conclude that the Corinthian church could literally *know again* the comfort of Christ through the *marks or characters* made by Paul in a letter to them; to read what Paul wrote was to acknowledge or, by definition, to admit or own without doubt the truth of a fact, position or principle that Paul wished to communicate.

5. *Ephesians 3:3-4*. "...(as I wrote afore in few words, Whereby when ye *read*, ye *may understand* my *knowledge* in the mystery of Christ)..."
Conclusion: Paul *wrote* to the church at Ephesus what *he knew* of the grace and fullness of God by Divine Revelation so the Gentiles there might literally *know again*, through *reading*, what *Paul knew* of "the mystery of Christ."

6. *Acts 15:30-31*. When Paul and Barnabas and Silas went to Antioch, Syria and Cilicia, they *read* the epistle from the church at Jerusalem and (the church at Antioch) "rejoiced for the consolation."
Conclusion: Reading aloud a letter on the liberty and law of the gospel brought great delight and gladness (consolation) to the church at Antioch.

B. READING
1. *II Corinthians 3:12-16* (14) "...For until this day remaineth the same vail untaken away in the *reading* of the old testament, which vail is done away in Christ." (& vs. 15) "But even unto this day when Moses is *read*, the vail is upon their heart. Nevertheless, when it (their heart) shall turn to the Lord, the vail shall be taken away." (by the Spirit of the Lord)
Conclusion: The "Children of Israel" may read with understanding the Old Testament once "the law of the Spirit of life in Christ" rules in their heart. (Rom. 8:2)

C. SPEAK
1. *Psalm 119:172*. "My tongue shall *speak of thy word:* for all thy commandments are righteousness."
Conclusion: If the primary sense of read is to speak, then the biblical purpose of speaking from

either reading or remembrance should embrace and publish God's Word and righteousness. (See also Zech. 8:16; Mal. 2:6; II Cor. 12:6)

D. UTTER
1. *I Corinthians 14:9*. "So likewise ye, except ye *utter* by the tongue *words* easy to be understood, how shall it be known what is spoken? for ye shall speak into the air."
Conclusion: We read here that when anyone "gives forth" (Greek rendering of *utter*) the "sound of the Gospel," that the "words" (defined as *something thought and said* in the Greek) should be "easy to be understood." Hence, whatever is both *thought* and *declared* in words should readily give understanding.

E. PRONOUNCE
1. *Judges 12:6*. "...for he (the Ephraimite) could not *frame* to *pronounce* it (Shibboleth) right. Then they took him, and slew him..."
Conclusion: A proper command over the principles or articulate sounds and combinations of sounds necessary to pronounce or render a word properly could mean life or death.

2. *Jeremiah 36:16-18*. (17) "And they asked Baruch, saying, tell us now, how didst thou write all these words at his mouth? Then Baruch answered them, He *pronounced* all these *words* unto me with his mouth, and I wrote them with *ink* in the *book*."
Conclusion: In obedience to God's command, Jeremiah *articulately dictated* God's warnings to Baruch, the scribe, who recorded God's thoughts for Israel and Judah *to know* and *heed*.

F. SOUNDS
1. *I Corinthians 14:7*. "...and even things without life giving *sound*, whether pipe or harp, except they give a distinction in the sounds, how shall it be known what is piped or harped?"
Conclusion: The Biblical purpose of any useful sound is lost unless it be uttered distinctly, separately, without blending or blurring.

G. WORD
1. *Acts 17:11*. "These were more noble than those in Thessalonica, in that they *received the word* with all *readiness of mind*, and *searched* the Scriptures daily, whether those things were so."
Conclusion: This passage suggests the sublimely Biblical disposition necessary to becoming a skillful reader, one who not only searches the Scriptures closely with a view to discover the truth, but is positively cheerful and prompt to do so, being free from reluctance or hindrance through Christ.

BIBLICAL SOURCE AND ORIGIN OF READING

Genesis 1:1,3. "In the beginning God created the heavens and the earth." "And God *said*, Let there be light: and there was light."

Conclusion: When God spoke, the Word of God became the basis of all real enlightenment (Let there be light). When the Word of God was written, reading had its Biblical source and origin.

SUMMARY

The following ten statements summarize some of the conclusions concerning the Biblical purpose of *reading* as a result of 4 R-ing the subject:

1. To effect obedience to God's Word (Ex. 24:7)
2. To govern in the fear of God (Deut. 17:18-19)
3. To bring consolation—delight and gladness (Acts 15:31)
4. To know again what others have known of the will and promises of God through reason applied to Revelation (Eph. 3:3-4)
5. To give understanding (I Cor. 14:9)
6. To be *ready* to search the Scriptures daily (Acts 17:11)
7. To speak of God's Word and righteousness (Psa. 119:172)
8. To comprehend the promises of God in the Old Testament (II Cor. 3:14)
9. To receive a blessing (Rev. 1:3)
10. To utter God's words so distinctly, as to give Biblical intelligence (Neh. 8:7-8)

COURSE GOALS FOR READING

The following four statements are suggested course goals and objectives for the Principle Approach to reading for grades K-6.

1. To read, write, spell and speak the articulate phonetic sounds and combination of sounds of letters, with their names, found in English words and sentences.

2. To know again the principles and ideas expounded in the Word of God through the English Bible.

3. To take possession of the English language, especially the vocabulary of American Christian and civil liberty, in order to properly govern oneself and be ready to control one's home, church and expanding spheres of civil government in the fear of God through "the perfect law of liberty"— the Bible.

4. To teach how literacy goes with individual liberty as the Gospel moved westward on the Chain of Christianity.

YOUR READING PROGRAM

Literacy is defined as a state of being literate or able to read and write and, subsequently, learned or educated in literature and science. Illiteracy is a state of being illiterate or inept, unable to read and write, hence, ignorant of letters or books, untaught, unlearned.[1]

The problem of illiteracy has reached the level of a national disaster. It has been documented that at least 50% of America's population over age 25 are functionally illiterate.[2] Imagine, half of the adult population, inclusive of newlyweds, young parents, management trainees and young citizens, cannot read and master such reading matter as newspapers, job applications, driving and service manuals.

Illiteracy invites dependence and slavery, both spiritual and political. Literacy is essential to achieving and maintaining a free, separate and distinct existence as Americans and as Christians.

---

1. *Webster's Collegiate Dictionary*, 1936; and *An American Dictionary of the English Language*, Noah Webster, 1828, reprinted in 1967 by the Foundation for American Christian Education, San Francisco.

2. Samuel Blumenfeld, *The New Illiterates and How You Can Keep Your Child From Becoming One*, Arlington House, 1974, Chapter 1.

In the light of these observations this article addresses the following concerns: the gravity of the reading problem in America; the Biblical significance and governmental importance of the ability to read; literacy and the Word of God in early American education; the history of the "look-say," sight vocabulary, whole-word approach to reading which has prepared a character to embrace socialism and to delight in irreverence, and has produced a dependent mentality followed by a loss of individual liberty and private property. As an alternative to the "look-say" method of reading, the Principle Approach to teaching reading in the context of "intensive phonics" versus sight-reading or token phonetics will be introduced. Lastly, the Christian home and school administrator is entreated to take the leadership in his school's reading program and to know the total function and significance of reading in the entire curriculum.

THE PROBLEM OF ILLITERACY IN AMERICA

"The teaching of reading—all over the United States, in all the schools, in all the textbooks—is totally wrong and flies in the face of all logic and common sense ... Johnny couldn't read ... for the simple reason that nobody ever showed him how."[3] With this observation, Rudolf Flesch declared war on the whole-word, look-say method of reading in his book *Why Johnny Can't Read*, published in 1955. Mr. Flesch was challenged by nearly all the professional educators and education psychologists, but to parents his observations rang true. Twelve years later, a 1968 U.S. Census estimated that over 50% of the population over 25 had less than a 12th grade education, while noting that such items as driving manuals and tax returns are written at about the 11th grade level or higher. In addition, the national government even acknowledged the problem of illiteracy in 1969, when they established the "Right-to-Read Program," citing the fact that one out of four students nationwide had reading deficiencies; that there were more than three million illiterates in the adult population; and that one half of all unemployed youths between ages 16 and 21 are functionally illiterate. The U.S. Armed Forces tabulated that nearly 70% of the youths entering the armed forces fell below the 7th grade level in reading and academic ability, consequently the military had to start remedial reading and writing programs in order to get recruits to merely read the training manuals necessary to carry out basic military functions.[4]

Even Walter Cronkite became alarmed over the illiteracy of the T.V. viewer. Writing in Signature Magazine, May 1970, he noted how T.V. is being watched by millions of viewers who do not read at all or seldom read newspapers or news magazines. He acknowledged that viewers depend upon evening news broadcasts to inform them through sight and sound and pictures and concluded: "The result of all this is a genuine crisis in communications. Since a democracy (sic) cannot flourish if its people are not adequately informed on the issues, the problem becomes one of the nation's survival."[5]

The ability to read is a key to our survival as a free nation with a Christian form of government as well as the survival of the individual American Christian as a free and independent man in relationship to other men and nations. I also submit that the ability to read is basic to the progress and defense of the Gospel of our Lord Jesus Christ. (See Ex. 24:7; Deut. 17:18-19; I Tim. 4:13)

It has been said that "reading is not merely *a*

basic subject in school; it is *the* basic subject."[6] Reading is the key to the 4 R's, the ability to research, reason, relate and record principles from the Word of God.

If a person does not or cannot read well he will not master the Bible, history, literature, or any other subject of record. In arithmetic, for example, poor readers are easily bewildered by word problems. As our common schools produce functionally illiterate students, the standards for academic achievement and entrance into college are lowered. Thus, as a result of the past fifty years of a sight-reading, look-say, ideographic approach to reading, America is being populated by an appalling number of ignorant, inept, and inert youths and adults.

THE BIBLICAL SIGNIFICANCE AND GOVERNMENTAL IMPORTANCE OF READING

How important is the ability to read from a Christian point of view? Do the Scriptures confirm the significance of reading to receive the blessings of God and to forward God's grace and purpose for men and nations? Of what importance is reading to the government of God through Christ in the hearts of individuals and with regard to their nation?

In *II Kings 22:8* we read that Hilkiah, the high priest, found the book of the law while the house of the Lord was being repaired. This copy of the Pentateuch was probably recovered from the cornerstone of Solomon's temple while the "breaches in the house" were being rebuilt. Hilkiah gave the book of the law to Shaphan, the scribe, who read it to King Josiah. Josiah in turn, called all the people of Judah together (*II Kings 23:2*) and "read in their ears all the covenant which was found in the house of the Lord." King Josiah made a covenant with the Lord on behalf of Judah and "all the people stood to the covenant." As a result of reading the books of the law, the people voluntarily stood and joined with King Josiah "to walk after the Lord to keep his commandments, and his testimonies, and his statutes, with all their hearts, and all their soul, to perform the words of this covenant that were written in this book: ..." Thus, Judah came under the blessing and government of God's law for a time through the reading and publishing of God's will for His people.

In *Acts 8:30* the Ethiopian Eunuch was reading

---

3. Rudolf Flesch, *Why Johnny Can't Read and What You Can Do About it*, Harper & Row, Publishers, 1955, p. 9.

4. Blumenfeld, *op. cit.*, pp. 16-17.

5. *Ibid.*

6. Arthur S. Trace, *Reading Without Dick and Jane*, H. Regency Co., 1965, p. 1.

the prophet Esaias and Philip was used to open the Eunuch's understanding and lead him to the redemption and control of God by faith in the Lord Jesus Christ followed by believer's baptism.

Revelation 1:3 declares the Revelation of Jesus Christ where God's blessing comes by reading: "Blessed is he that readeth and they that hear the words of this prophecy, and keep those things which are written therein: for the time is at hand."

Literacy goes with liberty and the capacity of the individual to be properly self-governed. Literacy is allied to both the liberty wherewith Christ has made us free from the bondage of sin and death and the liberty we enjoy under the umbrella of constitutional and civil law in America. The Biblical basis of Christian liberty and self-government, or the government of God in the inward man, is the foundation of the American Christian conviction that our rights or "just claims" to life, liberty and property are God-given, not civil government granted. Hence, as American Christians we conceive of civil government as a government of settled, known, and established written laws which only a literate people can write as well as fulfill in order to preserve and perpetuate their stewardship of God's property. The ability to read and write can be the means to enjoying Christian liberty and preserving our civil or political liberty. Illiteracy can keep a people in both spiritual darkness and under political tyranny and bondage or impel them into ignorance, then dependence, then bondage.

Literacy is one of the keys to liberty and freedom. Most educators are promoting reading methods which are robbing the people of the ability to reason biblically and governmentally, thereby keeping them in ignorance of both the Law and the Gospel which are the basis of our Christian form of government and the greatest liberty the individual has ever enjoyed in the history of the world.

LITERACY AND THE INFLUENCE OF THE WORD OF GOD IN EARLY AMERICAN EDUCATION

It has been documented that "adult male literacy in the American colonies seems to have run from 70% to virtually 100%, on the basis of signatures on deeds, wills, militia rolls, and voting rosters."[7] How do we account for this? One scholar of America's Christian history and literature offered the following reasons for such a high degree of literacy produced by our early colonial education.

"(Colonial Americans) read exceptionally well. Broadsides and newspapers had a high school reading level. Every colony published at least one newspaper. The people read and knew exactly what was being proposed by the British Parliament. They advised their representatives in the respective colonial assemblies.

"The colonists wrote with amazing skill. They wrote to each other and to friends in England, Ireland, and Europe to inform them of their position on principles. They spoke with effectiveness and convinced each other of the necessity of Independence. They understood principles and reasoned from them to each event or infringement of their privileges and responsibilities.

"The HOLY BIBLE has been documented as the single greatest reason for the *reading, writing, speaking,* and *reasoning* ability of our American colonists . . . If the Holy Bible so influenced the education of the vast majority of our Americans 200 years ago, let us put it back as an *educational* textbook and restore the quality of literacy we once had—allowing us to establish the first Christian Constitution the world has known, with the greatest outpouring of Christian evangelical effort ever witnessed."[8]

The research of such a secular historian and educator as Mr. Lawrence A. Cremin, Professor of Education and Director of the Institute of Philosophy and Politics of Education at Columbia University, also confirms the influence of the BIBLE as the "single greatest reason for the reading, writing, speaking and reasoning ability of our American Colonists." Some of Mr. Cremin's conclusions are as follows:

"Above all, however, the colonists were acquainted with the Bible itself, principally in the Geneva Version but increasingly in the King James Version. The Bible was read and recited, quoted and consulted, early committed to memory and constantly searched for meaning. Deemed universally relevant, it remained throughout the century the most important cultural influence in the lives of Anglo-Americans.[9]

"In the teaching of reading, a family might use a textbook like Edmund Coot's *The English Schoole-Maister* (1596); or a simple hornbook or ABC,

---

7. Lawrence A. Cremin, *American Education, The Colonial Experience, 1607-1783,* Harper & Row, Publishers, 1970, p. 546.

8. Rosalie J. Slater, "Restoring American Christian Education To Our Schools," *American Christian History Literature Program,* Foundation for American Christian Education, San Francisco.

9. Cremin, *op. cit.,* p. 40.

which presented the alphabet, a few syllables combining a consonant with a vowel, and a prayer or grace, usually the Lord's Prayer or the Apostles' Creed; . . . This was equally true of the Bible itself, which was frequently used as a reading text. Doubtless many a colonial youngster learned to read by mastering the letters and syllables phonetically and then hearing Scriptural passages again and again, with the reader pointing to each word until the relationship between the printed and oral passages became manifest."[10]

"*The Bible itself*, particularly the Geneva edition of 1560 and the Authorized Version of 1611, *is the single most important primary source for the intellectual history of colonial America.*"[11]

Scholars like Mr. Cremin may not acknowledge the Bible as the inspired, inerrant Word of God. However, his observations constitute a challenge to American Christian parents, teachers and administrators to take the leadership, as only we can, in restoring the Word of God, the Holy Bible, to the classroom as the source, origin and inspiration of our philosophy of education, methods and curriculum.

We know that one of the reasons local, community-centered common schools were established in Colonial times was to teach children how to read the Bible and comprehend the laws of the land. The Colonists desired a high degree of literacy in order to read the Scriptures and promulgate the Gospel. They used their Bibles to achieve literacy, consequently producing generations of Bible-believing, Bible-living, independent self-governing citizens. Should we do less?

A BRIEF HISTORY OF THE LOOK-SAY METHOD OF READING

Mr. Samuel Blumenfeld has documented the fact that the first look-say primer—or Dick and Jane reading series in America—was used and promoted as early as 1836 and was hailed as the best method of teaching reading by Horace Mann, the father of progressive education.[12] The highlights of this fascinating story are as follows:

Rev. Thomas H. Gallaudet, a graduate of Yale in 1805 and a student of theology at Andover, was the Director of the American Asylum at Hartford, Connecticut, for the Education of the Deaf and Dumb from 1817-1830. Gallaudet brought forth the system of sight-reading by teaching a deaf and dumb child to read by first having him learn a sight-vocabulary of about 50 words before teaching him the letters. He used pictures and whole words to teach deaf-mutes as they could not learn a sound-system of reading. The written words (a sound-symbol) of normal man's spoken language was taught to deaf-mutes as ideographs rather than phono-graphs.[13] Thus, students learned the meaning of *cat* by a picture and a word, giving rise to the sight-reading of whole words whose meanings are conveyed by pictures.

Gallaudet's success in teaching reading to deaf-mutes encouraged him to advance this method to normal students who could see and hear. Thus, Rev. Gallaudet became the first person in America to introduce a whole-word method with extensive use of pictures to represent words and meanings without mastering the sounds of letters and combinations of letters. He then published a "Mother's Primer" for normal schools which was the first Dick and Jane reader in America. Gallaudet's Primer, like the current Dick and Jane readers, emphasized the look-say, ideographic approach to reading and made sounds and oral explanations of letters secondary. Mr. Blumenfeld even documents the fact that Gallaudet's "Mother's Primer," published in 1836, used the names *Jane* for the little girl, *Spot* for the dog and *Frank* for the little boy. The Primer's first line was "Frank had a dog, his name was Spot."

Horace Mann, the acclaimed Secretary of the Massachusetts Board of Education from 1837 to 1848, endorsed Gallaudet's new method of teaching reading and attacked the teaching of the alphabet and letter sounds in his 2nd Annual Report issued in 1838. Mann and his wife subsequently toured Europe in 1843, visiting England, Scotland, Ireland, France and Holland and then spent six weeks visiting schools in Prussia and Saxony (a province of Germany). Upon his return he wrote his famous 7th Annual Report of 1884, praising Prussia's compulsory, state-controlled, secular educational system and criticized the Boston School system, renewing his attack on the phonetic approach to reading. "I am satisfied that our greatest error in teaching children to read lies in beginning with the alphabet;" he declared, " . . . being persuaded that no thorough reform will ever be effected in our schools until this practice is abolished."[14]

It is interesting to note that Horace Mann

---

10. Cremin, *op. cit.*, pp. 129-130.

11. Cremin, *op. cit.*, p. 587.

12. Blumenfeld, *op. cit.*, Chap. 7.

13. Ideograph: (idiogram) N. A picture of pictorial symbol (not phonetic) to represent an idea rather than a word. *Webster's Collegiate Dictionary*, 1946.

14. Blumenfeld, *op. cit.*, pp. 147-148.

praised a philosophy of education practiced in Prussia that was based upon a philosophy of government that subsequently produced a Bismark, a Kaiser, and a Hitler while indoctrinating and enculturating into its youth the character to embrace and support such "leaders."

Horace Mann's attack on the Boston School system and the alphabetic approach to teaching reading did not go unanswered. The Association of Masters, representing 31 Boston Schoolmasters, experimented with and evaluated the whole-word, sight-reading method praised by Mr. Mann. One of the masters was chosen to write a brilliant and challenging critique of Mann's 7th Report. The response of the masters, published in 1844, is well worth studying.[15]

This brief account of a fascinating period of reading "reform" in American education suggests several things. First, the look-say sight vocabulary, whole-word method of teaching reading advanced by Rev. Gallaudet for the deaf and dumb is producing generations of nearly aphonic, inarticulate, frustrated speakers and readers. As the Report of the Boston Schoolmasters demonstrated, advocates of the look-say method must learn thousands of ideograms for all new words. The phonetic approach teaches principles, a few key sounds (as few as 44 in some intensive phonetic methods) which provide the foundation for pronouncing, reading, writing and correctly spelling thousands of words. Otherwise, students grow up learning whole words or even phrases without knowing the relationship of the words to their letters and sounds or that letters have anything to do with pronunciation. But there is an alternative, as hundreds of Christian home and day schools in America are proving with great success.

THE PRINCIPLE APPROACH TO TEACHING READING

What is the Principle Approach to teaching reading which develops Christian character and scholarship? Consider some of the historical characteristics of Western education.

Historically, some of the most important goals and aims of traditional American education were to train children to function as adults in a free society; to develop men and women whose minds were trained to function independently by mastering all the analytical skills required to exercise an independent judgment. These goals required attentiveness, concentration, silence, "a room full of minds at work." Such mental work required solitary concentration. But this emphasis was to be radically changed.

One hundred years after Horace Mann, progressive secular educators such as John Dewey, George S. Counts, and William Kilpatrick advanced a philosophy of education which transformed the classroom into a noisy workshop where children were doing things together, making each classroom a little society and a group-oriented learning center. The new goal was not to train the individual to be independent and to exercise self-government and sound judgment, but to develop the child's social character and consciousness, his social interests and interdependence among men. This took a new curriculum to produce a character for socialism and modernism.[16] In addition, the historic method of phonetic reading was disputed and cast out as too tedious, dull and slow. The whole-word, sight-reading, Dick and Jane readers were substituted in enormous volume and with great fanfare but with devastating and even sinister effect upon the level of literacy in America.

Even now some Christian teachers may believe that an approach or text that uses *a* phonetic approach is enough. It *isn't* enough! The Principle Approach to reading requires what may best be called *intensive phonetics*. It should also be understood that a school's reading program is a reflection of a philosophy of government and character development. In fact, reading is a researching, reasoning, relating and recording process. Our method of teaching reading either promotes the use of principles as a basis of life and living or uses an environmental or progressive approach.

An INTENSIVE PHONICS method should have the following characteristics. It should develop the ability of the mind to *analyze* (resolve things into their parts or principles or elements) based upon specific principles which the student has mastered. When this analytical or reasoning process is implanted in the minds of youth in early childhood, it influences *every* subject in the curriculum and develops the scholarship necessary to promote and defend the Gospel as well as our liberty and property under the laws of the land. A child gains confidence by learning that he can master the difficult words by reducing them to their simpler parts. The child's mind becomes accustomed (familiar with, by use and by habits formed by practice) to the process of intellectual analysis and reasoning from the same simple principles worked over and over again in *each* subject.

---

15. *Ibid.*, Appendix II, pp. 315-351.

16. For excellent documentation on this point see: Paul W. Shafer and John Howland Snow, *The Turning of the Tides*, The Long House, New Canaan, Conn., 1962.

The child knows he is mastering each subject in terms of its principles. A mastery of the principles of phonics gives a mastery of thousands of words, over 90% of the English language. Forgetting a word or how to read or pronounce a word is not a threat. The student may forget, but he has the principal sounds of the alphabet and the combinations of sounds, i.e., the principles of phonic analysis, by which he can analyze the words he might have forgotten.

In contrast, the contemporary look-say, guess-the-word, and token phonetics approach relies on memorizing word-forms or the structure of words. It relies upon a pictographic or hierographic method of learning as used in learning Chinese by its characters which represent whole words. A method of word-guessing depends upon memorization and repetition which can be both boring and tedious. No mastery of specifics is required and no feeling of definite achievement is produced. No sense of dominion, independence or confidence results. Reasoning skills are minimized. The use of meaning clues often becomes ridiculous and time consuming. The look-say method has an impressionistic emphasis and minimized the ability to reason from principal sounds. Perhaps the greatest concern is that this method produces a quality of character that tends to be violent, discouraged, frustrated and provokes a feeling of being trapped and useless. Students who are inept at reading and writing become so disappointed and so dependent upon sensory experience that they are encouraged to seek drugs to provide a contrived and artificial enlightening of the mind.

Intensive phonetics, however, can produce a character for independence. This approach can liberate and give one a sense of dominion and confidence over new words, new material and provide the ability to grow and be in command of words, ideas and all the rich heritage of Christian history, literature, science, music, etc.

An intensive phonetic method of reading is consistent with the American Christian principle of property whereby the property of one's mind, identity and talents is preserved as private as far as other men are concerned and held in stewardship where God, His will, is concerned. On the contrary, reading methods which produce illiteracy tend to bring one's mind, identity and talents in obedience to and dependence upon society and opinion makers, and subject to "philosophy and vain deceit, after the rudiments of the world, and not after Christ." (*Colossians 2:8*) Mastering the principles of reading, writing, speaking and spelling develops a unity of principle with a diversity of expression and individuality which cannot be easily controlled. Reading methods responsible for producing functional illiterates develop a uniformity and conformity which is easily controlled because it is dependent.

Which of these opposing views of life and living do we see surfacing and parading about today as a result of the reading programs promoted so intensely in American Schools for the last 50 years? Do we see a character ripe for and actually embracing socialism and modernism, which is non-reflective and externally oriented and easily controlled; or a character which is the express image of Christ, which preserves and defends the Gospel and demonstrates the sovereignty of God in each aspect of life and living while exercising a practical, intelligent, literate stewardship over all spheres of life—civil, religious, educational, economic, social?

AMERICAN CHRISTIAN ADMINISTRATIVE LEADERSHIP IN THE READING PROGRAM

Every parent and Christian school administrator should know how to teach the reading method used in his school. Neither parents nor administrators should turn over the reading program to a teacher without knowing what the program produces in terms of literacy, character, and scholarship. Do we know what our teachers are teaching? Does the rest of the faculty know how to read phonetically and are they teaching the vocabulary of their subject phonetically, thus supporting and promoting the same principles of reading that the elementary and high school English teachers teach in depth?

We must understand the total function and importance of the reading program to the entire curriculum because "Reading is not merely *a* basic subject in school; it is *the* basic subject." Be certain that your reading program is producing the character and scholarship necessary to articulate and perpetuate Christ and Christianity in America and is able to defend and perpetuate America's heritage of Christian character, property and self-government under a limited, constitutional Christian form of government.

LITTLE PATRIOTS SERIES KINDERGARTEN PROGRAM

Developed over 15 years by reading and linguistic specialist Dr. Guyla Nelson and Master Kindergarten teacher, Miss Saundra Scovell, the *LITTLE PATRIOTS SERIES* stands unique among kindergarten programs available to Christian teachers and parents. Its content and methodology are based upon Biblical principles which account for its unusual success.

The most outstanding educational feature of the *LITTLE PATRIOTS SERIES* is its structured, analytical approach to teaching the American language. Identified from research are six basic categories of one-syllable words and the consistent, orderly rules that govern each. When mastered, these phonetic rules become the basis for a student's progression to the multi-syllable vocabulary of our language. In the process, these rules are applied not only to reading but to spelling as well.

Unlike other programs, which call themselves "phonics-based," the *LITTLE PATRIOTS SERIES* does not rely on "sight" techniques to memorize difficult words. Rather, since every word falls into one of the six categories, students can reason from and apply consistent rules to all of the words they encounter. The result — the *LITTLE PATRIOTS SERIES* has been producing outstanding readers, spellers, and thinkers for more than a decade! Families in almost every state and several foreign countries are reaping the results of this tremendous curriculum.

PHONICS FOR LITTLE PATRIOTS

Leading to understanding of the six categories of single-syllable words, the phonics curriculum, the foundation and hub for all language instruction, sets forth the principles that unlock the mysteries of sounds, letters, and words. PHONICS FOR LITTLE PATRIOTS provides the tools necessary for mastering the skills of reading, writing, and spelling.

LITTLE PATRIOTS READ

Beginning students can learn to read effectively without needing classroom reading groups. The phonics principles learned by the children are applied here in the reading of words, phrases, and sentences — all in preparation for reading the stories in the LITTLE PATRIOTS READERS.

KINDERGARTEN READERS

Six illustrated readers, each emphasizing one-syllable words from one of the six categories of the American language, contain over 540 interesting, Biblical, family-oriented, character-building stories. Kindergarten phonics instruction finds its culmination in the successful reading of these stories.

LITTLE PATRIOTS WRITE

These handwriting exercises provide opportunity for the students to develop, improve, and display skill in handwriting. Handwriting can be an important factor in developing the character traits of self-discipline and doing careful work.

LITTLE PATRIOTS SPELL

Also keyed to the six basic categories of the American language are the six volumes of kindergarten student spellers. Students progress step by step through these spellers, learning by principles how to spell one-syllable words while developing the ability to reason and spell with confidence and accuracy.

PHONICS/SPELLING MANUAL, PART 1

This comprehensive, 486-page Teacher's Manual is truly everything you need to know about phonics. Included are tips for teachers, visualized rules, and a structured phonetic analysis of approximately 3,000 one-syllable words. While not mandatory for teaching phonics, it is highly recommended that teachers and parents invest in this manual. It will pay for itself ten-fold in savings of teacher/parent preparation time and improved quality of instruction.

Part 2, available for Fall '86, follows the same approach for advanced phonics instruction (multisyllable words), grades 1-8.

For Brochures, Prices, and Additional Information, write or call MILE-HI PUBLISHERS, 980 South Upham, Denver, CO, 80286, (303) 992-5833 or 992-1557.

WRITING ROAD TO READING

THE SPALDING METHOD

"A classroom teacher can learn and can teach the Spalding method correctly by studying this ONE book (*The Writing Road to Reading* by Romalda Bishop Spalding). What distinguishes this method is its direct use of the complete phonics along with the rules of English spelling and writing from the sounds of spoken words.

"English has 70 common phonograms (25 letters and 45 *fixed* combinations of 2, 3 and 4 letters) to say on paper the 45 basic sounds used in speaking it. Under the Spalding method a beginning class starts learning fifty-four of these phonograms by saying their sounds and writing them. Then they write, from dictation, as they say the sounds of the most used 150 words, write original sentences to show meanings, and within two months, start reading good books.

HEARING, SAYING, WRITING AND SPEAKING AT THE SAME TIME

"The great advantages of learning words by writing them from dictation are that this connects at once the written symbols to their spoken sounds, and that all children can learn *because* every avenue into the mind is used. They HEAR the teacher say the word and each child HEARS himself say each sound while he *uses his mind* in saying it and in directing his hand to WRITE it. He SEES what he has written as he then READS it. No other way can fix sooner or more securely in his memory the words he can write, and so can read at a glance, thus building his sight vocabulary.

PROBLEMS OF INATTENTION VANISH

"... It gives an understanding of the logical basis of the written language. Each day's new words are taught to the whole class. All must produce, do mental work to write and read, and problems of discipline or inattention vanish under each child's desire to learn. The average first grade class knows the 70 phonograms, writes at least 700 words before June, and reads many times that many. The second and upper grades learn more words rapidly by the same method. Classroom reading is not confined to basal readers, but is centered on interesting books of real literature, which educate.

RULES OF SPELLING

"There are 28 simple rules of spelling which often determine which phonogram or spelling is used. They are taught as facts about the language as they occur in the spelling of a word. They are thus learned from examples, rather than memorized separately.

MENTAL WORK—NO GAMES

"The Spalding method is so direct and well organized that the children use only paper and pencil AND THEIR MINDS. No games, devices, workbooks, or films are needed. The direct use of their minds to work and learn, and to produce on paper, is far more interesting and instructive to all children. Their enthusiasm in every class is inspiring to teachers and parents. This comes from the careful order and the insight with which Mrs. Spalding built her method to arouse in children their natural eagerness to learn and use their latent capacity for mental work..."

(Spalding Education Foundation)

For copies of *The Writing Road to Reading*, phonogram cards, spelling notebooks, and additional information write:

Spalding Education Foundation
2301 W. Dunlap Ave., Suite 105
Phoenix, Arizona 85021

The Reading Reform Foundation
949 Market Street, #436
Tacoma, Washington 94802

Oma Riggs, Inc.
P.O. Box 2108
Portland, Oregon 97208–2108

See also AMERICAN CHRISTIAN KINDERGARTEN, by Lois Wehrman Miller, p. 173 in this *Guide*.

ELEMENTARY SCHOOL CURRICULUM

AN AMERICAN CHRISTIAN KINDERGARTEN

BY LOIS WEHRMAN MILLER

●

AMERICAN CHRISTIAN HISTORY

BY RUTH J. SMITH

●

ARITHMETIC
FROM THE PRINCIPLE APPROACH

BY JAMES V. KILKENNY

AMERICAN CHRISTIAN KINDERGARTEN

BY LOIS WEHRMAN MILLER
Former Master Teacher
American Heritage Christian Schools
Hayward, California

CONTENTS

AMERICAN CHRISTIAN KINDERGARTEN CURRICULUM

PREFACE

Can a teacher inspire children of kindergarten age with a love for learning many new things? Can a kindergarten teacher develop in her students a deeper sense of awe, wonder and appreciation of God's Creation? Can young children learn God's principles and laws and how they apply to what they are learning?

Can five-year-olds be taught to sit properly, write and give a recitation? Can they learn study skills and take responsibility for small amounts of homework, as well as their own personal notebooks?

Can they learn the first principles of reading, spelling, America's Christian history, natural science, American literature and other subjects?

The Principle Approach to American Christian Education was used successfully by the writer for eight years to give positive answers to these questions, and to prepare kindergarten children in a Christian day school with the character and eagerness to fulfill their God-given potential.

Parents and teachers who have used this approach are raising up students with the foundational skills for unlimited learning, the capacity for Christian self-government, and a distinctly American Christian character. These children delight in their Creator, His Word and His world. They respect authority and moral standards, live to please God, and are a joy to people around them. I am not describing the exceptional class, but typical youngsters, whose growth I have witnessed in years of experience working with committed and supportive parents.

This method may be used with one- to four-year-olds, too, or expanded into the upper grades. Many parents have testified that they, too, enjoyed learning while they helped their children learn.

The following course outline includes some very simple but necessary details and explanations because the author believes that other parents and teachers, like herself, may have come from contemporary "progressive" educational backgrounds, and need help to establish constructive classroom control, and to instruct children through America's historic method of Biblical reasoning.

The beginning teacher who is first using this approach may not discern the subtle, though pervasive aspects of evolutionary thinking, progressive education and liberal theology which have become so common today. Therefore, this overview offers well-defined instructions and expectations for student conduct and achievement, not only to guide the teacher but to provide practical American Christian standards by which to measure student progress in various subjects.

May the curriculum and recommendations that follow be only the beginning of the parent's or teacher's independent study, preparation and application of the rudiments and Biblical truths of American Christian education.

MY PHILOSOPHY OF EDUCATION

Before embracing a choice of curriculum or methods, the teacher should articulate her personal educational philosophy so that all decisions, curriculum and governmental methods will be consistent with her presuppositions. Here is the author's interpretation of the philosophy that was demonstrated in the beginning of our nation through historic American Christian philosophy.

Education is Christian when the Word of God is used as the primary authority for the origin and purpose for all subjects and of all discipline.

Education is American Christian when it is built upon the Christian idea of God, man and government as practiced by the Pilgrims, declared by the colonial American pastors, pedagogues, Puritans, and patriots, and extended into America's civil government and economy by the people.

American Christian education is based upon Biblical reasoning and governmental principles emphasized in first century Christianity, and expressed in America's first two hundred years. For example, some of the truths which govern the student, as well as the emphasis of the subjects, are the Biblical principles of individual worth, local self-government, character, personal property (especially the property of the conscience), and voluntary consent.

American Christian education focuses on cultivating the individual heart, mind, and character needed to maintain a Christian Republic. This provides opportunity for the teacher to help the student to apply his knowledge to the government of himself, and then to extend it into his home, church, community and nation. This approach purposes to develop in students a mind and temper, redeemed by the Spirit of Christ, and the manners and habits required for a useful life of service to God, man and country.

THE METHOD IS THE PRINCIPLE APPROACH

The Principle Approach is "America's historic Christian method of Biblical reasoning which makes the Truths of God's Word the basis of every subject in the school curriculum."[1] With this method, an American Christian curriculum is developed by researching, reasoning, relating, and recording the rudiments of each subject, their Biblical origin, Biblical purpose, and place in the Chain of Christianity. A wholistic approach is used to expand and unify the subjects.[2]

● THE TEACHER IS THE KEY

The teacher is not subservient or secondary to the textbooks but an example of an independent, productive self-teaching thinker who is capable of reflective reasoning. As a student of the Bible, she should be willing to research the Biblical principles, Christian history, and literature of the subjects and learn how to identify the seven Biblical principles of America's Christian history and government in education.[3] She should train the student in the art of reasoning with the ultimate goal of reasoning from the Bible.

THE NOTEBOOK IS THE TOOL

In the American Christian curriculum the teacher uses the notebook to record what she has researched, reasoned and related concerning the subject. The student's notebook reflects his own individual labor as he applies his mind to the teacher's directions and instruction. The notebook is the child's property which he learns to value as he organizes its contents, keeps it clean and neat, and remembers to bring it to class. The child's attitude toward his daily assignments is reflected in his written work. The notebook shows the student's character qualities: care or carelessness; order or disorder.

A PROVIDENTIAL VIEW IS NECESSARY

In applying this philosophy to the classroom the American Christian teacher accepts God as Creator and Designer of each individual, and as the Sovereign, Providential God of all that He creates. As an American Christian educator she rejects evolutionary, progressive and pagan interpretations of school curriculum and methods of teaching.

---

1. *T/L.*, p. 88.
2. *Ibid*, pp. 108-110. See also p. 183 for an example of a wholistic approach to teaching arithmetic.
3. *Ibid*, pp. 111-112.

Specific American Christian ideas and themes can be taught to the kindergarten student through the curriculum and classroom government.[4] By the end of the year the student can be trained to respect:

1. *The authority of God and His Word*, for all subjects and for all government—from self to civil.
2. *The authority of parents and teacher* as representatives of God and His Word.
3. *The Christian individuality of each student* as unique and valuable in God's plan of history. He can appreciate others' individuality and show concern for their needs.
4. *The principle of Christian self-government.* He can develop the capacity for self-government by:

   a. using the Bible as a standard for knowing right and wrong;

   b. realizing that God is interested first and foremost in the internal attitudes of the heart. Outward expression is important, but secondary;

   c. recognizing that each student is in control of his own eyes, mouth, hands, and body;

   d. learning that a home, school, church, and civil government can be governed by Biblical principles.
5. *The principle of Christian character* as illustrated by biographies from the Bible, America's Christian history and literature and practiced through the student's daily work and play.
6. *Individual property, including the property of conscience*, by:

   a. recognizing each individual as God's property, made "in His image," and accountable to his Creator-Maker;

   b. caring for his own property and allowing others to care for theirs;

   c. training his conscience in the Law of God and also respecting others' expression of their conscience in understanding Biblical standards and principles.
7. *The rudiments of each subject* by learning the first principles, or elements, and the rules which govern them.
8. *The liberty to become self-teaching* through mastering the first principles of the English language.[5]

---

4. Government is defined by Webster's 1828 Dictionary as direction, regulation, control and restraint. The purpose of external laws is to encourage individual internal control and allow each student the liberty to learn.

5. The teacher should not under-estimate the natural capacity of the five-year-old to achieve these end-of-year goals, nor should she over-estimate his God-given maturation level.

INTRODUCTION TO THE SUBJECT OVERVIEWS

Kindergarten curriculum overviews for fourteen specific subjects follow this article. Through her personal classroom teaching experience, the author is convinced that the content of these overviews is within the capacity of any five-year-old child who is developed physically, mentally, and emotionally enough to enter, and continue, kindergarten training.

The teaching material in the subject overviews provides a well-balanced foundation for academic and character training. If the teacher prefers to teach more in any subject area, she may explain and amplify further, but care must be taken not to neglect the most basic subjects. If the teacher prefers to teach less than the entire curriculum, she may choose limited subjects or selected portions of study. It is still possible for the child to be successful in first grade if a limited and partial curriculum is taught. However, his skills may not be as well-balanced as they would be if the whole curriculum were used. In any case, the teacher should be sure to include a thorough literacy program and instruction in basic Bible reasoning in order to provide the minimum foundation for his American Christian education. The kindergarten curriculum *is important* because once the child enters first grade there will not be the same opportunity to lay the foundations in such a full, unhurried, and enjoyable way.

Any parent or instructor should be capable of teaching the curriculum in the subject overviews. It may be necessary to learn how to be more imaginative and flexible, or how to expand on seemingly simple truths in order to broaden understanding from a child's viewpoint. This overview provides some examples of how to do this. The teacher, as an example of a self-teaching student, should continue to read and research the subjects, collect pictures for her files, acquire books for use, and find other supporting materials.

THE PACE

The content of the subject overviews consists of simple principles, ideas and facts to be presented during the week and reviewed day by day. The weekly presentation gives opportunity to use a variety of methods of introduction, presentation, and review. Because this course of study challenges and "stretches" the mind, there are times when a student, or students, may not comprehend the material being taught. This may be due to some childish fear, immaturity, or perhaps the teacher's inadequate explanation of a particular point.

The weekly presentation not only creates an interesting format but allows the teacher great freedom, and takes away frustration or pressure when students do not understand or have been distracted. The teacher knows she will succeed at a later time. The thorough weekly treatment of a subject makes the pupil feel at home with an idea while he is acquiring skill in using it and lets him do this before his attention is shifted to another idea. Moving on prematurely disturbs the pupil and makes for failure.

All subjects cannot be taught every day. Subjects such as history, geography, and science may be alternated, or they may be taught in a cluster of days. Art is often used to illustrate another subject so it may sometimes be used in that subject's time slot. With few exceptions, Bible, literacy, mathematics, and literature should be taught each day. However, in one instance, the teacher replaced Friday's math class with art because that period furnished the perfect clean-up time for a full-length, well-taught art class.

Occasionally forfeiting a main subject class does no harm. In fact, it may give refreshment from the routines of weekly work. There are also times when a subject may take only a few minutes and, after that, the class may go on to another topic. Thus, several subjects sometimes can be covered in one time slot.

For example, the discussion of George Washington as the "Father of Our Country" may require a few minutes only, for three days out of the week. Often during the year, the concept may be referred to as it is related to other facts in history and in other subjects.

A time rhythm, or cycle, may be used effectively with this curriculum. With this rhythm the teacher repeats the subject by review and further study. It may be every three weeks, or every three months. For example, when studying fractions the student can first learn what the word *fraction* means, then learn that two halves make a whole. About three months later the teacher can review what was learned about fractions, then teach how four fourths make a whole. A later review on fractions can include eight eighths.

In literacy class the time rhythm, or cycle, can be used to teach a specific area of emphasis such as spelling, reading, or writing. This method allows for testing, review, and daily improvement while it eliminates a fragmented feeling of jumping from one topic to another in literacy and avoids a sense of uncertainty as to what is being accomplished.

This teaching technique keeps the work from becoming too heavy and burdensome for a young child. It also allows the youngster to develop and mature and thus be ready for greater comprehension when the teacher returns to the subject. Furthermore, it renews the child's interest and promotes a good attitude towards learning.

TESTS AND TESTING

American Christian education emphasizes the need for a standard to measure and report achievement. A test is one way to provide that standard as the student is compared, or tested, by the standard. The young kindergarten child should be trained how to work toward, achieve and accomplish the specific goals which the teacher sets forth as standards for testing.

WHY TEST

"What is a test?" the five-year-old may ask.

"A test tells me what is inside your mind so that I can help you to learn. You must tell (or write) what you know—so *I* know what *you* know," the teacher answers.

It is easy to assume that all the students are understanding and retaining what is being taught. Unless five-year-old students are tested individually to find if there are some who do not understand, the teacher will be covering too much material—or she may be over-teaching on something already learned.

The young child must be challenged and encouraged, not discouraged, by meeting the standard of tests. Since the teacher is "mind stretching" she must be sure to set reasonable standards for achievement which will be basic, clear, and well-taught. She can allow for immature, childish mistakes which do not affect overall comprehension of an idea or fact. The five-year-old will learn that from the beginning of the year the teacher is not expecting perfection but to continually improve and keep reaching for higher achievements that represent small but obtainable steps.

About two-thirds of the academic tests will be *oral*. Written tests include dictation of phonograms, spelling words, music notation, art work, handwriting and arithmetic.

Oral testing in kindergarten, in addition to showing the teacher what the student knows, also teaches a child to learn by listening to others. The listening audience is taught how to "talk" and think internally while concentrating on a student's memory work or answers to questions. A receptive and appreciative audience is not allowed to laugh or make fun, but will be encouraged to clap as an acceptable response to their classmates' presentations. The performer develops confidence as he learns the elements of speech-making and what to do in case he doesn't know an answer. He finds that it is no disgrace, but that he must rise above his ignorance. Failure to answer correctly has no ill effect as long as the teacher's expectations have not been excessive.

Tests, such as historical quotes, songs, Bible verses and poems may be used for school programs. In fact, recitation of almost any learning is appropriate when, for example, performing for an assembly of parents at school or for the elderly in a convalescent home. Washington's Rules of Civility, the names of the planets, or counting by 10's to 100 can be incorporated into a performance which will help the child to retain facts, demonstrate self-government, and provide a way for him to bring happiness to others.

The teacher can use the testing in place of negative discipline. Idle minutes before recess, while desks are being cleared, belongings gathered or put away, can be an enjoyable time for one or more students to say a rhyme, count, or review phonograms.

In an American Christian kindergarten the internal qualities developed through testing are most important. The subject matter tested should be clear, simple and well-taught. Satisfactory achievement requires that the student have a good attitude, the necessary work skills and the needed qualities of Christian character and Christian self-government. The teacher realizes that she is working with a sin-nature which is lazy; therefore, she must be firm as well as gentle.

Testing should increase, not decrease, a love for learning. It is possible to get too concerned with testing and dull the spirit and attitude of students and teacher. If the instructor keeps a record book at hand, and quizzes students who are "ready," one or a few at a time, testing will come naturally and be accomplished without waiting until the end of the quarter. For example, one Mother Goose rhyme could be recited and "passed" even in the first week of school.

REPORT CARD

A report card gives the student a sense of achievement and when he "passes a test," it is like an adult who makes a list of work to do and crosses out the thing accomplished. In both cases, the individual no longer needs to think about the accomplished task but goes on to other things.

To help the teacher develop her own report card, a suggested format is submitted from the author's experience. The report card may be divided into two sections as follows:

Christian self-government (Evidence of Christian character and Christian conscience):

Deportment[6]
Industry[7]
Care of Property[8]

Academic (Evidence of Christian scholarship by reading, researching, reasoning, relating and recording):

Bible
Literacy (reading, writing, spelling, grammar and speech)
American Christian Literature
Mathematics
Science
Music
Art
Physical Training

GRADING

The kindergarten student needs a very simple grading system. A grade of satisfactory (S) or unsatisfactory (U) is sufficient. Traditional letter grades are too complicated and a source of unnecessary labor for a kindergarten teacher, particularly in oral testing. There is also the problem of how to challenge an immature child to want good grades without developing a certain arrogance. The child who receives simple grades such as S and U in kindergarten will have no difficulty adjusting to the traditional letter grades in first grade. By then he will understand what a standard is and how he may work to reach it.

Grading academic tests, and Christian self-government, will help to indicate the student's strengths and weaknesses. The parent and teacher will become aware of specific needs or weaknesses by the end of the year and may, or may not, feel the child will be successful in first grade. If there are "unsatisfactory" marks at year end and the child continues on to first grade, the parent and teacher need to watch the student carefully during the first month. If necessary, the child may promptly return to kindergarten, to mature and to strengthen the needed skills.

---

6. The manner of acting in relation to the duties of life. (Webster 1828)

7. Habitual diligence, bodily and mental. (Webster's 1828) The emphasis is on a good attitude toward work, taking responsibility with a determination to achieve.

8. Personal, others, and school property.

How to Use the Subject Overviews

BIBLICAL PURPOSE

This part establishes a Biblical purpose for the subject, specifically how and why a particular discipline is used in and by God's Word. For example, a Biblical purpose of literacy is to know the Law of God and what God requires of man. (See p. 174) In most cases, there is a great deal more Scripture pertaining to the subject, but, of necessity, the number of verses is limited. Verses, or portions of verses, may be memorized by the students. More often, the teacher will use the Scripture for her own personal background study, and may also incorporate phrases, portions of verses, or entire Bible verses, when teaching the lessons. (See "Preface to the Constitution," paragraph 3, p. 190)

BASIC PREMISES

This section helps the teacher to think through The Principle Approach to the subject recognizing that each subject reveals some aspect of the principles and practice of America's Christian History and Government. The teacher should consider these presuppositions and teach them whenever appropriate, at the age level or capability of the child.

NOTEBOOK

The author gives examples of what can be recorded in the student's notebook. Individual teachers will vary the content of their students' notebooks.

VOCABULARY

A list of key words basic to each subject has been compiled from the course of study. These are a reminder to teachers that certain terms need to be explained and taught whenever possible. From the suggestions in this list the teacher should be more aware of the need to explain vocabulary words. She will discover how vocabulary is used to bring interest and variety to her teaching and to challenge the student to *think*, not just hear or say words, without knowing their meaning. Other words should be added to the instructor's list as she teaches the subject matter. Year by year, the student will build on his basic understanding of subject vocabulary.

CURRICULUM

This section identifies the first principles, ideas, facts, and rules of each subject and a distinctive American Christian emphasis. For clarification, occasional examples are given. The material is for a school year's work so it will have to be broken down for quarters, weeks and days.

It is recommended that parents and teachers use all or selected aspects of the curriculum for oral or written tests and quizzes, as appropriate.

SPECIAL RESOURCES

Suggested supplementary books, or audiovisual materials are listed. Generally available in public libraries, new or used book stores, these sources will help the reader begin to research background material, find pictures to show the students, explain the vocabulary or choose a book to read aloud.

BIBLE

BIBLICAL PURPOSE

The Bible is the Word of God. It reveals the need for a Savior, enlightens the understanding, cultivates a Christian conscience, and brings joy to the heart.

Romans 7:7: "I had not known sin, but by the law; . . ."

Psalm 119:11: "Thy word have I hid in mine heart, that I might not sin against thee."

Psalm 119:130: "The entrance of thy words giveth light: it giveth understanding unto the simple."

Acts 24:16: "Herein do I exercise myself to have always a conscience void of offense toward God and toward men."

II Timothy 3:15: "And from a child thou has known the holy scriptures, which are able to make thee wise unto salvation through faith with us in Christ Jesus."

Romans 5:8: ". . . Christ died for us."

Jeremiah 15:16: "Thy word was unto me the joy and rejoicing of mine heart."

Psalm 1:2: "But his delight is in the law of the Lord: and in his law doth he meditate day and night."

BASIC PREMISES

God's Written Word, the authority for every aspect of life and the foundation for understanding all other subjects in the curriculum, is used to study who God is and what is His will for man. It is important to learn to read and think about what the Bible says in order to become more Godly and to learn how to govern ourselves as Christians and as Americans.

NOTEBOOK

Pictures of Bible stories, characters, themes or illustrations of Bible truths and Bible memory verses may be included.

VOCABULARY

Bible, version, Testament, manuscript, translate, scribe, scroll, law, covenant, inspiration, forever, eternal, everlasting, meditation, sin, conscience, judge, obedient, will, obey, God, Jesus, Holy Spirit, heaven, hell, angels, Satan and other words used in daily teaching should be explained.

CURRICULUM

The Bible as God's Word. It is *"all the counsel of God."* (Acts 20:27) It reveals the nature of sin and tells us how to live in obedience to God. The Bible tells us the way to heaven.

Suggested Bible memory verses: Psalm 119:11, 18, 46, 73, 89, 105; or other teacher selected references.

Learn the number of books in the Bible, its two divisions, at least the first five books in the Old Testament and the first four books in the New.

Teach who God is and what He does. God is a sovereign, providential God, an ever-present Spirit, Who is great, good, loving, caring, forgiving, everywhere, and the only judge of what truth is. He is our Creator; all laws for righteous living were made by Him. Illustrate these truths with Bible verses, stories, and hymns. Memorize "God is great, God is good, Let us thank Him for our food. Amen."

Prepare lessons on the Biblical accounts of the birth of Jesus and His resurrection with emphasis on individual salvation. Learn to define the words sin and salvation. Memorize John 3:16, 17, 18.

Explain and illustrate what prayer is from Scripture. The teacher also provides an example of how to pray (Thank you, Lord, for the Bible, etc). The student learns by repeating the teacher's example and finally is able to pray two or three sentences on a subject of his choice.

Explain how to witness to others of Christ "in the heart," of the Bible as God's Word, and of God as creator of all individuals and nature.

Teach the Ten Commandments (Exodus 20) and the "New Commandment." (Mark 12:30, 31) The student learns at least five out of the Ten commandments, and the "New commandment."

Read and study verse by verse John 1:1-14 and John 3:1-18. Analyze the words, phrases, and verses from teacher's boardwork while student marks the sounds and syllables in his copy of John. The sounds of the words are taught, and the meaning explained. Therefore, this is not "sight word" reading but learning to read by reading the familiar. The emphasis is on a practical application of the use of the phonics and the discipline of following along while the class reads together in the rhythm of speech. The student reads John 1:1-12 as a "speech." (See *Speech* overview, *Guide*, p. 175)

Memorize the first stanza of "Praise to God for Learning to Read" by Isaac Watts.

Teach how to walk, sit, sing and listen in church or chapel. Student comes into chapel quietly, looks at the speaker or song leader, and is not a "busy body."

Tell the story of how our elected representatives encouraged Americans to read, pray and know the Bible throughout America's Christian history. (See *Teaching and Learning*, "Step 5, Study of Concepts," pp. 338-342 for "The Story of the First American Bible Printed in the United States, 1782," and *The Bible and the Constitution*, pp. xix-xxv, for the story of how 1983 was declared "The Year of the Bible.")

SPECIAL RESOURCES

Field, Rachel. *Prayer for a Child*, New York: MacMillan Publishing Co., Inc., 1944. This book is an example of children's prayers.

Gospel According to St. John, the large-print paperback book (03570). May be ordered from American Bible Society, Dept. O, 1865 Broadway, New York, NY 10023. The child can learn to "take notes" by marking his own book as the instructor separates the syllables with a vertical line and places the Spalding markings over the phonograms.

Hunt, P. J. *The History of Our Bible*, Ladybird Books, Ltd., 1971. (Out of print)

Watts, Isaac. *Divine Songs in Easy Language for the Use of Children*. Order from Fairfax Christian Bookstore, P.O. Box 6941, Tyler, TX 75711.

THE AMERICAN CHRISTIAN PHILOSOPHY OF EDUCATION APPLIED TO BEGINNING READING

There are four elements in the American Christian approach to the teaching of reading:

1. Approaching the subject governmentally—understanding the Biblical purpose and governing principles or laws that order the English language.

2. Cultivating the character for Christian self-government, independence and productivity through the reading program.

3. Emphasizing the inward man as primary and causative to the use of the physical senses.

4. Applying the Principle Approach—America's historic Christian method of Biblical reasoning with the 4 R's.

APPROACHING THE SUBJECT GOVERNMENTALLY

The child should learn the Biblical purpose of reading. (p. 152) He needs to demonstrate Christian self-government as he strives for mastery of the language. In order to learn to read, the student must grasp the principles of English—the phonetic sounds and their symbols, then apply the rules which govern words and sentences.

CULTIVATING CHRISTIAN CHARACTER, INDEPENDENCE AND PRODUCTIVITY

Reading, like any subject in the curriculum, should be a discipline to "enlighten the understanding, correct the temper, and form manners and habits of youth" so that the student will be equipped for "usefulness in his future station." (Webster's 1828 Dictionary definition of *education*) Every subject requires a certain character in order to take possession of the principles and ideas inherent in the discipline. For example, a character formed by habits of diligence, concentration, initiative, confidence and patience is required to maintain correct writing posture, proper formation of letters, clear and certain enunciation of sounds, and to consistently reason from spelling rules to write words and sentences correctly.

The subject matter requires individual accountability, independence and productivity. Challenging the student to "give a reason" for why a word is pronounced and spelled a specific way is *work*. The reading curriculum is a vehicle to teach a student to ". . . rejoice in his labor, this is the gift of God." (Eccl. 5:19) As students labor individually and collectively to learn how to read, there are opportunities to develop other qualities of character such as thrift, steadfastness, faithfulness, brotherly love and Christian care.

EMPHASIZING THE INWARD MAN AS PRIMARY AND CAUSATIVE

Our philosophy of education is based upon the Christian view of man and the Christian approach—internal—to learning. (*T/L*, p. 92) Therefore, the senses of seeing, hearing, speaking and touching (writing) are perceived as of secondary importance to the development of the student's reasoning ability and affections. External teaching aids such as flash cards, blackboards, charts, and pictures to illustrate the meanings of words, are used to teach reflective reasoning and not simply to stimulate, condition, or motivate the student to learn.

APPLYING THE PRINCIPLE APPROACH TO READING

Reading is a researching, reasoning, relating and recording process. The reading program should develop the student's capacity to *analyze*—to resolve things into their principles or elements. This reasoning skill cultivates a sense of and capacity for dominion. Analyzing of letters and their sounds helps to internalize the reading of words and to build mental pictures which the words communicate to "the mind's eye."

Reading programs that teach word recognition by clue of context or memorizing the shape or structure of a word are inconsistent with the Principle Approach. However, words which are read *phonetically* do become "sight words," words that are said upon sight without having to analyze individual syllables, letters or sounds.

It has been my experience that though a five-year-old may require more patience, need more review, and progress more slowly than an older student, he is ready to learn the rudiments of reading with facility and success. Specifically he is ready to learn how to sit and hold a pencil; how to write precisely and say each letter. He can learn how letters represent sounds; and how to write sounds and words from dictation. In fact, he or she can learn how to read, write and spell commonly used words.

PRACTICE READERS

Young students need practice readers to develop proficiency in applying learned principles. The readers should be challenging but not so difficult as to discourage. The content should be interesting, demonstrate a wholesome, child-like attitude toward life, and be consistent with the Christian idea of man and government. Therefore, common basal readers, or graded readers which are very limited in vocabulary and meaning, are not appropriate for class work. (See *T/L*, pp. 99-100) The use of practice readers may be compared to the piano student's need to practice scales and exercises. The elements of music are reinforced and the skills are practiced. Each step of practice work is discontinued as the student masters the skill.

TEACHING READING

THE SPALDING METHOD

The Writing Road to Reading by Romalda Spalding presents a method of teaching reading principles in keeping with the philosophy of American Christian education. The author has found the Spalding method harmonious with the Principle Approach during eight years of teaching kindergarten students, and through instruction received in five training courses, two taught by Mrs. Spalding.

The Spalding method recognizes that the basic *principles* of the English language are the phonetic sounds, or phonics, written down in the alphabetic characters, or letters. As the student learns the phonetic sounds of the letters, and the rules to govern the use of the sounds, he can read words. When he has learned the foundational principles and their rules, he will be able to read unlimited numbers of words.[9]

---

9. In the article entitled *Your Reading Program* (p. 153), James Rose explains how Americans, since the 1820's, began to abandon this principled way of learning to read, and started using the method currently known as "look-say," which bypasses the necessity of learning phonics for a presumably easier way of memorizing the *appearance* of words. If a young student learns to read without mastering the basic sounds, he only seems to be reading. The truth is that he has memorized the sounds of certain *whole words*, and may never truly learn to read English if he has no knowledge of its basic principles—the phonetic sounds.

The Principle Approach to American Christian education prepares the teacher to identify the Biblical purpose of reading, and the Spalding method provides an opportunity to learn who God is by taking literary possession of God's Word and subsequently dominion over His world. The Spalding method equips all students, who are capable of learning to read, with the tools to take dominion over reading.

LITERACY

The Spalding literacy program is based upon the reading and writing of phonograms and spelling words, and in learning to read, write, spell, speak, and reason with a precisely taught method. This intensive phonetic approach emphasizes the spelling of sounds and words, with the rules of spelling practically applied at the same time. The student learns to read and spell the *seventy symbols*, or *phonograms*, which represent the *forty-five basic speech sounds* in the English language. These sounds provide the foundation for learning to spell the most commonly used English words.

The instructor has unlimited opportunity to teach the skills of reasoning and reflective thinking through the use of the spelling words. The student, without any need for "readiness" training, begins immediately to learn the principles of our English language, and their practical application.

AUTHORITATIVE STANDARDS AND RULES

Simple rules are taught in order to govern the formation and use of phonograms, words, sentences and paragraphs. Clear, high standards are presented through the teacher's precise and exact direction. As the child learns to yield to these standards, it gives the teacher the opportunity to deal with any petty arrogance and pride. Since the youngster is striving for standards, he is in competition with himself, not his "peers," and must be graded according to his own ability. Consistent standards help to cultivate unity, as well as concern for others' needs, as students strive for common goals instead of competing for "peer approval."

AVENUES TO THE MIND

Four of the God-given senses are used as the student learns how to spell, speak, read and write. These faculties facilitate listening, speaking, reading and writing. As the child learns to read, research, reason, relate and record, his faculties serve as avenues to the heart and mind.

INTERNAL IS FIRST

The student's notebook and daily writing assignments help him concentrate while he is listening and speaking. The written record also helps the teacher to judge internal character qualities through tests, homework, and other assignments.

SELF-GOVERNMENT INHERENT

The student must concentrate on reasoning and producing organized, careful work in order to succeed in the Spalding method of learning to read and spell. Consistent, daily work in each of these areas develops self-government as the student writes, speaks, spells, or follows the teacher's precise directions. He also must learn to check or edit his own daily work, which provides opportunities to practice self-government and responsibility for correction and self-improvement.

INDIVIDUAL PROPERTY

As a child takes possession of basic principles, his handwriting, sentences and stories will gradually reflect his own uniqueness as his knowledge and confidence in the rudiments of literacy grow. His internal property—his own knowledge, talents and skills—will be expressed externally in his personal notebook and writing.

CHARACTER DEVELOPMENT

Through the daily classwork and assignments, the teacher will be able to train the student in Christian character qualities and identify those traits that need refining. Opportunities to demonstrate faith and steadfastness, diligence and industry, and love and concern for others will be seen throughout the reading and writing program.

A LIST OF 1700 WORDS

The extended Ayres' list of 1700 spelling words provides a foundation for applying the phonograms and their rules and a basis for planning simple, orderly lessons. The teacher should define these terms, use them in sentences, and teach children to read and use the same words in sentences.

EDUCATIONAL INDEPENDENCE

The Writing Road to Reading enables a student to become educationally independent by developing the reading, writing, speaking and spelling skills needed for unlimited learning in all subjects. Application of this method also provides a foundation for reasoning governmentally by God's Word. The teacher can rejoice in a solid achievement— laying the foundation for an independent, self-governing, productive Christian citizen who is a credit to his home, his church, and his nation.

LITERACY
(Reading, Writing, Spelling, Grammar and Speech)

BIBLICAL PURPOSE

God has given us His written Word so that we might learn from the Scriptures, and have hope for the future. The Word is in a form that each can read, and thus become accountable to God. In answering every man, speech is to be gracious and fitly spoken.

Romans 15:4: "For whatsoever things were written aforetime were written for our learning, that we through . . . the scriptures might have hope."
II Timothy 4:13: ". . . give attendance to reading . . ."
Nehemiah 8:3: "So they read in the book in the law of God distinctly, and gave the sense, and caused them to understand the reading."
Colossians 4:6: "Let your speech be always with grace . . . that ye may know how ye ought to answer every man."

BASIC PREMISES

Reading and writing are so important to God that He chose to speak to man through His written Word, the Bible. God can reach the heart and thus communicate with man through the use of the unique ability he has given man to read and write. Accepting the responsibility to read the Bible for himself is the only way for an American to advance both Christian and Constitutional liberty. Biblical literacy promotes individual accountability to God for a fruitful, productive, independent Christian life. (See also, *Curriculum* section of this *Guide*, pp. 148-158, on "Your Reading Program" and "How to 4 R Reading")

NOTEBOOK

A record of classwork in writing and spelling may be filed under the appropriate dividers.

VOCABULARY

Words will include spelling words, vocabulary from practice readers, and words used to explain other subjects of the curriculum.

CURRICULUM

READING
Teach how to read:

25 *one-letter* phonograms. (The term "phonogram" will refer to the 70 phonograms listed in Romalda Spalding's book *The Writing Road to Reading*) See "Special Resources."

25 out of the 45 phonograms with *more than* one letter. When testing individuals, the teacher shows the student all of the phonogram flash cards which she has had opportunity to teach—or which the student may have learned outside the classroom. She places the correctly read phonograms in one stack. Giving the student an opportunity to choose which 25 he can read will encourage, rather than discourage, his efforts to learn more. This method seems to open the student's mind, rather than cause a "mental block" that hinders learning the remainder of the phonograms.

Teach 88 A-H spelling words listed in *The Writing Road to Reading*.

Teach to the end of Lesson XX in the *McGuffey Primer*.

WRITING
Instruct students in the following:

The correct way of holding pencil and paper.

The correct body posture for writing.

Correct formation of lower case letters and the numbers 0-9.

How to write capital letters for student's name and capitals needed for proper nouns and a new sentence.

Correct formation of student's first and last name.

Proper spacing between letters and words.

How to write a comma, period, and question mark.

Correct posture when using the blackboard to write letters or numbers.

Correct use of chalk when using the blackboard.

Correct use of the blackboard eraser.

SPELLING
The Instructor teaches how to write, BY DICTATION:

25 *one-letter* phonograms.

20 out of the 45 phonograms with *more than one letter.* The teacher gives out all the sounds which she has taught, or the child has had opportunity to learn outside the classroom. The student writes the sounds which he knows and makes a dash, if unknown, to keep order and continuity. The teacher counts the correctly written phonograms to meet the standard of 20.

50 out of the 88 spelling words listed in section A-H of *The Writing Road to Reading*.

One each of two-, three-, and four-word sentences using any of the first twenty spelling words in the A-H list in *The Writing Road to Reading*.

The Teacher instructs how to write, BY MEMORY:

The five vowels.
Student's own first and last name.

GRAMMAR
The teacher should teach how to:

Recognize a question or a declarative sentence.

Capitalize sentences and proper nouns.

Use the period, question mark, and comma.

Begin letter writing by making special occasion cards.

Address envelopes.

Use similes in speech. (See pp. 47-48 in Stevenson's *The Home Book of Verse for Young Folk* in "Special Resources" section. The recommended use is two lines per week; one half of the poem is sufficient)

Diagram a two-word sentence.

Name nouns in the spelling word list.

Name simple verbs in the list.

Change singular nouns in the list into plural nouns.

Learn five simple compound words.

Learn the purpose of a dictionary.

SPEECH
The teacher should teach how to:

Pronounce phonograms, spelling words and simple sentences correctly, clearly and distinctly.

Use correct posture when speaking.

Read smoothly, with correct word emphasis and phrasing in the "rhythm of speech."

Use correct speech and posture during oral testing of Bible verses, poems, counting, and when giving historical or scientific facts.

Present poems, songs, historical quotes and simple plays to audiences.

Give John 1:1-12 (or other teacher-selected portion) as a "speech" using "notes." (The teacher demonstrates how to write the "notes" by writing the verse number and the first two or three words of each verse. Keeping in mind the purpose of a speaker's notes, the teacher writes the fewest words possible which are needed to bring the verse to mind. The student follows the teacher's blackboard example and writes his own "notes" on his paper, leaving one line space between each verse for added clarity. When giving the "speech" he may stand behind a chair using the back of the chair for a "podium," resting his hands and his paper on it. He should hold his paper with his right hand and use his left thumb to mark his verse place. He should be required to *read* the words at the beginning of each verse. He should then look at the audience in between the reading of his "notes." This method will teach him confidence in basic speech techniques.)

SPECIAL RESOURCES

McGuffey's Eclectic Primer, Christian School Edition. P.O. Box 6941, Tyler, TX 75711: Fairfax Christian Bookstore. Phone (214) 581-0677.

Original McGuffey's Eclectic Series, Mott Media, Inc., 1000 East Huron Street, Milford, MI 48042.

Spalding, Romalda, *The Writing Road to Reading*, N.Y.: William Morrow Co., 1969. Order from the Reading Reform Foundation, 7054 East Indian School Road, Scottsdale, AZ 95921.

Spelling Wide-spaced composition books. Order from Chaminade University Bookstore, 3140 Waialae Avenue, Honolulu, HI 96816.

Stevenson, Burton, *The Home Book of Verse for Young Folks*, Fairfax Christian Bookstore, P.O. Box 6941, Tyler, TX 75711. Telephone (214) 581-0677.

Webster's 1828 Dictionary: *Noah Webster's First Edition of An American Dictionary of the English Language*. San Francisco: Foundation for American Christian Education, 1967.

AMERICAN CHRISTIAN HISTORY AND GOVERNMENT

BIBLICAL PURPOSE

The Biblical purpose for teaching the influence of Christ, His Story of Christian and civil liberty, is to enable the student to "remember the works of the Lord" in establishing our nation. Illustrating and talking about God's Providence helps students to recognize and esteem the sovereignty of God over man, nations and civil government.

Psalm 77:11: "I will remember the works of the Lord: surely I will remember thy wonders of old. I will meditate also of all thy work, and talk of thy doings."

I Chronicles 29:11, 12: "Thine, O Lord, is the greatness, and the power, and the glory, and the victory, and the majesty: for all that is in the heaven and the earth is thine; thine is the kingdom, O Lord, and thou art exalted as head above all. Both riches and honour come of thee, and thou reignest over all; and in thine hand is power and might; and in thine hand it is to make great, and to give strength unto all."

BASIC PREMISES

Christian history is God's story of individual men, events, and nations—links on the Chain of Christianity. which reveal divine cause and effect and identify the Hand of God or His "eternal purpose and executive power."

When men and nations obey God and His laws, the result is *good* history. Each student who does what is "right in God's sight" and becomes a strong link in God's plan for men and nations is not only a good steward, but helps to maintain—and restore—America's Christian history and government.

NOTEBOOK

The notebook section can include pictures on topics of study such as historical scenes, the President's picture, and American symbols. A section on "Me" will illustrate the child's individuality as he contributes to history. It will include fingerprints, footprints, handprints, hair sample, etc.

VOCABULARY

Words discussed will include: history, cause, effect, nation, United States, America, republic, founding fathers, laws, life, liberty, property, self-government, civil government, Constitution, president, executive, indivisible, unity with union, plan, execute, judge, symbol, flag, and other terms used in stories, quotations or songs as appropriate.

CURRICULUM

Modern-day kindergartens have not accepted an academic curriculum for young children. But, as can be demonstrated, it is possible to lay foundations for many of the subjects which the students will be learning throughout the Elementary years. And, children love to learn when properly inspired. Here are some of the Leading Ideas,

Principles, Names, Dates, and Places which we have taught kindergartners about America's Christian history and government.

AMERICAN CHRISTIAN HISTORY AND GOVERNMENT

Since this subject will be taught throughout school years as a *Providential Approach* to history, and as *the Hand of God in American History*, it will be important to identify *God* as our *Author of Liberty*. We will be singing these words in our national anthem.

History means *Christian History* or *His Story*. History is the story of *how Christ brings liberty*—both internally (spiritually) and externally (through laws that limit the power of civil government).

INDIVIDUALS IN THE HISTORY OF LIBERTY

Christopher Columbus, a Link in the History of Liberty. Columbus believed that God had prepared him to sail West to find new lands for Liberty.

The Pilgrims: God prepared the Pilgrims to sail across the sea to America and to bring the Bible and government to the New World. John Robinson, their pastor, had taught them to be self-governed. Pastor Robinson's *Biblical rules* prepared the Pilgrims to write the Mayflower Compact—"for the Glory of God and the Advancement of the Christian Faith." The Mayflower Compact is our first document of self-government. Kindergarten children today can learn the same rules which pastor John Robinson taught his Pilgrims. (See *Christian History*, pp. 198-201)

George Washington, our first President of the United States of America. We teach some of his specific contributions to America and we learn his character qualities. The children can learn some of the same *Rules of Civility* which young George Washington learned. (Refer to *Miller* and *Wilbur* under Special Resources)

Office of Chief Executive is the office of the President of the United States. We teach children the name of our current President. They also learn the names and a few facts about our first six presidents: George Washington, John Adams, Thomas Jefferson, James Madison, James Monroe, and John Quincy Adams.

LEADING IDEAS IN AMERICAN GOVERNMENT

America is a *government of laws*. These laws come from God's individual responsibility for all of their actions—from how they act towards their classmates—to how they apply themselves to what they are learning. They come to know that *Local Self-Government* means *Individual Responsibility* in all things; it is *Local* because it is *where we can SEE Self-Government working.*

The Christian Principle of American Political Union:

Kindergarten is a wonderful place to teach *voluntary union*. We do many activities in voluntary union. We share a *unity* of goals, principles, ideals. We love to *work together* to accomplish them. This principle can be taught as an aspect of learning to work individually, locally, at Christian Self-Government. Sometimes we work alone. Sometimes we work together. America was founded on the principle of Voluntary Union.

MEMORY WORK FROM OUR HISTORY

In addition to our patriotic songs and poems and stories, we also learn some specific memory passages from our Documents of Liberty:

Our Pledge to the American Flag.

Words from the Mayflower Compact: "To the Glory of God and the Advancement of the Christian Faith..."

Speeches: i.e., Patrick Henry—"Give me Liberty or give me death."

Declaration of Independence: "We hold these Truths to be self-evident..."

Preamble to the United States Constitution.

Washington's Farewell Address: "...the Constitution ... is sacredly obligatory upon all..."

Kindergarten teachers will find many other historical passages which they may want to teach a class that is particularly eager to learn.

SPECIAL RESOURCES

Dalgeish, Alice and Leo Politi, *The Columbus Story*, N.Y., Charles Scribner's Son, 1955.

d'Aulaire, Ingri and Edgar Parin, *George Washington*, Garden City, N.Y., Doubleday & Co., Inc., 1936.

Hall, Verna M., *Christian History of the Constitution*, the excerpt on Bradford's "History 'of Plimoth Plantation,'" pp. 185-240, Foundation for American Christian Education, San Francisco, American Revolution Bicentennial Edition, 1975.

Hobbs, Carolyn, *Squanto by 'Aunt Carolyn,'* P.O. Box 643, Milton, Florida; Gospel Projects, Inc., 1981.

McGovern, Ann, *If You Sailed on The Mayflower*, N.Y., Scholastic Book Services, 1964.

Miller, Llwellyn, *The Encyclopedia of Etiquette,*

N.Y., Crown Publisher, Inc., 1967. (See pp. 89-94 for Washington's "Rules of Civility") This book is found in public libraries.

Wilbur, William H., *The Making of George Washington*, 435 North Lee St., Alexandria, VA 22314; Patriotic Education, Inc. (See pp. 111-118 for "Rules of Civility")

Weisgard, Leonard, *The Plymouth Thanksgiving*, Garden City, N.Y., Doubleday and Co., 1967.

PHYSICAL GEOGRAPHY

BIBLICAL PURPOSE

Physical Geography, as defined by Professor Arnold Guyot, testifies that God created and shaped the earth for *His Story*. God placed land, waters, and atmosphere, in order to historically advance the *History of Liberty*. "'The physical world has no meaning except by and for the *moral* world . . . all for the great purpose of the education of man, and the realization of the plans of Mercy for His sake.'" (*Teaching and Learning*, p. 142)

Psalm 95:4, 5: "In his hand are the deep places of the earth; the strength of the hills is his also. The sea is his, and he made it: and his hands formed the dry land."

Psalm 119:90: "Thy faithfulness is unto all generations: thou hast established the earth, and it abideth."

Psalm 115:16: " . . . The earth hath he given to the children of men."

Isaiah 45:18: "For thus saith the Lord that created the heavens: God himself that formed the earth and made it: he hath established it, he created it not in vain, he formed it to be inhabited. I am the Lord and there is none else."

BASIC PREMISES

The earth is the place which God made for man to live, and where history (Christ His Story) of man and nations takes place. Each individual should glorify God by carefully governing his private property while living on the earth.

NOTEBOOK

A few maps of continents may be colored and the names identified. For example, the map of Africa has a distinct outline and is a good one to use first. There is no need for the youngster to strain to color a difficult continent such as Europe or Asia. The child is capable of labeling the Nile River during the last part of the school year.

Other appropriate pictures of terms or places may be used, such as a picture of a globe, mountains, or some specific geographical location under discussion.

VOCABULARY

Terms include: geography, globe, compass, map, North Star, north, east, south, west, continent, ocean, sea, sea level, river, lake, mountain, mountain pass, valley, lowland, highland, island.

CURRICULUM

Show on a map the geographical location of place names in Bible stories, historical stories, or in any other study.

Teach the following areas of geography:

The general directions of east, west, north and south. (The Mother Goose rhyme, "Mr. East," may be learned at this time.)

The direction of north on maps.

The name and place of the six inhabited continents.

The name and identification of one river in each of six continents. (These may not be, in every case, the most important river in the continent but must be one that students are capable of remembering. For example, the Murray River is the longest in Australia, but the Darling River can be remembered much more easily. In Asia, for instance, the Ob River is a name more easily retained.)

The names and locations on the map of three oceans: Atlantic, Pacific and Indian.

Name and identify a mountain chain nearest the student's home.

Name and locate on a U.S. map the student's own state and town.

SPECIAL RESOURCES

Maps with clear, defined lines large enough for viewing. A world map, United States map, and a globe are useful.

Branley, Franklyn M., *North, South, East, and West*, New York: Harper and Row, 1966.

Dang, Katherine, *An American Christian Approach to Geography*, p. 257 of this *Guide*.

Rinkoff, Barbara, *A Map Is A Picture*, New York: Thomas Y. Crowell Co., 1962.

Watson, Jane Werner, *The First Golden Geography*, New York, Golden Press, 1955.

AMERICAN CHRISTIAN LITERATURE

BIBLICAL PURPOSE

Students are instructed to think upon things (words and pictures) that are true, honest, just, pure, lovely and of good report so that they will be prepared to manifest outwardly the result of reading and reflecting upon wholesome literature.

Philippians 4:8: "…whatsoever things are true, … honest, … just, … pure, … lovely, and of good report, … think on these things."

Proverbs 23:7: "For as he thinketh in his heart, so is he."

BASIC PREMISES

Wholesome literature is used to train the child to listen carefully, to concentrate, to use the "inward eye of the imagination," and to think reflectively. A happy, child-like spirit is encouraged as teacher and student delight in rhymes and stories containing descriptive words which use alliteration, rhythm and pictorial images to challenge the "mind's eye" and to edify the conscience and heart.

Mother Goose rhymes, fairy tales, and fables have helped to develop literacy and the imagination through the years and cause the student to think about his own experience and the quality of life around him. Through this kind of literature the student is also taught to mentally contend with evil and prepare himself to make wise choices later in life. Memorizing portions of what is read helps train the mind to organize and structure thoughts and remember details of the character and settings. Alliteration in poems (repetition of similar sounds in the first letters of adjoining words) encourages clear, crisp enunciation.

The five-year-old can learn to distinguish between what is true and what is pretend, between reality and unreality, and he can be taught to think imaginatively and constructively. He can learn to enjoy the humor produced by alliteration, rhymes or repetition. As he develops his mind and imagination, he is preparing himself for a life of Christian faith.

Literature provides opportunities to teach the seven Biblical principles of America's Christian history, and encourages seven loves as explained by Rosalie Slater in "The Christian History Literature Program" for grades K-12, pp. 330 and 331 of this *Guide*.

NOTEBOOK

Pictures illustrating the stories, poems or vocabulary words discussed in class may be filed in the notebook.

VOCABULARY

Terms include: literature, poem, Mother Goose rhyme, nursery rhyme, fairy tale, fable, setting, character, plot and theme. An unlimited vocabulary may be developed from the poems and stories selected for use, an especially timely and important emphasis as the pupil's thoughts and feelings are quickened through reading aloud.

CURRICULUM

The student must practice Christian self-government while being taught during literature class. He should demonstrate a growing capacity to reason and reflect when answering questions. He should sit quietly, look toward the teacher.

The following kinds of literature are taught in kindergarten: lullabies, nursery rhymes, Mother Goose rhymes, poems such as those in Stevenson's "A Child's Garden of Verses," fairy tales and fables. The child should memorize at least twenty Mother Goose rhymes and identify questions in three of the rhymes. For a comprehensive overview of the entire K-12 literature program, see pp. 343-351.

SPECIAL RESOURCES

Fujikawa, Gyo, *Fairy Tales and Fables*, N.Y.: Putnam Publishing Group, 1970.

Gag, Wanda, *Millions of Cats*, N.Y.: Coward, McCann & Geoghegan, 1928.

Galdone, Paul, *The Gingerbread Boy*, N.Y.: The Seabury Press, 1975. (Also by the same author: *Henny Penny*, 1968; *The Little Red Hen*, 1973; *Three Aesop Fox Fables*, 1971, Houghton Mifflin Co.)

Perkins, Lucy Fitch, *The Dutch Twins*, N.Y.: Walker & Co., 1911.

Piper, Watty, *The Little Engine That Could*, Platt, 1976.

Potter, Beatrix, *Peter Rabbit* (many publications).

Slater, Rosalie, *The Christian History Literature Program*, pp. 323-392 of this *Guide*.

Stevenson, Robert Louis, *A Child's Garden of Verses*, illustrated by Gyo Fujikawa, New York: Grosset and Dunlap.

Wright, Blanche Fisher, *The Real Mother Goose*, Chicago: Rand McNally & Co., 1916.

MATHEMATICS

BIBLICAL PURPOSE

Mathematics will reveal the character and nature of God in the infinity of numbers and the perfect system of order marked by a precision and dependability far beyond the ability of man to duplicate. The understanding of mathematics is necessary to know how to care for God's creation and maintain our own personal property.

Colossians 1:16, 17: "For by him (Christ) were all things created, that are in heaven, and that are in earth, visible and invisible."

Malachi 3:6: "For I am the Lord, I change not."

Genesis 1:26: "And God said, let us make man in our image, after our likeness: and let them have dominion over the fish of the sea, and over the fowl of the air, and over the cattle, and over all the earth, and over every creeping thing that creepeth upon the earth."

BASIC PREMISES

Mathematics should bring about a spirit of worship and glorify God as His orderly, unchangeable mathematical laws are recognized. *Psalm 9:1:* "I will praise thee, O Lord, with my whole heart; I will shew forth all thy marvellous works." As we recognize the character of God through His universal laws, we can trust Him to guide and care for us in the future. (See also, Jim Kilkenny's "Teaching Arithmetic from the Principle Approach," on p. 229 of this *Guide*)

NOTEBOOK

Important papers which demonstrate what is learned in class should be filed.

VOCABULARY

The meaning of number names and mathematical symbols should be explained including such common vocabulary words as over, under, behind, before, beside, between, top, bottom, ahead, after, next, above, in front of, backward, and forward. The teacher will need to define the specific terms identified in each section of the following curriculum overviews.

CURRICULUM

During the following course of studies, a simplified history of numerals may be taught including the fact that the word digit means finger; that our number system is based on ten (we have ten "fingers" and toes); that we call our number system "Arabic," after the Arab people who brought the Hindu numbers to Europe.

Bible stories containing number illustrations can be useful. For example, *Gen. 6:16:* "*A* window shalt thou make to the ark..." reveals there was only *one* window in Noah's Ark.

Mother Goose rhymes and other poems can be used to teach counting and the meaning of numbers as suggested in the math skills chart on page 182.

Instruct students in the following:

Arithmetic:
Vocabulary: number, numeral, digit, cardinal, ordinal, and each number used in counting.

Identify numerals out of order: 1 through 20.

Count by 1's from 1 to 100, with and without objects.

Count by 2's, 3's, 4's, 6's to 12; 5's to 100; 10's to 100, with and without objects; and 100's to 1000.

Count objects by ordinal numbers: first to twentieth.

Write the nine numerals with correct form.

Write numerals by 1's to 200; 2's to 12; 5's to 100; 10's to 100; 100's to 1000.

Read and write a number line from 0 to 20.

Say own phone number and write it.

Find hymn numbers in hymnbook.

Roman Numerals:
Vocabulary: Rome, Roman.
Count to XII on a clock with Roman numerals.
Write Roman numerals I, II, III.

Addition and Subtraction:
Vocabulary: add, sum, plus, "and," altogether, in all, total, subtract, minus, less, difference, "from," "take away," equal, sign.

Introduce the use of the number line in addition and subtraction.

Add zero to any number selected from 0 to 100.

Add one to numbers 1 to 19.

Add two to even numbers: 0 to 10.

Subtract zero from any number selected from 0 to 100.

Subtract one from any number 1 to 19.

Demonstrate that two halves equal one whole. Also four fourths and eight eighths equal one whole.

Read: 1/2, 1/4, 1/8.

Divide 2, 4, 6, 8 objects in half.

Divide (draw or cut) symmetrical things in half.

Money:

Vocabulary: dollar sign, cents sign, bank, check, credit card, and the names of both coin and common circulating paper money.

Identify penny, nickel, dime, quarter, and dollar.

Teach the penny value of nickel, dime, quarter, and dollar.

Estimate cost of articles from personal, school or family property.

Decimals:

Vocabulary: dollar sign, cents sign, decimal point.

Read figures out of order: $ .01 to $ .20.

Graphs:

Vocabulary: thermometer, temperature and degrees.

Read and draw a thermometer.

Estimate body temperature: "*about* 100 degrees."

Estimate the following weather guides of temperature: "0°F., very cold"; "100°F., hot"; "about 60°-70°F., pleasant temperature, if not raining."

Scale Drawing:

Explain how to draw to scale and how to draw very simple designs by following the teacher's large chalkboard design drawn to scale.

Algebra:

Explain the vocabulary of equation, representation, and horizontal. Very simple equations may be introduced. For example: $4 + 4 = N$; $3 + N = 4$, where N = number.

Geometry:

Vocabulary: left, right, horizontal, vertical, parallel, straight line, line segment, point, square corner, center of a rectangle, symmetrical, circle, square, triangle, rectangle.

Identify and draw a circle, square, rectangle, and triangle.

Correctly use the ruler to draw line segments from point to point.

SPECIAL RESOURCES

Allen, Robert, *Numbers: A First Counting Book*, N.Y.: Platt and Munk, 1968.

Gibbons, Gail, *Clocks and How They Go*, N.Y.: Harper & Row, 1979.

Hoban, Tana, *Circles, Triangles and Squares*, N.Y.: MacMillan Publishing Co., 1974. (Also *Count and See*, 1972, by the same author and publisher)

Kilkenny, James, *Teaching Arithmetic From The Principle Approach*, p. 229 of this *Guide*.

INTRODUCTION TO THE
FIRST NINE-WEEK MATH SKILL CHART

A plan for teaching math skills for the first nine weeks is explained on page 182. This chart is a week by week schedule for counting, number reasoning, reading and writing numbers, estimation of measurements and identifying and drawing geometrical shapes. It also includes the use of addition flash cards and the illustration of numbers from the Bible and Mother Goose rhymes.

The weekly math skill chart is to be divided into daily lessons. It is impractical to attempt to cover all eleven areas in one day's lesson. For example, use Monday through Wednesday of the first week to introduce the number line and the one-hundred space chart, then teach how to count and read the numerals one, two and three, and how to write and comprehend the meaning of the numeral one. On Thursday, the 12-inch ruler, a yardstick, and the straight line and point are introduced as vocabulary. Friday's lesson may be a review of the week's work. Biblical stories and Mother Goose rhymes may be used during any or all lessons to illustrate the number *one*. During art class, straight lines and points, with and without the ruler, may be used for training children how to hold the ruler correctly.

The math chart emphasizes the need to take time to expand, amplify and review the understanding of simple mathematical facts and skills. It is important to proceed carefully and precisely. Recognition of numbers or shapes by rote does not necessarily denote comprehension. For example, a child may identify a triangle by sight, but he should also be able to explain that a triangle has three sides and three angles. He can learn to observe triangular shapes in nature and in his everyday school surroundings.

Math Skills for the First Nine Weeks

SKILLS	WEEK 1	WEEK 2	WEEK 3	WEEK 4	WEEK 5	WEEK 6	WEEK 7	WEEK 8	WEEK 9	WEEK 10
Counting by memory	#1,2,3	Review	#1,2,3,4,5,6,7	Review	#1,2,3,4,5,6,7,8,9,10	Review	Review	Review	Review	Review
Number meaning	#1	#2,3	#4	#5	#6	#7	#8	#9	#10	Review
Number writing	#1	Review 1	#4	#7	#6	Review #1, 4,6	Review #7	#0,8,9	#2,3,5	Review
Read out of order	#1,2,3	Review	#1,2,3,4,5,6,7	Review	#1,2,3,4,5,6,7,8,9,10	Review	Review	Review	Review	Review
Write in correct space on 100-space chart	#1	—	#1,4 (new chart)	#1,4,7 (new chart)	#1,4,6,7 (new chart)	—	—	—	—	#1,2,3,4,5,6,7,8,9,10
Estimation	Introduces foot, ruler, yardstick .	Inch	Foot	Yard	Review	Review	Review	Review	Review	Review
Identify	Straight line, point	circle	triangle	square	rectangle	Review	Review	Review	Review	Review
Drawing in art class	Straight line from point to point	circle	point to point triangle	point to point square	point to point rectangle	Make circle inside square	Make circle inside square	Review	Review	Review
Student Flash Cards to read (Teacher made)	—	$1+1=2$ $2+1=3$	$3+1=4$	$4+1=5$	$5+1=6$	$6+1=7$	$7+1=8$	$8+1=9$	$9+1=10$	Review
Biblical illustrations	#1 Ex. 2:1-10 Luke 15:3-7	#2 Gen. 1:16 I Sam. 20:4-17 #3 Gen. 4:1 Luke 24:23-35	#4 Gen. 4:2 Gen. 5:32	#5 I Sam. 17:32-52	#6 Ex. 20:9,11 Ruth 3:15-17 Isa. 6:2	#7 Josh. 6:1-21 Gen. 2:1-3 Ex. 23:12	#8 II Chron. 34:1-28	#9 Luke 17:11-19	#10 Ex. 20 Ex. 7:7-12	Review
Mother Goose Number Rhymes	#1 Humpty Dumpty Little Tommy-Tittlemouse	Two Pigeons (#2) Three Wise Men of Gotham (#3) Three Blind Mice (#3) Baa Baa Black Sheep (1 + 1 + 1 = 3)			One, Two Buckle My Shoe (# 1-10) Over in the Meadow I Caught a Hare					

WHOLISTIC APPROACH

Approach mathematics, as every subject in the curriculum, wholistically, by working from the whole, complete picture or view of a subject to its component parts. This approach is similar to the way the head of a family (or classroom) might plan a vacation to another state. Before the trip begins, the driver would do well to build anticipation for what the travelers will see and do along the way and what they may expect to find and accomplish at the journey's end. A road map provides a fine *overview of the whole excursion*, a tool to discuss what roads will be traveled to the destination, what towns and natural or historical landmarks will be observed, where the family will stop and explore along the way, and even how each person can keep an interesting record of what they observe and learn on the trip. Applying this metaphor to arithmetic, counting may be introduced wholistically with a number line, a straight line divided into ten equal parts numbered from zero to ten. The instructor would count the numbers on the line together and explain what each student can learn to do with this simple tool — to add by counting forward and to subtract by counting backward. (See p. 232 for further explanation and illustration of the number line by James Kilkenny)

ONE HUNDRED SPACE CHART

The completed one hundred space chart (ten spaces vertically and ten columns of spaces horizontally) *with numbers written in*, should be displayed and explained first. This simple tool provides the needed boundaries when students are learning to write their numbers. The numbers are written to the right, horizontally, the direction we read. The chart helps the student to comprehend patterns, sequence, and the orderliness of our number notation system. When presenting the writing of the numbers 1 - 10 during the first quarter, the teacher may want to use only the first ten horizontal blocks to simulate the number line. Beginning with number 11, it is suggested that the entire form be gradually filled in line by line.

TEACHING ZERO

In my plan, adding by one is begun immediately because one is the basis for counting. Zero is introduced with the number line and is defined as the absence of objects to be counted. Zero may also be introduced as a place-holder when writing numbers past nineteen. Furthermore, the student can be taught to write by tens to one hundred (or more) and then to write by tens in the vertical spaces of an individual hundred-space chart.

ESTIMATION

According to some mathematics professors, the ability to estimate is greatly lacking in schools today. During the first nine weeks, estimation, with an emphasis on reasoning, is begun. The young student can estimate an inch between his thumb and parallel second finger. He can estimate a foot (12 inches) by the distance between the extended fingers of the two hands as he holds his wrists close to his ribs. A practical, more accurate foot measurement is twice the length of a dollar bill. An average size child can estimate a yard from fingertip to fingertip when stretching his hands out to either side. He can be shown how adults have traditionally measured yards of fabric by the distance from their nose to the fingers of one outstretched arm. Reasoning can be further challenged by comparing the measurement of a large man's foot to a 12-inch ruler, or a 36-inch waist to a yard stick. Discussion of the original historical background of each measurement will help the child to reason as he learns.

EXAMPLES OF LESSONS

Most teachers (even those of long experience need reminding) are amazed at the interest young children show when every day, ordinary illustrations and simple unpretentious methods of teaching are used. As an aid to the first year teacher, and to encourage the experienced instructor in this type of teaching, a suggested narration for three sample lessons follows:

Expanding the understanding of the number "1": The teacher asks each student to raise his hand when he sees *one* article in the classroom which he would like to show his classmates. When all hands are raised, the teacher gives permission for each student to carefully bring that "one" article to his desk.[10] She tells the class when all are seated and ready that she will choose students first who followed her directions well and have indicated readiness by a raised hand. Each child who is chosen to

---

10. This is one of the many times that Christian self-government can be explained and illustrated. The teacher can say that only "work noises" are acceptable. As the student learns that certain noises accompany real work, his reasoning becomes more clear than it would in response to the usual teacher direction to "work quietly." It helps him view work as more positve and important than just quietness (which can lead to a mind in "neutral").

come before the class holds up the article and says: "This is ONE (name of article)."

This activity is not with the intent to make a game out of the lesson, but is to provide a concrete example of reasoning as "one" is illustrated to the whole class. It gives practice in constructing a sentence from a model while giving a practical illustration of the number. This exercise helps the mind and body to work together and is an excellent way to revive an interest in learning when the physical muscles are tired and the mind is becoming lethargic. If the articles are brought to their desks in an orderly manner, it can be good practice in self-government. If the goal is to develop reasoning capacity, this exercise can lengthen the child's period of concentration.

Introducing the word "numeral," and the meaning and notation of "2". The teacher writes the word "cat" on the board. Teacher and students reason and reflect on the meaning of a real, live cat. Two toy cats are then shown to the class. The teacher talks about how she will soon write a numeral to represent how many cats there are (pretending they are alive). She then writes a "2" and explains that there are "two cats." It is a numeral that represents the two cats. She then calls two children to come to the front of the room. She asks the class to tell her what to write to represent the number of children standing in front of the class.[11] She explains that the name of the numeral gives a picture of how many things to see inside the mind.

This lesson suggests a traditional order for learning: 1. *Use of concrete objects.* All five senses are to be used for the purpose of reaching the inward person—the mind and affections. 2. *Use of written symbols*—writing down "semi-concrete" numbers and symbols to represent the operations of numbers. 3. *Use of the mind only.* This skill draws, or separates, "abstract" numbers from the paper to be reduced, or comprehended in the mind only.

Another lesson on the meaning of meaning of "2." The teacher holds up one piece of chalk. "Look at this piece of chalk," the teacher says. "Now, close your eyes. Think of *two* pieces of chalk. Open your eyes. Did you see this piece of chalk and another one like it when you saw a picture inside your mind?" (Teacher points with pointer and counts on the number line to 2) "I will write a '2' on the board." (Teacher may refer to the "2" on the number line and then write a "2" on the board) "Now, who would like to bring *one* book to the front of the room?" (One child is selected) "Please close your eyes and think of 'one book' that is like _____ has in his hands. Open your eyes. Did you see *two* books like this book?" (The teacher continues on with the lesson)

SCIENCE

BIBLICAL PURPOSE

A correct view of the "science" of nature confirms God's power in His magnificent workmanship and creation and should bring praise to the Creator. The student needs to understand the primary laws of the universe in order to have proper dominion over every living thing.

Genesis 1:1: "In the beginning God created the heaven and the earth."
Romans 1:19: "For the invisible things of him from the creation of the world are clearly seen, being understood by the things that are made, even his eternal power and Godhead; so that they are without excuse."
Psalm 69:34: "Let the heaven and earth praise him, the seas, and everything that moveth therein."
Psalm 103:22: "Bless the Lord, all his works in all places of his dominion..."
Genesis 1:28: "...have dominion...over every living thing that moveth upon the earth."

BASIC PREMISES

God, as Creator of all life, gives each of His creations a unique individuality. Man has a special individuality, above all other creatures. He is given a soul, emotions and reasoning ability to discern right and wrong. Made in God's image, he has the ability to communicate with God and is accountable to his Maker. Man also has the responsibility to have dominion over himself and the rest of creation. Therefore, he must learn all that he can about God's laws of the universe. As he observes, compares, and reflects on creation, he will discern intelligent order, obvious design and the purposeful planning of an Almighty God, and thus bring praise, honor and glory to the Creator.

NOTEBOOK

Include pictures from magazines, brochures, advertisements or posters that pertain to some

---

11. The teacher can use the governmental term *represent* with discretion. Often, new vocabulary and especially difficult words, may be introduced to young children by using the term along with a few definitive words. As time goes on, with further explanation, a more comprehensive definition will be learned.

aspect of the curriculum overview.

VOCABULARY

Terms to include: day, night, evening, morning, noon, sunrise, sunset, spring, summer, fall, autumn, winter; skeleton, skull, spine, limbs, brain, eyes, ears, tongue, nose, skin; roots, stem, leaves, conservation; balance of nature; gravity, magnet. Teach the names of the months; the solar system and names of the planets and weather (snow, sleet, hail, etc.).

CURRICULUM

Stories can be told to illustrate Christian character and a productive life that glorifies God's providence and individuality. Consider books under "Special Resources": Latham, *Carry On, Mr. Bowditch*, and Tiner's *Johannes Kepler* and *Isaac Newton*.

Teach about God as Creator of the universe, and of all the creatures on the earth. Identify God's orderliness, design and planning in small things. See references to Hawes' *Bees and Beelines*, and Goldin's *Spider Silk*. The teacher can show pictures, read books aloud, and instruct in the following subjects:

The meaning of the words "solar system" (sun, planets that go around the sun).

The nine planets in order (Mercury, Venus, Earth, Mars, Jupiter, Saturn, Uranus, Neptune, Pluto).

The meaning of the word "gravity."

The two metals that a magnet will attract: iron and steel.

The seven days of the week; twelve months of the year; four seasons of the year.

The three parts of plants: root, stem, leaves.

Teach God's Principle of Individuality by collecting and examining the diversity of structure, design, or form among the same kind of leaves, bills of birds, seeds, etc. Consider books such as Hornblow's *Fish Do The Strangest Things* and Selsam's *The Amazing Dandelion* under "Special Resources."

Through a study on the differences in animals the children can learn the five classes of invertebrate animals: fish, mammals, reptiles, birds, and amphibians.

Study how to take care of specific things including certain plants, pets, or insects.

Learn the three main body skeleton parts: skull, spine, limbs. (See David Holmes, *The Principle Approach to Human Anatomy, Physiology*, p. 451

of this *Guide* for elementary curriculum suggestions)

Learn the five main groups of food: breads and cereals, meat and eggs, vegetables, fruits, milk and cheese.

Study the distinct differences in the way God created man, and the way animals are made. Emphasize man's unique soul, his being "made in the image of God," and his responsibility for dominion over the "earth."

Learn the three elements of earth: land, water, atmosphere.

Learn the formula for water (H_2O).

Do experiments that show scientific principles which govern the land, water and atmosphere.

SPECIAL RESOURCES

Branley, Franklyn M., *Air Is All Around Us*, N.Y.: Thomas Y. Crowell, 1962. (Other books by Branley include *Floating and Sinking*, 1967; *What Makes Day and Night?*, 1961; and *Mickey's Magnet*, 1956)

Coleman, William, *Counting Stars*, Minneapolis, MN: Bethany House Publishers, 1981. (Teacher selected stories) Also Coleman's *My Magnificent Machines*, 1978, and *More About My Magnificent Machine*, 1980.

Conklin, Gladys, *I Like Caterpillars*, N.Y.: Holiday House, 1958. Also *I Like Butterflies*, 1960, and *I Watch Flies*, 1977.

Latham, Jean Lee, *Carry On Mr. Bowditch*, Boston: Houghton Mifflin Company, 1955. (Nathaniel Bowditch was the Father of American Mathematics. See pp. 367 and 246 in this *Guide*)

Dang, Katherine, *American Christian Approach to Geography*, 1986, p. 257 of this *Guide*.

Garelick, May, *What's Inside?*, N.Y.: William R. Scott, Inc., 1965.

Goldin, Augustam, *Spider Silk*, N.Y.: Harper and Row, 1964.

Goudey, Alice E., *Houses From the Sea*, N.Y.: Charles Scribner's Sons, 1959. (Also consider *The Day We Saw the Sun Come Up*, 1961, and *Red Legs*, 1966)

Gish, Duane, *Those Terrible Lizards*, San Diego: Master Book Publishers, 1977.

Hawes, Judy, *Bees and Beelines*, N.Y.: Thomas Y. Crowell, 1964. (Another book by Hawes, *Ladybug, Fly Away Home*, 1967)

Hornblow, Leonora and Arthur, *Birds Do the Strangest Things*, N.Y.: Random House, 1965. (Other books by Hornblow, *Fish Do the Strangest Things*, 1966, and *Reptiles Do the Strangest Things*, 1970)

McGuire, Leslie, *You: How Your Body Works*, N.Y.: Platt and Munk, 1974.

Oxford Scientific Films, *The Spider's Web*, N.Y.: G.P. Putnam's Sons, 1978. (Also recommended: *The Butterfly Cycle*, 1977, and *Bees and Honey*, 1977)

Podendorf, Illa, *Seasons*, Chicago: Children's Press, 1955.

Rockwell, Anne and Harlow, *The Toolbox*, N.Y.: MacMillan Publishing.

Selsam, Millicent, *The Amazing Dandelion*, N.Y.: William Morrow and Co., 1977; *Seeds and More Seeds*, N.Y.: Harper and Row, 1959; *When An Animal Grows*, Harper and Row, 1960; and *The Carrot and Other Root Vegetables*, 1971.

Terres, John K., *The Audubon Book of True Nature Stories*, N.Y.: Thomas Y. Crowell Co., 1958.

Tiner, John Hudson, *Johannes Kepler*, Milford, Michigan: Mott Media, 1977 (*Isaac Newton*).

Udry, Janice May, *A Tree is Nice*, Harper and Row, 1956.

MUSIC

BIBLICAL PURPOSE

Music is to be sung with grace and understanding unto the Lord. God, the King, is to be praised. Music is also used to teach and admonish one another.

Psalm 104:33: "I will sing unto the Lord as long as I live: I will sing praise to my God while I have my being."

Colossians 3:16: "Let the word of Christ dwell in you richly in all wisdom teaching and admonishing one another in psalms and hymns and spiritual songs, singing with grace in your heart to the Lord."

Psalm 47:7: "For God is the King of all the earth: sing ye praises with understanding."

BASIC PREMISES

Music plays an important part in preparing the heart for hearing the Word of God. Although there are differences in individual musical ability, each individual is accountable to "sing unto the Lord" from within with the best of his talent. In order to sing or play music he must submit to God's principles of melody, harmony and rhythm.

Plan performances before other classes, convalescent homes, or audiences on special occasions. These programs provide an opportunity to emphasize the importance of having an unselfish attitude and to discover that God will bless the "cheerful giver." It is an excellent time to cultivate Christian self-government and such character traits as diligence and concern for others. The student learns that unity is necessary in order to produce an organized and orderly program. There is the joy of voluntarily sharing the student's inner property of song with the audience. Certainly an important reward is recording the music and words within the mind of the participant.

NOTEBOOK FILING

Include in the notebook:
1. Notation of music notes and symbols
2. Pictures of musical instruments
3. Illustrations of various songs

VOCABULARY

Terms include: music, vocal, instrumental, sound, piano, organ, percussion, string, brass, woodwind, and additional terms used in the following curriculum (see especially "Theory").

CURRICULUM

ATTITUDE, USE AND RESPONSIBILITY

Attitude: Psalm 34:1 or similar verses may be used.

Use: Psalm 104:33 or other verses can illustrate the attitude of praise. The story of David playing for Saul can illustrate the use of music to speak to someone's heart to prepare for God's spirit.

Responsibility: Some individuals are more talented than others, but all have the responsibility of using what God has given. Acknowledge the student who has a teachable spirit and is willing to use his ability to produce music.

THEORY

Explain use of terms: melody, harmony, rhythm, note, rest, octave, chord, scale, measure, pitch, tone, tempo, treble, bass, piano (p), pianissimo (pp), forte (f), fortissimo (ff), staccato, legato, crescendo, decrescendo.

Identify and take notation of treble clef, bass clef, rests, and whole, half, quarter, and eighth notes.

Identify time signatures.

Listen to demonstration of tones using do, re, mi, fa, sol.

Listen to demonstration of rhythms. Repeat rhythms.

Sing do, mi, sol; sing do, re, mi, fa, sol.

Identify pitches of high and low sounds.

SINGING

See theory section for basic theory.

Study the parts of the body used to speak and sing: larynx, vocal cords, lips, tongue, teeth, lungs.

Songs which teach Christian individuality, self-government, and character should be taught. These may be found in hymn books, children's song books or children's records.

Mother Goose and other traditional children's songs can be found in libraries or book stores. For example, *A Collection of 50 Songs for Children* is from a public library.

Instruction in the use of the hymn book. Show how to find a song number, how to read a hymn and how to sing the stanzas.

The student should individually sing at least two specified songs each quarter.

Performance of talent should be given to others through special music programs.

LISTENING

See special theory section for basic theory.

The ear and the eardrum, as the parts of the body used to listen, are studied.

The student learns to balance his individual talent by willingly blending his voice with others in a choir.

Principles of sound should be studied. Simple science experiments such as feeling the vibrations of an alarm ringing, hearing echoes on a cliff or making a tin-can telephone can be found in encyclopedias or library science books.

Listen to rhythms of sound, such as falling rain, feet walking, and a clock ticking. Listen to the pitch of sounds around us.

Animal songs and calls will reinforce the individuality of creation, develop a joy and appreciation of nature, and show how everything that has breath can praise the Lord. (Psalm 150:6) See under Special Resources, *If I Were A Bird*, by G. Conklin.

INSTRUMENTS

Study the four main groups of instruments: string, woodwind, brass, percussion. Identify by sight and sound, at least one instrument in each of the four main groups. Hear and observe how a piano and/or organ make musical tones.

Listen to a phonograph record or audio tape of Prokofiev's *Peter and the Wolf*, Saint-Saëns' *Car-nival of the Animals*, Rimsky Korsakov's *Flight of the Bumble Bee*, Strauss' *Blue Danube*, Debussy's *Clair de Lune* and *La Mer*, Schubert's *March Militaire*, Sousa's marches, and well-known hymns.

COMPOSERS

Use stories from lives of composers to demonstrate: 1) God's principle of individuality, and 2) qualities of Christian character demonstrated. For example, the self-government which Mozart needed in order to compose at age five. Bach showed Christian character in using his life to compose church music to praise God.

SPECIAL RESOURCES

Branley, Franklyn, *High Sounds, Low Sounds*, N.Y.: Harper & Row, 1967.

Conklin, Gladys, *If I Were A Bird*, N.Y.: Holiday House, 1965.

de Angeli, Marguerite, *Marguerite de Angeli's Book of Favorite Hymns*, N.Y.: Doubleday and Co., Inc., 1963.

Graham, Mary Nancy, *A Collection of 50 Songs for Children*, Racine, Wis.: Whitman Publishing Co., 1964.

Hawkinson, John and Martha Faulhaber, *Music and Instruments for Children to Make*. Book One, Chicago: Albert Whitman & Co., n.d. (about 1970).

Perkins, Al, *The Ear Book*, N.Y.: Random House, 1968.

Spier, Peter, *The Star-Spangled Banner*, Garden City, N.Y.: Doubleday and Co., Inc., 1973.

Voigt, Erna, *Peter and the Wolf*, Boston: David R. Godine, Pub., 1980.

ART

BIBLICAL PURPOSE

God's handiwork reveals the love of God and is worthy of man's close observation, reflection and representation in art.

Psalm 19:1: "The heavens declare the glory of God; and the firmament sheweth his handiwork."

Ecclesiastes 3:11: "He hath made every thing beautiful in his time..."

Philippians 4:8: "... whatsoever things are lovely... think on these things."

Proverbs 23:7: "For as a man thinketh in his heart, so is he."

BASIC PREMISES

The precise detail of form, outline, color, texture, line and space is shown in God's Handiwork. It is a demonstration of God's Omnipotence, Orderliness and Precision in every detail. The student, as one of God's most beautiful creations made in His image, should feel great satisfaction and worthiness as he shows some artistic imagination. Art class should develop accuracy in observation and description of nature as well as man-made artistry. Learning self-government in skillfully using art materials will quicken the mind and hands to express outwardly what the *inner eye* records. The memory is trained as the eye sees shape, size and texture, and holds them within until they are drawn, painted or sculptured. Step by step the teacher's directions strengthen student listening ability. When the student records his own art work it becomes his personal property. Christian self-government can be practiced throughout all areas of art.

CURRICULUM

Use and Care of Property: Teach the skills of how to use and care for scissors, crayons, paint and paint brushes, glue, ruler, chalk. Instruct how to get materials and work area ready, how to clean up, and put things back in order. Emphasize self-government, order, and responsibility in all areas.

Colors: Identify the eight colors (hues): (red, yellow, blue, green, orange, purple, black, brown). Name the primary colors (hues) (red, yellow, blue). Use the rainbow to illustrate colors.

Drawing: Teach how to draw straight lines from point to point, and lines to form a triangle, square, rectangle, circle, and ellipse. Instruct how to draw land-sky division, sun, moon, stars, clouds, trees, grass, snow, mountains, hills, lakes, rivers, streams, boats, ships, canoes, fish, birds, insects, butterflies, houses, telephone poles, fences, airplanes, shadows, silhouettes, etc. Allow at least one lesson for each item before that item is combined with drawings from previous lessons.

Teach how to draw perspective by drawing a road, sidewalk, path, river, railroad track, and telephone poles going into the distance.

Draw various tails, eyes, ears, beaks, and tracks of animals. God's Principle of Individuality is clearly applicable in these lessons. (See "Special Resources," Earle's *Birds and Their Beaks*, Van Gelder's *Whose Nose is This?*, Yela's *Whose Eye Am I?*, and Headstrom's *Identifying Animal Tracks*)

Study the human body in conjunction with science. The internal workings are studied so that the external art expressions will be more accurate. Trace a human skeleton. A human skeleton may also be drawn with ellipses and circles. The student may practice drawing a variety of eyes, ears, noses, mouths to portray different expressions. Discuss internal heart attitudes and the facial expressions produced.

Painting: The same topics as listed under "Drawing" can be rendered with watercolor, chalk or crayons. A rainbow can be painted with wet colored chalk.

Sculpture: Basic three-dimensional shapes such as a cube, cylinder, and pyramid can be used for teacher directed instruction.

Printmaking: Use kitchen utensils or articles from nature. For example, a pastry blender or pine cones.

Lettering: Make a picture poster with simple lettering.

Craftsmanship: Teach a basic stitch for sewing. Crafts such as stitchery, weaving, and woodwork could include weaving paper placemats and a simple woodwork project using hammer and nails. The skills for using hammer and nails may be practiced with shingle nails used on a soft wood stump.

Architecture: A building may be designed with building blocks or clay. Columns, steps, and other parts of building can be made from clay and the purposes of designs discussed. Thomas Jefferson's influence on American architecture may be taught with history.

Historical Art: Stories from Dennis' *Benjamin West and His Cat Grimalkin* may be told when painting is begun: how Benjamin made a brush from the hairs of the cat's tail fascinates children. Examples of American historical art can be studied as follows: Edward Savage's *The Landing of Christopher Columbus*, John Trumbull's *The Declaration of Independence*, and Gilbert Stuart's *George Washington*.

SPECIAL RESOURCES

Brodatz, Phil, *Textures*, N.Y.: Dover Publications, 1966.

Emberley, Ed, *Ed Emberley's Great Thumbprint Drawing Book*, Boston: Little, Brown and Co., 1977.

Earle, *Birds and Their Beaks*, N.Y.: Wm. Morrow & Sons, 1965.

Epstein, Sam and Beryl, *The First Book of Printing*, Franklin Watts, Inc.

Feininger, Andreas, *The Anatomy of Nature*, N.Y.: Dover Publications, Inc., 1956. (Also by

Feininger: *Leaves*, 1977)

Freeman, Don, *A Rainbow of My Own*, The Viking Press, 1966.

Glubok, Shirley, *The Art of Colonial America*, N.Y.: MacMillan Publishing Co., 1970.

Headstrom, Richard, *Identifying Animal Tracks*, N.Y.: Dover Publications, Inc., 1971.

Henry, Marguerite and Wesley Dennis, *Benjamin West and His Cat Grimalkin*, Indianapolis: The Bobbs Merrill Co., Inc., 1947. (Benjamin West was the Father of American Painting)

Hoban, Tana, *Shapes and Things*, N.Y.: MacMillan Publishing Co., 1970. Also *Circles, Triangles and Squares, Is It Red? Is It Yellow?*

Hawkinson, John, *Collect, Print and Paint from Nature*, Chicago: Albert Whitman & Co., 1961. (Also by Hawkinson: *More to Collect and Paint from Nature*, 1964, and *Paint a Rainbow*, 1970)

Rubenstone, Jessie, *Crochet for Beginners*, N.Y.: J. B. Lippincott Co., 1974, and *Knitting for Beginners*, Harper and Row.

Turner, Alta R., *Finger Weaving: Indian Braiding*, N.Y.: Sterling Publishing Co., n.d. (See other books in "Little Craft" series)

Van Gelder, Dr. Richard, *Whose Nose is This?*, N.Y.: Walker & Co., 1974.

Yela, *Whose Eye Am I?*, N.Y.: Harper and Row, 1968.

Zolotow, Charlotte, *Flocks of Birds*, N.Y.: Abelhard-Schuman, 1965.

PHYSICAL TRAINING

BIBLICAL PURPOSE AND GOALS

God intended that each child's body be the special place, or temple, of the Holy Spirit. Stewardship of the body acknowledges the intricate planning of the Creator and demonstrates the desire to keep the outward body worthy of the indwelling Christ. It also shows respect for Jesus giving His life for our eternal life. The individual must be willing to be an example in well doing, knowing that God will give the reward.

I Corinthians 6:19-20: " ... Know ye not that your body is the temple of the Holy Spirit...ye are not your own ... For ye are bought with a price; therefore, glorify God in your body and in your spirit which are God's."

I Timothy 4:12: "Let no man despise thy youth: but be thou an example of the believers, in word, in conversation, in charity, in spirit, in faith, in purity."

Galatians 6:9: "And let us not be weary in well doing; for in due season we shall reap, if we faint not."

BASIC PREMISES

Each child is taught how to strengthen his body by teacher-directed exercises and use of playground equipment and class games. Through these activities he is able to practice Christian self-government and Christian character. He begins to understand his own individuality as he works to play well enough to enjoy the game or skill. He then can respect others who have special abilities in certain physical skills. Games also cultivate healthy attitudes toward those who lose or fail to achieve the standard. When the student personally fails, he can learn to watch his attitude and cultivate inner strength to practice a skill until he masters it.

Traditional childhood games teach the student to listen to instructions and to use his eyes and ears in coordination with body movement. He must remember details and perform in spite of distractions. He must govern his actions and be truthful in following the rules. Since decisions are often made quickly in physical training and sometimes in the midst of emotion, it is excellent training for important choices in life.

Throughout physical training the student is practicing the three Biblical functions of government: he is planning, doing, and judging—the legislative, executive and judicial functions. If he is weak in any of these areas, it will show in outward demonstration.

VOCABULARY

Include the names of games, the words used for game directions; the words employed during the playing of games should be explained. The students should know the names of the body members engaged in physical training. The following words should be understood: between, around, follow, lead, right, left, up, down, over, under, in, out, opposite, "it."

CURRICULUM

Simple instructions should be given on how to safely use play equipment and how to climb, swing, pedal, balance, dangle, push, pull, rock, lift, drop, crawl, dig, jump, kick, throw, catch, walk, run, skip, hop, gallop, and tip-toe. Appropriate grading is on the use of each piece of playground equipment. Even though the child can be helped with any of the above activities with which he is having trouble, a good one to select for grading is running done with determination and enthusiasm.

The teacher directs body exercises, teaches skills used in organized games, and leads in children's group games, which include singing games, tag games, relays and circle games. The child may be graded on having a good attitude during participation, following the teacher's instructions, and showing respect for others who have a difficult time or "lose" in a game.

Instruction may be given in the beginning skills and rules of baseball, football, soccer, basketball, tennis, volley ball, skating, archery, bowling, quoits, tug of war, and checkers. The student may be graded in the throwing, catching, and bouncing of a large ball.

SPECIAL RESOURCES

Berends, Polly Berrien, *Games to Play with the Very Young*, N.Y.: Random House, 1967.

Green, Mary McBurney, *Is It Hard? Is It Easy?*, Reading, MA: Addison-Wesley Publishing Co., 1960.

Prudden, Bonnie, *How to Keep Your Child Fit from Birth to Six*, N.Y.: The Dial Press, 1983.

PREFACE TO THE CLASSROOM CONSTITUTION

School rules are *written* as a Classroom Constitution in order to establish the teacher's authority and to clearly define how the student is expected to govern himself. This instrument enables teacher, parents, and student(s) to work together to maintain settled, known and established standards of classroom government.

The teacher uses the constitution to instruct and train the student in *written law* and the Christian self-government and character required to fulfill the rules. The student's responsibility increases as the teacher consistently clarifies to him how to be accountable for his own application of the standards of the constitution. The teacher keeps in mind the capability of a five-year-old but does not underestimate his intelligence—nor his sin nature. Little irregularities or small wrong-doings, which may seem insignificant are not indulged by the American Christian teacher.[12] She seeks to clarify the problem to the student, address the inner heart attitude, and hold the child accountable for small steps toward Christian self-government.

To keep closer to the standard of God's Word, the teacher should reinforce rules with the use of Bible verses, phrases, principles and discipline. For example, she may say: " 'Do all things without murmurings and disputing,' the Bible tells us." She may remind a student who is keeping another child from learning: "God has said in His Word, 'Don't be a busybody.' " Use of verbatim Scripture references is not usually necessary for this age as it can distract from the thought intended.

In the following Kindergarten Constitution the rules are organized around the idea that all laws are for the protection of each individual's *life, liberty* and *property.*

A SAMPLE CLASSROOM CONSTITUTION FOR KINDERGARTEN

BIBLICAL PURPOSE

Psalm 119:34: "Give me understanding, and I shall keep thy law: yea I shall observe it with my whole heart."

BASIC PREMISE

God is the highest authority in the classroom and the Bible is the manual for that authority. The teacher, by parental consent, is a delegated authority and is accountable to God and the parents for training the child to live by Biblical principles. The student is taught to be responsible for his own practical application of Biblical truth. *All classroom laws are intended for the protection of each individual's life, liberty, and property.*

---

12. A parent or teacher influenced by "evolutionary" or "progressive education" teachings may believe that the child will "evolve" or "blossom" into a better person, if his wrong-doings are ignored. Consider John Locke on discipline, p. 398, *CHOC.*

RULES FOR CLASSROOM GOVERNMENT:

LIFE

"Protect life: do not hurt or harm yourself or another student."

1. Follow classroom safety rules. The student should come into the classroom quietly and put his clothes, books, lunch and homework in their proper place.

2. Follow playground safety rules. The teacher will explain proper safety rules for each piece of playground equipment and for the general play area.

LIBERTY

"Protect the liberty to learn: Govern yourself: do not keep yourself or another student from learning."

1. Each student works to reach standards set by the teacher. He does the following:

a. Participates in class work.

b. Learns the use of the notebook to record his work.

c. Is accountable to complete all homework assignments.

d. Works to master the knowledge required for passing tests in each subject.

2. Each student is to be prepared for daily work with the following:

a. Two pencils, sharp at the beginning of the day and with a usable eraser.

b. Three-ring notebook, with two lined and two unlined papers placed behind the division labeled "Paper."

c. Books which were taken home overnight and books to be used for that day's classes are to be placed on the desk for the teacher's quick check. An example of teacher's specific directions may be: Bible—left side of desk; library book—right side; reading book—middle of the desk.

d. Homework assignments: Written work should be in the front of the notebook and then placed in the teacher's homework desk tray at the beginning of the school day. A student should raise his hand during attendance check if he did not do his homework. If a family emergency conflicted with the parental 10-15 minute homework help, then the parent should place a note at the beginning of the student's notebook so that the child may give it to the teacher. (If possible, have the student substitute some kind of work that he can do on his own for ten minutes in order for him to maintain the pattern of doing homework.)

3. Each student is to follow rules for classroom government:

a. The student should give attention to the teacher's directions for looking, listening, and concentrating.

b. He should face the front of the room, except when instructed to do otherwise, or for other practical reasons.

c. The student should always look at the teacher when she is teaching and at the board when the teacher is writing on it and at any student who is performing in front of the class, except when instructed to do otherwise.

d. The student should not play with clothing, pencils or any articles which may distract from learning.

e. The student should train himself to use the bathroom at specified times so that his learning, and that of others, is not interrupted. Required bathroom time is at the beginning of the first recess and during the ten minutes preceding the last noon bell. The student assumes responsibility for determining his own bathroom needs during the afternoon recess. Emergencies will require a "make-up time" of sitting at the desk during recess, and discussing how to meet his needs in the future, if the problem is other than illness.

4. Parents and students should take a "business-like," responsible attitude towards attendance at school.

a. Acceptable absences are illness, bereavement and medical appointments.

b. Any medical appointment should be scheduled as late in the day as possible. Especially avoid scheduling during the first hour.

c. Since kindergarten teaching sessions usually cannot be duplicated for "make-up," the parent should spend extra time going over the weekly overview. (This is the one-page paper which the teacher has the student put in his notebook each Friday. It gives a short description of the subject matter to be covered the following week and is filed under "Overviews") The parent should give special attention to the subjects missed during an absence.

d. The student should bring in advance a parental note of explanation for a planned absence. In other cases, the note should be brought the day following the absence.

PROPERTY

"Protect property: Take care of your own property and allow others to take care of their property."

1. The student should care for his notebook, clothing, books, supplies, and any other property.

2. The student should care for any school prop-

erty with which he is entrusted.

3. If the student brings his own property to play with during recess, he should take care of it. He will be encouraged, but not required, to let others play with his property, providing that they, too, take proper care of it.

4. The student must respect the property of a *name*. This includes:

a. His own name—an extension of his special identity and individuality.

b. Other student's names.

c. God's name:

1) As a holy, righteous God—not using His name "in vain."

2) As Creator of all things beautiful—not using profane or irreverent "body words."

5. The student should take care of his property of *time*.

CLASSROOM DISCIPLINE

God's law and love demand that we *"train up the child in the way he should go".* (Proverbs 22:6) Hence, the teacher instructs, corrects or punishes the student in order to train him to voluntarily consent to the government of God through Christ by the Holy Spirit and to obey his parents or teachers.

There are methods of discipline which may be appropriate to use. A student may be denied the privilege of participating in a certain activity because he has interrupted the lesson. He may be told to cover his face at his desk, allowing him only to listen, or be asked to place his finger over his lips to help him remember not to talk. He may be told to repeat an action, such as walking slowly, until it is correctly done or directed to sit down on the playground until he can "think about" the proper way to play without getting into trouble.

A student can also be trained to ask forgiveness for a clear, overt offense to others. Biblical principles involved in giving and receiving offenses, making restitution, and praying together may be discussed when appropriate.

Paddling, the Biblical use of a "rod," is used to impress, with pain, the need to obey authority and the law. It is primarily used to correct rebellion or a willful attitude as opposed to ignorance. The teacher is sensitive to the limitations of a five-year-old's comprehension, and cares that explanations and instructions have been clearly presented. A "rod," either a paddle or a thin narrow stick, is used in place of the hand, which is never used. The student's modesty is always respected whenever a rod is used. The teacher seeks to balance corporal punishment with thinking and reasoning about the need to obey just law and authority.[13]

---

13. The author recommends two excellent resources on child training or discipline: *Under Loving Command* by Al and Pat Fabrizio, Sheva Press, P.O. Box 183, Palo Alto, CA 94302, and *What the Bible Says About Child Training*, by Richard Fugate, Aletheia Publishers, Tempe, AZ 85281.

SCHEDULING THE KINDERGARTEN DAY

The five-year-old needs a schedule that is consistent enough to provide regularity and security. He wants to know what is ahead so that he can anticipate the teacher's requirements. A uniform routine is most important at the beginning of school, after each recess, and when special teachers come to the room. If there is a schedule change, a brief explanation usually frees the child from anxiety.

Aware of the child's physical and emotional needs, the teacher may occasionally change the regular schedule. She may lighten the intensity of learning by inserting a creative, expressive type of project if the regular lesson becomes too tedious or weary to teacher or students. At times when a five-year-old's attention seems irretrievable, the teacher may announce recess early. Whenever students are especially receptive to the subject matter and concentrating hard, it may be appropriate to *continue* instruction for five, ten, or more minutes.

The kindergarten schedule should offer contrasts in methods of teaching, body position, and placement of subjects. Examples are: alternating practice in reading and writing, sitting on the floor during literature time to rest the muscles used in a chair, changing from teacher-directed learning to student demonstration, and inserting music or exercises between subjects. Contrasts will provide a flexible classroom rhythm, bring refreshment to the mind and body, and encourage good learning.

The five-year-old is physically most capable of attentive listening, careful work, and good concentration during the first 60-90 minutes of the day. This prime learning time should emphasize the teaching of literacy. During the day, as his ability to concentrate decreases, the student should have work that requires shorter periods of intense attention and reasoning. In the afternoon, graded papers may be filed in the notebook. Science projects which require drawing, cutting, or pasting will revive interest. Individual blackboard participation or other more active methods of learning can help to capture waning student attention.

At the beginning of the year the usual 20-minute subject periods may be shorter, and the participation more active. As the year progresses, training in study skills will help the student to lengthen the time spent on each subject.

An experienced teacher of young children knows that many minutes must be allowed for line-forming, hand-washing, and other essential routines. The American Christian teacher will not look on these things as tedious, unimportant jobs but as a chance to teach principles of order, diligence and self-government.

A kindergarten student's most productive learning is teacher-directed and teacher-supervised. However, he should be trained how to study on his own. He can exercise a degree of self-study and self-government when the teacher has an emergency interruption or when the student gets his work done ahead of others. The first grade teacher, not the kindergarten instructor, will benefit most from such training and discipline.

A basic schedule, used in a kindergarten day school room and adapted to minor changes each year, follows this article.

A SUGGESTED SCHEDULE

Preparation for Daily Work

Bible Instruction (the usual time for *each subject* is 15-20 minutes)

Reading, Writing, Speaking and Spelling

Break

Music Singing, Listening and Theory

Literature Time

Mathematics

Break

Geography, Science, History, Art or Notebook Filing

Break

Homework Instruction

Quiet Time*

Dismissal

*Quiet time is an opportunity to read aloud and discuss quietly and informally stories and pictures from interesting, pictorial books just before dismissing class. This time is an alternative to closing the day with frantic, frustrating minutes of cleaning up and gathering everything to go home. After Homework Instructions, questions on assignments answered, notices or announcements for parents issued, and books and personal articles assembled, let the last few minutes be instructive, interesting and orderly without tumult. Frequently, the children will be ready to recall these times to parents more than the structured periods of learning.

THE FIRST DAY

On his first day of school every kindergarten child must be told what is expected of him in a school schedule, that he needs to learn to read, to learn subject matter to prove to others that he has learned, and to enjoy his success and accomplishment at learning. All of this can be accomplished in the first day's introduction to the first week's overview (see next article).

After the child learns to say the sounds of the letters a, c, d and f on the flashcards, the teacher can remind him that he is *reading*.

The teacher has demonstrated writing by writing the first four sounds on the board, introduced the clock face beginning at "2 on the clock," and has the class practice positioning their paper, hands, and body for learning to write correctly. The student has written during math class when he counted "one" and wrote the numeral "1" in the first space in the 100-space chart. Students learn that "all straight lines begin at the top" and have practiced this at the board and on a practice paper, before writing in the chart.

During Bible, discuss the meaning of the name Bible and explain Psalm 119:11: *"Thy word have I hid in mine heart."* Describing "the heart" emphasizes the fact that God sees and knows what goes on inside each individual. Each child may be called in front of the class and his attractive "first day" clothing (so important to a child) is mentioned in detail. Then the teacher talks about how

God sees it all, but is interested even more in the inside of the child. Through this topic the child has learned a verse, has felt special and important, and has learned something that will be emphasized in his American Christian classroom.

"Old Mother Goose" poem can be used for literature. By the end of the class, it can be memorized by using a great variety of ways to review. The words "Christian self-government" can be taught by explaining how to come to literature class demonstrating self-government. Its meaning can be reiterated during the day and, if the child learns to say it and tell the meaning in his own words, will delight himself and others with this big word after his day at school.

During literature the teacher can begin to train the child to "see pictures in the mind" by closing his eyes while she reads about Mother Goose. She asks him to dress his mind's picture of Mother Goose in a red dress like Mary's, socks like Johnnie's and shoes like the teacher's. This gives importance to the individual, while teaching the child how to observe and to imagine details of what he sees or hears.

In history class the teacher can show the world map as the word "history" is talked about. The globe, in comparison to the map, will bring in the topic of geography. The three basic elements of the earth's make-up—land, water, and air—can also be explained. The child can learn these facts and delight his elders with this knowledge at the end of his school day.

Learning how to open and close his notebook safely is an important lesson. Each student can also learn to value his property because the teacher has talked about the notebook with respect and has called it his special property, with some explanation of the meaning of property.

Of course, details of how to walk in and out of class, when to use the bathroom, and the order of a daily schedule are introduced. In a day school classroom there are many things students must be taught to use properly. The teacher need not explain all these things the first day, but should follow up as soon as possible so the child can assume responsibility for his own needs.

Explain *why* a student has certain rules such as working quietly, not talking, or wiping his shoes when coming in from recess. The time and effort to give a reason for some rules helps to free the teacher from frequent "policing" and helps the child learn to govern his own actions.

At the end of the first day both teacher and pupils can remember, with pleasure, these accomplishments. The child coming home from day school will be carrying his precious notebook with

the cards of the four sounds so he can prove he can read. He will have inside (no dividers yet), in the front of his notebook, his one hundred chart with the number "1" written in the first space. He may have a picture of a world map, globe, or Old Mother Goose. He will have in his mind a Bible verse, a few science and history facts, and a rhyme. He certainly has good proof that he is an important individual in an important place.

SUGGESTED LESSON OVERVIEW
FOR FIRST WEEK OF SCHOOL

The following curriculum outline constitutes summary lesson plans for five days for a full day program.

Bible: The Bible is God's Word. It is God talking to us by the words on the paper. The Bible tells us about God. "The Word of God will endure (live) forever." Psalm 119:11 says: "Thy Word have I hid in my heart that I might not sin against thee."

Reading, Writing, Spelling and Speaking: Discuss the beginning of language. God talked to Adam. Genesis 3. Adam gave names to everything in the garden. Genesis 2:20. How do you think Adam would have called and talked to the animals? Of all God's creation, only men, women, boys and girls talk in real languages, and read, write and spell. Introduce the "2 on the clock" sounds of the "Spalding Method" with flash cards for letters a c d f g o qu.

Practice making these basic lines which will be used to write the letters later:

Practice the correct sitting position. Hold the pencil correctly. Slant paper like the writing arm. Bend from hips. Feet flat on floor.

Math: Numbers are important to God. Matthew 10:30 tells us that the very hairs on our head are numbered. Psalm 139:17 says that if we should try to count God's thoughts they would be more in number than the sand.

Counting 1, 2, 3 will be worked with this week. The numbers are each individual. They look different. They sound different. They mean something different. The children will be illustrating this by examples. They will write the numeral "1" but not the other two. They will read the numbers 1, 2 and 3 as the teacher writes on the board.

American Christian Literature: The story of "Old Mother Goose," "Humpty Dumpty," "Hey Diddle Diddle" and a few more of the most common Mother Goose rhymes will be read and discussed. Talk about stories being told from generation to generation. The emphasis is upon listening, concentrating and developing the inner mind. Reasoning and vocabulary will be emphasized. Read the story: "The Gingerbread Boy."

American Christian History: History means "His story—God's story." It is the story of God and of people, events, and nations.

Geography: The earth is the Lord's. It was made by God for His people. (Psalm 24:1) The globe is a picture of the earth. A map is a picture of a globe all flattened out upon paper.

Science: God and His handiworks can be seen all around us. (Romans 1:20) The earth is made of land, water and atmosphere.

HOMEWORK

Wednesday evening: Count three hairs on his own head. Notice how many more there are. Count other things—to three (3).

Thursday evening: Tell what "history" means. Tell of what the earth is made.

THE KINDERGARTEN NOTEBOOK

The kindergarten notebook is a three-ring binder used to record the student's productivity and progress. It represents the application of time, labor and intellect to his academic studies. It shows how he has learned and recorded the simple principles and facts of each subject.

PURPOSE OF THE NOTEBOOK

This binder is an external physical means employed for an internal mental and spiritual end. It is used to strengthen Christian character, develop good work habits, and to record information which reflects the student's understanding and progress. Seeking to follow simple directions while striving to attain academic standards will often expose attitudes of the child's heart, and provide opportunities for the teacher to correct wrong attitudes. Filing papers according to the specific subjects, which is a good work skill, requires a student to think and reason in an organized manner. The basic foundational notebook skills learned by the student will give him liberty to use this skill in the future. (See also the *Curriculum* section of this *Guide,* the "Notebook Approach," p. 138)

PROPERTY EMPHASIS

The need to protect and maintain the notebook gives it high value as personal property. Each student is responsible for bringing his notebook back and forth to school in his tote bag. The student is also the steward of any parental notes, overviews and homework which are enclosed within the notebook.

PROVIDES PLACE FOR PAPERS

The three-ring binder provides a secure place for the student to keep his daily papers. It is also a temporary location for special homework papers, office messages, and teacher-parent notes. The binder eliminates the problem of loose "take-home papers" which may not reach their destination. It provides the student an appropriate way to display the "fruits of his labor" to his parents, and to his guests at home. A student can delight in leafing through his notebook privately, and take pleasure in remembering the work on the individual pages.

GOOD ATTITUDE DEVELOPED

The student must voluntarily consent to the direction of the teacher in order to maintain and improve his successful use of the notebook and be willing to practice patience in the application of Christian self-government.

ORGANIZING AND USING THE NOTEBOOK

After eight years of successful notebook use with kindergarten students, the author has learned some practical ways to organize and use the binder. The teacher who applies these suggestions must not be overwhelmed or frustrated by unrealistic expectations. She must take into account the immature student's limited ability to attend to his property. The child must be encouraged, as well as trained, in order to improve his ability to maintain his notebook. Perfection will not come all at once!

Notebook Binder: The parent should select a notebook binder which the student can open or close by himself. The rings should be about 1 1/2 inches across so that there is sufficient room for nine to ten weeks' work (one quarter).

Dividers: Twelve dividers, with tabs for the name of each section, are recommended as within the capability and comprehension of the young student to use. Suggested divider headings are (extra) *Paper, Weekly Overviews, Literacy* (includes reading, spelling, grammar and speech), *Bible, Mathematics, Literature, Science, History, Geography, Music, Art, and Homework*. After the teacher records in her grade book that the homework has been turned in and puts some identifying mark on the paper, the student files it under the last divider of his notebook. The order suggested is for the purpose of practicality. At this age utilitarian arrangement is more important than alphabetical sequence. The students should put the dividers in, one at a time, when needed. This helps the child to comprehend proper placement of his papers and develops his reasoning ability as he learns to file.

Paper: Lined, unlined or other 8 1/2 by 11 inch paper is used. For certain projects in art, science or history, 17 inch wide paper may be folded back to the edge of the notebook rings. At homework time each evening the student should replenish, if needed, the two sheets of lined paper and two sheets of unlined paper, which are filed behind the "Paper" division and used for the daily work. This responsibility provides opportunity to practice consistent dependability, an important work skill. It also eliminates the heavy bulk and the confusion caused by too much unused paper.

Name, Date and Title: The student's first name may be written between the first two horizontal lines beginning next to the red margin line. A simplified date (for example: 9-17-87) can begin at the middle of the same line. The class subject title is not written.

At the beginning of the kindergarten year, and until the time when the letters and numbers are properly taught, the teacher should write the student's name and date. Whenever necessary, a teacher-written title will help to explain a drawing or other assignment that is not self-explanatory. Of course, the student will write his own title as soon as he is able. The first day of May is an appropriate time to begin using the correct month name instead of the month's number in the simplified date.

Some Papers Not Filed: All papers need not be filed for the record. For example, do not file work assigned for the teacher's information when identifying some specific need or problem, nor occasional lessons which need special re-teaching. Handwriting lessons may be included when appropriate. The on-going practice paper used from day to day at certain times during the year need not be filed.

Quarterly Clearing: The parent should remove each quarter's work from the binder before the next nine-weeks begin. This keeps the notebook from becoming too bulky to handle. With only the binder, the dividers, and a fresh start, the student is encouraged to improve his notebook maintenance.

A Year's Record: At the end of the school year the child can help his parent compile the entire year's work into one binder. Most students and their parents will value this record and cherish it even more in the years to come. A mother of a Kindergarten student gave this testimony: "To have before me such an accurate account of my son's first school year is truly overwhelming. Having it all together, I am certainly proud to see my boy's great achievements in his first year."

FACILITIES AND EQUIPMENT

TEACHER'S STUDY AREA

A. Desk for work and for supplies.

B. Bookcase for books and notebooks (6' by 3' or larger).

C. Appropriate family books and encyclopedias.

CLASSROOM AREA

A. Desks.
  1. Teacher's desk.
  a. Drawer room for notebooks, teacher's books and file folder/records on each student. (Lock for desk if room is used for other purposes.)
  b. Space on desk top for books used daily.
  c. Filing tray or trays on desk top for pupil's homework and for teacher's use.
  2. Student's individual desks. (Tables are not appropriate for more than one student. Individuals need to care for their own property. Learning disadvantages, such as seeing letters and words in reversal form, are also present when in close proximity at a table.)
B. Chairs.

1. Teacher's desk chair and chair for literature reading-aloud time.

2. Students' chairs which are conducive to healthy posture.

C. Clear acrylic desk pad. (Extremely helpful for quick "filing" and for safe-guarding notes, reminders, etc.)

D. Teacher's daily plan book, grade book, and three-ring notebooks for various needs.

E. Blackboard and Supplies.

1. For teacher's and student's use. (Be sure blackboard height is correct)

2. Pointer and chalk.

3. Erasers. (At least one for every two students.)

F. File cabinet for picture file.

G. Bulletin board or wall space for pictures and teaching charts, etc.

H. World globe and map; United States map. (Very clear, distinct and simple marking)

LOIS WEHRMAN MILLER

After receiving a Master's Degree in Religious Education and teaching a wide variety of instructional materials for 20 years in public and private schools, I have learned by contrast and practice to value the results of American Christian education.

In 1976 God providentially led me to James Rose, Headmaster of a pilot and demonstration school for the Principle Approach to American Christian education and government. My assignment was to learn how to implement this philosophy and methodology on the kindergarten level. It was quickly apparent to me that the Principle Approach embraced Biblical wisdom, intelligence, and effective teaching methods and curriculum.

In childhood, my parents expected me to learn to think independently—to reason to a conclusion on my own. As an adult, my ability to reason Biblically matured through the example of my husband's expository preaching. And as I learned to apply the Principle Approach daily, the Word of God became more clear, profound and relevant to the diversity of subjects and children I was teaching.

The seven principles of America's Christian history, as presented in Rosalie J. Slater's book,

Teaching and Learning America's Christian History, were practical and effective truths to explain and illustrate to children. It was most rewarding to teach young children the concepts of individual worth, regard for private property, how to reason and use one's mind, and the overall authority of God's Word. Rather than teaching blind patriotism, I was promoting a lively sense of Christian liberty and making a contribution as a Christian citizen. Finally, it was a blessing to me to study the Hand of God in history; I was developing a personal enjoyment of history and government.

God was gracious during those first few years of developing an American Christian curriculum. I was thankful for the tutoring of pioneers in the work: Verna Hall, Rosalie Slater, James Rose and my fellow laborers. I was urged to teach that which "rings true" by checking all things against what I already knew to be Biblical and correct. Month by month, I was able to build upon each step. Few changes have been made since those early years, but the teaching has become more exact, in-depth, and enhanced with more illustrations, stories, and practical Bible truths.

The students had grasped the principles of the subjects and had the liberty to continue learning—and enjoying it! Each child had become a more knowledgeable young citizen, better grounded and appreciative of Christian self- and civil government. Many had accepted the challenge to love the Lord with all their heart, soul, and mind.

I was personally satisfied to know that I had helped to train boys and girls in sound moral and ethical character, some with a personal relationship with Jesus already, and the rest better prepared to open their hearts to God's saving grace.

It is my desire to be able to help other teachers successfully train their students to reason from God's Word and live in harmony with Biblical principles. I would like to have a part in helping to produce expository preachers for the pulpit, expository teachers for the Sunday School and Day School, and better readers and thinkers for the audiences of these preachers and teachers. I would like to be a part of the restoration of the Bible as the daily book of self-government for American Christians and as the "political textbook" for our nation's statesmen.

AMERICAN CHRISTIAN HISTORY

BY RUTH J. SMITH
Director
The Pilgrim Institute
Granger, Indiana

CONTENTS

Teaching America's Christian History In The Elementary School

INTRODUCTION

God commands us to remember all He has done for us as individuals and nations. (Deut. 7:18; 8:2; Josh. 4:1-9) Noah Webster tells us that *to remember is to have in the mind an idea which had been in the mind before, and which recurs to the mind without effort.* Indeed, as Emma Willard observed, "...if we expect that memory will treasure up the objects of attention," it would help to acknowledge that "Each individual is to himself the centre of his own world and the more intimately he connects his knowledge with himself, the better will it be remembered..."[1] Hence, if we individually rejoice upon every remembrance of the grace of God in our *personal* history and world, we do err in forgetting God's Providence—His immediate, sovereign care and supervision—in our *nation's* unique history.

Today, the study of history has become a study of dates, facts, names, and events, with no consideration for their cause and effect. This approach to history has produced students who regard history as *dull* and *boring* and who have some knowledge of *facts* (or effects) of history, but no understanding of the *cause* of history and the individual's importance in His Story. Studying history with an effort to determine the cause and effect of events gives *life* to the subject.

The individual Christian must determine what is the cause of all events in his own personal history and his nation's history. Rev. S. W. Foljambe declares a causal relationship in his Annual Election Sermon, January 5, 1876, "It has been said that history is the biography of communities; in another, and profounder, sense, it is the autobiography of him 'who worketh all things after the counsel of his own will' (Eph. 1:11), and who is graciously timing all events in the interests of his Christ, and of the kingdom of God on earth."[2]

Recognizing God as the cause of events of history will make our study of history truly Christian. How we must grieve the Holy Spirit if we attribute history to other than the true source!

A study of history from the premise that God is in control will cause the individual to recognize that God has a plan for each individual and nation. After Christ brought Christianity, Christianity

---

1. Emma Willard, *CHOC*, p. 405.

2. *C/P*, p. 47a.

203

through God's divine direction moved westward with its effect in civil liberty. This westward march of Christianity produced America, the world's first Christian Republic established with a Christian form of government.

In many classrooms, history loses its identity when it is blended into a social studies course. The teaching of social studies produces an individual who has no mastery of history and who has a philosophy based upon man as causative with a great emphasis upon societies rather than the individual. As early as 1876, the Centennial of American Independence, Rev. Foljambe cautioned Americans against a failure to study Providential history: "The more thoroughly a nation deals with its history, the more decidedly will it recognize and own an overruling Providence therein, and the more religious a nation will it become; while the more superficially it deals with its history, seeing only secondary causes and human agencies, the more irreligious will it be.[3]

The failure to teach history produces an irreligious people who attribute all advancement to man's efforts. History studied from original source documents enables individuals to see God's Hand moving to fulfill His plan and purpose and to therefore give God, not man, the glory.

American Christians must *again*, as our forefathers did, recognize that America is the direct result of Christianity and its relationship to all areas of life, including the sphere of civil government. American Christians must recognize the link between internal Christian liberty and external religious and civil liberty. If the foundations of our nation are to be restored, these premises must become an integral part of the teacher's philosophy of history and government and thus direct how and what he teaches in the classroom.

The directions for *Teaching America's Christian History in the Elementary School* given here have been developed for parents and teachers who already have some understanding of the American Christian philosophy of history, government, and education.

CHAIN OF CHRISTIANITY

History records the evidence of God's use of individual men and nations to move Christianity westward. This westward movement produced America and her Christian form of government. The links on the Chain of Christianity are the individual men and nations used by God to move the Gospel westward and the effect of Christianity in the civil sphere. For further study of the Chain of Christianity, see *Rudiments Handbook*, pages 47-76, *Teaching and Learning America's Christian History*, pages 158-179, and their references to *Christian History*.

COURSE OBJECTIVES

1. To recognize the Providential Hand of God in all events, past, present, and future.

2. To recognize the importance of each individual in God's plan of history.

3. To teach the major links on the Chain of Christianity.

4. To teach the Biblical principles of government which formed our Christian Constitutional Republic, i.e., God's Principle of Individuality, The Christian Principle of Self-Government, etc.

5. To learn to reason from cause to effect in historic events.

6. To recognize the stewardship responsibility of the American Christian for our nation.

DEVELOPING THE ELEMENTARY CHRISTIAN HISTORY PROGRAM

The Principle Approach to American Christian Education requires the parent/teacher to prepare himself internally to teach America's Christian History in the elementary school through his development of a Biblical philosophy of history and government. Such preparation comes by reasoning, relating, and recording the explicit evidence of those Biblical principles and key links advanced by the Hand of God on the Chain of Christianity. The parent/teacher's own notebook will reflect his mastery of America's Christian History, and the student's notebook will reflect the

3. *C/P*, p. 46b.

student's mastery of that which is taught. (See page 212)

The parent and teacher can readily and practically use the following charts and contents of this Elementary Christian History program by understanding the approach as follows:

1. Each year should begin with the following rudiments:
   a. Concise definitions of history, government, Providence, Chain of Christianity.
   b. Biblical and historic examples of the Providential Approach to history. For aid in developing, see p. 26.
   c. Explanation and overview of the Chain of Christianity.

These elements will be simplified or deepened according to the age of the child. See pages 207 and 208 for aid in developing.

Caution: Do not oversimplify. The kindergarten child can understand such words as history, government, and Providence.

2. Nine major links of the Chain of Christianity are studied each year. See Chart A, page 206.

3. The seed of each link—the primary, recurring principle(s) and idea(s)—is presented in kindergarten and expanded through the elementary grades. See Chart B, page 206. This expansion assures that the student will have been introduced to the major events of history in the context of one major theme—the Chain of Christianity Moving Westward.

4. In the Christian home or day school, the Headmaster should develop an overview of major points of emphasis for each grade. A Suggested Overview is given on page 207. This allows a needed diversity of emphasis within the grades but assures a unity of philosophy and method to reach the desired goals. In the home school, the parent should develop an overview for the number of years in which the child is to be taught in the home school.

5. Prepare an overview of one year to determine the number of days or weeks to be spent on each link and its expansion. The length of time spent on each link will vary within the year, and from year to year. For example, one might spend one or two weeks on most links but six to eight weeks on just one. See page 207.

6. Develop and record in your notebook a mastery of the individual links on the Chain of Christianity. For an overview of each link, see page 208. For a suggestion on expanding the first year of one link, *Pilgrim, Seed of Our American Christian Republic*, see page 212. Additional syllabi are being prepared by the Pilgrim Institute, which will give direction for expanding each of the nine major links included in this Elementary History Program.

7. Prepare daily lesson plans. Include the following aspects in each lesson plan:
   a. Goal(s)—The teacher should establish a particular goal or goals to be accomplished. These may embrace one or more of the course objectives given on page 204. Webster defines a goal as "the end or final purpose; the end … which a person aims to reach or accomplish."
   b. Content—Identify the principles and ideas to be taught, with supporting historic facts.
   c. Identify any one or more of the seven governmental principles to be taught. (See *Teaching and Learning*, p. 111)
   d. Methodology—Include any notes to be recorded by the student(s), and identify the source of any materials to be read, etc.
   e. Assignments to be given.
   For further direction and examples, see page 222.

8. Teaching Suggestions:
   a. A bulletin board reflecting the Chain of Christianity's westward movement should be developed for the classroom. Suggestions: Place a time line above the chalk board which includes all of the links of the Chain of Christianity which are to be taught that year. This will prove an excellent tool for teaching in other classes, as the teacher can teach the child the historic setting for the life of a specific author, scientist, or mathematician.
   b. Do not become encumbered by a continuing outline, i.e., an outline beginning in September and continuing throughout the school year. Make each day, few days, or an individual link on the Chain of Christianity a complete and separate lesson, which teaches at least one principle or idea that is related to the whole of the Chain of Christianity.
   c. Be careful that history prior to Christ does not become simply a narrative of Bible stories without identifying the cause and effect in the sphere of individual liberty and civil government.

CHART A
CHAIN OF CHRISTIANITY

| CREATION | MOSES and the Law | CHRIST Focal Point of History | PAUL Christianity Begins Its Westward March | BIBLE in English | COLUMBUS Link to the New World | PILGRIM Seed of our Christian Republic | PATRIOT First Christian Republic | PIONEER Westward Movement and Falling Away |

Nine major links on the Chain of Christianity are studied each year in the elementary school. These links have been derived from the more complete chart on page 6A, *Christian History of the Constitution.*

CHART B
CHAIN OF CHRISTIANITY
Expanding the Links Through
the Elementary School

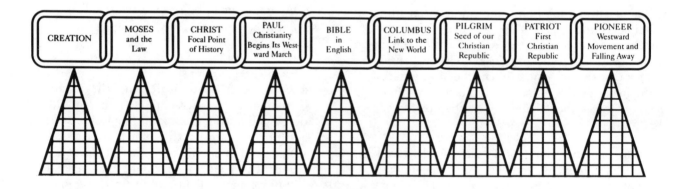

| CREATION | MOSES and the Law | CHRIST Focal Point of History | PAUL Christianity Begins Its Westward March | BIBLE in English | COLUMBUS Link to the New World | PILGRIM Seed of our Christian Republic | PATRIOT First Christian Republic | PIONEER Westward Movement and Falling Away |

Each link on the Chain is studied each year, with the seed of the link being presented in kindergarten and expanded through the elementary grades. This allows the teacher to review the materials learned in previous year(s) and build upon that foundation. By building the elementary history program upon expanding links, the student will complete his elementary education with a great mastery of Christianity's effect upon the domestic, ecclesiastical, and civil sphere, i.e., the relationship between internal Christian liberty and external religious and civil liberty.

The question is often asked: How can we teach the same link each year without being repetitious? The Suggested Overview on page 208 gives ideas for expanding each link through the elementary years without repetition. The basis for this approach is the Principle Approach to American Christian Education. See *Teaching and Learning America's Christianity History*, p. 108, "How Can the Same Principle be Taught in Every Grade?," and p. 112, "Principles Expanded Through the Grades."

CHART C: SUGGESTED OVERVIEW
KINDERGARTEN-SIXTH GRADE
CHAIN OF CHRISTIANITY

	CREATION	MOSES and the Law	CHRIST Focal Point of History	PAUL Westward Movement	BIBLE in English	CHRISTOPHER COLUMBUS Link to the New World	PILGRIM Seed of our Christian Republic	PATRIOT First Christian Republic	PIONEER Westward Movement & Falling Away
FIRST YEAR (Kindergarten)	God's Principle of Individuality — God as Creator — Christian Individuality	Moses Preserved by God — Infancy	Jesus: Birth and Reason for Coming	Story of Paul	John Wycliffe	Biography of Columbus	Thanksgiving Story	George Washington Father of our Country	Abraham Lincoln
SECOND YEAR (First Grade)	Man is God's Property ************** Geographic Individuals	Moses Preserved by God for His purpose as First Historian and First Lawgiver — First 40 Years	Jesus Christ — The basis for Christian self-government	Christianity moves Westward to Europe — Macedonian call	John Wycliffe ************** William Tyndale	Biog. of Columbus	America's Heritage of Christian Character — Brotherly love & Christian care	George Washington Father of our Country	Abraham Lincoln
THIRD YEAR (Second Grade)	God's Character Revealed in Creation — Infinity, Diversity, Individuality	Moses Prepared to Lead Children of Israel from Captivity — Last 80 years — Prin. of Representation. Deut. 1	Jesus coming changed history B.C. – A.D.	Paul's internal change — from persecutor to missionary	Geneva Bible	Providential Preparation of Columbus — Marco Polo's voyages	America's Heritage of Christian Character — Faith and Steadfastness — Diligence and Industry	Declaration of Independence — America declares herself an individual nation	Lewis and Clark
FOURTH YEAR (Third Grade)	Origin & dispersion of the Races — Noah's 3 sons	Ten Commandments — Dual Form of Government	Christ came to fulfill the law Matt. 5:17-20	Paul on Mars Hill	King James Bible	Providence of God — Prince Henry and Navigational Instruments — America Preserved until He had a people ready	Providence of God — Bible — Holland — John Smith — Squanto	God's Providence in American Revolution	State History
FIFTH YEAR (Fourth Grade)	Establishment of Civil Gov't. Gen. 9:6	Ten Commandments — God's law the basis of civil law	Law and the Gospel – the basis of our Government.	Purpose of God's law as identified by Paul	Magna Charta — Individual rights protected by written law	Origin of the name America ************** Cabot's claim to North America	Voluntary Consent: Key to Self-Government — Mayflower Compact	Samuel Adams — Christian Patriot	Noah Webster
SIXTH YEAR (Fifth Grade)	Christian Idea of Man and Gov't/ Pagan Idea of Man and Gov't	Hebrew Republic vs. Monarchy I Sam. 8	"In the fullness of time Christ came" — Greece & Rome prepared the soil for Christianity	Purpose of civil government as declared in Paul's writings	Bible — Basis of Reformation	Mexico and Canada claimed by Spain/France	Contrast Jamestown/ Plymouth	Patriotic Letters — Committees of Correspondence ************** Boston Patriots and Boston Tea Party	Herbert Hoover
SEVENTH YEAR (Sixth Grade)	Creation vs. Evolution	Distinctives of Moral law, Ritual law, Civil law	Two Systems of Law — Roman Civil Law — English Common Law — External/ Internal	New Testament Church — "a little republic"	Bible and the Constitution	Contribution of Columbus to Westward Movement	Communism vs. Free Enterprise	Our Constitution: Law of the Land ************** Republic vs. Democracy — Prin. of Rep.; 3 branches of gov't.; Dual Form of gov't.	Ronald Reagan American Federalism

This overview has been developed with the intent of building line upon line, precept upon precept. The foundation must be laid carefully year by year. To build the proper foundation, each teacher must begin with the primary level and expand in the following years. If the student(s) to be taught is in the upper elementary grades, the teacher may combine the concepts of more than one year, thus expanding more quickly to the appropriate grade level. When implementing in a school, all teachers would begin with the first year and expand in subsequent years.

OVERVIEW OF NINE LINKS

The elementary school years provide the opportunity for building a solid foundation for the student's development of a philosophy of history and government and the interpretation of all events of history from Biblical principles. The nine links selected as the central points of emphasis for *Teaching America's Christian History in the Elementary School* are the major steps which link Christianity's westward march. As the student masters these nine links, he will be adequately prepared to interpret the cause and effect of events which surround these major links and many current events.

The individual teacher or headmaster may wish to add other specific links to the overview prepared for his particular classroom setting.

Following are additional leading ideas, teaching suggestions, resources available, and suggested student materials which will aid the teacher in developing the nine links given in the overview on page 206.

THE FIRST LINK:
CREATION

LEADING IDEAS:
Character and attributes of God
  • revealed in creation
  • teaches the child "the fear of the Lord" which is the "beginning of knowledge"
Nature and character of man
  • "Who made me?"
  • "Why was I made?"

Christian vs. pagan idea of man and government

DEVELOPING THE TEACHER'S NOTEBOOK:
  Teaching and Learning, pp. 113-115
  • "Christian Individuality"
  • "Geographic Individuals"
  Teaching and Learning, p. 230
  • "Man is God's Property"
  Rudiments Handbook, pp. 7-8; 33-47

THE SECOND LINK:
MOSES
and the Law

LEADING IDEAS:
Providential preservation and preparation of Moses for His purpose as first historian and first lawgiver

Ten commandments
  • Evidence of a dual form of government
    –first four commandments deal with man's relationship to God
    –last six commandments deal with man's relationship to man
  • Restated in New Testament in the two great commandments of Matthew 22:37-40

Relationship of Old Testament Law to the New Testament (Gal. 3:24)

Distinction of Moral Law, Ritual Law, and Civil Law

DEVELOPING THE TEACHER'S NOTEBOOK:
  Rudiments Handbook, pp. 9-29; 48-54
  Teaching and Learning, pp. 158-159

THE THIRD LINK

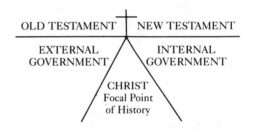

FOCAL—"Belonging to a focus."
FOCUS—"A central point; point of concentration."

Greece and Rome provided the setting for Christ's coming. This included both negative and positive preparations.

DEVELOPING THE TEACHER'S NOTEBOOK:
  Teaching and Learning, pp. 159-166
  Rudiments Handbook, pp. 55-62
  Self Government With Union, pp. 92-126

THE FOURTH LINK:
PAUL
The Westward Movement

"One of the most important steps for America's Christian History occurred in Acts 16 when the Apostle Paul, heeding the Macedonian Cry, turned westward to the Continent of Europe. At Philippi, 'which is the chief city of that part of Macedonia, and a colony' Paul found his first European convert in Lydia 'a seller of purple, of the city of Thyatira.' Lydia's words after her baptism have significance for the new life now opened up for women—a life whose unique role and contribution comes to particular fruition in the United States of America.

"'And when she was baptized, and her household, she besought us, saying, If ye have judged me to be faithful to the Lord, come into my house, and abide there. And she constrained us.' (Acts 16:15)

"Reverends W.J. Conybeare and J.S. Howson, in their *The Life and Epistles of Saint Paul*, American Edition of 1869, say this:

"Thus the Gospel had obtained a home in Europe . . . and nothing could be more calm and tranquil than its first beginnings on the shore of that continent, which it has long overspread. The scenes by the river-side, and in the house of Lydia, are beautiful prophecies of the holy influence which women, elevated by Christianity to their true position, and enabled by Divine grace to wear 'the ornament of a meek and quiet spirit,' have now for centuries exerted over domestic happiness and the growth of piety and peace."[4]

DEVELOPING THE TEACHER'S NOTEBOOK:
- Study the book of Acts for the life and testimony of Paul and Lydia.
- Research the Epistles of Paul to identify the purpose of law and civil government. Consider Matthew Henry's Commentary on the Pauline Epistles.
Christian History of the Constitution, pp. 16-17

THE FIFTH LINK:
The Bible in English

The history of the Bible is the history of civil liberty. Only as the Bible is placed in the hands of the individual can the individual be properly self-governed. As the individual learned to be self-governed, a change was reflected in the civil sphere. To understand the history of civil liberty, it is essential to study the history of the Bible.

It is difficult for American Christians to imagine a time when the Bible was not readily available to the individual. The beautiful story of the individuals who, committed to fulfilling God's purpose in their lives, faced persecution and martyrdom to make the Scriptures available must be reclaimed by American Christians.

Each Bible in the history of the Bible in En-

glish has a unique contribution.

DEVELOPING THE TEACHER'S NOTEBOOK:
Teaching and Learning, pp. 166-168; 173; 332-342
Christian History of the Constitution, pp. 28A-36
Rudiments Handbook, p. 65

THE SIXTH LINK:
CHRISTOPHER COLUMBUS
Link to the New World

LEADING IDEAS:
The Providence of God preserved the mainland of North America until He had a people prepared to establish the fullest expression of a Christian civilization.

Christopher Columbus recognized that God had a distinct, unique purpose for His life.

Christopher Columbus provided the leadership needed to establish a colony. The lack of individual self-government was reflected in the difficulties of the colony.

DEVELOPING THE TEACHER'S NOTEBOOK:
Christian History of the American Revolution, p. XXV
Journals of Christopher Columbus, translated by Samuel Eliot Morison
Life of Christopher Columbus, by Washington Irving

BOOKS FOR CLASSROOM USE:
Columbus, by Ingri and Edgar Parin d'Aulaire, Doubleday & Company, Inc., Garden City, New York
Meet Christopher Columbus, by James T. de Kay, Step-Up Books, Random House Inc., New York
Christopher Columbus and the Discovery of the New World, by Josephine Pollard, reprinted by Pilgrim Institute, Granger, Indiana

THE SEVENTH LINK:
PILGRIM
Seed of Our Christian Republic

In the Pilgrim is the seed of our American Christian Republic. This seed included the complete plant of a nation. God had providentially prepared the Pilgrim with the Christian Character, Self-Government, Economics, Education, and Unity which were needed to produce a Christian nation.

DEVELOPING THE TEACHER'S NOTEBOOK:
See the expansion of the Seventh Link, p. 211

---

4. Rosalie J. Slater's Literature Syllabus, "Abigail Adams, First Lady of Faith and Courage."

Teaching and Learning, pp. 177-179; 189-198; 215-224
Christian History of the Constitution, pp. 151-247
Rudiments Handbook, pp. 71-76

THE EIGHTH LINK:
PATRIOT
First Christian Republic

In Noah Webster's *Federal Catechism*, he declares the advantages of a representative republic over other forms of government.

Q. Is there another and better form of government than any of these? (i.e. monarchy, aristocracy, and democracy)

A. There is. A *representative republic*, in which the people freely choose deputies to make laws for them, is much the best form of government hitherto invented.

Q. What are the peculiar advantages of representative government?

A. When deputies or representatives are chosen to make laws, they will commonly consult the interest of the people who choose them; and if they do not, the people can choose others in their room. Besides, the deputies coming from all parts of a state bring together all the knowledge and information necessary to show the true interest of the whole state; at the same time, being but few in number, they can hear arguments and debate peaceably on a subject. But the great security of such a government is that the men who make laws, are to be governed by them; so that they are not apt to do wrong willfully. When men make laws for themselves, as well as for their neighbors, they are led by their own interests to make *good* laws.

Q. Which of the forms or kinds of government is adopted by the American States?

A. The states are all governed by constitutions that fall under the name of representative republics. The people choose deputies to act for them in making laws; and in general, the deputies, when assembled, have as full power to make and repeal laws, as the whole body of freemen would have, if they were collected for the same purpose.

Q. By what name may we call the United States, in their political capacity?

A. A federal representative republic.

As Christianity moved westward with its fullest expression in civil government, history records the unique contributions of many individuals who deserve our attention. George Washington, father of our country and Samuel Adams, father of the Revolution, are only two of the many who should be restored to a place of veneration in the hearts of the American Christian.

The home training of George Washington by his father and mother produced the character to be commander-in-chief in the American Revolution, President of the Constitutional Convention, and First President of the American Christian Republic.

Samuel Adams, recognizing the importance of educating the individual in Biblical principles of government, directed the Committees of Correspondence in accomplishing this great task.

DEVELOPING THE TEACHER'S NOTEBOOK:
The Making of George Washington, William H. Wilbur, available through Patriotic Education, Inc., Alexandria, Virginia
The Life of George Washington, Washington Irving
Christian History of the American Revolution, see Index of Leading Ideas
Teaching and Learning, pp. 250-259; 262-268 and referenced pages in *Christian History of the Constitution*

BOOKS FOR CLASSROOM USE:
George Washington, by Ingri and Edgar Parin d'Aulaire, Doubleday & Company, Inc., Garden City, New York
Meet George Washington, by Joan Heilbroner, Step-Up Books, Random House Inc., New York
The Life of George Washington, by Josephine Pollard, reprint of 1893 edition by Mile-Hi Publishers, Denver, Colorado

THE NINTH LINK:
PIONEER
Westward Movement and Falling Away

As the Pioneer moved westward, he carried with him the Bible, Noah Webster's "blue-backed" Speller, and an internalization of Biblical principles of self- and civil government. A nation had been established on the basis of individual self-government and an understanding of American Political Union (American Federalism)—The question now is, "Can we keep it?"

At this writing, almost two hundred years have passed since the confirmation of the union of thirteen diverse colonies. During those years there has been continual testing of our character and capacity for self-government and our understanding of American Political Union (American Federalism).

DEVELOPING THE TEACHER'S NOTEBOOK:

A mastery of the seven principles of America's Christian History and Government will provide the basis for interpretation of this period in history.

Abraham Lincoln, The Man and His Faith, by G. Frederick Owen, Tyndale House Publishers, Inc., Wheaton, Illinois

The Memoirs of Herbert Hoover, The Macmillan Company, New York

BOOKS FOR CLASSROOM USE:

Abraham Lincoln, by Ingri and Edgar Parin d'Aulaire, Doubleday and Company, Inc., Garden City, New York

Meet Abraham Lincoln, by Barbara Cary, Step-Up Books, Random House, New York

Noah Webster, Father of the Dictionary, Isabel Proudfit, reprinted by Pilgrim Institute, Granger, Indiana

The Herbert Hoover Story, by Catherine Owens Peare, Thomas Y. Crowell Company, New York

EXPANDING THE SEVENTH LINK

THE PILGRIM SEED OF OUR CHRISTIAN REPUBLIC

Seed—that from which any thing springs; first principle, original . . .

In the parable of the sower (Luke 8:4-18), the seed was planted in diverse types of soils. The seeds which fell on good ground grew and brought forth fruit, "some an hundredfold, some sixtyfold, some thirtyfold." As the Word of God was planted in the hearts of the people of England, history records that some fell upon "good ground." From this seed came forth "a peculiar people" who, "without tarrying for any," claimed the truths of God's Word for all spheres of life. Transplanted to the shore of North America, the seed had the liberty to grow into its fullest expression—the American Christian Constitutional Republic.

Until recent years, historians have venerated the Pilgrim Fathers and their contribution as the seed which produced our Christian form of government. It is this recognition of Biblical principles of self- and civil government as proclaimed and practiced by the Pilgrims which must be restored to present and future generations. It is the responsibility of each generation to declare the works of God as manifested in America and "teach them diligently to thy children."

The following statements recognize the Pilgrim as the "Seed of Our Christian Republic":

"Our popular government lay in embryo on board the Mayflower, all-environed with its only possible preservatives, popular intelligence and popular virtue. The idea born there, and embodied in a civil constitution . . . grew with the growth of the colonies, gradually expelling from the thoughts and affections of the people all other theories of civil government, until finally it enthroned itself in the national mind, and then embodied itself in our national government."[5]

Historian Thomas Armitage describes this small band of Separatists and their journey: "The passage of the *Mayflower* over the Atlantic was long and rough. Often before its bosom had been torn by keels seeking the golden fleece for kings, but now the kings themselves were on board this frail craft, bringing the golden fleece with them, and the old deep had all that she could do to bear this load of royalty safely over. Stern as she was, the men borne on her waves were sterner. More than a new empire was intrusted to her care, a new freedom. 'What ailed thee, O sea?' When this historic ship came to her moorings, not unlike the vessel tossed on Galilee, she was freighted with principles, convictions, institutions and laws. These should first govern a quarter of the globe here, and then go back to the Old World to effect its regeneration and shape its future. The Pilgrims knew not that the King of all men was so signally with them in the bark, and would send them forth as the fishers of Gennesaret were sent, on an errand of revolution. In intellect, conscience, and true soul-greatness, these quiet founders of a new nation were highly gifted, so that song and story will send their names down to the end of time on

---

5. Wellman, *CHOC*, p. 147.

the bead-roll of fame. The monarchs of the earth have already raised their crowns in reverence to their greatness, and they are canonized in the moral forces which impelled and followed them.

"Imperial bombast in James I had chuckled over this band of strong-souled ones. He 'had peppered them soundly,' as he loved to boast, and 'harried them' out of his land in the bitterness of their grief; but when their sturdy feet pressed Plymouth Rock they had a conscience void of offense toward Holland, England and God. An invisible hand had guided the helm of the *Mayflower* to a rock from which, in a wintry storm, a group of simple-hearted heroes, with bare heads, could proclaim a Church without a bishop and a State without a king."[6]

Timothy Dwight, President of Yale College, declared "we boast of the religion of the Puritans, and assert, what no one can deny, that the Pilgrim Fathers shaped the model which has given the form to our free institutions and government, and acknowledge the town of Plymouth to have been the birthplace of our nation."[7]

By 1620 and the planting of Plymouth Colony, the Word of God had been carefully searched for principles of government. The following principles reveal the extent of Biblical reasoning concerning the Christian idea of man and government which had transpired in the hearts and lives of this Pilgrim congregation and constitute seven

---

6. Glen Jaspers and Ruth Smith, *Restoring America's Heritage of Pastoral Leadership* (Granger, Indiana, Pilgrim Institute, 1982), pp. 3-4.

7. Nathaniel Morton, *New England's Memorial*, sixth edition (Boston: Congregational Board of Publication, 1855), p. xvi.

great exchanges in modern history:

• The infallibility of church organization had been exchanged for the infallibility of the Bible.

• The sovereignty of king or pope had been exchanged for sovereignty of the individual governed by God.

• Sovereignty as being external had been exchanged for the recognition of the sovereignty of God within the individual.

• An adherence to a class structure was exchanged for the recognition of equality before God's law and the reflection of this equality in civil law.

• Limited freedom of the individual as a grant from government was exchanged for the recognition of certain God-given rights, i.e., life, liberty, and property.

• The flow of power changed direction from *top down* to the people choosing their own representatives.

• Compulsory uniformity was exchanged for the acknowledgement of diversity with unity.

• As the seed of Biblical principles of government was planted in the heart of the Pilgrim, it began to grow first in his life, then extended itself into his congregation and colony, and from there flourished into thirteen diverse colonies united as one nation *under God*.

PREPARATION OF TEACHER'S NOTEBOOK

The first step in the teacher's preparation is to read the Pilgrim story. The primary work for studying the Pilgrim history is William Bradford's *History of Plimoth Plantation*. This memorable work records the trials, sufferings, struggles and victories of the first permanent settlement in America. Miss Verna Hall has included fifty-five pages from Bradford's history in *The Christian History of the Constitution of the United States of America: Christian Self-Government*, pages 185-240. (The complete edition of *Bradford's History* is about 500 pages)

During the first reading, you should note the following particular highlights of the Pilgrim story:
1. Chronological events, with their cause and effect
2. Providence of God
3. Character of the Pilgrims
4. Biblical principles of government

You may find it helpful to highlight your copy of *Bradford's History*, make notations in the margin, or record leading ideas as you complete your first reading.

You will next research and record in *your*

notebook the essential elements of the Pilgrim story for teaching your students. The primary source for developing your Teacher's Notebook is Miss Rosalie Slater's work in *Teaching and Learning America's Christian History: The Principle Approach.* The following section will guide you to the *Christian History of the Constitution* and *Teaching and Learning* volumes, give suggestions for further research in first source documents, make suggestions for books which may be read to the students and books which are available for classroom use, give specific teaching suggestions for making the Pilgrim story a treasure for you and the students, and give selected samples of specific lesson plans prepared by teachers using this approach in their elementary classrooms.

As America's Christian History is restored in the American Christian home and classroom, you will be able to expand and deepen your teaching of the Pilgrims. The suggestions made in this *Guide* are not to limit the teacher but to give direction as you begin preparing your Teacher's Notebook.

FIRST YEAR
THE THANKSGIVING STORY

"Make a joyful noise unto the LORD, all ye lands, Serve the Lord with gladness: come before his presence with singing. Know ye that the LORD he is God: it is he that hath made us, and not we ourselves; we are his people, and the sheep of his pasture. Enter into his gates with thanksgiving, and into his courts with praise: be thankful unto him, and bless his name. For the Lord is good; his mercy is everlasting; and his truth endureth to all generations." *Psalm 100.*

God—creator, sovereign of the universe, infinite in His wisdom, sustainer of all His creation—providentially brought to this land a "peculiar people," who with thankful hearts recognized God's almighty hand in all the events of their lives. Setting apart particular times and days of thanksgiving to God was an essential element of the Pilgrim's life and living.

Thanksgiving—"A public celebration of divine goodness; also, a day set apart for religious services, specially to acknowledge the goodness of God, either in any remarkable deliverance from calamities or danger, or in the ordinary dispensation of his bounties. The practice of appointing an annual *thanksgiving* originated in New England."

A CHRONOLOGY OF EVENTS CONSIDERING THEIR CAUSE AND EFFECT

The following section is a guide for the Teacher's researching, reasoning, relating and recording the essential elements of *Bradford's History.* To appreciate and understand the truths of the Thanksgiving Story, the teacher and student must recognize God's Providence in bringing forth a *peculiar people* who *without tarrying for any* carried the seed of a Christian Republic to the New World. Here the individual was protected that he might have *a conscience void of offence toward God, and toward men.* The Thanksgiving Story cannot be appreciated without its historic context. The following references from *Christian History* (CHOC) and *Teaching and Learning* (T/L), with the questions, will help the teacher and student to identify God's Providence in preparing the Pilgrim's character for the events that brought Christian liberty and self-government to America.

THE PURITAN BECOMES A PILGRIM

Read CHOC, p. 185.
1. What internal change first took place? What caused this change?
2. How did this affect the Pilgrim's external actions?
3. What was the effect in the ecclesiastic and civil sphere?
4. As they saw "further into things by the light of ye word of God," what step did they next take?
5. How did this reflect their study of the New Testament? See CHOC, pp. 16-17, 20.
6. How does this reflect their Biblical understanding of voluntary consent?
7. What form of church government was re-established by the Pilgrim?
8. What is a Puritan? See *Webster's Dictionary* and CHOC, pp. 48-50, 182.
9. What is a Pilgrim? In what sphere was he a Separatist? See CHOC, p. 182.

DEPARTURE INTO HOLLAND

Read CHOC, pp. 189-191.
1. What particular hardships did they face in Holland?
2. How were they able to have victory over these?
3. What relationship did the Pilgrims have with the Dutch?

REMOVAL FROM HOLLAND

Read CHOC, pp. 191-194.

Note the five reasons Bradford gives for their removal. How is the hope and zeal for "propagating & advancing ye gospell of ye kingdom of Christ" reiterated in the Mayflower Compact and later documents of America's Christian History?

PREPARATION FOR DEPARTURE

Read CHOC, pp. 194-197.

A patent was obtained for Virginia and an agreement was reached with the merchant venturers. This agreement required all things be held in common for seven years and the merchants were to be repaid from this common stock. The agents concluded this agreement with the merchants, "in some things contrary to their order & comission, and without giving them notice of ye same; yea, it was conceled least it should make any furder delay; which was ye cause afterward of much trouble & contention."

THEIR DEPARTURE FROM HOLLAND

Read CHOC, pp. 198-201.

1. How does Pastor Robinson endeavor to prepare the Pilgrims for their voyage? See CHOC, p. 184.
2. How does Pastor Robinson's letter reflect the relationship of internal to external?
3. Relate the sequence of ideas in Pastor Robinson's letter to Neander's statement on Christian Character, found in *Teaching and Learning*, p. 123.
4. How does the order of Pastor Robinson's letter reflect his understanding of "the flow of power and force in society?"

"Being thus put to sea they had not gone farr, but Mr. Reinolds ye mr. of ye leser ship complained that he found his ship so leak as he durst not put further to sea till she was mended. So ye mr. of ye biger ship (caled Mr. Jonas) being consulted with, they both resolved to put into Dartmouth & have her ther searched & mended, which accordingly was done, to their great charg & losse of time and a faire winde. She was hear thorowly searcht from steme to sterne, some leaks were found & mended, and now it was conceived by the workmen & all, that she was sufficiente, & they might proceede without either fear or danger. So with good hopes from hence, they put to sea againe, conceiving they should goe comfortably on, not looking for any more lets of this kind; but it fell out otherwise, for after they were gone to sea againe above 100. leagues without the Lands

End, houlding company togeather all this while, the mr. of ye small ship complained his ship was so leake as he must beare up or sinke at sea, for they could scarce free her with much pumping. So they came to consultation againe, and resolved both ships to bear up backe againe & put into Plimoth, which accordingly was done. But no speciall leake could be founde, but it was judged to be ye generall weaknes of ye shipe, and that shee would not prove sufficiente for the voiage. Upon which it was resolved to dismise her & parte of ye companie, and proceede with ye other shipe. The which (though it was greevous, & caused great discouragmente) was put in execution. So after they had tooke out such provission as ye other ship could well stow, and concluded both what number and what persons to send bak, they made another sad parting, ye one ship going backe for London, and ye other was to proceede on her voiage. Those that went bak were for the most parte such as were willing so to doe, either out of some discontente, or feare they conceived of ye ill success of ye vioage, seeing so many croses befale, & the year time so farr spente; but others, in regarde of their owne weaknes, and charge of many yonge children, were thought least usefull, and most unfite to bear ye brunte of this hard adventure; unto which worke of God, and judgmente of their brethren, they were contented to submite. And thus, like Gedions armie, this small number was devided, as if ye Lord by this worke of his providence thought these few to many for ye great worke he had to doe. But here by the way let me show, how afterward it was found yt the leaknes of this ship was partly by being over masted, and too much pressed with sayles; for after she was sould & put into her old trime, she made many viages & performed her service very sufficiently, to ye great profite of her owners. But more espetially, by the cuning & deceite of ye mr. & his company, who were hired to stay a whole year in ye cuntrie, and now fancying dislike & fearing wante of victeles, they ploted this strategem to free them selves; as afterwards was knowne, & by some of them confessed ...".[8]

Read CHOC, pp. 201-203.

Although Bradford does not identify the names of these two ships, historians of the next generation identify the *Speedwell* and *Mayflower*.

---

8. Bradford's History "Of Plimoth Plantation," from the original manuscript 1901 edition (Boston: Wright & Potter Printing Co.), pp. 83-85.

"... SEPTR: 6. These troubls being blowne over, and now all being compacte togeather in one shipe, they put to sea againe with a prosperus winde, which continued diverce days togeather, which was some incouragemente unto them; yet according to ye usuall maner many were afflicted with sea-sicknes. And I may not omite hear a spetiall worke of Gods providence. Ther was a proud & very profane yonge man, one of ye sea-men, of a lustie, able body, which made him the more hauty; he would allway be contemning ye poore people in their sicknes, & cursing them dayly with greeous execrations, and did not let to tell them, that he hoped to help to cast halfe of them over board before they came to their jurneys end, and to make mery with what they had; and if he were by any gently reproved, he would curse and swear most bitterly. But it plased God before they came halfe seas over, to smite this yong man with a greeveous disease, of which he dyed in a desperate maner, and so was him selfe ye first yt was throwne overbord. Thus his curses light on his owne head; and it was an astonishmente to all his fellows, for they noted it to be ye just hand of God upon him."[9]

OF THEIR ARRIVAL IN CAPE COD

"Being thus passed ye vast ocean, and a sea of troubles before in their preparation (as may be remembred by yt which went before), they had now no freinds to wellcome them, nor inns to entertaine or refresh their weatherbeaten bodys, no houses or much less townes to repaire too, to seeke for succoure. It is recorded in scripture as a mercie to ye apostle & his shipwraked company, yt the barbarians shewed them no smale kindnes in refreshing them, but these savage barbarians, when they mette with them (as after will appeare) were readier to fill their sids full of arrows then otherwise. And for ye season it was winter, and they that know ye winters of yt cuntrie know them to be sharp & violent, & subjecte to cruell & feirce stormes, deangerous to travill to known places, much more to serch an unknown coast. Besids, what could they see but a hidious & deso-late wildernes, full of wild beasts & wild men? and what multituds ther might be of them they knew not. Neither could they, as it were, goe up to ye tope of Pisgah, to vew from this willdernes a more goodly cuntrie to feed their hops; for which way soever they turnd their eys (save upward to ye heavens) they could have litle solace or content in respecte of any outward objects ... What could

now sustaine them but ye spirite of God & his grace? May not & ought not the children of these fathers rightly say: Our faithers were Englishmen which came over this great ocean, and were ready to perish in this willdernes; but they cried unto ye Lord, and he heard their voyce, and looked on their adversitie, &c. Let them therfore praise ye Lord, because he is good, & his mercies endure for ever. Yea, let them which have been redeemed of ye Lord, shew how he hath delivered them from ye hand of ye oppressour. When they wan-dered in ye deserte willdernes out of ye way, and found no citie to dwell in, both hungrie, & thirstie, their sowle was overwhelmed in them. Let them confess before ye Lord his loving kindnes, and his wonderfull works before ye sons of men." (CHOC, pp. 202-203)

Read CHOC, pp. 203-205.
1. How does the Mayflower Compact reflect the Pilgrim's understanding of government by volun-tary consent? Can this be seen in the actual Com-pact as well as in its purpose for being written?
2. Why does Bradford state "that shuch an acte by them done ... might be as firme as any patent, and in some respects more sure"?
3. How does this brief Compact evidence their thorough understanding of the purpose of civil government?
4. What evidences the Pilgrim's understanding of the relationship between God's law and civil law?

CORN HILL

"After this, ye shalop being got ready, they set out againe for ye better discovery of this place, & ye mr. of ye ship desired to goe him selfe, so ther went some 30. men, but found it to be no harbor for ships but only for boats; ther was allso found 2. of their houses covered with matts, & sundrie of their implements in them, but ye people were rune away & could not be seen; also ther was found more of their corne, & of their beans of var-ious collours. The corne & beans they brought away, purposing to give them full satisfaction when they should meete with any of them (as about some 6. months afterward they did, to their good contente). And here is to be noted a spetiall providence of God, and a great mercie to this poore people, that hear they gott seed to plant them corne ye next year, or els they might have starved, for they had none, nor any liklyhood to get any (50) till ye season had beene past (as ye sequell did manyfest). Neither is it lickly they had had this, if ye first viage had not been made, for the ground was now all covered with snow, & hard

9. *Ibid*, pp. 90-91.

frozen. But the Lord is never wanting unto his in their greatest needs; let his holy name have all ye praise."[10]

THE FIRST ENCOUNTER

"The month of November being spente in these affairs & much foule weather falling in, the 6. of Desember: they sente out their shallop againe with 10. of their principall men, & some sea men, upon further discovery, intending to circulate that deepe baye of Cap-codd. The weather was very could, & it frose so hard as ye sprea of ye sea lighting on their coats, they were as if they had been glased; yet *that night* betimes they gott downe into ye botome of ye bay, and as they drue nere ye shore they saw some 10. or 12. Indeans very busie aboute some thing . . . When *morning* was come they devided their company, some to coaste along ye shore in ye boate, and the rest marched throw ye woods to see ye land, if any fit place might be for their dwelling. They came allso to ye place wher they saw the Indans ye night before, & found they had been cuting up a great fish like a grampus, being some 2. inches thike of fate like a hogg, some peeces wher of they had left by ye way; . . . So they ranged up and doune all yt day, but found no people, nor any place they liked. When ye sune grue low, they hasted out of ye woods to meete with their shallop, to whom they made signes to come to them into a *creeke* hardby, the which they did at highwater; . . . So they made them a barricado (as usually they did every night) with loggs, staks, & thike pine bowes, ye height of a man, leaving it open to leeward, partly to shelter them from ye could & wind (making their fire in ye midle, & lying round aboute it), and partly to defend them from any sudden assaults of ye savags, if they should surround them. So being very weary, they betooke them to rest. But aboute *midnight*, (51) they heard a hideous & great crie, and their sentinell caled, 'Arme, arme'; so they bestired them & stood to their armes & shote of a cupple of moskets, and then the noys seased. They concluded it was a companie of wolves, or such like willd beasts; for one of ye sea men tould them he had often heard shuch a noyse in New-found land. So they rested till about 5. of ye clock in the *morning*; for ye tide, & ther purpos to goe from thence, made them be stiring betimes. So after praier they prepared for breakfast, and it being day dawning, it was thought best to be carring things downe to ye boate. But some said it was not best to carrie ye armes downe, others said they would be the readier, for they had laped them up in their coats from ye dew. But some 3. or 4. would not cary theirs till they wente them selves, yet as it fell out, ye water being not high enough, they layed them downe on ye banke side, & came up to breakfast. But presently, all on ye sudain, they heard a great & strange crie, which they knew to be the same voyces they heard in ye night, though they varied their notes, & one of their company being abroad came runing in, & cried 'Men, Indeans, Indeans'; and withall, their arowes came flying amongst them. Their men rane with all speed to recover their armes, as by ye good providence of God they did. In ye mean time, of those that were ther ready, tow muskets were discharged at them & 2. more stood ready in ye enterance of ther randevoue, but were comanded not to shoote till they could take full aime at them; & ye other 2. charged againe with all speed, for ther were only 4. had armes ther, & defended ye baricado which was first assalted. The crie of ye Indeans was dreadfull, espetially when they saw ther men rune out of ye randevoue towourds ye shallop, to recover their armes, the Indeans wheeling aboute upon them. But some runing out with coats of malle on, & cutlasses in their hands, they soone got their armes, & let flye amongs them, and quickly stopped their violence. Yet ther was a lustie man, and no less valiante, stood behind a tree within halfe a musket shot, and let his arrows flie at them. He was seen shoot 3. arrowes, which were all avoyded. He stood 3. shot of a musket, till one taking full aime at him, and made ye barke or splinters of ye tree fly about his ears, after which he gave an extraordinary shrike, and away they wente all of them. They left some to keep ye shalop, and followed them aboute a quarter of a mille, and shouted once or twise, and shot of 2. or 3. peces, & so returned. This they did, that they might conceive that they were not (52) affrade of them or any way discouraged. Thus it pleased God to vanquish their enimies, and give them deliverance; and by his spetiall providence so to dispose that not any one of them were either hurte, or hitt, though their arrows came close by them, & on every side of them, and sundry of their coats, which hunge up in ye barricado, were shot throw & throw. Afterwards they gave God sollamne thanks & praise for their deliverance, & gathered up a bundle of their arrows, & sente them into England afterward by ye mr. of ye ship, and called that place ye first encounter."[11]

---

10. *Ibid*, pp. 100-101.

11. *Ibid*, pp. 101-104.

THE FIRST NEW ENGLAND SABBATH

"From hence they departed, & costed all along, but discerned no place likly for harbor; & therfore hasted to a place that their pillote, . . . did assure them was a good harbor, which he had been in, and they might fetch it before night; of which they were glad, for it begane to be foule weather. After some houres sailing, it begane to snow & raine, & about ye midle of ye afternoone, ye wind increased, & ye sea became very rough, and they broake their rudder, & it was as much as 2. men could doe to steere her with a cupple of oares. But their pillott had them be of good cheere, for he saw ye harbor; but ye storm increasing, & night drawing on, they bore what saile they could to gett in, while they could see. But herwith they broake their mast in 3. peeces, & their saill fell over bord, in a very grown sea, so as they had like to have been cast away; yet by Gods mercie they recovered them selves, & having ye floud with them, struck into ye harbore. But when it came too, ye pillott was deceived in ye place, and said, ye Lord be mercifull unto them, for his eys never saw yt place before; & he & the mr. mate would have rune her ashore, in a cove full of breakers, before ye winde. But a lusty seaman which steered, bad those which rowed, if they were men, about with her, or ells they were all cast away; the which they did with speed. So he bid them be of good cheere & row lustly, for ther was a faire sound before them, & he doubted not but they should find one place or other wher they might ride in saftie. And though it was *very darke*, and rained sore, yet in ye end they gott under ye lee of a smalle iland, and remained ther all yt night in saftie. But they knew not this to be an iland till morning, but were devided in their minds; some would keepe ye boate for fear they might be amongst ye Indians; others were so weake and could, they could not endure, but got a shore, & with much adoe got fire, (all things being so wett,) and ye rest were glad to come to them; for after midnight ye wind shifted to the (53) north-west, & it frose hard. But though this had been a day & night of much trouble & danger unto them, yet God gave them a *morning* of comforte & refreshing (as usually he doth to his children), for ye next day was a faire sunshinig day, and they found them sellvs to be on an iland secure from ye Indeans, wher they might drie their stufe, fixe their peeces, & rest them selves, and gave God thanks for his mercies, in their manifould deliverances. And this being the *last day of ye weeke* they prepared ther to keepe ye *Sabath*. On *Munday* they sounded ye harbor, and founde it fitt for shipping; and marched into ye land, & found diverse cornfeilds, & litle runing brooks, a place (as they supposed) fitt for situation; at least it was ye best they could find, and ye season, & their presente necessitie, made them glad to accepte of it. So they returned to their shipp againe with this news to ye rest of their people, which did much comforte their harts."[12]

ARRIVAL AT PLYMOUTH

"On ye 15. of Desemr: they wayed anchor to goe to ye place they had discovered, & came within 2. leagues of it, but were faine to bear up againe; but ye 16. day ye winde came faire, and they arrived safe in this harbor. And after wards tooke better view of ye place, and resolved wher to pitch their dwelling; and ye 25. day begane to erecte ye first house for comone use to receive them and their goods."[13]

THE FIRST DIFFICULT WINTER

Read CHOC, pp. 205-206.

In spite of the many difficulties of the first winter, when the Mayflower returned to England *not one Pilgrim went back.*

1. How had God providentially prepared Cape Cod for the Pilgrims?
2. What evidence of Christian character was demonstrated during the first winter of want, sickness, and death?

The Pilgrims' relations with the Indians reflects their recognition that each individual had independent value. The friendship with Samoset, Squanto, and Chief Massasoit demonstrated the unity with diversity which existed from the first settlement of Plymouth and became the basis for our dual form of government.

1621-1623

Read CHOC, pp. 207-208.

With the aid of Squanto, the settlers planted their crops, established trade with the Indians, and explored the neighborhood. They farmed, fished, and hunted, laying up stores for the winter of 1621.

When they gathered the fruit of their labors, the Pilgrims rejoiced in their small harvest. As was the character of the Pilgrims, they set apart a time of Thanksgiving. Chief Massasoit and his men were invited to join them. Edward Winslow records this first Thanksgiving feast in a letter of

---

12. *Ibid*, pp. 101-104.
13. *Ibid*, p. 107.

the 11th of December, 1621, to a friend.

"Referring you for further satisfaction to our more large Relations You shall understand, that in this little time, that a few of us have beene here, we have built seaven dwelling houses, and foure for the use of the Plantation, and have made preparation for divers others. We set the last Spring some twentie Acres of *Indian* Corne, and sowed some six Acres of Barly & Pease, and according to the manner of the *Indians*, we manured our ground with Herings or rather Shadds, which we have in great abundance, and rake with great care at our doores. Our Corne did prove well, & God be praysed, we had a good increase of *Indian* Corne, and our Barly indifferent good, but our Pease not worth the gathering, for we feared they were too late sowne, they came up very well, and blossomed, but the Sunne parched them in the blossome; our harvest being gotten in, our Governour sent foure men on fowling, that so we might after a more speciall manner rejoyce together, after we had gathered the fruit of our labours; they foure in one day killed as much fowle, as with a little helpe beside, served the Company almost a weeke, at which time amongst other Recreations, we exercised our Armes, many of the *Indians* coming amongst us, and amongst the rest their greatest King *Massasoyt*, with some nintie men, whom for three dayes we entertained and feasted and they went out and killed five Deere, which they brought to the Plantation and bestowed on our Governour, and upon the Captaine, and others. And although it be not always so plentifull, as it was at this time with us, yet by the goodnesse of God, we are so farre from want, that we often wish you partakers of our plentie."[14]

Read CHOC, pp. 208-212.
After the first small harvest, the Pilgrims began to feel the inadequacies of collective farming. What had appeared as a liberal harvest fast became less than adequate as new settlers arrived without adequate provisions. The Pilgrims' love and care for the new settlers was upheld by their faith in the Lord to supply. Their faith was often tested during those first years but proved steadfast in spite of the famine and want.

ESTABLISHED FREE ENTERPRISE

Read CHOC, pp. 213-214.
Two winters wherein food was rationed were adequate for the Governor and the wise men amongst them to recognize they must lay aside collective farming and establish individual farming.
1. What Biblical principles of economics had been reasoned by the Pilgrims?
2. How will a study of Bradford's history help us to recognize the error of socialism today?

GOD'S BLESSING ON THEIR LABORS

Read CHOC, pp. 214-215.
Bradford records the truth that man must be obedient to God's commands and then the Lord gives the increase. After they laid aside collective farming and began to practice individual enterprise, they saw hopes of the greatest harvest. Yet God controls the winds and weather. After they united for a day of prayer, God saw fit to give a speedy answer. The gentle rain revived the crop providing "a fruitfull and liberall harvest, to their no small comforte and rejoycing."

AMERICA'S HISTORIC THANKSGIVING DAY ESTABLISHED

Following God's *mercie* upon their efforts, "they also sett aparte a day of thanksgiveing." Acknowledging the Hand of God in our nation is part of our unique heritage of America's Christian History. The truths of God's story as it relates to His blessing upon America must be restored by the American Christian that the heritage of God-given liberty might continue to future generations.

14. Mourts *Relation*, pp. 60-61.

SEVEN PRINCIPLES
IDENTIFIED IN THE PILGRIM STORY

The following Biblical principles of government are identified in *Teaching and Learning America's Christian History* by Rosalie J. Slater and may be readily documented in Bradford's *History of Plimoth Plantation*. These principles and ideas governed the infant colony and became the foundation of our American Christian Republic. Specific suggestions are submitted to guide the teacher in teaching these principles to the child through the Pilgrim Story.

I. GOD'S PRINCIPLE OF INDIVIDUALITY
T/L: pp. 113-117; Key: pp. 141-183

As the Bible was placed in the hands of the individual, a "peculiar people" in the "North parts" of England "became inlightened by the word of God." As they began to identify who God is, their idea of man and government changed. They soon learned that each individual was unique before God and that God had a plan and purpose for each individual to further His Story.

God being the source of all power, His power flows into society through the individual. This gives each individual an independent value.

The Pilgrims' recognition of individual value was demonstrated in the treatment of the strangers on board the Mayflower, the treaty with the Indians, and their care and concern for one another.

II. THE CHRISTIAN PRINCIPLE OF SELF-GOVERNMENT
T/L: pp. 119-121; Key: pp. 184-209

Since each individual has an independent value, the individual must be governed by God and be obedient to Him. The Pilgrim first recognized the need for self-government in his personal life. (CHOC, p. 185)

The Pilgrim soon realized that the national church could not be reformed by legislation. He discerned the local self-government of the first century churches, "shook of this yoake of antichristian bondage, and as the Lords free people, joyned themselves ... into a church estate." (CHOC, p. 185)

The Pilgrim carried this principle of local self-government in his heart to New England where he extended it into the civil sphere. (CHOC, pp. 198-201; 204)

III. AMERICA'S HERITAGE OF CHRISTIAN CHARACTER
T/L: pp. 123-124; Key: pp. 210-224

As the divine power of the Gospel caused the Pilgrim to be governed by God, he began to reform his life. The Pilgrims gave us the foundation of Christian Character which is demanded by a Christian Republic.

IV. "CONSCIENCE IS THE MOST SACRED OF ALL PROPERTY"
T/L: pp. 125-127; Key: pp. 225-239

Recognizing that man is God's property, the Pilgrim was a good steward of all that God gave him, both internal and external. To have a "conscience void of offence before God," they laid aside a national church and established a church by voluntary association. (CHOC, p. 185) In the name of God, they established a civil government based upon voluntary consent. (CHOC, p. 204) Realizing the injustice of collectivism, they established an economic system which demanded the productivity of the individual. (CHOC, pp. 213-215)

V. THE CHRISTIAN FORM OF OUR GOVERNMENT
T/L: pp. 129-130; Key: pp. 240-249

The Pilgrim considered both the spirit (internal) and the letter (external) as they established a Christian form of government. This was the basis of our Constitution.

VI. HOW THE SEED OF LOCAL SELF-GOVERNMENT IS PLANTED
T/L: pp. 131-133; Key: pp. 250-261

The Pilgrim first established self-government in his own life. He then extended Biblical principles into his local church government and civil government.

VII. THE CHRISTIAN PRINCIPLE OF AMERICAN POLITICAL UNION
T/L: pp. 135-136; Key: pp. 262-268

As the primitive church demonstrated Christian unity (CHOC, pp. 16-17), the Pilgrim extended Christian unity into the civil sphere. Pastor John Robinson admonished the Pilgrims that their diversity should not produce "contrariety." (CHOC, pp. 198-201) The second of the great commandments—*love thy neighbor as thyself*—can only be accomplished as we individually practice the first commandment—*to love the Lord thy God with all thy heart, and with all thy soul, and with all thy mind.*

THANKSGIVING DAY OUR AMERICAN CHRISTIAN HERITAGE

The *Lincoln Library of Essential Information* identifies Thanksgiving Day as follows:

"In the United States, a day set apart annually and appointed by the president and by the governors of the various states for giving thanks to God for the favors and mercies of the year past. It is essentially a harvest festival and owes its origin to the Pilgrim Fathers. Despite the lean harvest of the summer of 1621, Governor Bradford decreed a day of thanksgiving and rejoicing after the scanty crop had been gathered in."[15]

On October 3, 1789 George Washington gave the following Thanksgiving Day Proclamation:

BY THE PRESIDENT OF THE UNITED STATES OF AMERICA.

Whereas it is the duty of all Nations to acknowledge the providence of Almighty God, to obey his will, to be grateful for his benefits, and humble to implore his protection and favor—and whereas both Houses of Congress have by their joint committee requested me to recommend to the People of the United States a day of public thanksgiving and prayer to be offered by acknowledging with grateful hearts the many signal favors of Almighty God especially by affording them an opportunity peaceably to establish a form of government for their safety and happiness.

Now, therefore, I do recommend and assign Thursday the 26th day of November next to be devoted by the People of these Nations to the service of that great and glorious Being, who is the beneficent Author of all the good that was, that is, or that will be—That we may then all unite in rendering unto him our sincere and humble thanks for his kind care and protection of the People of this country previous to their becoming a Nation—for the signal and manifold mercies, and the favorable interpositions of his providence, which we experienced in the course and conclusion of the late war—for the great degree of tranquillity, union, and plenty, which we have since enjoyed—for the peaceable and rational manner in which we have been enabled to establish constitutions of government for our safety and happiness, and particularly the national One now lately instituted—for the civil and religious liberty with which we are blessed, and the means we have of acquiring and diffusing useful knowledge and in general for all the great and various favors which he hath been pleased to confer upon us.

And also that we may then unite in most humbly offering our prayers and supplications to the great Lord and Ruler of Nations, and beseech him to pardon our national and other transgressions—to enable us all, whether in public or private stations, to perform our several and relative duties properly and punctually—to render our national government a blessing to all the People, by constantly being a government of wise, just, and constitutional laws discreetly and faithfully executed and obeyed—to protect and guide all Sovereigns and Nations (especially such as have shewn kindness unto us) and to bless them with good government, peace, and concord—To promote the knowledge and practice of true religion and virtue, and the increase of science among them and Us—and generally to grant unto all mankind such a degree of temporal prosperity as he alone knows to be best.

Given under my hand at the City of New York the third day of October in the year of our Lord 1789.

G. Washington

Days of Thanksgiving were called throughout the Colonial Period and by the end of the Revolutionary War most states declared an annual day of Thanksgiving. President Lincoln declared August 6, 1863 "as a day for national thanksgiving, praise and prayer."

"In December 1941, through a joint resolution adopted by the United States Senate and House of Representatives and signed by President Roosevelt, the fourth Thursday of November was officially designated as the date for Thanksgiving Day."[16]

HONOR AND PRESERVE AMERICA'S THANKSGIVING DAY

Acknowledging the Hand of God in American History

---

15. *Lincoln Library of Essential Information* (Buffalo: The Frontier Press Co., 1953), p. 2074.

16. *Ibid.*

"Thanksgiving is the only truly American holiday. It is significant that its Christian basis has particular reference to our nation's founding. It has been customary to commemorate this holiday with school programs reminding us of the circumstances surrounding our first Christian settlement.

"Thanksgiving Day Programs should be a part of every American Christian home, every American Christian church, and every American Christian school for the Christian History of America begins with the story of this small remnant of primitive Christians—the Pilgrims—and of their efforts to carry out *Christ His Story* in their lives as they labored for His glory in this new land."[17]

For suggestions in developing a Thanksgiving Day Program for your home, church, or school, see *Teaching and Learning*, pages 271-273.

TEACHING SUGGESTIONS FOR THE ELEMENTARY SCHOOL

Each teacher must determine the particular classroom technique which best allows for developing the leading ideas and principles which he desires to emphasize. It is essential that each unit of study (i.e., each link on the Chain of Christianity) embrace the methodology of researching, reasoning, relating, and recording on the part of the teacher and student. Miss Rosalie Slater of the Foundation for American Christian Education developed the following suggestions for teaching the Pilgrim Story in the Elementary School. These suggestions are included, with permission, to provide ideas which will give variety and interest to the classroom.

I. TEACHER PREPARATION: Learning the Pilgrim Story

A. KNOW BRADFORD'S HISTORY OF THE PILGRIMS

1. Bradford is the primary sourcebook of the Pilgrims.
2. Bradford documents the Gospel purpose of the Pilgrims.
3. Bradford illustrates the Biblical principles—the Hand of God in American History.

B. KNOW THE CHRISTIAN HISTORY PRINCIPLES
1. Begin your own *Teacher Notebook* on the Pilgrim Story.
2. Use the 4 R's to organize your study.
1st R = *Research*—Find each principle in the Bible.
2nd R = *Reason* from the principles into the Pilgrim Story.
3rd R = *Relate* the principles to your own life.
4th R = *Record* the fruitage of your study.
3. Select what you will teach of the Pilgrim Story

II. TEACHER PRESENTATION: Teaching the Pilgrim Story

A. INTRODUCING STUDENTS TO PILGRIM STORY
1. Have students begin individual *Student Notebooks* or Pilgrim Story books.
2. Present first principles, write statements of principles.
3. Introduce individual Pilgrims.
4. Present *Leading Ideas* of Pilgrim Story.
5. Present an *Overview* of what they will study.

B. BEGIN STUDY OF THE PILGRIMS: Research
1. Teacher tells, reads to class.
2. Students read as a class.
3. Students do individual reading.

C. ORGANIZING INFORMATION: Relating
1. Identify Principles in Pilgrim Story.
2. Relate Leading Ideas studied.
3. Recall facts which support principles/leading ideas.

D. MAKING THE PILGRIM STORY YOUR OWN PROPERTY: Recording
1. Write the Pilgrim Story from dictation by teacher.
2. Highlight God's Hand in the story.
3. Describe individuals whom God used.
4. Summarize the facts which are important.
5. Why is the Pilgrim Story important to us?

III. STUDENT ACTIVITIES: Expanding our knowledge of the Pilgrims

A. MAPWORK:
1. Class map, i.e., Smith's map of New England 1614; or map of Europe and America tracing Pilgrim travels; or tracing CHAIN OF CHRISTIANITY from Asia
2. Individual maps for notebooks

B. ART AND CONSTRUCTION
1. Model of the Pilgrim ship Mayflower (made

---

17. *T/L*, p. 271.

outside of class time)
2. Model of Plymouth Plantation or Pilgrim homes
3. Drawings of important historic events

C. DRAMATIZATION AND MEMORIZATION
1. Memorize Pilgrim poems or passages from Bradford.
2. Dramatize some aspects of Pilgrim Story.
3. Present individual Pilgrims in costume with their story.

D. COMPOSITION
1. Write a diary: choose individual Pilgrim character.
2. Write a Pilgrim play as a class.
3. Write an individual Pilgrim story illustrating principles, leading ideas, and supported by facts.

ANNOTATED BIBLIOGRAPHY FOR THE ELEMENTARY CLASSROOM

CHILDREN'S BOOKS:

The Plymouth Thanksgiving written and illustrated by Leonard Weisgard, Doubleday and Company, Inc., 1967. Mr. Weisgard's research of Bradford's writings makes this book a pleasure to read to the younger student. He recognized God's hand in the Pilgrim Story and provided a fine narrative of the events through the harvest of 1621.

Squanto, written by Carolyn Hobbs and illustrated by Pat Roland, Gospel Projects, Inc., 1981. "Aunt Carolyn" recounts God's Providence in Squanto's captivity in England where he learned to speak English, and his return to America where he became the special friend of the Pilgrims. This picture story book provides an opportunity to demonstrate to the young child the Providence of God in America's Christian History. *Squanto* may be ordered from *Children's Bible Club*, P.O. Box 643, Milton, Florida, 32570.

Meet the Pilgrim Fathers, by Elizabeth Payne, Step-Up Books, Random House, 1966. The primary reader will have the opportunity to read for himself the difficulties found by the Separatists in England and Holland, and the many hardships which faced this small band as they voyaged to the New World and established Plymouth colony. Elizabeth Payne has been thorough in her work for children, while maintaining the simplicity of style which will be enjoyed by the early reader.

Margaret Pumphrey's *Pilgrim Stories*, revised and expanded by Elvajean Hall, Houghton Mifflin Company, 1968. Beginning with the Pilgrim congregation in Scrooby and ending with the second winter in Plymouth and the arrival of the Fortune, Elvajean Hall has provided an excellent book to be read by the elementary student. The student will read with anticipation the many trials and tribulations which this small congregation faced and the faith which carried them through. *Pilgrim Stories* is currently out of print, but may be found in the library or a used book store.

DEVELOPING A LESSON PLAN

After researching and recording his mastery of the nine links, the teacher must develop specific lesson plans. Each lesson plan should include the goal(s), principles and ideas with supporting facts, methodology, and assignments. (See *Approach*, p. 205)

Following are two examples of lesson plans for teaching the Seventh Link, *The Pilgrim*. The first example is for Kindergarten and the second example is for a multi-grade classroom of first through fifth. These two examples demonstrate the diversity which results from the teacher's individual expression and mastery of the Pilgrim Story.

FIRST EXAMPLE

The following general lesson plan was prepared by Jeanette Smith for the Kindergarten class of the Pilgrim Christian Academy. The Kindergarten history class met each day for fifteen minutes. It would take approximately four weeks to cover this link on the Chain of Christianity.

1. Goals:
   • To show God's Hand in the forming of our nation
   • To give evidence of individual contributions

to the Plymouth Colony
- To reveal the relationship of the Bible and the establishment of our nation

2. Content:

Relate the Pilgrim Story with emphasis on the following main points:
- The Pilgrims dearly loved the Word of God and desired to have their own church.
- They did not have liberty of conscience in England and sought a country in which they could have liberty.
- The Pilgrims lived for a time in Holland and then came to live in America.
- The Pilgrims wrote the Mayflower Compact, establishing self-government in their colony.
- The difficulties of building the colony in the New World were great, but God provided help for them.
- After they had survived a drought, they had a special day of Thanksgiving for all God had done for them.

3. Three of the seven governmental principles to be illustrated in the Pilgrim Story are as follows:
- God's Principle of Individuality
- Christian Principle of Self-Government
- Conscience is the Most Sacred of all Property

4. Methodology:

Teach the lessons requiring the students to reason and relate through answering questions orally.

The following exercises would be done during the class:
- Locate on the map or globe, England, Holland, North America, and Cape Cod.
- Outline maps of England and Cape Cod.
- Color a picture of the dress which identifies the Dutch people.
- Color a picture of the North American Indian.
- Color a picture of the Pilgrim.

The students may write one sentence which describes the specific event of the Pilgrim Story identified in the picture.

SECOND EXAMPLE

Lynn Meier prepared the following lessons for the elementary classroom, Grades 1-5, at the Pilgrim Christian Academy. The class met for twenty minutes each day.

The reader will find a record of the notes taken by the students, written assignments, and tests. With students in multiple grades, the teacher must account for the diverse ability in reasoning, relating, and recording both in the quantity and depth of written work expected. The following example demonstrates how a teacher can handle this diversity of ability without the necessity of teaching each grade separately.

Specific detail is given for each of seven days to aid in discerning what can be accomplished during one class time.

FAITH AND STEADFASTNESS

Goal: To develop faith and steadfastness (which are elements of Christian character) in the student's life, he must first understand what faith and steadfastness are, and then be given models to follow, in this case the Pilgrims.

Background: Before beginning this study of faith and steadfastness, the students should already understand the relationship of internal to external. Christian character begins in the heart and is then revealed in the actions.

DAY 1 - Give the definition of faith and reason with the students concerning its meaning.
- Notes: definition of faith from 1828 *Dictionary*. (See p. 224 under "Recording Student Notes")
- Read the Biblical definition of faith in Hebrews 11:1.

DAY 2 - Give the definition of steadfastness and relate to the individual's life or the external effect of internal faith.
- Notes: definition of steadfastness, relation of faith and steadfastness—internal to external. (See p. 224)
- Read I Corinthians 15:58 and relate to the definition of steadfastness.
- Assignment #1: (See p. 224)

DAY 3 - Review definitions and Biblical examples of faith and steadfastness.
- *Tell* the story of the Pilgrims' persecution in England and their decision to leave their homeland. Reason with the students as to the identification of faith and steadfastness in this story.
- Notes: Trials/Faith and Steadfastness in leaving England. (See p. 224)

DAY 4 - Relate the difficulties which the Pilgrims faced in Holland.
- Notes: Trials/Faith and Steadfastness in Holland. (See p. 224)

DAY 5 - Review the Pilgrim's reasons for leaving England.

- Relate the Pilgrims' reasons for leaving Holland.
- Relate the difficulties of the voyage to the New World.
- Notes: Trials/Faith and Steadfastness in going to the New World.
- Assignment #2:

DAY 6 - Tell the story of the first winter in New England and the difficulties that were faced and overcome by the Pilgrims.
- Reason with the students concerning the character qualities of faith and steadfastness in their individual lives and relate to the nation.
- Notes: Trials/Faith and Steadfastness in the New World.
- Review for test.

DAY 7 - Test

RECORDING STUDENT NOTES

First and Second Grades copy only the portions of the notes that are italicized. Third through Fifth Grades copy all notes.

FAITH
Faith is belief in the truth which God has given us. Hebrews 11:1.
"Now faith is the substance of things hoped for, the evidence of things not seen."

STEADFASTNESS
Steadfastness is firmness of mind. I Corinthians 15:58.
"Therefore, my beloved brethren, be ye steadfast, unmoveable, always abounding in the work of the Lord, forasmuch as ye know that your labour is not in vain in the Lord."
Faith in the heart will be shown by steadfastness.

TRIALS
When they left England, *the Pilgrims had to leave their country, land, jobs, homes, friends, and families.*

In Holland they had:
1. *A new language* to learn.
2. *New customs* to learn.
3. *Poverty* instead of plenty.

FAITH AND STEADFASTNESS
"These things did not dismay them ... for *their desires were set on the ways of God.*"
—William Bradford

By God's help they got the victory.

In Holland, their life was very hard.
In going to the New World, there were great dangers and many difficulties.
During the first winter in New England, one half of the people died.
They took their difficulties very cheerfully and with courage.
They knew they could overcome difficulties by God's help, if they were patient and trusted in Him.
Even though the Captain of the Mayflower offered to take them back at no cost, *none of the Pilgrims returned to England.*

ASSIGNMENTS

Assignment #1

Students answer only the questions indicated by an (x) for their grade.

1	2	3	4	5	
x	x	x	x	x	1. What is faith?
x	x	x	x	x	2. What is steadfastness?
x	x	x	x	x	3. How will faith be shown?
		x	x	x	4. What Bible verse teaches what faith is?
		x	x	x	5. Where does the Bible teach a person to be steadfast?

Assignment #2

Students answer all questions, but older students should give more complete, thorough answers.
1. Describe some of the difficulties the Pilgrims faced in Holland.
2. How did their faith help them face and overcome these difficulties?
3. Describe the difficulties the Pilgrims had in traveling to the New World.
4. How did their faith help them in these difficulties?

TEST

Students answer only the questions indicated by an (x) for their grade.

1	2	3	4	5	
x	x	x	x	x	1. What is Christian character?
	x	x	x	x	2. Where does Christian character begin?
	x	x	x	x	3. Where will Christian character be shown?
x	x	x	x	x	4. What is faith?
x	x	x	x	x	5. What is steadfastness?
			x	x	6. How are faith and steadfastness shown?

x x x x x 7. Describe the difficulties the Pilgrims had in England and how their faith and steadfastness were shown.

x x 8. Describe the difficulties the Pilgrims had in Holland and how their faith and steadfastness were shown.

x x x x 9. Describe the difficulties the Pilgrims had on the Mayflower and how their faith and steadfastness were shown.

x x x x x 10. Describe the difficulties the Pilgrims had during the first winter in New England and how their faith and steadfastness were shown.

BIBLIOGRAPHY

The following volumes are resources for expanding the teacher's mastery of the Pilgrim Story:

Bradford, William, *History of Plimoth Plantation*, edited by Samuel Morison.

Bradford, Winslow, *Mourt's Relation: A Journal of the Pilgrims of Plymouth*, edited by Jordan D. Fiore. Reprinted by Plymouth Rock Foundation, Plymouth, Mass., 1985.

Bradford, John, *The Pilgrim Fathers of New England and Their Puritan Successors*, 1898.

Fleming, Thomas, *One Small Candle—The Pilgrim's First Year in America*, W. W. Norton & Company.

Fountain, David, *The Mayflower Pilgrims and Their Pastor*, distributed by Reiner Publications.

Mather, Cotton, *Lives of Bradford and Winthrop*, Old South Leaflet #77.

RUTH J. SMITH

HOME NURTURE AND EXAMPLE

As a young girl growing up on an Iowa farm, I had no idea that God was preparing me to help educate Americans about their nation's Christian history. Dedicated Christian parents instilled a respect and love for God through daily Bible reading, prayer, and Biblical standards of conduct. Then the evangelical pastor of our local church made the gospel so individual and convicting that I accepted Christ as my personal Lord and Savior.

Those years on a Midwest farm, which at first lacked the conveniences of running water and electricity, taught me the value of hard work and of a family working together and governing itself to achieve a common objective. I discovered the pleasure of planting a garden or field, and learned what it meant to patiently pursue all of the steps that are needed to assure that crops will grow and that the harvest would bring forth sufficient plenty to feed a large family.

From my mother I learned the skills that a young lady needs to become an effective homemaker, but which many girls are no longer taught, such as sewing, baking, canning, meal preparation and cleaning—which together with Christian char-acter are vital to running a self-sufficient, self-governing home. More important still, when my father went to be with the Lord, Mother demonstrated the tenacity of Christian womanhood in keeping her family together, and provided an example of steadfastness and diligence that her children have never forgotten.

After high school in Iowa and college in Tennessee, the Lord sent me a young man named Allen Smith who became my husband, and gave stability, faithfulness and quiet direction to our lives as we established a home and assumed the responsibility of being parents to three daughters.

GOD REVEALS AMERICA'S CHRISTIAN HISTORY

Although formal education had prepared me for a position in the business world, God had something more significant in store. In the late 60's and early 70's, my husband and I were on the staff of South Sheridan Baptist Church in Denver, Colorado, where I taught part time at the church-sponsored Silver State Baptist School. Each Sunday evening the church offered a training program for adults, where we were first introduced to the Biblical principles of government, and the idea that America has a Christian history. The texts included *The Christian History of the Constitution of the United States of America* by Verna M. Hall, and *Teaching and Learning America's Christian History* by Rosalie J. Slater. These books were so rewarding and important to me that I studied them eagerly.

In 1973 we moved back to Iowa, where my brother, Glen Jaspers, served as a pastor. I worked with him to establish Central Iowa Christian Academy, teaching America's Christian history at every level from elementary through high school. Miss Hall and Miss Slater, of the Foundation for American Christian Education, patiently guided and tutored me during those years of mastering the history and literature of my curriculum.

The more I studied and taught, the more opportunities God providentially provided to share with others, not only in the classroom, but in seminars. I became convinced of the great ignorance of our land concerning God's Hand in all that He had produced in this country, and of each American Christian's responsibility to contribute to the restoration of our nation through the Christian home, church and school.

"ONE SMALL CANDLE"

In particular, my husband and I became con-vinced that something more was needed than the 40-minute lectures I had been giving at seminars conducted by others; and in 1979 Dr. Jaspers and we united to found the Pilgrim Institute, to restore American Christian Education and preserve America's Providential history—to provide serious, in-depth educational opportunities for a generation suffering the consequence of a people who had forgotten God and His mighty works.

Since that time, God has continued to open doors, and the Pilgrim Institute ministry now includes teacher training institutes, educational seminars, a correspondence program, consultation service, an elementary and secondary demonstration school, and a four-year collegiate program.

God's work of refining is not yet accomplished, of course; but we share this testimony in the hope that it will be an encouragement to others to remember and restore the victorious faith of America's first century Pilgrims who were persuaded that, as William Bradford declared, "out of small beginnings greater things have been produced by his hand that made all things of nothing, and gives being to all things that are; and as one small candle may light a thousand, so the light here kindled has shown to many, yea in some sort to our whole nation; let the glorious name of Jehovah have all the praise." (*History of Plimoth Plantation*, Commonwealth Edition, 1898, p. 332)

ARITHMETIC
FROM THE PRINCIPLE APPROACH

BY JAMES V. KILKENNY

Principal
Christian Heritage School
Tyler, Texas

CONTENTS

TEACHING ARITHMETIC FROM THE PRINCIPLE APPROACH

INTRODUCTION

Arithmetic, what is it? Every high school student has studied the subject for nine or ten years and many are skilled in its operations. But are the relationships between the various operations understood? The science or art of arithmetic is often perceived as an endless jumble of facts, and its operations are often taught and performed mechanically and by rote. The result is a lack of definition and therefore a lack of the ability to reason from the first principles of the subject and to apply these principles to the problems of everyday living.

This condition can be corrected by teaching arithmetic from the Principle Approach; that is by teaching from the whole of a subject to its parts, by defining the subject, its vocabulary and its first principles, and by teaching the students to reason from these principles in all of their work. This method will produce arithmetic students who have confidence, creativity and skill with numbers. There is a great distinction between learning by rote and learning by reason. A student who is taught to reason from definitions of terms, principles and rules will develop a mastery of his subject and will not be limited to solving only those problems for which he has memorized the formulae.

Three other essential aspects of the Principle Approach are:

1. To teach the Biblical source and origin, end, and purpose of the subject;

2. To teach how God has Providentially given understanding of the subject and used it in the history of liberty (the Chain of Christianity);

3. To teach the relationship between the subject and the seven principles of government.

The student who gains the understanding of these four aspects will master arithmetic and be inspired to use his mastery "for the glory of God and advancement of the Christian faith."[1]

The organization of an arithmetic course should follow the essential form of arithmetic itself. This form, in its beautiful simplicity, has been fully diagrammed on Mr. Darold Booton's *Counting Chart*, the primary source from which these notes have been reasoned.[2] (see p. 232) The Counting Chart illustrates that arithmetic proceeds from the Trini-

---

1. Mayflower Compact.

2. From *Algebra I: A Principle Approach*, by Darold Booton, Jr., Christian Heritage Academy, 1136 Southwest 48th Street, Oklahoma City, Oklahoma 73109, private distribution, 1983-84 school year, page 5. See p. 425 of this *Guide* for Mr. Booton's curriculum overview on "Teaching Algebra from the Principle Approach."

tarian nature of God because Trinity implies counting — one, two, three — and all of the operations of arithmetic are forms of counting (either forward or backward). This fact is the unifying principle of arithmetic. Within it is the answer to the first question of this introduction: "Arithmetic, what is it?" The word "arithmetic" comes from the Greek word *arithmeo,* to number, and arithmetic is simply numbering or counting.

DEFINITION OF ARITHMETIC

Arithmetic is, "The science of numbers, or the art of computation. The various operations of arithmetic are performed by addition, subtraction, multiplication and division." (Webster's, 1828) A concise form of this definition that even the youngest student will understand is this:

ALL ARITHMETIC IS COUNTING

Mr. Booton's counting chart,[3] shown below, and the following numberlines, add to this concise definition the following three concepts:
1. Arithmetic (i.e., counting) is derived from the nature and character of God.
2. Counting forward includes addition and multiplication.
3. Counting backward includes subtraction and division.

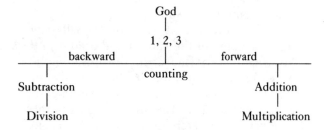

It is logically apparent that counting may be forward or backward, yet it is this simple fact that is the basis of the definitions of the four operations of arithmetic:

Counting
- forward
  1. Addition is counting forward on the number line.
  2. Multiplication is a short method of counting many additions of the same number.
- backward
  3. Subtraction is counting backward on the number line.
  4. Division is a short method of counting many subtractions of the same number.

Following is an example of each operation performed by counting. Note the great importance of

---

3. *Ibid.*

identifying the starting point and the direction of counting.

Addition: to solve 3 + 5, start at 3 on the number line and count forward 5 units ending on the answer, 8.

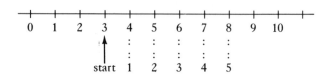

Subtraction: to solve 8 − 5, start at 8 on the number line and count backward 5 units ending on the answer, 3.

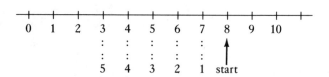

Multiplication: to solve 3 x 2, start at 0 on the number line and count forward 2 units three times ending on the answer, 6.

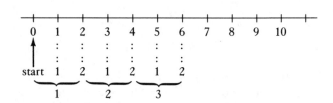

Another form of this example is:
$$3 \times 2 = 2 + 2 + 2 = 6$$

Division: to solve 6 ÷ 3, start at 6 on the number line and count backward 3 units as often as possible. The number of 3-unit segments is the answer, 2.

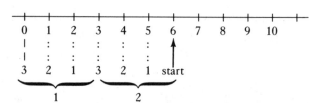

Another form of this example is:

```
        2
    3 | 6
      −3  (first subtraction)
        3
      −3  (second subtraction)
        0
```

Great confidence is instilled by this simple understanding of the whole of the subject, its beginning, middle, and end. Children should be reminded daily of the unity of this subject – all arithmetic is one process: COUNTING; even as they systematically consider the diverse techniques of counting and their seemingly infinite applications. Actually, the science or art of arithmetic provides great insight into the infinite. For example, a line may theoretically be divided in half infinitely many times; parallel lines may be extended infinitely in either direction and never cross; and, of course, the concept of counting on and on into infinity is fascinating.

THE LANGUAGE OF ARITHMETIC: DEFINITIONS

Mastery of the language of arithmetic is essential to true understanding of the subject. Many drill-sheet masters of addition, subtraction, multiplication, and division stand speechless when asked to explain either the nature of these operations or their own methods. This limitation reduces their knowledge of the subject to the significance of a parlor trick, which, although a fascinating skill, does little to form a Christian world view or even to produce facility of practical application.

This fact was amusingly illustrated by the reaction of an eighth grader, who had learned the definition of arithmetic during his first month in Christian Heritage School. With a self-satisfied grin, he told of a former classmate from another school who could not answer the question, "What is arithmetic?" nor could he explain the operations, or even define "unit" or "number." As he reported this story, the pleasure and confidence that came with his new found knowledge of the language of arithmetic was shining in his eyes.

Arithmetic has its own language and the first step to learning that language is to learn its vocabulary, beginning with the words of the definition: "Arithmetic is the *science* of *numbers*, or the *art* of *computation*. The various *operations* of arithmetic are performed by *addition, subtraction, multiplication* and *division*." (Webster's 1828)

SCIENCE: "... knowledge ... a collection of the general principles or leading truths relating to any subject ..."
NUMBER: "The designation of a unit in reference to other units ..."
UNIT: "... a single thing or person; ..."
ART: "skill"
COMPUTATION: "... numbering, ... the process by which different sums or particulars are numbered, ..." [The operations of arithmetic are methods of computation.]
COUNT: The etymology is the same as that of compute, from the Latin *computo*, "to think, count, reckon; to cast up. The sense is probably to cast or throw together." The definition is, "to number; to tell or name one by one, or by small numbers, for ascertaining the whole number of units in a collection; as, to *count* the years, days, and hours of a man's life; to count the stars."
OPERATION: "process"

(For definitions of addition, subtraction, multiplication, and division, see page 232)

● This simple research of the definition of arithmetic was all done in Webster's 1828 Dictionary. Further research in the same source will reveal a much greater detail and depth of the subject, but the student who has done even this much research will gain the confidence of knowing the boundaries of his study: that it comprises both a science and an art; that in all of its aspects it deals with numbering or counting; and that a number is a designation of one or more units.

Research into vocabulary is the first step to the study of each part of arithmetic. For example, the following vocabulary is necessary to the understanding of Arabic notation and numeration:

NOTATION: "... the expressing of numbers and quantities by figures, signs or characters ..."
NUMERATION: "... notation; the art of expressing in characters any number proposed in words or of expressing in words any number proposed in characters; the act or art of writing or reading numbers."
FIGURE: "In *arithmetic*, a character denoting a number; as 2, 7, 9."
DIGIT: "In *arithmetic*, any integer under 10; so called from counting on the fingers. Thus, 1, 2, 3, 4, 5, 6, 7, 8, 9, are digits."

(The terms figure and digit are synonymous.)
VALUE: "The *value* of a figure (or number) is the number of units it expresses."[4]
ORDER: "The order of a figure is the place it occupies in a number."[5] (The first six *orders* are: units, tens, hundreds, thousands, ten thousands, hundred thousands.)

---

4. This definition is taken from *Ray's New Practical Arithmetic*, facsimile edition, published by Mott Media, Milford, Michigan, 1985, p. 15. Many of Ray's definitions are more pertinent to arithmetic than Webster's.

5. *Ibid.*, page 10.

PERIOD: "... different orders are grouped into *periods* of three orders each. The first twelve periods are: unit, thousand, million, billion, trillion, quadrillion, quintillion, sextillion, septillion, octillion, nonillion, decillion."[6]

A student who has learned this vocabulary is prepared to understand such instructions as: "In the Arabic System of notation, 'Ten units of any order make a unit of the next higher order;'" "The value of a figure depends upon the place (order) it occupies."; "The different orders are grouped into periods of three orders each."; "Each period is composed of units, tens, hundreds of that period."

He should be able to follow these directions for reading numbers in the Arabic system:

1. Begin at the right, and point off the number

6. *Ibid.*, page 15.

into periods of three figures each.

2. Begin at the left, and read each period as a number composed of hundreds, tens, and units, giving the name of the period.

As the student learns to read and write numbers in the Arabic system of notation, he should also be learning to explain his method, that is, to be fluent in the language of the subject.

This fluency should be carried on into the teaching of the operations so that, for example, the student could intelligently discuss division in terms of the divisor, dividend, and quotient; and he could understand that to divide a fraction he must, "multiply the dividend by the divisor with its terms inverted."

Just as fluency in a foreign language comes slowly and with daily practice, a fluency in arithmetic can be developed, and this fluency is essential to a mastery of the subject.

BIBLICAL SOURCE AND ORIGIN OF ARITHMETIC

"God created the heaven and the earth," (Genesis 1:1) but He did not create the principles of arithmetic. This startling observation was made by Mr. Darold Booton, when he was Master Teacher at Christian Heritage Academy in Oklahoma City.* As he explained, the principles of arithmetic are not created because they are inherent in the nature and character of God. Of course God is not a created being. He has always existed, and before creation He was able to count His thoughts, time, the Three Persons of the Divine Trinity, etc. Since God has always been able to count, the principles of arithmetic have always existed. Mr. Booton's reasoning is quoted below:

1. The idea of 'one' has always existed as an attribute of God's nature.
2. Since God is a Trinity, the idea of 'three' has always existed.
3. The idea of 'two' has always existed because there was a Second Person of the Trinity (Jesus Christ)."

These three facts suggest the idea of counting—

*Mr. Booton is presently instructor of Mathematics at Pilgrim Institute Collegiate Program, Granger, Indiana.

counting forward and backward."[7]

This reasoning shows clearly the derivation of arithmetic in its fullest definition from both the Unity of God and His Trinitarian nature. It remains to search the Scripture to see if God is revealed there as the Three in One. Since the Scriptural evidence has been thoroughly considered by Mr. Gordon C. Olson, his work is quoted here. (For full discussion and documentation see *The Truth Shall Make You Free*)

THE TRUTH ABOUT THE NATURE
AND CHARACTER OF GOD

"A. The Godhead are revealed in the Bible as a Trinity of Personal Spiritual Beings, living in an endless duration of time, who have the ability of intellectual activity, who experience emotional reactions, and who possess moral freedom, or the power of self-determination or free will.

"1. A Trinity of Personalities of equal endowments and attributes, who are in absolute oneness of purpose and activity, designated Father, Son, and Holy Spirit: Ep.

7. *Algebra I: A Principle Approach, op. cit.*, page 5.

4:4-6; Lk. 3:21-22; Mt. 28:19.

"2. Yet A Divine Unity of Personalities – A compound oneness.

    a. The Old Testament emphasizes the unity of God: Ex. 20:3; De. 4:35, 39; 6:4; Is. 44:6. The word "one" (De. 6:4, quoted by the Lord Jesus, Mk. 12:29) in the Hebrew means "united," indicating a compound unity or a unity of parts rather than a simple unity.

    (b. and c. omitted)

"By making these comparisons (citations omitted), our Lord conveyed the idea that the oneness that exists among the Members of the Godhead is a moral or voluntary oneness of character and relationship, a united continuous choice to live in the realm of perfect love or true benevolence in all moral relations and responsibilities. The concept of salvation is elevated thereby and the profound nature of the glorious trinity somewhat exposed to our limited vision.

"Evidently from the foregoing, it is proper to refer to the Godhead in both the plural and the singular. The plural is proper because there are three Personalities so distinct that They may perform specific functions and actions separately. And yet there is a profound unity among the Members of the Godhead. Evidently this is a compound unity, as in Gen. 1:1 and 1:27, where the plural "Elohim" for God acted together in creation in such a manner that a singular verb could be used. We must, it appears, lean away from an elementary concept of unity into the realm of compound unity."[8]

ARITHMETIC DERIVED FROM GOD'S ATTRIBUTES

Mr. Olson also documents both: the metaphysical attributes of God (eternity of being, omnipresence, omniscience, or a knowledge of all that is knowable, and omnipotence); and His attributes of character (love, holiness, righteousness, lovingkindness, mercy, and wisdom or "the benevolent use of the abilities of personality,"[9] truthfulness, and faithfulness or unchangeableness).

The particular inherent attributes of God from which arithmetic is derived are: Unity, which suggests the idea of one or of the unit; Trinity, which suggests the idea of counting – one, two, three; Endless duration of time,[10] which suggests the idea of counting units of time to eternity past and to eternity future (i.e., counting forward and counting backward); Eternity of being,[11] which again suggests the infinity of arithmetic; and Unchangeableness,[12] which suggests that each operation of arithmetic results in only one correct answer. (Unchangeableness in arithmetic is called the closure property, which is reasoned from the fact that arithmetic presupposes the counting of real things, and is not a mental fabrication. It originates in the counting of the persons of the Trinity.) Both James 1:17 (which declares that with God there "is no variableness, neither shadow of turning.") and Hebrews 13:8 ("Jesus Christ the same yesterday, and today and for ever.") are particularly powerful expressions of God's unchanging character.

In summary, arithmetic – which is counting – is derived from the nature and character of God, specifically with respect to: the concept of one ("The Lord our God is one Lord." Deut. 6:4); the concept of counting (First Person, Second Person, and Third Person of the Trinity); the concept of the possibility of counting forward and backward to infinity (endless duration); the concept that arithmetic always existed (eternity of being); and the concept that there is one correct answer (unchangeableness or the closure property).

In conclusion, the answer to the question, "What is the Biblical source and origin of arithmetic?" is that arithmetic is derived from the nature and character of God.

8. *The Truth Shall Make You Free*, by Gordon C. Olson, Bible Research Fellowship, Inc., 2624 Hawthorne, Franklin Park, Illinois 60131, 1980.

9. *Ibid.*

10. *Ibid.*, Isa. 57:15; Psa. 102:24-27; 95:10-11; Zeph. 3:5; Zech. 1:12; Heb. 13:8; Rev. 1:8.

11. *Ibid.*, Gen. 21:33; *Deut. 33:27;* Psa. 9:7; 41:13; *90:2;* 93:2; 103:17; Isa. 26:4; 40:28; 44:6; 48:12; *Rom. 1:20;* 16:26; *Heb. 9:14;* Rev. 4:8.

12. *Ibid.*, Deut. 7:9; Psa. 102:25-27; *Lam. 3:23;* Mal. 3:6; I Cor. 1:9; *10:13;* II Tim. 2:13; *Heb. 13:8; Jas. 1:17;* I Pet. 4:19; Rev. 1:5,6; 5:9,10.

THE BIBLICAL END
AND PURPOSE OF ARITHMETIC

The Biblical end and purpose of arithmetic is twofold: (1) to know God; and (2) to make Him known.[13]

TO KNOW GOD

In Scripture, numerical terms often express concepts of God's nature and character, of His ways and providential acts, and of His plans and purposes – concepts that without a number system would be beyond the power of the human mind to grasp. For example: "And I will make thy seed as the dust of the earth: so that if a man can *number* the dust of the earth, then shall thy seed also be *numbered*." (Genesis 13:16) This example demonstrates that understanding of arithmetic enhances the knowledge of God as revealed in His Word.

Arithmetic also contributes to "understanding of the second of God's two Books – the Book of Nature."[14] Psalm 19 confirms that, "The heavens declare the glory of God; and the firmament sheweth His handywork." Romans 1:20 explains that, "the invisible things of Him from the creation of the world are clearly seen, being understood by the things that are made (nature), even His eternal power and Godhead;..." Arithmetic is the primary tool for the study of nature; and, since all of nature reveals God, arithmetic is a primary tool in coming to know God.

TO MAKE HIM KNOWN

God's people are His ambassadors; they represent Him. To the extent that they embody God's character and His ways, He is made known through them. By mastering arithmetic, an individual may more fully demonstrate the character of God, especially in two areas: (1) dominion, and (2) justice.

DOMINION

All arithmetic is counting, and counting is "the act of numbering." (Webster's 1828) The radical sense of "number" is "to speak, name, or tell," and "number may be applied to name, as the

Spaniards use *nombre* for name and the French word written with the same letters is *number*." (Webster's 1828) This etymology of the word "number," together with its first definition ("The designation of a unit in reference to other units, or in reckoning, counting, enumerating; ..." [Webster's 1828]), gives an interesting insight into Genesis 2:20. "Adam gave names to all cattle, and to the fowl of the air, and to every beast of the field; ..." It is apparent that Adam was giving consideration to each individual, making himself aware of each one as unique and distinct, in order to obey the command to "have dominion (in the sense of superintending care) ... over every living thing." (Genesis 1:28) The dominion of God Himself also takes the form of a superintending care. He "bringeth out their host [the stars] by *number*; he calleth them all by *names*... not one faileth." (Isaiah 40:26) This "naming" or "numbering" in order to exercise dominion is a Biblical purpose of arithmetic.

The life of Jesus demonstrates this lordship and dominion through a loving superintendence and care of the individual, and He taught that "If a man have a *hundred* sheep, and *one* of them be gone astray, doth he not leave the *ninety* and *nine*, ..." (Matthew 18:12) This is a clear example of counting as a tool of dominion (as well as of the value of the individual).

Again, a Biblical purpose of arithmetic is its use as a tool of dominion, and, without this tool, it would be difficult or impossible to superintend and care for the God-given responsibilities of life. It is in this role that mathematics is called "the language of science," and arithmetic is the foundation of all the other branches of mathematics. None of the vast varieties of the work of the world, either in planning, doing, or evaluating, could be done without arithmetic. It is an essential tool of dominion.

Following is a brief list of Scriptures exemplifying each of the three categories that show the application of counting to take dominion:
1. Counting of Individual Objects or Groups – "So teach us to *number* our days, that we may apply our hearts unto wisdom." (Psa. 90:12)
2. Counting of Equal Parts (i.e. Fractions) – "And he gave him *tithes* [tenths] of all." (Gen. 14:20)

---

13. Quotation from Joy Dawson, well-known Bible teacher.

14. *Teaching Algebra from the Principle Approach*, Darold Booton, Jr., page 10.

236

3. Counting of Units of Measure – "And this is the fashion which thou shalt make of it: The *length* of the ark shall be *three hundred cubits*, the *breadth* of it *fifty cubits*, and the *height* of it *thirty cubits*." (geometric units) (Gen. 6:15)

JUSTICE

Another purpose of arithmetic is to establish just trade relationships. Leviticus 19:35-36 gives a good example of this use of arithmetic in establishing standard units of measure for trade.

"Ye shall do no unrighteousness in judgment, in *meteyard*, in *weight*, or in *measure*. Just *balances*, just *weights*, a just *ephah*, and a just *hin* shall ye have: I am the Lord your God, which brought you out of the land of Egypt."

Proverbs 20:10 expresses God's feeling toward the misuse of standard units of measure: "Divers weights, and divers measures, both of them are alike abomination to the Lord."

In short, Christ's ambassadors will make Him known more perfectly by having dominion and control of their own lives and responsibilities and by dealing justly with others. Since arithmetic is a necessary tool for both dominion and justice, it is a necessary tool to make God known.

THE RUDIMENTS OF ARITHMETIC
(FIRST PRINCIPLES)

The rudiments or first principles of arithmetic are: (1) Counting, (2) Order and Magnitude, (3) Representation, and (4) The Plan for Solving Problems.

These principles of arithmetic and those of algebra are identical because "Algebra ... is a species of universal arithmetic, in which letters and signs are employed to abridge and generalize all processes involving numbers."[15] "The processes of algebra, in general, are only those of arithmetic extended, or rendered more comprehensive by the aid of letters taken in combination with figures."[16] Therefore, the principles of arithmetic listed here are a reflection of those presented by Mr. Booton.[17]

THE PRINCIPLE OF COUNTING

Counting, the first principle of arithmetic, is discussed more fully above under the heading, "Definition of Arithmetic." The child learning to count to ten is receiving the seed that contains the whole subject. By definition, each of the four operations (addition, multiplication, subtraction, and division) is a method of counting.

A corollary to this principle is the order of operations, i.e., when two or more operations are indicated, multiplication and division must be done before addition and subtraction. For example, if one boy in a group of six had 75 sea shells, and the other five had 50 shells each, the total could be expressed: 75 + 5 x 50. If this expression is worked from left to right (75 + 5 x 50 = 80 x 50 = 4000) the result is clearly a wrong answer. Since multiplication is counting additions of the same number, the meaning of 5 x 50 is 50 added 5 times. When the multiplication is done before the addition (75 + 5 x 50 = 75 + 250 = 325) the result is correct. This answer can be proved by adding 75 + 50 + 50 + 50 + 50 + 50 = 325.

This analysis demonstrates that the order of operations is inherent in the structure of arithmetic. It is not a mere convention or rule of thumb, but is an essential characteristic of the counting operations.

Children should learn the order of operations when they learn multiplication and division. Again, Mr. Booton's Counting Chart provides a simple, logical illustration for teaching this concept. Note the arrow above the label "Order of Operations" on the following Counting Chart. It indicates that in any given series of operations, the lowest level on the Chart (x & ÷) must be performed before the next level (+ & −).

---

15. *Elements of Algebra*, Charles Davies, SSD, A.S. Barnes & Co., 1866, page 11.

16. *New Elementary Algebra*, Benjamin Greenleaf, Robert S. Davis and Co., Boston, 1862, page 17.

17. *Teaching Algebra from the Principle Approach*, Darold Booton, Jr.

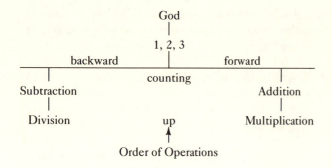

God
|
1, 2, 3
backward   forward
counting
Subtraction   Addition
Division   up   Multiplication

Order of Operations

"Each level of operation results from counting the preceding operation"[18] and, in solving an expression made up of several operations, start at the lowest level indicated on the Counting Chart and work upward, doing all the operations at each level before going up to the next level.

Again, counting, including the operations and the order of operations, is the first principle of arithmetic.

THE PRINCIPLE OF ORDER AND MAGNITUDE

The principle of order and magnitude is the source of two essentials of arithmetic: (1) the numbers of the number line; (2) units of measure.

Order is, "Regular disposition or methodical arrangement of things."

Magnitude is, "Extent of dimensions or parts; bulk, size; applied to things that have length, breadth, and thickness." (Foregoing definitions from Webster's 1828 Dictionary)

THE NUMBERS OF THE NUMBER LINE

The principle of order and magnitude is the source of number, "the designation of a unit in reference to other units." (Webster's 1828) A number (with the exception of one) is a collection of units and each number is related to all other numbers by order and magnitude. The number line is therefore an expression of this principle, because on it each number is methodically arranged by size, after a smaller number and before a larger.

UNITS OF MEASURE

A simple form of measurement is comparison: one is taller or shorter, heavier or lighter, warmer or cooler, than another. Measurement is a comparison based on the principle of order and magnitude. To measure implies to place in a "methodical arrangement" (order) by "size" (mag-

nitude), to determine if one is greater, smaller, or equal to another.

The various systems of measurement are based on the establishment of a unit of comparison, or, as Webster's fourteenth definition of "measure" states, "any quantity assumed as one or unity, to which the ratio of the other homogeneous or similar quantities is expressed." The cubit is an example. God told Noah, "The length of the ark shall be three hundred *cubits*." (Gen. 6:15) The unit of measure he used, the cubit, is the distance from the elbow to the fingertips. (For the average man today, this distance is eighteen inches. Webster's 1828 states that in Noah's day it was probably twenty-two inches.) Two other examples are the inch and the foot. An inch is equal to the length of three barley corns; a foot, to the length of a man's foot. When children are taught the principle of order and magnitude as the basis of measurement, they instantly understand the necessity of a standardized system of weights and measures.

The relationship of measurement to arithmetic is simply that arithmetic is counting and measurement is counting units of measure.

An exercise to introduce measurement to children is described in the book, *Benjamin West and His Cat Grimalkin*, when young Benjamin makes a new signboard for his father's inn. "With a piece of hemp Benjamin took the measurements of the old weathered sign. Then he sawed some boards and set to work sanding them."[19] Benjamin apparently used one length of cord to equal the length of the sign, and another for the width. Students may be given the assignment of making a sign, even out of paper, using string to make their measurements. Counting units can be demonstrated by making one sign twice or three times the length or width of another.

It is important for students to understand that both the numbers of the numberline and units of measure flow from the principle of order and magnitude.

THE PRINCIPLE OF REPRESENTATION

Represent is defined by Webster as, "To supply the place of; to act as a substitute for another." The principle of representation is the source of the various systems of notation. Notation is, "the expressing of numbers and quantities by figures, signs, or characters appropriate for the purpose." (Webster's 1828) The Arabic system of notation uses figures to represent numbers; the Roman system, letters.

---

18. *Ibid.*

19. *Benjamin West and His Cat Grimalkin*, Marguerite Henry, Bobbs-Merrill Co., Inc., Indianapolis, Indiana, 1947, page 126.

Problems involving all of the four basic operations of arithmetic are most easily solved in the Arabic system of notation, because of its properties, especially that of place value. Children who understand the principle of representation, i.e., that a given number may be represented in various ways, are quick to perceive the unique value of the Arabic system and to master its uses. For example, the number one thousand in Roman is M; in Arabic, 1,000. It is clearly easier to write the number in Roman, but it is also clear that it is much easier to add, subtract, multiply or divide in Arabic.

The primary skill taught under this principle is numeration: "In *arithmetic*, notation; the art of expressing in characters any number proposed in words, or of expressing in words any number proposed in characters; the act or art of writing or reading numbers." (Webster's 1828) The rules and practice of at least the following three systems of notation should be mastered: Roman; Arabic; and tally (i.e. a series of four slashes and a crosshatch [౹౹౹౹]. The student who masters various systems of notation is able to see the underlying principle of each system and to reason effectively in its application.

This effect was delightfully illustrated by the seven year old students in my classroom. They had briefly considered Mayan, Egyptian, Chinese, and Roman notation and taken notes on each system. One day as I was writing notes on the board for the class to copy into their notebooks, I noticed one of the boys lagging. When I asked him why, the boy sitting behind him blurted out with amused indignation, "Mr. Kilkenny, he's writing all the numbers in Chinese notation." The culprit had taken a child's history of arithmetic out of the library and set about to master Chinese notation. To the children in this second grade class, the Arabic system (with its nine figures, each given a value by the place it occupies in a number, and its zero to fill the vacant orders) is literally child's play.

The expression, "Arithmetic is the language of science," is given added meaning in light of the definition of numeration. Each system of notation is, in a sense, a distinct, written language, and in a language, "Articulate sounds are represented by letters, marks, or characters which form words." (Webster's 1828 Dictionary) Representation therefore may be identified as a principle both of language and of arithmetic.

Professor Charles Davies has explained the logic of the use of notation in the science of arithmetic and the *necessity* of understanding that figures ultimately *represent real things*, and are *not a reality in themselves*. His explanation is quoted below.

"In the science of numbers, the ten characters, called figures, are the alphabet of the arithmetical language; the combinations of these characters constitute the pure language of arithmetic; and the principles of numbers which are unfolded by means of this, in connection with our common language, constitute the science.

"In arithmetic, all quantity is regarded as consisting of parts, which can be numbered exactly or approximately, and in this respect, possesses all the properties of numbers. Propositions, therefore, concerning numbers, have this remarkable peculiarity, that they are propositions concerning all quantities whatever.

"In the various uses which we make of these symbols [figures], and the processes of reasoning carried on by means of them, the mind insensibly comes to regard them as *things*, and not as mere signs; and we constantly predicate of them the properties of things in general, without pausing to inquire what kind of thing is implied. All this we are at liberty to do, since symbols being the representatives of quantity in general, there is no necessity of keeping the idea of *quantity* continually alive in the mind; and the processes of thought may, without danger, be allowed to rest on the symbols themselves, and therefore, become to that extent, merely mechanical. But when we look back and see on what the reasoning is based, and how the processes have been conducted, we shall find that every step was taken on the supposition that we were actually dealing with *things*, and not with *symbols*; and that without this understanding of the language, the whole system is without signification, and fails."[20]

THE PRINCIPLE OF THE PLAN FOR SOLVING PROBLEMS

The principle of Isaiah 33:22, " For the Lord is our *judge*, the Lord is our *lawgiver*, the Lord is our *king*; he will save us," controls every human act. Each act must first be conceived or planned, then executed or carried out, and finally judged or evaluated. This truth, applied to civil government, suggests three distinct governmental functions, and when combined with the recognition of man's finite condition, gives rise to the separation of powers. In arithmetic, this truth provides *The Plan for Solving Problems.*

20. *Elements of Algebra*, Charles Davies, S.S.D., A. S. Barnes & Co., 1866, pages 11-13.

This principle is applied both in simplifying numerical expressions by performing the operations of arithmetic and in solving practical questions (commonly called word problems).

For example, in order to simplify the expression 596 − 387, one must: first, *plan* to write the subtrahend under the minuend placing figures of the same order in a column; second, the operation must be *done*; third, the difference must be *judged* for correctness either by seeing if it works in a practical situation or by adding the difference to the subtrahend to prove the problem (if the sum equals the minuend, the difference is correct). Of course, with practice the planning and doing become so nearly simultaneous that planning is not easily recognized as a part of problem solving. However, planning is an inherent part of the process and must be taught.

Practical questions provide excellent opportunities to teach the plan for solving problems. The first step, *plan*, should be performed by explaining each step of the solution without mentioning any of the given amounts. The second step, *application*, is simply to do the indicated operations. The third step, *check*, is to answer the specific question, checking to be sure it actually solves the problem. (Note that one practical question will take a full page of notebook paper.)

Following is an example of the practical question format:

PRACTICAL QUESTION

"A locomotive has 391 miles to run in 11 hours: after running 139 miles in 4 hours, at what rate per hour must the remaining distance be run?"[21]

Plan

Step 1: Subtract the miles already run from the total miles.
Step 2: Subtract the hours already run from the total hours.
Step 3: Divide the remaining distance by the remaining time.
Conclusion: the quotient will equal the rate per hour at which the remaining distance must be run.

Application

Step 1:   391 miles
           − 139 miles
            252 miles

Step 2:   11 hours
           − 4 hours
             7 hours

Step 3:   36 m.p.h.
            7 hrs. | 252 miles

Check

The remaining distance must be run at 36 m.p.h. This answer can be checked by proving the operations in each step.

Practical questions should also be used to teach the plan for solving problems to beginners, but the questions must be much easier. For example:

PRACTICAL QUESTION

"I saw three saucers of milk, and three cats drinking from each saucer. How many cats did I see?"[22]

Plan

(It is often helpful for beginners to draw illustrations.[23])

Geoffrey Strout

This problem can be solved by any one of three methods: (1) by counting; (2) by adding the number of cats at each saucer; (3) by multiplying the number of cats at each saucer by the number of saucers.

Application

(1) Counting: 1, 2, 3, 4, 5, 6, 7, 8, 9, cats
(2) Adding: 3 + 3 + 3 = 9 cats
(3) Multiplication: 3 x 3 = 9 cats

Check

I saw 9 cats. [This answer can be checked by reviewing the applications.]

The greatest usefulness of arithmetic is its application to practical situations, and yet the expression, "I'm not good at word problems," is very common. If students were to do one practical question each day using the suggested format, they would become "good at word problems." They would probably even enjoy them.

---

21. *The Principles of Arithmetic Analyzed and Practically Applied, For Advanced Students*, Joseph Ray, MD, Sargent, Wilson, & Hinkle, Cincinnati, 1856, page 54.

22. *Wentworth's Primary Arithmetic*, G.A. Wentworth and E.M. Reed, Ginn and Company, Boston, 1892.

23. Illustration by Geoffrey Strout, third grade, Christian Heritage School, Tyler, Texas, 1985.

Practical questions that require two or more operations are best even for the youngest students. For example:

PRACTICAL QUESTION

"George owed me 19 cents: he gave me 2 oranges, worth 5 cents each, and the remainder in money: how much money did I get?"[24]

Plan

Step 1: Multiply the cost per orange by the number of oranges.
Step 2: Subtract the product of step 1 from the total debt George owed me.
Conclusion: The difference will be how much money I received.

---

24. *Ray's New Primary Arithmetic*, Joseph Ray, originally published by Van Antwerp Bragg and Co., 1877, reprinted by Mott Media, Milford, Michigan, 1985, page 55.

Application

Step 1:   5 cents
          x 2
           10 cents

Step 2:   19 cents
         − 10 cents
            9 cents

Check

I received 9 cents.

(For suggestions on teaching, see the section entitled, "How to Determine Operations to Solve Practical Questions" on page 242.)

Students who learn The Principle of the Plan for Solving Problems will gain a practical mastery of arithmetic.

COURSE GOALS FOR ARITHMETIC

GENERAL GOALS

The general goal for arithmetic is to teach the following concepts as revealed in the discipline:

1. The knowledge of God: of His nature which is Trinitarian and infinite and exists in an endless duration of time; and of His character which never changes.

2. The knowledge of creation through arithmetic, "the language of science," to be used in obedience to the command to take dominion of the earth.

3. An American Christian philosophy of history identifying both the significance of arithmetic on the Chain of Christianity Moving Westward and the individuals who contributed to it.

SPECIFIC GOALS

1. To impart understanding of the nature of the subject, i.e. *counting*. As expressed in *Ray's Higher Arithmetic*, "... the analytic method of solution ... [is] preferred to mere formal and irrational directions; for no true development of the intellectual powers or satisfactory knowledge of any science can be attained, unless the *spirit of every operation*

is clearly seen through its form."[25]

2. To train the reasoning abilities. "One of the principal benefits of the study of mathematics is to teach the learner how to reason with elegance and exactness."[26] To train the pupil in governmental thinking, i.e. from cause to effect, or "to methods of reasoning; rather than in mere methods of operating."[27]

3. To impart mastery of the vocabulary, the skills, and the applications of arithmetic, especially the interpreting and solving of practical questions.

(The above quotations from nineteenth century teachers have been used to illustrate that the Principle Approach to arithmetic is not new. It is America's historic method of Biblical reasoning. Our task is not to create a new method, but to return to the method that produced liberty in our nation.)

---

25. *The Principles of Arithmetic*, Joseph Ray, MD, Sargent, Wilson, & Hinkle, Cincinnati, 1856, page iv.
26. *New Elementary Algebra*, Benjamin Greenleaf, A.M., Robert S. Davis and Co., 1862, page iii.
27. *The Complete Algebra*, Edward Olney, Sheldon and Co., New York, 1870, page v.

Arithmetic is the foundation of all mathematics. Mathematics is defined as "The science of quantity, the science which treats of magnitude and number, or of whatever can be measured or numbered... Arithmetic, geometry, algebra, trigonometry, and conic sections, are branches of *mathematics*." (Webster's 1828) This guide deals specifically with the branch of mathematics called arithmetic—i.e., counting or "The science of numbers or the art of computation."

Arithmetic is divided here into "Skills of Counting" and "Categories of Application" (i.e., three categories which include everything that can be counted).

I. Skills of Counting
    A. Oral (by 1's, 2's, 3's, etc.)
    B. Written
        1. Words (One, Two, Three, Etc.)
        2. Systems of Notation
            a. Roman (The Seven Letters and The Rules Governing Their Values)
            b. Arabic
                i. The Ten Figures and The Rules Governing Their Values
                ii. The Operations ($+$, $-$, x, $\div$) (Note that the operations are a unique feature of the Arabic system of notation, and that without them the science or art of arithmetic would be greatly hampered.)

II. Categories of Application
    A. Counting Individual Objects or Individual Groups
    B. Counting Equal Parts (i.e., Fractions, Decimal Fractions, Percent, and Interest)
    C. Counting Units of Measure
        1. Geometric Units
            a. Line (such as inches, feet, yards, miles, etc.)
            b. Area (such as square inches, square feet, etc.)
            c. Volume or Capacity (such as cubic inches, etc.)
            d. Angle (i.e. Degree, such as 30°, 60°, 90°, 180°, etc.)
        2. Physical Units
            a. Weight (such as ounces and pounds)
            b. Mass
            c. Temperature (such as degrees Fahrenheit etc.)
        3. Chronological Units
            a. Clock (seconds, minutes, hours, etc.)
            b. Calendar (days, weeks, months, years, decades, centuries, millenia, etc.)
    4. Monetary Units
        a. United States Money
        b. Foreign Money

Note: Unit Conversion (i.e., inches to feet, hours to minutes, etc.) and Compound Units (i.e., m.p.h., p.s.i., etc.) must be included in the teaching of Units of Measure.

The arithmetic course is organized around the structure of the subject – i.e., counting. The first concepts to be taught are: counting, forward and backward; notation and numeration; and the operations defined as counting. These concepts are then applied to the counting of: individuals and groups; equal parts; and units of measure. The student should be able to relate all the arithmetic he learns to these few simple concepts. The understanding of these basics provides the tool for problem solving and makes arithmetic useful and practical. Without an understanding of these basics, arithmetic is a discrete collection of unrelated facts which is both confusing and virtually useless.

Shawn Nelson, a seven-year-old student at Christian Heritage School, Tyler, Texas, 1985, wrote the following description of the organization of arithmetic.

"All arithmetic is counting forward and backward on the number line. There are two ways to count forward, addition and multiplication, which is counting many additions of the same number. There are two ways of counting backward, subtraction and division, which is counting many subtractions of the same number. So it is very easy to do arithmetic when you know all these simple ways of counting forward and backward.

"There are three simple classes that can be counted. The first class is individuals or groups. The second class is equal parts which are called fractions. The third class is units of measure. These three classes are easy to learn and count."

Shawn was able to write this skillful description because she knows the elements of the subject.

HOW TO DETERMINE OPERATIONS
TO SOLVE PRACTICAL QUESTIONS

Following is an example of reasoning from the basics of the numberline to determine the operations needed to solve a practical question.

"If a man travels 28 miles a day, how many miles will he travel in 152 days?"[28]

The needed operation may be determined by: first, identifying the given number on which to start counting; second, identifying the direction of counting. (Note that counting *forward* is counting toward *larger* numbers; counting *backward* is counting toward *smaller* numbers)

The given starting point in this question is 28. Since 28 is repeated 152 times, the result will be greater than 28, that is, forward on the number-line. Therefore the problem may be solved by addition; and, since it involves many additions of the same number, it may also be solved by multiplication.

This method is a key in determining which operations to apply in any problem. Once the direction of counting is identified, the needed operations will be known and problem solving will become a simple matter of working these operations.

Since problem solving is the most important use of arithmetic, and since the key to problem solving is knowledge of the basics of counting, understanding of the structure of arithmetic is more important than memorizing number facts. The arithmetic course is therefore organized around the structure of the subject and the students learn the number facts as tools for the important work of problem solving.

The strong tendency for the teacher is to spend the greater part of his classroom time drilling number facts, whereas his most important work is to impart knowledge of the structure and form of the subject. Daily answering of practical questions according to the format described above under the heading, "The Principle of the Plan for Solving Problems" helps the student gain mastery of basic structure.

The following tables from *Primary Arithmetic* by Samuel Hamilton, PhD., American Book Company, 1907, contain, in a concise form, all the addition and subtraction facts. Children are encouraged by seeing how simple and logical these facts are.

TABLE OF COMBINATIONS IN ADDITION

In addition there are 45 different combinations of figures, taken two at a time, and 17 different sums or amounts. Use these combinations for drill frequently:

---

28. *Ray's Modern Practical Arithmetic*, American Book Company, New York, 1903, page 45.

```
1    2        2  3            3  4        3  4  5
1    1        2  1            2  1        3  2  1
2    3        4  4            5  5        6  6  6

4  5  6            4  5  6  7        5  6  7  8
3  2  1            4  3  2  1        4  3  2  1
7  7  7            8  8  8  8        9  9  9  9

5  6  7  8  9                       6  7  8  9
5  4  3  2  1                       5  4  3  2
10 10 10 10 10                      11 11 11 11

6  7  8  9            7  8  9        7  8  9
6  5  4  3            6  5  4        7  6  5
12 12 12 12         13 13 13       14 14 14

8  9            8  9            9            9
7  6            8  7            8            9
15 15          16 16          17           18
```

TABLE OF COMBINATIONS IN SUBTRACTION

In subtraction there are 45 different combinations of figures, taken two at a time. Use these combinations for drill frequently:

```
9   9   9   9   9   9   9   9   9
1   2   3   4   5   6   7   8   9
8   7   6   5   4   3   2   1   0

8   8   8   8   8   8   8   8   7
1   2   3   4   5   6   7   8   1
7   6   5   4   3   2   1   0   6

7   7   7   7   7   7   6   6   6
2   3   4   5   6   7   1   2   3
5   4   3   2   1   0   5   4   3

6   6   6   5   5   5   5   5   4
4   5   6   1   2   3   4   5   1
2   1   0   4   3   2   1   0   3

4   4   4   3   3   3   2   2   1
2   3   4   1   2   3   1   2   1
2   1   0   2   1   0   1   0   0
```

SUMMARY

In summary, the basic structure or skeleton of arithmetic is counting forward and backward on the number line. There are three categories that can be counted: individuals and groups; equal parts; and units of measure. Whether he is beginning or advanced, the student who knows the nature of the counting operations, as well as the category to which each operation is being applied, is a student who has mastery of the facts he has learned.

TABLE OF THE SKILLS OF COUNTING

The following Table of Skills of arithmetic and

suggested grade levels for each skill is idealistically designed to schedule the teaching and learning of the basics of arithmetic into K through 4th grade, although in practice this subject may not be mastered until the end of the 8th grade. WARNING—the "suggested grade levels" for the teaching of particular skills are given here only to indicate a general plan for course organization. The teacher must carefully judge each individual student or class to determine the skills to be taught. This determination is based not on age or grade level but on the students' level of understanding. Students of every age must master all the rudimentary principles of the subject. Older students will usually learn these principles quickly, but the principles to be taught are the same for young and old.

TABLE OF SKILLS

K	1	2	3	4
ORAL COUNTING:				
1's, 5's, 10's to 100	1's, 2's, 3's, 5's, 10's to 100	1's, 2's, 3's, 4's, 5's, 10's to 100	1's, 2's, 3's, 4's, 5's, 6's, 7's, 8's, 10's to 100	1's through 12's to 100
WRITTEN COUNTING: (Words: one, two, three, etc.):				
one to one-thousand	one to one-thousand	one to nine hundred, ninety-nine thousand	one to nine hundred ninety-nine million	one to nine hundred ninety-nine decillion
ROMAN NOTATION (Letters):				
Value of I, V, X and I to XII	Same as K	I to XXIX	I to C	I to MMM
ARABIC NOTATION (Figures):				
1 to 100 place value and numeration	1 to 1000	1 to 999,000	1 to 999,000,000	1 to 999 decillion
OPERATIONS:				
Addition, subtraction with borrowing or carrying	Addition, subtraction with borrowing & carrying: multiply & divide with one place multipliers and divisors	Addition, subtraction with borrowing & carrying to 999,000; multiplication with two place multipliers; division with one place divisors	Addition, subtraction with borrowing & carrying to 999 million; multiplication with three place multipliers; division with two place divisors	Addition, subtraction with borrowing & carrying to 999 decillion; multiplication with four place multipliers and division with four place divisors

CATEGORIES OF APPLICATION

The categories of application are outlined above under the heading "Course Overviews." The teacher must blend the teaching of skills with the teaching of their practical application to these categories. Of course the teaching of fractions, decimals, the ruler, the thermometer, the clock, the calendar, money, angles, etc. is commonplace, even universal. But the teaching of arithmetic as counting and of each of these concepts as a function of counting is unique. It is reasoning from the whole to the part, from the principle to its application.

Even the youngest students, when they approach the subject from the aspect of counting, are confidently able to add and subtract fractions, calculate area and volume, and perform many other operations that are usually not presented to beginners.

Grade levels for the teaching of these categories are not listed here so that the teacher will not be robbed of the joy of seeing how much of this subject his students will master when they have grasped its principles.

Many students will achieve a mastery of Roman and Arabic notation much sooner than is indicated on the Table of Skills. By the end of the Fall of 1986, all twenty second grade students in my class were able to fluently read and write Roman notation of such numbers as MDCCLXXXVII. They also read and wrote Arabic notation of such numbers as 54, 360, 278, 001, 405, 697, 540, 090, 000, 416, 275, 001. Whenever a visitor would come to the classroom, they would vie with each other for the privilege of exhibiting their skill with numbers.

They also enjoyed competing with each other in *mental arithmetic*, producing instant solutions to such expressions as: $12 - 3 + 6$. Of course, this facility came with daily oral practice of the operations. Mental arithmetic is the favorite classroom activity of these students, and it is a very important method in the development of arithmetic skills.

In order to master these skills, the students must first understand the systems they are using, then they must have daily practice.

HOW TO ORGANIZE THE ARITHMETIC COURSE

The arithmetic course may be divided into three sections: (1) Beginning (K-2); (2) Development (3-5); and (3) Mastery (6-8).

SECTION 1, BEGINNING ARITHMETIC (K-2)

The elements of beginning arithmetic are taught in the following order:

A. Define arithmetic and some of its vocabulary. (See p. 232 and following) Most students will be familiar with counting and may be encouraged to realize that they already have the seed of the whole subject.

B. Introduction
   1. Teach the Scriptural origin and purpose of arithmetic (see p. 234 and following and p. 236 and following)
   2. Present an overview of arithmetic in the history of liberty (see p. 246)

C. The Counting Chart (see p. 232 and following)
   1. Count forward and backward on the number line
   2. Define arithmetic and addition, subtraction, multiplication, and division as *counting* processes
   3. Thoroughly teach the Counting Chart and have the students draw it in their notes

D. Oral Counting
   1's, 2's, 3's, 4's, 5's, and 10's to 100

E. Notation and Numeration (see p. 239 and following)
   1. Teach Roman notation
   2. Teach Arabic notation

F. Operations ($+$, $-$, x, $\div$)

G. Categories of Application (see page 242)

H. Daily Practical Question (see page 240) and Daily Practice Sheets ($+$, $-$, x, $\div$)

The teacher should be careful not to get bogged down on points A, B, and C. Mastery of these points will grow through constantly identifying and reasoning from them in the teaching of points D through H. For the beginner, the first emphasis should be on notation and numeration, and there must be a great deal of oral practice of the operations.

Again, the key to organizing the arithmetic course is to understand the complete list of the Skills of Counting (see pp. 242 and 244) and to organize the course around these skills, applying them to the Categories of Application. (see pp. 242 and 244)

SECTION 2, DEVELOPMENT OF ARITHMETIC (3-5)

A. Review
   1. Definitions of arithmetic and its terms (p. 232 and following)
   2. Scriptural origin and purpose of arithmetic (p. 234 and following and p. 236 and following)
   3. Overview of arithmetic in the history of liberty (p. 246)
   4. The Counting Chart with definitions of operations and the order of operations (pp. 232 and 237)
   5. Notation and numeration (pp. 233 and 239)
      a. Roman notation
      b. Arabic notation

B. The Teaching Plan
   1. Teach addition, subtraction, multiplication and division through each of the following sections and subsections
      a. Individuals and groups
      b. Equal parts (fractions)
      c. Units of measure
         (1) Geometric units
         (2) Physical units
         (3) Chronological units
         (4) Monetary units
   2. Teach unit conversion through all the units
   3. Assign a daily practical question and a daily practice sheet ($+$, $-$, x, $\div$).

The emphasis in Beginning Arithmetic is to lay a foundation by relating every operation to counting. This process should produce reasoning students. By the third grade, the number facts should be ingrained to the degree that the emphasis can begin to shift to the operations and practical questions applying the operations to the Categories of Application.

The Teaching Plan for Development of Arithmetic given above may at first seem inadequate for an entire course of study, but in reality it will take a great deal of time to teach the operations through the Categories of Application and the students will be greatly challenged. (This same plan will also apply to algebra, teaching addition, subtraction, multiplication, and division of polynomials)

In summary, the plan for organizing the Development of Arithmetic is simply to teach addition, subtraction, multiplication, and division of each of the Categories to which counting skills may be applied.

SECTION 3, MASTERY OF ARITHMETIC (6-8)

A. Review
(Points A and B of Section 2 above)
B. Teach the following
1. Percentage and interest
2. Factoring
3. Ratio and proportion
4. Involution (exponentiation)
5. Evolution (radicals)
6. Geometric units
   a. Measurement of surfaces (triangle, quadrilateral, trapezoid, etc.)
   b. Measurement of solids (cube, pyramid, cone, sphere, etc.)

ARITHMETIC AND THE HISTORY OF LIBERTY

The key to teaching the Providential view of history in a subject is to consider its *origin* in Asia, *development* in Europe and *liberty* in America. Arithmetic follows the pattern perfectly.

ORIGIN

All of the ancient nations seem to have had a knowledge of counting. This knowledge was based on counting the fingers. Among some primitive people, ten is the largest number known. The relationship of numbers to the fingers apparently produced various base ten systems of numeration. For example, the Roman "V" may represent an open hand, thumb extended. "X" may represent two "V's," "placed apex to apex."[29]

Practical arithmetic, or the art of computation, became highly developed among some ancient Asian nations. By the use of an abacus or other instrument, large numbers were efficiently combined and separated; but there was no understanding of the theory or science of numbers.

With the development of the Arabic system of notation, the operations became possible and the science of numbers began to progress. The Arabian arithmetic was called *algorism*. Webster's 1828 Dictionary defines algorism as, "an Arabic term, signifying numerical computation, or the six operations of arithmetic." (The six operations are: addition, subtraction, multiplication, division, evolution, and involution)

DEVELOPMENT

The general use and development of algoristic arithmetic (i.e., Arabic notation and the operations) began with men of science, and particularly astronomers in Europe and was adopted by the merchants of Italy. From Italy, it spread rapidly through the rest of Europe. The chief improvements subsequently introduced into the early Italian algorism were (i) the simplification of the four fundamental processes; (ii) the introduction of signs for addition, subtraction, equality, and (though not so important) for multiplication and division; (iii) the invention of logarithms; and (iv) the use of decimals.[30]

Decimal notation for fractions was developed in the early 1600's.

LIBERTY

One of the basic doctrines of American civil government is that: "All men are created equal." This truth is embodied in a people who value, not nobility of birth, but nobility of character. Accordingly, arithmetic, "the science of numbers or art of computation," in America has been used to produce liberty for the individual. An outstanding example of this attitude contrasted with the contemporary European attitude is described in the introduction to "Early American Philippine Trade: The Journal of Nathaniel Bowditch," American mathematician, navigator, and astronomer, as follows:

"The class distinctions on European ships between officers and crew were lacking on American ships. Of the crew of the Astera, every literate member eventually became a captain or chief mate.

---

29. *A Short Account of the History of Mathematics*, by W. W. Rouse Ball, Dover, New York, republished 1960, page 122.

30. *Ibid.*, page 188.

"Strong contrasts can be made between the selective processes which operated in the assignment of responsibilities in a typical American private trading vessel and those that operated in ships operated by a European monopoly such as the East India company. In the American vessel talent, skill and experience were paramount considerations, but in a typical East Indian ship, social class ties, political backing and outright purchase were the main determinants of one's position. In an East Indian ship, officers and crew were socially, functionally, and permanently separated.

"American crews were also given economic interest in a voyage. On the Astera 35 boxes of indigo and 141 bags of sugar were from 'adventures' of the crew."[13]

Nathaniel Bowditch is a fine example of the use of arithmetic to produce liberty for the individual. This liberty is characterized by personal advancement, productivity, dignity, and even

---

31. *Early American - Philippine Trade: The Journal of Nathaniel Bowditch in Manila, 1796* by Nathaniel Bowditch, edited and with an introduction by Thomas R. McHale and Mary C. McHale, Yale University, Southeast Asia Studies, New Haven, Connecticut, 1962, Distributed by: The Celler Bookshop, 18090 Wyoming, Detroit, Michigan (original in Boston Public Library).

safety. One of the great driving forces of his life was grief over the loss of men at sea caused by bad navigation and bad arithmetic. He labored to produce and to teach a system of arithmetic and of navigation to safeguard "the life, liberty and the pursuit of happiness" of the individual seamen.

Every man who sailed with Bowditch, whether seaman, gunner, cabin boy, or cook, returned from the voyage with a knowledge of navigation superior to that of many European naval officers, and these men were able to become officers on the merchant ships of Salem and to make this small port a leader in the world trade of the day. One can imagine Captain Prince asking why a mathematician, astronomer, and navigator of such stature would spend time teaching these ignorant men; and Nathaniel Bowditch answering simply, "Because they are worth it!"

This short answer simply states the spirit of America, a spirit that can be traced in the history of each academic discipline and in the lives of the men and women dedicated to those disciplines.

Every student of arithmetic should read *Carry On, Mr. Bowditch* by Jean Lee Latham, and be inspired with a love of liberty, and, perhaps be encouraged to research further the Providential history of arithmetic.

ARITHMETIC AND THE SEVEN PRINCIPLES OF AMERICA'S CHRISTIAN HISTORY AND GOVERNMENT

The Seven Principles are governmental principles and are not in themselves principles of arithmetic. Each of them, however, is clearly illustrated in arithmetic as well as in the other subjects. There is great value in teaching our students how the principles of history and government are illustrated in the various subjects, so that these Principles of American Christian History and Government will be securely planted in their minds and hearts.

The process of researching arithmetic through Scripture, history, and the Seven Principles helps produce in the teacher and his students a unified Christian world view. This process of researching, reasoning, relating, and recording distinguishes American Christian scholarship in the subject, and

inspires teacher and student with vision and goals in the fields of study to which arithmetic is foundational.

Following are explanations of how arithmetic illustrates each of the Seven Principles.

1. GOD'S PRINCIPLE OF INDIVIDUALITY

Arithmetic is "revelational of God's infinity." This subject, more clearly than any other, conceptualizes infinity.

Arithmetic is "revelational of ... God's diversity." Each number is unique and distinct, different from every other number without being contrary to any.

Arithmetic is "revelational of ... God's individuality." Each number on the number line is one, whole, and complete in itself, "having a separate or distinct existence" (Webster's 1828). Also, each operation has one and only one answer (i.e., closure property).

"God maintains the identity and individuality" of every number, just as He "maintains the identity and individuality of everything which he created."

2. THE CHRISTIAN PRINCIPLE OF SELF-GOVERNMENT

Self-government implies internal freedom to choose correctly, i.e., according to God's principles for governing individuals. (John 8:36; Phil. 2:13; Rom. 8:11, 14, 26; 6:18, 22)

Just as a man whose "Reason" is submitted to God may use that "Reason" to govern self, family, village, city, province, and kingdom; so arithmetic, when governed by its first principles, will produce correct answers to all problems from the most simple to the most complex. As the individual governs himself by right principle rightly applied, his thoughts and actions will be right and the flow of force and power will extend to the nation. Arithmetic provides a tangible illustration of this fact.

3. AMERICA'S HERITAGE OF CHRISTIAN CHARACTER

The stamp or mark which characterizes arithmetic is counting. When the student is true to this character in the sense of reasoning from counting in any given problem, his applications will be accurate, direct, and correct. If he loses sight of this character and follows rote memory of unintelligible formulas, the result is confusion, mistake, and discouragement.

Therefore, arithmetic provides a clear illustration of the third principle in that, when America as a nation remembers its heritage of Christian character of faith and steadfastness, brotherly love and Christian care, diligence and industry, and liberty of conscience, it is on the road to fulfilling its God-given purpose. When it forgets, it follows the road to destruction.

4. CONSCIENCE IS THE MOST SACRED OF ALL PROPERTY

More valuable than life itself is to have "a conscience void of offense toward God, and toward men." (Acts 24:16) The one who violates his own conscience loses his integrity and his self-worth.

Arithmetic too is useless and worthless when the integrity of its reality is violated. An arithmetic based on false premises is worse than useless, it is destructive. The most valuable property of arithmetic is to be rightly reasoned from the true principles of the subject.

5. THE CHRISTIAN FORM OF OUR GOVERNMENT

The internal aspects of the Christian form of our government are: Christian Self-government, Property, and Voluntary Union, each of which is listed as a separate principle and is discussed under its own heading.

The external aspects are:
1. Representation, which is also a principle of arithmetic and is explained above in "The Rudiments (First Principles) of Arithmetic." (See pp. 237-239)
2. The Separation of Powers, (i.e., into legislative, executive and judicial which is the governmental name for the principle in arithmetic called "The Plan for Solving Problems." (See p. 239)
3. Our Dual Form of Government, i.e., the federal - state system, reflects our vertical relationships to God (federal), and horizontal relationships to neighbors (state). This principle is illustrated in that arithmetic derives from God's nature and character (vertical) and is universal in its applications (horizontal).

6. HOW THE SEED OF LOCAL SELF-GOVERNMENT IS PLANTED

The seed of liberty is the Word of God planted in the heart of the individual. From this seed has sprung the American Christian Republic.

Arithmetic illustrates the seed principle because numbering or counting is the seed of arithmetic and from this seed grows the whole subject of mathematics.

7. THE CHRISTIAN PRINCIPLE OF AMERICAN POLITICAL UNION

This principle is characterized by voluntary consent to form a union of diverse individuals. The union is based on common principles and a common purpose. In 1774, the world was amazed to observe the unity of heart and spirit exhibited as the thirteen colonies arose in support of Boston. It was this unity which produced the Union.

Arithmetic illustrates this principle in that

diverse numbers of the number line are brought into a unity with union through the principles of the subject. Arithmetic is a whole, unified subject composed of unique and distinct numbers brought into unity through common principles.

RESOURCES

THE PROPER USE OF TEXTBOOKS

A teacher must teach a subject from his own understanding of that subject. This premise is true both in the home and in the school. The most deadening way to "teach" is to hand a textbook or workbook to a student with instructions to sit down and do a certain lesson or a certain number of pages per day. This method impedes both the imparting of a love of the subject, and the wonderful fellowship of teacher and student together learning the works of God.

The teacher who is deficient in a subject that he must teach has an opportunity to demonstrate love of learning and self-education. He can no more impart the knowledge of some learned textbook writer than David could slay Goliath with Saul's armor. Each teacher must use his own sling and five smooth stones, his own knowledge, ability to learn and to "lead in advance of others."

One method of "leading in advance" is to choose a textbook and do every lesson, every assignment, before requiring the student to do it. The teacher who uses this method will discover a camaraderie with the student. He will understand the intellectual difficulties to be overcome because he will have overcome them himself. He will be able to explain his own reasoning, and, in so doing, he will share his life with his student. Having done the work himself, the teacher will not become either a hard taskmaster or too soft. Finally, the teacher and student will have a common sense of accomplishment, "Look what we have learned!"

(Note: The term "teacher" in this *Guide* includes both school teacher and home teacher. The parent who is a home teacher has this advantage over the school teacher: an established, strong relationship with the student whereby the home teacher knows immediately when his students understand and when they don't. The school teacher must begin each year by building relationships with his students.)

STANDARDS FOR EVALUATION OF ARITHMETIC BOOKS

1. *Statement of Principles and Rules*: The first standard by which to evaluate an arithmetic text is its method. Many textbooks do not give statements of principles or rules, but only give countless examples, exercises, and drills. This method tends to produce students who have difficulty with mathematical concepts and applications, even though they may know the number facts. In contrast, the Principle Approach method is clearly stated in the following quotation from the Preface to *Ray's Practical Arithmetic*:

"Every principle is clearly explained by an analysis or solution of a simple example from which a rule is devised. The application of the rule to the solution of problems of gradually increasing difficulty completes the presentation of the subject.

"The exercises have been constructed with a view to affording the mental discipline necessary to strengthen the reasoning power and to giving the pupil a mastery over the problems that are sure to present themselves in the common walks of life."

Notice that Ray's method is to *explain a principle, analyze the principle, derive a rule*, and, finally, *assign exercises* to which the principles and rules may be applied.

The first standard for textbook evaluation is therefore: "Does the book state principles and rules?"

2. *Overall Organization*: The logical organization of an arithmetic course is:
I. Skills of Counting
  A. Oral
  B. Written (notation and numeration)
  C. Operations
II. Categories of Application
  A. Counting Individual objects or individual groups
  B. Counting Equal parts
  C. Counting Units of measure
Course organization is a standard by which to evaluate textbooks, and the teacher who understands the organization of arithmetic can pick and choose useful exercises and statements of principle from books that fail to measure up to standards one and two.

3. *Are Scripture References Inherent to Arithmetic?* Another standard by which to evaluate textbooks distributed by Christian publishers is their use of Scripture. Is the Scriptural foundation and use of the subject identified, or are the Scripture references tacked on to each chapter as a pious exercise that bears little or no relationship to the nature of the subject?

The teacher should do his own study of the Scriptural origin and purpose of the subject so that he will be able to intelligently apply this standard.

RECOMMENDED TEXT

The area in which the teacher may be most in need of help is in forming concise statements of principle and of rules. *Ray's Arithmetic* is most helpful for these statements, and the *Ray's* series is being republished by:

Mott Media
1000 East Huron
Milford, Michigan 48042
Phone: (313) 685-8773
Toll free: (800) 521-4350

Mott is also publishing answer keys and teaching guides to *Ray's*.

The series includes *Primary*, *Intellectual*, *Practical*, and *Higher* arithmetics. Children should start in the *Primary* and move to *Intellectual*, but the teacher will need *Practical* which gives definitions of terms and statements of principles and rules not found in the first two books.

Some teachers also feel the need for published exercises. It is a simple matter to make up exercises when the principle being taught has been clearly defined but exercises from any text or exercise book may be used effectively.

ANNOTATED BIBLIOGRAPHY

Ball, W. W. Rouse, *A Short Account of the History of Mathematics*, Dover Publications, Inc., New York, republished 1960.

Booton Jr., Darold, *Algebra I: A Principle Approach*, Christian Heritage Academy, 1136 Southwest 48th Street, Oklahoma City, Oklahoma 73109, private distribution, 1983-84 school year. It is Mr. Booton who identified the principles of arithmetic. His algebra text has not been distributed to the public to date.

Booton Jr., Darold, "Teaching Algebra from the Principle Approach," reprinted in this *Guide*, page 425.

Bowditch, Nathaniel, *Early American - Philippine Trade: The Journal of Nathaniel Bowditch in Manila, 1796*, edited and with an introduction by Thomas R. McHale and Mary C. McHale, Yale University, Southeast Asia Studies, New Haven, Connecticut, 1962; Distributed by: the Celler Bookshop, 18090 Wyoming, Detroit, Michigan (original in Boston Public Library).

Davies, Charles, SSD, *Elements of Algebra*, A.S. Barnes & Co., 1866. Excellent philosophical foundation.

Greenleaf, Benjamin, *New Elementary Algebra*, Robert S. Davis and Co., Boston, 1862.

Hamilton, Samuel, Ph.D., *Primary Arithmetic*, American Book Company, New York, 1907.

Henry, Marguerite, *Benjamin West and His Cat Grimalkin*, Bobbs-Merrill Co., Inc., Indianapolis, Indiana, 1947. An excellent work of literature.

Latham, Jean Lee, *Carry On, Mr. Bowditch*, Houghton Mifflin Co., Boston, 1955. Required reading for all arithmetic students.

Olney, Edward, *The Complete Algebra*, Sheldon & Co., New York, 1870.

Olson, Gordon C., *The Truth Shall Make You Free*, Bible Research Fellowship, Inc., 2624 Hawthorne, Franklin Park, Illinois 60131, 1980. This book provides a solid theological foundation for the study of every subject.

Ray, Joseph, MD, *The Principles of Arithmetic Analyzed and Practically Applied, For Advanced Students*, Sargent, Wilson, & Hinkle, Cincinnati, 1856. See comments under THE PROPER USE OF TEXTBOOKS, p. 249.

Ray, Joseph, MD, *Ray's Modern Practical Arithmetic*, American Book Company, New York, 1903. Also see comments under THE PROPER USE OF TEXTBOOKS, p.249.

Wentworth, G.A. and Reed, E.M., *Wentworth's Primary Arithmetic*, Ginn and Company, Boston, 1892. Excellent practical questions and exercises for beginners.

JAMES V. KILKENNY

¿QUIERES UNA BIBLIA?

In 1977 I left a career in public education and began to work with Youth With A Mission (YWAM) distributing Bibles in Mexico. Together with our family of six children, my wife, Barbara, and I joined a team of young missionaries to spend the summer in tents on a hillside overlooking the Pacific Ocean near Rosarito, Baja California. Every day we filled our backpacks with Spanish New Testaments, boarded our blue Ford station wagon, and set out on the dusty trails that pass for roads there, dropping off team members with their Bibles at intervals along the way. After working for two full summers and one Easter Week, we had systematically visited every hovel, every rancheria, every mansion and every modest home in Ensenada, in all the area between Ensenada and Tijuana, and in large sections of Tijuana. We went to the home of the Police Chief of Tijuana; we went to huts in the city garbage dump. At every door we said, "¿Quieres una Biblia? No cuesta nada." ("Do you want a Bible? It's free.") We talked with people, we prayed with them, we told them that the Bible would teach them of God and of how they should live so that all of their many needs would be met. Many of these people wept in gratitude as they sensed the Hand of God reaching out through us to touch their lives.

At the end of this time our minds were satisfied that every home there had received a Bible. We stood rejoicing on an Ensenada hilltop overlooking the harbor, the city, and the surrounding hills. Every family within that vista had received the Precious Word of God.

What were we to do now? We began to consider some questions: "Specifically, how is the Bible to affect the lives of these people? How might it transform their homes and churches, their economy and civil government? How might these people be set at liberty by the Word of God?" We both had been teachers for many years, but our effectiveness with students had seemed to be limited. At this time we heard Miss Verna Hall and Miss Rosalie Slater speak on the subject of American Christian History and the Principle Approach. Although I did not then fully grasp their philosophy, or the significance of the phrase, "think governmentally," I began to understand that a Biblical view of government might address our questions, and I told Barbara that, if I ever were to teach again, I would use the Principle

Approach. Within two months we were asked by the American Director of YWAM to start a Principle Approach school.

As we began, we did not realize how completely our minds, as teachers, were "conformed to this world." (Romans 12:2) We did not know that in order for us to produce a Principle Approach school we ourselves must first be "transformed by the renewing of the mind." (Romans 12:2) However, we blithely proceeded to open class in September 1979 on the open mezzanine of the YWAM missionary training center in Solvang, California, with twenty-five students and four teachers. Since the teachers were within hearing of each other, and since the lobby below was filled with people at regular intervals, we had great external obstacles as well as the internal ones.

The Lord in His mercy showed us the way to surmount the internal obstacles caused by our blind acceptance of false presuppositions about education. In February 1980 it was made possible for us to attend a two week seminar at the Foundation for American Christian Education (F.A.C.E.) in San Francisco with Miss Hall and Miss Slater, who taught us every day from nine A.M. to nine P.M., breaking only for meals. Between lectures we seminar students crowded around them for questions and discussion. By the end they were showing signs of physical weariness, but our presuppositions had been examined and changed. We had begun to "prove what is that good, and acceptable and perfect, will of God" (Romans 12:2) concerning self and civil government; we had begun to consider the Hand of God in history; and we had begun to formulate our own expression of an American Christian philosophy of education and government.

The true relationship between God and government has been beautifully described in the following passage from David Gregg's "Makers of the American Republic": "The church, in teaching American citizens, begins with God. The first essential is to get into right relation with God, to get His law written on the heart and incorporated in the life. Institutions must harmonize with His will, and so must rulers, and so must voters." (*T/L*, page 41)

The external obstacles, caused by the lack of adequate school facilities, were later diminished when, after one year in Solvang, we moved to Tyler, Texas, to an old, deserted school, having twelve classrooms, a library room, offices, a gymnasium, and a playing field. Each teacher now had his own classroom to restore, both internally and externally: internally, by dealing with his own character and scholarship; externally, by scrub-

bing, painting, waxing, etc. We determined to establish Christian Heritage School as a demonstration and pilot school for the Principle Approach as well as a teacher training institution. We now have one hundred students in kindergarten through twelfth grade and a number of student teachers.

Our vision for the future is to send out teams of teachers to establish Principle Approach schools and to teach Biblical self- and civil government and the Hand of God in history in all of the states and nations of North and South America. In this way, we believe that the hope set before the people of Baja California can become a reality for them as it can for all those who embrace these truths.

By bringing materials to enlighten our minds and individuals to help and guide us, the Holy Spirit has led us step by step. The development of the "Guide to Teaching Arithmetic" is one fruit of His leading. Mr. James Rose of The American Christian History Institute and Mrs. Ruth Smith of Pilgrim Institute have both worked faithfully and diligently to train both Barbara and me and the C.H.S. staff. We are greatly indebted to them as well as to Miss Hall and Miss Slater of F.A.C.E. for their diligence in teaching and learning and for their constant encouragement.

In 1981 we met Mr. Darold Booton, Jr., the author of the "Guide to Teaching Algebra" and he began to explain the principles of algebra to me. On one occasion while we were having dinner in a restaurant, Mr. Booton, in his minuscule handwriting, drew the counting chart and wrote the definitions of the operations on the back of a 3 x 5 card. As I thought it through, the information on that card became the foundation for my understanding of the principles of arithmetic. That year I was teaching first year algebra in the high school as well as a self-contained third grade. I taught the rudiments of algebra, as defined by Mr. Booton, to the high school students and then simplified these principles, applying them to arithmetic, and teaching them to the third grade.

Providentially, Barbara picked up an old arithmetic text book at a flea market. The book was *Ray's Practical Arithmetic* and from it I began to learn how to clearly articulate directions for the operations. For example, to subtract, first write the number of smaller value under the number of greater value placing figures of the same order in a column. Students are usually taught this procedure by example. They cannot explain it nor has it been explained to them. They have no vocabulary by which to express it verbally. Therefore, the character of one who is able to understand and to communicate is not being developed in them.

Mr. Rose and Mrs. Smith then began encouraging me to produce a "Guide to Teaching Arithmetic." The summer of 1984 was spent writing, and a first draft was sent off to Mr. Rose. When it came back with editorial suggestions, I realized that a great deal more research and analysis was needed, so I continued to work. The present *Guide* is the result of that second effort.

This "Guide to Teaching Arithmetic" represents a small effort to restore American Christian Liberty. If our nation or any nation is to live in liberty, the rudiments of every subject of study must be identified and the contribution of that study to the history of liberty appreciated. The minds of the children must be convinced, their hearts inspired, and their character formed. By the grace of God, let us gladly pursue the hope that He has set before us, and, as we labor, trust that we shall see the Salvation of our God.

ELEMENTARY AND HIGH SCHOOL CURRICULUM

GEOGRAPHY
AN AMERICAN CHRISTIAN APPROACH
BY KATHERINE DANG

•

RUDIMENTS OF AMERICA'S CHRISTIAN HISTORY AND GOVERNMENT – STUDENT HANDBOOK
BY BETH BALLENGER, KATHERINE DANG, & JAMES B. ROSE

•

SENIOR HIGH SCHOOL AMERICAN HISTORY
BY KATHERINE DANG

•

THE CHRISTIAN HISTORY LITERATURE PROGRAM
BY ROSALIE JUNE SLATER

•

THE PRINCIPLE APPROACH TO
AMERICAN CHRISTIAN ECONOMICS
BY CHARLES HULL WOLFE

•

ALGEBRA
FROM THE PRINCIPLE APPROACH
BY DAROLD BOOTON

•

AMERICAN CHRISTIAN APPROACH TO
NATURAL SCIENCE AND HUMAN ANATOMY / PHYSIOLOGY
BY DAVID HOLMES

•

TYPING
BY BARBARA ROSE

GEOGRAPHY
AN AMERICAN CHRISTIAN APPROACH

BY KATHERINE DANG

Administrative Director
Chinese Christian Schools
San Leandro, California

CONTENTS

AN AMERICAN CHRISTIAN APPROACH TO TEACHING AND LEARNING GEOGRAPHY

As an American Christian alternative to the atheistic philosophy and subject of Social Studies, the following distinctives, goals, overview and lesson are offered. These have been constructed from a study of the Bible and *Physical Geography* by Arnold Guyot, Swiss-born Christian scholar and Geographer, 1807-1884.[1]

Teaching the course requires independent study by the instructor, and permits his individual expression of the truths within the subject. Truth discovered through original scholarship will supplant all the familiarly secular, or pagan, presumptions concerning Geography.

DEFINITIONS AND DISTINCTIONS

Geography: A description of the earth or terrestrial globe, particularly of the divisions of its surface, natural and artificial, and of the positions of the several countries, kingdoms, states, cities, etc.

As a science, geography includes the doctrine or knowledge of the astronomical circles or divisions of the sphere, by which the relative position of places on the globe may be ascertained, and usually treatises of geography contain some account of the inhabitants of the earth, of their government, manners, etc., and an account of the principal animals, plants, and minerals. (Noah Webster, 1828 *American Dictionary of the English Language*)

Christian Geography: The view that the earth's origins, ends and purposes are of Christ and are for His glory.

American Christian Geography: The knowledge of geography as it pertains to the individual's proper relation to, and government of, material property with regard to God's will on earth.

"Thy will be done on earth as it is in heaven." — *Luke 11*

COURSE GOALS

1. To begin, a careful study of physical geography or the "Geography of Nature," leading to the

---

1. Arnold Guyot, *Physical Geography*, 1872. Reprint available from American Christian History Institute, 1093 Beechwood Street, Camarillo, CA. 93010; $8.00 includes shipping. See also excerpts from *CHOC*, pp. 3-5, 436; *T/L*, pp. 142-153, 156-157.

conclusion that "the great geographical constituents of our planet – the solid land, the ocean and the atmosphere – are mutually dependent and connected by incessant action and reaction upon one another; and hence that the Earth is really a wonderful mechanism in all parts of which work together harmoniously to accomplish the purpose assigned to it by an All-Wise Creator." (Arnold Guyot, 1872. See *Christian History*, p. 5)

2. To promote a view of the Earth as "the abode of Man, the scene of his activity, and the means of his moral development"; to view the Earth as the "theatre of human societies," with a recognition that the Geography of Nature is significantly linked to the Geography of Man – a relationship which is foundational to the study of history. (See *Teaching and Learning*, pp. 142, 144)

3. To prepare students for comprehending America's Christian history and government by laying a foundation of Christian geography – the Hand of God in the affairs of men and nations through His geographic creation.

4. To enlighten students with the geography of their own state, county, and city, in order to accept their stewardship to properly govern each sphere.

5. To introduce and develop techniques of map work and to teach the drawing of forms of continents, nations, and states and their physical features.

THE BIBLICAL PURPOSE FOR TEACHING AND LEARNING GEOGRAPHY

"And God said, Let us make man in our image, after our likeness; and let them have dominion over the fowl of the air, and over the cattle; and over all the earth, and over every creeping thing that creepeth upon the earth." *Genesis 1:26*

God made earth for man. Hence, the primary, practical subjects of geography are the study of earth and the study of earth in relationship to man. Before man can rule *in* nature and *over* nature, he must be enlightened in the laws which govern nature, and he must understand the causes of all phenomena belonging to nature. Man has a need to comprehend earth in its universal setting as well as the primary global relationships existing between its integral parts – both of the physical and political aspects of earth. Man is in dominion when he is possessing, exercising, and administering the prescribed, predetermined and preexisting laws God ordained for governing the physical and political aspects of earth.

It has been Biblical scholarship alone that enabled individuals to advance man's knowledge in all of the arts and science. As students are equipped with the rudiments of physical and political geography, then is each prepared to maintain and advance the dominion God intends him to have upon earth. The purpose for studying geography is not for any establishment of a utopia, but rather for the ascertaining of the nature of God, the Creator, and the discovering of His laws so that men may obey those laws.

"And hath made of one blood all nations of men to dwell on all the face of the earth, and hath determined the times before appointed, and the bounds of their habitation.
"That they should seek the Lord, if haply they might feel after him, and find him, though he is not far from every one of us;
"For in Him we live, and move, and have our being..." – *Acts 17:26-28*

As God created earth for man's dominion and enjoyment, so is man made for God's good pleasure. Those things pertaining to earth and man stem directly from those things which pertain to God's relationship with individual men and nations. Adam and Eve were removed from the perfect habitation of the Garden of Eden and turned over to an accursed earth when they first removed themselves from God's law and surrendered themselves to the law of sin and disobedience. History reveals how nations are blessed, or cursed, according to their adherence, or inadherence, to divine law.

The subject of geography is fundamental to the wisdom individuals must exercise in order to accomplish God's purpose for them upon earth.

"Thy will be done in earth as it is in heaven..." *Matthew 6:10*

COURSE OVERVIEW

As all subjects taught from the Principle Approach, geography should be taught wholistically. That is, the completeness of the subject is presented regardless of the level at which it may be taught, whether to kindergarten children or to college and university students. The content of such a geography curriculum is perceived as consisting of what Guyot defines as the *Geography of Nature* and the *Geography of Man*. Within each of these two major studies are found four basic divisions of study. A year's overview of geography would be as follows:

The year's overview is further expanded into a

THE GEOGRAPHY OF NATURE
(First Semester)

The Earth	The Constituents of the Globe	Organic Life	Provisions Providence
• in the Universe • in the Solar System • the Terrestrial Globe	• land • water • atmosphere	• vegetable • animal	• food, raiment, shelter • metals, minerals and gems

THE GEOGRAPHY OF MAN
(Second Semester)

The Human Family	The Continents of Nature	The Continents of History	State Geography
• races • cultures	• Australia • Africa • South America	• Asia • Europe • North America	• physical structure • products • industry and commerce • civil government

general curriculum outline for intensive daily instruction on the junior or senior high school level. Do not be overwhelmed by the minutia of detail in the outline that follows. Always start with the overall philosophy, the rudiments of the particular subject matter or topic, and the simplest lessons, then amplify the subject as the time and understanding of the teacher and student permit.

CURRICULUM OUTLINE
See Charts on Pages 269 and 270

I. Introduction: The Nature of Geography
   A. by definition
      1. science of the globe or the general existence of the present life of the globe
      2. study of the mutual exchanges of the forces of nature
      3. study of the interchanges of different portions of physical nature upon organized beings, upon man in particular, and upon the successive development of human societies
   B. subject of
      1. the Earth – as a unique, an individual organization with a definite structure and with a definite purpose
      2. the three geographical elements of the globe and their characteristics:
         a. land
         b. water
         c. atmosphere
      3. the character of organic life supported by the globe
      4. the mutual relations between the globe and organic life
   C. the Earth is studied from two points of view
      1. the Earth itself – as a masterpiece of Divine Workmanship, perfect in all its parts and conditions; this is called the Geography of Nature
      2. the Earth's purpose – as the dwelling place of man, the scene or setting of his activity, and the means of man's moral development
   D. the Geography of Nature
      1. physiography – simple description of the surface of the globe
         a. the extent and character of the land
         b. the distribution and extent of waters
         c. climate and productions in different parts of the Earth
      2. physical geography
         a. describes Nature
         b. discovers the laws which govern Nature and investigates the relations between them, with causes and consequences noted
      3. conclusions drawn from a study of the Geography of Nature
         a. that our planet with the land, ocean, and atmosphere are mutually depen-

dent and connected by continual and unceasing action and reaction upon one another
  b. that the Earth is a wonderful mechanism, all parts working harmoniously to accomplish the purpose designed to it by an All-Wise Creator
  c. that the harmony and peace of the Laws of Nature is God's text for human government
E. the Geography of Man
  1. the Continents of Nature in the education of mankind
    a. Australia
    b. Africa
    c. South America
  2. the Continents of History, forms and functions
    a. Asia
    b. Europe
    c. North America

II. The Earth
  A. the Earth in Scripture (*Nave's Topical Index*)
  B. the Earth in the Universe
    1. the Universe (*Webster,* 1828)
    2. the heavens
      a. by definition (*Webster,* 1828)
      b. creation of the physical heavens as recorded in Scripture
      c. as revelation of God
      d. the Earth in the heavens, *Job* 16:7
      e. the contents of the heavens
        i. heavenly bodies
        ii. solar system – sun, planets, and comets
        iii. fixed stars
      f. magnitude of the heavens
  C. the Earth in the solar system
    1. bodies composing the solar system
      a. sun
      b. planets
      c. satellites
      d. distances of planets from the sun
    2. movements within the solar system
      a. rotary motion
      b. revolutionary motion
    3. planetary orbits
      a. perihelion
      b. aphelion
      c. conclusion: the Earth's orbit moderates the cold of winter and the heat of summer in the most populous zone of the globe
    4. solstices and equinoxes

  5. advantages in the conditions of the Earth in the solar system
    a. conditions are intermediate between extreme heat and extreme cold
    b. a slightly elliptical orbit
    c. largest of the smaller planets
    d. conclusion: the Earth is better fitted than any other member of the solar system for sustaining organic life: vegetable, animal, and human.
  D. the Terrestrial Globe
    1. form of the Earth
    2. dimensions of the Earth
    3. geographic circles
      a. great circles – equator, and meridians
      b. small circles – parallels
    4. climatic circles
      a. tropics
      b. polars
    5. surface measurements
      a. latitude
      b. longitude
      c. Prime Meridian
      d. the relationships between longitude and time
    6. time on the globe
    7. temperatures of the globe
      a. evidences of internal heat
        i. thermal or warm springs
        ii. Artesian wells and mines
        iii. active volcanoes
        iv. conclusion: at some place within the Earth, there exists enough heat to melt solid rock.
      b. results of internal heat – volcanic phenomena
        i. nature and formation of volcanoes
        ii. volcanic products
        iii. height of volcanoes
        iv. amount of matter ejected
        v. stages of volcanic activity
        vi. position of volcanoes on the globe
    8. earthquakes
      a. defined
      b. earthquakes in Scripture (*Nave's Topical Index*)
        i. sources and origin
        ii. secondary causes of earthquakes, internal, physical pressure
        iii. prophecies of earthquakes
        iv. instances of earthquakes in the Bible
      c. three kinds of earthquake movements
        i. wave-like motion
        ii. vertical motion
        iii. rotary motion or whirling motion

d. velocity of earthquakes – 23 or 32 miles per minute

e. duration of earthquakes

f. distribution of earthquakes on the globe

III. The Three Great Geographical Elements of the Globe – Unity with diversity.

A. the land

1. land masses on the globe

a. proportion of land to water on the globe – 27:72

b. division of lands upon the globe

c. position of land masses on the globe

d. zone of fracture

2. grand terrestrial contrasts

a. northern and southern worlds

i. northern continents and their positions on the globe

ii. southern continents and their positions on the globe

b. eastern and western worlds – three pairs of continents

i. Asia and Australia

ii. Europe and Africa

iii. North America and South America

c. continental and oceanic worlds

i. northeastern hemisphere

ii. southwestern hemisphere

d. relative areas and positions of land masses

3. the horizontal forms of the continents

a. the horizontal form – the surface aspect

i. the peculiar figure of the continents

ii. the peculiar outline of the continents, following the contact of land with water

b. the peculiar continental outlines

i. the most highly civilized nations are from well-articulated continents

ii. continents with little articulation have played less a part in human history

c. the peculiar figures of the continents

i. a common fundamental figure – every continent has a figure more or less triangular

ii. a common law of structure is indicated

4. the vertical forms of continents

a. the vertical form – the solid aspect of the continents

i. general relief

ii. altitude

b. the importance of a study of relief forms

i. altitude affects climate and organic life of a continent

ii. altitude controls the drainage of the continent

iii. altitude influences the character of winds and their direction

iv. altitude influences the distribution of rain in a continent

c. the forms of relief

i. plains: alluvial, undulating, marine

ii. plateaus

iii. mountains: mountain peak, chains, systems and zones; mountains by folding and mountains by fracture

iv. valleys: longitudinal and transverse

5. islands

6. general laws of continental relief (see p. 270)

a. *the typical structure of continents:* a primary highland region upon one side, a secondary one on the opposite side, trending towards the primary, and a depression between the two.

b. *contrasting plans in the Old and New Worlds:* in the New World the north-south direction prevails alone: all the great lines of elevation extending in that direction. In the Old World the east-west direction predominates, but is repeatedly intersected by the other.

c. *the continental reliefs as a whole:* begin with vast low plains about the Arctic Circle, and increase in altitude towards the equatorial regions.

d. *dominant form of relief:* in general, each continent has one dominant form of relief, which gives it a special character, exerting a powerful influence upon its climate, and upon its functions both in nature and in human history.

i. the Americas – continents of low plains and fertile basins

ii. Africa – continent of plateaus, inferior in moisture, superior in temperature and development of animal life

iii. Europe – continent of mountains

iv. Asia – the fullest type of all the others; all the forms of relief on the grandest scale, in nearly equal proportions and in great variety of combinations: plains in the north and west, plateaus in the center, and mountains in the south

  e. *summary:* all the long, gentle slopes descend toward the Atlantic Ocean and its prolongation, the Arctic; while all the short and rapid slopes are directed towards the Pacific, and its dependent, the Indian Ocean, the highest lands being adjacent to the shores of the greatest oceans.

B. the water
  1. the second great geographical element of the globe
    a. function of water on the globe
      i. disintegrates and rearranges the materials of the Earth's crust
      ii. the main agent in shaping solid land
      iii. carries on the processes of vegetable and animal life; it forms the larger part of all organized bodies.
    b. nature and character of water
    c. the sea – the great reservoir of terrestrial waters
    d. the diverse conditions of terrestrial waters
      i. oceanic
      ii. continental
      iii. atmospheric
  2. oceanic waters
    a. ocean basins – forms and positions
      i. Pacific
      ii. Atlantic
      iii. Indian
      iv. others: Arctic and Antarctic
    b. branches of ocean basins or coast waters
      i. inland seas
      ii. border seas
      iii. gulfs and bays
    c. movements of oceanic waters
      i. waves
      ii. tides
      iii. currents
    d. temperature of ocean waters
    e. marine life
    f. the bottom of the sea – convex as the surface
    g. islands of the oceans
      i. Pacific islands
      ii. Atlantic islands
      iii. Indian islands
    h. conclusions:
      i. the three great ocean basins of the globe possess marked identities and diversities in sizes and forms, branches, islands, expressing distinct plans and purposes
      ii. the union of the three diverse oceans on the whole globe help facilitate man's movement from east to west – the three having one overall purpose
      iii. the identities of ocean movements are caused by the action and reaction of particular natural forces upon one another.
  3. continental waters
    a. rivers
      i. sources – springs form the source of most rivers
      ii. formation of river systems
      iii. the amount of water transported by streams dependent upon two factors: the amount of rainfall upon the area drained and the rate of evaporation in proportion to rainfall throughout the basin
      iv. three agencies served by rivers: active and powerful forces of erosion, reconstruction and general levelling
    b. rapids and cataracts and falls
    c. lakes
      i. mountain lakes
      ii. lakes in plains
      iii. reservoirs
      iv. salt lakes
C. the atmosphere
  1. the atmosphere – the vast ocean of air at the bottom of which we live, enveloping both land and water of the globe
  2. purpose
    a. absorbs heat and vapors caused by the action of the sun upon the surface of land and water
    b. through winds, carries invisible moisture and fertilizing rains from the sea to parched lands on the continents
  3. physical characteristics
    a. composition
    b. elasticity
    c. weight
    d. density
  4. the relation of atmosphere to organic life
    a. the right proportions of heat, oxygen, watery vapor are requisite for vitality and development
    b. the atmosphere is the universal medi-

ator between land and sea, organic
and inorganic life
5. winds
  a. definition: winds are air currents
  b. physical characteristic: invisible and
    intangible, *John* 3:8.
  c. source of wind, *Jonah* 4:8
  d. production of winds
    i. when the air over any place is
      more heated than that around, it is
      expanded and rises
    ii. the surrounding air rushes in to
      take its place
    iii. whirlwinds
  f. velocity of winds
  g. quality of winds are affected and
    determined by the lands over which
    they pass: pestilential winds
  h. purpose for winds
    i. necessary to purify the atmosphere
    ii. raise and transport clouds from
      seas to fertilize the land
    iii. serve to convey man over the
      ocean, as the highway of the globe
    iv. encourages the westward move-
      ment of man
6. rain
  a. spontaneous evaporation is continu-
    ally produced by the sun and air from
    the waters of the ocean and land
    i. evaporation
    ii. fog
    iii. clouds
  b. rain, snow and hail – the falling of
    accumulated water vapors in clouds
    returning, through rivers, to the ocean
    i. rain in Scripture
    ii. hail in Scripture
    iii. snow in Scripture
  c. height of clouds
  d. quantity of rain
  e. thunderstorms
7. temperature of the atmosphere and the
  climatic regions of the globe

IV. The Character of Organic Life Supported by
the Globe
  A. vegetation, refer to Scriptures
    1. species most important are those which
      furnish food for men and animals
      a. grains
      b. fruits
      c. roots
      d. grasses
    2. species used for clothing of men
      a. flax

      b. hemp
      c. cotton
    3. each grand division of the world has
      many peculiar vegetables which are na-
      tive to it; the geographical situation of
      vegetation depends upon temeprature,
      moisture, and soil of countries (at-
      mospheric, water, and land conditions)
    4. vegetation of polar, frozen and cold
      regions of the globe
    5. vegetation of temperate, and warm
      regions
    6. vegetation of the tropical and equatorial
      regions
  B. animal life, refer to Scriptures
    1. variety of forms, size, strengths, uses
      revelational of God's wisdom and good-
      ness, providing animals adapted to every
      climate and soil
    2. domestic animals
      a. supply man with milk and milk
        products
      b. feed man with flesh
      c. clothe man with skins, wool, and hair
    3. situation of animals regulated by climate
      and soil: each climatic zone is marked by
      residence of animals special to it
      a. *Torrid Zone* – remarkable luxuriance
        in animal as well as plant life, with the
        largest and most beautiful, fiercest
        and most dangerous animals upon the
        globe
        i. elephant
        ii. rhinoceros
        iii. lion
        iv. tiger
        v. panther
        vi. leopard
        vii. hyena
        viii. jaguar
        ix. puma
        x. tapir
        xi. boa constrictor
        xii. asp
        xiii. vampire
        xiv. tarantula
        xv. scorpion
        xvi. termites
        xvii. peacock
        xviii. ostrich
        xix. orangutan
      b. some animals subsist in almost all lati-
        tudes where cultivation is practicable
        i. the most useful domestic animals:
          ox, horse, swine
        ii. sheep

iii. dog
iv. cat
v. goat
vi. fox
vii. hare
viii. bear
ix. squirrel
x. rat
xi. mouse
xii. weasel
 c. the temperature of the ocean is so uniform, that the various tribes of fish distribute themselves through all latitudes more readily and extensively than land animals
 d. birds migrate from temperate zones during winter to the warm region
 e. tropical seas
  i. fish shine with brilliant colors
  ii. flying fish
  iii. shark
  iv. shell-fish
  v. oyster
  vi. forests of red coral

C. provisions for human life and social progress
 1. minerals
 2. metals
 3. forests

D. the human family: character and nature of the three stock races
 1. Hamitic
 2. Semitic
 3. Japhetic

V. The Continents of Nature
 A. Australia, the Continent of Antiquity
  1. general character
   a. the only subtropical continent
   b. the smallest continent
   c. the most isolated continent
   d. the only continent which preserves ancient forms of plants and animals
  2. physical structure
   a. general plan
    i. greatly resembles Southern Africa in its general plan of structure
    ii. differs from Southern Africa in that it consists mainly of low plains and the surface of the northern portion being generally the more elevated
   b. primary highlands – the Great Dividing Range
   c. secondary highlands
    i. Darling Range
    ii. Hamersley Range
    iii. western plateaus
   c. central depression – a great plain and deserts
  3. climate
  4. vegetation unique to Australia
  5. animals unique to Australia
  6. people
   a. physical character
   b. spiritual character of natives
    i. no dominion over creation or their environment because they have no dominion over their own darkness and their own natures
    ii. exist as animals
    iii. natural resources not harnassed and mastered for his benefit
    iv. conclusion: example of man fallen afar from God

 B. Africa, the Continent of Animal Life
  1. physical geography
   a. structure – characterized by a combination of the plan of the Old World (Asia-Europe) with that of the New World (North America and South America)
    i. North Africa
    ii. South Africa
   b. rivers
   c. lakes
  2. climate, vegetation and animal life
   a. climate – hottest and driest of all the continents
   b. animal life
   c. people
    i. native country of Negroes – occupying nearly all the continent south of the Sahara
    ii. Caucasians occupy lands north of the Sahara and along the Mediterranean coasts

 C. South America, the Continent of Vegetation
  1. physical structure
   a. primary highlands – the Andes Mountains
   b. secondary highlands
    i. Brazilian highlands
    ii. Guiana highlands
   c. central depression – one vast alluvial plain
  2. rivers
   a. Amazon River System
   b. Parana-Paraguay System
   c. Orinoco River System
  3. climate – because the larger part of

South America is near the Equator,
South America is a very warm continent
4. vegetation and animals
  a. because it is so warm and moist,
     South America has more luxuriant
     vegetation than any other continent
     on the globe
       i. tropical rainforests
       ii. llanos
       iii. pampas
       iv. Andes slopes
  b. cultivated lands and crops
       i. warm regions – along the coasts
          and in the high valleys of the An-
          des, inhabited by Caucasians
       ii. cool regions – southern countries
          and valleys of the Andes
5. native people
  a. race – Mongoloid, Indians
  b. character
       i. savages
       ii. feed mainly on fruits of forests and
          fish from streams

VI. The Continents of History
  A. Asia
    1. physical character
      a. largest continent and most centrally
         located
      b. irregular coastline of 33,000 miles
      c. 17,000,000 square miles, 1/11 of
         Earth's surface
      d. one enormous triangle
    2. the double-continent, Asia-Europe
      a. natural separation – Ural Mountains,
         Caspian and Black Seas
      b. common features
         i. primary and secondary features
            extend east to west
         ii. secondary feature near the center
            of the continent
         iii. highlands include several separate
            mountain systems and plateaus
         iv. central depressions are chiefly
            plateaus and small compared with
            the great plains between the sec-
            ondary feature and the sea
    3. Asia's two parts
      a. Eastern Asia
      b. Western Asia
    4. rivers and lakes
    5. climate and vegetation
      a. climate controlled by mountains shut
         out tropic winds in the north
      b. winds control the plains and deserts,
         east of the Caspian Sea

c. mountains and winds are responsible
   for the uneven distribution of moisture in Asia
    6. vegetation
    7. animal life – rich and varied
    8. people
      a. Caucasoid
      b. Mongoloid
  B. Europe
    1. characteristic structure
      a. smallest continent
      b. extreme irregularity, penetrated
         extensively by the sea
      c. primary highlands
         i. Alps
         ii. Balkans
         iii. Pyrenees
         iv. Cantabrian
      d. secondary highlands – divides High
         from Low Europe
         i. Carpathian
         ii. Sudetic
         iii. Riesen
         iv. low ranges to shores of the North
            Sea
      e. central depressions
         i. low plateaus, mountain ranges and
            small plains
         ii. small enclosed basins peculiarly
            characteristic of Central Europe
    2. contrasting divisions
      a. high Europe
      b. low Europe
         i. Scandinavian peninsula
         ii. British Isles
    3. rivers and lakes
    4. climate – temperate
    5. vegetation and animal life
    6. people – Aryan, Germanic, Frankish,
       and Anglo-Saxon
  C. North America, the fullest Expression of a
     Christian Civilization
    1. the New World as a whole
      a. shows a unity of structure, one com-
         mon plan
      b. in each America, the main axis
         extends unbroken through the entire
         length of the continent
         i. primary axis lies near the western
            shores
         ii. secondary axis lies near the east-
            ern shores
         iii. vast low plains occupy the interior
      c. diversity in
         i. details of structure
         ii. climate

      iii. purpose
   2. physical structure of North America
     a. primary highland – Pacific Highlands
       i. Cascades
       ii. Sierra Nevadas
       iii. Rocky Mountains
     b. secondary highland – Atlantic
       Highlands
       i. Piedmont Plateau – Great Smokey
         Mountains
       ii. Allegheny – Appalachian
         Mountains
       iii. Blue Ridge
       iv. Green Mountains
       v. White Mountains
       vi. Plateau of Labrador
     c. central depression – Great Central
       Plain
       i. MacKenzie-Hudson Bay
       ii. St. Lawrence – Mississippi
       iii. easy pathways from the sea to
         nearly all valuable parts of the in-
         terior of the continent
     d. largest fresh water lakes on the globe
   4. climate, vegetation and animal life
   5. historical purpose and function
     a. provision made everywhere for mu-
       tual exchange and intercourse into a
       common life, a uniting of one entire
       population
     b. not designed to give birth to a new
       civilization but to receive one, ready
       made
     c. encouraged expansion throughout its
       territory and fusion into one nation
     d. invites the Indo-European race to
       new fields of activities

VII. The forms of the States of America – identified
and drawn
   A. New England
   B. Mid-Atlantic
   C. South Atlantic
   D. Gulf States
   E. Central States
   F. Pacific States
   G. Alaska
   H. Hawaii

VIII. Physical Geography of the Student's Home
State

PREPARING A GEOGRAPHY LESSON

Individual lessons are drawn from the Curriculum Outline. The details and depth of the individual lessons are dependent upon the particular
capacity of the teacher to reason with his students.
Each lesson ought to be clear and useful and make
conclusive statements or point out truths relative
to the subject or topic discussed. Each lesson is
foundational to future lessons.

Consider the diagram on p. 273, *The Three
Constituents of the Globe*, as one example and explanation of how to construct an introductory lesson to the rudiments of geography.

EXPLANATION OF SAMPLE LESSON

Geography, taught at the simplest level,
requires no more than eight lessons a year, two
each quarter, without having to sacrifice any
essential part of the whole of Geography. For, at
least the rudiments of the eight given subdivisions
will have been introduced. The teacher is at
liberty to repeat, review in whole, or in part, amplify or modify, illustrate, and make assignments,
or give exercises, from each lesson he has laid
down, as frequently as necessary.

Any helps toward student comprehension and
mastery of the lessons by way of supplementary
materials from art, photography, literature, texts,
periodicals, classroom activities, and class excur-
sions, ought to be researched and used. The
teacher seeks to enable his students to make intelligent use of what they are taught. Regardless of
age, or grade level, the teacher endeavors to meet
the students where they are relative to their reasoning capacity, and, then, to lead them step by
step to higher levels of thought and reflection, to
thus increase their capacity to reason.

CONCLUSIONS AND APPLICATIONS FROM
THE INTRODUCTORY LESSON PLAN

The sample lesson on page 269 suggests how a
lesson that introduces the second subdivision of *The
Geography of Nature*, specifically "The Constituents
of the Globe," might be studied and presented.
The following conclusions and applications may be
drawn from the introductory lesson:

I

Genesis 1:1-2: The first mention of land, water,
and atmosphere in the Scriptures is found in the
first two verses of Genesis. The origin and im-
mediacy of their place in Scripture causes reflection upon their primary and essential significance
in God's overall plan for earth. Land, water, and
atmosphere are the vital elements of the physical
nature of earth.

COURSE OUTLINE

I. THE GEOGRAPHY OF NATURE

"The study of the earth itself as a masterpiece of Divine workmanship, perfect in all its parts and conditions." – *Arnold Guyot*

A. THE EARTH AS A WHOLE	B. THE THREE GREAT CONSTITUENTS OF THE GLOBE	C. THE CHARACTER OF ORGANIC LIFE SUPPORTED BY THE GLOBE	D. THE PROVISIONS FOR HUMAN LIFE AND SOCIAL PROGRESS

1. The earth in the universe
2. The earth in the solar system
3. The terrestrial globe:
  a. geographic circles
  b. latitude and longitude
  c. time meridians
  d. volcanoes
  e. earthquakes
	1. Land – Continents & Islands
	  a. landmasses as a whole
	    • two groups of continents
	    • three pairs of continents
	  b. horizontal relief
	    • length of coastlines
	    • peninsulas
	  c. vertical relief
	    • plains
	    • plateaus
	    • mountains
	    • valleys
	  d. typical structure of
	    continents
	  e. islands
	    • continental
	    • oceanic
	
	2. Water
	  a. properties of water
	  b. continental waters
	    • rivers
	    • lakes
	    • reservoirs
	    • cataracts and waterfalls
	  c. oceanic waters
	    • ocean basins
	    • coast waters
	    • movements of
	
	3. Atmosphere
	  a. physical properties
	  b. function of the earth's
	    atmosphere
	  c. relationship to organic life
	    of the earth
	  d. evaporation and
	    precipitation
	  e. winds
	  f. temperature and climate
		1. Vegetable life
		  a. in the different climatic
		    latitudes
		  b. in the different altitudes
		  c. in the Northern
		    Continents
		  d. in the Southern
		    Continents
		2. Animal life
		  a. in the Northern
		    Continents
		  b. in the Southern
		    Continents
			1. Food, raiment, and shelter
			2. Minerals employed in the arts
			3. Occupations of man
			  a. agriculture
			  b. grazing
			  c. lumbering
			  d. mining
			  e. lapidary
			  f. manufacturing, commerce
			    and trade

II. THE GEOGRAPHY OF MAN

"The earth as the dwelling place of man, the scene of man's activities, and the means of his moral development." – *Arnold Guyot*

A. THE HUMAN FAMILY	B. PHYSICAL STRUCTURE AND INDIVIDUALITY OF THE SOUTHERN CONTINENTS	C. PHYSICAL STRUCTURE AND INDIVIDUALITY OF THE NORTHERN CONTINENTS	D. STATE GEOGRAPHY

1. Races of mankind
  a. Hamitic
  b. Semitic
  c. Japhetic
2. Nations of man
  a. monarchies
  b. republics
3. Unity and diversity of
  cultures
	1. Australia, the "Continent of
	  Antiquity."
	2. Africa, the "Continent of
	  Animal Life."
	3. South America, the "Con-
	  tinent of Vegetation."
		1. Asia, the "Continent of
		  Origins."
		2. Europe, the "Continent of
		  Christian Development."
		3. North America, the "Fullest
		  Expression of a Christian
		  Civilization" – Christian
		  Civil Government
			1. Physical structure
			2. Products of the soil
			3. Arts and manufactures
			4. Industry, commerce and trade
			5. Major cities and counties
			6. Local self-government
			  a. towns
			  b. cities
			  c. counties
			  d. state

COURSE OUTLINE
THE TYPICAL STRUCTURE OF CONTINENTS

CONTINENT	PRIMARY HIGHLAND	CENTRAL DEPRESSION	SECONDARY HIGHLAND
Australia, the Continent of Antiquity	Great Dividing Range	Great Sandy Desert Great Victoria Desert Gibson Desert	Hamersley Range Darling Range Leopold Range
Africa, the Continent of Animal Life: *South Africa*	Drakensberg Mountains Ethiopian Plateau	Congo Basin Plateau Region	Camerouns
Africa, the Continent of Animal Life: *North Africa*	Atlas Mountains	Sahara Desert	Kong Mountains
South America, the Continent of Vegetation	Andes Mountains	Llanos La Plata Gran Chaco Pampas Selvas Patagonia	Guiana Highlands Brazilian Highlands
Asia, the Continent of Origins	Himalayas Thian Shan Kun Lun Hindu Kush	Siberian Plains Kirghiz Steppes	Altai Mountains Great Khinghan Mountains
Europe, the Continent of Development	Caucasus Carpathian Balkans Alps Dinaric Cantabrian Apennines Pyrenees	European Plains	Scandinavian Highlands Ural Mountains
North America, the Continent of "the Fullest Expression of a Christian Civilization"	Rocky Mountains Cascades Sierra Nevadas	Great Central Plain	Plateau of Labrador Appalachian Mountains

II

Leading Idea: One or more leading ideas control any given lesson. Following tangents or distractions away from leading ideas permit confusion to overthrow and undermine the lesson. Notes given to students on the chalkboard, whether in the form of outlines, charts or diagrams, need to be free from the clutter of extraneous verbiage and put on the chalkboard with order and logical progression of thought. Notes are the practical demonstrations of good reasoning.

III

The First Principles of Land, Water and Atmosphere: The sample lesson deals with land, water and atmosphere at the most basic level. The first principles, or rudiments, of each constituent of the globe may be deduced from the definitions of heaven, earth and water given in Webster's 1828 *American Dictionary of the English Language.*

More important than copying the definition verbatim as notes, is that the student record and comprehend *heaven* as: 1) a region of space, 2) above and around us, 3) where the sun, moon and stars appear to us, 4) embodying air, the most necessary for human life, in the aerial heaven, the lowest of the three heavens revealed to us in the Scriptures. In the same manner of deduction, *earth* is made known as: 1) dry- 2) solid- and 3) fixed part of the globe. Points deduced as pertaining to *water* may be: 1) a fluid, 2) the most abundant of fluids on earth, 3) excepting air, the most necessary for living beings, 4) stored in the earth in inexhaustible quantities, 5) springs, streams and rivers bring to the surface water from within the earth, 6) Three-fifths of the globe's surface is covered with oceanic waters, and 7) evaporation and precipitation bring water into the atmosphere and onto the land.

Further inferences could naturally be drawn from these primary ones. They are to be documented as original notes or points to be made for the students as needed, at another time, in a review lesson, or with an assignment or exercise.

Divisions: Land, water, and atmosphere each have their own particular divisions of study for which other lessons may be constructed. The more detailed and in depth the study of a topic, the greater will be the number of individual lessons required to make the study complete. The teacher is essentially in control of the curriculum he chooses to teach.

For example, an introductory lesson on the four divisions of the earth's atmosphere would deal with the main distinctions between, and individual characteristics of, each of the layers of the atmosphere, from troposphere to ionosphere. A teacher may choose, then, to proceed with four more separate lessons, one for each of the four atmospheric layers.

IV

"And God made the firmament, and divided the waters which were under the firmament from the waters which were above the firmament: and it was so.

"And God called the firmament Heaven. And the evening and the morning were the second day.

"And God said, Let the waters under the heaven be gathered together under one place, and let the dry land appear: and it was so.

"And God called the dry land Earth; and the gathering together of the waters called he Seas: and God saw that it was good." *Genesis 1:7-10*

"The great geographical constituents of our planet – the solid land, the ocean, and the atmosphere – are mutually dependent and connected by incessant action and reaction upon one another; and hence, that the Earth is really a wonderful mechanism, all parts of which work together harmoniously to accomplish the purpose assigned to it by an All-wise Creator." Arnold Guyot, *Physical Geography:* p. 2

In the process of making conclusions and applications, Biblical inferences relative to functions and purposes with regard to land, water, and atmosphere are documented. Arnold Guyot's observation and statement concerning the mutuality of forces and influences of each upon the other is validated by Revelation as recorded in *Genesis 1:7-10*

V

"*Of rain and evaporation.* The manner in which the earth is watered, and by which water is exhaled for the purpose of being diffused over the earth, furnishes us with *striking proof of Divine wisdom and goodness.* Rain is produced by collections of vapor in the air, and falling in small drops, supplies the food of plants without injuring them

by force in falling. Rain proceeds from clouds which obscure the sun, but as the light of the sun is necessary to mature plants which are the principal food of man, it is the order of Providence that a small portion of time is required to supply the water requisite to promote vegetation. On the other hand water is exhaled from the ocean, from rivers, coldness and land in fine, invisible, imperceptible particles in clear weather so that agricultural labors are not interrupted; and while the farmer is plowing his field, making his hay or reaping his grain, evaporation is raising water into the atmosphere to furnish new supplies for distribution over the earth." Noah Webster

An *American Christian perspective* of Geography, of which Noah Webster's discussion, "of rain and evaporation," is an example, comprehends and relates God's Providence in the subject of geography, or the Hand of God in the affairs of earth and man. Webster discloses not only how a knowledge of geography "furnishes us with striking proof of Divine wisdom and goodness," but suggests the American Christian idea of the *individual's responsibility* to take dominion over the property of his time, labor and land in relation to God's Kingdom on earth.

VI

"The heaven, even the heavens, are the Lord's, but the earth hath he given to the children of men." *Psalm 115:16*

"For thus saith the Lord who created the heavens, God himself who formed the earth and made it; he hath established it, he created it not in vain, he formed it to be inhabited; I am the Lord, and there is none else." *Isaiah 45:18*

The Scriptures in *Psalm 115:16* and *Isaiah 45:18* are among others which confirm the fact of *design* and *purpose* concerning the globe and its three constituents.

VII

"And Moses stretched out his hand over the sea; and the Lord caused the sea to go back by a strong east wind all that night, and made the sea dry land, and the waters were divided." *Exodus 14:21*

"But the Lord sent out a great wind into the sea, and there was a mighty tempest in the sea, so that the ship was like to be broken." *Jonah 1:4*

Further reflection upon the Scriptures reveals

the action and interaction of land, water, and atmosphere originating in the Mind of God and controlled by the power of God for the sake of men and nations.

To make the best conclusions and applications which are relevant to the topic under discussion, it is necessary to return to and think upon the Biblical purposes and themes which are to govern the entire course overview.

Lessons which are concise, coherent, and complete are clearly the most effective and successful lessons with regard to student comprehension and mastery of a subject. Good economy of time and material by way of individual lessons, as described above, are to enable the better teaching of the *whole subject* to individuals *at all levels* of instruction. Only time, experience, and practice, along with individual Biblical scholarship, can result in efficient and proficient teaching.

INSTRUCTIONS FOR MAP WORK

Map work is essentially a geographical essay. The physical and political features ought to be clearly distinguished and delineated. A great deal of labor and care is required to make a map readable, without blemish of smear and disfigurements. A good map may take on the average of 3-6 hours of student time, concentration, and patience. Be sure students know what is exactly required and what is not permissible each time.

Tools:
1. #2 lead pencil
2. a set of colored pencils (soft tips recommended) or a set of fine-tip felt pens
3. ink pen – black ink only or black fine-tip felt pen
4. a ruler or straight edge

Outlining:
1. Map work is mainly outlining and lettering. There is no filling-in of areas with solid coloring. At times straight vertical or horizontal lines may be drawn to cover specific territories; however, these lines are drawn only if they do not distract from the labeling and over-all purpose of the map assignment.
2. All shorelines of lakes, coastlines of seas and oceans, and rivers are always outlined with blue. Rivers are outlined along only *one side* of the drawn line.
3. Lands along oceans and around lakes are always outlined. Borders between nations or territories should be drawn (if not already printed on the map) with black ink or fine-tip felt pen, in either solid or dashed lines, then to be outlined on *both sides* according to the directions given.

4. Outlining may be of two styles:
a. following along the exact course of the printed lines
b. by making quick motions perpendicular to the printed lines (appearing like caterpillar hairs)

In both cases, there is not to be any visible space between the printed or drawn lines and the outlining. Both require steady pressure and control upon the pencil.

Printing:
1. All labeling is printed (manuscript).
2. Printing is *never* in lead or colored pencil. Printing must be in black ink or black fine-tip felt pen.
3. Printing is always in upper case lettering, no lower is used *except* when the typewriter is used. Size of printed lettering may vary, but it is always in capital letters.
4. Printing is to be straight and even on the map. Lettering may be on a slant on the map, but always even.
5. Print of the title is to be enlarged in proportion to all other lettering on the map.
6. Print the names of rivers along the direction of flow. The names should not be extended off to the side, apart from the river, if it can be avoided.
7. All letters should be closed. No gaps should be visible between lines that ought to be connected.
8. Size and style of lettering should be consistent throughout the map.

Mountains:
1. When mountains need to be drawn and labeled, be careful that they are not drawn out of proportion to the size of the map. For clarity they ought not to be clustered peaks huddled together into a tight ball. Keep the drawn mountains (upside down V's) loosely joined and evenly dispersed for the sake of readability, aesthetics, and easy labeling.
2. Mountains are to be drawn with black ink or felt tip pen. When drawn with black ink, outline with brown pencil. When drawn with felt-pen, black or brown may be used for outlining.

Keys:
1. When a key is required, whether boxed or linear, the boxes or lines should be all of equal dimensions and centered. The lines are to be straight and even with the page.
2. Never use the edge of the map as a straight

line. Draw all the lines in completely drawn key boxes, or squares if you have chosen to draw them.

Grading:

Map grade is based on neatness, cleanliness, spacing, readability, and artistic composition (color coordination included). There cannot be signs of lead penciling. Lead pencil marks should be thoroughly cleaned and erased. Accuracy in labeling and identifying places, spelling and following directions are also critical conditions to be considered before a map is regarded as well done.

THE THREE CONSTITUENTS OF THE GLOBE
INTRODUCTORY LESSON PLAN

GENESIS 1:1-2.

In the Beginning God created the *heaven* and the *earth*. And the earth was without form, and void; and darkness was upon the face of the deep. And the Spirit of God moved upon the face of the *water*.

LEADING IDEA
The three constituents of the globe are land, water and atmosphere.

THE FIRST PRINCIPLES OF LAND, WATER AND ATMOSPHERE

Heaven	Earth	Water
The *region of expanse* which *surrounds the earth,* and which appears *above* and *around us,* like an immense arch or vault, in which are seen the *sun, moon and stars.*	*Dry* land…the *solid* matter which constitutes the *fixed* part of the surface of the globe.	The *fluid* or *moveable* part of the globe.
Atmospheric *air; the most necessary* for living beings in nature.		The *most abundant fluid* and *most necessary* for living beings of any in nature, except air.
The Hebrews acknowledged three heavens; *the air* or aerial heavens; *the firmament* in which the stars are supposed to be placed; and the heaven of heavens, *the residence of Jehovah.*		It is *reposited in the earth* in *inexhaustible quantities,* where it is preserved fresh and cool, and from which it issues in *springs,* which form *streams* and *rivers.*
		The great reservoirs of water on the globe are the *oceans, seas* and *lakes,* which cover more than *three-fifths of its surface,* and from which it is raised by *evaporation,* and uniting with the air in the state of vapor, is wafted over the earth, ready to be *precipitated* in the form of rain, snow or hail.
Divisions: troposphere stratosphere mesosphere ionosphere	*Divisions:* continents islands	*Divisions:* oceanic waters continental waters

KATHERINE DANG

When I allow myself to dwell on it, the thought of my being a teacher of America's Christian History and Government does seem peculiar. I am an American-born, Chinese Christian. It was a dear Southern Baptist, Caucasian, elderly woman who led me slowly from my dark ignorance of God and Jesus Christ into the Light of the Gospel. The Lord opened my eyes and my heart to Christ's salvation when I was age nine. A knowledge of Christ and of His wisdom came to dispel the darkness of my life; and the seemingly strangeness of my individuality began to make sense and have purpose.

My public school education was typical of its day, as it was embodied with curriculum which led into the eventual issues that erupted into cries for civil rights and campus rebellions, while cynicism for the American establishment mounted within both Christian and secular circles. At the University of California in Berkeley, I majored in history, selecting courses in Medieval History, Italian Renaissance History, California History, Art History, British History, Black History and courses in Classics, all of which left me totally insecure and feeling absolutely incompetent to teach history in any Christian day school. For at the start of my

sophomore college year, I had submitted to God's call upon my life, resolved that with His help, I might do something to remove the embarrassment I felt over the poor scholarship I thought existed in Christian education which could not produce a superior, practical alternative to evolution and its implications in all areas of social and political concerns. I was a Chinese Christian, being schooled by socialists, aspiring to be an educator for the churches of America. I had been well-taught in the language of socialism and discovered the futility in defending Christianity in socialistic terms. In my ignorance, I hardly realized what an embarrassment I would prove myself to be in that first year of teaching at American Heritage Christian Schools.

It was not enough to work hard and be sincere when one's philosophy of government was a mixture of Christian and socialistic doctrines. To be politically conservative was only to be issue-centered and to reason from one's emotions. I had set government off to the side as a "secular" subject and in my ambivalence, I would only prepare generations to be suited for Christian socialism, at best, and these generations would, by degrees, exchange America's Christian form of government for pagan centralization and the tyranny of the State.

I used what was available to me in the form of textbooks, guides, and consultations with the Headmaster, Mr. James Rose. I leaned heavily upon the out-dated textbooks once used by public schools. American Heritage had only been in existence for two years, and in its innocence it entrusted me with Geography, eighth and eleventh grade U.S. History, Ancient History, and Rudiments. The days vacillated between anxiety attacks from panic and abiding calms that would come from prayer within the private closet of my heart. While I taught myself the subjects, it was "hit-and-miss" practice-teaching in the classroom. I knew I could do better teaching English, but no one else was to know this as I "bluffed" my way through the first year of teaching.

My ambivalence over "secular" and "sacred" subjects began to be displaced with the concept of "Christ over all" and "in all," at a three-week institute provided me by the Foundation for American Christian Education in the summer after my first year of teaching. Miss Verna Hall and Miss Rosalie Slater led several of us through a concentrated study of America's Christian history and government. I repented as it dawned upon me how wrong I had been. I had been the very problem I had vowed to correct. It became clear what it was I must do: work to build my teaching upon the foundation of my own Christian scholarship and Christian character with the purpose of promoting Christ's Gospel and His principles of self- and civil government to men and nations. And, then, there came the constant strivings for more maturity of understanding and self-expression.

The nine years I spent with American Heritage were years spent in liberty with which to reason, to labor, and to learn. The pastor and headmaster were always supportive and available for help and encouragement. There was freedom to expound upon principles and opinions, to experiment with applications, and to exchange concepts with others of like mind in an atmosphere of Christian grace, love, and hospitality. Mistakes and misunderstandings were mutually forgiven. There, also, I struggled with how I should articulate my learning in a manner which would develop the American Christian character and scholarship of my students. The years at American Heritage came to a conclusion as God moved to establish Chinese Christian Schools.

The pastor of my church is not Chinese, but he has a God-given affinity and love for the Chinese. He has been the pastor of the Bay Area Chinese Bible Church for the past nineteen years. It was quite consistent with his burden for his church when he proposed the establishment of Chinese Christian Schools eleven years ago. His burden became mine as well. It is his spiritual vision and patient leadership which brought Chinese Christian Schools into existence in 1979.

As Christ, His Story, moves westward, I can see what Christian character and Chinese scholarship God is developing in the Chinese for China's sake. Multitudes of Chinese from various parts of the Far East are coming upon America's western shores. I have a privilege in helping educate a vital Chinese Christian leadership which will support and promote the Gospel through its local churches and local civil governments. Might not the words of Charles Bancroft hold true:

"... As the heart in the human body receives the current of blood from all parts of the system, and, having revitalized it, returns it with fresh elements of strength, so America adopts the children of all lands only to return a manhood ennobled by a sense of its own dignity through the practice of a system of self-government which improves the condition and promotes the interest of each while it produces harm to none." (*CHOC*, p. 8)

RUDIMENTS OF AMERICA'S CHRISTIAN HISTORY AND GOVERNMENT
STUDENT HANDBOOK

BY BETH BALLINGER, KATHERINE DANG & JAMES B. ROSE

RUDIMENTS OF CHRISTIAN HISTORY STUDENT HANDBOOK

INTRODUCTION

The first student handbook ever designed to identify specifically the relationship between creation, Christ, Christianity and America's Christian history and government was printed in 1968 by Rosalie J. Slater and Verna M. Hall of the Foundation for American Christian Education, San Francisco. Entitled *Rudiments of America's Christian History and Government*, this compact 76 page "Student Handbook" was intended primarily for junior high and senior high school students who had not yet been introduced to the Christian history, Biblical principles, and sacred purpose of American self- and civil government. The Handbook has also been used at the freshman college level for the same purposes. Administrators have used it to teach their faculty while some parents and teachers used it to instruct themselves and elementary school-age children in their own heritage of Christian character and civil government.

The book was compiled and written to be used with The Holy Bible, *The Christian History of the Constitution*, *Teaching and Learning America's Christian History*, Noah Webster's *1828 Dictionary*, and the paperback book, *Evolution and the Modern Christian*, by Henry M. Morris.

PURPOSE OF COURSE

The declared purposes of the *Rudiments* course (pp. 1-2) are to help both teachers and students of Christian schools (in or outside of the home) to 1. remember the "purpose for which America was established ... , what America is all about"; 2. to reveal "that the history of Christianity and the history of America cannot be separated"; 3. to "restore the Christian writing and Biblical reasoning" of the Founding Father generation; and 4. to learn to "appreciate the sacred trust of Christian government..."

The course develops two major themes in the westward march of Christianity—character and government. The philosophy or body of wisdom that distinguishes the purpose of this book is Biblical, historical, political, educational and particularly governmental. (See *Guide*, p. 20)

The book has been successfully used on the senior high school level to achieve more specific aims as explained by Miss Katherine Dang from her own years of experience teaching "Rudiments":

1. To implant the Christian idea of man and government, based upon the significance and dignity of the individual, who is accountable for his own character and actions before God. The student is to discern between that which is pagan and that which is Christian, first within himself, and then in others.

2. To cultivate Christian scholarship, the ability to reason from the revelation of Scripture.

3. To inspire productivity—in quality as well as in quantity—which stems only from Christian character. Each student will research and examine the high caliber and industry of individuals whom God used to forward His purpose and plan for men and nations.

4. To enable each student to claim and forward his heritage of the American Christian Republic; to maintain and preserve its institutions so that the Gospel may flow freely to reach individuals for Christ. The student will put his labor into researching, reasoning, relating and recording "The Chain of Christianity moving Westward."

THE PACE

Those instructors who have had the best results teaching *Rudiments* have taken a full school year, on a *daily basis*, to enlighten themselves and then their students in the first principles of a truly inspiring religious and political heritage which most Christians have forgotten.

The lessons and questions in this little volume may be divided into four practical units of study over a period of eight to nine months as follows:
1. pp. 1-30 –1st quarter
2. pp. 31-47–2nd quarter
3. pp. 48-65–3rd quarter
4. p. 66   –4th quarter

TEACHING SUGGESTIONS

NOTEBOOK APPROACH: The Handbook is not designed as a workbook to record or complete someone else's reasoning. It is intended to effect a transition from a workbook approach to a self-teaching notebook. Experience has shown that a separate notebook—preferably a three-ring binder with paper and dividers—is a superior instrument for reflective thinking as well as for individual reformation.

The *Rudiments* Handbook leads to at least four other texts which open up a vast range of spiritual and intellectual ideas important to individual and

national happiness. Therefore, students are urged to first write their answers to questions given in the Handbook on a separate sheet of paper for clarity, completeness and neatness, before transferring their prose to the Student Handbook. (The how and why of using Notebook Methodology is explained on p. 138 of this *Guide*)

LEARN THE VOCABULARY: Most of the excerpts reprinted in the Handbook are drawn from literature written before 1900 by exceptionally literate, thoughtful, and scholarly men and women. Therefore, any teacher and student of this little volume is urged to develop the habit of underlining and defining the rich vocabulary of the authors, and to record the appropriate definition(s) from Webster's 1828 Dictionary in the margins of the Handbook or in their notebooks.

Some conscientious teachers either make a list of key words from certain paragraphs or pages, define them concisely, and give these to students to memorize and reason from, or simply list the terms students should define for themselves before reasoning through a reading assignment.

The reasons why Webster's 1828 Dictionary is used to define 19th century terms are explained by Miss Rosalie Slater on pages 9-10 of the "green" pages in the facsimile edition and also on page 7 of this *Guide*. The capacity of the student to comprehend the enduring ideas presented in the Handbook is tied to understanding the precise historic vocabulary of liberty.

READ AND REASON TOGETHER: The teacher needs to be prepared to show how principles and ideas from the text are deduced and to outline and use them to answer both oral and written questions. Hence, teachers are encouraged to read and reason from the text(s) with their students.

PARAPHRASE: Comprehension can be further advanced by paraphrasing the paragraphs, or sentences, of the author's work. To paraphrase does not mean to merely condense and repeat what another says, but to literally "unfold the sense of the author *with more clearness and particularity than it is expressed in his own words.*" Hence, *definitions* of the terms used by an author are essential to interpreting another's sentiments through paraphrase. The object is not simply to enable a student to arrive at answers to questions but to show his *path of reasoning*.

COURSE OVERVIEW

The following course overview has been constructed from the notes of three teachers: Miss Belinda Ballenger, Miss Katherine Dang, and Mr. James Rose. These individuals have collectively devoted nearly 30 years to teaching the principles and ideas in the *Rudiments* Handbook to children in grades 7-12. This outline will identify the leading ideas and questions to be taught. Specific page references to this *Guide* and the volumes used with the *Rudiments* course will provide the necessary resources and documentation to develop the enumerated themes.

The books referenced for further reading and research and the abbreviations used to refer the reader to them are as follows:

Rudiments "Student Handbook" — *RUDIMENTS*
The Christian History of the Constitution— *CHOC*
Teaching and Learning America's Christian History— *T/L*
Noah Webster's 1828 Dictionary—*WEBSTER'S 1828*
Guide to American Christian Education— *GUIDE*

ANNOTATED OUTLINE

COURSE OUTLINE

I. Introducing Rudiments of America's Christian History and Government

A. Purpose of the Rudiments Course (*Rudiments*, pp. 1-2 and foregoing introduction)

B. Introduce the Principle Approach: "America's historic Christian method of Biblical reasoning" and the 4 R's (*T/L*, pp. 88-89; *Guide*, pp. 5, 15, 16)

II. Identifying the Christian Idea of Man and Government (*Rudiments*, pp. 7-29)

A. Overview of the seven Biblical principles identified in Noah Webster's "Letters to a Young Gentleman Commencing His Education," 1823.
 1. *T/L*, pp. 61-63
 2. *Guide*, "Recapitulation" of the seven principles, p. 77
 3. *Guide*, p. 29

B. Study the character and contribution of Noah Webster in the fields of education and government
 1. *Rudiments*, pp. 3-6
 2. *T/L*, pp. 280-301
 3. *Webster's 1828*, "Green Pages"—biography on Webster

COMMENTARY

I. Introduction

To explain what Rudiments is all about, Belinda Ballenger writes the complete title of the course on a chalkboard, concisely defines each word, and then through paraphrasing and questions about each word, defines the purpose of the Handbook. The Principle Approach is *implicit* in the Rudiments Handbook as (1) a method of Biblical reasoning and (2) as the seven principles of our history and government. Introduce and explain briefly the 4 R's which students will learn in studying the book.

II. Identifying the Christian Idea of Man and Government

A. The Christian Idea of Man and Government is summarized by the seven principles of America's Christian history and government–truths that define the character necessary to maintain American Christian liberty and law. The study references will help you introduce and identify the first principles the student will discover in the Handbook and in the correlative texts.

B. Noah Webster is a splendid example of the kind of character and conscience God used to make an enduring difference in American education and government. His writings demonstrate American Biblical scholarship, how to think governmentally, and the character for productivity.

C. Teaching the Christian Idea of Man and Government through the seven principles and Webster's *"Letters"*

1. God's Principle of Individuality (*Guide*, p. 31)
   a. The Life and Testimony of Noah Webster (see II-B)
   b. Duties of the Christian parent, teacher and student in American Christian Education (*Rudiments*, pp. 7-9)
2. The Christian Principle of Self-Government (*Guide*, p. 36)
   a. Pagan vs. Christian view of man (*Rudiments*, p. 8); reason from revelation vs. reason unaided by revelation (*Guide*, p. 15)
   b. Who made me? Christian view of God (*Rudiments*, p. 8)
   c. Why was I made? Christian view of man (*Rudiments*, p. 8)
   d. What is my duty? Christian view of government (Eccl. 12:13-14, *Rudiments*, p. 8)

   e. The spirit and letter of the Ten Commandments (*Rudiments* appendix of Handbook)
   f. Christ's Two Commandments confirm and consolidate the Ten Commandments (*Rudiments*, pp. 12-13)

3. America's Heritage of Christian Character: "conflict within and without" (*Guide*, p. 39)

   a. "What consists of real worth or dignity of character?" (*Rudiments*, pp.16-17)
   b. The attributes of Christ in God and their opposites (*Rudiments*, p. 17)
   c. Dueling: The test of character in giving and taking offense (*Rudiments*, pp. 18-19)

   d. Furnishing one's mind: the making and molding of Christian character through the correct choice of literature (*Rudiments*, p. 19; *Guide*, p. 380; Phil. 4:8-10)

C. Imbedded in Noah Webster's 1823 "Letter" are the seven principles (the Rudiments) of America's Christian history and government. The letter illustrates how the Founding Fathers reasoned from these truths.

1. Webster's life and Christian testimony confirm that God works through individuals. God glorifies His own infinite individuality and sovereign ability to renew man's mind, enabling man to have dominion over himself, his home, and over the "bounds" of that man's "habitation" (Acts 17:26)
2. These pages help to define man's individual accountability to God for His commandments to respect one's parents, to apply reason to God's revelation, and to consequently demonstrate Christian self-government.

d. Two contrasting views of man (Christian vs. Pagan) may be discussed here in the context of three fundamental questions. The Biblical answers to each question may then be used to expose the opposite, ungodly view of God, man and government.

e-f. The importance of the Ten Commandments and Christ's two commandments to Christian self-government is confirmed by each individual who repents of specific sins revealed by God's moral law and, then, voluntarily yields by Grace to the "law of the *spirit* of Christ." (Rom 8:2)

3. These pages provide an opportunity to define exactly the character of God expressed by men when they become "partakers of the divine nature" through the "knowledge of God, and of Jesus our Lord."

Parents and teachers can also use this section to establish a standard of worth apart from that which is deemed popular by "peer" pressure.

c. Webster's advice on "dueling" or "the giving and receiving of offences" provide convicting descriptions of one form of cowardice in contrast to a proper fear of God.

d. Webster contrasts two classes of readers in this section—those who relish novelty and amusements in contrast to readers who cherish instruction and elevation of character. (Phil. 4:12)

e. Theatrical entertainment: TV, movies, etc. "strong attractions . . . for the young and thoughtless" (*Rudiments*, pp. 19-20)

f. Importance of Christian character in government (*Rudiments*, pp. 22-26) and in education (*Rudiments*, pp. 28-29)

4. The Principle of American Christian Political Union (*Guide*, p. 69; Amos 3:3)

a. Why friendships are important (*Rudiments*, p. 20; *Guide*, p. 72)

b. What is a friend? (*Rudiments*, pp. 20-22)

c. Groups worth joining or avoiding (*Rudiments*, pp. 21-22)

d. Basis for being inclusive or exclusive in religion or politics (*Rudiments*, pp. 21-22)

5. Conscience—the "most sacred of all property" (*Guide*, p. 43)

a. The Biblical concept of property (*Guide*, p. 47; *Rudiments*, p. 23)

b. Why conscience is the most sacred property (*Rudiments*, pp. 23-24)

c. The Biblical reasoning of John Locke on property and civil government (*CHOC*, pp. 58, 71)

d. Property, suffrage, and representation: Who should vote and legislate in a Republic? (*Rudiments*, pp. 23-27)

6. The Christian Form of America's Government (*Guide*, p. 49)

a. The Law and the Gospel as the basis of America's form of civil government (*T/L*, pp. 245-248; *Rudiments*, pp. 26-27; *Guide*, p. 55)

b. The principle of representation (*T/L*, pp. 317-323; *Rudiments*, pp. 23-27; *Guide*, p. 53)

c. The importance of Christian character in a Republic (*Rudiments*, pp. 22, 25-27; *CHOC*, pp. 396-397)

d. Christian liberties and responsibilities of American Christian citizenship (*CHOC*, pp. 262, 364b, 365-370; *Rudiments*, pp. 22-27)

e. American Christian suffrage (*Rudiments*, pp. 26-27)

7. How the seed of local self-government is planted within the constituents of America's Christian Republic: (*Guide*, p. 58)

a. Home: (Deut. 6:6-12; *T/L*, pp. 23-29, 255)

e. Questioning whether the theater and stage (inclusive of modern TV and video) have ever been "a school of virtue," Webster challenges youth to cultivate only such entertainments as refine one's tastes and pleasures rather than debase them.

f. Webster explains why the character of the people in a republic is especially reflected in the representatives they elect to office.

4. Webster shows how to apply the American Christian principle of unity and union to help a youth discern the character of his friends and the company he keeps socially, religiously, and politically. This is an excellent discourse on when to unite and when to separate religiously, as Christians, or politically as Americans.

5. Presupposing a form of government and a free market that encourages productivity and private property, Webster argues for equal protection of property in a Republic but challenges whether citizens with no property should have "an equal right to legislate upon (the) property" of others.

d. Webster submits that republics should be founded upon both an equality of rights and a right to private property. He proceeds to define the legislative interests of citizens who earn *no* property in contrast with the interests of citizens who *do earn* modest estates and help support the expense of civil government.

6. Webster charges both the citizen and candidate running for office to possess the necessary character and conscience to maintain a republic. He explains the *consequences* of strictly observing or disgracefully neglecting the Biblical principles of character and representation in choosing men for public office.

7. The consequences of student rebellion upon themselves and the orderliness and reputation of a school are explained by Webster. The promise of superior academic progress based upon a *mastery of the rudiments* of a subject is also outlined.

b. Church: (I Tim. 3:15; Acts 1:8; *T/L*, pp. 38-51, 248-249)

c. School: (Acts 17:11; *Rudiments*, pp. 28-29; *T/L*, pp. 52-57)

D. History and the Individual (*Rudiments*, pp. 30-37)
1. Christian history is the "autobiography of Him 'Who worketh all things after the counsel of His own will'" (Eph. 1:11)
2. Christian vs. pagan views of history (*Guide*, p. 27)
3. The universal period of beginnings: Gen. 1-11
a. Emma Willard, Preface to "Universal History in Perspective": What history teaches (*Rudiments*, p. 33)
b. An historical commentary on Genesis 1-11

E. Evolutionary claims on the individual (*Rudiments*, pp. 38-41)
1. "Evolution and the Modern Christian" by Henry M. Morris
2. Two philosophies of life: Biblical vs. evolutionary
3. Evolutionary claims—the basis of "liberalism" in religion, politics and education
4. Specific questions for emphasis (*Rudiments*, pp. 38-41)

III. The Chain of Christianity Moving Westward: The Providential View of History (*Rudiments*, pp. 42-76)

A. God's Principle of Individuality: Key to the study of history (*Rudiments*, p. 42)

1. Arnold Guyot and Geographic Individualities (*Rudiments*, p. 42; *T/L*, pp. 142-153)
2. The Earth:
a. In Scripture (*Guide*, p. 260)
b. In the universe (*T/L*, p. 142)
c. Its purpose (*T/L*, pp. 142-143)
3. The Continents: Their form and function (*Rudiments*, pp. 42-46)
a. Southern Continents: continents of nature (*T/L*, pp. 145-149)
b. Northern Continents: continents of history (*T/L*, pp. 145, 149-153)

B. Tracing the Chain of Christianity link by link (*Rudiments*, pp. 47-76)

D. Miss Dang suggests that each definition of history on pages 30-31 be analyzed to discuss which ideas are opposed to or implicitly consistent with the Christian view of history.

3. Mrs. Willard's preface to "Universal History" challenges Americans to reflect upon faithfulness in practicing God's principles of individuality, self-government, character and unity of their last two centuries.

E. Read page 42, why "God's Principle of Individuality . . . delivers a staggering blow to evolution." Then, (from the assigned reading and the answers to the questions), outline the phrases, sentences and ideas that define and *contrast* the two views of life. This section is helpful in explaining why Christians often embrace liberal or socialistic ideas which contradict Biblical doctrine.

III. The Biblical basis and the importance of knowing "who *causes* the human events which have taken place" in history are explained in the *Guide*, p. 28.

A. The Providential View of History is an expression of God's Principle of Individuality. The relationship between God's Principle of Individuality and God's Providence in history is suggested on pages 27 and 203 of the *Guide*. The history and geography courses in the *Curriculum* section of the *Guide* will help in teaching this section. (pp. 201 and 257)
1-3. Arnold Guyot lays the geographic basis for how the continents, the climate and natural environment facilitate the westward movement of Christianity.

B. There are countless numbers of individual men, events and nations God used in history to unfold and

COURSE OUTLINE	COMMENTARY

advance liberty. Teaching just nine "links" in the Chain of Christianity each year in relation to America and the student today makes history easier to remember and comprehend. (See History section in *Guide*, p. 203)

1. The themes of character and government help highlight the lessons of history.

2. Consider: Would there be an America and the U.S. Constitution without Moses and the moral law?

1. Two major themes considered along the Chain of Christianity (*Rudiments*, p. 47)

2. Moses and the Moral Law—a lesson on how character is both demanded and developed simultaneously. (*Rudiments*, pp. 49-54)
   a. Three aspects of Hebrew law (*Rudiments*, pp. 48, 53)
   b. Character and contribution of Moses to God's government of men and nations. (*Rudiments*, pp. 49-54)

3. The virtues and vices—good or bad qualities—within the Greek and Roman character determined how the citizens were governed. Consider how "all things (qualities and conduct) work together" for God in His Providence. (Rom. 8:28)

3. Greece and Rome (*Rudiments*, pp. 56-60; *T/L*, pp. 159-166; *CHOC*, pp. 10-16)
   a. Negative and positive preparations for the Gospel (*Rudiments*, p. 59; *T/L*, pp. 164-165)
   b. Three forms of nation-making (*Rudiments*, p. 58)
   c. How character and national government are indivisible (*Rudiments*, p. 59)

4. Jesus Christ: Focal Point of History (*Rudiments*, p. 55; *Guide*, pp. 208 and 290)
   a. "all things become new" (II Cor. 5:17)
   b. "The world turned upside down" by Christianity (Acts 17:6)
   c. The Republicanism of Christianity (*CHOC*, pp. 27-28)
   d. "Memorials of a Christian life" by Augustus Neander (*T/L*, p. 215)
   e. Principles of America's Christian history and government predicated on the principles of primitive Christian church polity (*CHOC*, pp. 16-17)

4. The birth of Christian liberty and self-government through Jesus Christ gave rise to religious and, subsequently, civil liberty. Jesus Christ is the only One in Christian history who can transcribe God's Law from the "tables of stone" onto the "fleshly tables" of man's heart (II Cor. 3:3), thereby making the Word of God an internal standard for life and implanting the "perfect law of liberty" in the conscience.

5. Two systems of law: Roman and English (*Rudiments*, pp. 61-62); *T/L*, p. 165; *CHOC*, pp. 12-14)
   a. Roman civil law and English common law
   b. Roman character and law
   c. English character and law
   d. American Christian character and law

5. Roman and English theories of law contribute two necessary but different attitudes toward law today. 1) Roman civil law represents man-made law—the *letter* in all its demands and detail. 2) English common law represents laws or principles that existed prior to man writing them down. "Do unto others" (from Matt. 7:12), summarizes the *spirit* of English common law.

6. Reformation of Religion (*Rudiments*, pp. 62-65; *T/L*, pp. 166-172, 325)
   a. John Wycliffe, "Morning Star of the Reformation"
   b. Martin Luther, "Awakening of the Human Conscience"
   c. John Calvin, "The Truth Shall Make You Free"

6. When the Word of God became the "common property" of the individual, it provided the best definition and defense of his liberty. The history of the Reformation reveals how God worked through individuals to effect first a spiritual, then an ecclesiastical and, finally, a political reformation. Salvation and reformation are first individual and internal before the home, church and civil government are conformed (reformed) to Bible truth.

7. The Bible in English (*Rudiments*, p. 65; pp. 172, 332-342; *CHOC*, pp. 28a-36)
a. Wycliffe Bible—1380
b. Tyndale Bible—1526
c. Great Bible—1539
d. Geneva Bible—1559
e. King James Bible—1611
f. Aitken Bible—1882

8. English Constitutional Law: (*Rudiments*, pp. 66-68; *CHOC*, pp. 38-47; *T/L*, pp. 173-174, 344-346, 349-351)
a. Magna Charta—1215
b. Petition of Right—1628
c. English Bill of Rights—1689
d. American Bill of Rights—1789

9. Christian philosophers of the American Constitutional Republic (*Rudiments*, pp. 69-70)
a. John Locke—Philosopher of the American Revolution (*CHOC*, pp. 57-125; *T/L*, p. 175)
b. Charles Montesquieu—Government of laws, not men (*CHOC*, pp. 139-146; *T/L*, p. 175)
c. William Blackstone—Law of Nature as God's law (*CHOC*, pp. 139-146; *T/L*, p. 176)

10. The Pilgrims bring Christian character, and constitutional law and government to America. (*Rudiments*, pp. 71-72; *CHOC*, pp. 24-27, 48-50; *T/L*, p. 177)

11. The Parent Colonies (*Rudiments*, pp. 72-73; *CHOC*, p. 150a; *T/L*, pp. 177-178)
a. Jamestown: English representative government
b. Plymouth: Primitive Christianity and local self-government

12. The Mayflower Compact (*Rudiments*, pp. 74-76)
a. Pastor John Robinson's counsel to the Pilgrims (*CHOC*, pp. 198-201)
b. Pilgrims: seed bed of America's heritage of Christian character, self-government, property, and voluntary union (*Guide*, p. 74)

---

7. "The *Bible*, in the hearts and hands of people, is the enginery of human progress." Discover how the history of the English Bible is basic to the story of liberty—Christian, ecclesiastical and political. Consider how the Bible is the reason behind the "Seven Great Exchanges in Modern History." (*Guide* p. 68)

8. As each body of English law was written, the purpose of civil government was progressively constrained to protect individual, God-given rights and responsibilities. There were no major constitutional developments in England after the Magna Charta until God's Word came into the hands of the individual (1382).

9. The views of government declared by each Christian philosopher reflects an enlightened people whose ideas of God and man are rooted in the Bible. Discern the Biblical basis for each thinker's views of law and government.

10. The Pilgrims are the Founding Fathers and Mothers of American Christian character and government. The Pilgrim idea of voluntary reformation is contrasted with the English Puritans' view of reformation by compulsion.

11. Jamestown and Plymouth colonies are the external manifestation of two important views of self and civil government.

12. Pastor John Robinson counseled the Pilgrims concerning Christian civil government as well as Godly conduct. Discern the cause-effect relationship existing between Biblical church covenants, local civil compacts, and the state and national constitutions that came from the Pilgrims, a people "united for civil as well as for spiritual purposes."

SENIOR HIGH SCHOOL
AMERICAN HISTORY

BY KATHERINE DANG

Administrative Director
Chinese Christian Schools
San Leandro, California

CONTENTS

AMERICAN CHRISTIAN HISTORY CURRICULUM FOR SENIOR HIGH SCHOOL

AMERICA IN THE SETTING OF UNIVERSAL HISTORY

There is a Providence which superintends and overrules the actions of men and nations, making them subservient to the higher and nobler purpose of bringing liberty to individual men and women. History attests to mankind's unending struggle with one form of tyranny after another, and man's gradual progress toward freer institutions, a result of the increase in internal liberty experienced by individuals. That liberty which sets men free from sin's control also sets them free from the control of tyrants.

America, the freest nation in human history, is a link in God's continuing chain of events that is bringing to fruition Christ's glory and reign – first, spiritually, making His kingdom in the hearts of individual men, and then one day, politically, actually ruling and reigning upon the earth.

> "This nation (America) has in its keeping, 'the last word in human political institutions,' – the Republican form of Government." (*CHOC*, p. 1, Richard Frothingham.)

OUR CHRISTIAN FORM OF GOVERNMENT

In America, God established a form of civil government predicated upon the Christian liberty of the individual. While men enjoyed a measure of Christian liberty in earlier eras – for example, in ancient Israel and in England – in America, for the first time, individuals were at liberty to such degree that they could be responsible for their own regulation, direction, control and restraint in civil society. This exercise of individual responsibility began within their own homes, extended into their churches, and was expressed most fully in local self-government and in self-government with union.

The timeline on pp. 290, *America in the Setting of Universal History*, suggests how each of four major periods of history contributed in bringing liberty to the individual through that "perfect law of liberty," the Gospel of Jesus Christ.

AMERICA'S HERITAGE

"Thus, we find the spirit of progress traversing the whole course of human history, constantly advanc-

289

AMERICA IN THE SETTING OF UNIVERSAL HISTORY

JESUS CHRIST, "FOCAL POINT OF HISTORY
CAME IN THE FULLNESS OF TIME" (GAL. 4:4)

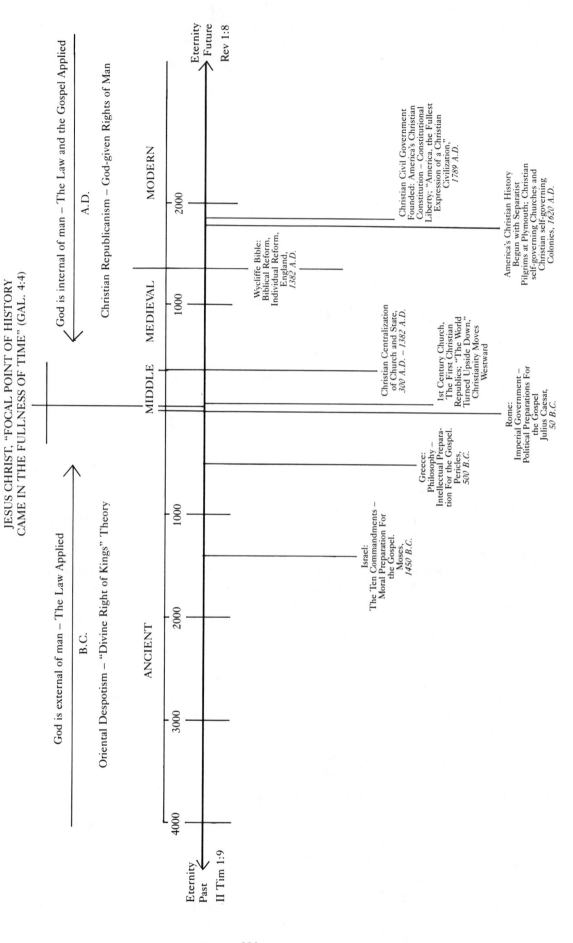

God is external of man – The Law Applied

B.C.

Oriental Despotism – "Divine Right of Kings" Theory

God is internal of man – The Law and the Gospel Applied

A.D.

Christian Republicanism – God-given Rights of Man

ANCIENT

MIDDLE   MEDIEVAL   MODERN

Eternity
Past
II Tim 1:9

Eternity
Future
Rev 1:8

4000   3000   2000   1000   1000   2000

Israel:
The Ten Commandments –
Moral Preparation For
the Gospel.
Moses,
1450 B.C.

Greece:
Philosophy –
Intellectual Prepara-
tion For the Gospel.
Pericles,
500 B.C.

Rome:
Imperial Government –
Political Preparations For
the Gospel
Julius Caesar,
50 B.C.

1st Century Church,
The First Christian
Republics; "The World
Turned Upside Down,"
Christianity Moves
Westward

Christian Centralization
of Church and State,
300 A.D. – 1382 A.D.

Wycliffe Bible:
Biblical Reform,
Individual Reform,
England,
1382 A.D.

America's Christian History
Begun with Separatist
Pilgrims at Plymouth; Christian
self-governing Churches and
Christian self-governing
Colonies, 1620 A.D.

Christian Civil Government
Founded: America's Christian
Constitution – Constitutional
Liberty; "America, the Fullest
Expression of a Christian
Civilization,"
1789 A.D.

ing through all the confusion of rising and falling states, of battle, seige and slaughter, of victory and defeat; through the varying fortunes and ultimate extinction of monarchy, republic, and empire; through barbaric irruption and desolations, feudal isolation, spiritual supremacy, the heroic rush and conflict of the Cross and the Crescent; amid the busy hum of industry, through the marts and behind the gliding heels of commerce; through the bloody conflict of commons, nobles, kings and kaisers to New Free America. There the Englishman, the German, the Frenchman, the Italian, the Scandinavian, the Asiatic, and the African all meet as equals. There they are free to speak, to think, and to act. They bring the common contributions of character, energy, and activity to the support and enlargement of a common country, and the spread of its influence and enlightenment through all the lands of their origin.

"As America is the common ground on which all the currents, hastening by lightning and by steam, seek again every quarter of the earth with kindly greeting, to renew the relations broken in the original separation of the races, and to cement, by exchanges mutually profitable, a new and better unity of mankind. As the heart in the human body receives the current of blood from all parts of the system, and, having revitalized it, returns it with fresh elements of strength, so America adopts the children of all lands through the practice of a system of self-government which improves the condition and promotes the interest of each while it produces harm to none." (*CHOC*, p. 8; Charles Bancroft.)*

---

*NOTE: see p. xiii or p. 305 for the full names of books referenced and the abbreviations used.

Six Themes
For America's Christian History

One may summarize America's Christian History with six major themes and time periods:

I. America, Reserved by God for Christian Self-Government, 1000-1620 A.D.
II. One Hundred Fifty Years of Local Self-Government Practiced, 1620-1770 A.D.
III. The American Christian Revolution, 1765-1783 A.D.
IV. The American Christian Constitution and

Republic, 1783-1789 A.D.
V. America, "the Fullest Expression of a Christian Civilization," 1789-1830 A.D.
VI. America's Falling Away: The Corruption and the Correction of a Christian Republic, 1830 A.D.-Present

Given four quarters to an academic year, the chart below will direct in the planning of lessons and topics for teaching.

Quarterly Overviews

FIRST QUARTER	SECOND QUARTER	THIRD QUARTER	FOURTH QUARTER
I. 1000 - 1620	III. 1765 - 1783	IV. 1783 - 1789	VI. 1830 - Present
II. 1620 - 1770		V. 1789 - 1830	

THEME I.

AMERICA, RESERVED BY GOD FOR CHRISTIAN SELF-GOVERNMENT, 1000-1620

Until God had prepared individuals ready to implement Christian civil government, the continent of North America was providentially closed for permanent settlement. The Separatist congregation, the tap root of New England, appeared in the northern parts of England in 1602. In 1620, the Pilgrims were ready to transplant New Testament Christian self- and civil government onto the shores God had reserved for their settlement and the further development of their liberties – both ecclesiastical and civil.

The original inhabitants of America, the American Indians, occupied the land, but never possessed it as their very own. Skilled in *living off the land and merging with it*, the American natives lacked the spiritual enlightenment and capacity which could free them to take dominion of the earth they lived upon. They were a part of nature, but not above it or able to control it. North America remained as wild, untamed and uncivilized as her inhabitants. It was a land whose resources remained untouched, uncultivated and ungoverned. No man, as yet, had dominion over her.

"And God blessed them, and God said unto them, Be fruitful and multiply, and replenish the earth, and subdue it; and have dominion over the fish of the sea, and over the fowl of the air, and over every living thing that moveth upon the earth." *Genesis 1:28*

TAKING DOMINION OVER THE LAND

"He that is nourished by the Acorns he picks up under an oak, or the Apples he gathered from the Trees in the wood, he certainly appropriated them to himself. No body can deny but the Nourishment is his. I ask then, When did they begin to be his? When he digested? Or when he eat? Or when he boiled? Or when he brought them home? Or when he pickt them up? And tis plain, if the first gathering made them not his, nothing else would. That *Labour* put a Distinction between them and common: That added something to them more than Nature, the common Mother of all, had done; and so they became his private Right . . . "

"*As much Land* as a Man Tills, Plants, Improves, Cultivates, and can use the Product of, so much is his *Property*. He by his Labour does, as it were, inclose it from the Common, . . . God, when he gave the World in common to all Mankind, commanded Man also to labour, and the Penury of his condition required it of him. God and his Reason commanded him to subdue the Earth, *ie*. to improve it for the Benefit of Life, and therein lay out something upon it that was his own, his Labour. He that in Obedience to this Command of God, subdued, tilled, and sowed any part of it, thereby annexed to it that was his *Property*, which another had no Title to, nor could without Injury take from him." (John Locke, *CHOC*, pp. 64, 65)

"The vast region which the flag of the United States protects was, two centuries and a half ago, the roaming of tribes and Indians . . . It was virtually a waste awaiting, in the order of Providence, the major influence of an incoming race, imbued with the spirit of a new civilization. The period referred to was an epoch in which there had been a providential preparation for great events in the heavens and the earth. It was also the period of the Reformation. This, in its essence, was the assertion of the principle of individuality, or of true spiritual freedom. . ." (Richard Frothingham; 1890; *CHOC*, p. 1)

292

THEME I.

AMERICA, RESERVED BY GOD FOR CHRISTIAN SELF-GOVERNMENT
1000 – 1620

KEY INDIVIDUALS	KEY EVENTS	KEY INSTITUTIONS	KEY DOCUMENTS, SPEECHES, SERMONS OR ESSAYS
Marco Polo	The Wycliffe Bible	Indian Nations of North America	Magna Charta
King Alfred	The Tyndale Bible	Latin Christianity	First Charter Granted for English Colonization
Archbishop Stephen Langton	The Spanish Armada	State Church of England	Mayflower Compact
John Wycliffe	The Geneva Bible	Separatist Christianity	Robinson's Letter to the Pilgrims
Prince Henry of Portugal	The King James Bible	Pilgrim Christianity	Pilgrim Treaty With the Indians
Christopher Columbus	Columbus' Discovery of the New World	Puritan Christianity	
John Cabot	European Exploration and Settlements in the New World		
William Tyndale	– Northmen – Spanish – French – Dutch – Swedish – Portuguese – English		
William Brewster			
John Robinson			
William Bradford			
John Smith			
Pocahontas			

293

Theme II.

One Hundred Fifty Years of Local Self-Government Practiced, 1620-1770

The sincere human effort to practice Christian self-government – the government of God through Christ's indwelling the individual – wrought out the local self-government witnessed in the American colonies, in which every person managed his own individual, internal affairs in the home, church, education and business, with varying degrees of civil liberty, as granted to each by England, their Mother Country.

The seed of local self-government – Christian self-government – was planted and cultivated in the three constituents of American republicanism: the home – the cradle of Christian character, the church – which quickens the Christian conscience, and the school – where Biblical scholarship is perpetuated to future generations.

Providence began to direct colonial affairs through internal, local concerns over common dangers – their fear of losing their collective rights and constitutional liberties as British citizens. By the Hand of God, an American political identity emerged.

COLONIAL CHRISTIAN EDUCATION

"At the time of the American Revolution, our Colonists had spent about one hundred and fifty years both learning and participating in the principle of self-government. The leadership from the pulpit, the knowledge of the Bible, and the opportunities afforded in Colonial government, all contributed to making our Forefathers and Mothers ready to 'assume among the powers of the earth, the separate and equal station' of a nation.

"... The colonists' familiarity with history ... extensive legal learning ... lucid exposition of constitutional principles, showing, indeed, that somehow, out into the American wilderness had been carried the very accent of cosmopolitan thought and speech."

"How did American education produce such a remarkable people – even before we became a nation?

"... From the time of the Pilgrims and Puritans, men had set the standard of God's Word before them to measure the tyranny and despotism of their times. American life began with the flight of men, women and children, who sought civil and religious liberty – a vision inspired by the Bible. The New World was to be the habitation of liberty and law. Literacy – the first promise of education – has always been associated with the Bible.

"The schools taught a classical education built upon the Bible. The primary purpose of early colleges was to turn out Christian men who knew God's Word thoroughly and could reason from its principles to civil government, economics, and all national concerns." (*B/C*, pp. 26, 27)

Theme II.
One Hundred Fifty Years of Local Self-Government Practiced
1620 – 1770

KEY INDIVIDUALS	KEY EVENTS	KEY INSTITUTIONS	KEY DOCUMENTS, SPEECHES, SERMONS OR ESSAYS
John Locke Charles Montesquieu William Blackstone Algernon Sidney	Acts of Tyranny Bacon's Rebellion The Great Awakening	Mercantilism Township County	John Locke, "Of Civil Government" "Of Paternal Power" "Of the Beginnings of Political Societies" "Of the Ends of Political Society & Government" "Of the Form of a Commonwealth"
Thomas Hooker John Witherspoon Jonathan Edwards	The French Armada The French and Indian War	Congregational Church Government Presbyterian Church Government	"Some Thoughts Concerning Education" (*CHOC*, pp. 50B-125)
John Winthrop William Penn	The Stamp Act Declaratory Act	Episcopal Church Government New England Colonial Government Middle Colonial Government Southern Colonial Government	"Spirit of Laws," by Charles Montesquieu (*CHOC*, pp. 131-138) Blackstone's Commentaries (*CHOC*, pp. 139-146)
George Washington Samuel Adams		Parliament Tory Party Whig Party	Fundamental Orders of Connecticut (*CHOC*, pp. 248B-257)
Phillis Wheatley		Stamp Act Congress Slave Trade and Market	Massachusetts' Body of Liberties (*CHOC*, pp. 257-261) Penn's Treaty with the Indians and "Great Law" (*CHOC*, p. 262A) Petition of Rights British Bill of Rights "On Liberty," by Samuel Adams (*CHOC*, p. 364B) "The Farmer's Letters" I-XII; by John Dickenson

THEME III.

THE AMERICAN CHRISTIAN REVOLUTION, 1765-1782

The American colonists patiently endured ten years of schemes by Crown and Parliament to enforce arbitrary supremacy and control through policies that steadily encroached upon lawfully established civil liberties.

Between the years 1765-1775, England and her colonies engaged in great Constitutional debates, which ultimately served only to reveal how irreconcilable were the principles of Britain with those of the colonies. The colonists stood together on the Biblical principle of civil government which concludes that the state is made for man, while British Crown and Parliament perversely held to the pagan principle of civil government which concludes that man is made for the state.

DEFENSIVE WAR

A war for independence ensued as a defensive measure by America against England's determination to force the American states to surrender lawful rights and liberties and submit to her supremacy and tyrannical rule. When all constitutional and peaceful measures had been exhausted, the colonies made their appeal to the first Law of Nature – the Law of Self-Preservation.

God raised up the leadership and provided the circumstances which effected the only true revolution in human history: slavery was truly exchanged for freedom, returning sovereignty to the self-governing individual. Victory at Yorktown virtually marked "the world turned upside down."

DIVINE INTERPOSITION

"The Revolution was not the result of any causes of any spirit that had suddenly arisen. It was the necessary consequence of the previous providential training – of moral and political forces which had long been at work in the minds of the people . . . It must have come sooner or later; but the attempt to deprive the Colonies of their representative system hastened the event. The passage of the Stamp Act and the Port Bill fell upon the minds of a spirited and jealous people as an act of oppression to be resisted. The presence of bodies of armed men, instead of producing the designed intimidation only served to arouse the spirit of the people, and cement the Colonies in a common bond, for mutual support and protection. . .

". . . It attained our national independence against all probabilities. Often, in the dark hours of the struggle, nothing saved the American cause from entire destruction but the divine interposition. It had its days of darkness, suffering, and reverses, when it seemed as if success were impossible. A country without resources, an army gathered on short enlistments, and without discipline, a Congress sometimes tardy in supplying the means of carrying on the war, were not the most encouraging conditions of success . . . God was as certainly in the lives of Washington, and Lafayette, and Marion, as he was in the lives of Moses, and Joshua, and Daniel; he was no more present at Megiddo and Jericho, than at White Plains and Valley Forge. The Battle was the Lord's and it could not be lost." (S.W. Foljambe, *C/P*, pp. 51, 52)

Theme III.
The American Christian Revolution
1765 – 1782

KEY INDIVIDUALS	KEY EVENTS	KEY INSTITUTIONS	KEY DOCUMENTS, SPEECHES, SERMONS OR ESSAYS
King George III	Boston Tea Party Boston Port Bill	First Continental Congress Second Continental Congress	John Locke, "Of Civil Government" "Of the State of War" "Of Slavery" "Of Usurpation" "Of Tyranny" "Of Dissolution of Government"
John Hancock John & Abigail Adams George & Martha Washington	Battle of Lexington & Concord Battle of Bunker Hill Battle of Trenton	Committees of Correspondence	
Benjamin Franklin John Paul Jones Robert Morris Thomas Jefferson Joseph Warren Paul Revere	Battle of Saratoga Battle of Long Island Battle of Yorktown Valley Forge Intolerable Acts		Artillery & Election Sermon, Rev. Howard Simeon (*ClP*, p. 193) Letter From the Boston Committees of Correspondence, 1773 (*ClP*, p. 457)
Marquis De Lafayette Gen. Baron Von Steubon Casimar Pulaski	The Aitkin Bible		Day of Prayer & Fasting, June 20, 1775, Proclamation (*ClP*, p. 505)
Samuel Adams			Declaration of Independence Virginia Declaration of Rights Declaration of Right to Bear Arms The Divine Goodness Displayed in the American Revolution, Rev. John Rogers (*ClP*, p. 52)

Theme IV.

The American Christian Constitution, 1782-1789

The American Revolution would have been in vain if it had not resulted in true union and an adequate general – or federal – government of the thirteen newly free and sovereign states of America. Without a strong union and a well-structured over-all government, the independent states would have dissolved and disintegrated, either through gradual annihilation of one another or from attacks by preying and meddling foreign forces.

Under the Articles of Confederation of 1782–1789, there were no provisions for the common defense nor were there enforceable laws for the common good with which to promote domestic tranquility and secure the blessings of liberty for which Americans had just paid dearly. It was a critical time when jealousy and self-interest of the states hindered voluntary union and effective cooperation for the good of the whole.

BALANCE OF POWER

But Providence worked by degrees to bring about timely issues that prompted a Constitutional Convention and a miraculous union bound by an American Christian Constitution – one government for a nation of diverse and independent states. This Constitution balanced national supremacy with states' sovereignty; and while making provision for one supreme law, it maintained inviolate local self-government. The Constitution was not a bundle of compromises between political factions and social classes, as some have maintained – rather, it articulated that perfect balance between liberty and law as reasoned through by the wisdom resulting from nearly two hundred years of education in the Biblical principles of self- and civil government – taught in the homes, churches and schools of colonial America.

CHARACTER FOR A REPUBLIC

"It was not enough that the country should become free from the domination of England: it was necessary that it should be united into a nation, and the numerous Colonies that had been converted into States should be formed into one Republic. This was a solemn hour in our history. The American cause needed men of far-sighted sagacity, of able statesmanship; it needed men of incorruptible patriotism, who would fill the offices of government, not in the interest of self, but of their country, – faithful at home, and just abroad." (Rev. J.W. Foljambe; *CIP*, p. 52)

"A study of the writings of George Washington, James Madison, Thomas Jefferson, Samuel Adams, Alexander Hamilton and others during the critical period of 1783 through 1786 reveals their concern for their nation and the necessity for establishing a Republic. In the history of mankind, such a republic as they structured had never been done. Was now the time to attempt it? These men thought so. They counted upon the Christian education of the people to understand and support such a venture. The success or failure of such an enterprise would depend upon the Christian character of the people and their understanding of the Biblical principle of self-government with union. God had provided such instruction for more than one hundred fifty years." (*BIC*, p. 32)

THEME IV.

THE AMERICAN CHRISTIAN CONSTITUTION
1782 – 1789

KEY INDIVIDUALS	KEY EVENTS	KEY INSTITUTIONS	KEY DOCUMENTS, SPEECHES, SERMONS OR ESSAYS
George Washington Alexander Hamilton James Madison John Jay Edmund Randolph William Patterson Benjamin Franklin James Wilson John Dickenson Roger Sherman Gouverneur Morris	Shay's Rebellion Domestic Problems Monetary Problems Treaty Problems Territorial Problems Ratification	Articles of Confederation Annapolis Convention Constitutional Convention Federalists Anti-Federalists	John Locke, *Of Civil Government* "Of the Ends of Political Society & Government" "Of Property" "Of the Forms of a Commonwealth" "Of the Extent of the Legislative Power" "Of the Legislative, Executive, & Federative Power of the Commonwealth" "Of the Subordination of the Powers of the Commonwealth" "Of Prerogative" The Constitution of the United States: Preamble Articles I, II, III, IV, V, VI, VII American Bill of Rights

THEME V.

AMERICA, "THE FULLEST EXPRESSION OF A CHRISTIAN CIVILIZATION," 1789-1830

The peace effected between the states by federal union, so secured to the individual his liberty and property that America prospered more rapidly than any nation ever had before. If America became the land of free states and free men whose every imagination for good grew unhindered and unrestrained in every field of endeavor in the arts and sciences, then it also became the inviting soil in which to plant the seeds of dying Old World institutions, hoping to renew themselves with American vivacity, and material resources.

Constitutional liberty promised a Christian resolution of Old World problems and social ills. Every freedom attained constitutionally for the people as a whole was preceded in America by some further development of Christian liberty in individual experience.

Westward went the Bible and constitutional government, carried by the pioneers – a new generation of Pilgrims. America became the model for would-be modern republics and free nations the world over.

But then, when the American Christian home, church and school wandered from their Biblical principles, the "tares" (false doctrines), which have always sought nourishment in individual Christians and free societies, began to sow their corruptive seeds and undermine the character so necessary to our Christian Republic. Americans exchanged the truth of God for a lie, and proceeded to *let* our Constitutional principles fall away and to *let* the notions of democratic socialism overrun her institutions.

"GREAT IS OUR LORD"

"The future chronicler of events, as he looks down on the unrolled scroll of time, will write down the period in which we live as part of the marvellous century in human story. The interest in history deepens as time advances, for it becomes more and more the record of intellectual and moral progress, of the advancing liberty and happiness of mankind. This is preeminently so with our history. It is the story of wonderful growth ... not by the might of our power, or the wisdom of our counsel, has this nation been built, or its resources developed. Has there been wisdom in our counsels? It was by the inspiration of the Almighty. Has wealth increased? God gave us power to get wealth (*Deut.* 8:18). Has freedom gained new victories? He led us in the ways of righteousness for his name's sake." *"He hath not dealt so with any nation" (Psa. 147:20).* (Rev. J.W. Foljambe; *C/P*, p. 53)

". . . But all this was far from ignoring the religious spirit in our national life, its guiding and impelling power in the lives of our people, and its formative influence in all their institutions and laws. If ever there has been a people who incorporated the Bible into themselves, and themselves into the Bible, – whose laws, customs, institutions and literature were permeated by the spirit of Christianity. . ." (*B/C*, p. 53)

THEME V.

AMERICA, "THE FULLEST EXPRESSION OF A CHRISTIAN CIVILIZATION" 1789 – 1830

KEY INDIVIDUALS	KEY EVENTS	KEY INSTITUTIONS	KEY DOCUMENTS, SPEECHES, SERMONS OR ESSAYS
George Washington	Whiskey Rebellion	Jeffersonian Democracy	Proclamation of Neutrality, 1794
John Adams	The French Revolution	Tariffs	
Thomas Jefferson		National Bank	Washington's Farewell Address
James Madison	Land Act of 1796	Party Politics	
James Monroe	Louisiana Purchase	Jacksonian Democracy	Jay Treaty
John Quincy Adams		Abolition	
	War of 1812	Nullification	The Monroe Doctrine, 1823
Noah Webster	Jay Treaty, 1814	Humanitarianism	
Horace Mann		State School Systems & Normal	"Letter to A Young Gentlemen
	Louisiana Purchase	Teachers College	Commencing His Education,"
Meriweather Lewis	Lewis & Clark Expedition		by Noah Webster, 1823
William Clark	Florida Purchase	Nationalism	
Jedidiah Smith	Missouri Compromise	Temperance Movements	
		Women's Suffrage	
Cyrus McCormick		Brook Farm	
Eli Whitney		American Labor Party	
Robert Fulton			
Henry Wadsworth Longfellow			
Benjamin West			
John S. Copley			
Charles Peale			
Rembrandt Peale			
Louisa May Alcott			
Henry Clay			
Andrew Jackson			
Washington Irving			

THEME VI.

AMERICA'S FALLING AWAY: THE CORRUPTION AND THE CORRECTION OF A CHRISTIAN REPUBLIC, 1830-PRESENT

As American Christians yielded to the temptations which accompany affluence and, as their vigilant determination to keep their liberties was gradually displaced by complacency and self-satisfaction, so they carelessly neglected the sacred trust of maintaining the spirit of the Constitution.

American Christians yielded their places of leadership in religion, education, and civil government. Through the medium of the state school, the Gospel of Christ was cast aside for a social gospel as *the* factor in shaping the character and conduct of oncoming generations. In the 1830's, the instructors trained in the normal schools were prepared to teach a non-sectarian, non-controversial, humanitarian curriculum.

A generation-and-a-half later, the progress of America's republic came to a halt with civil war – a bloody conflict which could not be prevented, for lack of Christian character and Biblical scholarship. Religious subversion, seen in various deviations from Biblical doctrine, was subtle and effective – a necessary first step in undermining America's Christian Republic. The training of character, once under the careful supervision of Christian teachers importing Scriptural truths concerning individual affections and actions, was surrendered to well-intentioned humanitarian hands, which molded a character ready to serve a secular social conscience, rather than a true Christian conscience.

EDUCATED CHARACTER FOR SOCIALISM

This erosion of character led to the deterioration of Constitutional liberty; and as the people lost their understanding of Constitutional principles and were taught collectivist ideas in the schools and colleges, socialism was free to take possession of every institution: the home, church, school, business, and civil government.

America's Civil War was the bitter consequence of the inability of men ruled by their passions to manage the affairs of the federal union. Issues overran principles and in the course of the conflict the national government gained powers which the Constitution's framers never intended, and which it has never given up. After the war, social ills and issues were resolved increasingly by social control through law, and centralization grew as local governments surrendered their spheres of authority and responsibility. The result was political subversion – a corruption and erosion of America's original system of government.

In turn, the federal official's intermeddling into local affairs became the foundation for America's intermeddling policies in international affairs. America's usual and normal practice at home became America's usual and normal practice abroad.

Educators committed to secularism and socialism gained control of the educational system, and shaped it to spread the doctrines in which they believed. Educational subversion – the undermining of America's traditional Christian approach to instruction – was put into operation through a national program for "progressive education" intended to foster generations of citizens who would bring America into conformity with international socialism.

For over one hundred years, this country has suffered afflictions, both individual and national, because American Christians forgot God's Hand in their history and forsook the Constitution He gave them through the dedication and sacrifice of their Founding Fathers.

RESTORING THE FOUNDATIONS

If a Christian republic should be built, and then fall away through corruption, may not Providence correct and restore it to even greater heights of Christian liberty, not only for its own citizens but for all mankind and for the greater glory of Christ?

Though the secular socialistic character of Americans and their institutions raises resistance to this nation's Christian history and form of civil government, Providence may, by degrees, bring to light the road to restoration – the path marked by remembrance, repentance, and return. American Christians must retell and relive the experiences of those first two hundred years before their country became the world's first Christian Republic, and then begin to rebuild their nation even as Nehe-

THEME VI.
AMERICA'S FALLING AWAY: THE CORRUPTION AND THE CORRECTION OF A CHRISTIAN REPUBLIC, 1830 – PRESENT

KEY INDIVIDUALS	KEY EVENTS	KEY INSTITUTIONS	KEY DOCUMENTS, SPEECHES, SERMONS OR ESSAYS
Abraham Lincoln	The American Civil War	Sectionalism	Emancipation Proclamation
Robert E. Lee	The Spanish American War	Manifest Destiny	13th-17th Amendments
Ulysses S. Grant	World War I	Nullification	
	World War II	Socialism	"Letter to Young Ladies," Lydia
George Washington Carver	The Cold War	Welfarism	Sigourney (*CHOC*, pp. 307-310)
Daniel Webster	The Korean War	Denominationalism	
John C. Calhoun	The Vietnam War	Conservatism	"Southern Colonies & Slavery"
Andrew Jackson	Grenada	Liberalism	(*CIP*, pp. 432-433)
Samuel F. B. Morse	The California Gold Rush	Civil Rights Movement	The Gettysburg Address
N. C. Wyeth		The New Deal	
Winslow Homer	Attack on Fort Sumter	Internal Revenue Service	Reconstruction Acts
Thomas Eakins	Battle of Gettysburg	The United Nations	
John Phillip Sousa	Sherman's March		Treaty of Peace at Versailles, 1919
Orville & Wilbur Wright	Impeachment of Andrew Johnson	Church Independents	The U.N. Charter, 1945
		Christian Day School and Home-	
Commodore Perry	The Union Pacific Railroad	School Movement	SALT Treaties
Horace Mann	Open Door Policy with China		
John Dewey	Panama Canal	Foundations for the Restoration of	
Woodrow Wilson		America	
Herbert Hoover	The Depression of 1929		
Franklin D. Roosevelt	Annexation of Alaska and Hawaii		
Ronald Wilson Reagan			
	The Equal Rights Amendment		

miah and his faithful band rebuilt the Jerusalem wall.

THE DANGERS BESETTING US

"Knowledge is power, but it may be power for evil as much as good; it has no moral quality in itself. The greatest danger of the Republic is its educated, experienced, cultivated, corrupt demagogues. Intelligence without religion is a dangerous pilot for the ship of state. Eliminate that element; take religious thought, sentiment, and aspirations from the atmosphere of our education, and men will soon become animalized, and this government sink beneath the green pool of its own corruption.

". . . No thoughtful man can close his eyes to the dangers which beset us, or be unmindful of the new issues constantly arising, demanding for their wise resolution the most unselfish and the purest patriotism with the most enlightened Christian conscientiousness . . .

". . . We are menaced by a growing spirit of materialism. The eagerness of men after material prosperity tends to a practical absorption in those ends. Thus we have the greed, the excitement, the infatuation, the extravagance, and the corruption, that, to so great an extent, characterize our times. The abounding iniquity of our day is a just cause of alarm. While we ought not to forget nor undervalue much that is noble, and true, and good, in the present time, nor regard the former days as in all respects better than these, we must admit that we are living in a period of shameful prevalent corruption and crime. Each daily paper brings its fresh installment of defalcations, fraudulent dealing, forgery, robbery, and murder. On every hand men are making void the law of God . . . there is a strengthening of bands of wickedness, and a breaking away from the restraints of law . . .

"It is true you cannot legislate evil out of the world, but by our impartial, rigorous justice you can make it too costly for practice, and by a wise and Christian legislation you may limit its reach and remove its temptations; and for this, in its most perfect measure, and to our utmost ability, the God of righteousness holds every man responsible . . . What our country needs in its leaders and legislators are the purest Christian principles, the loftiest personal character, the highest and most unselfish political aims; that they be men whom no gold can buy, no adulation of the people can mislead, and no spirit of ambition pervert." (S.W. Foljambe; *CIP*, pp. 53, 54)

SUGGESTED BIBLIOGRAPHY
FOR RESEARCH
AND LESSON PLANNING

The instructor will find the recommended readings below helpful in establishing his spiritual and academic position in teaching America's Christian History to Senior High School students. The readings articulate the spirit which should enliven all the facts which may be presented.

Only as present and future generations remember the Hand of God in America's history will they begin to return to the God of their fathers. It is in this spirit of true remembrance and repentance that the Foundation for American Christian Education made the following publications available:

The Bible and The Constitution, (B/C), 1983

The Christian History of the American Revolution – Consider and Ponder (C/P), pp. xxiii-xxxv

The Christian History of the Constitution (CHOC), pp. 1-15, 16; 405-406, 407

Rudiments of America's Christian History and Government, (Rudiments), pp. 30-37, 42-61

Teaching and Learning America's Christian History and Government, (T/L), pp. 141-157, 210-214, 215; 225-231; 311-316

Christian Self Government with Union, (GSG/U)

Resources which are useful for gathering factual accounts and overviews are textbooks such as:

American History in Verse, Burton Stevenson, Editor; Bob Jones University Press, 1932

Atlas of the United States; Hammond Inc.; Gemini Ed., 1984

Classroom Atlas; Rand McNally, 1979

Leading Facts of American History; D.H. Montgomery, Chautauqua Press, 1891

The Oxford History of the American People; Samuel Eliot Morison; Oxford University Press, 1965

The Quest of a Hemisphere; Donzella Cross Boyle, Western Islands, 1970

A Basic History of the United States; Clarence B. Carson, Western Goals, 1984

To guide the teacher in his studies, a bibliography relevant to each of the six major themes has been suggested for lesson preparations. It may not be possible or necessary to master all the content found under each of the themes; however, all that is needed at first is enough knowledge to prepare ordered and concise lessons that satisfactorily represent each theme. The references offer possible student reading and writing assignments. Some books may no longer be in print, but could be available at local college libraries.

BIBLIOGRAPHY

I. AMERICA, RESERVED BY GOD FOR CHRISTIAN SELF-GOV'T, 1000-1620	II. ONE HUNDRED FIFTY YEARS OF LOCAL SELF-GOVERNMENT, 1620-1770	III. THE AMERICAN CHRISTIAN REVOLUTION, 1765-1783
CHOC; pp. 16-40, 41; 150A-175	*CHOC*; pp. 48-50; 148-150; 150A; 176-314, 315; 413-417; 419-425; 50A-150, 391-395, 396-397; 398-404	*CHOC*; pp. 315-370; 372-390; 425-427
Self-Government With Union, (SGW/U); pp. 1-24	*B/C*; pp. 3-23, 24; 45-65	*C/P*; pp. 55-86; 191-210; 250-252, 253-254, 255; 300-313, 314; 352
T/L; pp. 158-179; 189-198; 215-224; 324-337, 338	*SGW/U*; pp. 301-329	*SGW/U*; pp. 330-585
Rudiments; pp. 62, 63-65	*C/P*; pp. 259-262; 275-310; 349-352; 357-422; 427-506; 46-50, 51; 89-182; 183-188, 189	*B/C*; pp. 24, 25-31, 32
Pocahontas, Grace Steele Woodward, Univ. of Oklahoma Press, 1969	*T/L*; pp. 198-203	*T/L*; pp. 227-239; 248; 250-268; 338, 339-342
Pocahontas, Ingri & Edgar Parin D'Aulaire; Doubleday, 1946	*Rudiments*; pp. 71-76	*Rudiments*; pp. 66-68
The Travels of Marco Polo	*The Making of George Washington*, William Wilbur; Patriotic Education Inc.; pp. 19-184	*The Making of George Washington*; pp. 185-205, 206
Admiral of the Ocean Sea, Samuel Eliot Morison; Little Brown & Co., 1942	*Old South Leaflets*, Old South Church, Boston:	*Lives of the Signers to the Declaration*; Rev. Charles A. Goodrich; William Reed & Co., 1829
Christopher Columbus, Piero Ventura; Camden House, 1977	"Words of John Robinson" "God's Promise to the Plantations," John Cotton	*The Farmer's & Monitor's Letters to the Inhabitants of the British Colonies*, Virginia Independence Bicentennial, Williamsburg, Va., 1969
Captain John Smith's America; John Lankford, Editor; Harper & Row, 1967	"Cotton Mather's Lives of Bradford and Winthrop" "The Day-Breaking of the Gospel with the Indians," John Eliot	*Old South Leaflets*, Old South Church Boston.
"The Settlement of Jamestown," John Smith; Old South Leaflet, Boston	"Bradford's Memoirs of Elder Brewster" "Winthrop's Letter on Liberty" "Winthrop's Conclusions" "The Humble Request, A Model of Christian Charity, 1630," John Winthrop "Lord Baltimore's Plantation in Maryland" "The Battle of Quebec," John Knox "The New York Declaration of 1764"	"Stamp Act Congress Declarations and Petitions, October, 1765" "The Boston Tea Party," Thomas Hutchinson "Paul Revere's Own Account of His Midnight Ride, April 18-19, 1775" "Layfayette in the American Revolution" "Battle Between the *Bon Homme* and the *Serapis*" "The Capture of Vincennes, 1779"

IV. THE AMERICAN CHRISTIAN CONSTITUTION, 1783-1789	V. AMERICA, "THE FULLEST EXPRESSION OF A CHRISTIAN CIVILIZATION," 1789-1830	VI. AMERICA'S FALLING AWAY, 1830-Present
CHOC; pp. 50A-150; 413-417; 528	*CHOC*; pp. 411-412	*CHOC*; pp. 371; 407-410
T/L; pp. 173, 174-176; 204-209; 240-247; 306-310; 317-323; 343-352; 353-354	*T/L*; pp. 276-279, 280-301	*T/L*; pp. 210-214, 215
B/C; pp. 32, 33-37, 38; Appendix, "Official Edition of Constitution Sent by Continental Congress to States for Ratification, September 28, 1787."	*C/P*; pp. 51, 52-54; 213-220, 221; 189, 190	*C/P*; pp. xxiii-xxxvi; 221-223, 224, 248, 249, 250; 255-256
Rudiments; pp. 69-70	*Rudiments*; pp. 3-29	*Rudiments*; pp. 1-2
The Making of George Washington; pp. 206, 207-221, 222	*B/C*; pp. 38, 39	*B/C*; pp. 39, 40-41
The Federalist Papers; James Madison, Alexander Hamilton, & John Jay	*The Making of George Washington*; pp. 222, 223-254	*Little Women*, Louisa May Alcott; 1868
Elementary Catechism on the Constitution of the United States, Arthur Stansbury; Hilliard, Gray, Little & Williams; Boston, 1828. (Reprint available from the American Christian History Institute)	*George Washington*, Ingri & Edgar Parin D'Aulaire; Doubleday & Co. 1936	*The Old South Leaflets*, Boston: "The First Lincoln-Douglas Debates" "The Fall of the Alamo" "Commodore Perry and Japan"
	"Washington's Farewell Address"	*Abraham Lincoln*; Ingri and Edgar Parin D'Aulaire; Doubleday, 1946
	Democracy in America; Alexis de Tocqueville	*The Glory and the Dream*; Michael A. Musmanno; The Long House, 1967
	Old South Leaflets, Boston: "The Monroe Doctrine" "Washington's Address to the Churches" "Washington's Legacy" "Letters of Washington and Lafayette"	*The Age of Jackson*; Arthur M. Schlesinger, Jr., 1945
		Addresses Upon the American Road, 1933-1938; Herbert Hoover; Charles Scribners, 1938
		The Memoirs of Herbert Hoover, 1874-1920, 1920-1933, & 1929-1941; Houghton & Mifflin Co., 1959
		The Coming of the New Deal; Arthur M. Schlesinger, Jr., 1959
		A Thousand Days, Arthur M. Schlesinger; Houghton & Mifflin Co., 1965
		The White House Years; Henry Kissinger; Little, Brown & Co., 1979
		The Reagans, Peter Hannaford; Coward-McCann, 1983
		Reagan, Lou Cannon; Putnam Publishing Group, 1982

LESSON PREPARATION, LECTURE TOPICS, STUDENT ASSIGNMENTS

THE FOUR APPROACHES

Within the range of each of the six themes or period divisions of the American Christian History course, are *key individuals, events, institutions* and *documents, sermons, and speeches or writings* which characterize the leading ideas of that period. Therefore, four approaches to each of the major themes may be used to emphasize particular aspects of the time under study.

These four approaches are: (1) the biographical sketch, the life and work of *one key individual*; (2) an *event* study, the origin of historical activities with their consequences upon later history; (3) the analysis of an *institution* in an effort to discern its philosophy and effects upon man and society as a whole; and, then, (4) the close reading of a recorded work (*document, sermon, speech* or *writing*), uncovering the operating principles.

PLANNING LESSONS

Both teacher and student may apply these four approaches throughout the course. The teacher may construct lectures and student research assignments around an individual, an event, an institution, or a literary work. Whatever the student is assigned to do for himself, it complements what the teacher has already discussed and reasoned through with the student in the classroom.

The teacher is *selective*, not exhaustive, about the time period he is teaching. He may use more than one of the four approaches in a manner such as to move with ease through the spans of time, maintaining continuity of the entire curriculum as well as sustaining student interest in the course.

To assist one in the researching, reasoning, relating and recording required of the four approaches to the study of history, one begins by organizing his findings upon a chart. For each approach there is a chart.

Now follows explanations of the four charts which may be used for planning and constructing lessons and assignments. After the explanation of each chart is an example or examples to illustrate what is meant. It is best in research to *use the words of the author or speaker* for more authoritative referencing. The task may seem tedious but is well rewarded by the elevation of thought, the expanded vocabulary and greater conviction or believability which results from using direct quotes and statements from the rich resources of America's Christian history and government.

The charts are examples of the type of research essential to begin good lesson planning; however, these are not to be given verbatim as lecture notes, nor need they be taught in their entirety. Teachers should be selective and decide from this research what must be communicated. The teacher decides what the student is to remember and recall with regard to the individual, the event, the institution, and/or the literary work under discussion and study. Aim at making the *ideas* clear, concise, and complete within themselves.

ORGANIZING LESSONS

As an example, from the research on one key individual, John Witherspoon, in the pages which follow, one may choose to organize his lessons from a variety of ways:

A. Develop four individual lessons for four separate occasions –
   1. "The Christian History of John Witherspoon"
   2. "The Influences Upon His Character"
   3. "The Character of John Witherspoon"
   4. "John Witherspoon's Contribution to the Chain of Christianity Moving Westward"

          or

B. Develop two lessons for two separate occasions –
   1. "The Christian History and Influences Upon John Witherspoon"
   2. "The Character of John Witherspoon and His Contribution to the Chain of Christianity"

          or

C. Develop one lesson from one of the following choices –
   1. "The Character of John Witherspoon and His Contribution to the Chain of Christianity"

          or

   2. "The Christian History of John Witherspoon, The Influences Upon

His Character and Contribution to the Chain of Christianity"

3. "The Contribution of John Witherspoon to the Chain of Christianity"

The teacher, in command of the content of his material, governs himself with practicality and versatility, taking into consideration the time available and his student's capability.

It is not necessary, but always enjoyable, to enrich the teaching of history with the poetic, imaginative and emotional qualities inherent in good literature. The bringing together of sentiment and intellect suitable to the topic will help remove from the subject of history the stigma which it holds for many individuals of being "dead and dry." Thus, at the conclusion of each example there is a poem selected to convey the appropriate spirit and feeling for the topic examined and charted. The poems or prose the teacher chooses to use ought to affirm his conclusions and inferences concerning the topic.

How to Study Key Individuals

In the research of a Key *Individual*, one might consider four areas of significance: (1) the time and historical setting into which Providence places that individual, (2) the influences responsible for his character development or training, (3) the attributes of his personality which are marked and prominent, and (4) the contribution the individual makes to forward the Gospel, or the Chain of Christianity Moving Westward.

On the chart for biographical sketches are the headings: "Christian History," "Christian Influences," "Christian Character," and "Christian Contribution."

Under "Christian History" one may write all those phrases and statements which depict the historical "setting" of an individual's life span, including the religious, mental, moral, social and emotional conditions of the time.

Under "Christian Influence" one would record phrases and statements which shed light on how such influences as the home, church, school, friends, associates and associations, literature, and circumstances affect the formation and strengthening of the individual's Christian character.

For "Christian Character" (or Personal Characteristics) one reads to discern and identify phrases and statements which describe and reveal Christian and peculiar attributes impressed by nature or acquired by training and habit. These are expressed in personal quotes, opinions, and the individual's reputation in society with regard to temperament, disposition, and inclinations.

When noting the "Christian Contribution" of an individual, give an account of his works—writings, speeches, services rendered and influences upon individuals and institutions. Include acclamations from contemporaries and subsequent historians, and how the person may have affected future individuals and events.

The following study of Rev. John Witherspoon consists of a few selected excerpts from one biographer. Your study could cover his entire life span.

310

KEY INDIVIDUAL
Reverend John Witherspoon 1722 – 1794

(M.E. Swanson, "Biographies," *Consider and Ponder*, pp. 570-573)

CHRISTIAN HISTORY	CHRISTIAN INFLUENCES	CHRISTIAN CHARACTER (and personal characteristics)	CHRISTIAN CONTRIBUTION
Born in South Yester, near Edinburgh, Scotland, the son of that town's pastor, the Rev. James Witherspoon; on his mother's side; it is said he could trace his ancestry back to John Knox . . . . . . the General Assembly of the Presbyterian Church insisted that the ecclesiastical authorities had the final word in regard to the appointment of ministers. Dr. Witherspoon was inaugurated on August 13, 1768. Dr. Witherspoon arrived at Philadelphia just as Congress was debating the resolution for independence. "great political crisis lying before the country" When the Congress declared May 17 as a day of fasting, Dr. Witherspoon preached a sermon (later published with a dedication to John Hancock) . . . *The Dominion of Providence over the Passions of Men*, a full discussion of the great political crises lying before the country, its causes and its cure After the war, he set about rebuilding the College of New Jersey, which had been closed during most of that time.	He attended grammar school at Haddington . . . At age thirteen, he was admitted to the University of Edinburgh where he received his M.A. in 1739 and his B.C. in 1743. In 1764, he was given a D.D. degree from the University of St. Andrews.	. . . intellectual precocity Of a sturdy build, with bushy eyebrows, and a soft Scotts "burr," he was an eloquent preacher and public speaker, gifted with a naturally commanding presence, rigorous intellect, and penetrating wit. A distinguished Presbyterian minister . . . Early in his ministry at Paisely, he had allied himself with the Church's Popular Party, becoming one of its most influential leaders. A major plank of the party was "the right to personal conscience," which Dr. Witherspoon heartily supported. Dr. Witherspoon defended the right of congregations to choose their own ministers. . . . full of activity and accomplishment this first half of Dr. Witherspoon's life. . . . he accepted the second invitation preferred to him by the Trustees of the College of New Jersey to become its President. He . . . lectured on four subjects: Eloquence and Comparative Taste and Criticism; Moral Philosophy; Chronology of History; and Divinity. Dr. Witherspoon was an accomplished linguist and is reported to have spoken French with "almost as much ease and eloquence as his own tongue." He believed in the necessity of a thorough mastery of the English language as he felt he was preparing his students for a life of public service. Learning as a mere adornment of the gentleman did not appeal to him. He felt that scholarship should have practical value to the living of life.	During the great debates at the Continental Congress in 1776, one of strongest voices in favor of independence . . . . . . to represent the State of New Jersey at Congress for the ensuing six years. – the only clergyman to sign the Declaration of Independence – and was President of the College of New Jersey. In 1743 he was licensed to preach and by 1745 was an ordained minister at Beith in Ayrshire . . . In 1757, the Church of Paisely called him to be its pastor and (1759) he was called to be moderator of the Synod of Glasgow and Ayr. . . . he introduced many improvements in the college curriculum, including new teaching methods. Teaching by lecture was one . . . He broadened the curriculum to include philosophy, Hebrew (which he taught), French, history, and oratory. . . . the philosophy of "common sense," which permeated American educational thought for a long period. As a result of all this fund-raising activity, the college debts soon were paid off and a small surplus remained. . . . under his aegis, there was a remarkable revival of religion at the College of New Jersey. When he arrived in the Colonies the Church was divided by various factions and, as a result, was in a stagnant state. Under his leadership, these factional differences were healed, the church institution became better organized, and best of all – ties of friendship were formed with the Congregational Church. Thus, revitalized, the Church began to grow and soon spread to the frontiers.

COLUMBIA

COLUMBIA, Columbia, to glory arise,
The queen of the world, and the child of the skies;
Thy genius commands thee; with rapture behold,
While ages on ages thy splendor unfold,
Thy reign is the last, and the noblest of time,
Most fruitful thy soil, most inviting thy clime;
Let the crimes of the east ne'er encrimson thy name,
Be freedom, and science, and virtue thy fame.

To conquest and slaughter let Europe aspire:
Whelm nations in blood, and wrap cities in fire;
Thy heroes the rights of mankind shall defend,
And triumph pursue them, and glory attend.
A world is thy realm: for a world be thy laws,
Enlarged as thine empire, and just as thy cause;
On Freedom's broad basis, that empire shall rise,
Extend with the main, and dissolve with the skies.

Fair Science her gates to thy sons shall unbar,
And the east see the morn hide the beams of her star.
New bards, and new sages, unrivaled shall soar
To fame unextinguished, when time is no more;
To thee, the last refuge of virtue designed,
Shall fly from all nations the best of mankind;
Here, grateful to Heaven, with transport shall bring
Their incense, more fragrant than odors of spring . . .

Thy fleets to all regions thy power shall display,
The nations admire and the ocean obey;
Each shore to thy glory its tribute unfold,
And the east and the south yield their spices and gold.
As the day-spring unbounded, thy splendor shall flow,
And earth's little kingdoms before thee shall bow;
While the ensigns of union, in triumph unfurled,
Hush the tumult of war and give peace to the world.

Thus, as down a lone valley, with cedars o'er-spread,
From war's dread confusion I pensively strayed,
The gloom from the face of fair heaven retired;
The winds ceased to murmur; the thunders expired;
Perfumes as of Eden flowed sweetly along,
And a voice as of angels, enchantingly sung:
"Columbia, Columbia, to glory arise,
The queen of the world, and the child of the skies."

TIMOTHY DWIGHT

(*AMERICAN HISTORY IN VERSE*, Burton Stevenson, Editor.)

How to Study Key Events

In charting the researches pertaining to *key events*, look for "Causes and Purposes," "Key Individuals," "Principles of Civil Government," and "Historical Significance."

"Causes and Purposes" account for the various secondary motives of men and nations, as well as for the primary causes traced to the Hand of Providence. There are always the plans of good men and the schemes of wicked men, and both serve the far greater purposes of God. These things are viewed in retrospect, through the eyes of the enlightened historian.

A list and description of the major individuals involved with carrying out the actions and reactions which constitute an event are recorded in the column marked "Key Individuals."

The activities of men and nations are expressions of either Biblical or pagan civil government. These activities are documented and noted as such in the next column – "Principles of Civil Government."

"Historical Significance" accounts for the end results and consequences accompanying the event. This is the concluding evaluation of the matter. Also, note the issues born out of the event. There will be the affirmation or the overthrowing of some principle, as well as the appearing of resolutions to issues and problems.

KEY EVENT

The Boston Port Bill, 1774

BY DAVID RAMSEY

(*Consider and Ponder*, pp. 460, 461)

CAUSES AND PURPOSES	KEY INDIVIDUALS	PRINCIPLES OF CIVIL GOVERNMENT	HISTORICAL SIGNIFICANCE
The minister who proposed this measure stated, in support of it, that the opposition to the authority of parliament had always originated in that colony, and had always been instigated by the seditious proceedings of the town of Boston; that it was therefore necessary to make an example of that town, which, by an unparalleled outrage had violated the freedom of commerce; and that Great Britain would be wanting in the protection she owed to her peaceable subjects, if she did not punish such an insult, in an exemplary manner. . . . making a pecuniary satisfaction would not be sufficient . . . it would be proper to take away, from Boston, the privilege of a port . . .	abettors of parliamentary supremacy Several natives and inhabitants of North America then residing in London	. . . disproportionate penalty *liberty:* the same principle of self-preservation, which justifies the breaking of the assassin's sword, uplifted for destruction, equally authorized the destruction of that tea, which was the vehicle of an unconstitutional tax, subverting of their liberties. *parliamentary supremacy:* . . . open defiance of that country (Great Britain) . . . treasonable intention to emancipate themselves from a state of colonial dependence. . . . the proceedings of Parliament against Boston were repugnant to every principle of law and justice.	The consequences resulting from this measure were the reverse of what were wished . . .

313

KEY EVENT

THE BOSTON PORT BILL, 1774

BY MERCY WARREN

(Consider and Ponder, pp. 389, 390)

CAUSES AND PURPOSES	KEY INDIVIDUALS	PRINCIPLES OF CIVIL GOVERNMENT	HISTORICAL SIGNIFICANCE
It was at this period that Lord North ushered into the house of commons the memorable bill for shutting up the port of Boston, also the bill for better regulating the government of Massachusetts. . . . though the cruelty and injustices of this step was warmly criminated, the minister and his party urged the necessity of strong measures, nor was it difficult to obtain a large majority to enforce them . . . in full force until satisfaction should be made for the loss of their teas; nor were any assurances given, that in case of submission and compliance, they should be repealed.	Lord North ushered into the house of commons the memorable bill . . . It was frequently observed, that the only melioration of the present evils was, that the recall of Mr. Hutchinson accompanied the bills, and his leaving the province at the same period the port-bill was to be put in operation, seemed to impress a dawn of hope from time, if not from his immediate successor. Every historical record will doubtless witness that he (Gov. Thomas Hutchinson) was the principal author of the sufferings of the unhappy Bostonians, previous to the convulsions which produced the revolution.	*arbitrary acts:* many thousands of the most loyal subjects of the house of Brunswick were at once cut off from the means of subsistence; poverty stared in the face of affluence, and a long train of evils threatened every rank. No discriminations were made. The innocent were equally involved with the real or imputed guilty. *brotherly love and Christian care:* but from the charitable donations of the other colonies, multitudes must have inevitably perished.	Several of the southern colonies remonstrated warmly against those novel proceedings towards Massachusetts, and considered it as a common cause.

KEY EVENT

THE BOSTON PORT BILL, 1774

BY VERNA HALL AND ROSALIE SLATER

(The Bible and the Constitution, p. 31)

CAUSES AND PURPOSES	KEY INDIVIDUALS	PRINCIPLES OF CIVIL GOVERNMENT	HISTORICAL SIGNIFICANCE
when Great Britain, counting on political divisions and colonial jealousies, closed the Port of Boston as a punitive response to the Boston Tea Party in 1773. On March 25, 1774, Parliament passed the Boston Port Bill to stop all trade into or out of the Port of Boston. . . . a measure to disrupt America	The first action of the colonies was to call for a Day of Fasting and Prayer for June 1, 1774, the day which the Boston Port blockade would take affect. Thus the colonies turned immediately "to seek divine direction and aid." "The Christian sympathy and generosity of our friends through the Continent cannot fail to inspire the inhabitants of this town with patience, resignation, and firmness, while we trust in the Supreme Ruler of the universe . . ." a people Biblically educated, practiced in self-government in church, town meeting, colonial assembly, conscious of the principles which they were living out in character and state constitution.	The Committee of Correspondence was instructed to the several colonies to acquaint them with the present state of the affairs of Boston. The response was *unprecedented* in history. It was the expansion at the individual, community and national level of the Christian charity which stunned the pagan world in the first century of Christianity. . . . the *cement of union* which was the *internal unity of heart, mind and character* of the colonists. *voluntary cooperation:* the cities and towns of the sister colonies responded to Boston with letters affirming their support and sending them whatever supplies they could. Every colony contributed something for a period of over six months – *voluntarily* – to strangers. *Christian association:* "We do for ourselves, and the inhabitants of the several colonies whom we represent, firmly agree and associate under the sacred ties of virtue, honor and love of our country." *Unity and union:* – united *internally* in Biblical principles, acting *externally* in accordance with those principles, in voluntary association. *American Federalism:* This action of the colonies exemplified self-government with union . . .	. . . test of the sincerity and depth of the Colonists' Biblical philosophy of government. The Christian charity action of the colonies stunned Great Britain. When in history had there ever been such an outpouring of political action and political uniting based upon Christian Constitutional principles? These letters seem to have been written by a Master Hand. . . . became the means of achieving American political union. The Association of the United Colonies was in effect the commencement of the American Union, a league of the continent, which first expressed the sovereign will of the people on the subject of their commercial relations with Britain. – a precursor of American Federalism. . . . first step toward political union under the duress of external economic and political threats.

HOW WE BECAME A NATION

(April 15, 1774)

When George the King would punish folk
   Who dared resist his angry will –
Resist him with their hearts of oak
That neither King nor Council broke –
   He told Lord North to mend his quill,
   And send his Parliament a Bill.

The Boston Port Bill was the thing
   He flourished in his royal hand;
A subtle lash with scorpion sting,
Across the seas he made it swing,
   And with its cruel thong he planned
   To quell the disobedient land.

His minions heard it sing, and bare
   The port of Boston felt his wrath;
They let no ship cast anchor there,
They summoned Hunger and Despair –
   And curses in an aftermath
   Followed their desolating path.

No coal might enter there, nor wood,
   Nor Holland flax, nor silk from France;
No drugs for dying pangs, no food
For any mother's little brood.
   "Now," said the King, "we have our chance,
   We'll lead the haughty knaves a dance."

No other flags lit up the bay,
   Like full-blown blossoms in the air,
Than where the British war-ships lay;
The wharves were idle; all the day
   The idle men, grown gaunt and spare,
   Saw trouble, pall-like, everywhere.

Then in across the meadow land,
   From lonely farm and hunter's tent,
From fertile field and fellow strand,
Pouring it out with lavish hand,
   The neighboring burghs their bounty sent,
   And laughed at King and Parliament.

To bring them succor, Marblehead
   Joyous her deep-sea fishing sought.
Her trees, with ringing stroke and tread,
Old many-rivered Newbury sped,
   And Groton in her granaries wrought,
   And generous flocks old Windham brought.

Rice from the Carolinas came,
   Iron from Pennsylvania's forge,
And, with a spirit all aflame,
Tobacco-leaf and corn and game
   The Midlands sent; and in his gorge
   The Colonies defied King George!

And Hartford hung, in black array,
   Her town-house, and at half-mast there
The flags flowed, and the bells all day
Tolled heavily; and far away
   In great Virginia's solemn air
   The House of Burgesses held prayer.

Down long glades of the forest floor
   The same thrill ran through every vein,
And down the long Atlantic's shore;
Its heat the tyrant's fetters tore
   And welded them through stress and strain
   Of long years to a mightier chain.

That mighty chain with links of steel
   Bound all the Old Thirteen at last,
Through one electric pulse to feel
The common woe, the common weal.
   And that great day the Port Bill passed
Made us a nation hard and fast.

HARRIET PRESCOTT SPOFFORD
(*AMERICAN HISTORY IN VERSE*, Burton Stevenson, Editor.)

HOW TO STUDY KEY INSTITUTIONS

It is the intent of the chart used to study *Key Institutions* to identify those true or false principles responsible for producing a particular character which warrants and, then, supports, some particular manner of governmental direction, control, regulation, and restraint – whether of the individual or of society as a whole.

Institutions – ecclesiastical, social or political – distinguish themselves by a set of distinctive, foundational precepts which may be noted as their *doctrine* (in a general sense, whatever is taught as being true). Institutions protect, promote, and perpetuate themselves by stamping their doctrine upon the physical, mental and moral character of individuals. This body of precepts instructs and trains future generations to carry on the existence of the institution.

Institutions govern their constituents either by pagan principles or by Biblical principles. The government of an institution is directly derived from its own particular supporting doctrine. The purer the doctrine upon one's heart and mind, the more Christian the influence upon character, and, thus, the more Biblical is the government of the institution.

KEY INSTITUTION

THE AMERICAN INDIAN

(*Leading Facts*, Montgomery, p. 10)

DOCTRINE	CHARACTER	GOVERNMENT
1. America, a hunting ground; a battle field to fight on 2. believed in a strict division of duties: *men*, hunt, fish, scalp *women*, farm the fields, build the wigwam or hut of bark, made the deerskin clothes for the family, carry furniture on their back whenever they move, cultivate the corn and tobacco 3. bound by customs handed down from forefathers 4. could not marry outside of the tribe, could not sit at whatever seat at a council, could not paint his face any color he chose 5. usually believed in a Great Spirit, all powerful, wise and good; believed in many inferior spirits, good and evil 6. worshipped evil spirits most, to avoid evil	1. *Physical:* tall, well-made; color resembling that of old copper; hair like a horse's mane, coarse, black and straight; eyes, small, black and deep set; high cheekbones 2. *Moral:* savage, but seldom degraded; northern more barbarous than those of the southwest; conscientious in his own standard of right and wrong; would not steal from his own tribe; would not lie to his friends; did not become a drunkard till the white man taught him; painted his feelings on his face rather than express in words; laughed, shouted, and seldom wept; died like warriors; tortured their captives, they wanted to see how much agony they could bear without crying out. The surest way for a prisoner to save his life was to show that he was not afraid to lose it; never failed to show respect for courage; a treacherous and cruel enemy, but a steadfast friend; could return good for good, but he knew nothing of returning good for evil	1. *Tribal,* primitive stage of society, America scantily covered with wandering tribes of savages, rude in morals and manners, narrow and monotonous in experience, sustaining life very much as do lower animals sustain it, by gathering wild fruits or slaying wild game, and waging warfare alike with powerful beasts and with rival tribes of men. 2. *Four Main Tribes:* Algonquin, the most numerous; Iroquois, ablest and most ferocious; Mobilean, in the Southeast; Natchez, in the Southwest. 3. Politically free, independent of external rule by another nation 4. Chief had little real power; all important matters decided by councils 5. Individuals socially enslaved to tradition and spiritual bondage to evil spirits

THE PEACE PIPE

On the Mountains of the Prairie,
On the great Red Pipe-stone Quarry,
Gitche Manito, the mighty,
He the Master of Life, descending,
On the red crags of the quarry
Stood erect, and called the nations,
Called the tribes of men together.

From his foot prints flowed a river,
Leaped into the light of morning,
O'er the precipice plunging downward
Gleamed like Ishkoodah, the comet.
And the Spirit, stooping earthward,
With his finger on the meadow
Traced a winding pathway for it,
Saying to it, "Run in this way!"

From the red stone of the quarry
With his hand he broke a fragment,
Moulded it into a pipe-head,
Shaped and fashioned it with figures;
From the margin of the river
Took a long reed for a pipe-stem,
With its dark green leaves upon it;
Filled the pipe with bark of willow,
With the bark of the red willow;
Breathed upon the neighboring forest,
Made its great boughs chafe together,
Till in the flame they burst and kindled;
And erect upon the mountains,
Gitche Manito, the mighty,
Smoked the calumet, the Peace-Pipe,
As a signal to the nations.

And the smoke rose slowly, slowly,
Through the tranquil air of morning,
First a single line of darkness,
Then a denser, bluer vapor,
Then a snow-white cloud unfolding,
Like the tree-tops of the forest,
Ever rising, rising, rising,
Till it touched the top of heaven,
Till it broke against the heaven,
And rolled outward all around it.

From the Vale of Tawasentha,
From the Valley of Wyoming,
From the groves of Tuscaloosa,
From the far-off Rocky Mountains,
From the Northern lakes and rivers
All the tribes beheld the signal,
Saw the distant smoke ascending,
The Pukwana of the Peace-Pipe.

And the Prophets of the nations
Said: "Behold it, the Pukwana!
By this signal from afar off,
Bending like a wand of willow,
Waving like a hand that beckons,
Gitche Manito, the mighty,
Calls the tribes of men together,
Calls the warriors to his council!"

Down the rivers, o'er the prairies,
Came the warriors of the nations,
Came the Delawares and Mohawks,
Came the Choctaws, and Camanches,
Came the Shoshonies and Blackfeet,
Came the Pawnees and Omahas,
Came the Mandans and Dacotahs,
Came the Hurons and Ojibways,
All the warriors drawn together

By the signal of the Peace-Pipe,
To the Mountains of the Prairie,
To the great Red Pipe-stone Quarry.

　　And they stood there on the meadow,
With their weapons and their war-gear,
Painted like the leaves of Autumn,
Painted like the sky of morning,
Wildly glaring at each other;
In their faces stern defiance,
In their hearts the feuds of ages,
The hereditary hatred,
The ancestral thirst of vengeance.

　　Gitche Manito, the mighty
The creator of the nations,
Looked upon them with compassion,
With paternal love and pity;
Looked upon their wrath and wrangling
But as quarrels among children,
But as feuds and fights of children!

　　Over them he stretched his right hand,
To subdue their stubborn natures,
To allay their thirst and fever,
By the shadow of his right hand;
Spake to them with voice majestic
As the sound of far-off waters,
Falling into deep abysses,
Warning, chiding, spake in this wise: –

　　"O my children! my poor children!
Listen to the words of wisdom,
Listen to the words of warning,
From the lips of the Great Spirit,
From the Master of Life, who made you!

　　"I have given you lands to hunt in,
I have given you streams to fish in,
I have given you bear and bison,
I have given you roe and reindeer,
I have given you brant and beaver,
Filled the marshes full of wild-fowl,
Filled the rivers full of fishes;
Why then are you not contented?
Why then will you hunt each other?

　　"I am weary of your quarrels,
Weary of your wars and bloodshed,
Weary of your prayers for vengeance,
Of your wranglings and dissensions;
All your strength is in your union,
All your danger is in discord;
Therefore be at peace henceforward,
And as brothers live together.

　　"I will send a Prophet to you,
A Deliverer of the nations,
Who shall guide you and shall teach you,
Who shall toil and suffer with you.
If you listen to his counsels,
You will multiply and prosper;
If his warnings pass unheeded,
You will fade away and perish!

　　"Bathe now in the stream before you,
Wash the war-paint from your faces,
Wash the blood-stains from your fingers,
Bury your war-clubs and your weapons,
Break the red stone from this quarry,
Mould and make it unto Peace-Pipes,
Take the reeds that grow beside you,
Deck them with your brightest feathers,
Smoke the calumet together,
And as brothers live henceforward!"

　　Then upon the ground the warriors
Threw their cloaks and shirts of deer-skin,
Threw their weapons and their war-gear,
Leaped into the rushing river,
Washed the war-paint from their faces.
Clear above them flowed the water,
Clear and limpid from the footprints
Of the Master of Life descending;
Dark below them flowed the water,
Soiled and stained with streaks of crimson,
As if blood were mingled with it!

　　From the river came the warriors,
Clean and washed from all their war-paint;
On the banks their clubs they buried,
Buried all their warlike weapons.
Gitche Manito, the mighty,
The Great Spirit, the creator,
Smiled upon his helpless children!

　　And in silence all the warriors
Broke the red stone of the quarry,
Smoothed and formed it into Peace-Pipes,
Broke the long reeds by the river,
Decked them with their brightest feathers,
And departed each one homeward,
While the Master of Life, ascending,
Through the opening of cloud-curtains,
Through the doorways of the heaven,
Vanished from before their faces,
In the smoke that rolled around him,
The Pukwana of the Peace-Pipe!

(*THE SONG OF HIAWATHA* by Henry Wadsworth Longfellow.)

HOW TO STUDY
KEY DOCUMENTS, SERMONS, SPEECHES, AND WRITINGS

Close examination and analysis of *key documents, sermons, speeches, and writings* from America's Christian history will uncover the underlying Biblical principles of history and government from which individuals are reasoning and upon which they are establishing their institutions of home, church, business, and civil governments. In order to discern the Biblical reasoning of American Christian scholarship, teachers and students will apply their knowledge of the seven principles from the *Teaching and Learning* volume by Miss Rosalie Slater.

When these seven principles of history and government have permeated the hearts and minds of men and women, they have been able to articulate and practice a distinctly Biblical philosophy of civil government, even when the heavy hand of tyranny has come upon them and threatened their religious and civil liberties.

An analysis of the recorded works in America's Christian history will affix in the minds of the teacher and student those principles operating in the lives of historians, ministers, statesmen, and orators.

As one takes the *Mayflower Compact*, the *first* written charter for civil self-government, and reads it closely, it is possible to identify the seven principles which set America apart as the world's first Christian republic. The text reads:

"In ye name of God, Amen. We whose names are underwriten, the loyall subjects of our dread soveraigne Lord, King James, by ye grace of God, of Great Britaine, France, & Ireland king, defender of ye faith, &c., haveing undertaken for ye glorie of God, and advancemente of ye Christian faith, and honour of our king & countrie, a voyage to plant ye first colonie in ye Northerne parts of Virginia, doe by these presents solemnly & mutualy in ye presence of God, and one of another, covenant & combine our selves togeather into a civill body politick, for our better ordering & preservation & furtherance of ye ends aforesaid; and by vertue hearof to enacte, constitute, and frame such just & equall lawes, ordinances, acts, constitutions, & offices, from time to time, as shall be thought most meete & convenient for ye generall good of ye Colonie, unto which we promise all due submission and obedience. In witnes wherof we have hereunder subscribed our names at Cap-Codd ye 11. of November. in ye year of ye raigne of our soveraigne lord, King James, of England, France & Ireland ye eighteenth and of Scotland ye fiftie fourth. Ano. Dom. 1620."

Applying the seven principles of America's Christian history and government may produce a chart as the one which follows.

KEY DOCUMENT

MAYFLOWER COMPACT, 1620
"AMERICA'S FIRST CHRISTIAN CONSTITUTION"

(*Christian History of the Constitution*, pp. 204-205; *Teaching and Learning*, pp. 111-112)

AMERICAN CHRISTIAN PRINCIPLES OF CIVIL GOVERNMENT IDENTIFIED	STATEMENTS
I. GOD'S PRINCIPLE OF INDIVIDUALITY – each man's own identity – each man self-responsible for his actions and government – each man's own integrity	"We whose names are underwritten . . ." " . . . we have hereunder subscribed our names . . ."
II. CHRISTIAN PRINCIPLE OF SELF-GOVERNMENT – self-governing, self-legislating – submission and obedience to laws of their own making – government by consent	" . . . covenant and combine ourselves together. . . for our better ordering and preservation . . ." " . . . to enacte, constitute, and frame such just and equall lawes, ordinances, acts, constitutions, and offices, from time to time, as shall be more meete and convenient for ye generall good of ye Colonie, unto which we promise all due submission and obedience."
III. AMERICA'S HERITAGE OF CHRISTIAN CHARACTER – faith – diligence and industry – liberty of conscience – brotherly love	"In ye name of God, Amen." " . . . undertaken, for ye glorie of God, and advancement of ye Christian faith, and honor of our king and countrie . . ." " . . . do . . . solemnly and mutualy in ye presence of God, and one of another, covenant and combine . . . for our better ordering and preservation and furthrance of ye ends aforesaid . . ."
IV. "CONSCIENCE – MOST SACRED OF ALL PROPERTY" – sacred trust of civil government – accountability before God	"solemnly. . . in ye presence of God . . . covenant and combine ourselves . . ."
V. THE CHRISTIAN FORM OF OUR GOVERNMENT – the law and the gospel as the foundation supremacy of law laws for the lawless – dual form of government self- and civil government local and national governments colony and crown – representation sovereignty in the electors officers to represent the will of the elector	" . . . for ye glorie of God, and advancement of the Christian faith . . . covenant and combine . . . into a civill body politick" "to enacte, constitute, and frame such just and equall lawes, ordinances, acts, constitutions, and offices . . ." " . . . the loyal subjects of our dread soveraigne Lord King James . . ." " . . . for ye glorie of God, and advancement of ye Christian faith, and honor of our king and countrie . . ." " . . . to enacte, constitute and frame . . . offices, from time to time."
VI. HOW THE SEED OF LOCAL SELF-GOVERNMENT IS PLANTED – truths of God's Word taught and practiced individually	" . . . advancemente of ye Christian faith . . ."
VII. THE CHRISTIAN PRINCIPLE OF AMERICAN POLITICAL UNION – unity and union – federal union – voluntary union of Christian self-governing individuals – fulfilling the Second Commandment of Christ	"solemnly and mutualy . . . covenant and combine ourselves into a civill body politick" "for our better ordering and preservation and furtherance of ye ends aforesaid." "for ye generall good of ye Colonie . . ."

THE WORD OF GOD TO LEYDEN CAME
(August, 1620)

The word of God to Leyden came,
    Dutch town by Zuyder Zee:
Rise up, my children of no name,
    My kings and priests to be.
There is an empire in the West,
    Which I will soon unfold;
A thousand harvests in her breast,
    Rocks ribbed with iron and gold.

Rise up, my children, time is ripe!
    Old things are passed away.
Bishops and kings from earth I wipe;
    Too long they've had their day.
A little ship have I prepared
    To bear you o'er the seas;
And in your souls my will declared
    Shall grow by slow degrees.

Beneath my throne the martyrs cry;
    I hear their voice, How long?
It mingles with their praises high,
    And with their victor song.
The thing they longed and waited for,
    But died without the sight;
So, this shall be! I wrong abhor,
    The world I'll now set right.

Leave, then, the hammer and the loom,
    You've other work to do;
For Freedom's commonwealth there's room,
    And you shall build it too.
I'm tired of bishops and their pride,
    I'm tired of kings as well;
Henceforth I take the people's side,
    And with the people dwell.

Tear off the mitre from the priest,
    And from the king his crown;
Let all my captives be released;
    Lift up, whom men cast down.
Their pastors let the people choose,
    And choose their rulers too;
Whom they select, I'll not refuse,
    But bless the work they do.

The Pilgrims rose, at this, God's word,
    And sailed the wintry seas:
With their own flesh nor blood conferred,
    Nor thought of wealth or ease.
They left the towers of Leyden town,
    They left the Zuyder Zee;
And where they cast their anchor down,
    Rose Freedom's realm to be.

JEREMIAH EAMES RANKIN

(*AMERICAN HISTORY IN VERSE*, Burton Stevenson, Editor.)

THE CHRISTIAN HISTORY LITERATURE PROGRAM

BY ROSALIE JUNE SLATER
Foundation for American Christian Education
San Francisco, California

THE PILGRIM FATHERS

Well worthy to be magnified are they
Who, with sad hearts, of friends and country took
A last farewell, their loved abodes forsook,
And hallowed ground in which their fathers lay;
Then to the new-found World explored their way,
That so a church, unforced, uncalled to brook
Ritual restraints, within some sheltering nook
Her Lord might worship and his word obey
In freedom. Men they were who could not bend;
Blest Pilgrims, surely, as they took for guide
A will by sovereign Conscience sanctified;
Blest while their Spirits from the woods ascend
Along a Galaxy that knows no end,
But in His glory who for Sinners died.

ECCLESIASTICAL SONNETS, William Wordsworth (1821–22)
The Poetical Works of Wordsworth, Cambridge Edition
Houghton Mifflin Company, Boston, 1982

CONTENTS

Poem: *The Pilgrim Fathers* by William Wordsworth

INTRODUCTION

In 1960 with the publication of *The Christian History of the Constitution of the United States of America: Christian Self-Government* compiled by Miss Verna M. Hall, American Christians had placed before them their Providential History. For the first time in almost one hundred years, we learned what we had not been taught before in our education:

Who we are as a people, beginning with the Pilgrims and Puritans

Where our principles of government come from in God's Word

What the founding generations understood as God's purpose for us as a nation

The myth that our Founding Fathers and Mothers had received an inferior education was dispelled as we recognized the superior quality of reasoning and writing which characterized our history and literature. One result of the re-publication of *America's Christian History* was to begin to translate the knowledge of our Providential History into the school curriculum. However, it soon became apparent that even Christian schools and colleges had accepted a *social* interpretation of American History. History was studied in the light of "only secondary causes and human agencies." History had therefore become *"irreligious."* What was needed was to restore our earlier conviction of the Sovereignty of God in history and in all subjects. We needed to learn our own history in the light of God's Hand in the history of all nations.

It is not difficult to see that as our nation turned away from its Christian History and allowed all subjects to become *secularized*, the field of Literature also suffered a decline. As the "handmaid" of History, the field of Literature deals with the consequences of history and deepens the *study of character*. Mrs. Mercy Warren, one of our first historians of the American Revolution wrote:

"History . . . requires a just knowledge of character, to investigate the sources of action." *Consider and Ponder*, page 358

As history, studied *superficially* in the Social Studies program, became more and more *socialized*, so also did the literature of the times become more and more concerned with the social character of men. Thus American education, in losing its knowledge of our Providential history, became more and more *irreligious*. It was in effect *producing a character for socialism* – a character less and less dependent on God, and more dependent on man; a character with less and less capacity for Christian self-government.

In short, our great heritage of the History and Literature of Liberty was removed from our national consciousness. Yet, we did not seem to miss it for we had also lost our capacity to read and understand those books of quality and worth which had helped build our character and our nation in the first place.

Since the 1960's, however, there has been a work of restoration occurring. Gradually, as American Christian educators in home and school have been willing to study and learn America's Christian History, there has been a return to our historic method of teaching. By incorporating the Principle Approach, our Biblical method of researching, reasoning, relating, and recording, into our educational program, there has been a resurgence of *vitality* in learning. Once again teachers are becoming masters of their subjects and helping to develop them, rather than continuing along as mere *textbook mechanics*. As the character of teachers is restored to the capacity for self-government we are witnessing students once again being properly educated to serve Christ and country.

The purpose of this article is to discuss the necessity for restoring Literature – the Literature of Liberty – to our American Christian homes and schools. An *Overview* of what is included in this study of Literature in its setting in the Chain of Christianity Moving Westward with "signs following" will first be given. We will also indicate the Levels of Learning Literature, that is: *when* the major aspects of the Christian History Literature Program can be studied. And finally, we will provide some examples of teaching and learning Literature, so that parents and teachers may adequately *prepare their own repertory* of excellent authors and books in order to present to students the History and Literature of Liberty.

Like all subjects in the Christian History Program the fundamental outcome lies in the field of *character development*. Charles de Montesquieu, an important thinker in the field of political liberty, wrote: "That the Law of Education ought to be relative the Principles of Government." Education is the key to government – to our political or civil liberty. For a nation's *form of government* is reflective of its *character for government*. Our study of America's Christian History indicates that it was the *quality* of Christian character demonstrated by our Founding generations which enabled us, as a self-governing people, to develop under God's guidance, an independent Constitutional Republic. As we let go the control of education, we let go the control of character, and we declined from a republic into a socialistic democracy.

If we are to restore "what the locusts have eaten" of our civil and religious liberties we must first begin to restore the *quality* and *capacity* of the American Christian character. This begins in the Christian home and school as we restore an educational methodology which requires much greater scholarship and productivity on the part of both teachers and students. The Christian History Literature Program, like all other subjects in the Christian History Program, makes the sincere effort to instruct students "in the art of self-government... in short of leading them in the study and practice of the exalted virtues of the Christian system..." *Christian History*, page xiv.

The "art of self-government" sprang from an understanding of the Christian Idea of Man and Government. It was "the assertion of the principle of individuality, or of true spiritual freedom," as a result of the period of the Reformation in Europe. As this idea travelled westward to American the importance of self-governing homes and churches required a deeper study of the Bible. It also required that those willing to *die* for "conscience sake" needed also to be willing to *live* and *produce* for the glory of God. No wonder a representative form of government developed in America, beginning with the *Mayflower Compact* and the charters of each colony.

As the thirteen colonies practiced the Biblical principles of the separation of the powers of government – the *legislative, executive* and *judicial* – in their local spheres, they were preparing for their role as a *national-federal* republic. And when, despite all Great Britian attempted to do to set these colonies one against another, when they came together in the First Continental Congress, it was in *voluntary unity*. This voluntary unity brought forth the American Political Union – a union which had been fashioned and prepared link by link throughout His Story.

OUR PHILOSOPHY
OF LITERATURE

If we define Literature as "the best expression of the best thought" we might agree that all that is written and all that is printed is not Literature. In fact today as printed matter has multiplied it seems to have grown less literary – for most of it is not the best expression of anything.

To agree upon what is "the best" must refer to one's view of *value* or *worth*. And this brings us to our *foundation* – "the basis or ground-work of anything; that on which anything stands, and by which it is supported." Noah Webster in his definition of this word included Paul's statement:

"For other foundation can no man lay than that which is laid, which is Jesus Christ." *1 Corinthians 3:11*

Clearly, if one lays Christ as the foundation of Literature, this will determine a *value* and *worth* not found in all that passes for the subject of Literature.

The Scriptures identify *value* and *worth* in the following words which are in themselves a "best expression of a best thought."

"Finally, brethren, whatsoever things are true, whatsoever things are honest, whatsoever things are just, whatsoever things are pure, whatsoever things are lovely, whatsoever things are of good report; if there be any virtue, and if there be any praise, think on these things." *Philippians 4:8*

Readers brought up in the study of Literature built upon this foundation will love the qualities identified by the Apostle Paul and will be repelled by their opposites, that which is false, dishonest, unjust, impure, unlovely, books of bad report in which there is no virtue and no praise, nothing of excellence or worth valuing.

The Christian History Program in Literature is an expression of "that liberty wherewith Christ hath made us free." *Internal* liberty was causative of *external* or civil liberty. It took some 1789 years on the Chain of Christianity moving westward for civil liberty to appear as our American Christian Constitutional Republic. For the first time the world came to know what it was like to live as self-governing individuals; what it was like to have property valued as sacred, including talent; what it was like to work on a voluntary basis with others and not to be compelled. America became visible in her history, and her literature confirmed what constituted a character and a conscience for Liberty.

What kind of books will be read in The Christian History Program as "we trace the nobler stream of liberty?" Many of the authors who wrote on Liberty will now be restored to our homes and schools for study. "The chief glory of a nation" wrote Dr. Samuel Johnson, "arises from its authors." Noah Webster, who quoted Dr. Johnson, and whose *An American Dictionary of the English Language* was to replace Dr. Johnson's *Dictionary of the English Language*, was the first American educator to place American writers alongside of English writers. Noah Webster knew that no other nation could surpass us in writings dealing with the subject of political liberty.

Even our youngest children can begin the study of the writings of our Pilgrims, Puritans, Patriots and Pioneers, as they developed the Literature of Liberty and identified the character needed to perpetuate and extend a Republic. Soon the "free and independent man" in America began to write about this Land of Liberty. American Independence found readers all over the world.

Our hope is to generate a love and appreciation for "whatsoever things" are "true," "honest," "just," "pure," "lovely," and "of good report" in our history and literature. Specifically the Christian History Literature Program should encourage the following:

SEVEN LOVES ENCOURAGED BY THE LITERATURE PROGRAM

#1 ## A LOVE FOR GOD

The study of both History and Literature should enhance our love for the Lord. "The more thoroughly a nation deals with its history, the more decidedly will it recognize and own an overruling Providence therein, and the more religious a nation will it become." *Consider and Ponder,* page 46

#2 ## A LOVE FOR GOD'S WRITTEN WORD – THE HOLY BIBLE

The Literature of the Bible, displayed in *"its matchless excellence,"* is unsurpassed by any era of literature. It "contains poetry more sublime than Homer," "patterns of character found in Prophets, Patriarchs, Apostles . . . and the glorious pattern of excellence, Jesus Christ." Every student of the Literature of the Bible is "a candidate for immortal existence." *Consider and Ponder,* pages 224–230

#3 ## A LOVE FOR HOME AND FAMILY

"If I had Leisure, I could dwell on the Importance of Piety & Religion, of Industry and Frugality, of Prudence, Economy, Regularity & an even Government, all of which are essential to the Well being of a Family." Samuel Adams to his Future Son-in-Law, 1780. *Consider and Ponder,* pages 71, 82

#4 ## A LOVE FOR AND APPRECIATION OF THE INDIVIDUAL

"History shows that the Christ-men and the Christ-women have always been the loyal men and women of the land, and the men and women who have inaugurated great and beneficial movements. Our national liberties were bought with their blood. This is an open and fearless statement, but it has as many verifications as there are races [people group] in our American nationality. Each race has contributed its heroes." Pastor David Gregg, *Teaching and Learning,* pages 43–44

#5 ## A LOVE FOR THE CHAIN OF CHRISTIANITY MOVING WESTWARD

"Driven by the persecution of centuries from the older world [Liberty] had come with Pilgrim and Puritan, and Cavalier and Quaker, to seek a shelter in the new . . . The dream of the Greek, the Hebrew's prophecy, the desire of the Roman, the Italian's prayer, the longing of the German mind, the hope of the French heart, the glory and honor of Old England herself . . . here in the heart of America they were safe . . . the time was already come when from these shores the light of a new Civilization should flash across the sea, and from this place a voice of triumph make the Old World tremble, when from her chosen refuge in the West the spirit of Liberty should go forth to meet the Rising Sun and set the people free!" *Oration at Valley Forge* by Henry Armitt Brown, 1878, *Consider and Ponder*, pages 66–67

#6 A LOVE FOR OUR OWN COUNTRY THE UNITED STATES OF AMERICA

"We demand America for Christ for the world's sake... The responsibility laid upon her, therefore, is a double one; first and supremely, to keep the fountains of her own intelligence and virtue and religion pure for the sake of the native-born in the land; and, second, to ply with all the forces of Christian learning and religion the thousands of un-evangelized who have come to her shores, that they may send back to their old homes... the blessed gospel of the Son of God to work as a regenerating and converting power in the different fatherlands across the sea... America taken for Christ means the nations of the world far and near taken for Christ; America a Christian nation means a mighty witness for God among all lands of the earth." David Gregg, *Teaching and Learning*, pages 44–45

#7 A LOVE OF CHRISTIAN SCHOLARSHIP AND LEARNING

Hail happy Land! the last and best Retreat
Of all that can exalt or bless Mankind!
New *Lockes* shall here the complex Thought unfold,
New *Miltons* soar on Fancy's ardent Wing,
And future *Newtons* to astonish'd Worlds
Great Nature's deepest Secrets shall reveal.
Even other *Handels* shall exalt the Soul
With Music's Charms above the starry Skies!
And other *Tullies* fill the ravish'd Ear
Of listening Senates, with their patriot Strains!

From *A Dialogue Spoken at Opening of the Public Grammar School at Wilmington*, October 26, 1773, *Consider and Ponder*, page 231

RESTORING THE GREATEST CLASSIC IN THE ENGLISH LANGUAGE

When young Timothy Dwight, grandson of Jonathan Edwards, gave the Commencement Address at Yale, in 1772, a college of which he would someday be president, he chose for his topic the following: *"A Dissertation on the History, Eloquence, and Poetry of the Bible," Consider and Ponder*, pages 224–230

From his background of Biblical and classical learning Dwight could speak authoritatively on his theme that the Bible surpassed every other writer in every literary expression. Some of his illustrative phrases described the Literature of the Bible "displayed as fine writing, compared to pagan or secular writers, contains poetry more sublime than Homer, more correct and tender than Virgil, contains eloquence greater than Cicero and Demosthenes, a divine morality unsurpassed by Plato, contains history more majestic and spirited than Livy and Robertson..." Index of Leading Ideas, *Consider and Ponder*, page 661a

In other words, Timothy Dwight, like so many of our founding pastors, statesmen and educators in the colonies, knew *all* Literature and could evaluate it correctly, because of his firm foundation in the Bible as Literature.

In the twentieth century we have seen a decline of academic education. And in this century we have been unable to study the appropriate masters of English and American Literature and that of other nations. Not only have we been unable to read well enough to enjoy our Literary heritage, but, we have not had a foundation for Literature in the Scriptures which would prepare us for that quality of writing.

Our foundation in the Literature of the Bible has been eroded by contemporary versions of the Scriptures. Influenced by our level of literacy we have sought modern words, simpler phrases, exact meanings, not realizing that the level of literature which produced our finest version of the Bible, was addressed to the *reflective* man or woman of God's creating and ability. To reflect in or to meditate on God's Word requires words capable of deeper shades of meaning than can be immediately grasped by exact translations. Our spiritual growth should allow for the unfoldment of God's Truth as we are ready for it. If words are deprived of their depth and wealth, we shall continue to impoverish ourselves in two ways. First, we shall deprive ourselves of spiritual effort to deepen our knowledge of the Word. Second, we shall be unable to read the Bible in its literary expression which, as one might know in God's infinite Wisdom and Grace, complements its doctrinal expression.

Consider for a moment what the Authorized Version achieved as a Literary manifestation! Consider also how God brought the English Language up to a high point – perhaps its highest – before the King James Version of 1611 appeared! Consider also that both English and American Literature were the beneficiary of this version! And finally, consider how men yearned to put the Word into its finest language as an honor to its Holy Author!

"The supreme literary excellence of the Authorized Version has made it the greatest of English classics. Owing to the superb beauty of its language, the Bible has had an importance in our literature which is unparalleled elsewhere. It has been said that its English 'lives on the ear like a music that can never be forgotten.'

"... It is almost impossible to exaggerate the influence of that Version on the English language and on English thought. The Bible made English Puritanism; and the Puritan tradition has fostered in the British and American peoples most of their best and distinctive qualities. From the Bible Milton and Bunyan took the inspiration of their poetry and allegory. In the Bible Cromwell and the Pilgrim Fathers found that which made them honourable, self-reliant, and steadfast. Bible in hand, Wesley and Whitefield transformed their country." John Drinkwater in *The Outline of Literature*, page 74

Both the Literature of England, and the Literature of America reflect the influence of the Bible in English. As Bishop Charles Wordsworth documents in his 1864 *"On Shakespeare's Knowledge and Use of the Bible,"* our greatest writers helped spread the doctrines of the Word, as they drew the Scriptures into their novels, short stories, essays, plays, and poetry. It is our hope with the introduction of The Christian History Literature Program, beginning with study of the Literature of the Bible itself in all grades, that we can once again raise up writers capable of recording the History and Character of Liberty – and honoring the Author of Liberty. It begins in the homes of America – especially in those homes schooling their own children. But our Christian schools must also become more determined to restore this quality of teaching so that American can return to her appointed path of Christian Constitutional Liberty.

CHARTING OUR COURSES OF STUDY

OVERVIEWS AND LEVELS OF LEARNING FOR THE CHRISTIAN HISTORY LITERATURE PROGRAM

The setting for all subjects in the Christian History Program can be found on the chart, page 6A in *Christian History*. Entitled the "Chain of Christianity Moves Westward with 'Signs Following,'" it records the impact of "that liberty wherewith Christ hath made us free" – civil as well as religious liberty. Against this backdrop of the History of Liberty, the Literature of Liberty has its setting and character.

Where do we begin in our study of the Literature of Liberty? How do we teach this program which is concerned with the Hand of God in History? Most educators would begin with the Elementary grades. Usually one begins with the earliest level of learning, working up year by year to the highest level. We believe, however, that in order to design our Literature curriculum according to a Biblically wholistic approach, we need first to look at the entire course of study. Only as we see how the Chain of Christianity moved westward with Christian Liberty can we understand the purpose for Literature in this context.

Historically, our setting relates to the impact of Jesus Christ upon the individual and then through the individual, on the nation. Thus we trace the appearing of both civil and religious liberty. So,

our first chart for the study of the Christian History Literature Program will not be Elementary Literature. That chart, Overview V, will be the last chart in our series. In this way teachers at all levels will once again be able to see the total program before they begin to teach at their particular age level. This should allow those who teach to learn much of the total program of Literature. They will then be teaching from a position of mastery rather than merely teaching from a limited perspective.

⌘ Our five Overview charts reflect the total Christian History Literature Program and can be found on pages 343 to 351.

⌘ OVERVIEW I – LEARNING THE LITERATURE OF THE BIBLE, *Source and Seedbed of Literature and Liberty.* Level of Learning, every grade, every semester, every year. See page 344.

⌘ OVERVIEW II – CONTRASTS BETWEEN THE PAGAN AND CHRISTIAN IDEA OF MAN AND GOVERNMENT IN LITERATURE. A two-year course for Junior High, Seventh and Eighth Grades. See page 345.

OVERVIEW III – TRACING THE NOBLER STREAM OF LIBERTY IN ENGLISH LITERATURE. A two-year course of study for the ninth and tenth grades. See pages 346 to 347.

OVERVIEW IV – THE LITERATURE OF THE AMERICAN CHRISTIAN REPUBLIC. A two-year course of study for eleventh and twelfth grades. See pages 348 to 350.

OVERVIEW V – RESTORING THE LITERATURE AND CHARACTER OF LIBERTY – *Elementary Years*. Level of Learning kindergarten through sixth grade. See page 351.

EXPLANATION OF THE COURSE OF STUDY

The following explanation of the Christian History Literature Program will expand upon the reasoning for this setting of Literature in the Chain of Christianity moving westward with ever greater liberty, opportunity and responsibility for the individual in both civil and religious spheres.

OVERVIEW I
LEARNING THE LITERATURE OF THE BIBLE, *Source and Seedbed of Literature and Liberty.* Every grade, every semester, every year. See chart, page 344.

As noted in the Level of Learning, the study of the Bible as Literature will come in every grade, in every semester, every year. The question may immediately arise: "How can I teach the Literature of the Bible if I have never studied it from that standpoint? We do teach our students the Bible as part of their curriculum." In order to help you think about the Bible as a Literary Classic we have given a brief introduction to teaching the Bible as Literature in the section of this article entitled *Planning Your Elementary Literature Program*. Whether you are introducing Kindergarten children to the appreciation and understanding of written language for the first time, or, whether you are preparing to teach High School students the influence of the Bible on Elizabethan Literature, it will be appropriate to have a standard for *Language, Style* and *Expression*. What better source than the King James Bible? Even the earlier 1560 Geneva Bible which the Pilgrims carried to America represents the period of the "flowering of the English language."

We can also see by the chart in Overview II, that if we were preparing to teach *Literary Types*, i.e. poetry, the essay, drama, the short story, the epic, or a biography, where could we find better sources of these forms of literature, than in the written Word of God? At the same time we can also deepen the knowledge of our students in those Literary Types unique to the Bible.

True, our Bible is not just a literary work, but it is, and should be, the finest literary expression of the English language. As we study the History and Literature of Liberty we learn of the influence of the English Bible on civil and religious liberty. Perhaps we find this influence directly in our documents of government like the *Mayflower Compact*, the *Fundamental Orders of Connecticut*, the *Declaration of Independence* and others. Or, perhaps our study of the influence of the Bible on English and American literature will be found in those memorable accounts of the aspiration and struggle for liberty in drama, poetry, or the short story and novel. This is the Character for Liberty.

In order to restore the great literature of every period in the History of Liberty, we must begin by restoring the study of the Bible as Literature. This will provide us with that most needed foundation in *Language, Style* and *Expression*, so that we can master all of the great worthwhile works of Literature which nourished us as a nation.

The Bible also provides us with an inspiring source of Literary types. The lyric poetry of the Psalms, the concise "moral essays" of the Proverbs, the dramas of God's dealings with man, and the parables or short stories recounted by our Lord, all these help set a unique standard of quality. The Bible's own literary types also prepare us to discern all literature from the perspective of man living without God, or, man living consciously in obedience or disobedience to God's principles.

OVERVIEW II
CONTRASTS BETWEEN THE PAGAN AND CHRISTIAN IDEA OF MAN AND GOVERNMENT IN LITERATURE. A two-year course for Junior High. See chart, page 345.

For the first year of the Junior High School program, turn to the chart on page 6A of *Christian History*. The study of Literature begins with a knowledge of Israel's History of Liberty. As we learn Moses' contribution to the Literature of the Old Testament, we shall also learn the standard of God's Law for nations. The History and Literature of Israel are a testimony of a chosen nation, and the consequences of accepting or turning away from God's Law as the basis of self- and civil government.

Against this backdrop we look at the three great nations God used to forward His story: "the Jews on the side of the religious element; the Greeks on the side of science and art; the Romans, as masters of the world, on the side of the political element. When the fulness of time was arrived and Christ appeared, – when the goal of history has thus been reached, – then it was, that through him, and by the power of the spirit that proceeded from him, – the might of Christianity, – all the threads, hitherto separated, of human development, were to be brought together and interwoven in one web." *Teaching and Learning*, page 160

We cannot study either history or literature without being conscious of the character of a people. Thus, as Hannah More, English evangelical writer, expressed it, the brilliance of the Greek mind, "the energy of her people, and the vigour of her character" led to a "natural bias towards corruption." Her pagan religion produced "extremes of tyranny and democracy." Her "devotedness to the arts, not only precipitated her own ruin, – but by the transplantation of those arts, encumbered with those vices, ultimately contributed to ruin Rome also." *Teaching and Learning*, page 161

Rome's centralization of government through law and conquest, "incorporation without representation," united at first the known world for the spread of Christianity, but the Roman method of nation-making failed to crush out "the spirit of personal independence" and "local self-government." Eventually the vast Union of the Roman empire "fell to pieces."

To what extent is our American world influenced by the pagan thinking? While we house many of our governmental activities in classical structures, did the principles of our American Republic originate in the Mediterranean world of Greece and Rome, or, did Christianity bring forth the first "little republics" from which our Pilgrims and Puritans would take their forms of church and civil government? We study ancient history and literature to identify the classical religions – those myths which still persist in some Western arts and sciences. Our students need to discern the relationship between what men worship and their governmental and literary expressions. Character is formed by the ideas and ideals that men contemplate.

In the Christian era a great novel becomes the background for those events which "turned the world upside down." Written by an American General, Lew Wallace, *Ben Hur, A Tale of the Christ*, presents the impact of Jesus Christ upon the world of Rome and Palestine. The Christian idea of man changes men's hearts and begins to move westward to change their forms of church and civil government. England, the last western outpost of Europe, becomes a focal point where the ideals of Christianity begin to penetrate feudalism and English chivalry.

The 2nd year of the Junior High School program concentrates upon the study of *Literary Types*, beginning with their origin in the Bible. Here many short classics are read and studied in relation to their contribution as Literature to the History of Liberty. This study also provides a fine introduction to the Senior High Program of English and American Literature.

OVERVIEW III
TRACING THE NOBLER STREAM OF LIBERTY IN ENGLISH LITERATURE.
A two-year course for ninth and tenth grades.
See chart, page 346.

In order to trace the Chain of Christianity moving Westward with the liberty and opportunity of the individual, we must study English history and literature *before* we study American history and literature. Only as we follow God's Story can we appreciate the first year of English Literature which emphasizes the *English Preparation for America*.

As the Anglo-Saxons invaded England in the 5th century they brought with them from Europe seeds of Christian self-government. The Anglo-Saxon way of life included a love of personal freedom, a respect for womanhood and home, "a fearless and enterprising spirit" willing to challenge danger. The Anglo-Saxon language, which today is predominant in our King James Bible, included words which conveyed their ideals of *love, home, faith, heroism, liberty*. The Anglo-Saxon gave our language its *masculine* qualities of strength, directness, simplicity. Refined by the currents of the Anglo-Norman invasion, the English strain prevailed, and we trace the development of the language through the Middle period of Wyclif and Chaucer, up to the flowering of the 1611 version of the Bible – prepared by God for the finest expression of English.

England's Preparation for America included also a character to establish colonies in the wilderness – bringing first English institutions of church and state. As the Bible's influence circulated through the British Isles some 200 years before the Pilgrims, so also, were efforts late in the 16th century to plant an English Colony. After Cabot's claims for England in 1497-8, Britain lagged behind other European powers in exploration. But, Sir Walter Raleigh persisted in his efforts to plant an English Colony. Only Americans can appreciate to the full this man of thought and action who wrote to Lord Cecil: "I shall yet live to see it an English nation." The territory to which Raleigh referred was of course Virginia – named for Elizabeth the virgin queen.

With the help of young Richard Hakluyt, pastor and geographer, whose classic work on *Principall Navigations, Voyages and Discoveries of the English Nation*, included a stirring account of the 1588 Providential Deliverance of England from the Spanish Armada, Raleigh secured a patent for Virginia. After several unsuccessful efforts Jamestown became the first permanent English colony in 1607 – desperately hanging on through extreme difficulties. Hakluyt's appeal to Queen Elizabeth for attention to English Western Planting was "That this Western discoverie will be greately for thinlargemente of the gospell of Christe, whereunto the princes of the Refourmed Relligion are chefely bounde, amongeste whom her Magestie ys principall."

English character is visible in English literature and as we watch the Hand of God preparing for the American Settlement, we also follow the English translations of the Bible, as well as watch the English nation become "a people of the Book." English Literature reflects the vitality of both Elizabethan and Puritan character as it was influenced by a Biblical perspective.

The second year of *Tracing the Nobler Stream of Liberty in English Literature* is a rich year of study including many writers who will be influential in America: John Bunyan's *Pilgrim's Progress*, John Locke and Algernon Sidney's essays on *Civil Government*, and Newton's writings on science. The 18th century identifies the age of prose in essay, oration, biography, novel and the newspaper. All of these literary forms will be expanded by the American Colonists who learn from their English heritage.

Our study of history is much enlivened by the contribution of Sir Walter Scott in his creation of the historical novel. Many of his major novels have Christian themes and illustrate Biblical principles. As a moralist, interested in the struggle for what is right, he peopled the minds of both Englishmen and Americans with characters for liberty. American author, James Fenimore Cooper, was inspired to write novels of American life and liberty because of the wide readership in America of the historical novels of Scott. This kind of reading takes teaching, for our early authors researched their history carefully and filled their writing with the detail of the plot, character and setting. In this second year of the study of English Literature, as we follow the nobler stream of liberty, our students should build upon an earlier introduction to Charles Dickens. Certainly the contrast of the French and American revolutions in *The Tale of Two Cities* could not be

more vivid. Our poverty in literature, stage and screen today stems from our ignorance of the great masterpieces of English and American Literature with some classics of French Literature.

Our final period of English Literature is to contrast the original Literature of Liberty with the Literature of Socialism. The return of Reformed religion in England during the twentieth century has had some effect upon the reprinting of many of the earlier English classics, i.e. the writings of John Bunyan, but also the writings of our American pastor Jonathan Edwards. Hopefully, there will be some who will paddle their literary canoes upstream and begin to return to English speaking peoples some of the quality of the Literature of Liberty which we once so richly enjoyed.

The study of English Literature in its chronological order of history, *before* the study of American Literature, enables us to appreciate God's preparation for America through the English language, the English Bible, English government, and certain aspects of English character.

OVERVIEW IV
THE LITERATURE OF THE
AMERICAN CHRISTIAN REPUBLIC.
A two-year course for eleventh and twelfth grades.
See chart, page 348.

The last two years of Senior High School allow our students to deepen their understanding of Providential History and accept their responsibilities for the stewardship of our nation, raised up under God to provide an asylum for civil and religious liberty – the translation of the Christian idea of man into government.

The Prologue and Preparation for America begins with the appearing of the handwritten Wyclif Bible. It was presented to the English people as a means of freeing them from injustices and tyrannies in both church and state. "Wycliff's Teutonic love of truth, of freedom, and of independence, . . . moved him to give his countrymen the open Scripture as their best safeguard and protection." The rise of the Lollard party, "in so far as it was a religious movement, marks the earliest break in the . . . continuity of Latin Christianity in England." *Christian History*, page 29

God's timing of events in "the discovery and preparation of this country" follows the impetus of the Bible in the hands of the individual. A new continent is needed for a new people being prepared with the Gospel. And these Biblical principles of civil and religious liberty will need a new land for their expression in government.

God's instrument for opening a highway across

the uncharted Atlantic Ocean is Christopher Columbus – who frees the Old World of its superstition regarding the dangers of navigation west. Since our American authors wrote of Liberty after the republic was established we have chosen two who wrote about our earliest period of history. William Prescott's biography of *Ferdinand and Isabella* gives us a picture of life in the *Spain of Columbus*. And Washington Irving, our first fruit of the New Republic, wrote his first biography about *Columbus.*

In our review of *Colonial Character* and its *Literature* we have a great variety of writers and the first appearing of those qualities which will identify America some one hundred and fifty years later. Sometimes we will be reading the vivid, forceful and picturesque style of Captain John Smith of Virginia. Perhaps we will be struck by the winning words or Gospel appeal of the Reverend Alexander Whitaker, Jamestown pastor who led the Princess Pocahontas to Christ. As we read the Christian History of each colony, Pilgrim, Puritan, Patriot or Pioneer, we will read history, love letters, satire, poetry, essays – all revealing how God was with our fathers and mothers as they endeavored to establish Christian government in the wilderness. Our first poetess, Anne Dudley Bradstreet, made the long voyage across the Atlantic only to find a mud village awaiting her in primitive Salem. Coming from the background of an educated Puritan society, where history and literature were available to her in an excellent Puritan library, she wrote of her first response to her new life: *"I found a new world and new manners, at which my heart rose. But after I was convinced it was the way of God, I submitted to it and joined the church at Boston."* Eight of Anne Bradstreet's children survived. Both her father and her husband served as governor of Massachusetts Bay Colony.

The American Indian was affected by Christianity, and in some cases had a definite role in the Colony. In Virginia, after her conversion, Pocahontas became a representative of the Colony at the English court. Harvard opened an Indian school, and John Eliot helped establish fourteen Praying Towns for the Indians, and translated the first American Bible into Algonquian. In Pennsylvania, even before he arrived, William Penn communicated with the Indians: "My Friends... The great God has written his law in our hearts, by which we are taught and commanded to love, and to help and to do good to one another... I shall shortly come to see you myself... In the meantime I have sent my commissioners to treat with you about land and a firm league of peace."

But, it is in the *Literature of the American Revolution* that we see the flowering of one hundred and fifty years of preparation by the Lord for our becoming a nation. From our rich heritage of the sermons of our pastors, from the political writings of our statesmen, from the letters of our women, and from verse, song, drama, we construct a picture of Revolutionary America. In this period we are introduced to the letters of George Washington as most representative of the spirit and character of the times.

After the establishment of the American Constitution we study the principles of our government in *The Federalist*. The westward expansion is traced in the writings of Washington Irving and in the novels of James Fenimore Cooper. *Leatherstocking* becomes an exciting example to the world of self-government – a Christian who loves the Lord and sees His laws at work in the American wilderness. In 1803 the *Louisiana Purchase* launched the Expeditions of Captains Lewis and Clark. Their *Journals* are read as living Literature of the geography and newly discovered Indian tribes.

The twelfth grade level of learning in American Literature is reflected in the Gospel and Constitutional government spreading across the continent. Our study of Regional Writers continues to identify the unity and diversity of our nation. The Civil War challenges that Union and the Christian idea of man in government. It also brings with it an aftermath of new writing – writing that reflects a falling away from God's moral absolutes. We identify these Nobel Laureates, but our students are presented with authors who continue to deal with the gold of Christian character in America. *Realism* need not be *materialism* but rather the persistence of those ideas and ideals which established our Republic. As a final review our students recall the stepping stones of Literature and Liberty which identify the American character and its Biblical sources.

For example:

The first section of the second year of The Literature of the American Christian Republic after Learning the Literature of the Bible, is *Christian Constitutional Government Reaches the Pacific*. This begins with a study of the opening of the Northwestern part of the continent, then called Old Oregon, a territory out of which our states of Oregon, Washington and Idaho were formed. Prior to 1830 a few American explorers, trappers or traders had carried their Bibles along with their guns to the far west. Among these was "Jedediah Smith who spent a month in 1824 at a post of the Flathead Indians in what is now western Montana." In 1831 a delegation of four Nez Perce Indians travelled from the Northwest to St. Louis, seeking information about Christianity and especially about the white man's *Book of Heaven*.

This Indian visit was one of a number of impulses which began serious interest in evangelization. Among Christ's most stalwart sons was Dr. Marcus Whitman who, along with his wife Narcissa, became part of the vanguard of western Pilgrims and Pioneers. Our teachers and students will not only have an opportunity to see the continuation of the Chain of Christianity moving westward with the Gospel of individual liberty in self- and civil government, but they will be able to read once again the records written by these Pilgrims and Pioneers themselves. As God brought the western territories of Oregon and California into the fold of the Union of American states, so did He also bring the men, women and children who would contribute to their growth and development under the principles of Christian Constitutional government.

Regional Writers of America will be studied as these identify both the unity and diversity of America. Sara Orne Jewett describes the Maine character in her short stories; Nathaniel Hawthorne and Herman Melville present different aspects of the New England character. We travel the *Oregon Trail* with Francis Parkman, and sail around the Horn to California with Richard Henry Dana in his *Two Years Before the Mast*. And some of the gold of California is discovered in short stories and poems by Bret Harte. Mark Twain is there too as a young journalist and author.

The Biblical issue of slavery was translated into more than a sectional dispute – it threatened to pull our nation asunder. At stake was the principle of the federation of states held together by our Christian Constitution. The Civil War was a tragic wound to the national conscience and God raised up noble men and women on both sides of the conflict. Our study in Literature of God's Preservation of the Union of the American States includes biographies of its leaders on both sides of the conflict, and the history of the period.

The years after the Civil War were difficult years – a *falling away* period from our Christian foundations. This is reflected in the "new" literature which was developed. For the most part those authors who accepted a negative, disillusioned view of America and her institutions also expressed in their writings a pagan idea of man as a "tragic hero" – a victim of his social, political, or economic environment. These authors reflected a world wide era of such writing. They also gave rise to a critical attack on America – the beginnings of a socialistic, evolutionary attitude towards our nation. Our foundations were being undermined.

Learning the Literature of the Bible as a standard for all Literature, we can approach modern writing from a Christian or pagan view. Much of modern writing reflects a return to the pagan values. As Dr. Leland Ryken defines the difference:

"Perhaps the distinction between Biblical and non-Biblical tragedy can be summed up by saying that in non-Biblical tragedy the tragic hero is, above all, the sympathetic tragic victim, while in Biblical tragedy he is the unsympathetic sinner. The appropriate response in the first case is, Isn't it too bad that all this happened to the tragic hero? The appropriate response to Biblical tragedy is, Isn't it too bad that he disobeyed God, when it might have been otherwise?" *The Literature of the Bible* by Leland Ryken, page 106

As we can select from the "new literature, and not violate the philosophy expressed in Philippians 4:8, we can contrast it with the literature written from a Biblical era of writing. The Nobel Prize for Literature did much to *internationalize* the standards of some American writers. As a nation we were beginning to disregard the principle expressed so well by George Washington and by Noah Webster of not reversing the Chain of Christianity. They urged us not to go back to the Old World, not to be influenced by her "folly, corruption and tyranny." This message was lost upon the group of young Americans who congregated on the Left Bank of the Seine River in Paris during the twentieth century.

As President George Washington wrote before the end of the eighteenth century:

"It is with indescribable regret, that I have seen the youth of the United States migrating to foreign countries, in order to acquire the higher branches of erudition... Although it would be injustice to many to pronounce the certainty of their imbibing maxims not congenial with republicanism, it must nevertheless be admitted, that a serious danger is encountered by sending abroad among other political systems those who have not well learned the value of their own." *Christian History*, page 417

Noah Webster, founding father of American scholarship and education, was even more critical of the influences of the Old World. He wrote:

"To receive indiscriminately the maxims of government, the manners and the literary taste of Europe and make them the ground on which to build our systems in America, must soon convince us that a durable and stately edifice can never be erected upon the mouldering pillars of antiquity. It is the business of Americans to select the wisdom of all nations, as the basis of her constitutions – to avoide their errours, – to prevent the introduction of foreign vices and corruptions and check the career of her own, – to embellish and improve the sciences, – to diffuse an uniformity and purity of language, – to add superior dignity to this infant Empire and to human nature." Page 11 facsimile reprint of Noah Webster's first edition of *An American Dictionary of the English Language*

But not all Americans subscribed to the literary, social, economic or political philosophy of the "new" literature. For while some "writers" were indulging new found "license" – other Americans were busy implementing the American Christian character in many fields of endeavor. We call this period of study *Twentieth Century Character as Literature*. For there are indeed two fountains rising in America – apparent in the post civil war era. One is from the sources mentioned above – man's government of man, thoroughly pagan – and submissive to evil's domineering. The other stream however is of the Pilgrim, Puritan, Patriot, and Pioneer strain.

As American Christian educators we select for our reading the record of those men and women who endeavored to make their lives count for something in this land of liberty. This is the Character for Liberty which is still so sorely needed today in our nation. These writings reflect the struggles which individuals always seem to have as they "fight the good fight" of faith in God and endeavor to contribute their talents to some field of endeavor which will bless others. As you look at this partial list you will see a Moses of the newly emancipated American Negro who, though born in abject poverty and slavery, endeavored to lead his people out of ignorance and incapacity, to positions of knowledge and ability to be truly self-governing Americans. It is the work of men like Booker T. Washington who paved the way for the progress of all peoples in America who accept themselves as individuals of value and worth and then prepare themselves for positions of responsibility and contribution. We also read of Hellen Keller, whose physical handicaps did not keep her from achievements in all the avenues which could have been denied to her had she accepted her limitations. And we read that incomparable biography of a mountain school-teacher in Appalachia, Jesse Stuart's *The Thread that Runs So True*. This is a literary teaching-treasure – that restores our faith that it is not money, or equipment, or the "environment" which makes teaching a success. Rather, it is the dogged determination and sacrifice of a teacher willing to make every effort to find the path of learning for his students to transform their lives – heart, mind and soul. Mr. Stuart's example should give encouragement to all who teach in home, school, church. He quotes Daniel Webster:

"If we work upon marble, it will perish; if we work upon brass, time will efface it; if we rear temples, they will crumble into dust; but if we work upon immortal minds, if we imbue them with principles, with just fear of God and love of our fellowmen, we engrave on those tablets something which will brighten to all eternity."

Equally satisfying to read in our Twentieth Century Character as Literature are the accounts of men like *Commander Richard Byrd*, whose explorations of both the North and South Poles open up for us the physical and mental challenges of extreme conditions. Byrd's five months *Alone* at Latitude 80° South remain an epic in personal courage and endurance. A whole new world of Pioneer-Pathfinder character is laid out for us as man begins to "subdue" the seventh continent of Antarctica.

The work of Americans is to demonstrate leadership in all fields – and to bless mankind by their ability to carry out their individual goals from the basis of a government derived from the Christian idea of man. Our twentieth century heritage of Character and Literature includes the masterpiece lived and written by Charles A. Lindbergh, *The Spirit of St. Louis.* In an age when collective scientific accomplishment often over shadows the work of the individual, this memorable account of the first New York to Paris flight by a 25-year-old aviator, in a monoplane, in 1927, begins the age of commercial aviation as a reality in the life of the world. When young Lindbergh landed in Paris after 33½ hours of flight over uncharted skypaths, Europe once again caught the vision of what America means in the history of the westward direction of liberty and responsibility – Christian self-government. Myron T. Herrick, our United States Ambassador to France, was present to witness the reception of this young American and he wrote in the Foreword to Lindbergh's first account of his flight:

"When Joan of Arc crowned her King at Rheims she became immortal. When Lafayette risked his all to help the struggling Americans he wrote his memory forever across a mighty continent. Shepherd boy David in five minutes achieved with his sling a place in history which has defied all time.

"These three shining names represent the triumph of the idealism of youth, and we would not speak of them with such reverence today had their motives been less pure or had they ever for an instant thought of themselves or their place in history.

"So it was with Lindbergh, and all the praise awarded him, judged by the rigid standards of history and precedent, he has merited. He was the instrument of a great ideal and one need not be fanatically religious to see in his success the guiding hand of providence...

"Lindbergh was not commissioned by our government any more than Lafayette was by his; in each case it has been merely left for statesmen to register and approve the vast consequences of his acts. Both arrived at the critical moment and both set in motion those imponderable forces which escape the standards of the politician's mind. Who shall say but that they were God-sent messengers of help, smiling defiance of their faith at an all too skeptical world...

"The way Lindbergh bore himself after getting here was but the continuation of his flight. He started with no purpose but to arrive. He remained with no desire but to serve. He sought nothing; he was offered all. No flaw marked any act or word, and he stood forth amidst clamor and crowds the very embodiment of fearless, kindly, cultivated, American youth – unspoiled, unspoilable. A nation which breeds such boys need never fear for its future – America vibrates with glowing pride at the thought that out from our country has come this fresh spirit of the air and that the whole world hails Lindbergh not only as a brave aviator but as an example of American idealism, character and conduct." Myron T. Herrick, *United States Embassy, Paris, June 16, 1927*

Our final section of The Literature of the American Christian Republic includes a review of the *Literature and Character of American Liberty*. This allows us to leave our students on a high plane of inspiration and challenge – as they go on to further prepare themselves for the opportunities for service and sacrifice which the Lord will open up to their talents – if they be willing. To restore a character which is able to perpetuate our American Christian Republic is a major goal in the Christian History Program.

OVERVIEW V
RESTORING THE LITERATURE AND CHARACTER OF LIBERTY – *Elementary Years.*
Kindergarten through sixth grade.
See chart, page 351.

We have now come back to our Christian History Literature Program for the Elementary Years after having followed the Chain of Christianity moving westward with liberty – from Asia, through Europe, and to America for what Professor Arnold Guyot called "the most complete expression of the Christian civilization." We can now design our Elementary curriculum in Literature to produce a character which can appreciate and perpetuate the blessings of liberty. We can also prepare our students for the Leading Ideas of Liberty they will encounter as they progress through the Christian History Literature Program.

The first study for any level of learning is *Learning the Literature of the Bible.* A discussion of how to introduce the Bible as Literature is given on page 377 of this article. Our Founding fathers and mothers grew up on the finest translations of the Word – the Geneva and King James Bibles. Our children can afford to do no less. This study of the Literature of the Bible will prepare them to read at a higher level of our heritage of English and American writers.

Parents can begin to teach their children our heritage of English and American poetry even before they reach formal school age. A fine researched collection is *The Oxford Nursery Rhyme Book,* assembled by Iona and Peter Opie, published by Oxford University Press, latest reprint 1967. Since Literature begins with the baby, the years at mother's and father's knee can be delightful learning experiences with "infant jingles, riddles, catches, tongue-trippers, baby games, toe names, maxims, alphabets, counting rhymes, prayers, lullabies." In fact, the Opies indicate: "The nursery rhyme book is the first book which the parent is actually able to *read* to the child without his attention flagging."

"The rhymes of Mother Goose free the fancy, charm the tongue and ear, delight the inward eye, and many of them are tiny masterpieces of word craftsmanship." So wrote Walter de la Mare, children's poet. *Mother Goose* is an excellent introduction to the hearing and speaking of the English language in ordered metre. Nor can we separate the History of England from the characters and verses of Mother Goose. There are several volumes which can become a resource for this kind of research: *The Real Personages of Mother Goose* by Katherine Elwes Thomas, or, *The Annotated Mother Goose,* with Notes by William S. Baring-Gould and Cecil Baring-Gould. Our favorite picture book of Mother Goose is that done by Margaret de Angeli, *Book of Nursery and Mother Goose Rhymes,* Doubleday, publishers. There is a softness and tenderness in Mrs. de Angeli's illustrations. She and her family visited England to check out all the historic spots and personages which become a part of our childhood memories of learning Mother Goose.

The children's poets begin with simple subjects and simple verse to progress to ballad and more complicated patterns. Once again the study of poetry during the elementary years allows teachers the opportunity of presenting some of our major poets with their individuality of style to young readers. This will help to restore the "inner eye and ear" of the mind and heart and open up many of the wonders of God's Creation to those who have eyes to see, and ears to hear.

Poetry about America's Christian History can be learned as we study the Links of Liberty during the Elementary Years. Bob Jones University Press in Greenville, South Carolina, has republished *American History in Verse*, edited by Burton Stevenson. This is a chronological collection of poetry beginning with *Columbus* and ending with World War I. With this volume in your home and school, you can follow the path of the Hand of God in our nation. There are some excellent selections by some of the major poets as well as some by minor poets who have caught the spirit and character of American history.

We can study the *Individuality of the Nations* in Literature through their folklore which usually has its origin in secular history. It is useful to know what children in other lands read as folk and fairy tales. However, another aspect of the Literature of nations is in the study of their *Heroes and Heroines of Liberty*. These volumes have become less and less available. But, if we are seeking to follow the Chain of Christianity westward to America we can usually come across some treasures in old bookstores, in book sales, and even in our own public library. One such volume we found was entitled *Magna Charta Stories*, copyrighted in 1898. The author's preface ended with these words:

"If the stories stimulate a love of history and add to the inspiration of freedom which should be the heritage of every American boy and girl, the aims of the writers and of the Editor will be met."

The book begins with the memorable struggle of the barons of England with King John to sign England's most important *Charter of Liberty* – the first document from which we as Americans trace the written down rights of the individual, and the first *limitation* of the power of government. How important for our children to know and love *Magna Charta* and its appearing! Today few school children could identify it as a major link in the History of Liberty and England's most important piece of paper.

Among those heroes and heroines which our children should come to know and respect from France are *Joan of Arc, Admiral Gaspard de Coligny,* and *Le Marquis de Lafayette.* Once again the resources for learning about these individuals have to be searched out. But, some books are available. In 1980 the Viking Press in New York reprinted an earlier classic, *Joan of Arc* written and illustrated by a Frenchman, Maurice de Monvel. This classic of some 55 pages traces the legendary story of the peasant girl whose love of God brought to her heavenly visions encouraging her to help her country by first urging the Dauphin of France to be officially crowned king, and by leading the armies of France against the English. Tried for heresy by the church hierarchy she was turned over to the English who burned her at the stake, 1431, in Rouen. Joan "died in the flames, the name of Jesus on her lips ... We are lost! We have burned a saint," cried the English, as they fled from the place. Years later the church reversed her status as a heretic, and elevated her to sainthood. But Joan's appearance and courage and faith gave to the French people a new feeling of unity and identity as a nation.

Many names like that of Paul Revere, John Jay, Matthew Fontaine Maury are known to us. But, do we know of the history of civil and religious forces which brought us these brave descendants of the people known as the Huguenots? As the Reformation proceeded in France in the 16th century the nobleman Gaspard de Coligny, Admiral of France, converted to the new faith. But France was not yet ready to include Protestantism or Biblical Christianity in its character or government. In a delightful little book, published in 1879 as part of Harper's School Classics, entitled *Gaspard de Coligny, Marquis de Chatillon,* by Walter Besant, we read the inscription of our Lord *"Greater love hath no man than this, that a man lay down his life for his friends."* John 15:13. Admiral Coligny was a martyr to religious liberty when he and countless others were murdered on St. Bartholomew's Day in 1572. But, the blood of the martyrs is the seed of liberty. Many countries benefitted from the flight of those remaining Huguenots. Louise, the daughter of Coligny, married William, Prince of Orange, whose battle for religious liberty in the Netherlands, prepared the way for the Pilgrims who found there a second home on their way to America.

Perhaps the most inspiring Link of Liberty from France is that of the young Marquis de Lafayette who offered "his services to a people who were struggling for freedom and independence" in America. General George Washington took this young Frenchman to his heart when he came to our shores. And Lafayette, whose blood was shed for American liberty, also helped bring us French assistance. His tragedy was to discover in France that there was no proper soil for republicanism. The departure of the Protestants had removed a Biblical base for a Christian Republic. The outbreak of the French Revolution brought personal suffering, imprisonment, and the threat of death to both Lafayette and his wife Adrienne. But their personal courage and faith allowed them to outlive the French Revolution. And Lafayette returned twice to America to receive the gratitude of the nation whom he helped achieve Independence. As our *Christian History Literature* program grows in acceptance we hope to republish a fine book entitled *The True Story of Lafayette, called the Friend of America*, by Elbridge S. Brooks, 1899.

Finally, as both history and literature combine to teach us once again of the Hand of God in our nation, we can learn the character of America by a better understanding of the persons, places, and events of Liberty. In this section of *History as Literature* we hope to republish Nathaniel Hawthorne's *Grandfather's Chair*, which contains true stories from New England's History and Biography. With background added of the events of history we hope that this volume, carefully read by parents and teachers with their students, using maps, illustrations, poetry and song, will begin to restore a true knowledge of particular names, dates, places where our History of Liberty was born, and the Character of Liberty formed.

The final selection of books for the Elementary Years are found when both teachers and students are invited to develop Notebook Studies on *America's European Heritage of Liberty*, see *Chart A*, page 354, and *America's Establishment of Liberty*, see *Chart B*, page 362. These studies represent a clear development of the Christian History principles in some Key Nations and Key Classics on the Chain of Christianity moving westward with the Character of Liberty. As we shall be discussing in this article how to prepare for the teaching of these books, we will not comment further on this section of the program.

Our prayer for this program is to once again inspire parents, teachers and students with the vision and purpose of America as the world's testimony of a nation whose foundation and character were once Biblical – a nation allowed by God to plant the first Christian Constitutional Republic.

CHARTS FOR
THE CHRISTIAN HISTORY
LITERATURE PROGRAM

TRACING THE NOBLER STREAM OF LIBERTY
ON THE CHAIN OF CHRISTIANITY MOVING WESTWARD

The Christian History Literature Program (Overview I)

Learning the Literature of the Bible, *Source and Seedbed of Literature and Liberty*

The King James Version of 1611 — Studies in the Old and New Testaments

LEVEL OF LEARNING
EVERY GRADE
ALL SEMESTERS
EVERY YEAR

The Language, Style and Expression of the Bible

LANGUAGE OF THE BIBLE FOR A GOD-CENTERED LIFE: righteousness, justice, purity, honesty, obedience, sincerity, reverence, worship, hope, faith, love, etc.

EXPRESSION OF THE BIBLE: "No single book has so profoundly affected universal expression as has the English Bible."
The Bible and English Literature, Edgar Witaker Work, D.D., page 27

STYLE OF THE BIBLE: the style of "highly gifted individuals."

A. B. Simpson: "Each man's message was colored by the complexion of his own mind...each has its unique colors, forms, fragrance and individuality." *Teaching and Learning*, page 154

Literary Types from the Bible

POETRY: "O taste and see that the Lord is good: Blessed is the man that trusteth in him." *Psalms 34:8*

ESSAY: "Train up a child in the way he should go, and when he is old, he will not depart from it." *Proverbs 22:6*

DRAMA: The Story of Joseph *Genesis*, Chapters 37–48

SHORT NARRATIVE OR SHORT STORY: The Parable of the Good Samaritan, *Luke 10:10-37*

EPIC OR LONG NARRATIVE: The Life of David *1st Samuel* Chapter 16–*1st Kings* Chapter 2

BIOGRAPHY: Jonah, *The Acts of the Apostles* ~~Moses, The Family: Nation Biblical Childhood -Rosalie Slater~~

Literary Types Unique to the Bible

PARALLELISM: of Hebrew Poetry
PROVERBS: concise moral truths
PASTORALS: shepherd literature
PARABLES: brief narratives of our Lord

Literary Elements from the Bible

HISTORICAL SETTINGS: The Garden of Eden, The Home of Potiphar the Egyptian, Solomon's Temple, The House of Peter, Lydia's Home in Philippi

CHARACTER STUDIES: Ruth, Esther, Stephen, Aquilla and Priscilla, The Apostles Paul, Peter, Timothy

PROVIDENTIAL PLOTS: Abraham and Isaac, Daniel in Babylon, Saul on the Damascus Road, John on Patmos

THEMES OR LEADING IDEAS: *Preparation, Protection, Direction, Deliverance*

INDIVIDUALITY OF WRITERS: *Prophets, Kings, Herdsmen, Soldiers, Fishermen, Scholars, Evangelists*

THE CHRISTIAN HISTORY LITERATURE PROGRAM (OVERVIEW II)

Contrasts Between the Pagan and Christian Idea of Man and Government in Literature

LEVEL OF LEARNING

JUNIOR HIGH 7TH AND 8TH GRADES

A TWO YEAR PROGRAM

*LEARNING THE LITERATURE OF THE BIBLE, *Source and Seedbed of Literature and Liberty*

PAGAN HISTORY AND LITERATURE

LEADING IDEAS

READINGS

CLASSICAL MYTHS THAT LIVE TODAY
A Christian View of Greek & Roman gods and goddesses

Nathaniel Hawthorne's *A Wonder Book*

PAGAN EPICS AND THEIR AUTHORS
The gold of Troy

The Walls of Windy Troy: A Biography of Heinrich Schliemann by Marjorie Brayer

Homer and the Greeks

Homer's *The Iliad; The Odyssey*
Padraic Collum's *The Children's Homer*

ROMAN PHILOSOPHERS
Pagan thinkers on statesmanship and life contrasted with Gospel

Seneca: *Epistles*
Cicero: *Essays, Letters*

CHRISTIAN HISTORY AND LITERATURE

LEADING IDEAS

READINGS

NOVELS SET IN THE CHRISTIAN ERA

Ben Hur; A Tale of the Christ by General Lew Wallace
Quo Vadis? by Henryk Sienkiewicz
The Robe by Lloyd C. Douglas

CHRISTIANITY AND ENGLISH CHIVALRY

Howard Pyle's *King Arthur and His Knights of the Round Table;*
Men of Iron
Alfred Lord Tennyson's *Idylls of the King*

LITERARY TYPES IN THE HISTORY OF LIBERTY

NOVEL: *A Tale of Two Cities* by Dickens
SPEECHES: James Otis, Patrick Henry, John Adams
BIOGRAPHY: *The Making of George Washington* by General Wilbur
AUTOBIOGRAPHY: Franklin's *Autobiography*

POEMS: *Patriotic*
ESSAYS: *The Farmer's Letters* by Dickinson
SHORT STORIES: *The Liberty Tree* by Hawthorne
DRAMA: *The Pilgrim Spirit* by Baker

*Studied every semester

THE CHRISTIAN HISTORY LITERATURE PROGRAM (OVERVIEW III)

Tracing the Nobler Stream of Liberty in English Literature—A Two-Year Program

*LEARNING THE LITERATURE OF THE BIBLE, *Source and Seedbed of Literature and Liberty*

ENGLISH PREPARATION FOR AMERICA

LEVEL OF LEARNING

NINTH GRADE 1ST YEAR PROGRAM

ANGLO-SAXON PERIOD 450–1050 A.D.

LEADING IDEAS

Our Anglo-Saxon Heritage of the English Bible; local self-government; Language; the Bible and Literature. Character of Alfred.

READINGS

Anglo-Saxon Epic: *Beowulf*
Anglo-Saxon Poetry: *Caedmon, Cynewulf*
Asser's *Life of King Alfred*
First History written in English: *The Anglo-Saxon Chronicle*

ANGLO-NORMAN PERIOD 1066–1350

LEADING IDEAS

The Norman Conquest brings Feudalism, French & centralized government. Magna Charta records the first protection of individual rights before the law. Character of William the Conqueror.

READINGS

Chivalry: Malory's *Morte d'Arthur, Robin Hood Legends*
Poetry: *The Pearl*
Period Novel: Scott's *Ivanhoe*

WYCLIF AND CHAUCER 1350–1400

LEADING IDEAS

Wyclif's translation of a Bible *"for the government of the people, by the people, for the people."* Chaucer writes about the individual in middle English.

READINGS

The Bible: Wyclif's Bible, (selections)
Allegory: William Langland's *Piers Plowman*
Chaucer's *Canterbury Tales* (selections)

THE ENGLISH REFORMATION 1400–1550

LEADING IDEAS

An age of wars; Reformation and spiritual freedom, Renaissance, study of Greek and Roman classics; opening of the New World.

READINGS

Thomas More's *Utopia*
John Foxe's *Book of Martyrs*
Coverdale's translation of *The Psalms*
Miracle and Mystery Plays: *Everyman*

THE ELIZABETHAN AGE 1550–1620

LEADING IDEAS

Age of nationalism, patriotism, peace. 1560 Geneva Bible. 1588 Defeat of Spanish Armada. Exploration and Colonization of the New World. 1611 King James Bible begins spread of individual liberty.

READINGS

Spencer's *Faery Queen*
Kingsley's *Westward Ho!*
Bacon's *Essays*
Hakluyt's *Voyages of the English Nation*
Shakespeare's *Tragedies, Histories*

THE PURITAN AGE 1620–1660

LEADING IDEAS

Puritan struggle for righteousness and liberty. Monarchy overthrown, Commonwealth established. Reform of national church. Pilgrims separate, flee to Holland, then to America.

READINGS

John Milton's *Poetry, Essays, Epic*
George Herbert's *Poems*
D'Aubigné's *Cromwell*

© ROSALIE JUNE SLATER, Foundation for American Christian Education, San Francisco, California

*Studied every semster

The Christian History Literature Program (Overview III)

Tracing the Nobler Stream of Liberty in English Literature—A Two-Year Program

*LEARNING THE LITERATURE OF THE BIBLE, *Source and Seedbed of Literature and Liberty*

BIBLICAL INFLUENCES ON ENGLISH LIFE AND LITERATURE

LEVEL OF LEARNING

TENTH GRADE 2ND YEAR PROGRAM

RESTORATION PERIOD 1660–1700

LEADING IDEAS

Internal influence of Puritanism on the life and character of the nation and on Literature. *External* reaction to Puritanism. Restoration of the monarchy.

READINGS

John Bunyan: *The Pilgrim's Progress, Grace Abounding, The Holy War*
John Locke, Algernon Sidney: *Essays on Civil Government*
Isaac Newton: *Letters on Science*

EIGHTEENTH CENTURY 1700–1800

LEADING IDEAS

Last of Stuart Kings. 1689 William & Mary, Bill of Rights, Toleration. Age of Prose, newspapers, magazines. Coffee Houses. Age of social progress. Liberty and property, taxation without representation. Loss of the American Colonies in the American Revolution.

READINGS

ESSAYS: Addison & Steele, *The Spectator*
ORATION: Burke's *Conciliation with the Colonies*
POETRY: Gray, Blake, Cowper, Burns, Watts
BIOGRAPHY: Boswell's *Life of Johnson*
HISTORY: Gibbon's *Decline and Fall of the Roman Empire*
NOVEL: Defoe, *Robinson Crusoe*

AGE OF ROMANTICISM 1800–1850

LEADING IDEAS

Age of Individualism and Revolution, God or man the source of Liberty? Adam Smith's capitalism in conflict with European Mercantilism. Reform of society internal or external? Decline of individual Christian character.

READINGS

DRAMA: Hannah More's *Sacred Dramas*
NOVELS: Scott, Austen, Jane Porter
POETRY: Wordsworth, Byron, Keats, Shelley
ESSAYS: Stevenson, Charles and Mary Lamb

VICTORIAN AGE 1850–1900

LEADING IDEAS

England established as a Constitutional Monarchy. Industrial Revolution and social injustice. Retreat of Christianity from market place. Rise of Evolution, Social Darwinism, Socialism.

READINGS

POETRY: Tennyson, Coleridge, Robert and Elizabeth Browning
ESSAYS: Stevenson, Macaulay, Carlyle
NOVELS: Dickens, Eliot, Stevenson, Thackeray, The Bronte Sisters
HISTORIAN: Carlyle

TWENTIETH CENTURY 1900–

LEADING IDEAS

Influences of Fabian Socialism in Literature. Rise of the Irish School of writers. Decline of Colonialism. Return of influence of the Reformed faith.

READINGS

NOVELS: Kipling, Conrad
POETRY: Kipling, Masefield, Noyes, Yeats
DRAMA: Galsworthy, Barrie, Shaw, Synge

---

*Studied every semester

THE CHRISTIAN HISTORY LITERATURE PROGRAM (OVERVIEW IV)

The Literature of the American Christian Republic—A Two-Year Program

*LEARNING THE LITERATURE OF THE BIBLE, *Source and Seedbed of Literature and Liberty*

PROLOGUE AND PREPARATION FOR AMERICA 1382–1607

LEADING IDEAS

READINGS

1382 Wyclif's English Bible launches the opening of the New World; 1492 Columbus; 1580 Virginia Voyages of Exploration

Yule: *The Travels of Marco Polo*
Prescott: *Ferdinand and Isabella*
Irving: *Life of Columbus*
Hakluyt: *Discourse on Western Planting*

COLONIAL CHARACTER AND LITERATURE 1607–1765

LEADING IDEAS

READINGS

Virginia: Virginia's first writer
Virginia's first convert
Virginia's first missionary

Captain John Smith: *Histories of Virginia, New England*
Grace Steele Woodward: *Pocahontas*
Alexander Whitaker: *Good News from Virginia*

Pilgrim Colony of Plymouth:
American Christian Classics

Gov. William Bradford: *History 'Of Plimoth Plantation'*
Edward Winslow: *Good News from New England*
Bradford & Winslow: *Mourt's Relation*

Puritan Colony of Massachusetts Bay:
First American Poet
American Metaphysical Poet

Gov. John Winthrop: *Love Letters, Journal*
Anne Bradstreet: *Poems*
Edward Taylor: *Poems*

Pennsylvania Colony of Religious Toleration
Proprietor and Founder

William Penn: *No Cross, No Crown*

Contributions from the Colonial Clergy

Thomas Hooker: *American Constitutionalist*
Jonathan Edwards: *American Theologian*
Cotton Mather: *American Biographer*
Samuel Sewall: *American Diarist*

Colonial Best Sellers

Music: *The Bay Psalm Book*
Education: *The New England Primer*
Manners: Nathaniel Ward's *The Simple Cobbler*
Theology: Michael Wigglesworth's *The Day of Doom*

*Studied every semester

THE CHRISTIAN HISTORY LITERATURE PROGRAM (OVERVIEW IV)

The Literature of the American Christian Republic—A Two-Year Program

*LEARNING THE LITERATURE OF THE BIBLE, *Source and Seedbed of Literature and Liberty*

LEVEL OF LEARNING

ELEVENTH GRADE 1ST YEAR PROGRAM

THE LITERATURE OF THE AMERICAN REVOLUTION 1765–1789

LEADING IDEAS	READINGS
Our pastors preached Biblical principles of Liberty. The church was the "morning star" of the state.	Sermons: *Artillery-Election Sermon* by Simeon Howard, *Law of Liberty* by Rev. John J. Zubly, *Fast Day Sermon to Morgan's Riflemen* by Daniel Batwell
The American State Papers reflected the Colonists' "familiarity with history...and constitutional principles."	Statesmen: James Otis, John Dickinson, John Adams, Samuel Adams, Thomas Jefferson, James Madison, etc.
The Literature of the American Revolution	The Writings of General George Washington, 1932 edition, edited by John C. Fitzpatrick
The Ladies in Literature	Abigail Adams: *Correspondence* Mercy Warren: *History, Dramas, Poetry* Phillis Wheatley: *Poetry*
Orations that contributed to Liberty	James Otis, Patrick Henry, John Adams
Poetry of the American Revolution	Freneau, Trumbull, Hopkinson, Barlow, Dwight
First American Drama	Royal Tyler: *The Contrast* (first comedy) William Dunlap: *Andre* James Nelson Barker: *The Indian Princess* first "Indian" play
Biography/Autobiography	Benjamin Franklin: *Autobiography*

FIRST FRUITS OF THE REPUBLIC 1787–1840

Classic of American Political Writing	*The Federalist,* Essays on the Constitution by Alexander Hamilton, James Madison, John Jay
America's first man of letters	Washington Irving: *The Sketch Book, A Tour on the Prairie, Life of Washington*
America's first poet	William Cullen Bryant: *Poems*
America's first novelist	James Fenimore Cooper: *The Deerslayer; The Spy*
Western Chroniclers and Literary Pioneers	*The Journals of Lewis and Clark*
A citizen by adoption celebrates America	James John Audubon, Ornithologist: *Delineations of American Scenery and Character*

*Studied every semester

349

THE CHRISTIAN HISTORY LITERATURE PROGRAM (OVERVIEW IV)

The Literature of the American Christian Republic—A Two-Year Program

*LEARNING THE LITERATURE OF THE BIBLE, *Source and Seedbed of Literature and Liberty*

CHRISTIAN CONSTITUTIONAL GOVERNMENT REACHES THE PACIFIC

NORTHWEST: The opening up of Old Oregon. Marcus and Narcissa Whitman, Pioneers and Missionaries

CALIFORNIA: The Providential History of a Republic. Christ's Forty-Niners

REGIONAL WRITERS OF AMERICA—19th Century

MAINE: Sarah Orne Jewett
NEW ENGLAND: Nathaniel Hawthorne, Herman Melville
THE SOUTH: Joel Chandler Harris, Mark Twain

MIDWEST: Willa Cather
WESTWARD: Francis Parkman, Richard Henry Dana
CALIFORNIA: Bret Harte, Mark Twain

GOD PRESERVES THE UNION OF AMERICAN STATES 1850–1870

American Christians fall away from our Biblical principles of government. A civil war between the states is fought. Slavery is the issue, Union is the principle.

ORATORS: Henry Clay, John C. Calhoun, Daniel Webster, Abraham Lincoln
BIOGRAPHIES: Abraham Lincoln, Robert E. Lee
POETRY: Lowell, Holmes, Lanier, Whittier, Whitman
NOVELIST: Louisa M. Alcott

THE "NEW" LITERATURE—Late 19th Century, Early 20th Century

NOVELISTS:
Frank Norris, Jack London, Upton Sinclair, Pearl Buck, Ernest Hemingway, William Faulkner, John Steinbeck

PLAYWRIGHTS: Maxwell Anderson, Thornton Wilder, Robert Sherwood
POETS: Emily Dickinson, Edgar Lee Masters, Edwin Arlington Robinson, Carl Sandburg, Robert Frost, T.S. Eliot

**Note: These writers will be identified, some selections read which do not contradict the philosophy of Philippians 4:8.*

TWENTIETH CENTURY CHARACTER AND LITERATURE

Booker T. Washington *Up From Slavery*
George Washington Carver *Biography*
Helen Keller *The Story of My Life*
Jesse Stuart *The Thread that Runs so True*

Commander Richard E. Byrd *Alone, Discovery*
Colonel Charles A. Lindbergh *The Spirit of St. Louis*
Captain Eddie Rickenbacker *Autobiography*
General Douglas MacArthur *Reminiscences*

REVIEWING THE LITERATURE AND CHARACTER OF AMERICAN LIBERTY

*Studied every semester

THE CHRISTIAN HISTORY LITERATURE PROGRAM (OVERVIEW V)

Restoring The Literature and Character of Liberty—Elementary Years

LEVEL OF LEARNING

KINDERGARDEN THROUGH SIXTH GRADE

*LEARNING THE LITERATURE OF THE BIBLE, *Source and Seedbed of Literature and Liberty*

OUR ENGLISH HERITAGE OF MOTHER GOOSE

Mother Goose, The Nursery Rhymes, and English History

AN INTRODUCTION TO ENGLISH AND AMERICAN POETRY

ENGLISH POETS: William Blake, Elizabeth and Robert Browning, Lord Byron, John Keats, Rudyard Kipling, John Masefield, Christina Rossetti, Percy Bysshe Shelley, Sir Walter Scott, William Shakespeare, Robert Louis Stevenson, Alfred Lord Tennyson, Ann and Jane Taylor, William Wordsworth

AMERICAN POETS: William Cullen Bryant, John Dickinson, Ralph Waldo Emerson, Eugene Field, Robert Frost, Oliver Wendell Holmes, Henry Wadsworth Longfellow, James Russell Lowell, Joaquin Miller, James Whitcomb Riley, John Greenleaf Whittier

THE INDIVIDUALITY OF THE NATIONS

FOLKLORE AND FAIRY TALES

Arabian: Kate Douglas Wiggin
Denmark: Hans Christian Andersen
England: Andrew Lang
France: Charles Perrault

Germany: The Grimm Brothers
Spain: Washington Irving
America: Joel Chandler Harris, Washington Irving

HEROES AND HEROINES OF LIBERTY

Joan of Arc Boutet de Monval 1896
Gaspard de Coligny, Huguenot Harper School Classic 1879
Lafayette, Friend of America Elbridge S. Brooks 1899

HISTORY AS LITERATURE

Columbus: *Christopher Columbus* Pollard
Jamestown: **John Smith, Man of Adventure* Mason
Plymouth: **Pilgrim Stories* Hall
Mass. Bay: *John Eliot, Apostle to the Indians*

The Whole History of Grandfather's Chair; True Stories from New England History and Biography by Nathaniel Hawthorne

AMERICA'S EUROPEAN HERITAGE OF LIBERTY

NOTEBOOK STUDIES

CHART A

Studying Key Nations and Classics on the Chain of Christianity Moving Westward with Individual Liberty

AMERICA'S ESTABLISHMENT OF LIBERTY

CHART B

Studying Key Classics of America's Christian History and Character

*Studied every semester   **reprint anticipated

America's European Heritage of Liberty

Studying Nations on the Chain of Christianity

As we turn to the chart on page 6A of *Christian History*, we note that a number of European nations contributed to the History of Liberty as Christianity affected the life of the nation to a greater or lesser degree. Later in our study of American History we shall learn about contributions from other continents, especially the continents of Asia and Africa. Europe, however, was the first continent as Christianity moved from Western Asia, to receive the impact of the Gospel, and where its effects were made visible—"signs following."

Arnold Guyot, first Professor of Geography, wrote about this "continent of development:"

"Europe is thus the most favored continent, considered with respect to the education of man, and the wise discipline it exercises upon him... Christian Europe beholds poetry, the arts, and the sublimest sciences, successively flourish, as in the bright days of pagan Greece... but Christianity has placed it on the solid foundation of truth." *Teaching and Learning*, p. 150

However, "the precious gifts of culture" developed in Europe were "not to remain the exclusive property of a small number of privileged men, nor of a single society, or one continent alone." The structure of church and state in Europe did not lend itself to spreading cultural or scientific benefits to all. As Guyot continued his study of the *"geographical march of history"* it was evident to him that *civil and religious liberty* needed to be developed before a more abundant life might be enjoyed by all. "The Christian principle is broader; it is universal, like the love of Christ. An important work remains, then, to be done; the work of diffusion and of propagation... To what people shall it belong to carry out this work into reality? The law of history replies, to a new people. And to what continent? The geographical march of civilization tells us, to a new continent west of the Old World— to America." *Teaching and Learning*, p. 151

America is twice blessed by Europe in her own History of Liberty for she received first, the benefits of the Gospel as it affected Europe, and later, she received the contributions of many individuals from these nations as they sought greater civil and religious liberty. As Charles Bancroft wrote of America's unique role in history:

"(Here) the Englishman, the German, the Frenchman, the Italian, the Scandinavian, the Asiatic, and the African all meet as equals. (Here) they are free to speak, to think, and to act. They bring the common contributions of character, energy and activity to the support and enlargement of a common country, and the spread of its influence and enlightenment through all the lands of their origin ... So America adopts the children of all lands only to return a manhood ennobled by a sense of its own dignity through the practice of a system of self-government which improves the condition and promotes the interest of each while it produces harm to none." *Christian History*, page 8

The following list of Key Nations and Key Classics have been selected for studying America's European Heritage. (See Chart A, p. 354) As materials are developed, and as books are reprinted, we hope to enlarge this list. Other nations will be added as we find satisfactory classics and can identify contributions to the historical effort for civil and religious freedom.

PREPARING TO TEACH KEY CLASSICS WITH THE PRINCIPLE APPROACH ELEMENTARY YEARS

Literature as the *handmaid of History "attends" or "accompanies" our study of Liberty. Literature reveals the character* of a nation. It also enables us to learn the *contributions* of nations and individuals to the History of Liberty.

We have a unique opportunity during the Elementary years to introduce students to *nations* on the Chain of Christianity. This study will help them to appreciate what Liberty has cost and why we in America have a responsibility to perpetuate and spread the blessings of civil and religious freedom to all nations.

The study of selected Key Classics and Key Nations enables us to put into practice the method of the Principle Approach: to *research, reason, relate* and *record* Biblical principles as they apply.

This study for the Elementary Years has two parts: one part deals with *nations* on the Chain of Christianity moving Westward; the other part deals with the development of *our own unique Christian character* in America as we see it unfold through particular historical periods.

And our study of the History of Liberty throughout the school years emphasizes the following aspects:

America's Heritage of Liberty as she received it from nations on the Chain of Christianity and also benefited from the character of individuals from those nations who came to America to contribute to the principles of self-government, productivity, and voluntary unity.

America's Establishment of Liberty, which indicates what we did with our Christian Heritage in forming, under God's Grace, our Constitutional Republic.

America's Legacy of Liberty, that which we bequeath to each succeeding generation and which we teach and preach to all nations.

PREPARING TO TEACH HANS BRINKER AS A KEY CLASSIC ON THE CHAIN OF CHRISTIANITY

Because of their love of Liberty American Authors of the nineteenth and even of the twentieth century were inspired to research and record the struggles for freedom in other lands. They recognized that each link on the Chain of Christianity had contributed to our own liberty. They wanted their readers to better understand and appreciate our own civil and religious freedom. Above all, they wished to inspire each new generation with a love of liberty and a character to perpetuate its blessings.

One student of the History of Liberty was John Lathrop Motley (1814–1877), American historian who became fascinated with the struggle for civil and religious freedom in the Netherlands. He also recognized Holland's struggles as related to our own. In fact he identified the westward influence of Christianity upon Holland, England and America, as "all links of one chain" in the History of Liberty.

"The rise of the Dutch Republic must ever be regarded as one of the leading events in modern times ... The lessons of history and the fate of free states can never be sufficiently pondered by those upon whom so large and heavy a responsibility for the maintenance of rational human freedom rests."

It may surprise Americans of today that one hundred years ago we read authors like Motley, and that his six-volume *The Rise of the Dutch Republic* was a part of many home libraries. One hundred years ago we still felt a deep responsibility for our Heritage of Liberty.

One American girl of Dutch ancestry was so inspired through her own reading of Motley that when asked to write a book for young people she decided to write about "the land of pluck" as she came to call Holland. The plot and the character of her story are fictional—but the setting is geographically true as are also the many historical references to the brave struggles of the Dutch people to free themselves from Spanish tyranny.

Published in 1865, *Hans Brinker, or The Silver*

AMERICA'S EUROPEAN HERITAGE OF LIBERTY

STUDYING KEY NATIONS AND CLASSICS ON THE CHAIN OF CHRISTIANITY

CHART A
Elementary Years

NOTEBOOK APPROACH with Syllabus for each book for Teacher *Researching, Reasoning, Relating* and *Recording* for Preparation and Presentation to students.

HERITAGE: ENGLAND, OUR MOTHER COUNTRY. The English Bible, English Common Law, the English Language, English Literature

BOOK
Magna Charta Stories edited by Arthur A. Gilman (1882) *(reprint anticipated)*

HERITAGE: SWITZERLAND AND LIBERTY. Heroes of the Reformation. Home of the Geneva Bible. Calvin's city of Biblical Law

BOOK
Heidi by Johanna Spyri

HERITAGE: THE NETHERLANDS AND LIBERTY. Holland's fight for civil and religious liberty. Second Home of Pilgrims

BOOKS
Hans Brinker, or, The Silver Skates by Mary Mapes Dodge

The Boys' Motley, or, The Rise of the Dutch Republic by Helen Ward Banks *(reprint anticipated)*

HERITAGE: FRANCE, FRIEND OF OUR LIBERTY. Home of Admiral Coligny and the Huguenots, French Explorers, Le Marquis de Lafayette

BOOKS
Joan of Arc by M. Bouter de Monvel

Coligny, Martyr of the Reformation *(in preparation)*

The True Story of Lafayette by Elbridge Brooks *(reprint anticipated)*

HERITAGE: ITALY AND LIBERTY. Birthplace of Marco Polo and Columbus, Home of the Arts

BOOKS
Stories of the Great Artists and Musicians

Pinocchio by Carlo Collodi

HERITAGE: GERMANY AND LIBERTY. Home of Christian Music

BOOKS
Johann Sebastian Bach by Opal Wheeler *(reprint anticipated)*

The Story of Siegfried by James Baldwin

HERITAGE: SPAIN AND LIBERTY. Home of Ferdinand and Isabella, Spanish Explorers of the New World

BOOKS
Tales of the Alhambra by Washington Irving

El Cid

Odyssey of Courage, The Story of Cabeza de Vaca by Maia Wojciechowska

HERITAGE: DENMARK AND LIBERTY. Home of the Viking Explorers

BOOKS
Lief the Lucky by Ingri and Parin d'Aulaire

Fairy Tales by Hans Christian Andersen

Skates, by Mary Mapes Dodge, became a classic upon its first reading. For almost a century children read and re-read this book. And many generations of parents, teachers and librarians enjoyed introducing the history and character of the Dutch people through this delightful family story.

Gradually, however, as American education became less and less literate, the reading of *Hans Brinker* and other classics of this quality began to disappear. Just at a time when the possibility of travel has become far more probable within the lifetime of most students, just at this point we as a nation have fallen to our level of greatest ignorance concerning both our own literature and history and that of other nations.

One reason why this delightful and informative book has not been included in modern education is that twenty-one of the forty-eight chapters in the book touch upon such subjects as Dutch art, architecture, music, history. Restoring *Hans Brinker* and other books which our children deserve to have taught to them requires first that parents and teachers take time to prepare themselves. This task is not difficult. In fact, it is most rewarding, and it is especially thrilling to discover the link between Holland, or the Netherlands, and our own history of liberty.

Key

Here is some of the background which our study of *America's Christian History* enables us now to *re-search* for the teaching of Key Nations and Key Classics on the Chain of Christianity. We will provide some Guidelines for Curriculum Development so that you can *record* in your notebook the essential elements which your students will want to learn in order to understand and enjoy this nation and classic.

PREPARATION OF TEACHER'S NOTEBOOK FOR HANS BRINKER

The following steps need to be taken for the preparation of your Teacher's Notebook for the researching and recording of a nation on the Chain of Christianity before presenting the book which will be studied as Literature by your class.

Since we regard Literature as the Character of a Nation we will look for that character as we first study the Setting or Location of where God placed a people. The following elements apply to the study of all nations on the Chain of Christianity:

Researching and Recording a Nation

1. The Geographic Individuality of a nation
   a) How does Guyot identify the continent on which this nation is found?
   b) What is the geographic location of this country on this particular continent?
   c) What are the geographic distinctions of this country?
   d) What has been the effect of geography on this country?

2. The Historic Individuality of a nation
   a) What is the history of liberty or oppression in this nation?
   b) What have been the contributions of this nation to the Chain of Christianity moving westward?

3. Form of Government in a nation
   a) What is the form of government in this nation?
   b) What documents of government are important to this nation?
   c) What governmental bodies does it have?
   d) What is the role of government in the life of the individual in this nation?

4. The Character of a nation
   a) What are the dominant qualities of character displayed in the history of this nation?
   b) Is it a homogeneous or a heterogenous people?
   c) Does it display a character of liberty? What aspects of the seven principles which form America's Character of Liberty does this nation demonstrate?

5. The Arts and Sciences of a nation
   a) What is the position and function of the sciences?
   b) What is the position and function of the arts in this nation?
   c) To what degree is the government involved in the arts and the development of the sciences?
   d) To what degree has Christianity affected the arts and sciences of this nation?

6. What is the economy of this nation?

7. What is the relationship of this nation to America?

REASONING AND RELATING A NATION AND ITS CHARACTER TO AMERICA AND THE CHAIN OF CHRISTIANITY MOVING WESTWARD WITH INDIVIDUAL LIBERTY

Reasoning and Relating a Nation to America

1. What is the relationship of a nation to America's history?

2. What contributions have individuals of this nation made to America?

3. What has been the influence of this nation upon American government, education, sciences, arts, etc.?

A First Reading of Hans Brinker

In order to help parents and teachers apply these steps to the study of *Hans Brinker* as a Key Classic in a Key Nation on the Chain of Christianity, let us make the following suggestions as guidelines for developing your own curriculum:

Your first reading of *Hans Brinker* will enable you to become familiar with a) the story, b) the setting of Holland or the Netherlands, c) the style of the author, or the way in which Mrs. Dodge puts together all the elements of setting, characterization, plot elements, and themes.

It is helpful to mark your book for easy reference. Some like a *color code*, with one color representing settings, another plot elements, or character, and so on. On a first reading you will want to record in your Notebook all the Dutch terms the author uses: names of persons, places, things, etc. You might decide to make page headings in your Notebook on particular subjects so that you can add to your information as you read. Perhaps you might like to use pages in the back of your copy of *Hans Brinker* where you can enter certain things which you want to find easily, i.e., references to God, to prayer, to Dutch customs, to artists, etc. After a first reading you will be ready to *Research* and *Record* some of the steps listed for the study of the nation.

Researching the Geographic Individuality of the Netherlands

Pages 141-149 in *T/L* describe the geographic individuality of the continent of Europe as "the continent of development." This gives us a clue to the nations in Europe. What kind of people should we expect to find in the Netherlands? This should be a country where things happen.

Where on the continent of development are the Netherlands located? *The National Geographic Atlas* provides both a map of the continent and a map of the nation and gives a short description of the outstanding geographical features of the land. You will want a map for your classroom, and perhaps you will want your students to have small notebook-sized maps too. It is good to see the nation in relation to the continent – and to the world. It is important to see the size of a nation in relation to America. It is hard for us to realize the size of the Netherlands in proportion to the size of the United States of America.

A resource for descriptive materials for your study is from the *Netherlands National Tourist Office*. Most large cities have this resource. If you are not in a large city look up the address in some city in your state and phone or write for their Teacher's Pack of materials. Over the years we have obtained many wonderful pamphlets, maps, and posters, giving up-to-date as well as historical, economic, and cultural information. Travel Bureaus are also a resource for you.

As soon as you begin to research the Dutch nation you will discover that you are looking at a unique and courageous people.

"One of the world's most densely populated nations fights an ongoing war with the sea for its land. One third lies below sea level, protected by dikes and canal systems whose prototypes appeared 800 years ago." *National Geographic Atlas of the World*, 1981, Fifth Edition.

The Dutch have a saying that "God created all the world except the Netherlands, which Dutchmen made." In fact "the life of the people in the Netherlands is to a large extent dominated by their struggle to keep the forces of water at bay. If they were to leave their country or give up the fight against these forces, it would be only a matter of time before the greater part of the Netherlands became uninhabitable." *The Netherlands: Land from Water.* Pamphlet.

Not only have the Dutch had to guard dike and dune against the sea, but they have also reclaimed land from the sea for agriculture. Fully 20% of the Netherlands has been reclaimed. No wonder Mary Mapes Dodge was fascinated by this "land of pluck."

"From time to time a nation is called upon to tackle a great task, regardless of the cost. A great mission endows a people with a new and powerful sense of awareness, inspiring it to devote itself to its task with enthusiasm. Such enthusiasm befits the descendants of a race that has ruled the sea not only with its admirals but also with its engineers."

(Dr. H. J. A. M. Schaepman, in a speech on the Zuyder Zee Reclamation Works in 1897)

*Researching the Historic
Individuality of the Netherlands*

Just as Mary Mapes Dodge found John Lothrop Motley's volumes on *The Rise of the Dutch Republic* most helpful, you too should seek out these books in your Library. Perhaps you can find a set in a second-hand book store. So eager were American educators for young people to learn this history that Helen Ward Banks in 1912 paraphrased Motley in a book entitled *The Boy's Motley, or, The Rise of the Dutch Republic*. Twenty chapters re-tell the History of Liberty in Holland, including the thrilling account of William of Orange who was the George Washington of his country and fought courageously against Spain and her efforts to curtail the Biblical liberty of his people.

In *Hans Brinker*, Mary Mapes Dodge includes the two chapters dealing with the siege of the cities of Haarlem and Leyden. When we consider the efforts that the Dutch people made to keep the sea from invading their land it is startling to learn that for the relief of Leyden they deliberately broke down dikes to let in the sea so that a fleet could sail over the land. The people of Leyden held out for months and many died of starvation. But at last their cruel Spanish besiegers were defeated and the Dutch fleet reached them. The Foundation for American Christian Education has reprinted Motley's chapter of this event to accompany our syllabus on *Hans Brinker*.

When we remember that Leyden is the city where the English Pilgrims spent eleven years on their way to America we marvel at the Lord's Providence in the deliverance of these brave and tolerant people. Isn't it important for us to know this Link in the History of Liberty? Can we afford to ignore it any longer? Let us prepare our youth to extend the blessings of liberty.

FORM OF GOVERNMENT
OF THE NETHERLANDS

It will not take much research to learn that the Netherlands is a constitutional monarchy with a King or Queen at its head. It has a parliamentary system and the States General has two chambers: an Upper House elected indirectly by the Provincial Councils, and a Lower House whose members are elected directly by the Dutch electorate. It would be good to identify for your students where the executive and legislative powers rest, and how their Court System works. Just the fact that "there is no trial by jury in the Netherlands" gives you as a teacher an opportunity to teach your students how this precious right came to us in our country. This is one of the goals for studying nations on the Chain of Christianity. They provide us with oppor-

tunities to learn how our heritage came to us and what liberties we enjoy under our unique Constitutional Republic.

THE CHARACTER OF
THE DUTCH PEOPLE

You will be able to derive the character of this people as you look at all aspects of their geography, history and religion. In the time of William of Orange there was a growing Protestantism due to the Reformation. Now the country is over 40% Roman Catholic. Dutch Reformed represents about 25% and fully one quarter of the country has no religion. What has happened to the Dutch people who fought so hard in 1575 for Biblical liberty? What efforts are being made today to preach civil and religious liberty?

THE ARTS OF THE NETHERLANDS

Holland today has much modern art and architecture. Van Gogh is widely acclaimed as their greatest artist. But there was a significant Dutch School of Art which was coincident with Holland's independence from Spain and Catholicism. The Reformation also brought about the painting of Rembrandt van Rijn, known as the Painter of the Bible. In this study of art we learn how the religious foundations of a country shape and form the arts. It provides us with an opportunity to become aware of the American schools of art and Christianity's influence upon them.

*Reasoning and Relating the Role
of the Netherlands to the United States*

We know that one of Holland's contributions to the Chain of Christianity was that of providing an asylum for refugees from all countries. "Holland was the most tolerant and liberal country in Europe. Holland was an asylum for all refugees. The Puritans from England, the Protestant Huguenots of France, the Jews expelled from Spain and Portugal, all found its doors open to them." (*Holland and the United States*, published by the Royal Netherlands Embassy)

From our study of William Bradford's *History 'Of Plimoth Plantation,'* we know that the Pilgrims were grateful for refuge in Holland. It was a "treasury" of preparation for them for the New World. But, as a Biblical people, there came a time when the Dutch liberalism became too much for them. The Pilgrims' first impulse for America was to protect their children from the irreligious influences in that pluralistic society and for their Christian education. In 1609, the Dutch sent an Englishman, Henry Hudson, to find a new route to the East Indies. He left the mark of his discoveries on America, chief

357

of which is the Hudson River. Our own Washington Irving picked up the Dutch influence in this area and wrote his Sleepy Hollow Stories, *The Legend of Sleepy Hollow*, and *Rip Van Winkle*.

The most famous real estate transaction was that of Peter Minuit who, in 1626, purchased Manhattan Island from the Indians for a reputed $24. This deal made Nieuw Amsterdam an official Dutch trading post.

There is considerable Dutch influence in our country. Consult your card catalog in the library and you may find some interesting paths to follow. How many Dutch products are imported today from the Netherlands? Do you grow Dutch tulips? Do you eat Dutch cheese? Do Delft tiles hang in your kitchen? There are some Christian links to our relationship to this country. Let us discover them. And what are we doing in evangelical outreach today in that nation? What can you and your students discover? What can we export of America's Christian history and government to this "land of pluck?"

READING FOR THE LITERARY ELEMENTS IN HANS BRINKER

Before presenting your students with the book *Hans Brinker*, you will need to read it a *second* time for the Literary Elements. Learning the *art of writing* from a study of the author's techniques is part of the Christian History Program in Literature. Recording *in the words of the author* will prepare you and your students to do your own writing at a later date – perhaps when you have finished studying the book. Let us now refresh our definitions of these Literary Elements by giving an illustration of each from the novel.

Setting:

The geographical, historical, physical, and sometimes spiritual background against which the action of the narrative takes place.

Example:

From Chapter 2: Dutch cities "a bewildering jungle of houses, bridges, churches, and ships, sprouting into masts, steeples, and trees"

The Country "lower than the level of the sea"; ditches, canals, ponds, rivers, lakes are everywhere"; "great flapping windmills"; "trees bobbed into fantastic shapes"

Characterization:

Character descriptions should identify Biblical qualities and show the consequences of choices.

Example:

From Chapter 1:

Hans: "He was fifteen years old . . . a solid, hearty-looking boy, with honest eyes and a brow that semed to bear a sign 'goodness within'"

From Chapter 7:

Dr. Boekman: "It was a face that one could never forget. Thin, and lank, though a born Dutchman, with stern, blue eyes, and queer compressed lips, that seemed to say 'No smiling permitted,' he certainly was not a very jolly or sociable looking personage."

Plot Elements:

That series of actions which move in a related sequence to an outcome. Plots which spring from character as the *internal cause* of events are most effective.

Example:

From Chapter 7: "But Hans was bidden, and that, too, by a voice he seldom disregarded – his own conscience.

"'Here comes the greatest doctor in the world,' whispered the voice. 'God has sent him; you have no right to buy skates when you might with the same money, purchase such aid for your father!'"

Themes:

The purposes, convictions, and leading ideas of the author and how they are expressed in the literary work.

Example:

From Author's Preface: "Should (this book) cause even one heart to feel a deeper trust in God's goodness and love, or aid any in weaving a life wherein, through knots and entanglements, the golden thread shall never be tarnished or broken, the prayer with which it was begun and ended will have been answered. M. M. D." *(Reference to Ecclesiastes 12:6)*

Style:

The individuality of the author and the literary techniques used to achieve the purposes for which the book was written.

Example:

From Chapter 8: "'We can stop at Haarlem, Jacob, and show your cousin the big organ,' said Peter van Holp, eagerly, 'and at Leyden, too, where there's no end to the sights; and spend a day and night at The Hague, for my married sister, who lives there, will be delighted to see us; and the next morning we can start for home.'"

(The trip was the author's *literary technique* for introducing her readers to the history and culture of Holland.)

Presentation of Hans Brinker to Your Students

To introduce your class to *Hans Brinker* and the study of the Netherlands, it is good to endeavor to inspire an interest and to have an appropriate setting for the subject in your classroom. Your Bulletin Board might display a chart, poster, or map of the nation to be studied on the Chain of Christianity. You might even have a chart with neatly printed questions, such as: What did the Dutch contribute to the Westward course of Liberty? What did the Dutch contribute to American History? What do we import from Holland? It is good to leave some things for your students to find, i.e., a Dutch flag, coins, pictures, or other objects. You might start with some prints of the Dutch School of Art, as referenced in *Hans Brinker;* or, perhaps you might want to introduce Rembrandt, the Biblical painter who was born in Leyden.

Be sure to have a map of Europe which shows the Netherlands. Also, contrast the size of this tiny nation with the United States. There are other resource maps.

Student Researching and Recording in Notebooks

Your introduction to the Netherlands should be worked out in your teacher's notebook so that you have some periodicals or books for them to research. Help them with their research by having some specific points to discover: Write down on the board for them to copy just what you want them to look for. When they bring in their reports summarize their findings on the board in sentences under specific subjects, i.e., government, the arts, geography, etc. What you write on the board will be copied into the notebooks as the result of class findings. But if some students have been able to write up additional materials, let them put these copied neatly, into their own notebooks. Essentially, your board work is to help them reason and relate what they are researching before recording.

After your study of the Netherlands you will then be ready to introduce them to the book *Hans Brinker, or, The Silver Skates.* Every student, of course, will have a copy of the novel. Let them look through the edition you have and enjoy the chapter heads, the illustrations and the book as a whole. Somewhere in their research you will want

to make a special study of the author and her influence in America in the field of children's literature, but it may not be just at this time. They should first meet her in her writing.

Read the first chapter together around the class out loud. Discuss the Literary Elements, and identify the *setting* in your discussion. Ask them what they think will be the *theme* of the book, or how they feel about the *characters* presented in the first chapter.

Never assign reading for the students which you do not do *with* them first. These books of more substance require reading and re-reading. So, it is helpful to read a chapter together and then let them record the literary elements you choose in the author's words, on practice paper first, before deciding what to copy into their notebooks. It takes longer, but you are teaching them how to Research, Reason, Relate and Record both Literature and History, as well as other subjects which these books present. It is a rich experience if you are willing to work at it, and the harvest is great.

ORGANIZING YOUR STUDENT READING OF HANS BRINKER

The Major Divisions of the Book

I.	Chapters 1–9	An introduction of all major elements of the story.
II.	Chapters 10–31	The skating journey of the seven boys from Broek to The Hague.
III.	Chapters 32–48	The story of The Silver Skates taken up again.

The first section of the book allows you to become familiar with the main characters of the book, the country and some of its customs, and the major themes of the story. In the last two chapters of this section, 8 and 9, you should record the names of the seven boys who are going to take the skating trip. They are almost all Dutch names and delightful to learn, i.e., Voostenwalbert Schimmelpennick. After each boy's name give some indication of his character. Also have your students record for each of the five Literary Elements those summary statements so that they are clear on the plot elements and the themes of the book.

Section II, the longest in the book, gives us an opportunity to learn many things about the country. You could list each city visited and summarize the boys' sight-seeing. You could take subjects, i.e., art, architecture, homes, and enter brief observations on them. You could identify historical points that they learn in their journey. Finally, you can summarize what events the boys are involved in—what happens to them. Or you could write up a class record of what you enjoyed most about this journey into Dutch history and culture.

Section III takes up the story again. How are the main characters affected by what takes place in the Brinker cottage? How does it seem that "all things work together for good" in the events that transpire? And how does the race come out?

You may want to read the final chapters out loud again, as a drama, after you have recorded what you want each student to have in Notebook form. At the end of a book study like this it is good to take each of the five Literary Elements and write a summary for each. For *Setting* you may discuss with your students how they would write a concluding paragraph or page on the settings they have read in this book. Now they can scan all their notebook records on setting. In *Characterization* you may wish to take a few characters in whom you saw change and summarize your observations. The *Plot Elements* can be briefly recorded by reviewing what has been written out as you were reading the book. *Themes* should not be hard to summarize and should provoke a lively discussion. And finally, the *Style* of the author will allow you to help the students identify Mrs. Dodge's most outstanding methods of telling her story and bringing in her themes. At the same time you might conclude this analysis by adding to what you have learned about her contributions to juvenile literature in the nineteenth century in America.

A book of the size and substance of *Hans Brinker* may take you a whole semester or longer to cover adequately. What you will have learned and accomplished by the end of the study will, of course, be measured by your own enthusiasm and preparation. Some classes may wish to present a program to culminate their reading and recording of this book. They could make reports on the country, read or act out some part of the book. Or perhaps indicate their plans for a trip to Holland and what they would need to do to prepare.

It may sometimes seem as if we are trying to do too much with this book and others we have listed. But these books which the Lord has Providentially brought to our attention, can be *teaching tools* so that we may enliven and enhance the reading habits of our students to take on books of more substance and challenge. Teachers and parents too will have the opportunity of "catching up on the classics" which they missed in home or school while they were growing up. This will help to build the unity of families and schools, and imbue our hearts and minds with the responsibilities which our American Christian Liberties require of us. We pray such a study will help grow back the character to perpetuate and propagate our Constitutional form of government.

HOLLAND AND AMERICA LINKS TO LIBERTY

"God has given both to great America and to little Holland a great task. May both nations stand together for the lofty ideals for which our forefathers lived and struggled." Preface, p. viii

These words were written by a Dutchman, Dr. D. Plooij, invited to America on the occasion of the 300th anniversary of the Dutch Reformed Church in America to lecture on the subject of *The Pilgrim Fathers from a Dutch Point of View:*

"Through two channels the Dutch influence reached this country... indirectly, through the Pilgrim Fathers; directly, through the Dutch settlers, their church, and form of government, on Manhattan... As a matter of fact, when I speak on the earliest history of the American nation, I am speaking at the same time on the history and on the noblest traditions of my own country; and whatever difference there may be between the simple and strong John Robinson, the spiritual founder of the civil as well as of the religious freedom of America, and our own Prince William of Orange, the Father of our Fatherland, of both of them it may be said that they lived and died for the religious and civil freedom of their people, and of the world. Both were men of deep religious convictions..." Introduction, pp. 3, 5

Dutch immigration to America contributed directly to our own history and literature. We have only to remember Washington Irving's charming *Rip Van Winkle* and his *Legend of Sleepy Hollow* to recall the Hudson River Valley, which became one of the homes of the settlers from the Land below the Sea. They also settled in Michigan.

America, made up of men and women from all nations, accepts their "contributions of character, energy and activity"—especially when these support the principles of "self-government which improves the condition and promotes the interest of each." *CHOC*, p. 8

AMERICA'S ESTABLISHMENT OF LIBERTY

KEY CLASSICS OF AMERICA'S CHRISTIAN HISTORY AND CHARACTER

We have endeavored to show with our study of *Hans Brinker* and the History of Liberty in the Netherlands, the Researching, Reasoning, Relating, and Recording of a Key Nation and Classic on the Chain of Christianity Moving Westward. This is the first aspect of the study of the Literature of Liberty. From it we should learn an appreciation of God's dealings with the men and nations contributing to *America's European Heritage of Liberty*.

Chart B which follows represents the second aspect of our study of the History of Liberty, or, *America's Establishment of Liberty*. This shows what we did with our Christian Heritage in forming our Constitutional Republic. So much depended upon the embodiment of Biblical principles in individual lives, carrying forward the seed of Christian self-government into new fields like science, commerce, the arts, and education.

For each of these books the Foundation for American Christian Education has prepared a syllabus available for purchase with the books listed. The syllabus is designed to help parents and teachers with research and curriculum construction. Suggested resources for the historical settings are given as well as information on partic-

ular fields, such as American Art, Architecture, Science, etc. Guidance is also provided for the development of individual teacher and student notebooks.

A brief survey is now presented so that you might be challenged to see the possibilities in each of these books, to learn the historical periods they represent and the character they portray. Perhaps you will then be encouraged to prepare to teach them in your home or school. Our format will include the exemplification of the Christian History Principles and the character to support our American Christian Republic.

All but one of the books described here touches upon the influence of the American Christian home. It is in the homes of our nation where the character and the philosophy of government is formed. As Pastor Phillips wrote: "The Christian home...forms the citizen, lays the foundation for civil and political character, prepares the social element and taste, and determines our national prosperity or adversity. We owe to the family, therefore, what we are as a nation as well as individuals." *Teaching and Learning* page 11. The seven principles identify our character and how we are governed–individually and as a nation.

America's Establishment of Liberty

CHART B
Elementary Years

NOTEBOOK APPROACH with Syllabus for each book for Teacher *Researching*, *Reasoning*, *Relating* and *Recording* for Preparation and Presentation to students.

SYLLABUS: PILGRIM-CHARACTER MOVES WESTWARD. Midwest Pioneer Life

BOOK
Little House in the Big Woods by Laura Ingalls Wilder

SYLLABUS: PATRIOTIC WOMEN IN THE AMERICAN REVOLUTION. Massachusetts and the Adams Family.

BOOK
Abigail Adams, First Lady of Faith and Courage by Evelyn Witter

SYLLABUS: WILLIAM PENN AND HIS PENNSYLVANIA COLONY OF RELIGIOUS TOLERATION. Benjamin West, Father of American Painting

BOOKS
Benjamin West and His Cat, Grimalkin by Marguerite Henry and Wesley Dennis

SYLLABUS: AMERICAN MEN OF SCIENCE. Nathaniel Bowditch, Father of American Mathematics

BOOKS
Carry On, Mr. Bowditch by Jean Lee Lathan

SYLLABUS: THE AMERICAN CHARACTER IN GOVERNMENT AND EDUCATION. Colonial Connecticut and Constitutional America

BOOKS
Noah Webster, Father of the Dictionary by Isabel Proudfit

SYLLABUS: THE NEW ENGLAND MIND AND CHARACTER. Concord, Massachusetts and the Civil War

BOOKS
Little Women by Louisa May Alcott

SYLLABUS: THE FREE AND INDEPENDENT MAN IN THE AMERICAN WILDERNESS. The French and Indian War in Upper New York

BOOKS
The Last of the Mohicans by James Fenimore Cooper

NOTE: Inasmuch as this is a Reading and Writing study, each school should examine these books to determine at what level of learning they can best be taught.

PREPARATION OF TEACHER'S NOTEBOOK FOR THE STUDY OF KEY CLASSICS OF AMERICA'S CHRISTIAN HISTORY AND CHARACTER

America's Establishment of Liberty is the exciting story of how a diverse people, in many geographical areas, produced during our Colonial times a unique character for a Republic. This section deals with those Key classics of America's Christian history and characer. The following steps are suggested for those parents and teachers who want to be well prepared to teach America's Christian History through Literature.

Researching and Recording the Historic and Geographic Individuality of the Classic to be taught

1. In what period of our history does this story take place?
   a) Is the story told as fiction or biography?
   b) Can we verify the factual parts of the book?
   c) How does this historic period fit into America's Christian History?
   d) Does this classic add to our understanding of the unity and diversity of America?
2. In what geographic location of America does this book have its setting?
   a) How well does the book identify geographic factors peculiar to its area?
   b) How much do these add to the effectiveness of the book?
   c) How much should geographic features be stressed for students?
3. What scientific, cultural, or economic facts can be learned from this book?

Reasoning and Relating the Principles of America's Christian Character as Exemplified in this Classic

   a) What are the outstanding character principles exemplified in this book?
   b) Can they be successfully related to the lives of individual Americans today?
   c) How do you as a teacher plan to help students to exemplify aspects of these American Christian priniples of character in the study of this book?

Reasoning and Recording this Classic's Leading Ideas

   a) What are the major themes of the author?
   b) Can you make a Biblical comparison between the ideas the author stresses and similar ideas expressed in the Word of God?

Researching and Recording the Literary Elements of Setting, Characterization, Plot Elements, Themes, and Style of Author

   a) How will you have your students develop their understanding of these Literary Elements in their notebooks?
   b) What will every student research and record?
   c) What particular aspects of the Literary study of this book provide opportunities for individual projects? for group projects?

Reasoning and Relating the contribution of this book to our understanding of American Liberty and Responsibility

   a) Could the character expressed in this book have been exemplified in any other country?
   b) What does this book reveal about living in an American Christian Republic?
   c) Would individuals living in other countries learn what elements contribute to successful Constitutional government by reading this book?

Researching and Recording the Author of this book

   a) What research will you do and what references will you provide for a biographical study of this author?
   b) Can you identify what this author has contributed to the Literature and Character of Liberty for student recording?
   c) Will you introduce your students to some other books by this same author for their outside reading? Are they books you have read?

TEACHING AMERICAN CHARACTER THROUGH LITERATURE WITH THE PRINCIPLES OF AMERICA'S CHRISTIAN HISTORY

KEY CLASSIC TO BE TAUGHT

Little House in the Big Woods,
    by Laura Ingalls Wilder, 1932
HISTORIC AND GEOGRAPHIC INDIVIDUALITY
    Nineteenth Century Midwest America
CHRISTIAN HISTORY PRINCIPLE EXEMPLIFIED
    The Christian Principle of Self-Government
LEADING IDEA IDENTIFIED
    The Pilgrim-Pioneer Character Moves
    Westward with Constitutionalism

As the tide of individuals and families moved westward across the American continent, the Christian principle of self-government was greatly in evidence. But the struggle was always to place it upon a Christian base so that it would not be merely man's government of man. We are sometimes tempted to believe contemporary pictures of out westward expansion as a period of violence and lawlessness. Yet as we research the seeds in the forming of our mid-western and western states and the building of towns and communities, we reason that only the stabilizing influences of Christianity could have kept the nation steadily building Constitutional government.

"The Christian church has been one of the most potent factors in the construction of the American Republic and one of the greatest bulwarks of its magnificent principles and institutions." *Teaching and Learning,* pages 39–40, Pastor David Gregg

The key was home example, and in the study of the Pilgrim-Pioneer character, we find this true of the Ingalls family. Father and Mother were examples of character. It was this character which made possible Pioneer life and its self-sufficiency.

Researching and Reproducing Pioneer Life

With firm, clear strokes of the pen, Mrs. Wilder recreates for us her first years in the Big Woods of Wisconsin. Her words and phrases are short and forceful. Her images are clear and convincing and we are transported back one hundred years or more when a man could "go to the north" walking for a whole month and "there was nothing but woods. There were no houses. There were no roads. There were no people. There were only trees and the wild animals who had their homes among them."

Pa and Ma and the three girls all had to work together in order to survive in this American wilderness. How many children of today would love to have their parents include them in helping to build the house, produce and preserve food, make clothing, sheets and blankets, and even provide playthings for themselves. Even the youngest children were allowed to watch, to learn, and to help as soon as they were able. Each step was patiently explained to them.

A major purpose for the study of this book is to encourage parents and teachers to help *recreate* some of the aspects of this Pioneer life for our present generations. Our children no longer can do things with their hands as earlier generations could. What processes, or activities, can you prepare and present to your class to help restore a knowledge of what it took to live and contribute to America's westward experience? A number of books have been specially written including *The Little House Cookbook, The Laura Ingalls Wilder Songbook,* and books of American needlework and woodwork. If we are to be successful in reproducing qualities of American Christian character needed for the survival of our Republic, our children must practice patience and excellence. As Samuel Adams reminded us, self-government is an "art" which is found "in the study and practice of the exalted virtues of the Christian system." *Christian History,* page xiv

What Should This Book Yield?

The teacher's notebook should include a study of the author, of pioneer life, and of how communities were started. There does not have to be a great amount of research but sufficient to help your students to record in their notebooks. Teach them and help them reason out on the blackboard just what they are able to write as background.

Recording Literary Elements

When you follow the writing instructions in the syllabus, emphasize the principle of self-government as it was visible in the various characters of the book. Each of the Literary Elements set forth: *Setting, Characterization, Plot Elements, Themes, Style* can be written into the notebooks with simple sentences. For example:

Setting: Laura lived in a little house made of logs. She lived with her family in the Big Woods of Wisconsin. There were no houses. There were no roads. There were no people. Wild animals lived in the Big Woods, etc.

Characterization: Laura's father showed her the wolves outside the house. Pa had to hunt and kill deer for food. Pa built a smoke house in the trunk of a hollow tree. Ma put hickory chips on the fire under the meat, etc.

Plot Elements: Getting ready for winter. They smoked the meat. They salted the fish in barrels. They stored the potatoes, carrots, beets, turnips, cabbages in the cellar. They hung red peppers, onions, and herbs in the attic, etc.

Themes: Can you help your class write a sentence about what Laura felt about her home? If you have already written some ideas down in your own notebook you can guide them as they reason, relate and record.

Style: Mrs. Wilder conveys her themes with graphic descriptions of just what this Pioneer family did. Even without the illustrations you should "see" this home, and "feel" its message. How does the author accomplish this? You may wish to discuss this and help make your class aware of the author's style.

KEY CLASSIC TO BE TAUGHT

Abigail Adams, First Lady of Faith and Courage,
   by Evelyn Witter, 1976
HISTORIC AND GEOGRAPHIC INDIVIDUALITY
   Massachusetts during the American
   Revolution and First Years of Nation
CHRISTIAN HISTORY PRINCIPLE EXEMPLIFIED
   America's Heritage of Christian Character
LEADING IDEA IDENTIFIED
   Patriotic Women in the American Revolution

This well-written little book describes the Adams family in our history, and most especially traces the life of an American Christian woman, Abigail Smith Adams. How should it be studied as both history and literature?

Our 24-page syllabus on Abigail Adams begins with the liberation of women through Christianity. It also provides us with some of the letters which Abigail and John wrote. Mrs. Adams was known as the "correspondent of the American Revolution." Because Abigail was a "reading" woman, her "writing" reflected principles with which the American colonists were concerned. When we read her letters we are reading from "original sources" and making friends with our past through coming to know the very individuals who made our history. We see the Hand of God in America.

Researching and Recording our Revolution

In order to understand the events that form a background to Abigail Smith Adams' life we need to know what they were about. Our syllabus has referenced these events into the Christian History books. This provides us with an opportunity to introduce our Elementary children to our Providential History. We prayed our way through the American Revolution. How thrilling to learn that on the very day the Militia of Lexington was gathered on the Common awaiting the arrival of British troops, the sister colony of Connecticut was on its knees holding a Day of Fasting and Prayer. No wonder the men on Lexington Green "held their fire." They did not start an aggressive war, but only returned fire when called upon to defend their homes and community.

And the *Boston Port Bill* became, under God's Providence, not an event to *separate* the colonies, but, rather, a means of uniting them. American Political Union came about through internal unity of principles. There are some key events mentioned in this book which our students should be able to identify and discuss. Do not let the children "slide by" the mention of these historic happenings without teaching them what they are all about.

Researching and Recording Colonial Home Life

Our Lord said of those who listened to His teachings: "Having eyes, see ye not?" He referred to *internal* seeing. But we today are not even alert to seeing *externally*. In the first chapter of the book *Abigail Adams*, the author devotes herself to describing the home in which Abigail lived and its furnishings. This is a fine chapter to practice with words and phrases. It provides us with an opportunity to learn how to "see" a colonial home of Massachusetts. In our syllabus there are some reference books on homes in America. We had such a variety of homes because of God's principle of individuality. This can begin your own preparation for future travel and visitation to historic American homes. Our God is a God of Detail and Design. We need to spend time looking at His Creation. We need also to spend time looking at what His children have made up from His Creation. Decorating and furnishing our homes can become an American Christian adventure. There are suggestions on how to record this study in our syllabus. We suggest you "record" a room from your own home too.

America's heritage of Christian character has had a unique expression in American womanhood. From the westward move of the Apostle Paul to the continent of Europe we have seen the role of woman become more important and it is especially critical to the perpetuation of a Republic. Abigail Smith Adams is a fine example of this principle as wife, mother, and First Lady.

Researching and Recording Contrasts

In your reading of *Abigail Adams* be prepared to help your students make the contrasts between a girl brought up in colonial Massachusetts and a girl brought up anywhere in America today. What do we need to restore to our young American Christians that has gone out of home training? How can this study begin to make us aware of how far we have fallen from our leadership role as Christians in a nation? On the other hand, what could our age provide for Abigail Adams which would make her role as an American Christian woman even more significant—provided she did not "drop" many of the activities which, Providentially, enabled her to contribute to our nation?

KEY CLASSIC TO BE TAUGHT

Benjamin West and His Cat Grimalkin,
    by M. Henry and W. Dennis, 1947
HISTORIC AND GEOGRAPHIC INDIVIDUALITY
    William Penn and His Pennsylvania Colony
    of Religious Toleration
CHRISTIAN HISTORY PRINCIPLE EXEMPLIFIED
    "Conscience is the Most Sacred of all
    Property"
LEADING IDEA IDENTIFIED
    Benjamin West, Father of American Painting

The principle of Conscience has always been associated with America's establishment and perhaps never so vividly as in the founding of the Parent Colony of Pennsylvania. This allows us to begin our research of William Penn, a man who suffered "for conscience sake" in England, and came to the New World with a love of liberty and a determination to extend religious toleration to all men. In America, though granted extensive acres by the King of England, Penn purchased the land from the Indians. In fact, this famous transaction was immortalized in a large oil painting more than a century later by another Pennsylvania Quaker, Benjamin West.

Today we know Benjamin West as the *Father of American Painting.* As we read this charming book we also learn of his struggles of conscience as he began to paint and draw. Quakers regarded pictures as "images"—and they believed that "images" offended God. Should Benjamin be "called off" his painting? This was a matter for the Friends Meeting to decide. What happened is left to the reader-researcher. But the life of Benjamin West is important to learn, especially when we realize that Quakers never took off their hats to anyone, even to the King of England. How this American artist maintained his loyalty to his nation and helped other struggling American painters is worthy of research. And he is especially dear to us because of the unusual relationship which Pennsylvania Quakers had to the Indians—and how these Indians helped Benjamin learn about color from the earth.

Researching and Recording the Parent
Colony of Pennsylvania

A goal of the Christian History Literature Program is to teach Elementary students the individuality of the Parent Colonies: Virginia, Plymouth, Massachusetts Bay, Connecticut, and Pennsylvania. Through literature we can catch the flavor and color of these settlements and learn their Christian History. Pennsylvania, a Middle Colony, includes such distinct individuals as Benjamin West and Benjamin Franklin, Charles Thomson, and John Dickinson. There were many diverse groups in Pennsylvania as well as the Quakers. Today we love to visit historic Philadelphia to see where our Documents of Liberty were written. During our Bicentennial of the American Constitution 1987–1991, the spotlight will again focus upon this most important historic and geographical area.

The study of Benjamin West as the Father of American Painting presents the opportunity to introduce Art in the History of Liberty. West brought changes to styles and subjects of Art in his day.

"Biblical, classical, and historical themes with moral content were the constant sources of West's paintings." Grose Evans, in *Benjamin West and the Taste of His Times,* 1959

Reasoning and Relating in Writing

As you record the Literary Elements of this book, it will be significant to identify those aspects that make the West's family Inn and their conduct as Quakers distinct from any other group of settlers. What words do the authors use or what descriptions do they give us to help us "see" this cozy farm in the American wilderness? Do your students know what a "door-latch" is and how it works? How can you help them understand the *internal* and *external* symbolism?

The food of colonial America differed from one section of the country to another. What kinds of foods did these Quakers serve? Do we have some of the same foods today? What will you record? Are there any resources for learning about tools and implements, lamps, cooking utensils, etc. for your class? Perhaps a local museum, or some family heirloom would provide you with examples. the importance of Notebooks in this study is to gain an idea of what early Pennsylvania was like. When the Elementary Years are over each child could have representative descriptions of many different colonial homes.

Of course, the most intriguing character in the book is the cat, Grimalkin. The authors have allowed him to remain a cat, but they portray a most unusual animal creature in whom we all delight. Can your students write an accurate description of Grimalkin which will document some of his interesting contributions to Benjamin? Have you practised writing such a description yourself so that you can help others wrestle with this challenge?

Most important of all is the idea of stepping back into history through making the acquaintance of a real personage. Let us pray "that something will happen to us" when we take this trip.

KEY CLASSIC TO BE TAUGHT

Carry On, Mr. Bowditch,
    by Jean Lee Latham, 1955
HISTORIC AND GEOGRAPHIC INDIVIDUALITY
    Salem, Massachusetts in our Constitutional
    Period
CHRISTIAN HISTORY PRINCIPLE EXEMPLIFIED
    How the Seed of Christian Self-Government is
    Planted
LEADING IDEA IDENTIFIED
    Nathaniel Bowditch, Father of American
    Mathematics

Nathaniel Bowditch is a good representative of this sixth principle of America's Christian History, for he, like his forebear Samuel Adams, taught his field of mathematics "by the vital force of distinc-

tive ideas and principles." (*T/L*, page 257) As the acknowledged Father of American Mathematics, he demonstrated how the seed of Christian self-government could be carried into a number of fields founded on mathematics, particularly the field of celestial navigation. In America the free and independent man began to explore every field, and even without the help of learned societies, or advanced equipment, began to make scientific investigations of God's universe.

By the end of his lifetime, Nathaniel Bowditch had received honors from almost every scientific society in Europe. But the character of Bowditch had been developed under Constitutional liberty and he educated himself, through the rigorous discipline of principles and then spent his lifetime translating these principles into practical use for other men. The United States Government still publishes *American Practical Navigator,* An Epitome of Navigation and Nautical Astronomy, originally by Nathaniel Bowditch, LL.D., H. O. No. 9, published by the Hydrographic Office under the Authority of the Secretary of the Navy. It is still studied in the United States Naval Academy as a text.

Bowditch's major work which brought him world-wide recognition was his translation of the Marquis La Place's great, incomprehensible *Mechanique Celeste*. This was a labor of about fourteen years in which Bowditch included all the contributions of those men upon whose work La Place had built his masterpiece, individuals neglected by La Place.

Researching and Recording Salem, Massachusetts

As a background for teaching the biography of Nathaniel Bowditch, parents and teachers can make a study of Salem, Massachusetts. Salem was one of America's short-water ports not to fall into the hands of the British during the American Revolution. And Salem built and supplied more ships and men for privateering than any other town in the colonies. Consequently, after the war, "the energy that had been shown in privateering found an outlet in a worldwide search for new markets." No wonder then that world trade had its beginnings on the small docks of Salem, where one might find a parrot or an elephant, as well as other cargoes from around the world, including the all-important pepper from the Dutch West Indies.

The success of the young captains and merchants of Salem brought them the wealth to build some of America's most beautiful homes – now a repository of the Federal Period of American Architecture. Chestnut Street, Salem, is a street you will some day want to visit as you study the distinctions of style and construction which characterized the homes of these "free and independent" Americans. To know and appreciate the homes of Salem is to be introduced to Samuel McIntire, a self-taught Christian architect and wood carver. His mark upon this town is truly beautiful, another example of planting the seed of Christian self-government in particular fields of endeavor. As teachers you will want to study the references given in the syllabus for Bowditch and introduce your students to this study of the work of McIntire as well as enlarge their horizon and knowledge of this particular period of American Architecture.

Researching, Relating, and Recording God's Providence in Bowditch's Life

This book provides us with a number of significant Providential events in the life of Nathaniel Bowditch. The study also brings to bear God's Providence in the life of an individual or a nation. After you have read the book yourself and studied the syllabus, you will discover how Nathaniel was able to educate himself while confined for nine years to his desk in the Ship's Chandlery. As we find in Bowditch's experience, there are no obstacles to God's development of an individual.

In the *Memoir* written by his son, Nathaniel Ingersoll Bowditch, 1839, is a comment on how Christian self-government often develops best when there is no visible means of help for the individual. Speaking of his father he said:

"Dr. Bowditch never considered that the obstacles in his path had the slightest tendency to retard his progress. On the contrary, he felt that they afforded him a foothold by which progress was rendered more sure and steady."

This attitude is so needed to encourage our youth to venture into new fields when they must go forward by the inspiration of their vision and with faith that by god's Grace they can accomplish. Bowditch was actually concerned that young people brought up "in the midst of ease and luxury" would have a disadvantage. They would lack the spur of necessity – or even of poverty – which he had endured – but which made him determined to educate himself and others. He was also appreciative of those who had helped him.

In the biography *Carry On, Mr. Bowditch*, the author explains how he learned to patiently teach the ordinary seaman the principles of celestial navigation:

"The men gathered round to listen . . . But teaching wasn't so easy. Time and again Nat ex-plained something in the simplest words he could think of – only to see a blank look on the man's face . . . He would bite back his impatience. Slowly, carefully, he'd explain again – and again. At last he'd see the man's eyes brighten. He'd hear the happy, 'Oh, yes! Simple isn't it.' Nat would grin. 'Yes – simple.'

"When he got back to his cabin, he would write down the explanation that had finally made sense to a man. Just so I won't forget it, if I ever have to explain that again! he told himself. After three weeks, he had quite a stack of notes. He was making a new notebook, he realized; a very different sort of notebook. All his other notebooks just said enough to explain things to him. But this notebook said everything he had to say to explain things to other men – to the men who sailed before the mast.

"One day Captain Prince called Nat to his cabin . . . Tell me, Mr. Bowditch, just what are you trying to do with the men during the dog watch?

"Teach them what they want to know, sir . . .

"But, Mr. Bowditch, why are you doing it?

"Nat was silent for a moment. 'Maybe, sir, it's because I want to pay a debt I owe to the men who helped me; men like Sam Smith and Dr. Bentley and Dr. Prince and Nathan Read. Maybe that's why. Or maybe it's just because of the men. We have good men before the mast, Captain Prince. Every man of them could be a first mate – if he knew navigation.'" Pages 110–111

Dr. Bowditch, as he came to be known, taught every man who sailed with him who "would show a disposition to learn." And every man who studied with him "attained at least the rank of first or second officer of a ship." so, with his book, *The American Practical Navigator*, Bowditch was instrumental in instructing thousands in the art of navigation and saving the lives of many more who were dependent upon accuracy in mathematics – in the tables upon which they depended for sailing.

The planting of the seed of Christian self-government in a new field is a goal of the Christian History Program. It takes discipline, self-denial, devotion to explore new fields and to open up God's principles in these fields that He might be glorified. The study of men like Nathaniel Bowditch can represent this challenge to your students as they consider and ponder how they will give their lives to the service of Christ and country.

"As long as ships shall sail, the needle point to the north, and the stars go through their wonted courses in the heavens, the name of Dr. Bowditch will be revered." – Salem Marine Society

KEY CLASSIC TO BE TAUGHT

Noah Webster, Father of the Dictionary,
> by Isabel Proudfit, 1942

HISTORIC AND GEOGRAPHIC INDIVIDUALITY
> Colonial Connecticut and Constitutional America

CHRISTIAN HISTORY PRINCIPLE EXEMPLIFIED
> The Christian Form of our Government

LEADING IDEA IDENTIFIED
> The American Character in Government and Education

It is most satisfying to think of Noah Webster as representative of the finest qualities of American Education inclusive of scholarship. In fact, Noah Webster is representative of all the Christian History Principles which define the *character* of our nation. This little book by Isabel Proudfit is most valuable as an introductory biography by a well-known author. For teachers and students there are additional materials to research in the Christian History books for a more complete understanding of this Founding Father of American Christian Education.

The Principle entitled The Christian Form of our Government is illustrative of Webster's own life from Colony to Constitution. Webster, a descendant of William Bradford, Pilgrim Governor of Plymouth Plantation, was raised in Connecticut, known as the Constitution State, because of Pastor Thomas Hooker's 1638 sermon which led to the writing of the first American Constitution. (See *Christian History,* pages 248–257) Webster had the opportunity of seeing government produced at the town-meeting level, for his father, and father's fathers before him, like most New Englanders, were active in local government.

Noah Webster demonstrated all aspects of our Christian form of government. He served in the legislative branches of state government. He wrote essays in support of our national Constitution and its division of powers. And he is the best representative of what both an *educator* and an *educated* American Christian should be.

Noah Webster's Tools of Constitutionalism

Preparing each generation to serve Christ and country, Noah Webster labored to produce the tools of *Literacy, Law, Literature.*

Literacy: In his blue-backed *American Spelling Book,* Webster produced a self-teaching tool so that every American might learn to read, write, and speak in the defense and promotion of Biblical principles of Liberty.

Law: Webster knew that in order to maintain our independence every American needed to know the Constitution of the United States of America. He included *A Federal Catechism* in one of the first editions of his spellers. He stated in his *History of the United States* "that the genuine source of correct republican principles is the BIBLE, particularly the New Testament or the Christian religion."

Literature: Noah Webster was the first American educator to place American authors alongside of English authors in the curriculum. "But I may go further, and affirm with truth, that our country has produced some of the best models of composition." Webster felt that in writings dealing with a philosophy of government we were unsurpassed. Many of the authors he noted appear in The Christian History Literature Program including *James Madison, John Jay,* and *Alexander Hamilton* of the *Federalist; George Washington; Washington Irving,* and many others.

Often called the "schoolmaster to the Republic," Noah Webster, like Samuel Adams and others, mastered the principles of many fields and indeed, began some new fields. He represents the quality of character which we need so desperately in American Education today. Webster was interested in everything and felt that free and independent men and women should learn as much as they could, for who could anticipate the fields into which the Lord might call them to serve!

The study of Noah Webster can inspire and challenge your students to prepare themselves to become effective stewards of American Christian Constitutional government.

KEY CLASSIC TO BE TAUGHT

Little Women,
> by Louisa M. Alcott, 1868

HISTORIC AND GEOGRAPHIC INDIVIDUALITY
> Concord, Massachusetts and the Civil War

CHRISTIAN HISTORY PRINCIPLE EXEMPLIFIED
> The Christian Principle of American Political Union

LEADING IDEA IDENTIFIED
> The New England Mind and Character

The Pilgrims and Puritans who came to America were a people of the Book—and that Book was the Bible. They were also a people who believed in the primary importance of the family as the basic institution of our nation. They would have agreed with Pastor S. Phillips when he wrote:

"We owe to the family, therefore, what we are as a nation as well as individuals." *Teaching and Learning,* page 11

As the Chain of Christianity moved to America, home became a "nursery" for freedom. Miss Verna M. Hall writes: "The remarkable Christian character of the Americans preceding and during the Revolution suggests that we look for its cause, that lessons for today can be learned. We find this cause rooted in the importance given the home and the church, with education supporting both." *Consider and Ponder,* Editor's Note, page 73

New England with its independent church was especially notable in its attachment to home and to education. And during the nineteenth century despite the trememdous growth and progress of the nation, the anchor of home held firm. Indeed, the American Home was perhaps the basic unifying force which kept North and South "one nation under God" despite the tragedy of the Civil War.

Little Women has its setting in Concord, Massachusetts during the Civil War. Written by Louisa M. Alcott (1832–1888) it presents one of the finest family pictures ever written – perhaps because it is based upon a real family – the Alcotts. It is also a very excellent representation of the New England Mind and Character, which the study of this novel allows us to explore.

Researching and Recording the Civil War

When Louisa M. Alcott persuaded herself that she could be spared from the support of her family to serve as a nurse to the embattled troops of the Union, she did not realize how precious *home* would be in that experience. The Civil War had just started, a year had gone by, but every New England town had watched "the home soldiers march away, down the Lexington and Concord road, past the gray stone walls behind which the fighting men of another war had taken cover... There is little that is to terrible as seeing strong, wholesome young men, every one of them beautiful in the flush of their high patriotism, as watching them go and knowing that they are surely to die.

"Louisa had all the desperate emotion which goes with such a sight, but most of what she felt, consciously, was a frantic desire to go also... She was young, she was very strong, she was a good nurse, as all of her family testified." *Invincible Louisa,* by Cornelia Meigs, page 98

Louisa's experiences and letters home became *Hospital Sketches,* published in 1863. They demonstrated that Miss Alcott, whose earlier books had been imaginative, "could write so truthfully and vividly about the war." (ibid., 133) During this wrenching time of service in the terribly inadequate "hospital" facilities of Washington, D.C., Miss Alcott came into her fullness of womanhood.

She was a hardworking nurse and a tender Christian comforter to the wounded and the dying. Perhaps it was in that grim crucible of heart-break, yearning to do more for these fine young men, that the importance of home and all its ties of individual identity transcended any locality and became a national necessity.

Louisa M. Alcott herself almost became a war casualty. She contracted a severe illness and her father had to come to Washington to bring her home. Providentially, with home care and nursing, after a long period of time, she recovered.

What should you know about the background of the Civil War which is consistent with America's Christian History?

Testing the Christian Principle of American Political Union

The Civil War was not a War Between the States over slavery, although slavery was the issue. Rather, it was a test of whether our national-federal Union of states could survive.

The principles of self-government with union had been forged link by link along the Chain of Christianity moving westward. Finally, in America, from the time of the Stamp Act Congress, the two principles began to act in harmony with each other. For the first time the colonies were put in the position of seeing the necessity for united action to protect the individuality of each colony. The *internal unity* of Biblical principles which bound them together during the American Revolution provided the *strength of union* which at last, under the Providential Leadership of General George Washington, brought forth Independence.

Some years later, faced with the inadequacy of the Articles of Confederation, they debated and discussed the principles of a national-federal union of states which would preserve the local self-government of each state in all but a few critical areas. Our Constitution of the United States of America was the result, proposed in 1787 and ratified in 1789.

The achievement of the American Union of states was a governmental miracle founded upon the Biblical unity of a people who had participated in government for more than one hundred and fifty years in preparation for a national union. But the arch-enemy of mankind, unsuccessful to prevent this union, now would endeavor to break it up. If it could not be broken from *without* – perhaps it could be broken from *within*.

Less than fifty years after our Constitutional Republic was established, voices were heard in the legislative halls of the states and in the national capitol. Our union of states was being threatened.

Here are some of the voices that were raised. From a southerner, the great Kentuckian, Henry Clay (1777–1852):

"Sir, our prosperity is unbounded – nay, Mr. President, I sometimes fear that it is in the wantonness of that prosperity that many of the threatening ills of the moment have arisen. Wild and erratic schemes have sprung up throughout the whole country, some of which have even found their way into legislative halls; and there is a restlessness existing among us which I fear will require the chastisement of Heaven to bring us back to a sense of the immeasurable benefits and blessings which have been bestowed upon us by Providence . . .

"And, Sir, I must take occasion here to say that, in my opinion, there is no right on the part of any one or more of the States to secede from the Union. War and dissolution of the Union are identical and inevitable, in my opinion . . .

"Mr. President, I am directly opposed to any purpose of secession or separation. I am for staying within the Union, and defying any portion of this confederacy to expel me or drive me out of the Union . . ." *The Consequences of Secession*

John Caldwell Calhoun (1783–1850), however, as a South Carolinian, felt otherwise. He believed that slavery and States' rights should be defended above the call to the obligations of the Union and patriotism.

Daniel Webster (1782–1852), a staunch New Englander, was one of the great debaters of the century, concerned with the threat of disintegration of our land. His most famous phrase: "Liberty and union, now and forever, one and inseparable."

In his Second Inaugural Address, President Abraham Lincoln in 1863 addressed the heart of the question, speaking of the two positions: "Both parties deprecated war, but one of them would make war rather than let the nation survive, and the other would accept war rather than let it perish, and the war came . . .

"Neither party expected for the war the magnitude or the duration which it has already attained. Neither anticipated that the cause of the conflict might cease when, or even before, the conflict itself should cease. Each looked for an easier triumph, and a result less fundamental and astounding. Both read the same Bible and pray to the same God, and each invokes His aid against the other. It may seem strange that any men should dare to ask a just God's assistance in wringing their bread from the sweat of other men's faces, but let us judge not that we be not judged. The prayer of both could not be answered. That of neither has been answered fully. The Almighty has His own purpose. Woe unto the world because of offenses, for it must needs be that offenses come, but woe to that man by whom the offense cometh. If we shall suppose that American slavery is one of those offenses which, in the providence of God, must needs come, but which having continued through His appointed time, He now wills to remove, and that He gives to both North and South this terrible war as the woe due to those by whom the offense came, shall we discern there any departure from those divine attributes which the believers in a living God always ascribe to Him. Fondly do we hope, fervently do we pray, that this mighty scourge of war may speedily pass away. Yet if God wills that it continue until all the wealth piled up by the bondsman's two hundred and fifty years of unrequited toil shall be sunk, and until every drop of blood drawn with the lash shall be paid by another drawn with the sword, as was said three thousand years ago, so still it must be said, that the judgments of the Lord are true and righteous altogether.

"With malice toward none, with charity for all, with firmness in the right as God gives us to see the right, let us finish the work we are in, to bind up the nation's wounds, to care for him who shall have borne the battle, and for his widow and his orphans, to do all which may achieve and cherish a just and a lasting peace among ourselves and with all nations."

The drastic consequences of the war between the states was not unity but disunity – and it has taken a return to Christian history, a restoration of Biblical principles in individual homes and families to bring back a vision of the original purpose for this nation as brought by our forefathers who came here for civil and religious liberty. Only Christian statesmen can hold our nation in that balanced position of a National-Federal Union of States, but the unity must first be *internal* before externally realized.

Relating and Recording a Study of Little Women
Little Women, one of the most successful American novels ever written, celebrates a New England family of girls, growing up in Concord, Massachusetts at the time of the Civil War. It is an excellent representation of the Christian principle of unity producing union. Because it is based upon a real family and their education in Christian living, it has more than a fictional interest.

We remember Concord in our history from the lines of this poem written by one of its most famous inhabitants, Ralph Waldo Emerson:

By the rude bridge that arched the flood
   Their flat to April's breeze unfurled,
Here once the embattled farmers stood,
   And fired the shot heard round the world.

Concord was also an intellectual center, "that fair small country of the mind," where a number of famous writers congregated, among them Henry David Thoreau and Nathaniel Hawthorne. The Alcott Family was well-known to many of the thinkers and preachers of their time. Their struggle under the constant threat of poverty was of concern and interest to all. They watched and sometimes helped as determination and resourcefulness won and "by God's assistance they prevailed and got ye victorie."

When Louisa May Alcott was asked by her publisher to write this book, what came about is described by her biographer, Mrs. Cornelia Meigs, as "a well-deserved blessing of Providence." Writing about a subject she knew, Miss Alcott brought into being a book of interest to both young men and young women, for it deals with all the interests of home, parental love and affection, ideals and aspirations, courtship, love and marriage, as well as a devotion to each other that kept them close in spite of trials and tribulations. With the publication of *Little Women* in 1869 Louisa May Alcott forever lifted the bondage of insufficiency from her own life and that of her family. And this book captures the heart of family living because it is centered in Christian principles and ideals.

"Without intending it, all the scenes she described seemed to center about the brown hillside house where they had begun to live when she was thirteen and where she had spent her happiest years. The games on the hills, the plays in the barn, the work, the small differences, all the ups and downs of their family life began to take their appointed places in the story. Louisa's fine, intrepid mother entered into the narrative, just as she had entered into everything else that any of her girls had done. The beautiful story of *Pilgrim's Progress*, which was the favorite of their early reading, interwove itself with many of the chapters as they developed. Of her father, Louisa did not seem able to say so much as of her mother. He was so unlike usual men that she felt herself not quite equal to the task of showing him to others, particularly to young readers, in all his true dignity and worth. Yet the beauty of his ideas slipped in somehow and gave the work a different aspect from that of any ordinary tale." *Invincible Louisa*, page 150

This book is a study in character development—

those internal battles which each individual must wage in dealing with disposition and temperament. Learning how to be good Pilgrims like *Christian* in Bunyan's *Pilgrim's Progress* is the challenge. How to put off the "old man" of selfishness and put on the "new man" or "new woman" in Christ is the goal.

In our day of the "self-centered generation" we suggest that special study be made of the individual characters to record their particular struggles and achievements. Plan you notebook so as to devote it to character studies of all the girls, of Mother, and of Laurie in particular, since he is the main male character.

Identify the Biblical character qualities which these girls earnestly sought to express. If you know *Pilgrim's Progress* well enough, indicate how the author has used this book to explain their individual trials.

Indicate the particular aspects of Christian womanhood and manhood which are expressed. Compare them to the young people of today.

Finally, take some of the activities or outings which the March family enjoyed and compare New England life and manners with ours today.

Record the main themes and leading ideas of the book and indicate which ones you regard as unique to America.

KEY CLASSIC TO BE TAUGHT

The Last of the Mohicans, or A Narrative of 1757,
   by James Fenimore Cooper, 1826
HISTORIC AND GEOGRAPHIC INDIVIDUALITY
   The French and Indian War in Upper
   New York State
CHRISTIAN HISTORY PRINCIPLE EXEMPLIFIED
   God's Principle of Individuality
LEADING IDEA IDENTIFIED
   The Free and Independent Man in the
   American Wilderness

James Fenimore Cooper, 1789–1851, was our first American novelist after we became a Republic. He was also the first to use themes of American history and to develop the uniqueness and individuality of the American Character.

Cooper's most famous contribution to Literature rests upon five novels called *The Leatherstocking Saga*, written at different times, but presenting "the most memorable character American Fiction" ever gave to the world. *Natty Bumppo*, an unlettered Christian frontiersman and scout, made a name for himself with both white and red men for his integrity and consistent Christian self-government. Called by various sobriquets which reflected his skills in the wilderness, he became *Hawkeye*,

Leatherstocking, La Langue Carabine, Pathfinder, Deerslayer.

Cooper had introduced both *Hawkeye* and his Indian friend, a noble Delaware by the name of *Chingachgook*, in his first Leatherstocking novel, *The Pioneers*, in 1823. Pleased with the reception he continued to develop these characters in the next book of the series, *The Last of the Mohicans*, in 1826. This novel proved to be the most popular of the five and in it we begin to see Hawkeye's Christian character appear, although it is in *The Deerlsayer* that it reaches its finest expression.

The setting of *The Last of the Mohicans* is the French and Indian War which actually began when young George Washington was sent by Virginia Governor Dinwiddie to negotiate with the French on the Ohio River in 1853. The struggle for North America was to take place on two continents. "Such was the complication of political interests," says Voltaire, "that a cannon-shot fired in America could give the signal that set Europe in a blaze."

Francis Parkman, 1823–1893, American historian who devoted the major portion of his writings to the conflict between England and France for America added: "It was not a cannon-shot, but a volley from the hunting-pieces of a few backwoodsmen, commanded by a Virginia youth, George Washington." Europe soon became aware of the young Virginian as the report of his *Journey into the Wilderness* was published. "The struggle that followed swept France from the North American continent. Yet a generation later the Ohio Valley belonged to neither France nor England. Ownership of a land, after all, depends not upon claim but upon control. And in control of the Ohio Valley was the new United States of America." (Introduction to *The Journal of Major George Washington*, facsimile Edition, published by the Colonial Williamsburg Foundation, 1959)

Researching and Recording Francis Parkman

The Christian History Literature Program has as a major goal the introduction of parents, teachers and eventually students, to those *original sources* of our history which make "history come alive." We also can come to know the historians who searched out and wrote from the original sources of our history. Francis Parkman is one of the most rewarding of our nineteenth century researchers and recorders of the struggle between France and England in America. And since this struggle is the setting for Cooper's novel *The Last of the Mohicans*, even a brief acquaintance with Parkman will be a revelation of how interesting history can become. The uniqueness of Parkman's work centers around the fact that, despite illness, he *visited personally* every place, every setting about which he wrote. He was no "armchair historian."

Samuel Eliot Morison, 1879–1976, most distinguished historian of the twentieth century, wrote of Parkman:

"In the summer of his freshman year (at Harvard), Frank made his first journey through the northern New England woods. That seems to have confirmed the love of the wilderness which he had acquired in childhood. 'I had a taste for the woods and the Indians... and it was this that turned my attention to forest themes. At one time I thought of writing the history of the Indians, with the Iroquois as a central point; but on reflection I preferred the French colonies as equally suiting my purpose, while offering at once more unity and more variety, as well as more interest to civilized readers.' It was early in his sophomore year, when he was only eighteen, that the two influences, academic and outdoors, became 'crystallized into a plan of writing the story of what was then known as the *"Old French War,"* that is, the war that ended in the conquest of Canada... My theme fascinated me, and I was haunted with wilderness images day and night.' Before long he 'enlarged the plan to include the whole course of the American conflict between France and England, or in other words, the history of the American forest.'" (Morison, Introduction to *The Parkman Reader,* 1955)

In the two volumes, *Montcalm and Wolfe*, 1884, which have special pertinence to Cooper's novel, Parkman states: "The plan of the work was formed in early youth; and though various causes have long delayed its execution, it has always been kept in view. Meanwhile, I have visited and examined every spot where events of any importance in connection with the contest took place, and I have observed with attention such scenes and persons as might help to illustrate those I meant to describe. In short, the subject has been studied as much from life and in the open air as at the library table."

When Parkman visited the ruins of Ft. William Henry, still standing in his day, from the records available he carefully reconstructed the appearance of the Fort, with accompanying drawing:

"Fort William Henry was an irregular bastioned square, formed by embankments of gravel surmounted by a rampart of heavy logs, laid in tiers crossed one upon another, the interstices filled with earth. The lake (Lake George) protected it on the north, the marsh on the east, and ditches with cheveaux-de-frise on the south and west. Seventeen cannon, great and small, besides several mortars and swivels, were mounted upon it; and a brave Scotch veteran, Lieutenant-Colonel Monro, of the thirty-fifth regiment, was in command.

"General Webb lay fourteen miles distant at Fort Edward, with twenty-six hundred men, chiefly provincials." Vol. 1, page 510

Between these two commanders there was an exchange of visits, letters and pleas, some reinforcements, and finally the fatal letter which broke the heart of Monro in Cooper's novel. As Parkman records it, General Webb had his aide-de-camp write Colonel Monro as follows:

"The General has ordered me to acquaint you he does not think it prudent to attempt a junction or to assist you till reinforced by the militia of the colonies, for the immediate march of which repeated expresses have been sent."

Webb was concerned about his own command, Fort Edward, and this is why he hesitated to help Monro.

"The letter then declared that the French were in complete possession of the road between the two forts, that a prisoner just brought in reported their force in men and cannon to be very great, and that, unless the militia came soon, Monro had better make what terms he could with the enemy."

While the chance that this letter would reach Monro were slim, the bearer was killed by the Indians and the letter taken to General Montcalm of the French forces. At the psychological moment Montcalm sent this letter down to the beleaguered English commander Monro with the hope that "General Webb's letter may induce the English to surrender the sooner." page 518

Of course Monro had no alternative and Montcalm is reputed to have given very generous terms. The most important agreement was that the English troops and their women and children were to march out of the fort unmolested by the Indians or French soldiers:

"Before signing the capitulation Montcalm called the Indian chiefs to council, and asked them to consent to the conditions, and promise to restrain their young warriors from any disorder. They approved everything and promised everything." And soon they disobeyed everything.

"The Marquis de Montcalm ran thither immediately, and used every means to restore tranquility: prayers, threats, caresses, interposition of the officers and interpreters who have some influence over these savages. We shall be but too happy

if we can prevent a massacre." page 521

Cooper is far less restrained in his judgment of Montcalm than Parkman. In the opening paragraph of Chapter xviii, the novelist portrays the villain in these words:

Why, anything:
An honorable murder if you will:
For naught I did in hate, but all in honor.
Othello

"The bloody and inhuman scene rather incidentally mentioned than described in the preceding chapter, is conspicuous in the pages of colonial history, by the merited title of 'The Massacre of William Henry.' It so far deepened the stain which a previous and very similar event had left upon the reputation of the French commander, that it was not entirely erased by his early and glorious death. It is now becoming obscured by time; and thousands, who know that Montcalm died like a hero on the plains of Abraham, have yet to learn how much he was deficient in that moral courage without which no man can be truly great. Pages might be written to prove, from this illustrious example, the defects of human excellence; to show how easy it is for generous sentiments, high courtesy, and chivalrous courage, to lose their influence beneath the chilling blight of selfishness, and to exhibit to the world a man who was great in all the minor attributes of character, but who was found wanting when it became necessary to prove how much principle is superior to policy. But the task would exceed our prerogatives; and, as history, like love, is so apt to surround her heroes with an atmosphere of imaginary brightness, it is probable that Louis de Saint Veran will be viewed by posterity only as the gallant defender of his country, while his cruel apathy on the shores of the Oswego and of the Horican (Lake George) will be forgotten."

Parkman characterized the French and Indian War against the English settlers as a critical chapter in the History of Liberty. It was, he stated: "English liberty versus French absolutism, Protestant freedom versus Catholic authority with victory to the forces of light and progress... A happier calamity never befell a people than the conquest of Canada by the British arms." *Parkman Reader*, pages 20, 270

Relating and Recording Cooper's Settings and Characters

James Fenimore Cooper's main setting is the American Wilderness itself and he indicates in the opening paragraph of *The Last of the Mohicans* that "the toils and dangers of the wilderness were to be encountered before the adverse hosts could meet." In other words the wilderness presented an even greater challenge than did "the terrific character of their merciless enemies," be those enemies savage Indians or troops from Europe–from France or England.

Cooper's descriptions of our American wilderness run like a golden thread through all his Leatherstocking novels. His skill allows us to forever possess the unspoiled wilderness of two hundred years ago. For the vast forests, the crystal lakes and roaring falls had not yet felt the devastation of man, and they still existed to glorify the Creator and speak of a magnificent freedom for those men and some women who were able to endure its "toils and dangers." Our author makes us pay attention to detail and that is why we as teachers must prepare ourselves to be "a guide in the wilderness" to our students who might otherwise get bogged down with Cooper's full wording. But the reward of learning to read and to "see" through the author's descriptions will be repaid when we make our own journeys into the beauties of America's natural wonders. We will *look* and *listen* more carefully and value what James Fenimore Cooper has restored to us as our heritage.

In brief form we will now identify the major settings for the action of the novel. As you can see they are in effect all aspects of the wilderness which pervades everything.

Settings	*Plot Elements*
I. On the Forest Trails between Forts Edward and William Henry	Magua, the vengeful Huron, leads his party astray, only to be discovered by Hawkeye
II. In the caves above Glenn's Falls	Hawkeye and his Indian friends prevail over Magua and his attackers
III. At Fort William Henry. Surrender, Massacre	Montcalm unable to restrain the fury of the Indians. Magua captures Alice and Cora
IV. In the Village of the Delawares with the Indian Patriarch, 100-year old Tamenund	Magua is finally cornered by Hawkeye and friends, but in the fight both Cora and Uncas are killed. Last scene is the Burial of each one.

Cooper's Characters

DAVID GAMUT, *Psalmodist,* carries the 26th edition of the *New England Psalm Book* into the wilderness. Like David, the "sweet singer of Israel," Gamut is pitted against his own Goliath of murderous Indians, deceitful French, and the terrors of the unknown. His only weapons are the Psalms of David set to music and sung in defiance of all that confronts him.

HAWKEYE, Scout, superior frontiersman, marksman and friend of Mohican Indians, Chingachgook and Uncas. The Indians also named him La Longue Carabine. He is the main character and is an example of the free and independent man who is a "believer in religion, and friend to the law and to the king."

CHINGACHGOOK, also Le Gros Serpent, a noble Mohican who has known Hawkeye all his life.

UNCAS, son of Chingachgook, last of the Mohicans, called Le Cerf Agile.

MAJOR DUNCAN HEYWARD, Aide to Colonel Monro, has been sent to escort Cora and Alice Monro to Fort William Henry.

GENERAL MONTCALM, Marquis Louis Joseph de Saint-Veran, the French commander who captures Fort William Henry.

COLONEL MONRO, Scotchman, and Commander of Fort William Henry.

ALICE MONRO, blonde, blue-eyed, younger daughter of Colonel Monro.

CORA MONRO, dark-haired, older sister of Alice.

MAGUA, the antagonist, a displaced Huron, whose smouldering hatred of Colonel Monro leads him to plot against the English. His nickname is Le Renard Subtil.

TAMENUND, the venerable patriarch of the Delaware Indians, whose wisdom and justice were revered by all. Cooper's description of this venerable warrior in chapter 28 includes the statement that he had the reputation "of holding secret communion with the Great Spirit."

Cooper's Treatment of the Indians

James Fenimore Cooper's representation of God's Principle of Individuality is best seen in his identification of the two races of White and Red men. Cooper found his references to the Indians from what he called "the school of Heckewelder," a Moravian Missionary who had spent years living among the tribes. In *The Deerslayer* our hero confesses to have been brought up by the Moravians and instructed in the Scriptures, although Deerslayer never learned how to read.

Cooper through his character of Hawkeye indicates that each race was distinct and had special "gifts" or customs. He also characterized the individual by his character, so Cooper presents both good and bad Indians and good and bad white men.

Throughout the Leatherstocking tales there are conversations with the Indians, Hawkeye's friends, about what has happened between the two races. In *The Last of the Mohicans*, Chingachgook describes to Hawkeye how it was when the Red men were first on the North American Continent:

"Then, Hawkeye, we were one people, and we were happy. The salt lake gave us its fish, the wood its deer, and the air its birds. We took wives who bore us children; we worshipped the Great Spirit; and we kept the Maguas beyond the sound of our songs of triumph...

"My tribe is the grandfather of nations, but I am an unmixed man. The blood of chiefs is in my veins, where it must stay forever. The Dutch landed, and gave my people the fire-water; they drank until the heavens and the earth seemed to meet, and they foolishly thought they had found the Great Spirit. Then they parted with their land. Foot by foot, they were driven back from the shores, until I, that am a chief and a sagamore, have never seen the sun shine but through the trees, and have never visited the graves of my fathers!" Chapter 3

Even Tamenund, the great Patriarch of the Lenape, echoes the same lament: "The pale-faces are masters of the earth, and the time of the redmen has not yet come again."

But Cooper has one message of hope to leave as Chingachgook mourns over the grave of his son:

"Why do my brothers mourn!" he said, regarding the dark race of dejected warriors by whom he was environed; "why do my daughters weep! that a young man has gone to the happy hunting-grounds; that a chief has filled his time with honor! He was good; he was dutiful; he was brave. Who can deny it? The Manitou had need of such a warrior, and He has called him away. As for me, the son and the father of Uncas, I am a blazed pine, in a clearing of the pale-faces. My race has gone from the shores of the salt lake, and the hills of the Delawares. But who can say that the Serpent of his tribe has forgotten his wisdom? I am alone—

"No, no," cried Hawkeye, who had been gazing with a yearning look at the rigid features of his friend, with something like his own self-command, but whose philosophy could endure no longer; "no, Sagamore, not alone. The gifts of our colors may be different, but God has so placed us as to journey in the same path. I have no kin, and I may also say, like you, no people. He was your son, and a redskin by nature; and it may be that your blood was nearer—but if ever I forget the lad who has so often fou't at my side in war, and slept at my side in peace, may He who made us all, whatever be our color or our gifts, forget me! The boy has left us for a time; but, Sagamore, you are not alone."

Chingachgook grasped the hand that, in the warmth of feeling, the scout had stretched across the fresh earth, and in that attitude of friendship these two sturdy and intrepid woodsmen bowed their heads together, while scalding tears fell to their feet, watering the grave of Uncas like drops of falling rain. Uncas was the last of the Mohicans.

This book is the first introduction to James Fenimore Cooper in Upper Elementary School. In High School he will be read again.

PLANNING YOUR ELEMENTARY LITERATURE PROGRAM

The chart which follows *Planning Your Elementary Program* enables you to develop a balanced program of Literature for your students. Even if you are teaching a multi-grade, with children of different levels of learning, you can still make plans so that you can read some books aloud to all of them, and at the same time, plan to teach different books for some of these levels. Actually, as perhaps you already know, the subject of Literature tends to *unite* rather than divide diverse ages of learners.

The Christian History Program for the Elementary Years is entitled *Restoring the Literature and Character of Liberty*. It is page 351.

OVERVIEW V. One goal of the program is to restore to our posterity how God was with our fathers, mothers and even some of the children, in the struggle to establish a Christian Constitutional Republic. Also, we are stewards of liberty, civil and religious, so we need to know what other nations have contributed to the Chain of Christianity moving Westward to America.

> *Religion, like a Pilgrim, westward bent,*
> *Knocking at all doors, ever as she went . . .*

On the chart for Planning your Individual Literature Program (see following page) the first area of study is *Learning the Literature of the Bible*. While the teaching and learning of the Bible as Literature may be new, you will soon find it to be foundational to all subjects, as well as to the character and self-government of your students. A short introduction to this program is given and reference made to OVERVIEW I where an outline of Learning the Literature of the Bible, *Source and Seedbed of Literature and Liberty* can be found.

The second area on your Planning Chart, *Soil Softeners*, is *not* on the Overview V chart, for it deals with your own selection of *special* books. As you discover books which you love and which you find can become *tools* to help you prepare the soil of the hearts and minds of your students you will choose those which will be appropriate. A Biblical approach to this critical area of feelings and attitudes basic to character development is presented.

The six remaining areas on your Planning Chart are discussed in the following pages. *What* you teach in literature and *how* you teach can develop certain skills, especially the 4th R of recording or writing. History can come alive if it has a compelling setting in language, style and expression of character. And the Notebook Studies of Key Classics in Europe and American can provide a

THE CHRISTIAN HISTORY LITERATURE PROGRAM

PLANNING YOUR ELEMENTARY PROGRAM (see Overview V)
AN INDIVIDUAL TEACHER PLAN FOR LITERATURE

LEARNING THE LITERATURE OF THE BIBLE	LITERATURE AND THE INDIVIDUAL: CHOOSING "SOIL SOFTENERS"	INTRODUCTION TO OUR HERITAGE OF ENGLISH AND AMERICAN POETRY	INDIVIDUALITY OF THE NATIONS: FOLK, FAIRY, ANIMAL STORIES
HISTORY AS LITERATURE Listening, Writing Skills	NOTEBOOK STUDY: KEY NATIONS AND CLASSICS. Writing Skills	NOTEBOOK STUDY: KEY CLASSICS OF AMERICAN CHARACTER. Writing	READING ALOUD CLASSICS Listening/Learning Skills

springboard for the introduction of many associated fields, such as geography, government, the arts, and the sciences.

Our hope is that your cup of Literature and Learning will overflow with enthusiasm as you prepare to teach books which can play a "life-changing" part in the development of the character of each rising generation.

LEARNING THE LITERATURE OF THE BIBLE: LANGUAGE, STYLE, EXPRESSION

LANGUAGE OF THE BIBLE

RESEARCHING: On the first page of his Introduction to the *1828 An American Dictionary of the English Language*, Noah Webster makes the Scriptural distinction between *animal sounds* and *human speech*. Discuss this with your students. Point them to the Genesis Two account of the beginning of language.

REASONING: What kind of language do we find in the Bible? Does it differ from language in other books? Why? From Genesis, Chapter One, find some words which characterize *God*, for example, the word *Good*, which in the Anglo-Saxon, means *God*. Look up this word in the 1828 Webster for a definition. Trace this word through your Bible Concordance. Take those aspects which would be appropriate for the age and learning level of your students.

RELATING: A second word which you might follow from Genesis One, is the governmental word *Let*. How is this word used in connection with God? Relate this word to your students' lives. Where do they encounter this word and how much does it have to do with their learning to develop their ability to be Christianly self-governed?

RECORDING: The words which you develop with your students on the Language of the Bible can be recorded in Bible Literature Notebooks. Remember that the word "record" also has the meaning of "testimony." You make a record of your character when you write and when you live out your life. (See page 102, *Teaching and Learning*)

STYLE OF THE BIBLE

RESEARCHING: God's Principle of Individuality is evident in the writers of the Bible—those men whom God chose to record the Revelation of the Word. (See page 154 of *T/L*) Our study of the Bible as Literature should enable us to distinguish both the man and God's message through him. Begin with the shorter books of the Bible, i.e., the Minor or shorter Prophets. For example: AMOS, a countryman, a shepherd, a dresser of sycamore trees, and a gatherer of wild figs, took God's message to the city. His country background was reflected in what he wrote. Read Amos, learn his message, identify his style. Do the same for some of the shorter books of the New Testament. Each study should identify both the man and his message.

REASONING: Discuss the principle that we write best about the things we know. David's experience as a shepherd accounts for the kind of writing he did. Find some examples in First Samuel and in Psalms. Identify this as a Leading Idea in the study of Literature. It also applies to our own writing.

RELATING: What characterizes our own individual style of expression? How do we speak or write? What kind of language do we use? Will the study of the Language, Style and Expression of the Bible be a help in improving our style? How was the speech of Jesus characterized in the Bible?

RECORDING: After you have studied particular writers in the Bible choose how you will record the style. This will depend upon the learning level of the children. It will also depend upon how much you have recorded in your own notebook. You may develop a method of studying writers of the Bible that you can add to year by year.

EXPRESSION OF THE BIBLE

RESEARCHING: Look up Webster's definition of the word *Expression*. Decide what you and your students have learned about Bible expression and language.

REASONING: Reasoning from the above, decide what kind of standard the Bible sets for Language, Style and Expression.

RELATING: Decide what should characterize our individual expression in speech and writing.

RECORDING: What kind of a record or impression are we leaving with people by our individual style of speaking and writing? Record our goals in this area.

In the other areas of Learning the Literature of the Bible continue in the same manner. Much will come out of your own individual study, and more and more ideas will be forthcoming as you begin to restore this foundation of all Literature.

Literature and the Individual: Choosing "Soil Softeners"

The Christian History Program in Literature is centered in the History and Character of Liberty. Our focus in both the philosophy and content is based upon the Chain of Christianity Moving Westward – the impact of the Gospel of Jesus Christ upon men and nations. In the methodology of the Literature Program, however, even as we are reconstructing a nations's character, we are very much concerned that we minister to individual students as they learn how to deal with their own dispositions and temperaments.

Each individual yearns to resolve his or her own identity and worth. Each of us wants to learn the answer to the same three questions which we have addressed to the nation:

WHO am I as an individual? What is my value or worth?

WHERE do my attitudes, feelings and convictions come from?

WHAT is the purpose for my life?

Just as the principles of America's Christian History lead into a consideration of the unique heritage of our nation – so these same principles can help us come to terms with our own character as we find the vision and leading for our future. Let us briefly state the seven Christian History Principles in terms of the individual and the nation.

The principles are found in *Teaching and Learning America's Christian History: The Principle Approach*, see Table of Contents Part II, and Part III. The principles are set forth twice, once for the Study Group Plan for Christian History, and once again for the Teacher's Guide for Christian History. There are two charts on pages 63 and 111 which show all of the principles.

Each of the seven principles guide us into a study of the text *The Christian History of the Constitution of the United States of America: Christian Self-Government* compiled by Verna M. Hall. Our first concern is to see the importance of these principles to America as they unfolded along the Chain of Christianity Moving Westward with the liberty of the individual.

THE "SOIL" TO BE SOFTENED

The Bible has the direction for successful teaching and learning as well as successful planting and reaping in the lives of students – and adults. The Bible has the prescription for working with the ingredients of our characters and dispositions – how we dispose of our feelings and attitudes, our talents and our time. For parents and teachers the Parable of the Sower has some helps. What can we learn from this parable which will help us select books to read to students with special needs and challenges?

Matthew 13:1–9 tells of the Sower of seeds who found four kinds of soils for seed sowing. The first three soils resisted productivity and growth. It was only the fourth soil which was "good ground" and brought forth fruit. Later in the same chapter our Lord explained that the Sower was indeed the messenger with "the word of the kingdom" and the soil represented different conditions of heart or character receptive to the seed. What analogy can we make from this parable to our work in dealing with our own character and temperament and that of our students?

It is obvious that you cannot plant seed on dry, hard, or unprepared soil. The same is true of the heart and mind. The heart and the mind need to be prepared for seed planting. In the parable of our Lord the seed was the Word of God or the message of the Gospel. In our classrooms and homes, we can also consider our academic teaching as the seed of those subjects which we have Biblically based upon principles from God's Word.

Books which help prepare the soil for what you want to teach can be called SOIL SOFTENERS. Every parent or teacher who has the discernment to begin to work with disposition and temperament – *character* – in themselves as well as in their children, should be ready to begin compassionately to select books in this area.

Webster has in his *1828 Dictionary* a number of pertinent definitions for the words SOFTEN, SOFTENING, SOFT-HEARTED. Let us first think of these meanings as dealing with our willingness to accept ourselves as God made us, of Biblical self-love, that love which enables us to "love our neighbors as ourselves."

GOD'S PRINCIPLE OF INDIVIDUALITY is a means of getting at the first question: WHO am I, and WHAT is my worth? (See page 65 or 113 of *T/L*)

In the *Statement of the Principle*, we learn that Individuality is a fundamental principle of God's Universe. It gives us some idea of God's Infinity and Diversity. From our Biblical research of Genesis, Chapter One, which deals with Creation, we see the imprint of God's principle of individuality, of distinction, on all things. While each created category was after its "own kind," each individuality of the "kind" was distinct. Each blade of grass is distinct from every other blade of grass, as is

THE EXPANDING PRINCIPLES OF AMERICA'S CHRISTIAN HISTORY

	THE INDIVIDUAL	THE NATION AMERICA
I. GOD'S PRINCIPLE OF INDIVIDUALITY Statement of Principle: 113-117 Key: 141-183	God made me "Special." What is my "well defined individuality?" How can I play my part in the "definite plan of the all-wise Creator?"	America is the nation whose Constitutional form of government is produced by the "free and independent man."
II. THE CHRISTIAN PRINCIPLE OF SELF-GOVERNMENT Statement of Principle: 119-121 Key: 184-209	I am learning to be self-governed." *I can of mine own self do nothing.*" But *"I can do all things through Christ which strengtheneth me."*	Local self-government is the essential principle in our Constitutional form of government.
III. AMERICA'S HERITAGE OF CHRISTIAN CHARACTER Statement of Principle: 123-124 Key: 210-224	"The whole life of the Christian is a conflict with the world, a conflict within and without." Neander	The Pilgrim heritage of Christian Character provided us with those unique qualities needed to establish the world's first Christian Republic.
IV. CONSCIENCE IS THE MOST SACRED OF ALL PROPERTY James Madison Statement of Principle: 125-127 Key: 225-239	I am God's property. "Take my life and let it be consecrated Lord, to Thee." Frances Ridley Havergale	Property and productivity are the individual's opportunity and responsibility protected by Constitutional law.
V. THE CHRISTIAN FORM OF OUR GOVERNMENT Statement of Principle: 129-130 Key: 240-249	"It is in the man of piety and inward principle that we may expect to find the *uncorrupted patriot*, the *useful citizen*, and the *invincible soldier*. God grant that in America *true religion* and *civil liberty* may be *inseparable.*"John Witherspoon, 1776	Representation, the separation of powers, the dual form of our government are all Biblical principles which find full expression in American government.
VI. HOW THE SEED OF LOCAL SELF-GOVERNMENT IS PLANTED Statement of Principle: 131-133 Key: 250-261	The seed of local self-government is planted by the individual in all fields of human endeavor: business, the arts and sciences, invention, education, etc.	Samuel Adams, American Christian statesman, worked on an individual basis to unite the colonies by the vital force of distinctive ideals and principles and through the "virtue of the people."
VII. THE CHRISTIAN PRINCIPLE OF AMERICAN POLITICAL UNION Statement of Principle: 135-136 Key: 262-268	Voluntary union is "a degree of freedom in the individual to engage in the various pursuits of life … unknown where centralization prevails, whether he chooses to act by himself or in association for civil or religious purposes." *CHOC*; p. 149	The cement of American Political Union was found in the unity with diversity which produced our National-Federal Constitution – self-government with union.

every petal of every flower, every mineral, rock or animal. Every aspect of God's Creation expresses the imprint of the infinite individuality of the Creator.

On page 155, in *T/L*, in the KEY to this principle, we see that God has made each one of us *special*. This specialness is not of our own doing, but it glorifies God's infinite individuality and diversity. As we consider the *internal* and *external* expressions of our own individuality, can we accept what God has already done in us?

On a paper write down the two headings on page 155 relating to the *internal* and *external*. Under one heading write down your physical attributes. Under the other heading write down your mental and spiritual qualities. As we learn to identify and accept our God-given individuality as an indication of God's distinct mark on our lives, we can prepare ourselves to accept the responsibility to develop those unique talents which He has given into our stewardship.

Just as the *Inward Identification* is the center of our individuality, the *heart* of man in which our Lord was especially interested, so Webster identifies it as "the seat of the affections and passions," "the seat of the understanding," and the "seat of the will." The heart is both the soil of *rebellion* and *obedience*, of *barrenness* and of *fruitfulness* for the Lord. This truth can be well documented throughout God's Written Word.

Books of all literary types can be useful SOIL SOFTENERS. Poetry, drama, short stories, novels, biographies and autobiographies, all can illustrate how individuals accepted the value and responsibility of their God-given individuality.

The Principle Approach which is being restored as the Biblical method of our Colonial and Founding Father generations, encourages teachers and parents to create a climate of Love and Affirmation with their children. Teach your children how to accept God's Principle of Individuality in their own lives as you have learned to accept this principle. Research your own books which can become SOIL SOFTENERS to support your children and students as they learn to be self-governed, as they accept the Christian life of "conflict with the world—a conflict within and without." Help them to see themselves as productive and fruitful for the Lord, and illustrate another precious principle of American life, so evident in our history: the ability to work with others for the accomplishment of worthwhile goals—in voluntary union.

Let us prepare the soil of our children's hearts to accept the seed of being a totally committed American Christian. Let us prepare the upcoming generations to be the rebuilders and restorers of America's Christian History and Government.

"And the fruit of righteousness is sown in peace of them that make peace." James 3:18

INTRODUCTION TO ENGLISH AND AMERICAN POETRY

We begin to learn our English Heritage of history and literature through the study of Mother Goose and the Nursery Rhymes. These can be started at home as soon as your child learns to speak. At school Kindergarten is a good place to begin the study of poetry. The memorization of Nursery Rhymes helps develop an appreciation for the regularity of metrical accent. Children learn to appreciate rhythmic sound. We can teach them to look at God's Universe and listen to the rhythm of sounds in nature. Parents and teachers will enjoy learning the Real Personages of Mother Goose in England's history, and they can share what seems appropriate.

Some poets hold special delight for young children and are found in collections like *The Home Book of Verse for Young Folks* edited by Burton E. Stevenson. Among these are the names of Jane and Ann Taylor, Christina Rossetti, William Blake, Eugene Field, Isaac Watts, Robert Louis Stevenson and others. Poets listed in OVERVIEW V, the Elementary Program, are available in collections dated from 1900, or in single volumes of each author.

An excellent way to teach American History is through poetry. Our 19th century poets loved to celebrate special events and to honor individuals in our history. *American History in Verse*, also edited by Mr. Stevenson, is in print by Bob Jones University, Greenville, South Carolina. You can follow our Calendar of Liberty throughout the school year, from Christopher Columbus' voyages, the Landing of the Pilgrims, the Patriots of the American Revolution, through the westward expansion of the Pioneers, into the history of the 19th and 20th centuries.

INDIVIDUALITY OF THE NATIONS: FOLK AND FAIRY TALES

The study of nations is the study of history and literature. Many of the collections of Folk and Fairy

Tales reflect individual nations. For example the following authors identify particular nations.

FRANCE: Charles Perrault

GERMANY: The Brothers Grimm

DENMARK: Hans Christian Andersen

ENGLAND: Andrew Lang, Joseph Jacobs

SPAIN: Washington Irving's *Tales from The Alhambra*

Fables, which are brief tales in prose or verse, with a moral, have long been a source of interest and instruction. Perhaps the earliest and most famous collection is that by the Greek slave, *Aesop*, who wrote around 500 B.C. *Jean de la Fontaine*, of France, published his first volume of *Fables* in 1668. And in America, *Joel Chandler Harris*, a Southerner, devised his *Uncle Remus Stories* during the last years of the 19th century and the first years of the 20th. Most of these authors can be found in reprint.

ANIMAL STORIES THAT TEACH

The individuality of nations is also reflected in the kinds of animals that are celebrated in literature. In many ways these animal stories complement the History of Liberty. For example we have the following books to draw upon for our selections:

Bob, Son of Battle by Alfred Ollivant, 1898, was the first novel with a dog hero—an English Sheepherding dog.

Greyfriars Bobby by Eleanor Arkinson, 1912, a Skye terrier of Scotland, whose fidelity in watching over his master's grave captured the heart and benevolence of the city of Edinburgh.

King of the Wind by Marguerite Henry is the story of an Arabian stallion, born in Africa, in the stables of the Sultan of Morocco. He was sent as a gift to Louis XV, the boy king of France. Godolphin the Arabian became one of the three great foundation sires of the Thoroughbred line, of which America's champion, Man o' War, was bred.

Almost every country has its unique animal, like the *St. Bernard* dogs of the French and Swiss alps. The original dogs went out from the St. Bernard Monastery searching out lost travellers in the alpine snows. Their story was filmed.

In America the *Morgan* horse became the father of a famous family of horses unique to the life of free men. The Morgan horse helped clear the land, drag logs, build bridges and cut roads through the wilderness. He could labor all day, then take part in races at night or he could pull a heavier load than any other horse. *Justin Morgan Had a Horse* is another Marguerite Henry classic. And *Mustang, Wild Spirit of the West*, also by Henry, is the true story of Wild Horse Annie, who fought for free ranges for the wild mustangs of the west.

Animal Stories that Teach is a study that enables us to see the kinds of animals representative of individuals and nations.

HISTORY AS LITERATURE

Some of the greatest writers in the world have endeavored to introduce children to the vitality of history. Sir Walter Scott wrote his *Grandfather Tales* as a history of England and Scotland for his little grandson. Charles Dickens wrote his *A Child's History of England* for his son, Charles. And our own Nathaniel Hawthorne wrote his *Grandfather's Chair* for young Americans as an introduction to the History of Liberty in Massachusetts. When Laurence observed to Grandfather that "Eliot's labors had done no good except to a few Indians of his time," Grandfather remarked:

"Laurence, if ever you should doubt that man is capable of disinterested zeal for his brother's good, then remember how the apostle Eliot toiled. And if you should feel your own self-interest pressing upon your heart too closely, then think of Eliot's Indian Bible. It is good for the world that such a man has lived and left this emblem of his life." Page 39 of *Grandfather's Chair*, 1901 edition of Standard Literature Series

Let us restore the treasures of history to the hearts and minds of each new generation.

READING ALOUD CLASSICS

Since we have already discussed how to teach Key Nations and Classics on the Chain of Christianity (see Chart A), and Learning Key Classics of American Character (see Chart B), we will conclude our suggestions for your Individual Teacher Plan for Elementary Years by discussing this last section.

As American Christian parents and teachers regain their ability to *read, research, reason, relate*, and *record*, once again, there will be no limitations upon what we can Read Aloud to our children except our own philosophy of literature as indicated by Philippians 4:8. Most individuals educated today have an *improverished* background in both history and literature. Adults have grown up without parental Reading Aloud, and they have missed being read to in school by inspired and inspiring teachers. But the Lord gives us every new day to restore "what the locusts have eaten." We can begin to read a little every day, a little more every week and month, so that after a year has gone by we will have added shelves to our home library. It is important to first read to ourselves what we will present to children and students. In this way the Lord can illuminate our hearts and minds so that we can *break out* many useful truths and help them reason and relate what they hear to their own lives and characters.

While there are some outstanding authors in the twentieth century, there has been such a reversal of the philosophy of writing for the young that we have to guard against modern tendencies. The effort to introduce young readers to all kinds of social problems, many of them abhorrent to Christian parents, needs to be replaced by providing fine books for young minds to feed upon. As we work for restoration of Biblical standards in literature we can influence others to accept Nathaniel Hawthorne's statement when he wrote:

"The author regards children as sacred, and would not for the world, cast anything into the fountain of a young heart, that might embitter and pollute its waters."

In our *A Family Program for Reading Aloud* we have discussed many classics. This part of the Elementary Literature Program is for the cultivation of Listening-Learning skills. Today these are difficult skills to cultivate because both children and adults are constantly drawn away from *reflective* learning to *objective* or *visual* learning. Listening enables us to develop our internal or mental vision. It requires concentration, and Readers need to help their Listeners by increasing the length, and depth of the classics they introduce – gradually. Most of the books of value and worth which help to shape and form our minds and characters are longer than the little books written for contemporary audiences. Also, vocabulary is much richer and much more

interesting in the earlier classics. But, with compassion, we as teachers can help our Listeners to grow in their ability to use their minds more by cultivating their ability to hear. Christian self-government often requires that we block out the competing noises, and especially that we exercise dominion over our thoughts which often, like the "wild ass ... snuffeth up the wind at her pleasure," and wanders off to graze in other pastures while we are reading. (Jeremiah 2:24)

In your Public Library, look up *The Scribners Illustrated Classics*. These were beautifully illustrated volumes published early in the century. Many of N.C. Wyeth's paintings are included in these delightful books which families used to enjoy reading together. These are rich, long books, and they will provide you with a bond of listening-learning experiences which you will not want to relinquish to any one else. Children brought up on the Reading Aloud of parents and teachers become individuals of greater mental capacity. They learn to value character as the foundation of Liberty.

Here are a few titles from the Scribner's list you may wish to read as a preparation for your family Reading Aloud or your school sessions with the Read Aloud classics:

The Arabian Knights,
    edited by Kate Douglas Wiggin

A Little Princess
    by Frances Hodgson Burnett

Robinson Crusoe
    by Daniel Defoe

The Children of Dickens
    by Samuel MacChord Crothers

The Little Shepherd of Kingdom Come
    by John Fox, Jr.

Lone Cowboy and *Smoky*
    by Will James

The Scottish Chiefs
    by Jane Porter

Twenty Thousand Leagues Under the Sea
    by Jules Verne

Rebecca of Sunnybrook Farm
    by Kate Douglas Wiggin

POETRY IN THE CHRISTIAN HISTORY LITERATURE PROGRAM

From the successful teaching of the poetry of the Bible we develop the inner ear which can respond to music and the sound of words. And the teaching of the traditional Mother Goose and Nursery Rhymes helps to put words together in a measured meter. Poetry, like music, should commence the listening, literary life of a child. It should be started when the babe is in Mother's and Father's arms. And it should be continued without a break by parents at home and teachers at school. Every aspect of life and living can include poetry so that it becomes as much a part of everyday life as work and play, food and rest, sunshine and rain.

Noah Webster's definition of *Music, Poetry,* and *Rime,* in his 1828 *An American Dictionary of the English Language* expresses the following ideas:

Music: "The art of combining sounds in a manner to please the ear." "Order, harmony in revolutions; as *music* of the spheres."

Poesy: "The art or skill of composing poems; as the heavenly gift of *poesy.* Poetry; metrical composition."

Rime: "In poetry the correspondence of sounds in the termination words of syllables of two verses, one of which succeeds the other immediately, or at no great distance."

Poetry and music have always been intertwined for good or for evil and thus it is natural to see them brought together in arriving at a definition of poetry. Many of our English and American poets have identified the relationship of *God* to poetry as the following verse from *The Singers* by Henry Wadsworth Longfellow:

God sent his Singers upon earth
With songs of sadness and of mirth,
That they might touch the hearts of men,
And bring them back to heaven again.

John Keats echoed the same conviction when he stated in his *Ode:*

Bards of Passion and of Mirth,
Ye have left your souls on earth!
Ye have souls in heaven too,
Double-lived in regions new.

If we read any of the lyrical *Psalms* from God's Word, we recognize where the inspiration for poetry comes from:

385

Psalm 121

I will lift up mine eyes unto the hills, from whence cometh my help.

My help cometh from the Lord, which made heaven and earth.

He will not suffer thy foot to be moved: he that keepeth thee will not slumber.

Behold, he that keepeth Israel shall neither slumber nor sleep.

The Lord is thy keeper: the Lord is thy shade upon thy right hand.

The sun shall not smite thee by day, nor the moon by night.

The Lord shall preserve thee from all evil: he shall preserve thy soul.

The Lord shall preserve thy going out and thy coming in from this time forth, and even for evermore.

As we learn Hebrew parallelism, which is "the basic poetic technique of Hebrew poetry," we shall see the effectiveness of "saying the same thing twice in different words but with the same grammatical structure." (Leland Ryken in *The Literature of the Bible*, page 122)

In *The Christian History Literature Program* we seek to measure the effective expression of the beautiful and the true by the standards of God's Word. Is the poem a violation of God's commands — of the letter or the spirit of the Word? Does it encourage the love of God? Is it in good taste? Taste is, according to Noah Webster, "the faculty of discerning beauty, order, congruity, proportion, symmetry, or whatever constitutes excellence, particularly in the fine arts and belles lettres." And finally, is it rhythmical? Does it convey the "music of the spheres," or the order of God's universe, governed by unchanging laws which have a rhythm to them, a rhythm that is multifarious in expression?

If we do not want our children to respond to worldly rhythms and patterns of sound, if we do not want them to march to "a different drummer," then let us plant God's meters in their heads and hearts by means of our selections of poetry.

AN AMERICAN POET YOU CAN ENJOY TODAY

Family reading aloud and the school study of English and American authors made us a well-read people — and this was an extension of our *Biblical literacy*. And the accessibility of those authors whose writings were an expression of our civil and religious heritage were readily available. Notable in homes and school were the little *Riverside Literature Series*, edited by Horace Scudder, and published by Houghton Mifflin. For almost one hundred years these paperbooks — some 283 titles — were read and loved.

However, as the level of education declined in our nation, we have gradually dropped almost all of these fine writers. And in so doing we have lost both our cultural and historical literacy. But let us now restore *what the locusts have eaten*.

Henry Wadsworth Longfellow (1807–1882) was called the Poet of Home and Hearth. While he held the Professorship of Modern Languages at Harvard for many years, and was a translator and interpreter of much foreign literature, it is for his American poetry that he is best remembered.

Today you can begin your study of Longfellow either from books which you check out of the library, or, from poems found in old books, or by ordering *The Complete Poetical Works of Longfellow*, Cambridge Edition, one volume, from Houghton Mifflin Publishing Company. They still publish *The Children's Longfellow* with shortened versions of some of his longer poems.

Among the shorter and best known of Longfellow's poems is *The Arrow and the Song*. It goes like this:

THE ARROW AND THE SONG

I shot an arrow into the air,
It fell to earth, I knew not where;
For, so swiftly it flew, the sight
Could not follow it in its flight.

I breathed a song into the air,
It fell to earth, I knew not where;
For who has sight so keen and strong,
That it can follow the flight of song?

Long, long afterward, in an oak
I found the arrow, still unbroke;
And the song, from beginning to end,
I found again in the heart of a friend.

In his poem entitled *A Psalm of Life*, sub-titled *What the Heart of the Young Man said to the Psalmist*, Longfellow's New England philosophy of life is evident. That "life is real! Life is earnest!" was representative of the men and women of that geographical area.

Lives of great men all remind us
We can make our lives sublime,
And, departing, leave behind us
Footprints on the sands of time;

Footprints, that perhaps another,
  Sailing o'er life's solemn main,
A forlorn and shipwrecked brother,
  Seeing, shall take heart again.

Let us then be up and doing,
  With a heart for any fate;
Still achieving, still pursuing,
  Learn to labor and to wait.

Longfellow took up residence in Cambridge, Massachusetts, where he lived in *Craigie House*, made famous by George Washington who had his Headquarters there during the siege of Boston, 1775–76. Close to the house Longfellow daily passed a "smithy" standing under a large horse chestnut tree. When the tree was cut down it was made into a chair and presented to Longfellow by the children of Cambridge. Here are some verses from his poem:

THE VILLAGE BLACKSMITH

Under a spreading chestnut-tree
  The village smithy stands;
The smith, a mighty man is he,
  With large and sinewy hands;
And the muscles of his brawny arms
  Are strong as iron bands.

His hair is crisp, and black, and long,
  His face is like the tan;
His brow is wet with honest sweat,
  He earns whate'er he can,
And looks the whole world in the face,
  For he owes not any man.

Toiling, – rejoicing, – sorrowing,
  Onward through life he goes;
Each morning sees some task begun,
  Each evening sees it close;
Something attempted, something done,
  Has earned a night's repose.

Thanks, thanks to thee, my worthy friend,
  For the lesson thou hast taught!
Thus at the flaming forge of life
  Our fortunes must be wrought;
Thus on its sounding anvil shaped
  Each burning deed and thought.

Longfellow wrote many long verse narratives that complement our history. Our love for the Pilgrims grows as we become familiar with *The Courtship of Miles Standish*. The theme of this poem is the romance of John Alden, an ancestor of Longfellow, and Priscilla Mullins. Perhaps you are familiar with the famous line which is put into the mouth of Priscilla when she rebukes John as he pleads the suit of Miles Standish: "Why don't you speak for yourself, John?" However, there are many memorable moments in the poem and one of the most moving occurs when the *Mayflower* returns to England in the spring of 1621, after half of the colony has perished. Written in *hexameters*, a line with six heavily accented beats, it has a lively pace. Here are a few lines of this Pilgrim story:

O strong hearts and true! not one went back in the
    Mayflower!
No, not one looked back, who had set his hand to
    this ploughing!

As the *Mayflower* sailed from the harbor, rounding the Gurnet, a headland, the Pilgrims watched. What thoughts crowded their minds?

Long in silence they watched the receding sail of
    the vessel,
Much endeared to them all, as something living
    and human;
Then, as if filled with the spirit, and wrapt in a
    vision prophetic,
Baring his hoary head, the excellent Elder of
    Plymouth
Said, "Let us pray!" and they prayed, and thanked
    the Lord and took courage.
Mournfully sobbed the waves at the base of the
    rock, and above them
Bowed and whispered the wheat on the hill of
    death, and their kindred
Seemed to awake in the graves, and to join in the
    prayer that they uttered.
Sun-illumined and white, on the eastern verge of
    the ocean
Gleamed the departing sail, like a marble slab in a
    graveyard;
Buried beneath it lay forever all hope of escaping.

Lo! as they turned to depart, they saw the
    form of an Indian,
Watching them from the hill; but while they spake
    with each other,
Pointing with outstretched hands, and saying,
    "Look!" he had vanished . . .

Throughout this poem Longfellow makes continual reference to the Scriptures with which the Pilgrims were familiar, employing many excellent examples of the Pilgrims' use of Biblical imagery.

387

Longfellow's longer poems included *Evangeline*, a French-Canadian romance set in Arcadie, and *The Song of Hiawatha*, his superb, legendary Indian poem, whose simple flowing rhythm enabled him to produce a work of "serenity and dignity." The metre of *Hiawatha* is borrowed from a Finnish collection of poems that Longfellow had studied. The lines are unrhymed, and are made up of trochees, that is, of feet consisting of a stressed syllable followed by an unstressed . . . Only an accomplished poet like Longfellow could have handled it so as to bring out the effects of which it is capable. His introduction of melodious Indian words and names that are almost little poems in themselves, together with his skillful use of alliteration and repetition, give the poem a serenity and dignity that recalls the golden age it depicts." (D. C. Browning in *The Children's Illustrated Classics* Edition of E. P. Dutton) The poem runs some 200 pages and covers Hiawatha's childhood, his fasting, his friends, his wooing, his picture-writing, his lamentation, the white man's foot, and Hiawatha's departure. Here is a sample of the rhythm from the Prologue:

THE SONG OF HIAWATHA
PROLOGUE

SHOULD you ask me, whence these stories?
Whence these legends and traditions,
With the odours of the forest,
With the dew and damp of meadows,
With the curling smoke of wigwams,
With the rushing of great rivers,
With their frequent repetitions,
And their wild reverberations,
As of thunder in the mountains?

I should answer, I should tell you:
. . .

Ye who love the haunts of Nature,
Love the sunshine of the meadow,
Love the shadow of the forest,
Love the wind among the branches,
And the rain-shower and the snowstorm,
And the rushing of great rivers
Through their palisades of pine-trees,
And the thunder in the mountains,
Whose innumerable echoes
Flap like eagles in their eyries;
Listen to these wild traditions,
To this Song of Hiawatha!

Ye who love a nation's legends,
Love the ballads of a people,
That like voices from afar off
Call to us to pause and listen,

Speak in tones so plain and childlike,
Scarcely can the ear distinguish
Whether they are sung or spoken;
Listen to this Indian Legend,
To this Song of Hiawatha!

Ye whose hearts are fresh and simple,
Who have faith in God and Nature,
Who believe, that in all ages
Every human heart is human,
That in even savage bosoms
There are longings, yearnings, strivings,
For the good they comprehend not,
That the feeble hands and helpless,
Groping blindly in the darkness,
Touch God's right hand in that darkness,
And are lifted up and strengthened;
Listen to this simple story,
To this Song of Hiawatha!

A beautifully illustrated, very short version of *Hiawatha* by Susan Jeffers, is available from E. P. Dutton, Inc., 2 Park Avenue, New York, N.Y. 10016. Write Customer Service for this trade edition.

Perhaps the most familiar poem of Henry Wadsworth Longfellow which children still recite, is his *Paul Revere's Ride*, which celebrates that famous night when Paul Revere and others rode to warn the inhabitants of Lexington and Concord that the "British were coming." This date is still celebrated in Boston, and every April 18th the lantern is hung in Old North Church to send the signal. The first lines begin:

Listen, my children, and you shall hear
Of the midnight ride of Paul Revere,
On the eighteenth of April, in Seventy-five
Hardly a man is now alive
Who remembers that famous day and year.

The final lines of the poem give "a cry of defiance" to tyrants in any age who try to impose their will on free men and women:

For, borne on the night-wind of the Past,
Through all our history, to the last,
In the hour of darkness and peril and need,
The people will waken and listen to hear
The hurrying hoof-beats of that steed,
And the midnight message of Paul Revere.

In our own day we, as American Christians, have had to wake up our nation to the infringements on our civil and religious liberties. There are many Paul Reveres still giving warning, and we need to rebuild a knowledge and awareness of those principles, persons, and places in our history which testify to our stand for the blessings of liberty. *Paul Revere's Ride* is a good poem to start with.

The Complete Poetical Works of Longfellow, a 689-page book, is still published by Houghton Mifflin Company. This poet, who gained the heart of the world, wrote a great variety of poetry. We memorize both his short ballads, and verses from his longer, historical poems, like *Evangeline, The Song of Hiawatha, The Courtship of Miles Standish, Tales of a Wayside Inn*. One historic poem, less known, but of interest to students of America's Christian History is entitled *Christus: A Mystery*. This trilogy was written over a period of time and may be said to have "dominated his literary life." The theme, essentially, was the persecution of Christ and Christianity. The triumph of the love of Christ despite all misconceptions of His mission on earth and among men is also predominate. Part I, *The Divine Tragedy*, deals with the period of Christ on earth. Part II,

The Golden Legend, deals with the Middle Ages, and Part III, *The New England Tragedies*, deals especially with the persecution of the Quakers in Puritan Massachusetts. How difficult it is to reflect upon "man's inhumanity to man," especially when it is Christian against Christian, against those who differ in doctrine and interpretation. In effect, it is a history of Christianity's reception among the Lord's own.

But, while *Christus* was on the heart of Longfellow most of his professional life, it was for his poems of Home and Hearthside that he was best remembered. Many literary critics of the 20th century have dismissed Longfellow as of little consequence as a poet. But, as we read and re-read his poems of Home and Family we know why his work should be restored to our own hearts and minds. One of the most endearing of these poems is *The Children's Hour*, reminding us how important it is that we reserve time to spend with our own—lest they grow up before we are aware!

THE CHILDREN'S HOUR

Between the dark and the daylight,
    When the night is beginning to lower,
Comes a pause in the day's occupations,
    that is known as the Children's Hour.

I hear in the chamber above me
    The patter of little feet,
The sound of a door that is opened,
    And voices soft and sweet.

From my study I see in the lamplight,
    Descending the broad hall stair,
Grave Alice, and laughing Allegra,
    And Edith with golden hair.

A whisper, and then a silence:
    Yet I know by their merry eyes
They are plotting and planning together
    To take me by surprise.

A sudden rush from the stairway,
    nA sudden raid from the hall!
By three doors left unguarded
    They enter my castle wall!

They climb up into my turret
    O'er the arms and back of my chair;
If I try to escape, they surround me;
    They seem to be everywhere.

They almost devour me with kisses,
    Their arms around me entwine,
Till I think of the Bishop of Bingen
    In his Mouse-Tower on the Rhine!

Do you think, O blue-eyed banditti,
    Because you have scaled the wall,
Such an old mustache as I am
    Is not a match for you all!

I have you fast in my fortress,
    And will not let you depart,
But put you down into the dungeon
    In the round-tower of my heart.

And there will I keep you forever,
    Yes, forever and a day,
Till the walls shall crumble to ruin,
    And moulder in dust away.

ROSALIE JUNE SLATER

A biographical sketch is only justified if it reveals the Providence of God in the development of a ministry. It is in this spirit that these developments are recorded. Actually, my Biblical and historical background was not appreciated until I learned *America's Christian History.* How significamt then to discover that I was a descendant of the Founders of Hartford, Connecticut. In effect, I was represented in the band of English Puritans who emigrated with their pastor, Thomas Hooker. His famous sermon of May 31, 1638 produced the Fundamental Orders of Connecticut, America's first Constitution. For three centuries my Slater ancestors busied themselves with the responsibilities of government—in both the Congregational churches and in the town meetings.

On my mother's side, hardy Dutch emigrants to Plymouth in the 1700's stayed long enough for Hannah Sturtevant to marry John Cotton, the local Pilgrim pastor. The rest of the family moved westward to Ohio and Illinois, to farm and industrialize and to intermarry with Scotch and French stock.

A heritage is, however, only as good as the influence it has upon succeeding generations. This was confirmed in my life when my father led me to Sunday School in Congregational New England where the inspiration of Bible study became a vital part of my life. Later, again through his good efforts for my life, while attending boarding school in Switzerland, I entered into a living relationship with Jesus Christ and dedicated my life to serve Him.

My mother's instructions in Literature and its relationship to character, prepared me to read before entering school. And our years in New England Academies gave me a foundation in Christian academics: a love for the learning of history, literature, languages, science and nature study, art, music and government. The emphasis in my education was upon researching and writing. Our school put out a literary journal and published the writings of students. Thus, weekly compositions and summer reading assignments were the norm and enabled me to be productive in my own education.

When family affairs took us to Europe for several years, in addition to our American studies which our father brought with us, we learned to appreciate our heritage of western civilization with its roots deep in Christianity. Travel and planned visitations by our parents to points of historical significance gave us insights about art, architecture, sculpture, music and their importance as expressions of the character of a people. More and more as we looked at America from other shores, we appreciated its unique legacy of liberty from Europe.

"LED BY THE HAND OF HISTORY"

Returning to America our family began its own westward trek. From small geographical states with a large history, we traveled to large territories – later arrivals into the union. In California the opportunity to study at Stanford University enabled me to earn a degree in Literature, yet, in my heart I was searching to find a ministry in which I could serve the Lord. In Chicago, working with George Read, teaching adults in the *Know Your Bible Better* program, led to a desire to teach youth. Returning to California to enroll in teacher education, I realized that the philosophy of education had been changed – that the future of perpetuating American Constitutional government was in jeopardy.

Benson J. Lossing (1813–1891), journalist and historian, urged us to specifically educate our youth "in the inheritance of those prerogatives which God alone can bestow, and which God alone can withhold." Lossing was concerned about the need to produce through education in the home and school, a character capable of supporting a Constitutional Republic. He wrote:

"Above all, let our youth be instructed in all that appertains to the vital principles of our Republic. To appreciate the blessings they enjoy, and to create in them those patriotic emotions, which shall constitute them ardent defenders in the hour of trial, it is necessary to be taught the price of their goodly heritage; the fearful cost of blood and treasure, suffering and woe, at which it was obtained. They should be led by the hand of history into every patriotic council; upon every battle field; through every scene of trial and hardship, of hope and despondency, of triumph and defeat, where our fathers acted and endured." (*C/P*, p. 255)

The "new" educational philosophy which I found in teacher education was in effect designed to *educate away* our republic. This was being accomplished through the social studies curriculum content and methodology. What we were developing was the dependent character of socialism – not the character of the free and independent American capable of self-government.

I understood this more clearly when I enrolled in the doctoral program in education at Stanford University. Teaching had led into curriculum development and teacher education. Traveling to the Soviet Union for the purpose of learning how a philosophy of education produces the character for the government of a nation, it was possible to relate this goal to American education. Without the presence in the curriculum of our original history and literature of liberty our students were not learning the "price of their goodly heritage; and the fearful cost" of establishing Constitutional government in America. Instead of becoming acquainted with our founding fathers and mothers and the ideas and ideals of the Colonial and Revolutionary periods of American History, our children were studying the cultural or anthropological approach to the forming of character. As our early Pilgrims, Puritans, Patriots and Pioneers looked to the internal sources of education – Christian homes, churches and schools – to form character, our modern socialists looked to the external environment of mankind.

But the Lord had a purpose in all of this. He was "pricking" my own conscience to awaken me to the dangers of all state-dominated education which begins by loosening the ties of family and religion. As I pondered my path in education, the command came: "Separate! Cut all ties with public education! Truly seek to serve the Lord!" A revival was needed in my life. My personal rededication to a merciful God enabled me to leave public education with a purified heart and mind. I had a vision to establish a school which would begin with a curriculum designed to teach the fundamentals of character as well as the basics of American history and literature.

A CHRISTIAN HISTORY MINISTRY

At this time, by God's Providence, I met Miss Verna M. Hall, whose ministry with America's Christian History was just beginning. Her first volume, *The Christian History of the Constitution of the United States of America, Christian Self-Government*, had just been published. What a joy to learn from her research and remarkable testimony. I loved *Christian History*! It spoke to my heart of that Biblical and historical heritage that belonged to every American – a heritage which was fast being dissipated through the socialization of education. I loved *Christian History*, after teaching from the complex and poorly written modern textbooks of history. The prose of *Christian History* was so clear! The truth was so apparent of the Hand of God in History – Christ His Story of men and nations. I believed with all my heart that *Christian History* could be taught through Biblical principles to the youngest child at home or in school. It had an appeal to the heart and mind that no American Christian could resist.

The newly awakened Christian school movement in America presented itself as a natural source of interest in America's Providential History. Miss Hall and I began to travel together, attending Christian school conferences and endeavoring to explore the readiness of private education to restore what public education was endeavoring to destroy. But, the inroads of progressive education had allowed the Christians to "fall away" from their original leadership in character, curriculum, and Constitutional government. They did not see how Christian History could be integrated with social studies. It was soon evident that Christian History could not be taught through a modern philosophy of education – no matter how Biblicized. In order to restore America's Christian History to the curriculum, it was necessary to first restore the original Biblical education which had enabled us to produce the character for Christian self-government and the world's first Christian republic.

Teaching and Learning America's Christian History – the seed of the Principle Approach, was written so that America's Christian History could be taught to the youngest child in home, church or school, through Biblical principles of character and self-government. We were reintroducing a basic method of Colonial and Constitutional education – learning to reason and to write from Biblical truths into all subjects of the curriculum.

At this time, Miss Hall and I established the Foundation for American Christian Education. We wanted a non-profit, tax-exempt foundation so that we could keep the Christian History books in perpetual publication. But, we also wanted to keep the cost of these books at a price which every American Christian could afford. It was also critical to raise funds for the continuing research of our history, and for the historic Christian method of Biblical and historical reasoning which we were beginning to find in our early American education. Secondly, we knew that in order to restore America's Christian History to its central position in the school curriculum, we must educate pastors, parents, principals, and teachers. Seminars for this purpose were given in San Francisco, and at schools across the nation. Thirdly, our goal was to cooperate with those individuals, or foundations engaged in ministries of mutual concern. One such cooperative effort was with John G. Talcott's

Plymouth Rock Foundation. Here for six years Pilgrim Seminars were given at the historic location where the original contribution to our philosophy of government and education began. We endeavored to reach Christian colleges and schools, as well as pastors and parents. From these small beginnings "one small candle" began to illuminate "a thousand."

It was then that we discovered Noah Webster to be the Founding Father of American scholarship and education. In him we found a character and a commitment to American Constitutional government which is still a vital requirement for successful education in America.

There was another critical "missing ingredient" in Christian education in America. It was Literature – literature which is indeed "the handmaid" of history. But, without the restoration first of America's Christian History, literature would only follow the path of the secular, progressive educators, as it was indeed doing. Beginning with our Pilgrim history and with William Bradford's *"History 'Of Plimoth Plantation,'"* we began to uncover the treasures which awaited us. Accordingly, *The Christian History Literature Program* began to appear. It has a two-fold purpose. First, to restore to homes in America the joys and riches of "reading aloud" together as a family. Secondly, we wished to restore the teaching of Literature to its chronology in the history of liberty – identifying the character of those nations on the Chain of Christianity who have contributed links to American Liberty.

We have much to repent of in American Christian education. By our "falling away" we have allowed "unrighteous" men and women to take over the leadership of this nation – in almost all fields. It will take courage for individuals to reclaim each field of study and action for the Lord. Many parents who have taken back the responsibility for the education of their children, are also restoring America's Christian History and Literature. As we put the suggestions of inadequacy behind us, and, instead, feed richly upon our heritage of history and literature, we shall be able to inspire and teach all those within our sphere of opportunity and ministry. What a joy to know that the victory belongs to the Lord – the victory over ignorance and the sin of forgetting God!

Wherefore seeing we also are compassed about with so great a cloud of witnesses,
let us lay aside every weight, and the sin which doth so easily beset us,
and let us run with patience the race that is set before us,
Looking unto Jesus the author and finisher of our faith;
who for the joy that was set before him endured the cross, despising the shame,
and is set down at the right hand of the throne of God.
(Hebrews 12:1,2)

392

THE PRINCIPLE APPROACH TO
AMERICAN CHRISTIAN ECONOMICS

BY CHARLES HULL WOLFE
President, American Renewal
Pacific Palisades, California

CONTENTS

The Principle Approach
to American
Christian Economics

INTRODUCTION

The young Americans we are educating today in our Christian homes and schools will be confronted as adults with an array of economic decisions which will have profound impact upon their personal lives and the life of their nation.

They will have to make decisions about how to make a living, and about how to spend and manage the money they earn. How will they utilize the vast job and entrepreneurial opportunities the American economy offers? How will they protect themselves against its dangers – such as unemployment and inflation?

Even before they enter the world of work, as students in high school and college, our children will discover the various political and economic systems, and will have to make decisions about the merits of socialism vs. capitalism, about a free market economy vs. a so-called mixed economy or, more correctly, a hampered market economy. Our young people should be prepared to give sound answers to such questions as "Which systems are the natural outcome of Biblical principles? Which oppose these principles? Which system will build

freedom, prosperity and justice? Which economic system is right for me and America?"

Again, when today's children become adults they will be obliged to make decisions concerning their personal relationships with their government, at local, state and national levels. Which economic benefits, payments or privileges should they accept as their rightful due, and which should they reject, for themselves, their families and their businesses, as Biblically unprincipled and immoral?

Which tax burdens and government regulations should they deem necessary and desirable from the perspective of sound principles? Which should they view as excessive and unprincipled? They will have to make decisions as citizens in choosing between candidates for elected office, and in evaluating proposed and existing legislation. Which candidates and which laws should they view as essentially sound in terms of economics, and which should they see as unsound – even unbiblical?

Once young people have made good decisions on these matters, how do they become effective in explaining their decisions, and why they have made them, in communicating with family, friends, neighbors, their entire community and their elected officials?

ECONOMIC LEADERS OF TOMORROW

Finally, young Christians who have been educated in America's Christian history and the Principle Approach, who have developed a strong, Christian character and a sense of their God-given dominion, are being prepared for positions of leadership – in the church, in education, in the media, in business, the professions and government. These Christian leaders of tomorrow should be at the head of a great crusade to restore America, and they should have the knowledge and convictions that can contribute to the restoration of the American economy, to the rebuilding of American productivity, the balancing of the central government's budget, and the reduction of the national debt.

To prepare our children to make these decisions and contributions, once they have reached adulthood, we must begin now to teach them basic economics. If we are consistent with the premises behind this book, we will want to teach them *Christian* economics, and more specifically, *American* Christian economics. In particular, we will want our young people to learn the *economic* implications of the seven Biblical principles of America's Christian history and government presented so clearly in Rosalie J. Slater's *Teaching and Learning America's Christian History*, and throughout this *Guide*. Fortunately, those who study the Principle Approach, as explained by Verna M. Hall, Rosalie J. Slater and James B. Rose already have the best possible preparation for a study of Christian economics: an understanding of the Biblical principles of civil government.

GOVERNMENT AND THE ECONOMY

There is a very close correlation, in any nation, between its civil government and its economy. As Verna Hall puts it, with surprising simplicity, "Government is the house in which the economy lives." Civil government either protects, or fails to protect, the private property, voluntary exchanges, sound currency and contractual agreements on which a prosperous free economy rests. Government, by its rightful or wrongful actions, either maximizes or minimizes the incentives that human beings need in order to live up to their economic potential – in working, saving, inventing, investing and in launching and managing enterprises.

Because of this close correlation between a nation's civil government and its economy, each of the seven Biblical principles of government presented by Miss Slater in her seminal work and amplified by Mr. Rose in this volume has direct and specific economic applications. These are explained in Diagram II and its accompanying text, "The Wheel of Progress in a Christian Free Economy," on p. 404.

As we present America's Christian principles of government to the children in our care, we should quite naturally explain some of their economic implications. And even before we do this, when we are focusing entirely on the personal use of governmental meanings of these principles, we are preparing children to grasp the economic meanings.

The approach to education presented in this book lends itself especially well to the teaching of economics because it not only emphasizes the principles of government but the providential approach to the history of each subject. This is exceedingly pertinent to a study of economics.

STUDYING ECONOMIC HISTORY

Just as the wisdom or folly of our individual economic decisions is confirmed in due time by our personal histories, so the soundness or unsoundness of the economic decisions of entire communities and countries is verified in their histories. The best teachers of economics are always good economic historians, and draw freely on historical economic experiences to illustrate their points.

The Principle Approach, embracing as it does universal history, from ancient to modern times (and using the Bible as its primary text), also lends itself nicely to the teaching of economics. Economic history, from a Christian perspective, begins with God's creation of the three basic factors of production as recorded in the first chapter of Genesis, (see Diagram I, p. 400) and the economic experiences of Adam and Eve, in enjoying the abundance of the Garden, then coping with scarcity once they were removed for disobedience.

As the teacher instructs from Old and New Testaments, explaining the Hand of God in history, the Biblical principles of government, or the Biblical origin and purpose of any subject, he should also look for the Biblical principles and examples that relate to economics. As our course overview indicates (p. 415), such a Bible study could include references not only to Adam and Eve but to his sons and to such figures as Noah, Solomon and Jeremiah, either as tool users or entrepreneurs or both.

History confirms the basic truth expressed in the lower half of the two diagrams on page 401 – that production in a Christian culture with great economic freedom generally has exceeded production in a secular culture with limited economic freedom, and thus has contributed more to man's material welfare or prosperity.

Since America began as a number of independent, "underdeveloped" and relatively impoverished colonies, was transformed into the world's most prosperous and productive nation, and currently is experiencing signs of a long-term economic decline, this country presents a superb economic case history. What caused its rapid economic rise? What prompted its relatively recent economic decline? What must be done to restore the American economy? By the time our children are ready for college, they should understand that the rise and fall of the American economy correlates with the degree to which the American people understood and practiced the Biblical principles of history and government and the related principles of economics as visualized in Diagram II, "The Wheel of Progress for a Christian Free Economy." (See p. 404)

Miss Hall, Miss Slater and Mr. Rose encourage far more detailed emphasis on the early colonial period than do most teachers of American history, and this also lends itself to the teaching of economics, since this initial period is so rich in economic instruction.

INSTRUCTIVE COLONIAL EXPERIENCES

The disastrous economic experiences of Jamestown, the first permanent English colony in North America, illustrate the dire consequences of a failure to practice sound Biblical principles![1] The second permanent English colony, established in Plymouth, also presents excellent economic lessons as we consider the near-starvation experienced by the Pilgrims in their first two years in the wilderness, under the communal agricultural system imposed upon them by the investors in their expedition, and the vast economic improvement resulting from their switch to individual, private agriculture in 1623.[2]

The misguided attempts of the government of Massachusetts Bay to regulate prices and wages are documented in Clarence Carson's book, "The American Tradition" (see Bibliography). The colo-

nial lessons reach a climax as we examine the inflation generated during the War for Independence as the Continental Congress, lacking the coercive power to collect taxes, was forced to pay the costs of war by issuing more and more paper money, which kept losing value until, at war's end, it was literally worthless.[3]

In turn, a study of the Constitution is incomplete without consideration of its economic provisions – how it limited the size and cost of national government, prevented it from intervening in the self-regulating free market, provided for a sound currency based on precious metals, and made possible a nation-wide common market by eliminating tariff barriers between the states. (See Bibliography: Clarence Carson, "A Basic History of the U.S.")

As our children discover how sound economic principles were implemented in America's first century under the Constitution, and how they have been rejected in the latter part of this century, they will learn what must be done to restore the nation's economic health.

OUR FORGOTTEN ECONOMIC MIRACLE

Shortly after the American free market economy was launched under the provisions of the Constitution, Americans began to amaze the world in the way they worked, saved, invented and invested – in the tools of production that multiply men's energies – and in how they worked together in voluntary union to form a winning economic team. In the relatively short span of one century from the framing of the Constitution, America was transformed from thirteen struggling, relatively poor, newly united colonies into the most productive and prosperous nation in the world.

By 1890, American workers, in the factories and on the farms, had more and better power tools per capita, and used these tools more effectively, than the people of any other nation – including Mother England, where the Industrial Revolution began. By the turn of the century, Americans were producing more (and in some ways, better) goods and services per capita than any other people. Thus they enjoyed the world's highest living standard.

They earned the money to buy the necessities of life with fewer work-hours than any other people. It meant that they could also enjoy more lux-

---

1. *CHOC*, pp. 162-163
2. *Ibid*, pp. 213-214. See also Charles Wolfe essay on "Pilgrims' Voluntary Union," p. 74, of this *Guide*.

3. For a concise account of the Colonial and pre-Revolutionary experience with money, see *C/P*, Index of Leading Ideas, p. 665, col. 2.

uries, and had more free time than other peoples – for instruction, recreation, to worship the Lord and serve others – and had more money to give their churches and charities, and to their foreign missionary efforts, which became the largest in the world.

Even though Americans were the world's highest paid workers, the quantity and quality of the goods they produced was so great in relation to their compensation, that many American products were competitively priced on world markets.

Because of the American people's failure to understand and apply the Biblical principles of government and economics on which our original prosperity was built, and their refusal to remember their Christian history and to learn its economic lessons, the natural growth of our economy has been stunted, its normal vitality has given way to semi-stagnation; and over the past few decades, for the first time in our national history, our standard of living has been falling.

Our Children's Economic Future

Unless radical changes are made in our government and economy, it will continue to fall, and our children will be poorer than we are, and their children will be poorer still, on average.

Today Americans are saving a smaller percentage of their personal incomes than the peoples of any other industrial nation; America is investing a smaller percentage of its Gross National Product in new tools of production than any other modern nation; Americans are losing their long-time pre-eminence as inventors of advanced tools of production; and as a consequence, the U.S. is experiencing the slowest productivity growth rate of any industrialized country.

HAMPERING INFLUENCES

While American productivity has declined, American wages have continued to rise, not only because of monetary inflation but because of un-principled governmental interventions in the economy, such as minimum wage laws and legislation granting labor unions the privilege of being *monopolies* (only one union allowed in an industry) and of using *coercion* to recruit members (if workers don't join the union, they can't get a job in a unionized firm). Worse yet, union restrictions typically hamper productivity.

Thus Americans are pricing themselves out of world markets, and losing jobs, especially in highly unionized industries such as coal, steel, cars, radio and TV set manufacturing.

America has three times more energy resources in the form of coal than the Middle East has in oil. We have half the world's known supply, but we are making scant use of it. One reason: American labor costs make our own coal so expensive, we are now importing coal from other countries.

Japanese steel mills are the world's most automated; they produce more steel per worker than the best U.S. mills, but American steelworkers are paid twice as much per hour. Thus the American steel industry is on the verge of extinction.

Look at the direct labor hours required to produce a color TV set: only 1.9 hours in Japan vs. 3.5 to 4.5 hours in the U.S. Look at the number of auto engines produced per day per employee: nine engines per day by Toyota in Japan vs. two engines per day by Ford in the U.S.

Currently, the most advanced U.S. auto factory builds a car in 43 man-hours, while a Japanese plant builds a car in 14 hours. The difference in economic efficiency is even more shocking when one considers that the American auto workers are paid over twice as much per hour, and their cars have far more defects traceable to worker errors.

IMITATING AMERICAN PRINCIPLES

What is especially interesting is that the Japanese make few claims for innovation: largely, they insist, they have *simply imitated the principles* and techniques on which America's original prosperity was built – principles and techniques which *grew out of our Christian culture*, and which Americans today have at least partly abandoned.

The Japanese have imitated "the Puritan work ethic" and "Yankee ingenuity." They have heeded the early American saying, "a penny saved is a penny earned." They have adopted the principle of *individual responsibility*, making each individual responsible for the quality of his own work, rather than relieving assembly line workers of that responsibility and placing it on the shoulders of "quality control" specialists. They also have adopted the American principle of *representative government* and applied it to the factory, giving workers a voice in the decision-making process in the plant.

Further, the Japanese have understood the principle that says "What truly benefits the workers also benefits the managers and owners, and vice versa." They have largely avoided the management-worker adversary relationship, encouraged by Marxist notions, and come together in a kind of *voluntary union* which includes almost complete job-assignment flexibility.

This means that *anyone* can do *any* job, within his competence, that needs to be done. (Compare that to an American auto plant: under its strict union rules, there are several hundred job classifications which encourage or even direct workers to say: "I can't do that, it's not my job!")

The most efficient plants in Japan – and in Europe – also have adopted the traditional American principle of *limited government* and applied it to the factory, strictly limiting the number of managers in relation to the number of workers, while American business and industry have become top-heavy with an excess of managers.

Thus it is obvious that American industry needs to be restored by a thorough understanding and expression of Biblical principles of economics. Our task as Christians seeking to apply the Truth to every aspect of life is to contribute to that restoration ourselves, and to so educate our children that they will be able to contribute further to the restoration of American industry.

Restoring American Welfare

This nation's welfare system also needs to be restored. Originally, following Christian principles, Americans depended on God and themselves for their economic welfare, and in turn on their families, their churches, their neighbors and on local charities – first private, then public. But during the last 50 years that pattern has been reversed, and ever higher percentages of Americans have been depending on the federal government, in whole or in part, for their economic welfare.

The American welfare state, rejecting as it did Biblical principles of government and economics, has encouraged a host of evils: a vast increase in government spending and taxes, a great decrease in the percentage of the federal budget devoted to national defense, huge deficits, inflation, an erosion of the family unit for those receiving welfare, and a growth in poverty. As scholar Charles Murray has written in *Losing Ground*, "We tried to provide more for the poor and produced more poor instead."

To a considerable extent, alternatives to federally-funded social programs will appear spontaneously, as misguided government efforts are reduced or eliminated, tax and inflation rates are lowered, and people are obliged to turn to God and their own God-given inner resources. But there also needs to be a conscious, deliberate move by Christian churches, para-church organizations and other private groups to respond to the economic needs which the federal government has tried, but failed, to meet.

While our children should learn about such private, non-profit activities, our chief economic objective should not be to relieve people in distress, but to prevent such distress from occurring, by raising up a generation of children with strong Christian character, an excellent basic education, and a knowledge of sound governmental and economic principles. In turn, these young people will become the leaders of tomorrow – in education, business, the media and government – and under God's Providence, they will find effective ways to restore the American economy, and make it far more free and far more productive.

Practical, principled guidance in this restoration process will be found in The Ten Pillars of Christian Economic Wisdom (p. 408), which reject the false notion that government can give us something for nothing, expose the evil in government creating "unearned" money out of thin air, and show the merit of the free market as the means of determining wages, and the importance of boosting productivity with better tools.

THE WANT-SATISFACTION CHAIN

Finally, as the teacher combines the insights from the Ten Pillars with the understanding of Diagrams I and II, and their accompanying texts, he will be able to shed considerable light on Diagram III, "The Want-Satisfaction Chain in Two Kinds of Societies" (p. 412). This diagram is adapted from one widely used by secular economists, but with major modifications which point to the solution of an otherwise unsolvable economic problem, called *the* basic economic problem today in the U.S. and most other countries: un-redeemed man appears to have *un*limited wants but *limited* human and natural resources with which to meet those wants, and thus seldom experiences real satisfaction.

This disparity – between what people want as consumers and their legitimate means of satisfying their wants – has plunged millions of Americans into debt, and many thousands into bankruptcy. This same gulf – between what Americans want from their central government, and their ability and willingness to pay for it in taxes – has plunged our government into debt (on which we and our children must pay the interest) and has created huge deficits (which could precipitate runaway inflation).

No economics text ever written sheds as much light on this deep-seated problem as the Bible. It tells us how unsaved men keep wanting and getting things but are never satisfied. As the author of the book of Ecclesiastes tells us, "I made me great works; I builded me houses . . . I made me pools of water . . . I got me servants . . . I gathered me also silver and gold . . . And whatsoever mine eyes desired I kept not from them ... Then I looked on all the works that my hands had wrought, and on the labor that I had labored to do: and behold, all was vanity and vexation of spirit, and there was no profit under the sun." (Eccl. 2:1, 6, 7, 8, 10, 11)

The same author sums it up, "All the labor of man is for his mouth, and yet the appetite is not filled." (Eccl. 6:7) But as man receives Christ, and grows in spiritual understanding, the carnal yearning for more and more things of this world is effectively *limited*, and at the same time, there is a growing faith in and understanding of God's *un*-limited ability to meet human needs. Thus the great gulf between man's wants and resources is narrowed.

GOD'S ANSWER

As believers internalize the instructions of the Master, in Matthew 6:24-34, and learn to trust God to clothe them even as he does "the grass of the field," seeking God first and letting the things they need be added, they find their once-unlimited wants are satisfied by a super-natural response to God's law and will. At the same time, as believ-

ers take to heart the Bible's powerful assurance that God is the great Provider – as they say with the Psalmist, "The Lord is my shepherd, I shall not want" (Psa. 23:1) and agree with Paul that "God shall supply all your needs according to his riches in glory by Christ Jesus" (Phil. 4:19) – then once-limited resources begin to enlarge, as men lay hold of God's unlimited provision for their needs and wants.

Only to the extent that this divine provision becomes a reality in the lives of America's citizens will they be willing to abandon their dependence on the welfare state, and do their part to limit our government and restore our economy.

COURSE OF STUDY

Diagrams I – IV, including the Ten Pillars of Christian Economic Wisdom, will now be explained in some detail. Beginning on p. 415, suggested definitions, course goals and overview for teaching the Principle Approach to American Christian Economics are introduced with recommendations on what and how the basic principles and ideas of economics may be introduced at various grade levels.

DIAGRAM I
THE RUDIMENTS OF GOD'S ECONOMY

God gives man everything he needs for his human welfare.

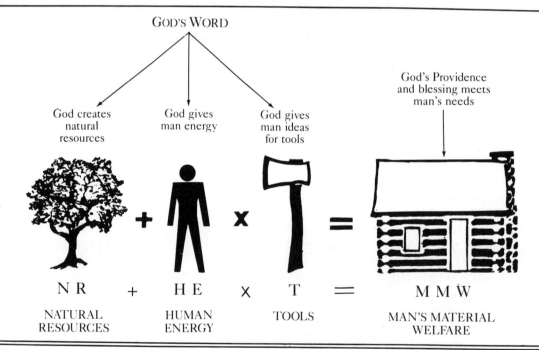

GOD'S WORD

God creates natural resources

God gives man energy

God gives man ideas for tools

God's Providence and blessing meets man's needs

| N R | + | H E | x | T | = | M M W |
| NATURAL RESOURCES | | HUMAN ENERGY | | TOOLS | | MAN'S MATERIAL WELFARE |

PRODUCTION

IN A SECULAR CULTURE WITH LIMITED ECONOMIC FREEDOM

LACKING A RELATIONSHIP WITH THE ALL-POWERFUL GOD, AND DEPRIVED OF THE INCENTIVES OF FREEDOM, MEN EXERT LESS ENERGY.

LACKING FAITH IN GOD'S PROVISION, MEN FIND FEWER NATURAL RESOURCES.

CUT OFF FROM THE BIBLE AND THE MIND OF CHRIST, MEN GET FEWER IDEAS FOR INVENTING NEW AND BETTER TOOLS.

NET RESULT: MAN'S MATERIAL WELFARE SUFFERS.

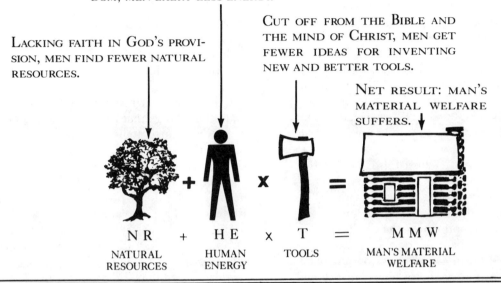

N R	+	H E	x	T	=	M M W
NATURAL RESOURCES		HUMAN ENERGY		TOOLS		MAN'S MATERIAL WELFARE

IN A CHRISTIAN CULTURE WITH GREAT ECONOMIC FREEDOM

TRUSTING IN THE OMNIPOTENT GOD, MEN "RENEW THEIR STRENGTH." IMPELLED BY THE INCENTIVES OF FREEDOM, THEY EXERT MORE ENERGY.

BELIEVING THAT GOD HAS PROVIDED ALL THAT IS NEEDED, MEN HAVE THE FAITH TO SEEK, FIND AND PROCESS ABUNDANT NATURAL RESOURCES.

LACKING A RELATIONSHIP WITH THE ALL-POWERFUL GOD, AND DEPRIVED OF THE INCENTIVES OF FREEDOM, MEN EXERT LESS ENERGY.

NET RESULT: MAN'S MATERIAL WELFARE IMPROVES.

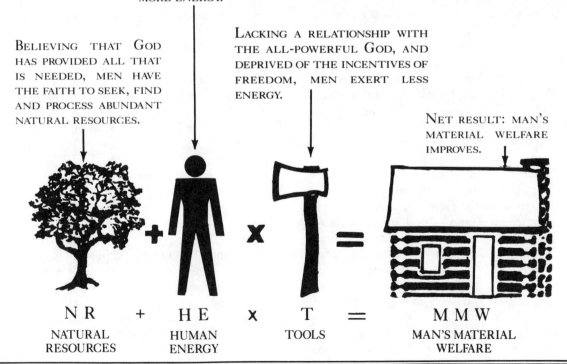

N R	+	H E	x	T	=	M M W
NATURAL RESOURCES		HUMAN ENERGY		TOOLS		MAN'S MATERIAL WELFARE

The Rudiments of God's Economy

From the very beginning God knew that the man He had created would have certain basic needs, such as food, clothing and shelter. And from the beginning, God created everything that man would require to meet those needs. This truth is illustrated in Diagram I, p. 401, which is also a basic formula for economic production, which determines man's material welfare or living standard.

God created *natural resources*, as the Bible declares at the outset, in the first chapter of Genesis. God created the earth with all its minerals, the sky with its sun, moon and stars, the water with its fish. He also created edible fowl, animals and cattle.

The first chapter of Genesis also tells us that God created man, and told him to "have dominion" (i.e., take control) over the earth with the labor of his hands and the "sweat of his brow." But man could not take control over the earth, or meet his needs, with his bare hands. No matter how much of his God-given *human energy* he might exert, with nothing but his bare hands, man could not produce enough to stay alive.

GOD GIVES IDEA FOR TOOLS

In order to take the natural resources God has created, and turn them into the food, clothing and shelter that man must have to survive, man must have tools to till the soil, to cut down trees and saw timber, to mine and refine minerals, and to tend sheep and weave wool. And so God gave man the ideas for inventing and making tools – tools for digging, cutting, weaving, pounding and carrying.

Most important, God gave man both intelligence and physical strength – the mental and muscular *energy* he would need to create and use tools, to transform God's natural resources into the goods that meet man's needs. Since Adam and his first son, Cain, were farmers, no doubt they created and used such tools as a digging stick or simple plow, to cut open the earth and plant the seeds that God had created, and some kind of sickle or cutting tool to harvest the grain once it was grown.

Since Adam's second son, Abel, was a shepherd, very likely he created and used such tools as a rod and staff (to guide the sheep and to strike any creature that would seek to harm them). In the Bible are many references to tools – hammers, axes and other tools made of iron (I Kings 6:7), plows drawn by oxen (I Kings 19:19), millstones

for grinding meal (Isa. 47:2), mortar and pestle for grinding grain by hand (Prov. 27:22), furnaces for refining silver and gold (Prov. 27:21), ovens, baking and frying pans for preparing food (Lev. 2:4, 5, 7) etc.

As Diagram I, and the formula (NR + HE x T = MMW) on page 401 indicates, God gave man everything he needed to provide for his human welfare – the natural resources, the human energy and the ideas for creating tools; but man still had to do the work, to take what he had been given and transform it into the food, clothing, shelter and other things that meet his human needs.

In Diagram I, tools are represented by an axe, but for thousands of years no one had such an efficient cutting tool as a steel-bladed axe, and in advanced industrial countries today, axes have been replaced by power saws. As Clark and Rimanoczy have explained in *How We Live*, "The usefulness of each tool is measured by the amount of time and energy it saves; by the increase in the quantity and (or) quality of the goods and services that can be produced through its use."

To a large extent, economic progress is externally the consequence of the development of better tools. In the beginning, Adam probably had only a simple wooden digging tool, and could only raise enough food for Eve and himself. (In some parts of the world today, farmers still seek to till the soil with such a crude instrument, and barely produce enough food to stay alive.)

BETTER TOOLS PRODUCE MORE

Later, a farmer with a wooden plow drawn by an ox proved more productive; he could raise enough food to feed *one* large family. (Archaeologists have found this was the kind of agricultural tool used by Abraham, and in some poor countries, such equipment is still in use.) Inventions flourished in the Christian free economy which developed in the late colonial and early federal periods in America; a farmer with a horse-drawn iron plow could raise enough food to feed *three* families.

In the 1800's in the United States, the nationwide free market economy made possible by the Constitution gave rise to one new agricultural invention after the other: the chilled steel plow, power reaper, steam thrasher, disc harrow, the first combine, then the first tractor. By the 1940's, one farmer with his tractor could raise enough food for *fourteen* families. Today, one farmer – with a much more advanced tractor and related tools – can raise enough food to feed *sixty* families!

His productivity is a result not only of better tools (which required his personal investment) but better use of those tools (which results when individuals are free to own their own farms and their own farm tools, and benefit from their own productivity). However, some key industries in our manufacturing sector, which for generations was the world's most efficient, no longer have the most advanced tools, and many of our factory workers are no longer using the tools they have with maximum efficiency, and so other countries – which have copied the economic principles on which our country was built – are now surpassing America in manufacturing such important products as steel, automobiles and television sets.

Jesus gave us an example of a man who worked with his hands to meet human needs, because He was a carpenter. The Apostle Paul was a tentmaker, and urged his followers "to work with your own hands," (I Thess. 4:11) and warned that "if any would not work, neither should he eat" (II Thess. 3:10). Much earlier, Solomon had advised, "Go to the ant, thou sluggard; consider her ways, and be wise." (Prov. 6:6)

The formula for man's material welfare applies all over the world, to every country; and in creating the earth, God was very just and fair in providing an abundance of natural resources in every continent. Yet the people in most parts of the world are poor; one-third of the world's population is almost constantly hungry. By comparison with the rest of the world, the people of America are very prosperous indeed.

Even when compared with most other industrial nations, such as England and the Soviet Union, America is a wealthy country. The best way to compare the real wealth of the people of one country with the wealth of the people of another is how many hours of work it takes a factory worker to earn the money needed to buy the same basic commodities in retail stores in that country. Following are the figures for March 1979, compiled by the National Federation of Independent Business, San Mateo, CA:

	Moscow	London	Washington
Bread (1 Kilogram)	18 min.	12 min.	8 min.
Milk (1 Liter)	18 min.	9 min.	7 min.
Men's leather shoes	33 hrs.	11 hrs.	8 hrs.
Car (Volga, Ford)	35 mos.	8.5 mos.	4.1 mos.

WEALTH AND POVERTY

The lower half of Diagram I explains why some countries (primarily those with a secular, worldly culture and limited economic freedom), are *poor*, while others (primarily those with a more godly culture and more economic freedom) are prosperous. While men and women in every country try to multiply their human energies with the help of tools in order to transform natural resources into useful goods and services, Christian free societies generally do it more efficiently than others.

The captions explain why such societies find and process more natural resources, release more human energy, and multiply that energy with more and better tools. The captions emphasize the primary importance of Christian faith and character in enlarging, vitalizing and improving the three factors of production. But the economic incentives of freedom are also important. To find and process natural resources such as oil and minerals is extremely costly. So is the protracted process of researching, developing and producing new and more efficient power tools. The profit motive provides individuals with the needed incentive in a Christian free economy based on individual enterprise.

History shows that in a Christian free economy, such as we have had in America, men tend to invent more and better tools, invest more in producing those tools, and use those tools more efficiently than in a secular society with limited economic freedom.

403

Diagram II
The Wheel of Progress in a Christian Economy

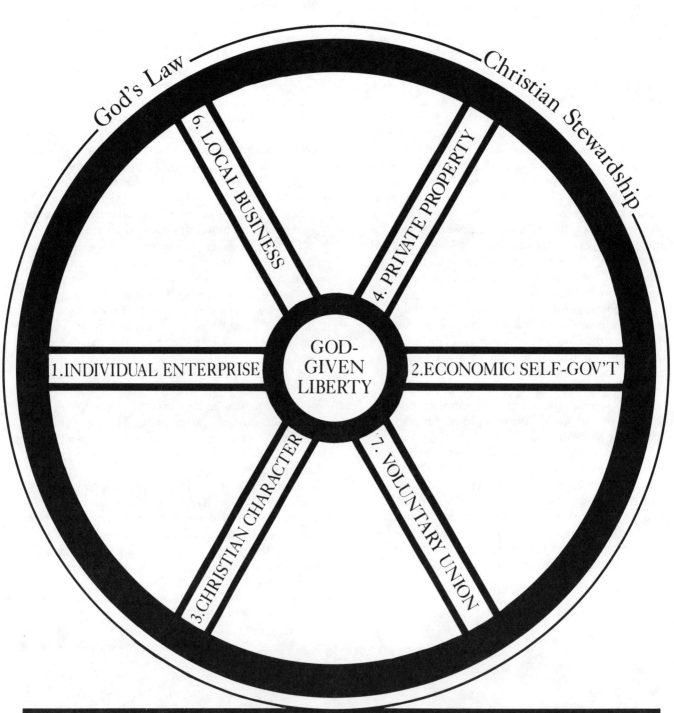

God's Law

Christian Stewardship

6. LOCAL BUSINESS

4. PRIVATE PROPERTY

1. INDIVIDUAL ENTERPRISE

GOD-GIVEN LIBERTY

2. ECONOMIC SELF-GOV'T

3. CHRISTIAN CHARACTER

7. VOLUNTARY UNION

5. A CHRISTIAN CONSTITUTIONAL FORM OF GOVERNMENT

THE WHEEL OF PROGRESS
IN A CHRISTIAN FREE ECONOMY

THE WHEEL OF PROGRESS
IN A CHRISTIAN FREE ECONOMY

Ever since the time of Abraham, when God revealed to man the idea for the wheel, it has contributed to progress in transportation; it has increased man's effectiveness in moving people and things toward desired destinations.

By the same token, the Biblical principles of history and government, when applied in the economic realm, reaching out like spokes from a hub of God-given liberty, and bound together by a rim of spiritual law and Christian stewardship, form a kind of wheel; and this wheel has contributed greatly to progress in moving man toward his economic destinations – more and better goods and services with less time and effort, under an economic system in keeping with God's will and wisdom: a Christian economy.

The liberty which God gives to man, as man yields to God's government, is first experienced internally, as freedom from sin, and then manifests itself externally in political freedom, the freedom of a Christian people to form and operate their own civil government, which in turn gives rise to economic freedom – a people's freedom to own their own property, to choose their own occupation, to keep the fruits of their labors, and to buy and sell in a free market, where wages and prices are determined not by government mandate but by voluntary exchanges of free men and women.

THE HUB OF LIBERTY

This God-given liberty expressing itself in the economic arena is the hub of the wheel of progress in a Christian economy. If the hub of the wheel is seen as freedom granted by man or the state, rather than by God Himself, then that freedom can readily be taken away, in whole or in part, and there is no reliable basis for a continuing, consistent free economy. But when the hub of the wheel is seen as God-given liberty, then the economy has a reliable center or core to which the various spokes – the Biblical principles of economics – can be securely attached.

Only a hub of economic liberty can give rise to the various spokes of this wheel; only when the economy begins with economic liberty do men have the freedom needed to practice individual enterprise and economic self-government, the freedom to fully develop Christian character and to exercise the rights and responsibilities of private property, the freedom to start and run one's own local business, and to come together in voluntary union to build a prosperous free market economy.

RIM OF STEWARDSHIP AND LAW

To form an effective, smooth-running wheel, these spokes must be bound together by the discipline of God's law and the practice of Christian stewardship, which together create a rim of responsibility which keep economic freedom under God's control.

In an economy – as in any society generally – the great challenge is not merely to maintain freedom but to maintain freedom with order, which means that people must be disciplined from within so they do not infringe upon the rights of others. To the extent that men understand and obey God's law in the economic realm, they will respect each other's property, they will not steal or cheat one another, they will abide by contracts, and when elected or appointed to positions in government, they will not use the power they have been granted to secretly erode the value of the people's money through inflation, or gradually restrict their economic freedom through excessive regulation.

To maintain economic freedom, individuals also must practice Christian stewardship. They not only must be industrious in earning money, but disciplined in saving it, wise in investing it, and obedient to God's law in how they share it with their church and with those in need. Especially, men and women must be good stewards in the sense of practising the self-denial necessary to restrain themselves from buying many things that would bring immediate gratification, in order to save and invest enough to provide for emergencies and their later years, without having to turn to government for assistance.

THE COMPLETE WHEEL

Put all the elements of the wheel together, a hub of God-given liberty, spokes formed from the Biblical principles of economics and a rim of responsibility based on God's law and Christian stewardship, and you have a splendid wheel of progress that will move individuals and an entire people forward in a Christian economy. That wheel, of course, must have a good road to run on – ideally, the road formed by a Christian Constitutional Republican form of government, which results from the understanding and application of the Biblical principles of government, explained in detail elsewhere in this book.

Now, let's take a look at that wheel, and examine its spokes – the Biblical principles of a Christian free economy, as visualized in Diagram II, p. 404, *The Wheel of Progress in a Christian Economy*.

1. *Individual enterprise* appeared in America because our country – its government and economy – were built on God's principle of individuality. Each man, woman and child is distinct, unique and important in an economic sense.

Each has special God-given talents as a producer, and individual desires as a customer. Each has individual *rights* (such as the right to enter an occupation of one's choice, to start one's own business, or to buy the goods one prefers).

Each one also has individual economic *responsibilities* (such as the duty to become economically self-reliant, and to voluntarily help others when they are in acute need through no fault of their own).

This principle opposes economic collectivism, under which government is more concerned with *groups* than with *individuals*, and *forces* people to join together in producing goods and in providing for their economic security. Rather, it encourages the system called individual enterprise, which applies the Bible principle, "As you sow, so shall you also reap."

2. *Economic self-government.* He who governs himself, by responding in his heart to the government of Jesus Christ, will control and direct his own economic actions responsibly. He will be a self-governing producer, not needing constant supervision from another person to assure the quality and quantity of his work.

He will be a self-governing customer, buying only what he needs and never spending in excess of his income. He will also be a self-governing saver, regularly saving some of his earnings to assure a strong economic future.

Such a person will also be a self-governing manufacturer or retailer, producing and selling quality goods and services, with due concern for the rights and needs of employees and customers. Such self-government gives rise to a free economy.

3. *Christian character.* America's original prosperity arose from the diligence and industry of its settlers, who trusted the Lord to provide for their needs – if they worked hard, put Him first, and let all things be added in God's good time. ("Seek ye first the kingdom of God and His righteousness and all these things will be added unto you.")

The problem of economic scarcity can only be solved as people have the faith to believe in God's unlimited resources, and the discipline to limit their wants and to maximize both their productive efforts and their savings. Christian character expresses itself in brotherly care for the needy, in trusting relationships between employers and employees, and in honest money – a government that does not secretly increase the "money supply" – i.e., create more and more paper money out of thin air.

4. *Private property.* A person's property is whatever he has the exclusive right to possess and control. To the Christian, property is first internal; his most precious possession is his conscience, which tells him what is right and wrong in the way he earns his living.

Property is also external. The God who owns everything delegates to man the temporary right to possess external property, and the obligation to use it conscientiously as God's steward. This property includes land, a home, money, wages and profits. It means a person owns his own labor.

Only as we enjoy property rights can we exercise our stewardship duties. This principle gives rise to private enterprise, based on individual liberty with responsibility.

5. *Christian Constitutional form of government.* Our unique form of government, based on Biblical principles, provides the road on which the wheel of economic progress can turn with great efficiency.

The American government, rooted in the Law and the Gospel, on the Christian idea of God and man, provided an environment of freedom with order in which production and exchange could flourish. Under the traditional American system, it was the duty of government to protect private property, to punish theft and fraud, but not to provide for the people's economic needs.

Under our Constitution, the government was meant to be strictly limited in its functions and cost – to have just enough power to guard the citizen's rights, but not the power to interfere with honest economic activities.

6. *Local business.* The seed of local self-govern-

ment is planted by individuals who assume responsibility for governing themselves, their homes, their churches and their local civil government. By the same token, small businesses (that may grow into large businesses) are started locally by the same kind of responsible individuals – people who do not depend on someone else to employ them, but who save their money, get an idea for serving others, become self-employed, win customers, and then employ others. This is how new jobs are created. This is how our economy grows.

7. *Voluntary union.* The same spirit of Christian brotherhood that brought the thirteen colonies into voluntary union more than 200 years ago also brought buyers and sellers, producers and consumers, into voluntary union across the nation through the American marketplace.

The Constitution created what became the world's largest "common market" or "free market," without tariff barriers. This allowed each person in each state to do what he could do best, and exchange it for the production of others, using honest money as the medium of exchange.

THE MARKET

When these Biblical principles are expressed by a group of people living in a community, they spontaneously form a "market." We see a market tangibly illustrated in a marketplace where people come together to buy and sell, a basic institution of local business that has existed since Old Testament times.

Sensing God's principle of individuality, people specialize – arrange for the division of labor. Each uses his private property to produce what he believes he can do best. Expressing Christian character, each person seeks to make a good product or render a useful service – one that will meet other peoples' needs – and each person trusts others to do the same.

Manifesting the principle of voluntary union, they come together in a spirit of cooperation and engage in voluntary exchange. All are free to offer any product or service they wish – unless government has determined that it will be extremely harmful to customers, and a law prohibits its sale. All also are free to offer their product or service at any price they wish, but they cannot force anyone to buy.

The whole process is non-coercive. Everyone who exchanges goods or services in a free market does so voluntarily, and everyone believes he benefits from the exchange. A producer sells only because he wants the money the customer is willing to pay more than he wants what he has produced. A customer buys only because he wants the producer's goods or service more than he wants the amount of money that the producer is charging.

Children should develop a growing understanding of the free market, how it works in a community, a nation, and in the world via international trade without tariff barriers. In chapter 5, "Social Cooperation and the Market," in her *Free Market Economics Syllabus*, Bettina B. Greaves offers a fascinating in-depth explanation of the market, of how it allows vast numbers of people to work together effectively in meeting each others' needs – in a wonderful way that would be impossible under centralized, authoritarian human direction.

Mrs. Greaves also explains how research might be assigned into the historical development of markets.

THE MARKET PRICE

In her next chapter is an excellent explanation of how prices are determined in a free market, by a process that resembles an auction. "The lower the price, the more would-be-buyers will be bidding, and the fewer, if any, owners, will be willing to sell. As the bids rise, less eager buyers will drop out of the bidding; more owners will enter the auction as higher prices make selling seem more advantageous. The object is to find the 'market price,' . . . the price at which the number of items offered and the number of items wanted are the same."

Children should understand that there is a sound principle behind this economic process that brings supply and demand into balance, and that just as over-priced products result in unsaleable merchandise, so over-priced labor results in unemployment. Students should also realize that the greater the supply of any particular kind of good or service (including the kind of service they can offer in the marketplace), the more the price will tend to go down; and the greater the demand for any kind of good or service, the more the price will tend to go up.

GOLD IS HONEST MONEY

As young people grow in their grasp of economics, they need to develop an understanding of money. Money is simply a response to a need that results from specialization – the need for a means of exchange. Children can readily understand that, historically, exchange began with barter, but that it is far more practical to have something generally accepted as a means of exchange that is relatively small, light and enduring.

True money is not a piece of paper with no inherent value, but a *commodity* – something of genuine value in the marketplace, whether cattle, coconuts, shells, silver or gold – all of which have been used as money. Note that in Old Testament times, money was silver or gold, a precious metal. This is money based on principle, and it was the only kind of money in which our Founding Fathers had confidence.

Paper money is convenient, but it is honest money only when each paper dollar is redeemable in a specified amount of precious metal. For most of America's history, our central government followed this practice; America was on the "gold standard," and there was never any prolonged inflation.

The fact that our central government was obliged to redeem all paper money on demand for a certain amount of gold served to discipline our government officials not to issue an excessive amount of paper dollars. Since we have abandoned the gold standard, the U.S. Treasury is no longer obliged to practice genuine self-government in issuing paper money. Our central government has continued to spend more than it collected in taxes, and has made up the difference by creating paper money out of thin air, thus generating inflation.

BASICS OF BANKING

Many years ago, as barter gave way to money exchanges, people looked for a safe place to store their money, and bankers offered this service for a fee. Gradually, banks began to act not only as warehouses for money but as intermediaries between savers who were willing to lend, and others who wanted to borrow.

As banking has become more complex, there have been increasing opportunities for banks to engage in ethically questionable practices, which Mrs. Greaves explains in her chapter on "Money, Credit and Banking." Certainly the entire field of money and banking presents special challenges for bankers, businessmen and government officials to express the truly honest, dependable qualities of Christian character.

TEN PILLARS OF CHRISTIAN ECONOMIC WISDOM

America's original prosperity resulted not only from the understanding and practice of basic economic principles, but from freedom from a variety of economic misconceptions, which have become prevalent in modern times. Such misconceptions are exposed and corrected in a statement we call The Ten Pillars of Christian Economic Wisdom, which we have adapted from a remarkably clear summary by Fred G. Clark and Richard S. Rimanoczy of the main ideas in their best-selling little book, "How We Live." (Their original "pillars" are shown in quotes.)

PILLAR NO. 1

Everything has a cost that must be paid.
Everything we need for our spiritual and material welfare comes from God; but we must use our God-given energies to transform God-created natural resources into useful goods.

"Nothing in our material world can come from nowhere or go nowhere, nor can it be free: Everything in our economic life has a source, a destination and a cost that must be paid."

Even in our spiritual life, everything has a cost that must be paid. Salvation is "free" only because it is a gift to us from Jesus, who paid the price. Spiritually and economically speaking, it is impossible to get something for nothing. A loving God does not give His creation a free lunch. "If any would not work, neither should he eat."

PILLAR NO. 2

God is the source of man's ability to produce.
The ultimate source of all good is God, and He empowers man to produce goods in order to "have dominion" over the earth.

"Government is never a source of goods. Everything produced is produced by the people, and everything that government gives to the people, it must first take from the people."

It is evil for government, when transferring goods from one group to another, not to disclose the source and extent of the sacrifice involved. As government increasingly takes from the most productive in order to give to the least productive, it violates the property rights protected by the Decalogue – "Thou shalt not steal" and "Thou shalt not covet thy neighbor's house." (Ex. 20:15, 19)

PILLAR NO. 3

Only earned money is honest; inflation is dishonest.

The *love* of money is evil, but money itself is simply a medium of exchange, something generally accepted in exchange for other things that man needs or wants.

"The only valuable money that government has to spend is that money taxed or borrowed out of the people's earnings. When government decides to spend more than it has thus received, that extra unearned money is created out of thin air, through the banks, and, when spent, takes on value only by reducing the value of all money, savings and insurance."

The earned money is "honest," the unearned money "dishonest." It is evil to dilute the value of the people's money except with their knowledge and consent; and a people with Christian character will not give their consent. Inflation existed even before the prophet Amos decried "making the shekel great" (i.e., adulterating silver with base metals); but a Christian people, determined to keep their government from spending more than it collects, could stop inflation once and for all.

PILLAR NO. 4

Wages should be determined by voluntary exchange in a free market.

In a Christian free economy, neither government nor any government-sanctioned institution will be allowed to control what people pay for goods or services. "The laborer is worthy of his wages," but those wages should not be determined arbitrarily by government or a labor union.

Instead, they should be determined by supply and demand through the free market, in which all exchanges are strictly voluntary: wages and prices must be mutually agreeable to buyers and sellers of good and services. If employees are allowed to force wages above the free market level, prices for the goods they produce will become so high that customers will not pay them, and unemployment will result.

"In our modern exchange economy, all payroll and employment come from customers, and the only worthwhile job security is customer security; if there are no customers, there can be no payroll and no jobs."

PILLAR NO. 5

Job security depends upon customer security.

"Customer security can be achieved by the worker only when he cooperates with management in doing the things that win and hold customers. Job security, therefore, is a partnership problem that can be solved only in a spirit of understanding and cooperation."

False social philosophies, such as Marxism and various forms of socialism, have created needless friction between employers and employees, often by misrepresenting the facts, exaggerating the size of profits and underestimating the percentage of corporate income paid out to employees. (Of the money available for distribution between owners and employees in a typical corporation, 90% goes to employees, 10% to owners.)

Employers and employees should work together in a spirit of brotherhood and trust; both should view customers as "neighbors" to be loved, by providing them with the best possible products and personal service.

PILLAR NO. 6

Wages must be related to productivity.

"Because wages are the principal cost of everything, widespread wage increases without corresponding increases in production, simply increases the cost of everybody's living." It is evil for employees to extort unearned wages which are added to the selling price of goods and becomes a burden on everybody.

It is also evil for government to set "minimum wages," which always create unemployment, especially for the least educated and least experienced workers. God gives His sanction to the free market, under which wages rise as high as possible without creating unemployment.

For those who are jobless because they are unskilled, private charity or private enterprise can provide needed training. "Give a man a fish and he can live for a day, teach him how to fish and he can live a lifetime." "The noblest charity is to prevent a man from accepting charity; the best alms are to enable a man to dispense with alms."

PILLAR NO. 7

Increasing output per worker benefits everybody.

"The greatest good for the greatest number means, in its material sense, the greatest productivity per worker."

The Christian way to increase wages is to increase output per worker—by working harder, smarter or more cooperatively, by introducing better management methods, and by increasing the quantity and quality of tools which the workers use.

It is evil for anyone to impede the production

from which material blessings flow. To maximize production, we must cultivate the character for Christian self-government and respect for private property in the home, church, and school, then maximize human incentives—to work, save, invent and invest—and reward workers according to their productivity. "As you sow, so shall you also reap."

PILLAR NO. 8

God created the three basic factors of production—natural resources, human energy and tools.

All productivity is based on three factors: 1) God-created natural resources, whose form, place and condition are changed by the expenditure of 2) God-given human energy (both muscular and mental), with the aid of 3) tools, which are based on ideas God imparts to increase human productivity. (The Clark-Rimanoczy 8th Pillar, with "God-given" added)

From a Christian and practical perspective, each factor is indispensable, and the mental aspect of human energy includes entrepreneurial and managerial skills and the gift of invention. It is evil to infer that there is any substitute for the natural resources which God provides, for conscientiously applied human energy, or for the tools which man must have to fulfill the Dominion Mandate.

PILLAR NO. 9

Tools are created when individuals deny themselves, save and invest.

"Tools are the only one of these three factors that man can increase without limit, and tools come into being in a free society only when there is a reward for the temporary self-denial that people must practice in order to channel part of their earnings away from purchases that produce immediate comfort and pleasure, and into new tools of production."

For a nation to build a maximum tool kit, it must be privately owned, and individual men and women must practice Christian self-government

and Christian character, to make possible the needed invention and investment. There must also be proper payment for the use of tools. People who invest in tools (by investing in American industry) not only increase productivity and wages, they create jobs.

Payment for those who *create* the jobs is just as morally worthy as payment for those who *do* the jobs. Even as "the laborer is worthy of his hire," so the inventor is worthy of his profit. Excessive taxes on profits hurt everyone.

PILLAR NO. 10

High productivity is the effect of a free people in competition with each other.

"The productivity of the tools — that is, the efficiency of the human energy applied in connection with their use — has always been highest in a competitive society in which the economic decisions are made by millions of progress-seeking individuals, rather than in a state-planned society in which those decisions are made by a handful of all-powerful people, regardless of how well-meaning, unselfish, sincere and intelligent these people may be."

Jesus said, "You shall know the truth, and the truth shall make you free" — free from sin, and free from the tyranny of a state-planned economy. In a Christian free society, people release more productive energy — not only in using tools but in inventing tools, and in discovering God-given natural resources.

In a Christian free society, men will also have more faith to make high-risk but God-guided investments, and will exhibit more entrepreneurial courage, even as Abraham "by faith when he was called out ... obeyed and went out, not knowing whither he went..." Most of all, in a Christian free economy, men and women will obey Jesus' command, "Seek ye first the kingdom of God and His righteousness, and all these things shall be added unto you." This is the ultimate secret of prosperity.

Diagram III

Two Economic Blessings of God's Word

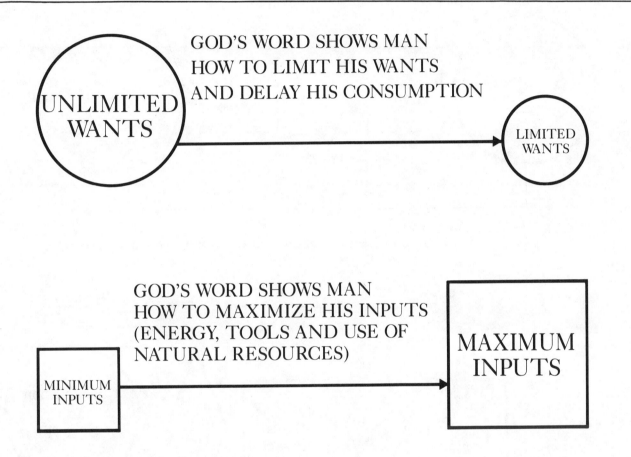

GOD'S WORD SHOWS MAN
HOW TO LIMIT HIS WANTS
AND DELAY HIS CONSUMPTION

UNLIMITED WANTS → LIMITED WANTS

GOD'S WORD SHOWS MAN
HOW TO MAXIMIZE HIS INPUTS
(ENERGY, TOOLS AND USE OF
NATURAL RESOURCES)

MINIMUM INPUTS → MAXIMUM INPUTS

DIAGRAM IV
THE WANT-SATISFACTION CHAIN IN TWO KINDS OF SOCIETIES

HOW CHRISTIAN FAITH, CHARACTER AND FREEDOM AFFECT WANTS, INPUTS AND ECONOMIC SATISFACTION

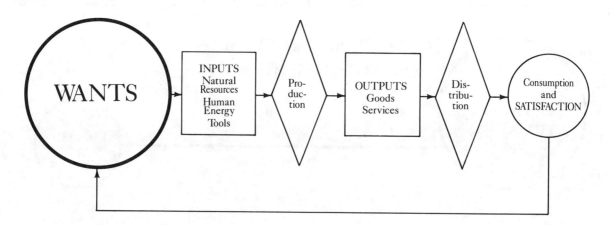

Want-Satisfaction Chain in a Secular Culture with Limited Economic Freedom

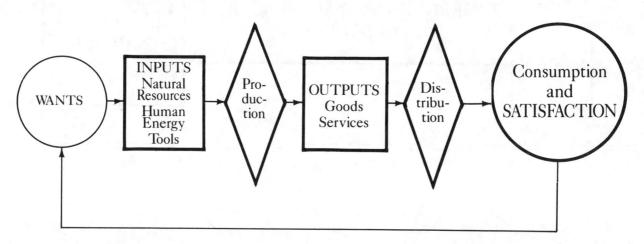

Want-Satisfaction Chain in a Christian Culture with a Free Economy

THE WANT-SATISFACTION CHAIN

Professional academic economists, such as those from the various university economic departments associated with the Joint Council on Economic Education (a private group, the dominant economic education organization that seeks to improve the teaching of economics in America's schools), generally agree that the basic economic problem is *scarcity* – the consequence of unlimited human wants and limited resources, resulting in limited human economic satisfaction.

Secular economic educators seek to instruct the upcoming generation with a curriculum that emphasizes this point, grade after grade, in different ways, from the first through the twelfth, simply by presenting *information* about it. By contrast, the Principle Approach says it is not enough merely to present information, there must be individual *transformation* – internal changes wrought by the power of the living Christ through the Word of God, the development of Christian character, and the internalization of Biblical principles of government and economics.

We begin by acknowledging that unredeemed, sinful man does appear to have virtually unlimited wants, and seems to have access only to limited resources – in terms of natural resources, human energy and ideas, and capital or tools. We also maintain that there is no merely human or secular answer to this problem.

Only as man receives Christ, and grows in spiritual understanding and Christian character, is the carnal yearning for more and more things of this world effectively limited, and the ability to delay consumption strengthened. And only as man receives Christ, and acknowledges God as the great Provider, will there be a growing faith in God's unlimited ability to meet legitimate human needs. Thus the great gulf between man's wants and resources is narrowed.

Diagram III, "Two Economic Blessings of God's Word" on p. 411 illustrates the truth that the Word of God shows man how to limit his wants and delay his consumption – not to devour the "seed corn," which is needed to grow next year's crop. Those who learn, with the Apostle Paul, "how to be abased," will rejoice while they live modestly, practicing self-denial without feeling self-pity. Besides, if they live in a free society, they know that those who are frugal for a time, save their money and invest it, will end up with greater wealth than those who "waste their substance in riotous living." (Luke 15:13)

Diagram III visualizes the fact that God's Word shows man how to maximize his economic inputs – his human energy, supply of tools, and his use of natural resources. As men receive Christ, study the Word, and are uplifted in prayer, then procrastination and sloth give way to diligent effort and willingness to perform even menial tasks, and God-given mental and physical energy is not dissipated by alcohol, drugs, or sensual indulgence. Turning with the mind of Christ in faith that God has an answer to every problem, men invent better tools of production. Certain that God in His Providence has provided well for man's needs, men are inspired to find and process more natural resources, and to discover practical uses for resources which, to uninspired men, have no value.

TWO KINDS OF SOCIETIES

Diagram IV, "The Want-Satisfaction Chain in Two Kinds of Societies," is really a more sophisticated and complete version of the lower part of page 401 – "Production in a Christian Culture." In a secular culture with limited economic freedom, men are unredeemed and undisciplined, human wants for goods and services loom large, but inputs in the production process (natural resources, human energy and tools) seem relatively small. Hence outputs of goods are also small, and so is the amount available for distribution and consumption, resulting in limited human satisfaction. And dissatisfaction is heightened by the carnal mind's envy and ingratitude.

What the chart does not show is the impact this materialistic sequence of economic activities tends to have on the uninformed and unprincipled citizens' view of government. Unless people possess strong Christian character and understand and practice sound economic principles, when their wants appear unlimited and their resources limited, they may turn to government, as if it were God, a source of good, and could satisfy their wants without cost or effort – not understanding Pillars #1 and #2 in the Ten Pillars of Christian Economic Wisdom, on pages 408–410. This false belief greatly contributes to the creation of the welfare state, with its high taxes and inflation, lowered productivity, and weakened, dependent welfare recipients.

By contrast, in a Christian culture with a free economy, Christian self-government and self-denial effectively limit man's wants, and enable him to delay his consumption, while Christian character maximizes man's productive efforts. Thus he saves more. And emboldened by the Lord, he is willing to invest his savings, and risk losing them, in order to generate new tools of production that will multiply his human energies. (How the internal individual qualities of Christian character give rise to external individual property is explained in Diagram 4a, "The Christian Principle of Private Property," p. 45.) Simultaneously, the incentives of individual economic liberty (freedom to keep the fruits of one's labors and investments in the form of wages, salaries, royalties and profits), also prompt men to exert more productive human energy, invent and invest in better tools, and to find and process more natural resources. This maximizes inputs.

Production – in fields, factories, warehouses, offices and shops – is maximized not only because inputs are increased but because the Christian character of individual workers, their voluntary union and cooperation, and their freedom from excessive restrictions on their productive efforts – imposed by over-intrusive government and monopolistic labor unions – greatly increases output per worker.

In turn, *outputs* of goods and services are increased, and more goods are available for distribution. One reason: the voluntary processes of the free market determine wages and prices; this keeps workers from pricing themselves out of the market, leaving untapped natural resources still in the ground, and unsold goods on retailers' shelves and showrooms. Another reason more goods are available for distribution in a Christian free society: who gets what is produced is determined voluntarily, according to the Biblical principle, "as you sow, so shall you also reap." Government is not engaged in an arbitrary, coercive redistribution process in which a sizeable part of the total labor force is not engaged in production but in redistributing what others have produced. (Because these redistributors are not producing, and because they themselves must be paid, much less is available for actual distribution and consumption.)

Net economic result in a Christian free society: there is more production and consumption, more money and goods available for charitable distribution, and more individual satisfaction. Since workers can produce the necessities of life with fewer hours of toil, some will choose not to consume more but to work less at economic production, and devote more time to other things, which also brings satisfaction. Satisfaction is further increased by the Christian conviction that gratitude is a Godly quality, and that men should continually praise their Creator, the Giver of all good, and thank the Lord for all worthwhile goods – material as well as spiritual.

WHY SOME IMMIGRANTS PROSPER

To be completely honest about economic outcomes in the real world, we must acknowledge that certain immigrant groups, especially Jews, Japanese and Chinese, have achieved well above average economic success in America, even though they were exceedingly poor on arrival. They were not Christians, they faced racial and religious prejudice, yet they flourished in the American free economy. Why? Because our Christian form of government and the economic system it permits and encourages, do in fact provide a remarkable measure of equal opportunity. And such groups as Jews, Japanese and Chinese, even before coming to America, developed highly productive cultural traits – deep parental concern for their children's schooling, determination to get the best possible higher education, refusal to have children outside of marriage, rejection of government welfare, willingness to work hard even at low-status jobs, and a disciplined commitment to save, invest and launch enterprises.

These traits, in their highest expression, were once widely manifested by Christians in America; but today, after generations of secular humanist public school education, which develops the character for socialism, the vast majority of nominal Christians in this country manifest less of the prosperity-producing traits than the most economically successful immigrant groups. If they can do that well, without Christ, by approximating traditional Christian characterisitcs, think how well born-again believers should do economically, once they begin to fully express the Principle Approach in every aspect of their lives!

414

THE PRINCIPLE APPROACH TO AMERICAN CHRISTIAN ECONOMICS

DEFINITIONS

Economics: Greek roots – house and law. "The management, regulation and government of a family or household . . . A frugal and judicious use of money, or management of public affairs." (Webster 1828 Dictionary)

The discipline that studies how men, by their choices and labor, use natural resources to produce goods and services to satisfy human needs and wants, with maximum efficiency; a study of the ways in which men produce, distribute and consume goods and services under different economic and governmental systems – how the economy is managed and regulated either by the coercive powers of a political elite or by the voluntary decisions of the entire citizenry, subject to laws against theft and fraud.

Christian Economics: The discipline that studies the application of Biblical principles or laws to the production, distribution and consumption of goods and services; how men choose to govern themselves, by God's law and love, to produce and exchange the things they want in a free society; how men use God-given natural resources, ideas and energy to meet their human needs and glorify Him.

American Christian Economics: Christian economics as it appeared historically and governmentally in the United States – in a society based upon individual liberty and stewardship, and a culture that encouraged invention, saving, private charity and a frugal and judicious use of money; the kind of economy made possible by a Christian form of government expressing itself in the United States Constitution, framed to protect private property, economic freedom, voluntary exchange, and a sound currency.

COURSE GOALS

1. To teach the rudiments (first principles) of God's economy.

2. To develop the Christian self-government and character needed to apply the principles of God's Word to resolve the spiritual and economic problem of unlimited wants and limited resources.

3. To value and practice the Biblical principles of individuality, local self-government, character, private property and voluntary exchange as the basis of a free market economy under a Christian form of civil government.

COURSE OVERVIEW

I.   The Rudiments of God's Economy
    A. Factors of production in a Christian culture
        1. God-given natural resources
        2. God-given energy
        3. God-given ideas for tools
        4. God's Providence in man's material welfare
    B. Factors of production in a secular culture in contrast with a Christian culture.

II. The Wheel of Progress in a Christian Economy
    A. The hub of God-given liberty
    B. The rim of stewardship under God's law
    C. The spokes:
        1. Individual enterprise
        2. Economic self-government
        3. Christian character
        4. Private property
        5. Local business
        6. Voluntary union
    D. The road bed: A Christian Constitutional form of government
    E. The free market
    F. Money

III. The Ten Pillars of Christian Economic Wisdom
    A. Everything has a cost that must be paid
    B. Only earned money is honest; inflation is dishonest
    C. Wages should be determined by voluntary exchange in a free market
    D. Job security depends upon customer security
    E. Wages must be related to productivity
    F. Increasing output per worker benefits everybody
    G. Tools are created when individuals deny themselves, save and invest
    H. High productivity is the effect of a free people in competition with others.

IV. The Want-Satisfaction Chain in Two Kinds of Societies
    A. Two economic blessings of God's Word
    B. How Christian faith, character and freedom affect economic satisfaction.

CURRICULUM SUGGESTIONS

INTRODUCING CHILDREN TO ECONOMIC IDEAS

Every child will differ in his interest in and ability to grasp economic ideas, but to give some general guidance regarding the concepts explained in the overview which might be introduced at different grade levels, we have prepared the following summary.

PRIMARY GRADES
K-3

There is no doubt that basic economic concepts can be presented to and grasped by small children in kindergarten and developed through the primary grades. For example, the five year old can understand the fact that people have wants for both goods and services, that these wants seem never-ending, that God gives people everything they need to satisfy their essential wants – but people must *work* to take the things God has given and change them into a form that meets their needs – for example, for food, clothing and shelter.

Again, the primary grade student can appreciate that in earlier times the family was a more complete, self-sufficient economic unit – that father, mother and their children, working on their family farm, produced most of what they needed for their own use, and did not have to buy much from others.

The small child also can comprehend that today there is more specialization, a greater division of labor (God's Principle of Individuality), and that now most of the things the family consumes are bought in the marketplace, where buyers and sellers come together voluntarily (God's principle of voluntary union.)

WHY DAD AND MOM WORK

The child in kindergarten or first grade also can grasp the fact that purchases in the marketplace require money income, and that is one reason Dad goes to work. He is a *producer*, is paid in money for producing goods or services for others (which is one way he serves them and shows his love for others).

Mother is also a producer. Whether or not she has a paid job, she is just as important economically as Dad; she is producing services in the home (which is one way she serves others, and shows her love for them). So are the children producers, when they straighten up their room, and help Mom or Dad with chores in the house or yard.

Jesus declared in John 5:7, "My Father worketh hitherto, and I work." Children can be taught that God is the source of all *good work* and that "they which have believed in God might be careful to maintain good works" through faith, because "these things are good and profitable unto men." (Titus 3:8) The right attitude toward work can be taught by the parent's example and through literature that conveys the proper spirit or consciousness of *work*. For example, the following poem could be committed to memory by parent and child:

WORK

Work!
Thank God for the might of it –
The ardor, the urge, the delight of it;
Work that springs from the heart's desire
Setting the brain and soul on fire.
Oh, what is so good as the heat of it?
And what is so glad as the beat of it?
And what is so kind as the stern command
Challenging brain and heart and hand?

Work!
Thank God for the swing of it
For the clamoring, hammering ring of it.
Passion and labor daily hurled
On the mighty anvils of the world.
Oh, what is so fierce as the flame of it?
And what is so huge as the aim of it?
Thundering on through dearth and doubt
Calling the plan of the Maker out.
Work, the Titan; Work, the friend,
Shaping the earth to a glorious end,
Draining the swamps and blasting the hills,
Doing whatever the Spirit wills –
Rending a continent apart
To answer the dream of the Master heart.
Thank God for a world where none may shirk.
Thank God for the splendor of work.

(Selected)

The Busy Man

If you want to get a favor done
   By some obliging friend,
And want a promise safe and sure
   On which you may depend
Don't go to him who always has
   Much leisure time to plan,
But if you want your favor done,
   Just ask the busy man.

The man of leisure never has
   A moment he can spare;
He's busy "putting off" until
   His friends are in despair;
But he whose every waking hour
   Is crowded full of work,
Forgets the art of wasting time –
   He cannot stop to shirk.

So when you want a favor done,
   And want it right away,
Go to the man who constantly
   Works twenty hours a day.

He'll find a moment, sure, somewhere
   That has not other use,
And fix you while the idle man
   Is framing an excuse.

                (Selected)

Children in the first few grades can also discover how *tools* multiply human energies, and make it possible to produce things that could not be made otherwise. They can see how Dad uses carpentry tools, how Mom uses kitchen and laundry tools, that a power saw will cut wood for the fireplaces far faster than a handsaw, and that to invent the power saw took more good ideas (which come from God), and to buy it took money (which requires the discipline of Christian character, in order to save).

Primary school children can draw their own versions of Diagram I, p. 401, or create variations by cutting out pictures from newspapers and magazines, both to show how progressively more advanced tools help create improved goods, and to illustrate the different kinds of resources and tools needed to produce food, clothing, shelter, means of transportation, etc.

At first, the child's economic thinking will focus on himself and others in his immediate world, at home and at school. Then he will look at people as members of groups, and by the second or third grade he will also see producers and customers as members of communities. Soon he will begin to envision an extended community of farmers and manufacturers distributing goods through the various retailers in town, some offering services rather than goods.

SELF-DISCIPLINE IN WANTS

In the first few grades, children can grasp the fact that even though God is the all-sufficient Provider, the family does not have enough money to buy everything that everyone wants, that we must exercise Christian self-discipline concerning our wants. We must ask God's guidance in making wise decisions as to what goods and services we will buy with our present income, and recognize that when we use our money to buy one thing we will not have it left to buy something else.

By the second or third grade, children can grasp in some detail the concept of specialization of labor, and begin "career education" – what people do in different occupations, the special skills and education needed, why some occupations pay more than others, and why specialization requires interdependence, voluntary exchange of goods and services, and the Christian character required to work well with others.

Before children are out of the primary grades, they should be taught to distinguish between goods and services produced by the private sector and those produced by government, that government is supported with income from taxes, that in a Christian country government's function should be restricted primarily to national defense and the protection of life, liberty and property – and that only by limiting government's services can we hold down taxes.

ELEMENTARY-INTERMEDIATE GRADES 4-8

By the time children leave the primary and enter the elementary grades, they should be ready to look at the economy of their nation, and grasp some relatively "adult" economic concepts. While they may have been introduced to Diagram II earlier (p. 404), by the fourth or fifth grade, they should be prepared to perceive with some clarity the application of the seven Biblical principles of government to economics, as explained in the text accompanying "The Wheel of Progress in a Christian Free Economy." (p. 405)

At first, children may need help from their teacher in understanding each spoke, the rim and the road on which the wheel rides. The concepts here are profound, and should be studied year after year, continuing through high school.

Fourth, fifth and sixth graders also can return to Diagram I (p. 401), especially the bottom half, with growing appreciation and comprehension. The lower part of Diagram I challenges the student to see why a Christian culture and a free economy are more productive than a secular culture with limited economic freedom.

The bottom of Diagram I can be examined with insights from Diagram II (p. 404), and it can be explained that this "Wheel of Economic Progress in a Christian Economy" has its opposite economic manifestation – spoke for spoke and point for point, in a wordly culture with restrictions on economic liberty – whether these are the moderate restrictions of the contemporary U.S. "mixed economy" (i.e., a mix of capitalism and socialism, really a hampered market economy), or the more severe restrictions of English or European socialism, or the virtual elimination of economic freedom under Marxist communism. (A comparison of economic systems is so important and challenging, it should continue throughout high school and college.)

STUDYING ECONOMIC HISTORY

In upper elementary grades, students also can dig deeper into economic history, and make comparisons of how wants, and the means of satisfying them, have changed. Between early colonial times and the present, how have tools – pounding, cutting, throwing, lifting and carrying tools – improved? What influence did Christianity in America exert on invention and investment of advanced tools, and especially agricultural tools? How did improved farm tools combine with private property and Christian character to make American farmers the most productive on earth?

In these grades, the study of geography also will focus more on economics, as children explore in a modern atlas the importance of different regions of the U.S., and of different nations of the world, in their contributions of natural resources, and their suitability for different kinds of agriculture, manufacturing and trade.

For boys and girls to grow in their understanding of the American economic system as a market economy, they must learn that *markets* are a key institution for deciding what to produce and to whom it should be marketed. Since customers are free to spend income as they wish, they are able to tell producers what they want produced.

Children also should learn that economic *competition* is essentially healthy, and must be undertaken in a Christian spirit – with each producer or distributor simply doing his best to serve customers, providing quality goods and services that respond to customers' needs and desires at the lowest possible prices.

At the same time, students should discover that the same principles of demand and supply that determine prices of goods in a free economy also determines wages and salaries, and that workers sell their services to employers in order to earn income with which to buy goods and services.

UNDERSTANDING ECONOMIC FREEDOM

In the sixth, seventh and eighth grades, boys and girls should be developing a good understanding of the *freedom* that characterizes a Christian free economy: the producer is free to own property and produce what he thinks customers will buy; the employee is free to sell his services to producers in exchange for wages or salary; the customer is free to buy what he wishes and thus direct what products and services will be offered; the inventor is free to create a new tool or product and seek patent protection for his invention; the investor is free to save his money and invest it in any enterprise which he thinks may prove profitable.

But our young people must also understand that in our time there have been increasing restrictions on these freedoms, and that even under ideal circumstances, for each of these economic rights or freedoms there is always an individual responsibility and often a risk, which points to the need for participants in a free economy to develop Christian faith and character.

At the sixth grade and Junior High levels, children should be ready to grasp the Ten Pillars of Christian Economic Wisdom (p. 408). There is so much substance and challenge in these Ten Pillars, they should be studied throughout the high school experience.

HIGH SCHOOL
GRADES 9-12

As young Christians advance through the high school years, and prepare to assume the responsibilities of adult citizenship, they need to understand the economic difficulties America faces today, and to consider how these can be resolved through the application of Biblical principles.

Their study of American history should cover the major negative changes in this century, beginning with the federal income tax and continuing with the Franklin Roosevelt "New Deal" and the Lyndon Johnson "Great Society" that transformed our free market economy and limited Constitutional government with balanced federal budgets into a hampered market economy and welfare state with huge year-after-year deficits.

At the high school level, young people should gain an understanding of social cooperation and voluntary union as manifested in the free market; of the entrepreneur and the profit and loss system; of labor, wages and employment; and of money, credit and banking. They should clarify and enlarge their developing understanding of the basic institutions of private property, markets and companies – and how they are organized through the private, individual, decentralized decision-making of producers and customers.

BASIC ECONOMIC BOOKS

In the last years of high school, students should be able to take economic items from newspapers or newsweeklies, and write thoughtful interpretations based on Biblical principles. And they should be able to explain in convincing detail the four diagrams in this presentation.

High School students should be able to explain how the insights in Diagrams III and IV (pp. 411 and 412) have been put to work by those American immigrant groups which have been most economically successful, and give specific explanations of how these insights could be applied by the entire American people today – how reduced wants would mean more personal savings, more investments, less government spending – and how the expression of Christian character, together with the increased incentives of lower tax rates, would boost production, lift living standards, and help balance the federal budget.

In senior high school, students also should study the economies of other countries, analyze the relationship between their religion, character, culture and civil government on one hand, and their standard of living on the other. Students should take special note of the role of civil government in each country's economy, the degree of economic freedom, and the success of the people in meeting their economic goals.

BIBLIOGRAPHY OF ECONOMIC REFERENCES

Bastiat, Frederic, *The Law*, Foundation for Economic Education, New York, 1979.

Bradford, William, *Of Plymouth Plantation*, Edited by Samuel Eliot Morison, The Modern Library, New York, 1952.

Campbell, Charles, *Economics and Freedom*, Haverford House, Pennsylvania, 1964.

Carson, Clarence B., *The American Tradition*, Foundation for Economic Education, New York, 1964.

———, *A Basic History of the United States*, Foundation for Economic Education, New York, 1983.

Chamberlain, John, *The Enterprising Americans*, Foundation for Economic Education, New York, 1963.

———, *The Roots of Capitalism*, Foundation for Economic Education, New York, 1959.

Chilton, David, *Productive Christians in An Age of Guilt Manipulators*, Institute for Christian Economics, Texas, 1981.

Clark, Fred and Richard Rimanoczy, *How We Live*, American Economic Foundation, Ohio, 1976.

Clawson, Elmer, *Our Economy: How It Works*, Addison-Wesley Publishing Co., California and Maine, 1980.

Fairchild, Fred and Thomas Shelly, *Understanding Our Free Economy*, D. Van Nostrand Co., New York, 1956.

Flick, Frank, *Two Worlds*, Flick-Reedy Educational Enterprises, Illinois, 1967.

Greaves, Bettina B., *Free Market Economics: A High School Syllabus*, Foundation for Economic Education, New York, 1975.

———, *Free Market Economics: A Basic Reader*, Foundation for Economic Education, New York, 1975.

Hartley, E. N., *Ironworks on the Saugus*, University of Oklahoma Press, Oklahoma, 1957.

Hazlitt, Henry, *Economics in One Lesson*, Foundation for Economic Education, New York, 1946.

Kershner, Howard, *God, Gold and Government*, Prentice-Hall, Inc., New Jersey, 1957.

Lindsell, Harold, *Free Enterprise: A Judeo-Christian Defense*, Tyndale House, Illinois, 1982.

Murray, Charles, *Losing Ground*, Basic Books, Inc., New York, 1984.

North, Gary, *The Dominion Covenant: An Economic Interpretation of the Bible*, Institute for Christian Economics, Texas, 1982.

———, *An Introduction to Christian Economics*, Institute for Christian Economics, Texas, 1974.

Novak, Michael, *The Spirit of Democratic Capitalism*, Simon and Schuster, New York, 1982.

Opitz, Edmund A., *Religion and Capitalism: Allies, Not Enemies*, Arlington House, New York, 1970.

Richardson, John R., *Christian Economics*, St. Thomas Press, Texas, 1966.

Ropke, William, *A Humane Economy: The Social Framework of the Free Market*, Henry Regnery, Chicago, 1960.

Rose, Tom, *Economics: Principles and Policy from a Christian Perspective*, Mott Media, Michigan, 1977.

Simon, William E., *A Time for Truth*, Berkley Books, New York, 1978.

Sowell, Thomas, *The Economics and Politics of Race*, William Morrow and Company, Inc., New York, 1983.

Taylor, E. L. Hebden, *Economics, Money and Banking: Christian Principles*, The Craig Press, New Jersey, 1968.

EDUCATIONAL ORGANIZATIONS THAT CAN HELP ENRICH YOUR TEACHING OF ECONOMICS

Achievement Basics
P.O. Box 26306
Denver, Colorado 80226
(303) 935-6343

Mrs. Elaine Wainwright, President, produces professional dramatized story cassettes with printed practice materials and sample forms which teach basic free-market economic concepts to children ages nine through young adult. Three levels of educational materials are offered: level one teaches individual productivity and right attitudes toward work; level two explains the stock market – principles of wise investment, business trends and career guidance; level three teaches simple bookkeeping, budgeting, profit and loss incentive, and entrepreneurship. An eight page Guide to assist parents in using these self-teaching resources comes with the package.

The Foundation for Economic Education
Irvington-on-Hudson, New York 10533

A leading organization for developing public understanding of the free market economy, FEE also appreciates the importance of a sound civil government as "the road on which the wheel of economic progress turns." Among the many fine books distributed by FEE is Verna M. Hall's *The Christian History of the Constitution of the United States*. An outstanding book published by FEE is *Free Market Economics: A Syllabus* by Bettina B. Greaves. In her preface she says, "The idea that led to this syllabus (for a high school economics text) was sparked many years ago by Rosalie Slater and Verna Hall on a visit to the Foundation." Mrs. Greaves also has published an excellent companion volume, *Free Market Economics: A Basic Reader*.

FEE conducts 2-day seminars in Irvington and at various locations around the country, and a special 2-week seminar every summer for serious stu-

dents and teachers. It publishes an excellent monthly journal, *The Freeman*.

The Free Enterprise Institute
17575 East Fulton Road
Ada, Michigan 49355
(616) 676-5178

This educational outreach of the Amway company produces films, videotapes and slide programs about the American free enterprise system, including an outstanding exposition of the MMW formula by Amway president Richard DeVos. The Institute also publishes a free *Resource Index*, a comprehensive catalogue of sound economic educational organizations and materials, both print and audio-visual, many grouped according to suggested grade level.

Junior Achievement, Inc.
National Headquarters Office
550 Summer Street
Stamford, CT 06901

Junior Achievement is best known for its local offices that provide volunteer business persons who help young people organize "companies" that simulate adult enterprises – providing youth with the challenges of creating, making and marketing an actual product of their choice. Junior Achievement also assists schools with economic education by offering "business consultants" who volunteer to come into the classroom on a regular basis for such courses as *Project Business*, a supplement to the so-called "social studies" course, which many schools conduct at the high school level, and *Applied Economics*, a 5-day-a-week course taught by the regular teacher with a once-a-week course.

The Mini-Society Program
c/o Dr. Marilyn Kourilsky
UCLA Graduate School of Education
210 Moore Hall
405 Hilgard Avenue
Los Angeles, California 90024

This highly effective instructional method offers three programs – Kinder-Economy (K-2), Mini-Society (3-6) and Max-Economy (7-12). They allow students to actually experience and then resolve economic problems through the creation and development of their own classroom economy. They are not a substitute for teaching Biblical principles of economics; the teacher does not teach in the conventional sense but creates a learning situation and de-briefs students after each session. However, it is an excellent means of helping children understand, in a clear and vivid way, such economic basics as scarcity, costs, prices, profits, supply, demand, competition, money, inflation and the challenges of entrepreneurship.

National Schools Committee for Economic Education
P.O. Box 326
143 Sound Beach Avenue
Old Greenwich, Connecticut 06870
(203) 636-4548

Creates educational materials for elementary through junior high school in the form of charts, pamphlets, comic strip characters and audio-visual aids to explain basic ideas about our economy and the value of free enterprise. Their materials are highly compatible with the economic primer *How We Live*, the MMW formula, and the Ten Pillars of Economic Wisdom. Example of a cartoon: a poster headed "Better Tools Mean More Work in Less Time," dramatizes the idea that a power saw cuts more fireplace logs than a handsaw. Examples of filmstrips: how young people go into the recording business; how a boy spends his summer washing windows to buy a bicycle; how two teenagers discover the tools and resources it takes to produce a shirt.

CHARLES HULL WOLFE

When I was nine years old, apparently I began to display some writing and speaking abilities which impressed my father, and I recall him saying one day, "When you grow up, I want you to use your talents to fight for our class!"

The remark puzzled me. The only class I could think of was my class in school. I said, "Dad, what do you mean, 'our class'?" My father, who was a gifted intellectual but not very good at communicating with children, said, "The proletariat, of course!"

That left me even more puzzled. I asked for a definition and he explained that our family belonged to the poverty class, that the American capitalist system held us in bondage, and that he wanted me, as an adult, to "fight for the poor." In all innocence, I blurted back, "But Dad, when I grow up, I don't want to be poor, I want to be rich!"

My Dad, a Marxist professor of economics at Columbia University, was so imbued with the notion that poor people are good and rich people are bad that he took my retort as a sign of a juvenile predisposition toward evil. I could see, instantly, from the hurt look on his face that he was deeply wounded.

Through my high school years, Dad continued in his attempts to persuade me of the merits of Marxism – a form of socialism built upon totally materialistic premises and a belief in the inevitability of a class struggle, culminating in a violent revolution that establishes "the dictatorship of the proletariat."

From time to time my Dad would apologize to me and my brothers for raising us in what he viewed as a despicably capitalist country, instead of the nation he most admired, the Soviet Union. Once I recall saying, "Dad, don't feel bad – I love America!" This he saw as gravely misguided patriotism, and it added to his distress.

Unfortunately for him, and his ambitions for his children, my father had allowed my mother to send me and my two brothers, for just a few years, to a Bible-teaching Sunday School; and my mother, while not especially articulate, either as a Christian or an anti-Marxist, had a strong Christian character and a love for all that was good in America. When my father was away, evening after evening, after our homework was done, my brothers and I would gather round the piano and sing with earnest enthusiasm while my mother played traditional evangelical hymns, and then those implicitly Christian patriotic songs that portray God as the "author of liberty," that petition Him to "shed His grace" on America, and that see a link between Christ and ourselves as conscientious citizens – "as He died to make men holy, let us live to make men free!"

While these influences did not prepare me to debate with my father, they seemed to provide a kind of temporary immunization against his Marxist rhetoric: I had a feeling that there was some positive relationship between Christianity and America, that Christian ideas were compatible with the American system, and that quite possibly this was not the case with the ideas that had spawned Marxist-Leninist Communism.

Then during my freshman year in college, when I was a great distance from my parents' home, and confronted with overwhelming physical and emotional difficulties, I was led to the Lord by a deeply thoughtful woman who was convinced that the Truth which is Christ applies to every aspect of life and society, and holds the answer to both personal and social problems. Among the anxieties I shared was my father's insistence that now, as a college student, I was mature enough either to join him as a crusading Marxist or to give him a well-reasoned explanation of why I was marching in an opposite direction.

"Is it right for me as a Christian to be a Marxist?" I asked this studious, insightful Christian woman. She did not answer my question directly, but told me how to get the answer: to read the basic works of Marx, including *Das Kapital*, make careful notes of all his key ideas, then make diligent use of a Bible concordance, to see how Marxist views stack up against the Word of God.

At the time, the Soviet Union was America's ally, Joseph Stalin was seen by an American President as "good old Joe," liberal clergymen tended to be Marxist sympathizers, and conservative ministers had little or nothing to say on the subject, so I was not at all sure what conclusion my study would produce.

As I finished my note-making from Marx's writings, and compared his ideas with those of the Scriptures, the answer became obvious: Marx espoused atheism, saw religion as an opiate, believed that matter is everything, and spirit nothing, rejected marriage and the traditional family, had no use for the private property, voluntary exchange and limited civil government espoused by Old and New Testaments, and was filled with envy toward the "capitalists" – those who had prospered and had the courage to risk their savings by investing them in enterprises which provided jobs, products and services for others.

I shared my study with my father. He commended me for doing my "homework" – a good job of reasoning and research; but he insisted that my foundational premise – that the Bible is true and the final authority – was unsound, and so rejected everything that I had concluded.

Continuing my college studies, I was convinced that I had identified Marxism as a false economic system – one that rejected God as the source of supply, and denied man his God-given freedom – but recognized that I had yet to identify a true economic system, from a Christian perspective. At the end of my first year's study of economics, the professor said we could write our term paper on any subject we chose, as long as it utilized what we had learned in class. I chose "The Economics of Jesus," a topic I had never even heard of before, and researched the entire New Testament, noting any statements or events with economic meaning.

To my surprise, my professor, though not a believer, gave me an A and said he had learned something about Christianity from my paper. Essentially, I concluded that Jesus commended an economic system built around individuals and not the State – good stewards who trusted their heavenly Father to meet their economic needs, who respected private property and voluntary exchange, who rejected unscrupulous money-making, and assumed personal responsibility for acts of charity, in the spirit of the Good Samaritan.

After college, my goal was to become a pastor, but I realized that I was not academically or spiritually ready. Instead, I launched an interim career in broadcasting and advertising, which gave me personal contact with executives of hundreds of corporations, and an insider's view of American business and the media.

At this time, my Marxist father, a protege of Columbia University's Rexford Tugwell (a leading figure in President Franklin Roosevelt's "brain trust") was helping to establish the Social Security System. When my Dad discovered I had entered the advertising business, he was shocked. Locked into Marxian ideology, he called me a "mental prostitute" and agreed with his ultra-liberal professor friends that I had "sold my mind to the highest bidders" – the so-called "capitalist exploiters of the innocent consumers." In turn he disowned me, refused ever to speak to me again.

From these experiences in advertising and with my father and his fellow academicians, I discovered the hostility which American socialists feel toward capitalism, and learned that there is more moral decency in American businessmen that most pastors, professors and journalists realize.

When I finally was ready to leave the advertising business and prepare to become a pastor, God in His Providence led me to the distinguished scholar, Verna M. Hall, who began to share with me America's Christian history and the Biblical principles on which our government and economy were built. I promptly became convinced that the ministry the Lord wanted me to pursue was not in the pulpit but in the press and the classroom – communicating and educating about America's political and economic system from a Scriptural perspective.

With Miss Hall's encouragement, I joined the Senior Staff of the Foundation for Economic Education, which espouses views in keeping with Christian principles. I went on to become President of the American Economic Foundation, then co-founder and Executive Director of Enterprise America – two organizations presenting economic truths and their applications to current issues simply and clearly to sizeable audiences.

During the last few years, my long-time friend, James Rose, the author of this book, asked me to lecture for the American Christian History Institute, presenting the Principle Approach to economics, a subject I continued to develop in lectures for the Mayflower Institute, the Association of Christian Schools International, and Pat Robertson's Freedom Council, which I served as National Education Consultant. Currently I am writing a book on the Christian History of the Constitution.

I believe that God has given me this array of experiences for a purpose: to help me grow in my own understanding of American economics, and to show me how urgent it is for American Christians to become more knowledgeable about economics from a Biblical perspective, in order to fulfill a mission which I believe God has given them – to advance Christian liberty and its effects – civil and economic freedom. In the process, they will do something else: they will lead in restoring America's economy.

ALGEBRA
FROM THE PRINCIPLE APPROACH

BY DAROLD BOOTON
Director of Admissions
The Pilgrim Institute, Collegiate Program
Granger, Indiana

CONTENTS

Teaching Algebra from the Principle Approach

PREFACE

As we begin to examine the science of mathematics from a Christian perspective, we gain a new way of looking at the universe by studying God's nature, character, and works. The science of mathematics is no longer a drably neutral assortment of unrelated facts but an exciting aspect of the divine creation, expressing fundamental, unifying principles.

Looking at the subject from the Principle Approach, we conclude that God is the Author of mathematics and has a purpose for it. The subject becomes far more satisfying because we start from a core of principles, and discover that initially we need master only a small body of information, from which we can gradually build.

This approach greatly simplifies things, and as we follow the methodology, we can teach our students to become independent—to ask their own questions and get their own answers.

Our presentation for teaching Algebra I is organized in the following manner:

1. The definitions of the vocabulary of mathematics are studied in the Scriptures to discover the subject's Biblical source and purpose.

2. The four principles of mathematics are deduced and explained from the above research.

3. An explanation follows as to how these four principles define the scope of the material to be covered and the method through which it is to be taught.

DEFINITIONS OF THE WORDS OF MATHEMATICS

Note: The following definitions are *selected* from Noah Webster's 1828 *American Dictionary of the English Language*.

MATHEMATICS, n. (L. *mathematics*, from Gr. *mathematiche*, from *manthano*, to learn)
The science of quantity; the science which treats of magnitude and number, or of whatever can be measured or numbered. This science is divided into *pure* or *speculative*, which considers quantity abstractly, without relation to matter; and *mixed*, which treats of magnitude as subsisting in material bodies, and is consequently interwoven with phys-

ical considerations. It is the peculiar excellence of *mathematics*, that its principles are demonstrable. Arithmetic, geometry, algebra, trigonometry, and conic sections, are branches of mathematics.

ARITHMETIC, n. (*arithmeo*, to number; *arithmetiche*, the art of numbering; *arithmos*, number; fom *rithmos*, number, rhythm, order, agreement) The science of numbers, or the art of computation. The various operations of arithmetic are performed by addition, subtraction, multiplication and division.

GEOMETRY, n. (*geometria*, *ge*, the earth; *metron*, measure)
Originally and properly, the art of measuring the earth, or any distances or dimensions on it. But geometry now denotes the science of magnitude in general, comprehending the doctrine and relations of whatever is susceptible of augmentation and diminution as the mensuration of lines, surfaces, solids, velocity, weight, etc., with their various relations.

ALGEBRA, n. (*al-jabr*, the reduction of parts to a whole, or fractions to whole numbers, from the verb, which signifies to consolidate)
The science of quantity in general, or universal arithmetic. Algebra is a general method of computation, in which signs and symbols, which are commonly the letters of the alphabet, are made to represents numbers and quantities. It takes an unknown quantity sought, as if granted; and, by means of one or more quantities given, proceeds till the quantity supposed is discovered, by some other known quantity to which it is equal.

TRIGONOMETRY, n. (*trigonos*, a triangle and *metreo*, to measure)
The measuring of triangles; the science of determining the sides and angles of triangles, by means of certain parts which are given. When this science is applied to the solution of plane triangles, it is called *plane* trigonometry; when its application is to spherical triangles, it is called *spherical* trigonometry.

MAGNITUDE, n. (L. *magnitudo*)
1. Extent of dimensions or parts; bulk; size; *applied* to things that have length, breadth or thickness.
2. Greatness, grandeur.

SCIENCE, n. (L. *scientia* from *scio*, to know; Sp. *ciencia;* It. *scienza; Scio* is probably a contracted word)

1. In *a general sense*, knowledge, or certain knowledge; the comprehension or understanding of truth or facts by the mind. The *science* of God must be perfect.
2. In *philosophy*, a collection of the general principles or leading truths relating to any subject. *Pure* science, as the mathematics, is built on self-evident truths; but the term science is also applied to other subjects founded on generally acknowledged truths, as *metaphysics*; or on experiment and observation, as *chemistry* and *natural philosophy*; or even to an assemblage of the general principles of an art, as the science of *agriculture*; the science of *navigation*. *Arts* relate to practice, as painting and sculpture.
—"A principle in *science* is a rule in art."—Playfair
3. Art derived from precepts or built on principles.
—"*Science* perfects genius."—Dryden
4. Any art or species of knowledge.
—"No *science* doth make known the first principles on which it buildeth."—Hooker
5. One of the seven liberal branches of knowledge, viz. grammar, logic, rhetoric, arithmetic, geometry, astronomy and music.
Note: Authors have not always been careful to use the terms *art* and *science* with due discrimination and precision. Music is an *art* as well as a *science*. In general, an *art* is that which depends on practice and performance, and *science* that which depends on abstract or speculative principles. The *theory* of music is a *science*; the *practice* of it an art.

NUMBER, n. (Fr. *nombre*; L. *numerus*; It. Sp. Port. *numero*; Arm. W. *niver*; Ir. *nuimhir*. I know not whether the elements are *Nm* or *Nb*. Probably the radical sense is to speak, name, or tell, as our word *tell*, in the other dialects, is to number. *Number* may be allied to *name*, as the Spaniards use *nombre* for name, and the French word written with the same letters, is *number*. Class Nm. No. 1.)
1. The designation of unit in reference to other units, or in reckoning, counting, enumerating; as, one is the first *number*; a simple *number*.
2. An assemblage of two or more units. Two is a *number* composed of one and one added. Five and three added make the *number* eight. *Number* may be applied to any collection or multitude of units or individuals, and therefore is indefinite, unless defined by the other words or by figures or signs of definite specification.
4. Multitude.
—"*Number* itself importeth not much in armies, where the men are of weak courage."—Bacon
8. In *mathematics*, number is variously distinguished. *Cardinal numbers* are those which express the amount of units; as 1. 2. 3. 4. 5. 6. 7. 8. 9. 10.

Ordinal numbers are those which express order; as first, second, third, fourth, etc.

Determinate number, is that referred to a given unit, as a ternary or three; an *indeterminate* number, is referred to unity in general, and called quantity.

Homogeneal numbers, are those referred to the same units; those referred to different units are termed *heterogeneal*.

Whole numbers, are called *integers*.

A *rational number*, is one commensurable with unity. A number incommensurable with unity, is termed *irrational* or *surd*.

A *prime* or *primitive number*, is divisible only by unity; as three, five, seven, etc.

A *perfect number*, is that whose aliquot parts added together, make the whole number, as 28, whose aliquot parts, 14. 7. 4. 2. 1. make the number 28.

An *imperfect number*, is that whose aliquot parts added together, make more or less than the number. This is abundant or defective; abundant, as 12, whose aliquot parts 6. 4. 3. 2. 1. make 16; or defective, as 16, whose aliquot parts, 8. 4. 2. 1. make 15 only.

A *square number*, is the product of a number multiplied by itself; as, 16 is the square number of 4.

A *cubic number*, is the product of a square number by its root; as, 27 is the product of the square number 9 by its root 3.

Golden number, the cycle of the moon, or revolution of 19 years, in which time the conjunctions, oppositions and other aspects of the moon are nearly the same as they were on the same days of the month 19 years before.

COUNT, vt. (Fr. *conter*, It. *contare*; Sp. Port. *contar*; Arm. *counto* or *contein*. *Qu* the root. The Fr. has *compter*, also from the L. *computo*; the Sp. and Port. *computar*, and the It. *computare*. The Eng. *count* is directly from *counter*; and *contare* from the L. *computo*.)
1. To number; to tell or name one by one, or by small numbers, for ascertaining the whole number of units in a collection, as, to *count* the years, days, and hours of man's life; to *count* the stars.
—"Who can *count* the dust of Jacob?"—Numb. 23
2. To reckon; to preserve a reckoning; to compute.
"Some tribes of rude nations *count* their years by the coming of certain birds among them at certain seasons, and leaving them at others."—Locke
3. To reckon; to place to an account; to ascribe or impute; to consider or esteem as belonging.

—"Abraham believed in God, and he *counted* it to him for righteousness."—Gen. 15
4. To esteem; to account; to reckon; to think, judge or consider.
—"I *count* them my enemies."—Psa. 139
—"Neither *count* I my life dear to myself."—Acts 20
—"I *count* all things loss."—Phil. 3
5. To impute; to charge.

ORDER, vt. 1. To regulate; to methodize; to systemize; to adjust; to subject to system in management and execution; as, to *order* domestic affairs with prudence.
2. To lead; to conduct; to subject to rules or laws.
—"To him that *ordereth* his conversation aright, will I show the salvation of God."—Psa. 50

OPERATION, n. (L. *operatio*.)
1. The act or process of operating; agency; the exertion of power, physical, mechanical or moral.
—"Speculative painting without the assistance of manual *operation*, can never attain to perfection."—Dryden
—"The pain and sickness caused by manna are the effects of its *operation* on the stomach."—Locke
2. Action, effect.
3. Process; manipulation; series of acts in experiments; as in chimistry or metallurgy.

ADDITION, n. (L. *additio* from *addo*)
1. The act of adding, opposed to subtraction, or diminution; as, a sum is increased by *addition*.
2. Any thing added, whether material or immaterial.
3. In *arithmetic*, the uniting of two or more numbers in one sum; also the rule or branch of arithmetic which treats of adding numbers. *Simple* addition is the joining of sums of the same denomination, as pounds to pounds, dollars to dollars. *Compound* addition is the joining of sums of different denominations, as dollars and cents.

SUBTRACTION, n. (L. *subtractio*)
1. The act or operation of taking a part from the rest.
2. In *arithmetic*, the taking of lesser numbers from a greater of the same kind or denomination; an operation by which is found the difference between two sums.

MULTIPLICATION, n. (L. *multiplicatio*)
1. The act of multiplying or of increasing number; as the *multiplication* of the human species by natural generation.

2. In *arithmetic*, a rule or operation by which any given number may be increased according to any number of times proposed. Thus 10 multiplied by 5 is increased to 50.

DIVISION, n. (L. *divisio*, from *divido*, *divisi*)
1. The act of dividing or separating into parts, an entire body.
2. The state of being divided.
3. That which divides or separates; that which keeps apart; partition.
4. The part separated from the rest by a partition or line, real or imaginary; as the *divisions* of a field.
9. Disunion; discord, variance; difference.
 —"There was *division* among the people."—Jn. 7
11. Distinction.
 —"I will put a *division* between my people and thy people."—Ex. 8
13. In *arithmetic*, the dividing of a number or quantity into any parts assigned; or the rule by which is found how many times one number is contained in another.

MEASURE, n. (Fr. *mesuse*; It. *misura*; Sp. *medida*; Arm. *musur* or *musul*; Ir. *meas*; W. *meidyr* and *mesur*; G. *mass*, measure, and *messen*, to measure; D. *maat*; Sw. *matt*; Dan. *maade*, measure, and mode; L. *mensura*, from *mensus*, with a causal *n*, the participle of *metior*, to measure; Eng. to mete; Gr. *metron*, *metreo*. With this correspond the Eng. *meet*, fit, proper, and *meet*, the verb; Sax. *gemet*, meet, fit; *metan* and *gemettan*, to meet or meet with, to find, to mete or measure, and to paint. The sense is to come to, to fall, to happen, and this sense is connected with that of stretching, extending, that is, reaching to; the latter gives the sense of *measure*. We find in Heb.—measure;—, to mete, to measure. This word in Ar.—, *madda*, signifies to stretch or extend, to draw out in length or time; as do other verbs with the same elements, under one of which we find the *meta* of the Latins. The Ch.—signifies to come to arrive, to reach, to be *mature*, and—, in Heb. Ch. and Eth. signifies to find, to come to. Now the Saxon verb unites itself the significations of all three of the oriental verbs.)
1. The whole extent or dimensions of a thing, including length, breadth and thickness.
 —"The *measure* thereof is longer than the earth and broader than sea."—Job 11
It is applied also to length or to breadth separately.
2. That by which extent or dimension is ascertained, either length, breadth, thickness, capacity, or amount; as, a rod or pole is a *measure* of five yards and a half; an inch, a foot, a yard, are *measures* of length; as gallon is a *measure* of capacity. Weights and *measures* should be uniform. Silver and gold are the common *measure* of value.
4. Determined extent or length; limit.
 —"Lord, make me to know my end, and the *measure* of my days."—Ps. 39
5. A rule by which any thing is adjusted or proportioned.
 —"God's goodness is the *measure* of his providence."—More
6. Proportion; quantity settled.
 —"I enter not into the particulars of the law of nature, or its *measures* of punishment; yet there is such a law."—Locke
14. In *geometry*, any quantity assumed as one or unity, to which the ratio of the other homogeneous or similar quantities is expressed.

REPRESENT, vt. (Fr. *representer*; L. *repraesento*; *re* and Low L. *praesento*, from *praesens*, present.)
1. To show or exhibit by resemblance.
 —"Before him burn
 Seven lamps, as in a zodiac, *representing*
 The heavenly fires."—Milton
5. To supply the place of; to act as a substitute for another. The parliament of Great Britain *represents* the nation. The Congress of the United States *represents* the people or nation. The senate is considered as *representing* the states in their corporate capacity.

SUBSTITUTE, vt. (Fr. *substituer*; It. *sustituire*; Sp. *substituir*; L. *substituo*; *sub* and *statuo*, to set.)
To put in the place of another.
 —"Some few verses are inserted or *substituted* in the room of others."—Congreve

NAME, vt. (Sax. *naman*, *nemnan*, Goth. *namnyan*, to call, to name, to invoke; D. *noemen*; G. *nennen*; Sw. *namna*; Dan. *naevner*.)
1. To set or give to any person or thing a sound or combination of sounds by which it may be known and distinguished; to call; to give an appellation to.
 —"She *named* the child Ichabod."—I. Sam. 6
 —"Thus was the building left
 Ridiculous, and the work confusion *named*."—Milton
3. To nominate; to designate for any purpose by name.
 —"Thou shalt anoint to me him whom I *name* to thee."—I Sam. 16

UNKNOWN, a. 1. Not known. The author of the invention is *unknown*.

2. Greater than is imagined.
4. Not having communication.

When we take the vocabulary of mathematics, which we have just presented, and examine it in the Scriptures, we not only learn more about our subject but more about the Bible itself and our Christian walk.

Here are our overall conclusions about the Biblical source and purpose of mathematics in general and algebra in particular.

BIBLICAL SOURCE AND PURPOSE OF MATHEMATICS

Genesis 1:5 " . . . and evening and morning were the *first* day."
CONCLUSION: When God began His creative work, He established the science of *quantity* and set forth an *order* of history which would be marked off in days, years, and millennia. Just as God was in control of the creation, He is in control of the march of time, and "when the fulness of time was come, God sent forth his Son, made of a woman, made under the law, to redeem them that were under the law . . ." Gal. 4:4, 5. His Son effected *unlimited* Spiritual Liberty, which eventually brought forth *greater* and *greater* degrees of Christian Civil Liberty in history.

BIBLICAL SOURCE AND PURPOSE OF ALGEBRA

Genesis 2:19 " . . . and God brought them (the animals) to Adam to see what *he would call them:* and whatever Adam called every living creature, *that was the name thereof.*" (i.e., this is the representative principle)
CONCLUSION: Although this passage has no direct reference to algebra as a mathematical science, it nevertheless concerns the principle considered in the study of algebra—the principle of representation. Therefore, it shows the *source* of algebra. Because God directed Adam to begin his work of taking dominion with *naming* and *calling* (the vocabulary of representation), it shows that the *purpose* of algebra is for dominion work.

The following statements summarize the Biblical End and Purpose of Mathematics as suggested *elsewhere* in the Scriptures:
1. To know the extent of God's superintending care over man and particularly His people. (Matt. 10:29-31, Gen. 18:23-33)
2. To exercise godly dominion in the earth. (Gen. 1:28)

3. To understand the second of God's two Books—the Book of Nature. (Psa. 19)
4. To apply our hearts to wisdom. (Psa. 90:12)
5. To understand the infinity of God and His works. (Rev. 5:11-14, Rev. 7:9-10)
6. To teach us that the unknown may be known—it is possible to know God. (Acts 17:22-31)

Now let's review in a more systematic way selected mathematical terms found in the Bible and consider what else they tell us about the Biblical purpose of algebra.

HOW THE VOCABULARY OF MATHEMATICS IS USED IN THE BIBLE

MATHEMATICS, (from *mathetes*—disciple, discipline)
The Bible does not contain the word *mathematics*, but because this word is derived from the Greek word *manthano*, to learn, it is possible to find what is said about this aspect of mathematics under other related words such as *mathetes*, disciple.
Matthew 10:24—"The *disciple* is not above his master, nor the servant above his lord."
Acts 11:26—"And when he had found him, he brought him unto Antioch. And it came to pass, that a whole year they assembled themselves with the church, and taught much people. And the *disciples* were called Christians first in Antioch."
CONCLUSION: Both *disciple* and *discipline* come from the same Latin root, *disco*—to learn. A disciple is under instruction and *discipline* means "To instruct or educate; to inform the mind . . . To instruct and govern . . . To advance and prepare by instruction." A conclusion which may be drawn from this is that mathematics is a discipline to advance our knowledge of the creation. The general character of mathematics is problem solving—learning things not previously known.

NUMBER, TELL, WHOLE, MULTITUDE
Genesis 15:5—"And he brought him forth abroad, and said, Look now toward heaven, and *tell* the stars, if thou be able to *number* them: and he said unto him, So shall thy seed be."
Psalms 48:12—"Walk about Zion, and go round about her: *tell* the towers thereof."
Romans 8:22—"For we know that the *whole* creation groaneth and travaileth in pain together until now."
Genesis 28:3—"And God Almighty bless thee, and make thee fruitful, and multiply thee, that thou mayest be a *multitude* of people."
CONCLUSION: These verses suggest that num-

bers and counting are used to investigate the universe, particularly the stars. Gen. 15:5 shows how counting is used to describe the coming of the Redeemer.

COUNT, ACCOUNT, RECKON
Genesis 15:6—"And he believed in the Lord; and he *counted* it to him for righteousness."

Psalms 139:18—"If I should count them, they are more in number than the sand: when I awake, I am still with thee."

Luke 14:28—"For which of you, intending to build a tower, sitteth not down first, and *counteth* the cost, whether he have sufficient to finish it?"

CONCLUSION: Luke 14:28 suggests the Principle of Problem Solving, because it implies planning, executing, and checking. The word *count* is used in the Bible to suggest the Doctrine of Imputation (see Gen. 15:6). *Counting* suggests discreteness and individuality.

ORDER
I Corinthians 14:40—"Let all things be done decently and in *order*."

CONCLUSION: Order is a characteristic of good government.

OPERATION
I Corinthians 12:6—And there are diversities of *operations*, but it is the same God which worketh all in all.

Colossians 2:12—"Buried with him in baptism, wherein also ye are risen with him through the faith of the *operation* of God, who hath raised him from the dead."

CONCLUSION: Operation means " . . . agency, the exertion of power . . . action, effect." The Bible speaks of "the operation of God", i.e., the exercise of His power. This suggests the principle of problem solving. The *operations* of arithmetic are used to solve certain kinds of problems.

ADDITION, ADD, INCREASE
II Peter 1:3-10—"According as his divine power hath given unto us all things that pertain unto life and godliness, through the knowledge of him that hath called us to glory and virtue: whereby are given unto us exceeding great and precious promises; that by these ye might be partakers of the divine nature, having escaped the corruption that is in the world through lust. And beside this, giving all diligence, *add* to your faith virtue; and to virtue, knowledge; and to knowledge, temperance; and to temperance, patience; and to patience, godliness; and to godliness, brotherly kindness; and to brotherly kindness, charity. For if these things

be in you, and abound, they make you that ye shall neither be barren nor unfruitful in the knowledge of our Lord Jesus Christ. But he that lacketh these things is blind and cannot see afar off, and hath forgotten that he was purged from his old sins. Wherefore the rather, brethren, give diligence to make your calling and election sure: for if ye do these things, ye shall never fall."

CONCLUSION: Peter uses *addition* to describe the marks of Christian Assurance.

SUBTRACTION, DECREASE, DIMINISH, ABATE
Genesis 8:5—"And the waters *decreased* continually until the tenth month: in the tenth month, on the first day of the month, were the tops of the mountains seen."

John 3:30—"He must increase, but I must *decrease*."

CONCLUSION: Decrease is used to describe the Christian's relationship to Christ.

MULTIPLY
Genesis 1:28—"And God blessed them, and God said unto them, Be fruitful, and *multiply*, and replenish the earth, and subdue it: and have dominion over the fish of the sea, and over the fowl of the air, and over every living thing that moveth upon the earth."

Acts 6:1—"And in those days, when the number of the disciples was *multiplied*, there arose a murmuring of the Grecians against the Hebrews, because their widows were neglected in the daily ministration."

CONCLUSION: The term *multiply* is used in connection with the idea of "dominion" and with the extension of Christ's kingdom.

DIVIDE, DIVISION, SEPARATE, PART
Genesis 1:4—"And God saw the light, that it was good: and God *divided* the light from the darkness."

Matthew 25:32—"And before him shall be gathered all nations: and he shall *separate* them one from another, as a shepherd *divideth* his sheep from the goats."

CONCLUSION: The term *division* is used to show distinction or difference.

DISTRIBUTION, DISTRIBUTE
Acts 4:35—"And laid them down at the apostles' feet: and *distribution* was made unto every man according as he had need."

Luke 18:22—"Now when Jesus heard these things, he said unto him, Yet lackest thou one thing: sell all that thou hast, and *distribute* unto the poor, and thou shalt have treasure in heaven:

and come, follow me."

CONCLUSION: In these passages *distribution* is used in connection with Christian charity.

UNKNOWN

Acts 17:23—"For as I passed by, and beheld your devotions, I found an altar with this inscription. TO THE *UNKNOWN* GOD Whom therefore ye ignorantly worship, him declare I unto you."

CONCLUSION: Paul says that the God who was *unknown* to them could be *known* by them. In the physical world mathematics is one tool for making "unknown" things "known."

The above conclusions were derived from a study of the vocabulary of mathematics and an inquiry into the Bible. This listing of words, references, and conclusions should not be considered complete and the reader is encouraged to do further research along these two lines. "These were more noble than those in Thessalonica, in that they received the word with all readiness of mind, and searched the scriptures daily, whether those things were so." *Acts 17:11*.

TERMS OF ALGEBRA I

This listing of terms was developed from a survey of several algebra texts. Familiarity with the vocabulary of algebra is necessary, if the student is to gain a mastery of the subject.

absolute value
add
added
addends
addition
algebra
algebraic addition
algebraic division
algebraic expression
algebraic multiplication
algebraic subtraction
apply
area
ascending order
associative
base
binomial
centimeter
change
check
circle
circumference
closure
coefficient

common
commutative
complementary angles
consecutive
consecutive integers
conversion
coordinate
count
counting numbers
cube (third power)
cube (geometric figure)
cubic units
decide
decreased by
define
degree
denominator
descending order
determine
difference
dimension
distributive
divide
divided by
dividend
division
divisor
dominion
doubled
equal
equality
equation
evaluate
even
exponent
exponentiation
extremes
factor
factoring
foot
formula
fraction
gallon
graph
greater than
greatest common factor
height
identity
inch
inclusion
inclusion symbol
increased by
inequality
integers
intercept
isosceles triangle

kilometer
law
least common denominator
least common multiple
length
less than
line
linear
linear equation
liter
mathematics
magnitude
means
measure
monomial
more than
multiple
multiplicand
multiplication
multiplied by
multiplier
name
name of point
natural number
negative
nesting
number
number line
number line addition
numerator
numerical expression
odd
opposites
order
order of operations
ordered pair
origin
ounce
parallelogram
parentheses
perimeter
pi
pint
plan for solving equations
plane
point
polynomial
positive
power
prime numbers
principal root
principle
property
proportion
quantity
quart

quotient
radical
rate
ratio
real numbers
reciprocal
rectangle
replace
represent
representation
root
rule
sign
similar
simple interest
simple polynomial form
simplify
slope
solution
solve
square (geometric figure)
square (second power)
square root
square units
substitute
substitution
subtract
subtraction
supplementary angles
symbol
term
term of operation
thickness
time
transformation
trapezoid
triangle
Trinity
tripled
twice
unit
unknown
variable
volume
whole numbers
width
yard

THE PRINCIPLES OF ALGEBRA

Counting and the Order of Operations

Foundational to all the operations of arithmetic is the process of counting because each may be described as a kind of counting. Counting is a first principle—a rudiment—of our number system. It is an idea derived from the nature of God, as revealed in the Bible.

It is important to know what the Bible teaches about God's nature, or individuality. A chief attribute of God's nature revealed in the Bible is one that we call *The Holy Trinity*.

If we were to investigate the whole body of Scripture, we would see that this doctrine is taught, because the Bible reveals that:

1. There is only *one* God.

2. There are *three* persons (the Father, the Son, and the Holy Spirit) who have personalities and each of whom is called God.

3. These three Persons are *distinct*. That is, they speak to one another, one sends the others, each is active in the things for which only God is responsible. The Spirit was active in creation (Gen. 1); The Son was active in creation (Col. 1:17); and the Father was active in creation (Isa. 44:24)—but only God creates (Heb. 3:4).

If we *relate* this to mathematics, we arrive at the following conclusions:

1. The idea of "one" has always existed as an attribute of God's Nature.

2. Since God is a Trinity the idea of "three" has always existed.

3. The idea of "two" has always existed because there is a Second Person of the Trinity (Jesus Christ).

These three facts suggest the idea of counting—counting forward and backward.

To help explain this more clearly, consider a diagram of the *Counting Chart*:

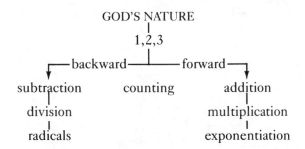

GOD'S NATURE

1,2,3

backward — forward

subtraction   counting   addition

division   multiplication

radicals   exponentiation

Each level of operation results from counting the preceding operation (*addition* is based on "counting numbers forward," *multiplication* is based on "counting additions," *exponentiation* is based on "counting multiplications," *subtraction* is based on "counting numbers backward," etc.).

If we extend our counting further we arrive at all the rest of the numbers which we called *integers*, that is, . . . -3, -2, -1, 0, 1, 2, 3, . . .

As we have seen, all the operations are based on counting. According to the chart, counting numbers forward is addition, and counting addi-

tions is multiplication. Counting numbers backward is subtraction, and counting subtractions is division.

This order among the operations suggested by the above chart indicates that there should be an ordering of the operations in an arithmetic expression. In an expression such as $3 + 2 \times 5$, the multiplication should be performed before the addition. The reason for this is that if we take the problem all the way back to counting, we would first have to rewrite the multiplication as multiple additions, then rewrite each of these additions as the counting of integers. Thus multiplication is done before addition. The full *Order of Operations* suggested by the chart is this (or see any standard algebra text):

THE ORDER OF OPERATIONS

1. Perform exponentiations and/or radicals. If the expressions are nested, work from the innermost outward.

2. Perform multiplication and/or division from left to right in the order that they appear in an expression.

3. Perform addition and/or subtraction from left to right in the order that they appear in the expression.

If an expression has inclusion, each of these should be simplified first (by the Order of Operations). Absolute value should be performed at the same time as inclusion. If the expression has nesting, then work from the innermost inclusion outward.

The Counting Chart and the Order of Operations represent the same thing.

The Principle of Order and Magnitude

THE PRINCIPLE OF
ORDER AND MAGNITUDE

One of God's activities as recorded in the Bible is measurement. Man is created in the image of God. For this reason man has ability to measure and to apply numbers to the universe in which he lives.

This principle suggests two things in regard to the study of algebra:

1. Numbers may be compared according to their *relative size*. That is, given two numbers

either they are *equal* or one is *larger* than the other. Numbers may be compared according to *Magnitude* or size (Order).

2. The length of a line may be compared to a given unit in such a way that its magnitude may be determined. This may also be extended to area, weight, etc., and under such cases as these the comparison is made with *real numbers*.

Words related to this idea are: measure, distance, weight, size, volume, mass, amount, quantity. Also words signifying units of measure are related: inch, cubit, foot, pound, mile, etc.

According to Webster (1828), *magnitude* is "extent of dimension or parts; bulk; size; applied to things that have length, breadth, and thickness."

This is a Biblical Principle:

1. Measurement is one of God's activities:

"God came from Teman, and the Holy One from Mount Paran . . . He stood, *and measured the earth*; he beheld, and drove asunder the nations; and the everlasting mountains were scattered, the perpetual hills did bow; his ways are everlasting." —*Habakkuk 3:3, 6*

"The way of the just is uprightness; thou, most upright, dost *weigh* the path of the just." —*Isaiah 26:7*

"For he looketh to the ends of the earth, and seeth under the whole heaven, to make the *weight* for the winds; and he *weigheth* the waters by measure." —*Job 28:24, 25*

"Behold the Lord God . . . Who hath measured the waters in the hollow of his hand, and meted out heaven with the span, and comprehended the dust of the earth in a measure, and weighed the mountains in scales, and the hills in a balance?" —*Isaiah 40:1, 12*

2. He commands us to measure various things and the measurement corresponds to numerical quantity.

+ The construction of the Tabernacle (Exodus 26, 27, 28).

+ The measurement of the Temple (Ezek.40).

3. Measurement is a way of comparing the *differences* between things. Differences between things are important because they help to emphasize God's diversity and individuality. Distinctions in magnitude make the *ordering* of quantities possible. "To order" means "to adjust," that is, to arrange according to size.

It is natural to expect that the number system is useful in the physical creation, because the one is an expression of the thoughts of God and the other is His work, so they should be consistent with each other.

THE PRINCIPLE OF SUBSTITUTION AND REPRESENTATION

One quantity or expression may represent or be substituted for another quantity of equal value in any given numerical or algebraic expression.

Words and expressions that suggest substitution and representation are: *put in the place of, change for, give place to, take the place of, instead of, in the behalf of, interchange, exchange.*

Substitution is a Biblical idea. One of the central teachings of the Bible about salvation is that Christ died a *substitutionary death.* He died *in the place of* His people. *Matthew 20:28* "Even as the Son of man came not to be ministered unto, but to minister, and to give his life a ransom *for* many." In this passage the word *for* indicates the principle of substitution. The word "for" in the Greek language of this passage is *anti* (pronounced AHN-ti) and means "in the place of," "instead of," "in the behalf of." That is, Christ substituted himself "in the place of" many. He *took* their place. *II Corinthians 5:21* "For he (God) hath made him who knew no sin to be sin *for* us; that we might be made the righteousness of God in him" demonstrates the same idea. Some other passages in the Bible that express this principle are:

Leviticus 1:4, the animal sacrifice is accepted in the place of the offerer.

John 15:13, Christ acts as a substitute for His people in order to bring them life.

Representation is similar to substitution, but as we shall see when we study these principles as related to algebra, they are not exactly the same. Representation is also a Scriptural principle. We see it in *I Timothy 2:5* "For there is one God, and *one mediator* between God and men, the man Christ Jesus." One thing that this means is that Christ *represents* His people to His Father in Heaven. Other passages that show this principle are:

Deuteronomy 18:18, the Prophet is God's representative to men.

Psalms 110:4, the priest represents men to God.

John 14:6-26, Christ represents the Father on earth. He promises to send the Holy Spirit, "another Comforter," to represent the Father and Himself when He returns to Heaven.

A key word for the idea of representation is "through" (in Greek *dia* (DEE-ah). This word *dia* is sometimes translated "by" in the King James Version of the Bible. The term "diameter" has this word in it. *Diameter* literally means "measure through" and in a circle it is the "measure through" the center of the circle. There are two passages in which this word is found: *Romans 1:8* "First, I thank my God *through* Jesus Christ for you all, that your faith is spoken of throughout the whole world," and *Colossians 3:17* "And whatsoever ye do in word or deed, do all in the name of the Lord Jesus, giving thanks to God and the Father *by* (through) him." In this last passage the idea of representation is expressed in two ways. First, whatever you do, do *in the name* of Christ, that is, as His representative. To act in another person's name is to be that person's representative. Second, "giving thanks to the Father *through* Him." Christ maintains the place of *Representative* for us in Heaven. He *represents* us to the Father in prayer.

The Plan for Solving Problems

The Plan is the three step approach to problem solving. It is:

THE PLAN

1. *Decide* what steps must be taken in order to eventually solve an equation or problem.
2. *Apply* these steps.
3. *Check* your result to see if it actually answers the equation and fits all the conditions of the problem.

This principle is suggested by the three governmental powers described in *Isaiah 33:22*, "For the Lord is our *judge*, the Lord is our *lawgiver*, the Lord is our *king*; he will save us." in that the legislative (lawgiver) suggests the formulation of the steps required to solve a particular problem, the executive (king) suggests putting these steps into effect, and the judicial (judge) suggests checking the results for correctness.

The above statement is only the bare statement of the principle. When a student applies this principle to solving a problem, he must research, reason, and relate. This includes reading the problem and identifying the key terms for the observations in the problem, the relationships in the problem, and the nature of the solution to the problem. The student must analyze the problem or work from the whole of the problem to its several parts. The actual approach he takes to the problem must depend upon the kind of problem (algebra, geometry, or arithmetic), however, each of the steps taken will fall into one of the three categories given in the statement of the principle.

Two other passages that suggest this principle

are *Luke 14:28, 29* and *Luke 14:31*.

The plan for solving problems applies to every sort of problem (simplification of numerical expressions, solution of equation, solution of word problems, etc.).

EXPLANATION OF THE COUNTING CHART AND THE ORDER OF OPERATIONS

The *Counting Chart*, which is described in the last section, and which is reproduced below, is used as a teaching tool because it demonstrates *The Order of Operations*, an important leading idea which results from *The Principle of Counting*. It is used as an aid for the student, giving him a visual demonstration to remind him of *when* and *why* certain things are performed. It shows why there is a distinction among the various operations of arithmetic and how these operations are related.

When the Counting Chart is introduced, it is shown in a form that is commensurate with the students' knowledge, and parts are added to it as they are introduced. When the chart is used to teach an idea, it is used to teach *only one* idea at a time. For example, at the beginning of an Algebra I course all of the chart is shown except exponentiation and radicals. This is because these operations are not introduced until later in the course. In the same manner the way in which *The Order of Operations* is expressed at any given time is complementary to the information given on the chart. The students are apprised of this limiting of the information given in order to avoid the misconception on their part that the teacher is "changing" the chart and the Order of Operations in a strictly arbitrary fashion. Three expressions of the Order of Operations are given: the elementary the intermediate and the final forms.

When the chart is first introduced it appears in this manner:

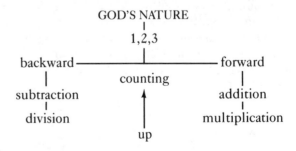

No mention is made of any operation beyond the four operations of arithmetic. The "up arrow" indicates that in performing the operations of arithmetic "up" is the direction that should be followed in the chart: Multiplication and division should be performed before addition and subtraction. It is pointed out to the student that this is not an arbitrary convention but a necessary feature of the number system and its operations, due to the fact that the numbers and the operations are extensions of *The Principle of Counting*.

The *elementary* and *intermediate* forms of the Order of Operations which are presented *with* the foregoing Counting Chart are:

THE ORDER OF OPERATIONS

1. Perform multiplication and/or division from left to right in the order that they appear in an expression.

2. Perform addition and/or subtraction from left to right in the order that they appear in the expression.

---

and

THE ORDER OF OPERATIONS

1. Perform multiplication and/or division from left to right in the order that they appear in an expression.

2. Perform addition and/or subtraction from left to right in the order that they appear in the expression.

If an expression has inclusion, each of these should be simplified first (by the Order of Operations). Absolute value should be performed at the same time as inclusion. If the expression has nesting, then work from the innermost inclusion outward.

The second expression above is presented after inclusion (i.e., parentheses, etc.) and absolute value are presented.

When exponentiation is reached in the study it is added to the chart and to the Order of Operations. When radical expressions are reached, the Counting Chart has this form:

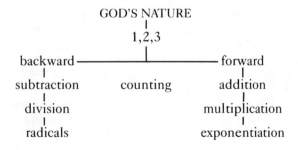

THE ORDER OF OPERATIONS

1. Perform exponentiations and/or radicals. If the expressions are nested, work from the innermost outward.

2. Perform multiplication and/or division from left to right in the order that they appear in an expression.

3. Perform addition and/or subtraction from left to right in the order that they appear in the expression.

If an expression has inclusion, each of these should be simplified first (by the Order of Operations). Absolute value should be performed at the same time as inclusion. If the expression has nesting, then work from the innermost inclusion outward.

The above expression of the Order of Operations is the *final* form.

What is taught with the chart.

As has been stated, when the chart is used to teach simplifying numerical expressions, it is shown with an "up arrow" and is used to show that this is the direction used when the Order of Operations is followed. When the chart is used to show the most efficient way to solve a linear equation a "down arrow" is used:

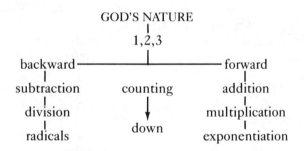

Solve *most efficiently* by cancelling *operations* in the downward direction:

Example:
3x + 7 = 28   cancel the *addition* of 7
3x + 7 − 7 = 28 − 7
3x = 21   cancel the *multiplication* of 3

3x ÷ 3 = 21 ÷ 3
x = 7, answer.

It is possible to *convert* from one operation to the other on the same level of the chart (subtraction to addition, division to multiplication, radical expression to exponentiation). This is accomplished by a procedure called "change and replace." On the chart it is shown as:

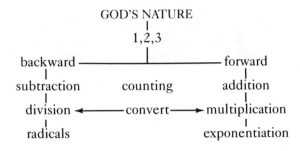

In the example of multiplication and division:

21/4 ÷ 7/2

Change the operation to its inverse on the chart. *Replace* the second number by its reciprocal.

21/4 × 2/7

The chart is used time after time in the teaching of algebra to tie the various topics together. The unifying principle in the case of the chart is the Principle of Counting and its particular expression is the Order of Operations. The chart embodies this expression thus making it useful for expanding the principles.

Expanding the Principles of
Elementary Mathematics Through Algebra — Part I

SUBJECT	
Numbers	counting numbers whole numbers integers real numbers rational and irrational numbers prime numbers

PRINCIPLES (THE INTERNAL)	
Counting — The Order of Operations	the operations of arithmetic (addition, subtraction, multiplication, division) exponentiation radicals counting chart the laws of exponents quadratic expressions and equations quadratic formula evaluating numerical expressions solving linear equations directed number arithmetic addition and subtraction conversion multiplication and division conversion

The Principle of Order and Magnitude	the number line
	the operations
	absolute value
	geometric representation of linear equations
	units of measure
	units of conversion
	length, area, volume
	ratio
	rate formulas
	   1. rate $\times$ time = distance
	   2. unit price $\times$ amount = extension
	   3. percent $\times$ amount = percentage

The Principle of Substitution and Representation	variables formulas solving equations
The Plan for Solving Problems	translating word expressions into algebraic expressions solving equations solving word problems

EXPANDING THE PRINCIPLES OF
ELEMENTARY MATHEMATICS THROUGH ALGEBRA — PART II

THE STRUCTURE OF THE NUMBER SYSTEM (THE EXTERNAL)

Properties that develop from the principles	*Properties of Operations*
	Closure
	Commutative for addition and multiplication
	Associative for addition and multiplication
	Distributive Property of Multiplication over Addition
	   1. Distributive Property 1
	   2. Distributive Property 2
	The Three Laws of Exponents
	   1. $a^m a^n = a^{m+n}$
	   2. $(ab)^n = a^n b^n$
	   3. $(a^m)^n = a^{mn}$
	Properties of Numbers
	Multiplication Property of Negative One
	Identity for addition (Addition Property of Zero)
	Identity for multiplication (Multiplication Property of One)
	Property of Opposites
	Multiplication Property of Zero
	Properties of Equality
	Transformation 1 — addition and subtraction
	Transformation 2 — multiplication and division

THE CHAIN OF CHRISTIANITY

	Original use of the Numbers (Genesis) Algebra in seed form in the garden of Eden: "... and brought them (the animals) to Adam to see what *he would call them:* and whatsoever Adam called every living creature, *that was the name thereof.*" Gen. 2:19 Muhammed ibn Musa al-Khowarizmi — *ilm al-jabr wa'l muqabalah* A.D. 820 Moors expelled from Spain c. 1100 Robert O'Chester — translated *ilm al-jabr* 1140 Leonardo Fibonacci *Liber Abaci* 1202 *Magna Carta* 1215 John Wycliffe — Bible translated into English 1384 Robert Record, *The Ground of Artes, The Castle of Knowledge, The Pathewaie of Knowledge, The Whetstone of Witte* 1542 Francisco Viete introduced the variable in algebra 1580 Thomas Harriot — early survey of Virginia and Carolinas 1585, *Artis Analyticæ Praxis, ad Æquationes Algebraicas nous...Methodo resoluendas* (introduced "<" and ">") 1631 Isaac Newton *Philosophiæ Naturalis Principia Mathematica* (mathematical description of laws of physics) 1687 *Arithmetica Universalis* (the theory of equations) 1707 Nathaniel Bowditch *The American Practical Navigator*, 1802

KEY TO EXPANDING THE PRINCIPLES OF ELEMENTARY MATHEMATICS THROUGH ALGEBRA

The chart entitled, *Expanding the Principles of Elementary Mathematics Through Algebra*, which precedes this section, is an attempt to explain where various topics "fit" in a Principle Approach algebra course. The following is an explanation of the chart.

NUMBERS

Numbers are the subject of algebra because algebra is "the science of quantity in general, or universal arithmetic . . . in which signs or symbols, . . . are made to represent numbers and quantities." The terms employed here to denote the numbers are used more for ease of explanation than necessity, since these terms have been arbitrarily chosen. They are used here because of their common usage and acceptance in mathematical literature—including instructional material.

THE INTERNAL AND EXTERNAL NATURE OF THE NUMBER SYSTEM

Mathematics has a dual nature—principle and structure. They are of *equal importance* to a proper understanding of algebra as a distinctive branch of mathematics. The principles given here suggest the *internal aspect* of the number system because they suggest the derivation of the numbers and their consequent operations from the Trinitarian nature of the Godhead, the activity of God in measuring, representing, and exercising power (the latter is called problem solving in mathematics). The implementation of mathematics in general and algebra in particular as a science and an art is predicated upon the command of God to man to "take dominion" of the earth for His greater glory. (Gen. 1:28)

The number system arising from the principles reflects a definite and identifiable character. This character is demonstrated in the *properties* of the number system. They, the properties, suggest, therefore, an *external aspect* of the number system. It is possible to draw the properties of the number system from the principles. For example, the Closure Property (i.e., when two real numbers are added, subtracted, multiplied, or divided validly, the result is a unique real number) is a reflection of the nature of these operations as *counting* procedures and counting by its nature is a discrete process producing a unique result.

In like manner, other properties, such as the commutative properties and the associative properties are reflections of the counting aspects of addition and multiplication.

Once the principles of the subject are introduced to the student, then they may be expanded using the topics suggested in the chart. Because the properties listed are expressions of the principles as well, they may be used in explanation. By teaching algebra in this manner it is possible to explain it as both a science ("universal arithmetic"—the study of properties) and an art ("a general method . . . in which symbols, . . . , are made to represent numbers and quantities. It takes an unknown quantity sought, . . . (and) proceed(s) till the quantity supposed is discovered . . .")

THE CHAIN OF CHRISTIANITY

No subject in the curriculum of an American Christian school can be divorced from its history without militating against the governmental and educational philosophy of the school. If students are to have a complete understanding of God's Hand in History, it is necessary that they be introduced to the Providential History of each subject.

In mathematics, this perspective or view of history resolves itself into these questions: How has mathematics been instrumental in the propagation of the Gospel of Christ with its corollary of internal Christian Liberty translated into the civil sphere? That is, how has mathematics aided the progress of the Gospel and its manifestation of Christian Civil Liberty? Another important question arising from the study of the Providential History of mathematics is this: How has Christian Civil Liberty aided the development of mathematics and advanced its usefulness in the lives of individuals?

The historical references given in this listing are some of the links in the "mathematical" Chain of Christianity. These references include people who were not Christians. The presupposition of the Providential view of history is that God raised up men in many nations and used them to identify and develop the mathematics that contributed to His plan for the advancement of mankind and the support of individual liberty.

1. Al-Khowarizmi wrote the first algebra book about AD 820. It was produced during a period of relative freedom during the Saracenic Empire (see Weaver). The Arabs were borrowers who took the work of others and improved it. Al-Khowarizmi based *ilm al-jabr* upon the mathematics of the Greeks.

2. The Moors (c. 1100) carried their culture and learning with them when they migrated across northern Africa and into the Iberian Peninsula (Spain). In time, they were expelled and the libra-

ries of their universities became accessible to European scholars. The learning of the Greeks and Arabs, which was unknown to the Europe of the dark ages, became available as scholars from every nation came to Spain to investigate the resources of this new learning. One of these scholars was Robert O'Chester of England who translated *ilm al-jabr* into Latin in 1140, thus making it available in Europe for the first time. This mathematical knowledge prepared Europe for the Age of Exploration beginning with Prince Henry the Navigator and Christopher Columbus.

3. Robert Record (c. 1542), who was a mathematician, poet, and physician, wrote several mathematics texts, including *Grovnd of Artes*, an arithmetic text, and *The Whetstone of Witte*, the first algebra book in English. Record lived during the period when mercantilism as an economic policy was gaining importance. Mercantilism required a certain amount of mathematical knowledge to render possible the accounting necessary for government as well as the private sector to keep track of business activity. Robert Record's texts met this need for mathematical preparation. As England's manufacturers proliferated and expanded, the need for raw materials increased. America was seen as a source of such materials and so colonists were sent to acquire them and send them back to England. The earliest colony for this type of enterprise was Jamestown.

4. Francois Viete (c. 1580) is significant to the advancement of algebra because of his recognition of the representative principle and thus the introduction of the variable in algebra.

5. Thomas Harriot (c. 1600) made further notational contributions to this developing branch of mathematics: He introduced the inequality signs in their present form. He was a member of a survey party led by Sir Richard Grenville prior to the settlement of Jamestown (see CHOC, pp. 152–153; Harriot is not mentioned here but was a member of the party). He wrote *A Brief Narrative of the New Found Land of Virginia*, a description of the geography and the people encountered during this expedition. It was published in 1558. This description encouraged interest in the settlement of what is now Virginia, and later, when William Brewster, William Bradford, and their pastor, John Robinson, began to consider the journey of the Pilgrims to America, they consulted this work (see Bartlett).

6. Isaac Newton's *Principia* (1687) was foundational to the branch of natural science known as mechanics, and mechanics is important to the study of celestial mechanics. This work shows how mathematics was used historically to gain an insight into the working of nature.

7. Nathaniel Bowditch (c. 1802), America's first mathematician, rendered the science of navigation more easily understood to the individual by compiling *The American Practical Navigator*, a self-teaching reference to celestial navigation. The modern version of this work is still in use today. This work aided the expansion of American commerce, and thus the growth of world trade. In turn this made possible the more effective propagation of the Gospel.

THE SEVEN PRINCIPLES OF HISTORY AND GOVERNMENT AS APPLIED TO MATHEMATICS

The following application of the Seven Principles of America's Christian History and Government is given merely to suggest the place of mathematics in God's plan for man.

It would be unwise to try to force these principles out of mathematics or to use mathematics instruction as a vehicle or platform for teaching them. To do so would rob the Seven Principles of their distinctive character as principles of America's Christian history and government. A subject (such as mathematics) should be *taught from* the system of principles peculiar to it. Webster would perhaps have said that mathematics should be taught "according to its real nature" (see T/L p. 286).

Mathematics should be *taught from* its principles, and taught *within* a distinctive system of principles of history and government which govern the educational philosophy of the school (i.e., the Seven Principles). This allows the student to understand historically the end and purpose of mathematics in the scheme of Providential history: How has mathematics aided the progress of the Gospel and of Christian civil liberty? and what place does a knowledge of mathematics have in an individual's life as he fulfills his duty to God in rendering the world about him subservient to Christ and thus to human happiness? Mathematics taught in this manner (i.e., from the perspective of the Principle Approach and Providential History) becomes not only a Christian subject, but an *American* Christian subject.

1. *God's Principle of Individuality*

God's Principle of Individuality is the background to the mathematical principles. It explains the diversity of the operations; the diversity of the properties of the operations (commutative, associative, distributive, etc.); and the diversity of the properties of the numbers (identity properties, multiplication property of -1, etc.). Mathematics is revelational of God's individuality, diversity, and infinity.

2. *The Christian Principle of Self-Government*

God's orderly government of the universe is seen through mathematics. Mathematical laws are not contradictory. The "Flow of Force and Power" is from the (internal) principles to the (external) properties.

3. *America's Heritage of Christian Character*

This principle is taught through the discipline of classroom instruction and the development of the notebook. It is exemplified through the lives of mathematicians (Bowditch, Banneker, etc.).

4. *"Conscience is the Most Sacred of All Property"*

Man is God's property—sent to do God's work. Man has been given dominion over the earth. (Gen. 1:28) Mathematics is a tool for this dominion work. Conscientious computations are necessary for the development and stewardship of economic property, and the advance of Christ's Kingdom.

5. *The Christian Form of Our Government*

Internal   Self-Government: See 2
                 Property: See 4
                 Political Union: See 7

External   Representation: The Principle of Representation and Substitution
                 Separation of Powers: The Plan for Solving Problems (1. Decide, 2. Apply, 3. Check)
                 Dual Form: *Mathematics* is one *Science* with many *branches*

6. *How the Seed of Local Self-Government Is Planted*

The Principle of Counting is the seed from which the number system, the operations, the properties, and the laws develop. This principle of counting is based upon the mathematical aspect of God's Nature (one God in three Persons—the Trinity). It applies to the physical world because of the Principle of Order and Magnitude.

7. *The Christian Principle of American Political Union—Unity With Union*

The principle of unity with union is demonstrated by the integrity (see Webster 1828) of mathematics. Mathematical principles, properties, and laws are consistent regardless of the branch of mathematics in which they are found. This principle, applied to mathematics, is the fulfillment of the promises of God's Principle of Individuality. Uniting or combining numbers into new numbers does not deny the identity or integrity of the integers involved and is necessary to make useful calculations. Again, all the branches of mathematics unite in operating according to fundamental principles.

A LESSON PLAN—CHRISTIAN HERITAGE ACADEMY
Teacher Preparation and Presentation
References
Algebra Text, p. 144

Course: Algebra I   *Teacher:* Booton   *Grade:* 9   *Date:*

PRINCIPLES	LEADING IDEAS	FACTS	METHOD
The Plan for Solving Problems Order of Operations (Counting)	The Plan for Solving Linear Equations	Examples: $5x - 7 = 63$ $8(x - 7) = 0$ $2(2x + 3) - 5 = 21$ $14(x + 5) + 19(2x - 5) = 1$ Others as needed Decide Apply Check *Terms* Linear Equations Transformation 1 and 2 Distributive Property 1	Explanation and Example Student Board Work Review of Vocabulary Assignment: p. 146 (1-25) Note: Assignment requires analysis of word problems for future word problem solutions.

This is one form for a lesson plan. It identifies the principles of the lesson, how they are expanded, and the methods. The principles here are the Principle of Counting (Order of Operations) and the Plan for Solving Problems and the leading idea is the Plan for Solving Linear Equations in one variable which is a particularized form of the plan.

THE CHAIN OF CHRISTIANITY MOVING WESTWARD

The history of mathematics is seen in the development of mathematics in relation to scientific development, invention, and discovery, and interpreted in the light of the development of Christianity:

Asia: The origin of the branches of mathematics.

Europe: The development of mathematics. (In the modern age under the influences of Christianity.)

America: The use of mathematics in the development of the technology that aided in the spreading of the Gospel and the advancing of Christian Liberty.

HOW TO IDENTIFY AND USE THE CHRISTIAN PRINCIPLES OF A SUBJECT

1. Begin by identifying the vocabulary of a subject. Use Webster 1828 because a) he intended to define words according to a Christian-Biblical standard; b) later dictionaries show evidence of the erosion of the meanings of the words we use.

2. Examine the subject for underlying principles.

3. Examine the Scriptures to see what they say about these principles: Are they Biblical principles?

4. Examine the subject for individual topics to be covered, relating each topic to one or more of the various principles which have been identified. These are the *leading ideas* of the subject and should be used to *expand* the principles.

5. After becoming grounded in the Providential View of history, the teacher can then begin to study the history of his subject to see how it has contributed to the westward progress of the Gospel. Then the teacher can study to see how the Gospel's manifestation of Christian civil liberty has contributed to the advance of his subject.

PREPARING A COURSE OF INSTRUCTION

1. Arrange the leading ideas according to their logical progression. This would be the material to cover for the year.

2. Divide this list into two equal parts or divide it at some logical breaking point. These two sections will be the first and second semesters. Further division will give quarters, weeks, and days.

3. Incorporate the material resulting from the historical research in order to show the place oc-cupied by this subject in the Chain of Christianity.

4. As you progress with the class through the year, adjust your schedule so that you will not run out of time at the end of the year, or be forced to spend too little time on some topics, or too much on others.

OBJECTIVES FOR ALGEBRA I

Mathematics is revelational of the created universe. It reveals certain aspects of God's nature because He is the Creator. We learn the following things from mathematics (T/L pp. 97-99):

1. God is unchangeable
2. God is orderly
3. God is systematic
4. God is precise
5. God is dependable
6. God is infinite.

GENERAL OBJECTIVES

1. A study of Algebra should aid the reasoning ability of students. In particular, it should help to make them more capable as Biblical reasoners. They should learn to reason from principle.

2. Mathematical skills are individual and not social; one object of Algebra is to encourage the student to better his or her mathematical skill.

3. This course is designed to cause the student to "think algebraically" which is the governmental way of thinking about the number system.

4. Algebra shows the connection between the concept of number and the created universe. It helps the student in fulfilling his responsibility to God to have dominion over the earth. (Gen. 1:28)

5. Studying Algebra historically reveals how God prepared man scientifically and mathematically, as well as spiritually and politically, for the foundation of America as a Christian Nation.

SPECIFIC OBJECTIVES

1. Students should gain an historical appreciation of the subject in its relationship to America.

2. Students should acquire a knowledge of the meanings of the terms that make up the vocabulary of Algebra.

3. They should gain basic skill in solving equations (linear and quadratic).

4. They should gain an ability to relate equation solving to problem (word problem) solving.

OVERVIEW OF THE YEAR IN ALGEBRA I

The references, *G4*, *S2*, etc., refer to the general (*G*) or specific (*S*) goals given the previous section entitled *Objectives for Algebra I.*

HISTORICAL MATERIAL

If America was to be founded as a Christian Nation, the men and women of Europe would need a mathematical and scientific preparation, as well as a spiritual and political preparation. *G5, S1*

1. Muhammed ibn Musa al-Khowarizmi—*ilm al-jabr wa'l muqabalah* AD 820. The first algebra book. Limited freedom in the Saracenic Empire made the writing of it possible (background *Mainstream of Human Progress*).

2. Introduction in Europe. Moors expelled. Robert O'Chester translates *ilm ad-jabr*, AD 1140. The introduction of Arabic learning into Europe. The mathematical preparation for the colonization of America begins.

3. Francois Viete (1580) and the identification of the Principle of Representation.

4. Robert Record (textbook writer, first algebra text in English) and Thomas Harriot (mathematician and explorer of Virginia) provide for the mathematical preparation for mercantilism and

thus for the settlement of Plimoth Plantation.

5. Isaac Newton—mathematical description of the laws of motion.

6. Nathaniel Bowditch—navigation renders the seas safer for travel and thus for the propagation of the Gospel.

This is one possible outline for an Algebra I course. Others are possible. After a topic is introduced, it is reviewed frequently in the homework that follows throughout the year. Students who have difficulty understanding a topic at first will have an opportunity to learn it later as they continue their work with it. We thank Mr. John Saxon of Rose State College, Midwest City, Oklahoma, for the re-introduction of this method in the teaching of mathematics through his algebra textbooks. (See Bibliography, also see *Symbolic Logic* by Lewis Carroll published in the late nineteenth century for another example of this technique.)

BIBLIOGRAPHY

Ball, W. W. Rouse. *A Short Account of the History of Mathematics*. New York: Dover, 1908.

Bartlett, Robert M. *The Pilgrim Way*. Philadelphia: Pilgrim Press, 1971.

Boettner, Loraine. *Studies in Theology*. Nutley, NJ: Presbyterian and Reformed Publishing Company, 1947.

Dodgson, Charles L. (Lewis Carroll). *Symbolic Logic and the Game of Logic*. New York: Dover, 1896.

Hall, Verna M. *The Christian History of the Constitution of the United States of America*. San Francisco: Foundation for American Christian Education, 1966.

Kline, Morris. *Why Johnny Can't Add: The Failure of the New Math*. New York: Vintage Books, 1973.

———. *Mathematics in Western Culture*. London: Oxford University Press, 1953.

North, Gary, ed. *Foundation of Christian Scholarship—Essays in the Van Til Perspective*. Vallecito, CA: Ross House Books, 1979.

Saxon, John. *Algebra I An Incremental Development*. Norman, OK: Grassdale, 1981.

———. *Algebra II An Incremental Development*. Norman, OK: Grassdale, 1984.

Slater, Rosalie J. *Teaching and Learning America's Christian History*. San Francisco: Foundation for American Christian Education, 1965.

Smith, David Eugene. *History of Mathematics*, 2 Vols. New York: Dover, 1923.

Weaver, Henry Grady. *The Mainspring of Human Progress*. Irvington-on-Hudson, NY: Foundation for Economic Education, 1947.

Webster, Noah. *First Edition of an American Dictionary of the English Language* 1828. Facsimile with introduction by Rosalie J. Slater, MA. San Francisco: Foundation for American Christian Education, 1967, 1984.

DAROLD BOOTON

I have taught school since 1972, all but the first year at Christian Heritage Academy in Oklahoma City.

In 1975, our Administrator, Mr. Ralph Bullard, attended a seminar conducted by the Plymouth Rock Foundation at which he was introduced to the Principle Approach. Upon his return he began to study and instruct the faculty in this approach, and has done so ever since.

In 1977, Miss Verna Hall and Miss Rosalie Slater of the Foundation for American Christian Education visited our school and suggested areas of study I could undertake. As a result, I traveled to Virginia and spent the summer researching the life and work of Nathaniel Bowditch, America's first mathematician.

Since then I have prepared curricula in Rudiments (a beginning course in the Christian foundation of history and government), Government, Economics and German. I have researched the principles of mathematics and have developed an approach to teaching algebra which has been explained in educational seminars in at least four states. I am currently engaged in writing a first-year algebra textbook which embodies the Principle Approach. Among other things, this textbook will show that we can learn much about God's nature from mathematics — that he is unchangeable, orderly, systematic, precise, dependable and infinite.

I recall my first experience student teaching in a large public high school. I wondered how the students could ever assume the responsibilities of citizens. They were not interested in school; they knew next to nothing; they weren't being prepared even to be economically productive.

A year later, when I began teaching in a Christian school, I observed much the same attitude among students who considered themselves Christians. It was natural that most of the students and teachers previously had been in a public school. They merely reflected their educational backgrounds. After some years, our Christian school began using a somewhat "traditional" approach, really just a return to the beginnings of the progressive system as it was sixty years ago. The result: students who could memorize lists of facts but could not reason.

A BETTER PRODUCT

Today our students are learning how to develop

tools for self-education. They are learning to reason from principles — infinitely better than learning facts by rote-drill exclusively. They are taking responsibility for their education and many are thinking about national issues on the basis of Biblical principles. Our graduates have taken places of responsibility in churches, in business, and in education. Some have taken active roles, standing for Christian principles in the election of local and national representatives. Graduates have gone on to college and majored in mathematics or related fields such as engineering or computer science. Some have gone on to receive advanced degrees. Others are working in industry or teaching mathematics in high school.

As a student and teacher, I am thoroughly pleased with the Principle Approach, both Biblically and educationally. I have seen it give students the tools of Biblical reasoning and writing. It gives me a method for developing a subject according to its true nature and relating how it falls under the dominion of Christ "in whom are hid all the treasures of wisdom and knowledge." The Principle Approach is relevant to the character of the teacher as well as to the student, for if the teacher does not have the character to be a Christian scholar, it is doubtful that he will be able to produce students who are Christian scholars. "The disciple is not above his master, but every one that is perfect shall be as his master." Luke 6:40

CHALLENGE TO TEACHER

For a teacher, the challenge of implementing the Principle Approach requires time in research, thought and writing in addition to ordinary classroom duties. In my case, I began looking up and recording mathematically related terms from Webster's 1828 dictionary. I have identified over three hundred such words, some of which are included here. Perhaps the most difficult task has been to reform the practical side of teaching along the theoretical lines suggested by this research. Naturally, complete mastery does not come at once, but God will bless each step we take in the right direction.

An American Christian Approach to
Natural Science
and Human
Anatomy / Physiology

by David Holmes
Chairman, Science Department
Christian Heritage Academy
Oklahoma City, Oklahoma

CONTENTS

PART I

THE AMERICAN CHRISTIAN PHILOSOPHY OF NATURAL SCIENCE

DEFINITIONS OF KEY TERMS

Before beginning a study of any subject, one must understand exactly what it is he is studying. The following definitions, from Webster's 1828 Dictionary, will help the reader understand more precisely what is going to be discussed. In turn, the key words in each definition should be defined to gain a greater knowledge of the subject of Natural Science.

Natural—Pertaining to nature; produced or affected by nature, or by the laws of growth, formation or motion impressed on bodies or beings by *divine power.*

Nature—Whatever is made or produced; a word that *comprehends all the works of God;* the universe.

Science—*Knowledge* or certain knowledge, the comprehension or *understanding of truth* or facts by the mind.

Natural History—In its most extensive sense, is the description of whatever is *created,* or of the whole universe, including the heavens and the earth, and all the productions of the earth. But, more generally, natural history is limited to a description of the earth and its productions, including zoology, botany, geology, mineralogy, meteorology, etc.

Natural Philosophy—The science of material natural bodies, of their properties, powers and motions. It is distinguished from intellectual and moral philosophy, which respect the mind or understanding of man and the qualities of actions. Natural philosophy comprehends mechanics, hydrostatics, optics, astronomy, chemistry, magnetism, electricity, galvanism, etc.

DISTINCTIVES OF THIS PHILOSOPHY OF SCIENCE

The following statement of philosophy was developed with the assistance of Miss Garnett Ingold, a teacher of natural science at Arvada Christian School, Colorado in connection with material being produced for the Pilgrim Institute. These statements will lay the foundation upon which the teacher may construct his curriculum and constitute an American Christian view of the subject.

According to Noah Webster, *Philosophy* is "the explanation of the reason of things, the collection of general laws or principles under which all the subordinate phenomena or facts relating to that subject are comprehended."

The philosophy is Christian because it pertains to Christ and will confirm an individual's faith in God. It will also reveal that God's Word is the basis for the subject and reveals the subject's Biblical origin and purpose.

The philosophy is American Christian for two basic reasons: 1) It relates the history of science and its purposes to the Chain of Christianity moving westward to America. 2) It shows that America's Christian form of government secured to the individual a high level of freedom that enabled American science and scientists to flourish. In turn, the practical applications of science increased American productivity, and the resulting prosperity allowed Americans to spread the Gospel around the world.

AMERICAN CHRISTIAN VIEW OF NATURAL SCIENCE
I

God is the creator who brought into existence all things from nothing.

BIBLICAL INDEX: Heb. 11:3; Gen. 1:1; Col. 1:16-18; Neh. 9:6; John 1:3

KEY TERMS: *Create*—"To produce; to bring into being from nothing; to cause to exist."

HISTORICAL STATEMENT:
"Mathematics and dynamics fail us, when we contemplate the earth, fitted for life but lifeless, and try to imagine the commencement of life upon it. This certainly did not take place by any action of chemistry or electricity, or crystalline grouping of molecules under the influence of force, or by any possible kind of fortuitous concourse of atoms. We must pause, face to face with the mystery and miracle of the creation of living creatures."

Lord Kelvin, 1824–1907, British mathematician and physicist

ELUCIDATION:
A belief in God as creator is the first step in establishing a proper understanding of science. This conviction takes away all questions about *how* the universe came into existence. God is of primary importance, and as *Colossians 1:16-18* states: "For by him were all things created, that are in heaven, and that are in earth, visible and invisible, whether they be thrones, or dominions, or principalities, or powers: all things were created by him, and for him: And he is before all things, and by him all things consist . . . that in all things he might have the preeminence."

II

All scientific laws and principles must be in submission to the laws of God as revealed in the Bible, the source and origin of all truth.

BIBLICAL INDEX: John 17:17; I Tim. 6:20-21; Col. 1:17

KEY TERMS:
Law—"That which governs or has a tendency to rule; that which has the power of controlling."
Principle—"A truth admitted either without proof, or considered as having been proved."
Submission—"Compliance with the commands or laws of a superior."
Source—"First cause, original, that which gives rise to anything."
Origin—"The first existence or beginning of anything."

HISTORICAL STATEMENT:
"I have been blamed by men of science, both in this country and in England, for quoting the Bible in confirmation of the doctrines of physical geography. The Bible, they say, was not written for scientific purposes, and is therefore of no authority in matters of science. I beg pardon! The Bible is the authority for everything it touches. What would you think of the historian who should refuse to consult the historical records of the Bible, because the Bible was not written for the purposes of history? The Bible is true and science is true, and therefore each, if truthfully read, but proves the truth of the other.

"The agents in the physical economy of our planet are ministers of Him who made both it and the Bible. The records which He has chosen to make through the agency of these ministers of His upon the crust of the earth are as true as the records which, by the hands of His prophets and servants, He has been pleased to make in the Book of life.

"They are both true; and when your men of science, with vain and hasty conceit, announce the discovery of disagreement between them rely upon it, the fault is not with the witness of His records, but with the worm who essays to interpret evidence which he does not understand."

Matthew Fontaine Maury, 1806–1873, American Oceanographer and Meteorologist, *Matthew Fontaine Maury, Scientist of the Sea*, by Frances Leigh Williams.

ELUCIDATION:
The Bible was not written to be a science text-

book, but is scientifically correct both in statement and in principle. Science should be viewed in the light of God's Word—our only source of absolute, unchanging truth. As stated in the foregoing quote by Mr. Maury, when there seems to be a disagreement between science and Biblical teaching, the Bible is not the one in error.

It should be noted that several aspects of the Principle Approach can be seen in this statement of philosophy. The first is learning to "think governmentally," that is in terms of who or what is in control. By learning to "think governmentally," the student of natural science will be better equipped to reason about the way certain phenomena occur. Secondly, the Principle Approach stresses reasoning from the internal to the external, from the cause to the effect. God's decrees revealed in God's Word is the unseen cause of the visible effects or scientific laws that we see governing the world around us. Lastly, God's Word is revealed as the Source and Origin of the course content. All scientific facts are not in the Bible but "all nature is revelational of God." (Job 12:7-10)

III

Man, created in God's image, is given the responsibility of subduing and having dominion over all the creation.

BIBLICAL INDEX: Gen. 1:28; Psa. 8:6; Heb. 2:8; Gen. 9:2

KEY TERMS:
Image (similitude)—"Likeness; resemblance; likeness in nature; qualities or appearance."
Responsibility—"The state of being accountable or answerable, as for a trust or office."
Subdue—"To conquer by force or the exertion of superior power, and bring into permanent subjection."
Dominion—"Sovereign or supreme authority, the power of governing and controlling."

HISTORICAL STATEMENT:
"Almighty God, Who has created man in Thine own image, and made him a living soul that he might seek after Thee, and have dominion over Thy creatures, teach us to study the works of Thy hands, that we may subdue the earth to our use, and strengthen the reason for Thy service..."
Confession made by
James Clerk Maxwell in his papers, 1831–1879, Scottish Mathematician and Physicist

ELUCIDATION:
Science should not be viewed as simply a body of knowledge to be memorized by a student. Man was not created as the animals but in the image of God with the responsibility of subduing and having dominion over all the earth. As we view science, we need to realize that its purpose is to help man subdue the earth for his own use under God's leadership. Science should meet the practical needs of men as they become proper stewards of the world God has given them. In viewing science we should not only see the facts but how they have been used to help meet the needs of man through the ages. This shows the Biblical purpose of natural science, which is to exercise dominion over the world God has given to us in a way pleasing to Him. It means that we should teach children the importance of responsibility and stewardship in every aspect of the science curriculum.

IV

God's providential Hand can be seen in the preparation of individuals to discover the scientific advancements needed for the movement of the Gospel westward.

BIBLICAL INDEX: Dan. 2:20-22; Amos 3:7; Deut. 29:29

KEY TERMS:
Providence—"The care and superintendence which God exercises over His creatures."
Preparation—"The act or operation of preparing or fitting for a particular purpose."
Discover—"To lay open to the view something before unseen or concealed."
Advancement—"The act of moving forward or proceeding."

HISTORICAL STATEMENT:
"I see how God let me be bound with Tycho through an unalterable fate and did not let me be separated from him by the most oppressive hardships."
Johann Kepler, 1571–1630, German, Founder of Physical Astronomy.

ELUCIDATION:
The Principle Approach to American Christian education will teach the relation of every subject to the Chain of Christianity moving westward. In science God's providential hand can be seen as individuals are prepared to discover the scientific advancements needed for the movement of the Gospel westward. There is an indisputable intertwining of the Gospel moving westward and the scientific events needed for its advancement. Even an unsaved science historian will tell you

that scientific discovery exploded after the Bible got into the hands of the common man.

Getting the Bible into the hands of the individual was itself a scientific event. Witness the invention of the printing press. The press needed certain types of metals, specific molding processes and ways to make paper and ink. The list could go on and on. Scientific advancements such as the printing press did not come about by accident but were providentially planned for just the right time in history.

The Principle Approach enables us to move far beyond the memorization of facts, and enables us to see things wholistically. As we study, we will see how science is related to the advancement of the Bible. We will discover how the geography and history of certain countries with their different forms of government mesh together to bring the Gospel to America's shores.

Science comes alive with purpose and meaning as it is seen in its proper perspective to the Gospel. As the teacher uncovers the history of science, it is no longer a boring part of the curriculum. The teacher and student will develop a better view of God and what He is accomplishing in His-story.

V

America is unique in the history of science. Its form of government assured the individual the liberty to pursue and enjoy the benefits of his own productivity.

BIBLICAL INDEX: II Cor. 3:17; Eccl. 9:10; Isa. 33:22; Deut. 1:9-18; Prov. 6:6-11; Deut. 8:18

KEY TERMS:
Unique—"Distinct, separate and individual in oneness and purpose."
Government—"Direction, regulation, control, or restraint."
Assure—"To confirm; to make certain or secure."
Liberty—"Freedom from restraint."
Benefit—"Advantage; profit; expressing whatever contributes to promote prosperity and personal happiness, or add value to property."

HISTORICAL STATEMENT:
"I proceed, in the next place, to enquire what mode of education we shall adopt so as to secure to the state all the advantages that are to be derived from the proper instruction of youth; and here I beg leave to remark that the only foundation for a useful education in a republic is to be laid in religion. Without this, there can be no virtue, and without virtue there can be no liberty, and liberty is the object and life of all republican governments."

Benjamin Rush, American Physician, *Thoughts Upon the Mode of Education Proper in a Republic*, Early American Imprints, 1786

ELUCIDATION:
The Principle Approach teaches the uniqueness of America in its relation to science. This uniqueness stems from America's heritage of religious and civil liberty, a direct result of a government based on Biblical principles.

When America developed the form of government necessary to insure liberty for the individual, science exploded — not for its own sake — but for the good of mankind. This explosion benefited Americans in various ways which allowed them to accomplish their Gospel purpose. They soon possessed agricultural, technical, and medical knowledge which they shared with less developed peoples as they spread the Gospel around the world. Americans also enjoyed an unprecedented level of prosperity which permitted them to send missionaries all over the globe.

Americans need to remember God's past dealings with them, as the Israelites did in Deuteronomy 8. In doing so, they will realize that their prosperity is not an accident but a gift from God. This remembrance brings new meaning and purpose to the study of science. It also suggests the need to teach children their responsibility for civil government, even in the science classroom. Without a proper view of government, the benefits of science to individuals will diminish, and so will American prosperity.

BIBLICAL PRINCIPLES WHICH APPLY
TO NATURAL SCIENCE

What is the Bible and how should it be used in the study of science?

Webster defines the Bible as: "The Book, by way of eminence; the sacred volume, in which are contained the verbally inspired, literally true, revelations of God, the principles of Christian faith, and the rules of practice." The Bible is our only source of absolute, unchanging truth. All other sources of truth have come about by the observations of men and may contain error.

The following is just a sampling of the Biblical principles which could apply to any aspect of natural science. These principles will also fit under one or more of the five statements of an American Christian philosophy of natural science. As the teacher studies the Scriptures, he will uncover other Biblical principles which may be added to the list.

1. God's Word, the Bible, is our absolute final authority. (II Tim. 3:16)
2. The basis for God's creation is His decrees.
a. Eternal—No beginning or end. (Rev. 1:8)
b. Holy—Perfect and free from sin. (Psa. 99:9)
c. Omniscient—Knows all things. (Psa. 44:21)
d. Omnipotent—Unlimited power and authority. (Matt. 28:28)
e. Omnipresent—Present in all places at the same time. (Acts 17:27)
f. Personal—Deals with each person individually. (John 5:24)
3. God personally and directly created all things from nothing. (Heb. 11:3; Neh. 9:6)
4. God created with a divine orderliness and design. (Gen. 1:31)
5. God created kinds with a diversity within the kinds. (Gen. 1:21)
6. God created man in His own image.
a. Man was created separate from all living things. (Gen. 2:7)
b. Man was commanded to subdue the earth, and to have dominion over all living things. (Gen. 1:27-18)
c. Each man is created separate, distinct, and unique, as a revelation of God's diversity and individuality. (I Cor. 12:4-12)
d. Man was created as a triune being, individually responsible and individually accountable to God for the choices he makes. (Gen. 2:7; Acts 17:24-26)
e. Man's life does not end with death. (Dan. 12:2)
f. God has a divine plan to bring man salvation. (John 3:16)
7. God has chosen to use certain men to uncover His scientific truths, based on His own timetable. (Psa. 8:6; Eccl. 3:1-8)
8. God's perfect creation is complete and was finished in six 24-hour days. (Ex. 20:11)

9. God's material creation is deteriorating because of the entrance of sin. (Gen. 3:15-21)
10. The devil is a "real" person and, along with his demons, governs the activities of the non-Christian world—this is with God's permission. (Eph. 2:2; Job 2:3-5)
11. God brought judgment on the world with a year-long universal flood. (Gen. 7:11; 8:13)
12. God uses His creation to teach eternal truths. (Prov. 6:6; 30:25)

Many times it is helpful to contrast the Christian idea of man and his world with the pagan view. The contrast not only confirms the Christian idea, but also suggests many assignments involving reasoning and relating during the course of study.

SATAN'S COUNTERFEIT PRINCIPLES

1. The Bible is a combination myth and history book, written by men.
2. God is very remote and limited, or there is no God at all.
3. The universe evolved from pre-existing matter.
4. There is no design or designer of the world.
5. There are no certain kinds; everything is continually changing.
6. Man is a product of evolution, a higher form of animal; he is not accountable to God and has no need for God.
7. The men of science made discoveries because of their own intelligence and luck.
8. The world developed over a long, slow evolutionary process.
9. The world is continually improving.
10. The devil and demons are not real beings.
11. There were many small local floods in the world's past history.
12. The physical world has no meaning beyond how it can be used by man.

THE SEVEN BIBLICAL PRINCIPLES OF AMERICA'S CHRISTIAN HISTORY AND GOVERNMENT APPLIED TO NATURAL SCIENCE

When I first began to research my subject (natural science), I had the notion that the ultimate goal of an American Christian school was to teach the seven principles in every discipline.

Because of this misconception, I spent about eight weeks one summer working on a curriculum that illustrated the seven principles. At the time I felt rather good about the process because several of the principles fit nicely; those that didn't, I forced just a little.

As I tried to teach the subject the next year, I became very uncomfortable about this approach until I finally realized that the seven principles are those of America's Christian history and government, and not the principles of natural science. As a result of my research, I was able to see that there were principles of my specific subject.

I am not trying to say that the seven principles have no place in the natural sciences. As I view these principles, I see they have at least a fourfold purpose in the natural sciences or, for that matter, in any subject. *First,* they are the schoolmaster of the one doing the research. They help set the bounds and guide the individual as he becomes the master of the subject. *Second,* the seven principles help to determine course content. If what the instructor is teaching is not consistent with them, he is not emphasizing the proper things. *Third,* they help determine the method or the way we teach. The method of instruction must be consistent with the content, or the approach will not have the desired results. *Fourth,* the subject will reflect some of the seven principles which are also expressed in other subjects of the curriculum. As I present a particular idea, and one of the principles is evident, I will bring it out in passing and show how it is seen in other subjects.

A close look at the principles of anatomy and physiology and the course goals on pages 467 and 468 will show most of the seven principles restated in other terms because they are Biblical and useful to other subjects. In the natural sciences, the easiest principles to stress are one, four and seven.

I am convinced, however, that *the teacher should stress the principles of his particular subject,* and not the seven principles. If each area of the entire curriculum is being presented wholistically, the student will come away with a love for each subject—*and* an understanding of the principles of America's Christian history.

PART II
THE PRINCIPLE APPROACH
TO HUMAN ANATOMY AND PHYSIOLOGY

HISTORICAL OVERVIEW:
ANATOMY AND PHYSIOLOGY
ON THE CHAIN OF CHRISTIANITY

A study of the history of any subject will reveal the Hand of God moving to bring about His predetermined will upon the earth. The curriculum will come to life with meaning and purpose as it is viewed from an American Christian historical perspective, and students will develop a better understanding of a sovereign God who has a purpose for them *and* the subject in His creation. Chronology is intended to be a springboard for further study into the history of anatomy and physiology.

An American Christian curriculum would be incomplete for any subject without including the Chain of Christianity moving westward. As applied to anatomy and physiology, the Chain of Christianity relates both to the power of the Gospel with its transforming power on the minds of men, and to the practical application of anatomy and physiology in the area of medicine.

The scientific revolution and the Reformation are linked in that they both developed *after* the English Bible was put into the hands of the people in 1382. The transforming power of the Gospel and the liberty which it brought allowed science to advance out of the Dark Ages. Students need to be taught that the Scriptures were fundamental to the scientific revolution.

It is no accident that the founding of America as a nation and the major medical advancements go hand in hand. America's purpose as a nation was to spread the Gospel. The medical advancements were needed to show Christ's love as missionaries shared the Gospel message. Areas of the world without Christianity were uncivilized and missionaries could show the love of Christ by many physical means, including medical care.

The chronology that follows demonstrates how anatomy and physiology are linked to the Scriptures and to the needs of a missionary. The list is not intended to be all-inclusive. Medicine has been included because it is the practical application of anatomy and physiology. The persons listed are not all of equal importance, and not all of them need to be included in your curriculum. An asterisk (*) will indicate those individuals who have made the most important contributions. Choose those persons who are best fitted to the goals of your course. Further study will reveal others who are not on the list but are just as worthy and should be included. This will be especially true of American men of science.

1550 B.C. — Moses and the relationship between the supernatural and anatomical phenomena.

400 B.C. — *Hippocrates—Father of modern medicine

350 B.C. — Praxagoras—Greek physician

320 B.C. — Herophilus—Greek anatomist

B.C. — Birth of Christ

25 A.D. — Luke—Beloved physician

170 A.D. — *Galen—Greek physician

980 A.D. — Avcenna—Persian physician

1275 A.D. — Mondino De-Luzzi—Italian anatomist

1382 A.D. — John Wycliff

1454 A.D. — Gutenburg Bible

1492 A.D. — Columbus

1497 A.D. — Jean Fernel—French physician

1500 A.D. — Leonardo DaVinci—Italian scientist and artist

1517 A.D. — Martin Luther

1520 A.D. — Paracelsus—Swiss physician

1537 A.D. — Michael Servetus—Circulation of blood in lungs

1540 A.D. — John Calvin

1543 A.D. — *Andreas Vesalius—Published *On the Fabric of the Human Body*

1559 A.D. — Fabricius—Italian physician

1560 A.D. — Bible is widely distributed

1588 A.D. — England—preserved from Spanish domination

1596 A.D. — Galileo Galilei—developed heat measurement

1604 A.D. — *Johann Kepler—described lens principle of the eye

1611 A.D. — Sanctorius—Italian physician

1620 A.D. — Pilgrims land

1630 A.D. — William Harvey—Circulation of the blood

1648 A.D. — Francesco Redi—Disproves spontaneous generation

1650 A.D. — Alfonso Borelli—Italian physiologist observed muscular action

1658 A.D. — Jan Swammerdam—Observed red corpuscles

1661 A.D. — Robert Boyle—British chemist

1661 A.D. — Malpighi—Account of capillary system

1665 A.D. — Richard Lower—English physician

1677 A.D. — *Anton van Leeuwenhoek—Observed spermatozoa

1721 A.D. — Zabdiel Boylston—American, did inoculations for smallpox in Boston

1735 A.D. — Carlous Linnaeus—Father of classification

1758 A.D. — James Lind—Scottish physician

1759 A.D. — Kaspar Wolf—German physiologist—father of modern embryology

1761 A.D. — Rene Antoine Reaumur—Father of pathology

1770 A.D. — *Benjamin Franklin—American—many areas of science

1771 A.D. — Luigi Galvani—Italian anatomist

1772 A.D. — Joseph Priestly—English chemist

1774 A.D. — *Antoine Lavoisier—Proved H_2O and CO_2 are produced in breathing

1776 A.D. — Declaration of Independence

1780 A.D. — *Benjamin Rush—American—Many areas of physiology

1787 A.D. — America's Constitution

1796 A.D. — Edward Jenner—Smallpox vaccination

1799 A.D. — Noah Webster—American—History of pestilential disease

1809 A.D. — Thomas Jefferson—American—Interested in many sciences

1810 A.D. — Jean Larrey—Developed local analgesis (Pain killer)

1812 A.D. — Adoniram Judson—First American Foreign Missionary

1819 A.D. — Dr. Scudder—First Medical Missionary

1820 A.D. — Georges Cuvier–French anatomist

1822 A.D. — *William Beaumont—American surgeon

1842 A.D. — Crawford Long—American—First used anesthetic

1842 A.D. — Oliver Wendell Holmes—American author and physician

1844 A.D. — William Morton—American dentist

1846 A.D. — William Procter, Jr.—Father of American pharmacy

1847 A.D. — *Ignaz Shmmelweiss—Hungarian physician

1851 A.D. — Claude Bernard—French physiologist

1866 A.D. —*Gregor Mendel—Established principles of heredity

1867 A.D. — Joseph Lister—Developed antiseptic surgery

1870 A.D. — Sir Patrick Manson—Father of tropical medicine

1876 A.D. — Robert Koch—Discovered anthrax bacillus

1885 A.D. —*Louis Pasteur—Developed treatment for rabies and the "germ theory of disease"

1894 A.D. — Shibasabuso Kitasoto—Discovered bubonic plague germ

1896 A.D. — Ronald Ross—American—Discovered cause of malaria

1900 A.D. —*Walter Reed—American—Discovered cause of yellow fever

DEVELOPMENT OF AN INDIVIDUAL PHYSICIAN ON THE CHAIN OF CHRISTIANITY MOVING WESTWARD

DR. BENJAMIN RUSH

Young people today need examples of individuals who have displayed true American Christian character. These men can be found in most areas of study. The Principle Approach encourages us to uncover these individuals and highlight not only their Christian character but also their place on the Chain of Christianity. These examples of character do not have to be Americans, but it is helpful to your goals as an American Christian educator if they are.

As the history of these men is developed, look for original sources such as their writings and not just what historians said about them. Also look for the oldest biographies available. More recent studies are likely to omit the providential perspective.

Our biography of Dr. Benjamin Rush includes sufficient materials to indicate what sort of things to look for when studying an individual. As a man of science, Rush *is* a fine example of American Christian character — a character that was interested in all aspects of life and made significant contributions to the quality of health, medicine, liberty and government in his nation. As you study the history of any subject, you will find many other examples worthy of further study.

BENJAMIN RUSH HERITAGE AND CHARACTER

Ancestry and Parentage:
"Benjamin Rush liked to trace his revolutionary spirit back to great-grandfather John Rush, who had commanded a cavalry unit in Oliver Cromwell's army. Later, John Rush turned Quaker, and in the intolerant atmosphere of the Restoration, seized an opportunity to immigrate, settling with his children and grandchildren in William Penn's new colony in 1683."[1]

Benjamin was born on the 4th of January 1746, the fourth of seven children born to John Rush and Susanna Hall Harvey Rush. John Rush was a gunsmith like his father before him. He lived an exemplary life and died in good standing, as a member of the Episcopal church, on July 26, 1751. Benjamin was then only five.

On his mother's side, Benjamin descended from ancestors also all from England. Susanna was emotionally strong and a religiously faithful mother. She was able to support the family, after her husband's death, by running a grocery. She changed the family to the Presbyterian church, led by Gilbert Tennent, an evangelical leader in the Great Awakening.[2]

School and College:
At the age of eight, Benjamin was sent off to a boarding school run by his mother's brother-in-law, Reverend Samuel Finley, a good friend of Gilbert Tennent. The Reverend Finley ran the school in connection with his ministry and his main objective was to prepare young men for the ministry. He also stressed Greek, Latin, literature, philosophy, mathematics, love of nature, and a good amount of Christian character.

---

1. *Benjamin Rush's Lectures on the Mind*, p. 6.
2. *The Autobiography of Benjamin Rush*, p. 24.

461

Benjamin left this school in the spring of 1759 when he was 15. He was admitted into the junior class at Jersey College, where Reverend Jacob Green was the president. Benjamin said of Green, "His mode of teaching inspired me with a love of knowledge, and that if I derived but little from his instructions, I was taught by him how to acquire it in the subsequent periods of my life. I learned from him to record in a book which he called 'Liber Selectorum' such passages in the classics as struck me most forcibly in reading them. By recording these passages, I was led afterwards to record facts and opinions. To this I owe perhaps in part the frequent use I have made of pen and ink."[3]

Life in Philadelphia and the Revolutionary Period:

"From the time of my settlement in Philadelphia in 1769 till 1775, I led a life of constant labor and self-denial. My shop was crowded with the poor in the morning and at meal times, and nearly every street and alley in the city was visited by me every day."[4] "While my days were thus employed in business, my evenings were devoted to study. I seldom went to bed before 12 o'clock, and many many times have I heard the watchmen cry 3 o'clock before I have put out my candle."[5]

Rush was elected professor of chemistry in the college of Philadelphia in August 1769. He continued as a spectator of events until the winter of 1775, when he decided to bear his share of the Revolution. In the winter of 1776 he was elected a member of the Committee of Inspection. He took his seat in the Continental Congress and was a signer of the Declaration of Independence. Rush later wrote a paper dealing with the character of each man who signed the Declaration of Independence. During this time he was in frequent contact with the leaders of the Revolution. While visiting General Washington, Rush remarked "I observed him to play with his pen and ink upon several small pieces of paper. One of them by accident fell upon the floor near my feet. I was struck with the inscription upon it. It was "Victory or Death."[6]

Rush remained in the Congress until 1777. He then served with the Philadelphia militia as surgeon and was in the 2nd battle of Trenton and the battle of Princeton. He later became the Physician General in Washington's army. He continually fought for more order in the hospitals and better care for the soldiers. He finally brought charges against the medical Director General, who was later asked to leave the service. It has been said that it was Rush's insistent requests for proper care of the troops, including inoculations, that allowed America finally to triumph in the Revolutionary War. He retired from the army to Princeton where he continued his medical practice.

VARIOUS ASPECTS OF RUSH'S CAREER AND WRITING

Rush, Salvation, and Christianity:

"My only hope of salvation is in the infinite transcendent love of God manifested to the world by the death of His Son upon the cross. Nothing but His blood will wash away my sins. I rely exclusively upon it. Come Lord Jesus! Come quickly! And take thy lost, but redeemed creature! I will believe and I will hope in Thy salvation! Amen and Amen!"[7]

"The Gospel of Jesus Christ prescribes the wisest rules for just conduct in every situation of life. Happy are they who are enabled to obey them in all situations."[8]

"There can be no true greatness that is not founded upon Christian principles, and the men of this world are great only in proportion as they assume certain Christian virtues."[9]

How God Was Directing America and Her National Purpose:

"Upon passage of the Declaration of Independence—Most of the men who had been active in bringing it about, were blind actors in the business. Not one man in a thousand contemplated or wished for the independence of our country in 1774, and but few of those who assented to it, foresaw the immense influence it would soon have upon the national and individual characters of the Americans. It would have been a truth if God had said it, that "the way of man is not in himself, and that it is not in man that walketh to direct his steps." (Jer. 10:23)[10]

Establishment of Schools:

"I proceed, in the next place, to enquire what mode of education we shall adopt so as to secure to the state all the advantages that are to be derived from the proper instruction of youth; and here I beg leave to remark that the only founda-

---

3. *Ibid.*, p. 36.
4. *Ibid.*, p. 83.
5. *Ibid.*, p. 84.
6. *Ibid.*, p. 124.

7. *Ibid.*, p. 166.
8. *Ibid.*, p. 165.
9. *Letters of Benjamin Rush*, Volume I, p. 574.
10. *Autobiography of Benjamin Rush*, p. 119.

tion for a useful education in a republic is to be laid in religion. Without this, there can be no virtue, and without virtue there can be no liberty, and liberty is the object and life of all republican governments.

"I must be excused in not agreeing with those modern writers who have opposed the use of the Bible as a school book ... I maintain that there is no book of its size in the whole world that contains half so much useful knowledge for the governments of states, or the direction of the affairs of individuals as the Bible.

"Next to the duty which young men owe to their *Creator*, I wish to see a *supreme regard to their country* ... Our country includes family, friends and property and should be preferred to them all ... Let him be taught to love his family, but let him be taught at the same time that he must forsake and even forget them when the welfare of his country requires it. He must watch for the state *as if its liberties depended upon his vigilance alone*, but he must do this in such a manner as not to defraud his creditors, or neglect his family."[11]

Property of Conscience:

"I am aware of the difficulty of opposing popular prejudices and that it is often much better to swim with the multitude down the stream, than to stem it alone. I am aware too of the fate of reformers in religion—politics and science. Many have lost their characters—their livings—and even their lives, by advancing things contrary to the established opinions of the world. But, should this be my case, I will not conceal my sentiments, nor resist what I look upon and feel to be the *sacred power of truth*."[12]

---

11. *Thoughts Upon the Mode of Education Proper in a Republic*, 1786. Early American Imprints, p. 36. (Emphasis added)
12. *Sermons To Gentlemen Upon Temperance*, 1772, Early American Imprints.

MEDICAL WRITINGS

On the Use of Tobacco:

"Were it possible for a being who had resided upon our globe, to visit the inhabitants of a planet, where reason governed, and to tell them that a vile weed was in general use among the inhabitants of the globe it had left, which afforded no nourishment—that this weed was cultivated with immense care—that it was an important article of commerce—that the want of it produced real misery—that its taste was extremely nauseous, that it was unfriendly to health and morals, and that its use was attended with a considerable loss of time and property, the account would be incredible, and the author of it would probably be excluded from society, for relating a story of so improbable a nature. In no one view, is it possible to contemplate the creature man in a more absurd and ridiculous light than in his attachment to tobacco."[13]

Effects on Health
1. Impairs the appetite
2. Prevents proper digesting of food
3. Promotes diseases of the nerves
4. Loss of teeth
5. Impairs speech

Effects on Morals
1. Causes thirst—alcohol
2. Promotes idleness
3. Neglect of cleanliness
4. Offensive to those who do not use it

On Eating:

"Food, therefore, may be said to be taken in too large a quantity, when you do not feel light and cheerful after it."[14]

---

13. *Observations Upon the Influence of the Habitual Use of Tobacco Upon Health, Morals and Property*, Early American Imprints.
14. *Sermons to Gentlemen on Temperance*, 1772.

APPLYING THE PRINCIPLE APPROACH TO HUMAN ANATOMY AND PHYSIOLOGY

Once I became convinced of the Principle Approach, I started to 4R my subjects. I will illustrate the method while developing the course. The first step is to identify the vocabulary and properties of the discipline.

DEFINITIONS AND PROPERTIES
OF THE SUBJECT

An abridged list of the vocabulary of this subject is given on pages 464-466. I shall introduce only a few key terms and italicize some of the words one could further define.

1. Human—belonging to *man* or mankind; pertaining or relating to the race of man; as a human *voice*; human *shape*; human *nature*; human *knowledge*; human *life*.

    a. Man—Mankind; the human race; the whole species of human beings; beings distinguished from animals by the powers of *reason* and *speech*, as well as by their *shape* and dignified aspect.

    b. Nature—The essence, essential qualities or *attributes* of a thing, which constitute what it is; as the nature of the soul, the nature of blood; the nature of a circle or an angle. When we speak of the nature of man, we understand the peculiar *constitution* of his body or *mind*, or the qualities of the species which distinguish him from animals. When we speak of the nature of a man, or of an individual of the race, we mean his particular qualities or constitution; either the peculiar *temperament* of his body, or the *affections* of his mind, his natural *appetites*, *passions*, *disposition* or *temper*.

2. Anatomy—The *doctrine* of the *structure* of the *body*. The art of dissecting, or artificially separating the different parts of a body to discover their *situation*, structure and *economy*.

    a. Doctrine—In a general sense, whatever is taught. Hence, a *principle* or position in any *science*; whatever is laid down as true by an instructor or master.

    b. Structure—Manner of *organization* of animals and vegetables.

    c. Organization—The act of forming or *arranging* the parts of a compound or *complex* body in a suitable manner for use or *service*.

    d. Body—The *frame* of an animal; the *material substance* of an animal, in distinction from the living principle of beasts, and the *soul* of man.

3. Physiology—According to the Greek, this word signifies a discourse or treatise of nature, but the moderns use the word in a more limited sense for the science of the *properties* and *functions* of animals and plants, comprehending what is common to all animals and plants, and what is peculiar to individuals and species.

    a. Property—a *peculiar quality* of any thing: that which is inherent in a subject, or *naturally essential* to it.

    b. Function—In a general sense, the *doing*, *executing* or *performing* of any thing.

    c. Essential—Necessary to the constitution or *existence* of a thing.

VOCABULARY OF PHYSIOLOGY AND ANATOMY

The following physiological and anatomical terms are a sample of the extensive vocabulary of these subjects. These words are listed for further research in such helpful books as *Naves Topical Bible*. This list is intended to help the teacher and student begin to identify the Biblical origin and purpose of the specific course content. Further research will require a comprehensive Bible concordance.

A
Abortion
Abstinence total
Adam
Adultery
Afflictions
Anatomy
Anger
Antediluvians
Appetite
Arm
Atrophy (of the hand)

B
Babes
Baldness
Barrenness
Birth
Blindness
Blood
Body
Boil
Bones
Breath

C
Cannibalism
Children (many sub-topics)
Cleanliness
Conception
Concupiscence
Conscience
Cooking
Cosmetics
Creation
Creature

D
Dead
Deafness
Demons
Depravity of man
Disease (many sub-topics)
Doctor

P
Pain
Palsy
Paralysis
Philosophy
Physician
Physiology
Plague
Power of Christ

R
Reproduction

S
Salvation
Sanitation
Scab (disease)
Science
Scurvy
Self (control)
Sensuality
Sin
Skin
Sorcery
Soul
Suicide
Sunstroke
Sweat

T
Teachers
Teaching
Tears
Teeth
Tumor
Twins

V
Vanity

W
Wen (tumor)
Witchcraft
Women
Word of God
Wounds

COURSE DESCRIPTION

Human anatomy and physiology will comprehend the study of the structure and function of the human body. Structure will include the complex *arranging* of the diverse parts of a body and how these *parts* work together *in unity* for the proper function of the whole. Structure will also include the basic substances of which the body is composed. The functioning of the body will include the specific properties of all the parts of a body and all the materials necessary to insure their proper performance. The word "human" implies that the study will be limited to mankind, but should include differences and responsibilities that are peculiar to man.

BIBLICAL ORIGIN AND PURPOSE OF HUMAN ANATOMY AND PHYSIOLOGY

After the vocabulary of the subject has been exhausted from Webster's 1828 Dictionary, the next step would be Biblical research. Take all the words listed in your vocabulary section and look up their Scriptural meanings. Include synonyms of words and terms that can be obtained from cross referencing the Bible. Look up applicable terms from *Naves Topical Bible*.

Here are some examples that reveal the Biblical origin of human anatomy and physiology.

Biblical Origin:
1. Job 10:11
"*Thou* hast clothed me with skin and flesh and hast fenced me with bones and sinews."
2. Acts 18:28
"For *in Him* we live, and move, and have our being; as certain also of your own poets have said, for we are also his offering."
3. Genesis 2:7
"And the *Lord God* formed man of the dust of the ground, and breathed into his nostrils the breath of life; and man became a living soul."
4. Job 38:36
"*Who* hath put wisdom in the inward parts? Or who hath given understanding to the heart?"
5. Psalms 94:9
"*He that planted* the ear, shall he not hear? *He that formed* the eye, shall he not see?"

CONCLUSIONS: The Bible makes the origin of man extremely clear. God is the Master Designer Who created man and physiologically equipped him so marvelously to live in this world. There is never a hint of any evolutionary process or of man being a higher form of animal. Man was created by God and in the image of God. This list of scriptures is only partial.

Biblical Purpose:
The following references from the Bible are selected from numerous passages that suggest *why* God wants man to know himself physiologically and to "keep under my body, and bring it into subjection" (I Cor. 9:27):

Genesis 1:28: "And God blessed them, and God said unto them, Be fruitful, and multiply, and replenish the earth, and subdue it; and have dominion over the fish of the sea, and over the fowl of the air, and over every living thing that moveth upon the earth."

CONCLUSION: Man is to have dominion over God's creation, including his own body and other created organisms which will have an effect on the health or soundness of man.

Psalms 139:14: "I will praise thee: for I am fearfully and wonderfully made: marvelous are thy works, and that my soul knoweth right well."

CONCLUSION: We are to praise God because of His marvelous creation.

Proverbs 14:30: "A sound heart is the life of the flesh: but envy the rottenness of the bones."

Proverbs 3:7-8: "Be not wise in thine own eyes: Fear the Lord, and depart from evil. It shall be health to thy navel, and marrow to thy bones."

CONCLUSION: We are to understand Scriptural admonitions as to what causes man to be healthy or unhealthy.

Proverbs 23:21: "For the drunkard and the glutton shall come to poverty: and drowsiness shall clothe a man with rags."

CONCLUSION: We are to be good stewards of the body God has given to us, so that we may work more effectively in His Kingdom.

Matthew 9:12: "But when Jesus heard that, he said unto them, They that be whole need not a physician, but they that are sick." (Matt. 8:14-17; Luke 10:34)

CONCLUSION: American Christians should follow the example of Jesus who always met physical as well as spiritual needs.

I Corinthians 6:18-20: "Flee fornication. Every sin that a man doeth is without the body; but he that committeth fornication sinneth against his own body. What? Know ye not that your body is the temple of the Holy Ghost which is in you which ye have of God, and ye are not your own? For ye are bought with a price; therefore, glorify God in your body, and in your spirit, which are God's."

CONCLUSION: We are to understand how the body works because it is the temple of the Holy Spirit and should not be defiled.

I Corinthians 9:27: "But I keep under my body, and bring it into subjection lest by any means, when I have preached to others, I myself should be a castaway."

CONCLUSION: We should learn areas of our physical nature which require Christian self-control so that we can keep our body under subjection.

RUDIMENTS OF HUMAN ANATOMY AND PHYSIOLOGY

As mentioned earlier, the principles of a discipline are the foundation of the subject. Any part of the course content taught should have a principle at its base. These truths come out of the course description, vocabulary, Biblical origin and purpose of the subject and a knowledge of its history. The principles are written on a high school level, but could easily be rendered for an elementary student.

BASIC PRINCIPLES

1. God created distinct elements, with specific arrangements and numbers of parts, so that they can work individually or in complex combinations to form all the material universe, and, especially, to perform those functions necessary for life. (Gen. 1:1; Gen. 2:7)

2. God's creation shows evidence of having a Master Designer, not the appearance of chance happenings. (Job 12:7-9; Rom. 1:20)

3. God's creation will show the evidence of great order, not chaos. (Gen. 1:31; I Cor. 14:40)

4. God's creation is complete and finished. Matter and energy can neither be created nor destroyed. The world is designed so that only transformation, conservation and preservation are now taking place. (Gen. 2:1-3; Ex. 20:11; Neh. 9:6; Heb. 1:2-3; II Pet. 3:7)

5. The creation is deteriorating because of the entrance of sin into the world. Processes in nature eventually go toward less order. Variations in God's original design, because of deterioration, will cause harmful effects. (Gen. 3:6, 14-19; Isa. 51:6; Rom. 8:20-22; Heb. 1:10-11)

6. Man must consume nutrients, break down these nutrients, then build bonds between the elements and molecules to make the materials necessary for growth, repair, energy and control. (Gen. 1:29-30; Psa. 104:14; Matt. 6:11; Gen. 9:3)

7. Life activities depend upon a constant supply of energy, obtained from the breakdown of bonds in food molecules. In man, this is accomplished by adding oxygen to food (respiration). (Gen. 1:29-30; Gen. 7:22; Acts 27:34; Eccl. 3:19; Lev. 17:11, 14)

8. Life can only come from pre-existing life, which

originated with the creative Hand of God. (Gen. 2:7; Psa. 33:6-9; Acts 17:25-28; Heb. 11:3; Rev. 10:6)

9. The individual or diverse parts of a body will work together with unity to make and benefit the whole. (I Cor. 12:12,18,24)

10. The information needed for all life and all life activities must be passed from cell to cell and from generation to generation. (Gen. 3:20; Eccl. 3:20)

11. Humans have been given the ability to conceive, reproduce, and grow. Reproduction insures both unity and diversity among humans. (Gen. 1:28, 4:1, 9:17; Eccl. 11:5)

12. God has chosen to use men to uncover truths about His creation, on a timetable according to His sovereign plans. (Dan. 2:22; Amos 3:7; Eph. 1:11)

13. God created man in His own image, distinct from all other creations, with a body, soul and a spirit. Man is now responsible to God as regarding salvation, good works, the subduing of the environment, and exercising a wise stewardship of that which God has given him. (Gen. 2:7; Rom. 10:9; Eph. 2:10; Gen. 1:28; Psa. 8:6-8; Psa. 24:1; Prov. 27:23; Prov. 27:26-27; Rom. 14:12; I Cor. 15:38-39)

14. All humans have a life span and will eventually die. (Eccl. 12:7; Heb. 9:27; I Pet. 1:24)

15. Compliance with Biblical principles will result in better health for the individual. (Ex. 15:26; Mark 6:31; Prov. 17:22; Prov. 23:21)

16. God has created within man a system of control by which he can interact and thereby have dominion over his environment. (Gen. 1:26,28; 2:19-20; 9:2)

17. Man has been created with the need for rest and will not function properly without an adequate amount. (Ex. 23:12; 34:21; Mark 6:31)

AMERICAN CHRISTIAN COURSE GOALS FOR HUMAN ANATOMY AND PHYSIOLOGY

The following course goals are deduced from the distinctives of an American Christian philosophy of Human Anatomy and Physiology. The goals listed are intended to be used at the high school level. Similar goals could apply to the elementary grades.

1. The student, during the course of the year, should grow in his praise of, knowledge about, humility towards, and reverence for God, the Creator and Controller of all things.

2. The student will understand that the course content will always be in submission to the Word of God, our only source of absolute, unchanging knowledge.

3. The student should understand that the Bible is to be believed by faith and, although it is not meant to be a scientific textbook, the Bible does present the science of creationism as the only framework from which to view the world and its processes.

4. The student should develop the ability to recognize America's heritage of Christian character as evidenced in the lives of the men of American science.

5. Through the events of science, the student should develop a better understanding of America's Gospel purpose as God's providential hand moves in the history of the subject to advance the chain of Christianity westward.

6. By using the notebook approach, the student should learn to research, reason, relate and record. This will involve diligence, industry, organization, completeness, neatness, regard for property, and a mastery of the subject on the student's part. These will be accomplished by adherence to classroom procedures and the meeting of requirements which will center around the notebook, assignments, and tests.

7. The student should master the principles and leading ideas of human anatomy and physiology and, by thinking governmentally, be able to use them to reason and to relate to various other subjects.

8. The student should recognize that as American Christians they are to be internally Spirit-controlled, that they may become stewards of the course content learned during the year.

9. Through the teaching of America's heritage of Christian character, as evidenced in the lives of the men of science, the student should recognize the uniqueness of America and the need to return to Biblical attitudes concerning such moral issues as abortion, humanism, evolution, euthanasia, purity of life and eugenics. "Establish Thy word to Thy servant, As that which produces reverence for Thee." (Psa. 119:38, ASV)

INTRODUCTION TO THE COURSE OVERVIEW

As indicated in the *Summary Overview* chart that follows, the elements of the course have been divided into three major groups, with a total of seventeen units. The units can be divided into four groups. This would allow the teacher to teach four units each of the first three weeks, five units the last nine weeks, and complete the course in one year.

The first two units are parts of the general introduction. The unit on philosophy would include a brief introduction to an American Christian philosophy of science, the basic teachings of creation and evolution, and a section on the scientific method. The second unit is entitled "What is Man?" and teaches the Biblical view of man, how he is different and what his responsibilities are.

The second major part of the overview teaches the component physical part of an individual. To understand how an individual functions one must know the parts from which he was created. A thorough understanding of chemical principles and cells will enable the student to understand the basic elements that constitute the study of human anatomy and physiology.

The last major section is the systems of the individual. Each system performs a specific function, which all together make up the complete physiological individual. For each system the student should understand the structure of the system, how it fulfills its purpose, and its proper care. As the teacher develops each unit, the principles previously taught should be reviewed.

HIGH SCHOOL COURSE OUTLINE

FIRST NINE WEEKS
I. Distinctives of an American Christian study of Human Anatomy and Physiology.
II. What is man, that Thou art mindful of him?
III. Basic Chemical Principles
IV. Cellular organization and function

SECOND NINE WEEKS
V. Skeletal System
VI. Muscular System

SUMMARY OVERVIEW

INTRODUCTION	COMPONENT PARTS	SYSTEMS
I. Distinctives of an American Christian study of human anatomy and physiology II. "What is man, that thou art mindful of him?"	III. Basic Chemical Principles IV. Cellular organization and function	STANDING AND MOVING V. Skeletal System VI. Muscular System USE OF ENERGY AND WASTE DISPOSAL VII. Digestive System VIII. Respiratory System IX. Circulatory System X. Urinary System COORDINATION AND CONTROL XI. Nervous System XII. Sensory System XIII. Endocrine System PROTECTION XIV. Integumentary System XV. Infectious Disease and Defense Systems PRODUCING NEW LIFE XVI. Human Genetics XVII. Reproduction, Embryology and Birth

VII. Digestive System
VIII. Respiratory System

HIGH SCHOOL
DAILY LESSON PLAN

The following *Sample Lesson Plan* demonstrates various aspects of the Principle Approach to human anatomy and physiology. The lesson format and methods are useful at any level with slight variations.

Every lesson should be consistent with an American Christian philosophy of science but does not have to stress all the principles. Each lesson should, however, reflect an aspect of one course goal and emphasize at least one principle or Biblical concept. Each day's lesson should teach at least *one complete* thought. Do not leave students wondering what is the point of a presentation. *(The Basic Principles listed by number on the Sample Lesson Plan are all found on pp. 467 and 468)*

The material in the demonstration can be covered in one to two 50-minute class periods. The first major emphasis would be respiration, including its origin, purpose and history. The second major emphasis should be the structure and purpose of the first two parts of the respiratory system, the nose and pharnyx.

It is not enough simply to write facts on the chalk board and ask the students to copy them. The facts should be presented so that the student must deduce the principles and leading ideas from them — or deduce the facts from the principles. This can be done very effectively with questions which will cause the students to begin reasoning. Some of these questions have been included in the methods column.

ELEMENTARY COURSE OVERVIEW

In teaching elementary human anatomy and physiology, use only a small portion of the high school course outline. Choose any of the sections as long as the content is viewed through the five statements of an American Christian philosophy to natural science (see pp. 454-456). Biblical principles should be stressed whenever applicable to course content. Goals for the American Christian classroom should be reviewed often and course content developed to help meet those goals. The Biblical origin and purpose of the course should be kept in view. Finally, the basic principles of the course should be stressed throughout the year.

EMPHASIS AT THE ELEMENTARY LEVEL

Depending upon the grade level and emphasis of the school, the science curriculum is usually 10-12 hours every nine weeks. Whatever the length of time, the major emphasis should be on *capturing the spirit* of the content and not getting bogged down in teaching facts. If nothing but facts are presented, students quickly lose their desire to understand how God's world works and their responsibility in that world.

The major emphasis at the elementary level is as follows:

1. To capture the majesty and greatness of God's creation
2. To begin to develop an idea of how science fits on the chain of Christianity
3. To see America's heritage of Christian character through the men studied
4. To learn the basic principles which apply to the subject being studied
5. To understand how the body works to accomplish the specific function being studied
6. To learn how to be a wise steward of that specific function from both a medical and spiritual perspective

ELEMENTARY COURSE OUTLINE
(GRADES 3–6)

The following course outline is divided into four nine-week periods. Each period indicates the basic principles of human anatomy and physiology to be emphasized. One or more of the seventeen principles is listed by number and correlated with those found on pages 467-468.

FIRST NINE WEEKS

I. Distinctives of an American Christian study of human anatomy and physiology
   A. American Christian philosophy of natural science (Briefly explain the ideas expressed in the

five statements of philosophy to let the students know the background for the study.) (Principles 12, 13, 15)

B. Definitions of key terms in course titles (Use as many as are needed to let students know what they are going to study. (Principle 3)

C. Science history and the Chain of Christianity moving westward (Brief introduction to: 1.) The place of the Bible in science history, 2.) The Chain of Christianity and 3.) the purpose of America. Begin a timeline to be developed and consulted throughout the year.) (Principle 12)

D. Definition of American Christian character traits (Develop a list of terms with proper definitions which can be reviewed during the year as traits of character are seen in the lives of the individuals you will study.) (Principle 13)

E. How and why information is obtained about God's creation

1. Explain the place of the Bible in science.

2. Explain the purpose of studying science (Basically, having dominion, stewardship, and helping others).

3. Give a brief introduction to the scientific method (Most books have a section on this. Choose one that will not be too involved or detailed.) (Principles 2 and 3)

II. What is man, that Thou art mindful of him? *Psalms 8:4*

A. How is man different from the other creations of God?

1. God's Principle of Individuality

2. Created in the image of God

3. Created a triune being

4. Created for a purpose

5. Set over God's creation

(These four areas should be described Scripturally and as many implications as desired can be made. As you research you will find other areas to include.) (Principles 13 & 16)

B. What is man, and how is he controlled? Is he:

1. Just chemicals?

2. Just cells?

(An overall view of the complexity of man and the "breath of life")

3. How is man controlled?

(Possible sections could include: intelligence; learned behavior; spirituality; carnality; satan; inate behavior. Stress again that man is a spiritual being.) (Principles 2, 8 and 16)

C. What are the responsibilities of man?

1. Glorify God

2. Salvation

3. Stewardship

4. Follow God's laws set forth in scripture (Principle 13)

SECOND NINE WEEKS

III. Nutrition and Digestion

A. Nutrients

1. Inorganic nutrients

a. Minerals

b. Vitamins

c. Water

2. Organic nutrients

a. Roughage

b. Fats

c. Proteins

d. Carbohydrates

(This section includes parts about what would be a good diet, calories, gluttony and other related topics.) (Principles 1, 6, and 15)

B. Digestion

1. Oral cavity

a. Teeth

b. Tongue

c. Saliva

2. To the stomach

a. Pharynx

b. Esophagus

c. Epiglottis

d. Stomach

(1) William Beaumont

(2) Gastric fluid

(3) Stomach muscles

3. Small intestine

a. Small intestine—size and location

b. Liver—gall bladder

c. What happens to food

4. Large intestine

a. Size and location

b. Purposes (Principles 6, 7 and 9)

C. Disorders and diseases of the digestive system

1. Vomiting

2. Food poisoning

3. Heartburn

4. Mumps

5. Ulcers

6. Vitamin and mineral deficiency diseases (Principles 5 and 2)

D. Life and work of Benjamin Rush (Principles 12 and 15)

THIRD NINE WEEKS

IV. Framework of the body—skin, skeleton and muscles

A. Skin

1. Purposes

a. Protection

b. Sensation
c. Heat control
d. Excretion
e. Absorption
f. Vitamin and hormone manufacture
2. Hair and nails
3. Oil and sweat glands
4. Skin color
5. Proper care of the skin
6. Skin diseases and disorders
a. Burns
b. Callouses
c. Ringworms
d. Warts
(Principles 2 and 12)
B. Skeletal Systems
1. Bones are living organs
2. Purposes
3. Structure of bones
4. Growth of a bone
5. Bone fractures
6. Learn names of a few bones
7. Joints
8. Proper care of bones
9. Fossils, missing links and evolution
(Principles 1, 3, 9, and 13)
C. Muscular Systems
1. Purpose of muscles
2. Muscle structure
3. Types of muscles
4. Proper care of muscles
5. Muscle disorders
a. Atrophy
b. Paralysis

c. Cramps
d. Spasms
e. Muscular Dystrophy
f. Convulsions
(Principles 2, 5, 9, 14, 17)

FOURTH NINE WEEKS

V. Sense Organs
A. Skin
1. Pain
2. Touch
3. Pressure
4. Heat
5. Cold
B. Smell
1. Structures and functions
2. Purposes
C. Taste (covered in digestion)
D. Sight
1. Structures and functions
2. How we see
3. Care of the eyes
4. Common defects in vision
5. Scriptural admonitions
E. The Ear
1. Structures and functions
2. How we hear
3. Balance
4. Care of the ears
5. Common defects in hearing
6. Scriptural admonitions
(Principles 2, 3, 9, 15 and 16)

SAMPLE LESSON PLAN

BASIC PRINCIPLES	LEADING IDEAS	FACTS	METHODS	REFERENCES AND ASSIGNMENTS
7. Life activities: depend upon a constant supply of energy, obtained from the breakdown of bonds in food molecules. In man, this is accomplished by adding oxygen to food.	Breathing with respiration includes how a person gets oxygen, how it is used for energy release, and how it is released.	I. What is Respiration? A. Definitions 1. Breathing—the mechanism by which oxygen is brought into an organism and carbon dioxide is released. 2. Respiration—the cellular process of oxygen use, energy liberation, and carbon dioxide release.	Introduce with questions. Why do we breathe? Lecture notes	
8. Life can only come from pre-existing life, which originated with the creative hand of God.	Only God can cause matter to live.	B. Biblical origin and purpose 1. Biblical origin of breathing can be seen in Genesis 2:7 and Acts 17:25. These speak of God giving the "breath of life."	Have students deduce the origin and purpose of respiration before I write them out.	Bible

472

BASIC PRINCIPLES	LEADING IDEAS	FACTS	METHODS	REFERENCES AND ASSIGNMENTS
7. Life activities depend upon a constant supply of energy, obtained from the breakdown of bonds in food molecules. In man, this is accomplished by adding oxygen to food.	The Biblical purpose of breathing is to supply oxygen for energy release and speaking.	2. Biblical purpose a. To give life (Gen. 2:7) b. Energy release (Job 41:21) c. Speech to praise God. (Psa. 150:6)		

12. God has chosen to use men to uncover the truths about His creation on a timetable according to His sovereign plan.	Robert Boyle showed importance of oxygen to life and to combustion.	C. History of respiration
		1. Robert Boyle—British Chemist (1627-1691)
		  a. Fourteenth son of the Earl of Cork
		  b. Entered Eton at age eight, at which time he was already speaking Greek and Latin
		  c. Helped form the Royal Society whose motto was "nullius in verba" (Nothing by mere authority). This was a large step in removing science from the hands of the philosophers such as Aristotle.
		  d. He performed the experiment with the candle, mouse and the bottle, showing air was essential to both.
		  e. He transformed alchemy into chemistry in 1661 with the publication of *The Skeptical Chemist*. In this book he said the material substance was not something mystical but real and could be understood.
		  f. He learned Hebrew and Aramic for Biblical studies, and wrote many essays on religion.
		  g. He also financed missionary work in the Orient.
		  h. In his will he founded the Boyle Lectures, not on science, but on the defense of Christianity against unbelievers.
			Identify all three men on student copy of Chain of Christianity Timeline: Boyle 1661, Priestly 1772, Lavoisier 1774.	Explain three aspects of Boyle's contribution to science.

Sample Lesson Plan (continued)

BASIC PRINCIPLES	LEADING IDEAS	FACTS	METHODS	REFERENCES AND ASSIGNMENTS
12. God has chosen to use men to uncover the truths about His creation on a timetable according to His sovereign plans.	Joseph Priestly discovered oxygen and noticed its importance to life.	2. Joseph Priestly—English Chemist (1733-1804) a. He grew up without a mother, was extremely small, sickly and had a speech impediment. b. He became interested in science because of visits with Benjamin Franklin. c. Priestly supported the American colonists. d. He dissolved CO_2 in water and is considered the father of the soft-drink industry. e. He discovered oxygen by heating mercury oxide. He then noticed that things burned brighter and mice became more vigorous. f. However, he believed in the phlogiston theory and did not fully appreciate his discovery.	Do demonstration experiment with candle in a jar partially filled with water, then put a cylinder over the candle into the water. Demonstrates candle needs air and % of oxygen in air. Demonstration of making oxygen with manganese dioxide. Show how materials burn brighter.	Explain the significance of the two demonstrations.
12. God has chosen to use men to uncover truths about His creation on a timetable according to His sovereign plans. 7. Life activities depend on a constant supply of energy, obtained from the breakdown of bonds in food molecules. In man this is accomplished by adding oxygen to food.	Antoine Lavoisier discovered the importance of oxygen.	3. Antoine Lavoisier—French Chemist (1743-1794) a. He is considered the father of modern chemistry because he stressed the need for accurate measurement and accurate records. b. He named oxygen and showed its importance to biological combustion and energy release. c. He was beheaded in 1794 by vengeful revolutionary leaders. Two years later the French were unveiling busts of him because of his great contributions.		What major character quality allowed Lavoisier to succeed? How could it help you? How would living in America have helped Lavoisier? Explain the significance of Lavoisier's contribution to science.

9. The individual or diverse parts of a body will work together with unity to make and benefit the whole.	The nose in man helps filter and warm air before it reaches the lungs.	II. The Pathway of air—structure and function.
		A. Nose
		  1. Construction
		    a. Two nasal cavities separated by the nasal septum
		    b. Palate forms floor of nose and roof of the mouth
		      (1) cleft palate—is when the bones of the palate do not grow together properly and an opening exists
		      (2) The uvula is a fleshy projection of the palate which helps keep food from entering the nasal cavities.
			Lecture—Have students come up with different purposes for the nose.
			
			Good time to mention proper self-acceptance and our physical features
				Draw, color and label respiratory structures from text.

BASIC PRINCIPLES	LEADING IDEAS	FACTS	METHODS	REFERENCES AND ASSIGNMENTS
		2. Purpose a. lined with ciliated mucous membrane to trap bacteria, dust and smoke. Sneeze expels foreign materials. b. Air warmed before going to lungs c. Contains organ of smell—discussed in later section. d. Helps modulate the voice in speaking	Ask questions so that students can deduce Principle #9.	Good resource: *Biology for Christian Schools.* Bob Jones University Press, 1980.
2. God's creation will show evidence of having a master designer, not the appearance of chance happenings.	The pharnyx serves as a central station for the activities of eating, breathing and balance.	B. Pharynx 1. Position—Cavity which extends from back of the nose to upper portion of esophagus. 2. Purpose—Contains seven openings. a. Two for nasal cavities b. Two for eustachian tubes c. Passageway for food from mouth (Num. 11:20) d. Opening of esophagus—to stomach e. Opening to larynx—to trachea for air (Isa. 2:22)	Lecture—Develop idea of design and purpose	Explain how pharynx works to help your body function properly.

BIBLIOGRAPHY

Autobiography of Benjamin Rush, edited by George Corner, Princeton University Press, 1948

Autobiography of Benjamin Rush, American Philosophical Society, London: Geoffrey Cumerlege, Oxford University Press

Benjamin Rush's Lectures On The Mind, edited, annotated, and introduced by Eric T. Carlson, M.D., Jeffrey L. Wollock and Patricia Noel, American Philosophical Society, Philadelphia, 1981

Brand, Paul and Yancey, Phillip, *Fearfully and Wonderfully Made*, Zondervan, 1980

————, *In His Image*, Zondervan, 1984

Carver, William, *The Course of Christian Missions*, Fleming H. Revell, 1932

Delrich, Harvey and Walch, J. Weston, *Human Anatomy*, Publishers, Portland, Maine (48 visual masters)

Early American Imprints. Micro-card Collection, Oklahoma University Library

Gish, Duane T., *Evolution: The Fossils Say No*, Creation-Life Publishers, 1972

Gardner, Eldon J., *History of Biology*, Burgess Publishing Co., 1960

Eddy, Sherwood, *Pathfinders of the World Missionary Crusade*, 1945

Hall, Verna, *The Christian History of the Constitution of the United States of America—Christian Self-Government*, Foundation for American Christian Education, San Francisco, 1960

————, *Christian History of the Constitution of the United States of America—Christian Self-Government With Union*, Foundation for American Christian Education, San Francisco, 1962

Haycock, Ruth C., *Bible Truth for School Subjects: Vol. III—Science/Mathematics*, Association of Christian Schools International, 1981

Jaffe, Benard, *Men of Science in America*, Simon and Schuster, 1944

McMillen, S. I., *None of These Diseases*, Fleming H. Revell Co., 1963

Morris, Henry, *Men of Science—Men of God*, Creation Life Publishers, 1974

————, *Scientific Creationism*, Creation-Life Publishers, 1974

————, *The Genesis Record*, Baker Book House, 1976

Nave, Orville J., *Naves Topical Bible*, MacDonald Publishing, 1974

Pinkston, William, Jr., *Biology for Christian Schools*, Bob Jones University Press, 1980

Schaeffer, Francis A., *How Should We Then Live*, 1976

Slater, Rosalie, J., *Teaching and Learning America's Christian History*, Foundation for American Christian Education, San Francisco, 1965

Sooter, Wilburn L., *The Eye—A Light Receiver*, Creation-Life Publishers, 1981

Steele, DeWitt, *Science: Order and Reality*, A Beka Book, 1980

Strong, James, *Strong's Exhaustive Concordance of the Bible*, Crusade Bible Publishers, Inc.

Thoughts Upon The Mode of Education Proper In A Republic, Benjamin Rush, Philadelphia, and numerous other selections from Early American Emprints—A Microcard Collection, Oklahoma University Library

Tiner, John Hudson, *When Science Fails*, Baker Book House, 1974

Webster, Noah, *American Dictionary of the English Language*, 1828, Facimilie Reprint, Foundation for American Christian Education, San Francisco, 1962

DAVID HOLMES

Applying the Principle Approach to my subject matter has been an extremely rewarding experience to me as a science teacher. I was trained in the "modern" approach to mathematics and the natural sciences. Teacher training at a state college did nothing to improve either my ability to teach or my knowledge of what to teach. The only basic tool I knew to use was the textbook and the accompanying teacher's guide. As I began to instruct in a Christian school, I knew that something was missing.

Year by year, I began to incorporate Scripture and creationism into my subject areas to make them more Christian. In the spring of 1977 Miss Verna M. Hall and Miss Rosalie J. Slater came to our school for an afternoon's visit. They outlined the American Christian philosophy of education. The Biblical truths presented in that short afternoon session began to work on my spirit and mind. I shared with Miss Hall and Miss Slater my decision to attend summer classes at a Christian college and was shocked at their reply. They felt that what I needed most was not more study for a Masters Degree, but more understanding of how to apply Biblical truths to my approach to teaching.

Miss Hall and Miss Slater did not try to tell me how to develop a curriculum, or that I was capable of developing a curriculum, or even where I could get any help. They did share some Scripture passages with me that have changed my educational experience. Among the verses were I Corinthians 2:16 and Philippians 2:5 which speak of our need to have the mind of Christ. This took away any thoughts of "I can't do this," or "I wasn't trained" or "I can't write" or any of the other excuses that I might give. So with the support of these ladies and the guidance of my administrator, Mr. Ralph Bullard, I began with the Lord's help to research my subjects in a new way.

I spent several years "wandering in the wilderness," not really knowing what direction to take. I spent much time trying to fit the seven principles of America's Christian history and government into my biology curriculum, until I saw this reflected a misunderstanding of the Principle Approach.

When I saw the Principle Approach as not only a philosophy of education but also a methodology, a way to teach, then the approach really came to life. The years of researching and recording had strengthened my curriculum to the point at which, with a few changes and a new methodology, I was ready to begin in earnest.

I can now honestly say the Principle Approach, and the challenges it offered, changed my life as a Christian and, especially, as a teacher. I was able to become a producer, a controller of my curriculum, and a master of both the history and principles of my subjects. I became a more dedicated teacher, for now I had a purpose, a plan, and a goal. I also had an approach to education that truly could make a difference, academically and spiritually, in my students.

As the Lord continued to work in my life, I began to see the results in the classroom because my own self-worth was being developed and my overall love of learning was being transferred to the students. As the curriculum improved and my mastery of the subject grew, the students no longer manifested the old discipline problems. Students became proud of producing their notebooks and enjoyed learning more.

If it were not for the Principle Approach, I truly believe I would have left the teaching profession and sought other employment. Of course, this approach produces its results only because it is soundly based on the Scriptures. The approach has worked in my life and the lives of my students because it pointed to God's Word, which in turn made me sensitive to the illumination of God's Spirit in my life and my teaching.

TYPING
AN AMERICAN CHRISTIAN APPROACH

BY BARBARA B. ROSE
Secretary
American Christian History Institute
Camarillo, California

CONTENTS

EDITOR'S NOTE: The following course overview is a summary of the method by which Mrs. James Rose taught typing to junior and senior high school students for three years from 1974 to 1977. Students met three days a week for 50 minutes a day. They mainly had access to manual typewriters, although a few IBM electric typewriters were also available. Despite the limited practice time and the modest tools available, most of the students became proficient typists and were able subsequently to put their skills to good use to prepare accurate and neatly typed manuscripts in high school and, later, for college and career assignments. It is hoped that the "first fruits" of Mrs. Rose's experience will quicken typing teachers and others skilled in the more modern word-processing keyboards and software to 4 R this subject in even greater depth.

TYPING
IN THE AMERICAN
CHRISTIAN CURRICULUM

INTRODUCTION

Christians generally recognize Gutenberg's invention of the printing press as a crucially important part of God's plan for spreading His Word. By the same token, the invention of the typewriter is part of a divine plan. Modern typography, such as used in preparing this book, simply links a typewriter keyboard, via a computer, to the current version of Gutenberg's printing press. Knowledge of such events on the Chain of Christianity should enhance the student's esteem for the wonderful works of God while it increases his appreciation of the subject and his desire to master the skills of typing.

To those who think of typing in a primarily secular way, simply as an acquired neuro-muscular skill, this may come as a surprise. We believe that typing in an American Christian curriculum can and should contribute to the advancement of individual Christian character, self-government and property as well as a knowledge of the basic skills of the subject.

It is certain that the subject of penmanship, as taught in grammar schools throughout the colonial and federal periods, made similar contributions. The teaching of proper penmanship, like the teaching of typing, demands individual effort and accountability; it requires self-government in the control of one's thinking, one's hand, and one's writing tools.

Noah Webster once declared that the purpose of curriculum is "to diffuse the principles of virtue and patriotism." It may be obvious that this can be done through the study of the Bible and of America's Christian history and government, but not so apparent that it also can be achieved, to some degree, by what may appear, on the surface, to be the development of a merely mechanical ability.

We are convinced, however, that the Principle Approach, and particularly the 4 R's, which were vital to our Forefathers in the teaching of handwriting can and should be used today to achieve the aims and goals of typewriting in an American Christian curriculum.

USING THE 4 R's

In teaching and learning typing, the teacher and student will apply the 4 R's as follows:

Research the Word of God to identify the Biblical basis and purpose for the subject of typewriting including its vocabulary and place on the Chain of Christianity.

Reason from Biblical truths to typing.

Relate Biblical principles, inclusive of God's principles of individuality, self-government, character and property to the inward posture and outward product of the student in typewriting.

Record (type) the student's application and demonstration of the rudiments of typing and its Biblical principles.

COURSE AIMS AND GOALS

Identify God, as revealed in His Word, as the principle (source origin, foundation) of type and typing.

Identify God's plan and purpose for typing on the Chain of Christiantiy moving westward and how typing benefits the individual in America.

Cultivate an understanding of the Biblical principles of America's Christian history and government as a means of glorifying God both internally and externally in the typed product.

Impart a knowledge of the basic principles and techniques of typing so that the student may achieve proficiency in the subject.

Glorify God by identifying His attributes in the typed product—orderliness, precision, perfection, et al.

Challenge the student to be an American Christian typist who will perpetuate a Christian philosophy of government in order to be free to write and publish whatever is true.

COURSE OVERVIEW

FIRST YEAR STUDENT:

Biblical origin and purpose for typewriting
Type and typewriting on the Chain of Christianity
God's Principles of individuality, self-government and property as related to typing and the student
Typewriter—its properties, parts and their function and purpose
Principles of typing—work area, posture, finger position (home keys), key stroking, etc.
Tabulation and margins
Sentence writing and paragraphs
Figures, symbols, fractions

Centering: horizontal and vertical
Typing grammar—punctuation, word division, spelling, capitalization
Typewritten applications: memos, letters; modified block, carbons, letter folding, envelopes; manuscripts, outline and footnotes.

SECOND YEAR STUDENT:

Review first year curriculum as necessary
Cutting stencils
Typing historical documents
Justifying
Tabulated reports

CHRISTIAN METHODOLOGY IN TEACHING TYPING

Christian methodology is concerned first with the internal, and concentrates on the student's *heart*–"for out of it are the issues of life"–and the *conscience*, a faculty which is to be "void of offense toward God and man." Learning (the knowledge of principles and facts received by instruction or study) is primarily an inward activity of the mind and heart. Therefore, the Christian method of teaching, as suggested by Miss Rosalie Slater in *Teaching and Learning*, p.92, would be to:

Inspire: "to infuse ideas into the mind by the Holy Spirit."

Consecrate: "to set apart, dedicate, or devote to the service and worship of God."

Cultivate: "to refine, improve by correction of faults; improve by labor and study."

Instruct: "to inform, to direct, to impart knowledge."

Since Christian education begins with salvation (the individual's acceptance of his sin condition and receiving, by faith, the Lord Jesus Christ as his Savior and Lord) instruction must first deal with the internal commitment of the individual to the government of Christ and His Word. The Biblical principles of American Christian education can only be comprehended by a Christian although they can bless and influence for good the unbelieving, also.

Christian methodology reasons from a Christian view of God, man and government. (See *Rudiments* section of this *Guide*, p. 24)

Christian methodology embraces the Principle Approach: *researching* the subject for first principles which can be applied by the student and searching the Word of God for the Biblical basis of the vocabulary of the subject; *reasoning* from and *relating* the rudiments and truths revealed in His

Story of typewriting to the student and the subject; and *recording* the student's application of learned principles.

THE METHODS USED
IN TEACHING TYPING INCLUDE:

1. *Lecture*: "to instruct by discourses." Lectures are given at the beginning of the term and throughout the year on the following subjects: Course goals; God, the Author of type; the vocabulary of typewriting; Christian principles of typewriting; history of type and typewriting on the Chain of Christianity; the property of one's time, tools and talents in typing; the principles of typing.

2. *Notebook*: A three-ring binder is used to delineate how the teacher and student demonstrate the 4 R's in typing. It enables the student to develop his own typing book of sample forms, typing problems and principles. It becomes a self-teaching textbook of lecture notes, class constitution, exams, daily work, check lists, progress chart, and American Christian history handouts. It reflects the student's management of the subject as well as his attitude and disposition. It testifies to the qualities of diligence, integrity, perseverance, responsibility—or their lack in the student. Through the notebook, the student becomes a steward of the knowledge and time given him and of his own time, labor and tools.

3. *Textbook*: A self-teaching typing textbook enables the student to review and proceed at his own pace. The teacher instructs the student in the history and principles of the subject, and assigns drills, problems and tests while providing demonstrations and tutorial assistance. The textbook used for this course was *College Typewriting*, 7th Edition by Lessenberry, Wanons and Duncan.

4. *Dictation*: The teacher dictates finger positions and combinations, whole words to develop word recognition, and Bible verses.

5. *Drill*: Learning by repetition cultivates a proficiency in stroke and finger placement, increases speed and develops rhythm.

6. *Handouts*: As Noah Webster observed, "In America it will be useful to furnish schools with additional essays, containing the history, geography, and transactions of the United States. Information on these subjects is necessary for youth, both in forming their habits and improving their minds. A love of our country, and an acquaintance with its true state, are indispensable; they should be acquired in early life. In the choice of pieces, I have been attentive to the political interests of America. I consider it a capital fault in all our schools, that the books generally used, contain subjects wholly uninteresting to our youth; while writings that marked the revolution ... which are calculated to impress interesting truths upon young minds, lie neglected and forgotten. Several of those masterly addresses of Congress, written at the commencement of the late revolution, contain such noble sentiments of liberty and patriotism, that I cannot help wishing to transfuse them into the breasts of the rising generation." (Noah Webster, *An American Selection of Lessons in Reading and Speaking*, Preface, 1809)

Students will use sections of State Papers, famous documents of America's Christian history, addresses and quotes of the Founding Fathers as well as patriotic poetry for typing practice.

THE BIBLICAL VOCABULARY
OF TYPING

Is typing mentioned in the Bible? No. However, by 4 R-ing the subject, two very enlightening observations may be made: 1) A surprising number of words in the Bible are directly related to the idea of type-writing and suggest the *Biblical derivations* of the purpose and function of the machine. 2) The vocabulary of typewriting lends itself to teaching Christian character through the discipline of learning to type.

Definitions of the basic vocabulary of typewriting are primarily from Webster's 1828 Dictionary unless otherwise noted.

Typewriting: (N) 1. The art, act, or process of using a typewriter. 2. Writing done on a typewriter. (Webster's New World Dictionary, 1974)

Typewriter: (N) [(*type* + *writer*) so named (1867), probably by C.L. Sholes who patented the first practical machine in 1868.] 1. a writing machine with a keyboard for reproducing letters, figures, etc. that resemble printed ones: when the keys are struck, raised letters, figures, etc. are pressed as against an inked ribbon, making an *impression* on an inserted piece of paper... (Webster's New World Dictionary, 1974)
Typewriter is "a machine which prints *characters* in sequence, performing the work of writing at a speed greater than is possible with the pen." (Encyclopedia Britannica, 1937)

Type: (N) (to beat, strike, impress) The *mark* of something; that which *represents* something else. A sign; a symbol; a figure of something to come;

483

as Abraham's sacrifice and the paschal lamb, were *types* of Christ.

A model or form of a letter in metal or other hard material; used in printing.

Type: (N) Printing—a rectangular piece of metal or, sometimes wood, with a raised letter, figure, etc. in reverse on its upper end, which when inked and pressed against a piece of paper or other material, as in a printing press, leaves an ink *impression* of its face. (Webster's New World Dictionary, 1974)

Write: (VT) To perform the act of forming *characters*, letters, or figures as representatives of sounds or ideas.

Typography: (N) The art of printing, or the operation of *impressing* letters and words on forms of types. (Greek: to type and write)

Typology: (N) The study of types, symbolic meaning or representation. (Webster's New World Dictionary, 1974)

A *type* (from the Greek "a blow or mark left by a blow; a pattern or impress") is a double representation in action, the literal being intended and planned to represent the spiritual. A type is a divine image of spiritual truth upon a literal event, person or thing... Typology as the divine inworking of God's purpose in Scripture is a means of making the Word of God relevant for every age and situation. Since Jesus Christ is the constant subject of all Scripture, His person and work are divinely *impressed* upon it in type, symbol and prophecy. (Unger's Bible Handbook, pp. 7–8)

Character: (N) A *mark* made by cutting or engraving, as on stone, metal...; hence a mark or figure made with a pen or style on paper...; a letter or figure used to form words, and communicate ideas. A *mark* or figure made by *stamping* or *impression*. The peculiar qualities impressed by nature (Christ) or habit on a person which distinguishes him from others; these constitute real character, and the qualities which he is supposed to express...

Mark: (VT) To stamp; to *impress;* to make a visible impression. (N) Any note or sign of distinction.

Marked: (PP) Impressed with any note or figure of distinction; distinguished by some *character.*

Impress: (N) A mark or indentation made by pressure.

The figure or *image* of anything made by pressure;

stamp; *likeness.* Mark of distinction; stamp; character to *imprint.*

Impression: (N) Mark; indentation; *stamp* made by pressure.

The effect which objects produce on the mind; *images* in the mind; idea.

Image: (N) A *representation* or similitude of any person or thing, formed of a material substance. Any copy, representation or *likeness.* An idea; a representation of any thing to the mind.

Likeness: (N) Resemblance in form; an *image*, picture or statue resembling a person or thing.

Representation: (N) The act of re-presenting, describing or showing. The standing in the place of another.

Stamp: (N) That which is marked; a mark *imprinted;* an impression. (VT) To impress; to imprint; to fix deeply; as to stamp virtuous principles on the heart. To fix a mark by impressing it; as a notion of the Deity stamped on the mind.

Imprint: (VT) To stamp letters and words on paper by means of *types;* to *print.*

Print: (VT) In general to take or form letters, characters or figures on paper, cloth or other material by impression. Thus letters are taken on paper by impressing it on types blackened with ink.

To form by impression.

To use or practice the art of *typography.*

Ensample: (N) An example; a pattern or model for imitation (I Pet. 5).

From the foregoing list of terms related to typing one can deduce the Biblical origin and purpose of the subject as suggested on p. 485.

Lessons for developing Christian character can also be deduced from an internal and external application of the words used in teaching typing. For example, character is defined as "to mark," "a figure made by stamping or impressing" such as an individual type font makes on paper. But character is also the "peculiar qualities impressed by nature or habit on a person which distinguished him from others." From these definitions, students were challenged not only to learn how to "make their mark" in typing but to consider the impression Christ and His Word can make upon their character as they learn the subject. In the same context, words such as mark, image, representation, likeness are also significant to the typed impression on the page.

BIBLICAL ORIGIN AND PURPOSE OF TYPING

The first explicit Biblical reference to the *mark* of something, that which represents something else, is in *Genesis 4:15*: "And the Lord said unto him, Therefore whosoever slayeth Cain, vengeance shall be taken on him sevenfold. And *the Lord set a mark* on Cain, lest any finding him should kill him."

The etymology of type suggests the idea of a sign or symbol represented by the *mark* of something. In Genesis 4:15, the Biblical origin or idea of type was established when God make an impression or mark on Cain to be read of all men.

In addition, Job declared in one of the oldest books of the Bible, "Oh that my words were now *written*! Oh, that they were *printed* in a book." (*Job 19:23*) Some chronologists put Job in the time of Solomon, around 965 B.C. Job clearly suggested in this reference the capacity then to form letters by impressing them on skins or papyrus with some inked instrument.

The Biblical end and purpose of typewriting is suggested in the following references:

Exodus 17:14: "And the Lord said unto Moses, *Write* this for a *memorial* in a book, and rehearse it in the ears of Joshua: for I will utterly put out the remembrance of Amalek from under heaven."

CONCLUSION: Writing is said to have been introduced about 3200 B.C., about 5000 years before the first practical typewriter was patented. But the Biblical purpose of writing, either by hand or with a machine, is for the purpose of remembrance, to preserve the memory of what God has done and commanded man to do. (Hab. 2:2)

Proverbs 3:3: "Let not mercy and truth forsake thee; bind them about thy neck: *write* them upon the *table* of thine heart."

CONCLUSION: Writing the spirit of God's mercy and truth upon one's consciousness or heart is effected by the Holy Spirit as we read and reflect upon the *printed* Word of God.

ADDITIONAL BIBLE REFERENCES

The following references further identify the vocabulary of type and typewriting. The student will observe that most of these references are not applicable to the typewriter as we know it today nor to the more sophisticated generations of electronic typewriters and the most advanced word-processing software for computers. However, as *type* literally refers to "the *mark* of something; that which represents something else," as well as a "sign, a symbol" of something apparent or to come, so the Bible reveals the spiritual, mental and literal *idea* of type or representations in numerous ways. *These Biblical images or ideas preceded and eventually gave rise to the invention of tools to impress external letters or characters which represent internal ideas.*

WRITE: (External)
Exodus 32:16: "And the tables were the work of God, and the *writing* was the *writing* of God, graven upon the tables." (Ex. 17:14, 34:27; Deut. 6:9, 17:18; Isa. 8:1; Jer. 30:2; Luke 10:20; John 1:45; Rom. 15:4; I John 2:1; Rev. 21:5)

WRITE: (Internal)
Jeremiah 31:33: "But this shall be the covenant that I will make with the house of Israel; After those days, saith the Lord, I will put my law in their inward parts, and *write* it in their hearts; and will be their God, and they shall be my people." (Heb. 8:10, 10:16; Prov. 3:3)

CHARACTER: (Internal—rendered as "expressed image" in the Greek)
Hebrews 1:3: "Who being the brightness of his glory, and *the express image of his person*, and upholding all things by the word of his power, when he had by himself purged out sins, sat down on the right hand of the majesty on high:…"

MARK: (External)
Genesis 4:15: "And the Lord said unto him, Therefore whosoever slayeth Cain, vengeance shall be taken on him sevenfold. And the Lord set a *mark* upon Cain, lest any finding him should kill him." (Ezek. 9:4,6; Rev. 13:16, 14:9, 11, 19:20)

MARK: (Internal)
Jeremiah 2:22: "For though thou wash thee with nitre, and take thee much soap, yet thine iniquity is *marked* before me, saith the Lord God." (Phil. 3:14; Eph. 4:22-24—The mark or impression of Christ upon the "new man")

IMAGE: (External)
Exodus 20:4: "Thou shalt not make unto thee any graven *image*, or any likeness of any thing that is in heaven above, or that is in the earth beneath …" (Isa. 44:9; Rev. 14:9)

IMAGE: (Internal)

I Corinthians 15:49: "And as we have borne the *image* of the earthly, we shall also bear the image of the heavenly." (Gen. 1:26, 27; Rom. 8:29)

LIKENESS: (External)

Romans 8:3: "For what the law could not do, in that it was weak through the flesh, God sending his own Son in the *likeness* of sinful flesh, and for sin, condemned sin in the flesh:" (Ex. 20:4)

LIKENESS: (Internal)

Romans 6:5: "For if we have been planted together in the *likeness* of his death, we shall be also in the *likeness* of his resurrection:" (Psa. 17:15)

REPRESENTATION OR AMBASSADOR: (Internal)

Ephesians 6:20: "For which I am an *ambassador* in bonds; that therein I may speak boldly, as I ought to speak."

AMBASSADOR: (External)

II Corinthians 5:20: "Now then we are *ambassadors* for Christ, as though God did beseech you by us; we pray you in Christ's *stead*, be ye reconciled to God."

PRINT: (External)

Job 19:23: "Oh that my words were now written! oh that they were *printed* in a book!" (Job 13:27; John 20:25)

ENSAMPLE: (External)

II Peter 2:6: "And turning the cities of Sodom and Gomorrha into ashes condemned them with an overthrow, making them an *ensample* unto those that after should live ungodly;"

ENSAMPLE: (Internal)

II Thessalonians 3:9: "Not because we have not power, but to make ourselves an *ensample* unto you to follow us." (I Cor. 10:11; Phil. 3:17; I Thess. 1:7)

THE RUDIMENTS OF TYPING

The rudiments of typewriting include an understanding of the typewriter and its parts, the work area, posture, finger position, stroke, paper insertion, carriage return, space bar, margins, tabulation procedures, horizontal and vertical centering. These are amplified in the following outline:

I.
TYPEWRITER AND ITS PARTS
A. Carriage Return Lever
B. Left Cylinder Knob
C. Left Carriage Release
D. Line-space Regulator
E. Left Margin Set
F. Right Margin Set
G. Paper Guide
H. Paper Table
I. Paper Bail and Scale
J. Platen or Cylinder
K. Paper Release
L. Right Carriage Release
M. Right Cylinder Knob

II.
WORK AREA
A. Desk is clear of all unneeded books and papers.
B. Typewriter is at the front edge of the table.
C. Book is on the right, propped up.

III.
POSTURE
A. Body is erect, back against chair.
B. Feet flat on floor, one in front of the other.
C. Fingers, curved on Home Keys.
D. Wrists downward, not touching the machine.
E. Elbows close to side.
F. Eyes on copy.

IV.
FINGER POSITION (QWERTY KEYBOARD)
A. Home Keys: A S D F / J K L ;
  4 3 2 1 / 1 2 3 4
B. First finger is index finger not thumb.

V.
STROKE
A. Stroke is firm, snappy, with quick release.
B. Action is in fingers; wrists and arms are still.
C. Snap the fingers slightly toward the palm when releasing.
D. Do not let the fingers follow the key all the way down.
E. Type the next key without pausing.

VI.
PAPER INSERTION
A. Adjust the paper guide to "0."
B. Place paper on left with long side facing front edge of table.
C. Pull paper bail forward with right hand.
D. Holding paper in left hand, thumb under sheet and finger tips on top, bring paper to the platen and drop it between the platen and paper table.
E. Bring right hand to right cylinder knob and twirl knob.
F. Push paper bail down to hold paper against the platen.

VII.
CARRIAGE RETURN

A. Operate carriage return lever with the left hand; fingers bracing one another.

B. Return carriage with a quick wrist and hand motion.

C. Drop the hand to typing position without letting it follow the carriage across the line.

D. Keep eyes on copy while operating carriage return.

VIII.
SPACE BAR

A. Strike space bar with a quick down-and-in motion of the right thumb.

B. Hold thumb close to space bar in readiness.

IX.
MARGINS

A. Measure width of paper on paper scale; divide by two to locate the center of the paper.

B. 50-space line: subtract 25 from center for left margin, add 25 to center for right margin.

C. 60-space line: subtract 30 from center for left margin, add 30 to center for right margin.

D. 70-space line: subtract 35 from center for left margin, add 35 to center for right margin.

E. For paragraph writing, the ringing of the bell is a cue to return the carriage, so set the right margin stop 7-10 spaces beyond the desired line ending so the bell will ring approximately 7-10 spaces before the point at which you want the line to end.

X.
TABULATION PROCEEDURE

A. Clear tab stops: move carriage to extreme left, depress tab clear key holding it down as you pull the carriage all the way to the right.

B. Set tab stops: move carriage to the desired position, depressing the tab set key. Repeat for exact tab stop.

C. Depress the tab bar (or key) until the carriage stops.

XI.
HORIZONTAL CENTERING

A. Clear margin and tab stops.

B. Set a tab stop at the center of the paper.

C. Backspace once for each *two* letters or spaces and type the line.

XII.
VERTICAL CENTERING

A. Count all lines to be centered (typed and blank lines).

B. Subtract total lines from 66 (full sheet) or 33 (half sheet).

C. Divide by two to find top and bottom margins; disregard any fractions.

D. Space down from top edge of paper one more than lines in top margin.

E. Center each line horizontally.

APPLYING THE BIBLICAL PRINCIPLES OF GOVERNMENT TO TYPEWRITING

God's Principle of Individuality and Property:

The statement of the principles, their Biblical basis and elucidation may be found in the *Rudiments* section of this *Guide*, pp. 31 and 43.

How does the *individual* in typing reflect God's Principle of Individuality and the Biblical principle of property?

The individual typist is viewed as created by God, unique and distinct from any other person. God's infinite diversity and individuality is reflected externally in each individual man's actions, conversation, voice, scent, prints, posture, and signature. (see p. 32) Internally, each individual is distinguished by separate and distinct thoughts, motives, attitudes, tastes, character, and conscience.

How the individual governs and exercises his internal, individual *property* will determine his ability as a typist and directly influence his typed product. For example, as the individual is inspired and consecrated to bring the inward man, the heart, under the government of God, there will be a corresponding godly effect on the posture, property and product of the typist, as the diagram "Individuality and Property in Typing" suggests at the bottom of the page.

Individuality and Property in Typing

INTERNAL ➤ (Causative)	EXTERNAL (Effect)
Conscience, attitude, disposition; feelings, motives, temperament; thoughts, concentration; patience, industry	Property of the machine; posture; use of time and work area; finger position and stroking; accuracy, and speed; form, outline and content of typed product

When God through the power of Christ is in control of the individual typist, the product will reveal God's attributes – orderliness, precision, perfection. (Luke 6:45) The inward man should express or exercise christian character, self-government, property and unity to achieve a product (external) that will glorify God.

How does the *subject* of typing reveal God's Principle of Individuality?

God is the source and origin of the idea of the subject. Typewriting has a purpose as described earlier. Furthermore, the Christian history of type and typewriting on the Chain of Christianity reveals how God used individual men, events and nations to fulfill His plan and purpose for the invention of type and printing.

God worked through individuals. For example:

1. Johann Gutenberg invented the art of printing from moveable cast type and printed the Gutenberg Bible in 1456.

2. "Typographic missionaries" disseminated the knowledge of the invention of type throughout Europe.

3. Reformation printers suffered persecution in order to publish the Bible.

4. Stephen Day brought printing to America in 1638.

5. Isaiah Thomas and other American revolutionary printers gave their lives and fortunes to the cause of American Christian independence.

6. Sholes, Glidden and Soulé invented the first practical typewriter in 1867.

7. In 1932, Dr. August Dvořak redesigned the keyboard and made typing faster, easier and far more simplified. (see p. 491)

God worked through nations and continents to advance literacy and liberty through printing. Asia was the continent of origins, where the idea of type was birthed. Europe, especially Germany and England, developed the art of printing. Eventually, the American Christian philosophy of government secured the fullest expression of Biblical liberty and literacy for the individual.

God's Principle of Individuality is also illustrated in the typewriter itself. It prints individual characters in sequence giving identity to each letter and number. The use of the machine gives form to letters, envelopes, footnotes, outlines and reports. There are over 2000 parts in a manual typewriter, each with a distinct function. The keyboard has no blends or blurs. Furthermore, the typewriter is the *tool of the individual.*

THE CHRISTIAN PRINCIPLE OF SELF-GOVERNMENT

The Christian Principle of Self-Government:
The statement of the principle is found on page 36 of this *Guide.*

The internal government of Christ in the life of the student will enable him to have dominion over the machine. The student will either be governed by his mistakes or he will pray to overcome them in the conscious power of Christ. (Phil. 4:13)

As the student brings his thoughts, attitudes, motives, and conscience into captivity to Christ and lets "that mind be in (him) which was also in Christ Jesus," he should produce a superior product. I can testify that when students who were faced with frustration in learning to type have stopped to pray and examine their thinking before God, they were able to achieve the speed and accuracy desired.

As important as speed and accuracy are in typing, so is the content. Students should be taught to be governed by the dictates of the Word of God so that the content of the typed product reveals things that are true, honest, just, pure, lovely, and of good report. (Phil. 4:8) The finished work will reflect the student's exercise of Christian self-government in how directions were followed or whether an assignment was executed "decently and in order." (I Cor. 14:40)

HISTORY OF TYPE AND THE TYPEWRITER ON THE CHAIN OF CHRISTIANITY

God is the source and origin of all His subjects and is sovereign over them. God prepared individuals as well as nations for the invention of type so that it could flourish and be used to perpetuate the Gospel of the Lord Jesus Christ "with signs following." (Mark 16:20)

An American Christian philosophy of typing deals with the end and purpose of the use of type on the Chain of Christianity. The development of type and the invention of the typewriter on the Chain of Christianity moving westward is the Hand of God in the history of the subject.

Links on the Chain are defined as men, events and nations in Christ, His Story, that reveal God's plan and purpose in bringing men to a knowledge of Himself and in bringing all things under His control. The Chain begins in Asia, continent of origins, with the Law and the Gospel. It moves to

Europe, the continent of development, when Paul was led by the Holy Spirit to obey the "Macedonian call." The Chain of moved to America, the fullest expression of Christianity, when the Pilgrims settled in 1620.

ASIA

Asia was the continent of origins for the invention of type. Specifically, most Christians would acknowledge that writing originated in Asia in order that the Word of God could become a written record of the Hand of God in the history of Israel. Consider that the following component parts necessary for the invention of typewriting originated in Asia: (1) Alphabet: "As far as the Old Testament is concerned, the important thing is that a simple alphabet language was divinely prepared to record the history of redemption instead of the unwieldly and cumbersome syllabic cuneiform scripts of Babylonia – Assyria, or the complex hieroglyphic writings of Egypt. Hebrew takes its origin from the old Phoenician alphabet..."[1] (2) "Paper" made of papyrus reeds was introduced in ancient Egypt circa 2600 B.C. The art of manufacturing paper began in China in the second century B.C. It was made from linen. In a battle with Arabs, 751 A.D., Chinese prisoners gave the idea to the Arabs who spread it to Greece in the 11th century. The Moors in Spain introduced paper making to Western Europe in the 12th century. (3) Ink was originally made from charcoal soot or lamp black and gum mixed in water.[2] It was further developed in Europe so that it could be finally applied to metal surfaces. Although the Chinese were the first printers from wood blocks in 868 A.D. and from movable type in 1041-1049 A.D., their discovery was not disseminated throughout Asia and Europe at that time due to the isolation of China from the rest of the world and the sedentary and servile characteristics of the people. It may also be observed that God did not bestow His blessings among people who were ignorant of the Gospel.

EUROPE

Europe, the continent of development, when Paul was led by the Holy spirit to obey the "Macedonian call." The Chain moved to America, the fullest expression of Christianity, when the Pilgrims settled in 1620.

down" by the Lord and now the Word of God had to be disseminated throughout the world.

God prepared men and events for the expansion of typography in the 15th century. For example, the Old World emphasis upon centralization of power was beginning to break up. The individual was becoming more free to invent. There was emerging a mental readiness for the printing of books quickened by greater intellectual activity. Paper for printing was abundant and easily procured. Ink and press metallurgy had been developed.

Johann Gutenberg, printer and inventor of movable type and metal cast letters, began his early experiments in 1444 in Mainz, Germany. *The Gutenburg Bible, printed in 1456, is credited with being the first major printed work.* The invention of printing in the 15th century confirmed its Christian purpose—the dissemination of the Gospel throughout the world.

"Typographic missionaries" carried the invention throughout Europe demonstrating the principle of individual enterprise and property.

William Caxton printed the first books in English in 1476 with the publication of *Canterbury Tales.* Printing in England became an instrument for promulgating forms of literature which prepared the way for the Word of God in English.

Typography eventually led the way to a great religious and intellectual upheaval. Half of the printed books in Europe were religious with the Bible being the favorite volume. Religious tracts circulated among individuals. In Germany, the most popular printed books were the Bible and the works of St. Augustine. In contrast, Latin and Greek classics were printed in Italy. Indeed, demand for the Bible far exceeded interest in the classics for hundreds of years.

The invention of type or printing goes hand in hand with the history of the English Bible. "The secular history of the Holy Scriptures is the sacred history of Printing. Between 1450 and 1877, an interval of four centuries and a quarter, the Bible shows the progress and comparative development of the art of printing in a manner that no other single book can; and Biblical bibliography proves that during the first forty years, at least, the Bible exceeded in amount of printing all other books put together..."[3]

"The art of printing, which was one of the providential preparations for the Reformation, became the mightiest lever of Protestantism (Christianity) and modern culture."[4]

1. *Unger's Bible Dictionary*, 1979 edition, p. 823.
2. *Ibid.*

3. Henry Stevens as quoted in Philip Schaff, *History of the Christian Church*, Vol. VII, p. 159.
4. *Ibid*, p. 245.

Prior to the invention of printing, Bibles were chained to the pulpit because of their rarity and the great expense in copying them. The invention of printing made Bibles cheaper and more abundant. "Previously, the price of a Bible was a year's wages."[5] Individuals were able to read the Word of God, lives were transformed, and individuals set at liberty through the saving knowledge of the Lord Jesus Christ.

The following observations may be made on the relation between the Bible and printing:

1. The Wycliffe Bible was produced in 1382, about 60 years prior to the invention of printing.

2. Erasmus' New Testament was printed in 1516.

3. Luther's *New Testament* of 1522 "made the Bible the (German) people's book in church, school and house."

4. Papal bulls prohibited printing of the Bible in German. John Foxe once said, "the Pope must abolish printing, or he must seek a new world to reign over, for by this printing the doctrine of the gospel soundeth to all nations and countries under heaven."[6]

5. William Tyndale's New Testament was printed in 1525. Prior to its publication, Tyndale had said "I defy the pope, and all his laws; and if God spare me I will one day make the boy that drives the plough in England to know more of Scriptures than the pope himself!" And, indeed, English bishops "saw in the circulation of the 'heretical' book the greatest threat to their power which had appeared in a thousand years."[7] Subsequently, Tyndale was martyred in 1536. (The story can be read in *Teaching and Learning*, pp. 334–337)

6. The Coverdale Bible was printed in 1535; the Great Bible in 1539; the Geneva Bible – the Bible of the Pilgrims, in 1560; and the King James Bible in 1611. (See *Christian History*, pp. 29–36)

In his book of martyrs, John Foxe states "… and here we have first to behold the admirable work of God's wisdom. For, as the first decay and ruin of the church began by rude ignorance and lack of knowledge in teachers, so, to restore the church again by doctrine and learning, *it pleased God to open to man the art of printing* shortly after the burning of John Huss and Jerome. Printing opened the church to the instruments and tools of learning and knowledge, which were good books and authors, who before lay hid and unknown.

The science of printing being found, immediately followed the grace of God, which stirred up good understandings to conceive the light of knowledge and of judgment; by which light through darkness began to be seen, and ignorance to be detected, truth to be discerned from error, and religion from superstition."[8]

As the art of printing disseminated the Word of God, Christian liberty and civil freedom were propagated. The freedom of the individual to read the word, to receive Christ as his Savior, and to worship God as he pleased finally brought about Christian institutions and a form of church government which allowed greater liberty for the individual. Civil government was subsequently limited to secure both civil and religious liberty. The genius of Christianity is that it gives rise to liberty in civil government. Thus the Chain of Christianity moving westward is the history of the printed Bible and individual liberty—internally and externally.

AMERICA

Printing came to America as did Christian liberty and our Christian form of government—Christian self-government. The King of England rejoiced that there was no printing machine in the Virginia colonies because *thought* could be more easily controlled.

Providentially the printing press was brought to Massachusetts in 1638 by a Puritan minister, Rev. Jesse Glover. Rev. Glover died during the crossing, but his wife and Stephen Daye established a printing business in Cambridge. The first book printed was the Bay Psalm Book, 1640.

Rev. John Eliot, pastor of the church in Roxbury, Massachusetts translated the Old and New Testament into the language of the Algonquin Indians and printed the first American Indian Bible in 1663. With his associate, Daniel Gookin, Eliot labored among the native Indians to instruct them in the Law of God and succeeded in establishing fourteen "Praying Towns" of self-governing Indians.

The Bible of the American Revolution printed in 1782 by Robert Aitken with the authorization of the Continental Congress reveals how important the Word of God was to the Founding Fathers. The Bible became "the great political textbook" of the patriots as they established the world's first Christian Republic based on Biblical principles of individual liberty, self-government, character, property, and unity with diversity.[9]

The great influence of the printed word in com-

5. Halley, *Bible Handbook*, p. 859.
6. M. d'Aubigne, *The Reformation in England*, Vol. II.
7. *Ibid*, Vol. I, pp. 246-247.

8. John Foxe, *Christian Martyrs of the World*, p. 54.
9. *T/L*, pp. 338-341.

municating the goals and principles of the American Revolution and in uniting the country is delineated through pamphlets, sermons, broadsides, newspapers and state papers printed by independent presses throughout the colonies. Isaiah Thomas and other Revolutionary printers gave their lives and fortunes to the cause of American Independence.

After the Constitution of the United States was adopted, there were years of enormous productivity and prosperity because the new nation's unique form of government protected individual liberty and private property and therefore encouraged greater individual enterprise and invention.

For example, the invention of the typewriter in America shows how individual liberty came to fruition. The first practical machine was invented in 1867 by Sholes, Glidden and Soulé. The typewriter revolutionized business and was thereby a support to free enterprise as well as a means to spread the Gospel.

It must be observed that in 1932 Dr. August Dvořak of Seattle, Washington, formerly Director of Research, University of Washington, invented a revised keyboard that increased the ease and speed of typing. The Dvořak system should be considered as a logical and more efficient alternative to the standard typewriter keyboard.[10]

---

10. Credit goes to Dr. Gary North, President of the Institute for Christian Economics in Texas, for providing the following information on the differences between the standard keyboard (QWERTY) and the simplified Dvořak keyboard.

"The improved keyboard was patented in 1936 by August Dvořak, professor and efficiency expert at the University of Washington. He used time and motion studies to develop a typewriter keyboard designed for speed, comfort and efficiency.

"Standard keyboard (QWERTY) has been in use since the typewriter was invented in 1873. *Its design was intended to slow down typists so keys would not jam on the crude early machines.*

"Problems of transition and training have prevented conversion from QWERTY to Dvořak. Over 30 million QWERTY keyboards are in use today; only a small number of Dvořaks.

"Differences between QWERTY and Dvořak:

–On Dvořak, the keyboard is arranged to reduce the movements of the typist. QWERTY typist's fingers travel 16 miles per eight hour day; Dvořak typist's travel one mile.

–On Dvořak, most frequently used keys are placed on the home row, where typist's fingers naturally fall. On QWERTY, 32 percent of typing is done on home row, just 100 common words can be typed using only the home row keys. On Dvořak, 70 percent of typing is on the home row, 3,000 words are typed on the home row only.

–On Dvořak, the keyboard is arranged for a natural rhythmic flow between right and left hand, with most of the typing done with the right hand. All vowels are on the left hand side of the home row; commonly used consonants on the right hand side.

–On Dvořak, logical arrangement means easier recall. It takes an average of 200 hours of training to achieve 40 words per minute on QWERTY; only 18-20 hours on the Dvořak."

For further information, contact Dvořak International Federation, 11 Pearl Street, Brandon, Vt. 05733.

Never before has the individual had such a useful tool to advance Christ, His story and liberty. Surely, Christians will perceive the typewriter and its more sophisticated counterpart, the word processor, as a tool for God, for good, and train future generations to take possession of the keyboard and the tools of printing in order to help advance "the fullest expression of a Christian civilization."

BIBLIOGRAPHY

Armitage, Thomas, *History of the Baptists*, Byran, Tahlor & Co., New York, 1887

D'Aubigne, J.H. Merle, *History of the Reformation in England*, The Banner of Truth Trust, London, 1971

Encyclopedia Britannica, 1937 edition

Fisher, George P., *History of the Reformation*, Charles Scribner's Sons, New York, 1884

Foxe, John, *Christian Martyrs of the World*, Moody Press, Chicago

Hall, Verna M., *The Christian History of the Constitution of the United States of America*, F.A.C.E., San Francisco, 1975

Halley, Henry H., *Halley's Bible Handbook*, Zondervan Publishing House, Grand Rapids, 1962

Schaff, Philip, *History of the Christian Church*, A,P & A reprint

Slater, Rosalie, J., *Teaching and Learning America's Christian History*, F.A.C.E., San Francisco, 1975

The Holy Bible, King James Edition

Thomas, Isaiah, *The History of Printing in America*, Imprint Society, Bane, Mass., 1970

Unger, Merrill F., *Unger's Bible Dictionary*, Moody Press, Chicago 1957

_____, *Unger's Bible Handbook*, Moody Press, Chicago, 1967

Webster's New World Dictionary, William Collins + World Publishing Co, Cleveland, 1974

Webster, Noah, *An American Dictionary of the English Language*, 1856

_____, *An American Selection of Lessons in Reading and Speaking*, 1809

_____, *History of the United States*, New Haven, 1833

Wroth, Lawrence, C., *The Colonial Printer*, The University Press of Virginia, Charlottesville, 1964

BARBARA B. ROSE

Giving thanks unto the Father, which hath
made us meet to be partakers of the inheritance of the saints in light:
Who hath delivered us from the power of darkness, and hath
translated us into the kingdom of his dear Son:
(Colossians 1:12,13)

Certainly these two verses describe what happened to me as a college graduate in 1964, when I was led out of spiritual darkenss and an erroneous secular political and educational philosophy, and introduced to the light of the Gospel and the principles of America's Christian History.

The *darkness* of my youth was no means total. God and the Bible were presented to me in my childhood home in California and I was taught by my mother, a woman of deep and abiding faith, that I could find the truth about many things in the Scriptures. My conservative parents also taught me a love for my country.

But throughout those years, I never knew the Scriptures well enough to gain a saving knowledge of Christ. I had not learned to extend the truths of the Bible to every aspect of life and living – to government, history, economics and education.

At the University of California, Santa Barbara, I majored in Political Science and minored in History. Like so many other students of my generation, I was led in the direction of secular rationalism and international relations. But all this time the Lord was preparing me for a closer relationship with Himself and a clearer vision of America's uniqueness.

In 1964, I met James B. Rose, a young executive in a small business in which my family and I had invested. Jim was already a serious student of America's Christian History. Our first date was to attend a weekly Bible class conducted by a pastor who was relating Biblical principles to the political events of the day. I was intrigued by this pastor's reasoning and relating and after that Bible study, Jim took me over to meet a friend, "Brother" Bill Hosmer. For three hours, Jim and Bill introduced me to America's Christian History. Much of what they said seemed indisputably true and inspirational, but some of their assertions ran against the secular liberalism with which I had been indoctrinated, and provoked warm discussions. When we finally concluded, I felt greatly inspired, and my attention had been turned away from a fuzzy-minded preoccupation with a social, evolutionary idea of events to a Providential view of history.

To me, history was a study of biographies and man's relation to man in various political and economic environments; but after that night, it became a fascinating illustration of God's Hand at work in the affairs of men or their failure to obey Him and to understand and implement His governing principles. America's Christian History also led me to value how God worked through my own Pilgrim ancestor, Richard Warren, a stranger until he became a Pilgrim. By God's grace, I was a stranger and was led to become a Pilgrim, too.

Subsequently, Jim and I attended a church started by Dr. Bob Wells, the patriot pastor who preached on our first date. Until then, I had never heard Christ's plan of salvation, but I was soon convinced that I was a sinner. I wanted and needed Christ as my Saviour and Lord. The translation from the *power of darkness* was complete. Christ's light replaced my ignorance of not only the Word of God but of God's Sovereignty in the lives of men and nations.

A short time later, Dr. Wells asked Jim to be the administrative assistant in his church in Southern California and I was hired to be secretary to the business administrator.

The church-school had the first pilot program for America's Christian History. One particularly outstanding teacher in the school was Nancy Willard, who pioneerred in teaching Christ, His Story, at the elementary level. She invited me to observe her at work in her fourth grade classroom, and then let me do practice teaching under her supervison – an inspiring and instructive experience.

As Jim Rose and I were drawn closer to the Lord and the Principle Approach to American Christian education, we were also drawn closer to one another. We were married in 1966, and two years later, moved back to the San Francisco Peninsula to minister in a new Principle Approach School starting in Hayward. Jim became the high school history teacher, then the Headmaster, and I taught two classes in typing from the Principle Approach and supervised student activities.

Over the eleven years we were there, the faculty developed the first demonstration school for this educational philosophy. Pastors, professors, administrators and teachers from around the country came to our school to be taught and Jim and I entertained them at our home. Often I had occasion to thank God for the day I had been Providentially prepared to be a hostess by my mother.

I have been privileged to sit in the presence of two Master Teachers – Verna Hall and Rosalie Slater. For over twenty years they have lovingly and patiently equipped me to apply the history and literature of liberty in my own life and in Jim's and my ministry. They have diligently helped us to restore our paths and show us how to "raise up the foundations of many generations." (*Isaiah* 58:12)

While Jim and I wanted children early in our marriage, God ordained that we wait for ten years. Those years were "divine delays" that permitted me to work closely with Jim as he developed the pilot school program and traveled about the country consulting with Principle Approach schools. Thus, we were in this ministry together, and I had a unique opportunity to assist and to teach, to help rebuild the foundations of American Christian character and education.

During this decade working with Jim, our lives were knit together in a common vision and the Hand of God was preparing us to train our own children with an understanding of the Principle Approach. As the Scripture tells us, "unto whomsoever much is given, of him shall be much required." (*Luke* 12:48) Since God had given us this gift of knowledge before having children, we were responsible for making it practical in the nurture of our four children when they arrived in God's timing. His love and Word spared us a dependency upon secular philosophies of child training and enabled us to approach the task with confidence and a conviction that "God hath not given us the spirit of fear, but of power, and of love, and of a sound mind." (*II Timothy* 1:7)

God has dealt graciously with his daughter. I am humbled to be called by Him, to have a godly and committed husband, four precious "jewels," and a ministry in American Christian education. How mighty is the Hand of God in the life of the believer. I am persuaded that "He which hath begun a good work in (us) will perform it until the day of Jesus Christ." (*Philippians 1:6*)

BIBLIOGRAPHY

Dang, Katherine. *A Sunday School Manual for the Oakland Chinese Bible Church.* Unpublished, 1977.

———. *An American Christian Approach to Teaching and Learning Universal History.* Unpublished, 1977.

Dewey, John. "My Pedagogic Creed" from *Three Thousand Years of Educational Wisdom.* Ed. Robert Ulich. Harvard University Press, 1959.

Gill, John. *An Exposition of the Old Testament.* Reprinted by the Primitive Baptist Library, 1979 edition, Vol. IV.

Hall, Verna M. *Christian History of the Constitution of United States of America: Christian Self-Government.* San Francisco: Foundation for American Christian Education, 1960 (also 1975 ed.).

———. *The Christian History of the Constitution of the United States of America: Christian Self-Government with Union.* San Francisco: Foundation for American Christian Education, 1962.

———. "The Hand of God in American History." Lecture, First Pilgrim Seminar, Plymouth, Massachusetts, November 18, 1971.

———. "The Providential Approach to History." Lecture, Second Pilgrim Seminar, Plymouth, Massachusetts, November 18, 1972.

———. *The Christian History of the American Revolution, Consider and Ponder.* San Francisco: Foundation for American Christian Education, 1975.

Hall, Verna M., and Rosalie J. Slater. *Rudiments of America's Christian History and Government.* San Francisco: Foundation for American Christian Education, 1968.

———. *The Bible and the Constitution of the United States of America.* San Francisco: Foundation for American Christian Education, 1983.

Hodge, Charle Rev. *What is Presbyterianism?* Philadelphia, Presbyterian Board of Publication, 1855.

Henry, Matthew. *Commentaries on the Bible.* Fleming Revell, Vol. 6, 1705.

Kevan, Ernest. *The Moral Law.* Sovereign Grace Publishers, 1971.

Punchard, George. *History of Congregationalism from about A.D. 250 to 1616.* Salem, 1841.

Robinson, John. "A Justification of Separation from the Church of England, 1610," from *History of Congregationalism from about A.D. 250 to 1616,* by George Punchard, 1841.

Seabury, William Jones. *An Introduction to the Study of (Protestant Episcopal) Ecclesiastical Polity.* New York: R. W. Crothers, 1911.

Slater, Rosalie J. *Teaching and Learning America's Christian History: The Principle Approach.* San Francisco: Foundation for American Christian Education, 1965.

Story, Joseph. *A Familiar Exposition of the Constitution of the United States,* 1840.

Vine, W. E. *An Expository Dictionary of New Testament Words.* Royal, 1939.

Webster, Noah. *First Edition of an American Dictionary of the English Language 1828.* Facsimile with Introduction by Rosalie J. Slater. San Francisco: Foundation for American Christian Education, 1967.

BIBLE INDEX

BY MARTIN G. SELBREDE

501